The President on Trial

The President on Trial

Prosecuting Hissène Habré

Edited by

SHARON WEILL

KIM THUY SEELINGER

KERSTIN BREE CARLSON

OXFORD
UNIVERSITY PRESS

OXFORD
UNIVERSITY PRESS

Great Clarendon Street, Oxford, OX2 6DP,
United Kingdom

Oxford University Press is a department of the University of Oxford.
It furthers the University's objective of excellence in research, scholarship,
and education by publishing worldwide. Oxford is a registered trade mark of
Oxford University Press in the UK and in certain other countries

First Edition published in 2020
Impression: 1

Published in the United States of America by Oxford University Press
198 Madison Avenue, New York, NY 10016, United States of America

British Library Cataloguing in Publication Data
Data available

Library of Congress Control Number: 2019955609

ISBN 978–0–19–885862–1

Printed and bound by
CPI Group (UK) Ltd, Croydon, CR0 4YY

Foreword

From 2013 through the middle of 2016, someone was abducting and raping little girls in the village of Kavumu, not far from my hospital in the Democratic Republic of the Congo. During those two years, over forty children aged from eighteen months to ten years of age were stolen from their homes in the middle of the night, raped, and left to be found by morning. The victims were so young and small that these experiences left them with serious injuries. Day after day, week after week, these children were brought to us at Panzi Hospital for surgery and counselling. As I stood over each child on the operating table, I felt an urgent desire to help their families and communities seek justice.

So, in addition to providing all the medical care and psychosocial support we could, my team also joined with legal experts and other human rights defenders to push the local authorities to investigate and prosecute these systematic crimes. It turned out the villagers of Kavumu all knew who was responsible: a member of the provincial parliament who controlled local militia and who was abusing children with impunity. It was not easy, but with strategic partnerships and survivors brave enough to testify against a powerful person, we were able to secure convictions for crimes against humanity.

This book tells a related tale. The story of Hissène Habré is well known throughout the African continent. Perhaps it started as a tale of a brilliant young politician who stood up to Gaddafi. It became the story of a Chadian president who became increasingly paranoid and repressive of political opposition at home, even while he was supported by powerful friends abroad. It ended with his trial not in the Hague but at the far end of the Sahel, in a Senegalese courtroom where he was convicted of war crimes, crimes against humanity, and acts of torture—including widespread sexual violence.

The lessons of the trial of Hissène Habré echo what we learned in a smaller scale in Kavumu. It shows the immense promise of national courts in addressing international crimes, despite daunting challenges. It also highlights the value of strategic partnerships to strengthen investigation and prosecution of these crimes, including between local and international actors. But most importantly, the Habré case demonstrates the boundless patience and power of survivors pursuing justice, however long it might take. Without the men and women who were willing to testify against their former president, there would never have been a case, much less a conviction.

This book is the first volume of its kind to present the historic trial of Hissène Habré from its many angles. The volume is brought to us by a stellar team of editors with complementary areas of expertise and attention. Sharon Weill and Kerstin Carlson combine their experience studying hybrid courts and the role of national tribunals in delivering justice for international crimes. Kim Thuy Seelinger brings her expertise in conflict-related sexual violence as well as her sensitivity to the experience of survivors, witnesses, and individual practitioners moving through the legal process. I commend the editors for showing profound respect for the African practitioners who personally delivered the case, by presenting their words and perspectives as the heart of the book. Their chapters are framed by historical and academic analysis that will be valuable to so many of us who are not lawyers or judges ourselves. This is truly a thoughtful, informative, and provocative volume that helps us look frankly at the Habré trial and the larger, complicated project of international criminal justice itself.

Despite its challenges, the Habré trial gives me great hope in the prospect of accountability for atrocity crimes. More importantly, the case should serve as an inspiration to survivors in other countries, including my own homeland. Impunity cannot stand—even for the powerful. With the courage of survivors and the efforts of serious jurists, we can reach justice together.

Dr Denis Mukwege
Director, Panzi Hospital—Bukavu, South Kivu,
Democratic Republic of the Congo
Nobel Peace Prize Co-Laureate, 2018

Acknowledgements

This book was written over three years and across three continents. We three editors accrued many debts: to the institutions that supported us in conducting this research and producing this book; to participants in the Extraordinary African Chambers (EAC) who gave generously of their time to meet with us and, for some, to write for this book; to our academic contributors who responded to the call to contextualize the EAC; to Oxford University Press and their anonymous reviewers for tightening the product; and to our families, who made do without us over some nights, weekends, and vacations. We are three women, professors, parents. We sometimes stopped to marvel at how we were accomplishing this joint effort, marked by each of our contributions yet far greater than any of us could have achieved on her own. So we would also like to acknowledge each other, and our collaboration.

This book could not have happened without the Center of Law and Society in Berkeley, which was where all the three of us met. We are also indebted to distant but constant advisors like Reed Brody, Elise Le Gall, Franck Petit, Olivier Bercault, and Ndeye Amy Ndiaye, who helped connect, check, and encourage us along the way. Together, we wish to thank those who supported our time and travel. We thank the France-Berkeley Fund and Social Science Matrix at the University of California, Berkeley and Sciences o Paris, for supporting Kim and Sharon to travel to Senegal with their research teams. We thank The George and Irina Schaeffer Center for the Study of Genocide, Human Rights and Conflict Prevention at the American University of Paris, which supported field research and the translation of many chapters in the book. We are also grateful for the Danish National Research Fund, which supported two of Kerstin's trips to Senegal, as well as the University of Southern Denmark, that supported Dakar research travel as well as Paris-based collaboration time. Finally, the Open Society Foundation contributed seed funds to support translation work.

The book also benefited from tremendous support from our students. Sharon's Sciences Po students included Emma Sanchez-Swaren, Sarah Cattin, Daria Pugliese, Anjali Suali and Lisa Staxang, who travelled with us for fieldwork in Dakar and coded extensive interview and field notes. Sara and Emma continue to work with us on the editing of the book and they did an excellent work along with Gabriel Green from the American University in Paris. These students worked with Kim's Berkeley Law students, who contributed desk research, fieldwork, and even translation: Elise Berdugo, Djenab Conde, Naomi Fenwick, John Hannon, Nicole Kaneza, Pearle Nwaezeigwe, Sanaz Payandeh, and Isabel Tule. Julia Uyttewaal lent tremendous editing, graphics and translation support first at Berkeley and then from Washington University in St Louis, where Matthew Ho also assisted with graphics.

For the translation of the numerous chapters written originally in French we want to thank our dear colleague Linda Martz of the American University of Paris. She translated many of our contributors' first-person accounts, keeping an eye on tone and personal style while simultaneously contending with specialist language.

Individually, Sharon thanks her students in the Capstone course at Sciences Po; The Paris School of International Affairs (PSIA) for hosting the workshop that we held prior to our first field work as well as Professor Bill Schabas and all the participants in the workshop; FIDH for their collaboration, specifically Clemence Bectarte, Florent Geel, and Anjali Suali; Professors Perelman and MuirWatt for facilitating the application to the Social Science Matrix grant at Sciences Po and encouraging the project. Special thanks to Eric Stover, who was the first who encouraged Sharon to work on this case and introduced her to Kim at the Human Rights Center in Berkeley. Heddy, for her energies, generosity and brilliant ideas including connecting Sharon with Olivier in Berkeley. And above all Sharon's thanks go for her love Bartolomeo Conti and their girls, Zoé and Maayane, who all give her light on a daily basis.

For her part, Kim thanks Alain Werner, Jacqueline Moudeina, Souleymane Guengueng, and Reed Brody for introducing her to the Habré case and so many of the direct actors in the trial. She is grateful to Naomi Fenwick and Khaled Alrabe, with whom she led an emergency *amicus curiae* effort in late 2015 and with whom she took a crash course in the Extraordinary African Chambers as a lawyer before engaging it as a researcher. For the broader project, Kim is indebted to Eric Stover, from the UC Berkeley Human Rights Center, for connecting her to Sharon Weill to launch the research that led to the book you hold in your hands today. The process was long but constantly rejuvenated by so many beloved students and professional researchers, noted above. No one supported Kim more than her infinitely patient family, Elvin Geng and Kaien Thuy. Thank you. Finally, Kim honors the Chadian women who travelled across the African continent and sat right in front of her in the trial chamber on 30 May 2016: When Judge Kam uttered Habré's verdict and sentence that morning, you stood up, raised your arms, and started singing out loud. May the justice pronounced that day in Senegal be with you in Chad.

Kerstin thanks iCourts at the University of Copenhagen and colleagues in the MOISL program and law department of the University of Southern Denmark for intellectual and financial support. Claudio checked all the equations. Kerstin's village of friends and family kept her kids while she travelled for research and conferences; she has no words. Finally, Kerstin thanks the kids in question, who are almost always good-natured about being kept, and proud of their mom's work.

Table of Contents

C. The Trial

D. Beyond the Courtroom

PART II: REFLECTIONS ON THE SIGNIFICANCE OF THE HABRÉ CASE AND BEYOND

A. Portraits, Positionality, Paradigms

List of Contributors

Kirsten Ainley, Associate Professor of International Relations, London School of Economics and Political Science.

Khaled Alrabe, Staff Attorney for the National Immigration Project and former researcher with the Human Rights Center, University of California, Berkeley.

Mahamat Hassan Abakar, Judge, President of the Chadian Truth Commission.

Aboubacry Ba, Technical adviser to Minister of Justice, in charge of registries; former clerk at the EAC.

Victor Băieşu, Legal Officer in the Trial Chamber of the Special Tribunal for Lebanon. Former Associate Trial Lawyer in the Office of the Prosecutor at the International Criminal Court and Legal Officer at the European Court of Human Rights.

Mounir Ballal, Lawyer of the Senegalese Bar, and court-appointed defence lawyer of Habré, before the EAC.

Olivier Bercault, Adjunct Professor, University of San Francisco. During the trial he gave testimony as an expert witness on behalf of the prosecutor; Human Rights Watch coordinator of the case (2000-2008).

Leïla Bourguiba, Legal Advisor for *Médecins Sans Frontières*. Former Legal Officer at the Pre-trial Chamber of the International Criminal Court (2006-2012) and at the French War crimes and Crimes against Humanity Unit within the *Tribunal de grande instance* of Paris (2012 -2018).

Kerstin Bree Carlson (co-editor), Associate Professor, University of Southern Denmark and The American University of Paris; Global Fellow at iCourts, University of Copenhagen.

Reed Brody, Senior Counsel with Human Rights Watch and architect of Chadian victims' long campaign for justice.

Gaëlle Carayon, Former Post Conflict Policy Advisor at Redress.

Hélène Cissé, Lawyer of the Senegalese Bar and at the International Criminal Court. She was a member of Habré's defence team in the first domestic proceedings before the Senegalese courts between 1999-2001.

Stephen Cody, Assistant Professor of Law, Suffolk University Law School.

Nancy Amoury Combs, Ernest W. Goodrich Professor of Law, Cabell Research Professor of Law, William & Mary Law School.

Sara Dezalay, Senior Lecturer, School of Law and Politics, Cardiff University.

Ngoundji Dieng, Senegalese Journalist for Senegalese daily, *The Quotidien*, society desk.

Mbacké Fall, Advisor to Senegal's Supreme Court and former EAC Prosecutor.

Naomi Fenwick, Assistant Federal Public Defender in Dallas, Texas, and former researcher with the Human Rights Center, University of California, Berkeley.

Élise Le Gall, Lawyer of the Paris Bar, International Criminal Law expert with the EAC Office of the Prosecutor.

Richard Goldstone, Former Chief Prosecutor to the International Criminal Tribunals for Rwanda (ICTR) and the former Yugoslavie (ICTY); former judge of the South African Supreme Court.

Souleymane Guengueng, Founder, Association of Victims of Political Repression in Chad and Civil Party in the Habre trial, and director of the Souleymane Guengueng Foundation.

Pierre Hazan, Transitional Justice Senior Advisor to the Centre for Humanitarian Dialogue (Geneva) and professor at the Media Academy in the University of Neuchâtel.

Dov Jacobs, Trial Lawyer at the International Criminal Court.

Jean Kandé, Judge, President of the Indicting Chamber of the Thiès Court of Appeal, Investigating and Coordinating judge of the Investigative Chamber of the EAC.

Mark Kersten, Digital Fellow, Montreal Institute for Genocide and Human, Rights Studies, Senior Consultant, Wayamo Foundation.

Jocelyn Getgen Kestenbaum, Associate Professor of Clinical Law, Benjamin N. Cardozo School of Law.

Ben Kioko, Former Legal Counsel to the Commission of the African Union and judge on the African Court on Human and People's Rights.

Fannie Lafontaine, Professor of Law at Laval University, Canada, and director of the Clinic for International Criminal and Humanitarian Law (CDIPH).

Emmanuelle Marchand Senior legal counsel at Civitas Maxima, Legal consultant for Civil Parties during the Habré trial.

Marcel Mendy, Journalist and author, former Coordinator of the EAC Communications Unit.

Jacqueline Moudeina, Victims' Legal Counsel before the EAC and former president of the Chadian Association for the Promotion and Defense of Human Rights.

Amy Ndiaye Ndeye, Lecturer at the Institute of Human Rights, Cheikh Anta Diop University of Dakar, Legal Advisor at the EAC Trial Chamber.

Franck Petit Deputy editor for Justiceinfo.net and former team leader for the Outreach Consortium on the EAC during the Hissein Habré trial.

William Schabas, Professor of International Law, School of Law, Middlesex University, and Professor of International Criminal Law and Human Rights, Leiden University.

Amadou Mokhtar Seck, International expert in financial and accounting management, EAC Administration and Finance Office.

Kim Thuy Seelinger (co-editor), Research Associate Professor, Brown School of Social Work, Public Health, and Social Policy; Visiting Professor of Law, Washington University in St. Louis. Former Director of the Sexual Violence Program at the Human Rights Center, University of California, Berkeley.

Patricia Viseur Sellers, Special Advisor for Gender to the International Criminal Court Office of the Prosecutor, former Legal Advisor for Gender at the International Criminal Tribunal for the former Yugoslavia (ICTY); visiting fellow at Oxford University.

Julien Seroussi, Social Scientist, Former analyst at the International Criminal Court and at the French War Crimes Investigative Unit.

Christoph Sperfeldt, Senior Research Fellow, Peter McMullin Centre on Statelessness, Melbourne Law School.

Eric Stover, Faculty Director of the Human Rights Center and Adjunct Professor of Law and Public Health, University of California, Berkeley.

Érick Sullivan, Lawyer, Deputy Director, International Criminal and Humanitarian Law Clinic, Law Faculty, Université Laval (Québec), Coordinator, Canadian Partnership for International Justice.

Jeanne Sulzer, Lawyer of the Paris bar, Former Head of the International Justice Desk, International Federation of Human Rights (FIDH).

Mia Swart, Visiting Professor, University of the Witwatersrand, Johannesburg, South Africa and Adjunct Professor, Faculty of Law, Hamad bin Khalifa University, Qatar.

Henri Thulliez, Lawyer of the Paris bar, Senior coordinator for Human Rights Watch.

Sarah Valentina Fall, Human Rights and Human Security program, Swiss Embassy in Dakar.

Manuel J Ventura, Associate Legal Officer in the Office of the Prosecutor at the International Residual Mechanism for Criminal Tribunals, Adjunct Fellow at the School of Law at Western Sydney University, and a Director of The Peace and Justice Initiative.

Ouagadeye Wafi, Prosecutor General to the Malian Supreme Court and former judge, EAC Appeals Chamber.

Sharon Weill (co-editor), Assistant Professor at The American University of Paris and Associate Researcher, CERI, Sciences Po Paris.

Alain Werner, Director of Civitas Maxima and Civil Parties Lawyer during the Habré Trial.

Sarah Williams, Professor, Faculty of Law, University of New South Wales, Sydney.

Liesbeth Zegveld, Professor of War Reparations at the University of Amsterdam and partner at the human rights law firm, Prakken d'Oliveira.

Hissène Habré on Trial

Mapping the Long Road to Justice

Sharon Weill, Kim Thuy Seelinger, and Kerstin Bree Carlson

By some accounts, the trial and conviction of Hissène Habré in 2015–2016 is the most significant achievement global criminal justice has enjoyed in the past decade. Simply creating a court and commencing a trial against a deposed head of state was an extraordinary and arguably unlikely success. Moreover, the ad hoc tribunal set up in Senegal exceeded expectations, working on time, within budget, with no murdered witnesses or self-dealing officials. The 2016 judgment of the Extraordinary African Chambers (hereafter EAC) found Habré guilty of war crimes, crimes against humanity, and torture—including several counts involving sexual violence committed by Habré's agents and Habré himself. The 2017 appeals judgment affirmed the conviction on all counts except for Habré's personal commission of rape, which was dismissed for procedural reasons, and affirmed Habré's life sentence. Despite fears that sympathetic African heads of state might push for his pardon, Habré remains, to this day, imprisoned in a dusty location at the southern tip of Dakar's peninsula, just behind the main bus terminal and surrounded by goats and chickens. It is a humble end for a man who once controlled the destiny of a nation and its peoples.

The judicial achievement of the EAC is particularly meaningful in the current climate, where we are witnessing a 'backlash' against international criminal justice. The optimistic days of the first ad hoc tribunals for Rwanda and the former Yugoslavia, built on the template of the Nuremberg and Tokyo tribunals and seeking the same normative and political reordering that those institutions heralded, has faded. The International Criminal Court (ICC), the first permanent international criminal tribunal, became operational in 2002. It quickly amassed a solid global membership (as of this writing, 122 states are members). Yet enthusiasm was short lived. The ICC has more recently encountered a series of political and operational hurdles that have led to what many now fear is an existential crisis for the institution. Some now advocate for local, hybrid tribunals as the best method for realizing the anti-impunity goals of global justice. The EAC, for the reasons named above, is the lodestar for such tribunals.

This book presents the Habré trial and its impact using a novel structure of first person accounts and academic analysis, presenting both local and international perspectives through distinct but inter-locking parts. It offers empirical source material followed by expert analysis designed to bring the reader closer both to the construction and work of the EAC as well as wider themes, practices, and challenges in international criminal law.

Sharon Weill, Kim Thuy Seelinger, and Kerstin Bree Carlson, *Hissène Habré on Trial* In: *The President on Trial*. First edition. Edited by: Sharon Weill, Kim Thuy Seelinger, and Kerstin Bree Carlson, Oxford University Press (2020). DOI: 10.1093/oso/9780198858621.003.0001

Impetus, objectives, structure

We the editors followed the case from 2015 onwards. We made several trips to Dakar, some taken alone, some together and some with students, in order to interview a spectrum of actors associated with the EAC. Convinced of the trial's significance, concerned that it would remain understudied by an anglophone audience, and wishing to bring local experience and knowledge out of Dakar and to the world, we conceived of the book's particular structure. We began with the driving idea that the richness, professionalism and critical inquiry that we saw all around us in Dakar should be shared with a wider audience. This is the genesis of the twenty-six actor testimonials that constitute Part I, the heart of the book.

Through chapters written by Senegalese, Chadian, and foreign experts who were directly involved in facilitating and operationalizing the Habré trial, we present the unfolding of the case against Habré in its chronological order, beginning with the 1990 regime change in Chad. Our contributors include judges, lawyers, administrators, victims' representatives, media and civil society leaders central to this case. This is the first time many of their personal reflections will be shared with an Anglophone audience. These voices are drawn from across the echelons of power, ideology, and status, including international judges and bureaucratic workers. We have tried to present the contributors' voices as we first heard them in our on-the-ground interviews. The process of writing and translating is necessarily transformative, however. People don't write as they speak, personality often doesn't translate, anecdotes disappear, and stories told 'off the record' cannot be shared. Nonetheless, we have endeavoured to present the contributors' voices as authentically as possible, so that the reader has a first person experience of the empirical data upon which research is based.

Our selection of authors for this part was driven by our own interdisciplinary backgrounds and interests, which dictated what is relevant and constructive to explain the process, the institution, and/or the development of international legal doctrine. Chance and timing also had some impact: administrators are busy, politicians feel more or less secure, and activists have sometimes moved on to the next engagement. Finally, we regret that some actors, such as Habré's chosen counsel and Senegalese and Chadian government officials, are missing. Nonetheless, we believe this book presents much of what was essential about the institution and how multiple persons and interests interacted in this process. It is our hope that readers will use this data to stimulate their own theorization and further inquiry.

In the second part of the book we situate the Habré case in its larger context. Many proponents of international criminal law and transitional justice ask what impact the EAC's design and jurisprudence can have for other prosecutions of international crimes. Should this model be replicated? Can it be? What can we learn from the EAC's work to design and strengthen future institutions? We wanted to explore those questions in the second part of the book, which is comprised of academics' and legal experts' chapters. We approached scholars mainly within the legal discipline based on the themes we found central to the case: procedural hybridity; international criminal law doctrine; victim and witness participation; and the future of international criminal justice and its challenges. Part II presents seventeen chapters offering paradigmatic samples of the theoretical and practice-oriented discussions accompanying the Habré trial.

When we had assembled Part II, however, it became clear that beyond our original thematic categories, new ways of seeing emerged. We have therefore grouped the chapters of Part II around what we identified as the authors' own positionality in relation to international criminal law, identifying four categories. To explain what we mean by using the term positionality, we offer this metaphor: A stone falls in a river on a summer day. Where do you look to capture this event? Do you follow the stone, as it descends in the water, observing its shape and its trajectory? Do you look rather at the ripples created by the stone, their height, density, when they hit the bank or move on down the river? Do you take account of the surrounding scenery, the trees, bushes, fields? Is there a hierarchy of where and what you observe to meaningfully describe and understand the event?

In Part II, we have grouped the chapters according to the authors' self positioning on the banks of the river of international criminal justice: the ones who are following the stone of articulated doctrine, the ones engaged with the ripples of impact on people and ideas, the ones who broaden their gaze to the bushes and trees around the river, and which include considerations of the wider political landscape, environment and potential participants and actors. We deliberately seek not to privilege any particular positionality, as we find each of these categories equally important to constructing a portrait of international criminal law.

The EAC: Overview of law, procedure, and structure

The EAC established in the Senegalese judiciary is sometimes referred to as a domestic court of an internationalized nature. We offer a brief overview of its structure and procedure here.

Common law and civil law are two dominant legal traditions. Both systems strive for justice, which in the context of legal accountability is punishment of the guilty and acquittal of the innocent for pre-defined crimes. Both systems require assurance of guilt to convict, a standard known as 'beyond a reasonable doubt' in common law traditions and '*conviction intime*' ('inner certainty') in civil law tradition. They diverge in terms of how they achieve this, ie in their procedure. Civil law prioritizes the *dossier*, a file established by the investigating judge, who is independent from the prosecution, and responsible for investigating and collecting both incriminating and exculpatory evidence for this file. The file should be available for the defendant to review, to add to, and to contest. Any interlocutory decision (ie, any determination made by the investigating judge) may be appealed to an appeals chamber that is operational solely for that purpose. Appeals decisions are final at this stage and cannot be reviewed (or otherwise reconsidered) by the trial chamber.

Victims who have suffered a direct injury can participate in the procedure as civil parties. This means that they can join the criminal procedure to make their own request regarding civil remedies, ie, reparations. They are permitted to participate in all stages beginning with the investigation, where they can propose witnesses, or even, as was the case against Habré, trigger the investigation itself. The investigation phase is decisive and can take years. At the end of the investigation, if there is enough evidence, an indictment is issued by the investigating judge. This indictment is final and passed to the prosecutor, who represents the state at the trial stage.

The trial judges, who are not the same as those who conducted the investigation, will review the investigation file prior to trial. Regardless, they start the inquiry afresh, which is to say that they are not bound by the conclusions of the investigating judge. With few procedural constraints, it is the president of the bench who directs the trial and the questioning of the accused and the witnesses. The accused is a central protagonist and almost never exercises his right to silence. The trial proceeds in two stages (1) the inquiry of the personality, where the path of the accused from childhood is reconstructed and (2) the establishment of the facts. The prosecutor, the civil parties, and the defence can question the accused and the witnesses. The defence will always have the last word. Appeals are made on the final decision and may be made by any party regardless of the outcome, i.e., the state can appeal acquittals. The appeal is a complete redo of the trial, where judges reconduct the entire trial, starting again from the investigation file (which cannot be modified after the conclusion of the investigation stage).

The EAC was a hybrid tribunal applying international criminal law doctrine and governed by Senegalese procedure, ie, civil law tradition with some adjustments. This is why victims were able to participate as parties before the EAC (standard in civil law traditions; unknown in common law), a development that many cite as critical to the capacity of international justice institutions to meaningfully address victims.

The EAC Statute defined the core crimes,[1] echoing the ICC's, and the penalties. It regulates some of the procedure, such as the constitution of civil parties (Article 14) as well as the grounds for appeal (Article 25), which are closer to common law procedures, like the ICC. Most of the rules of procedure remained undefined by the Statue, and here the Statute specified, in Article 16, that whatever is not included in the Statute shall be governed by Senegalese law. Institutionally, in Article 2 the Statute created four chambers. For the investigation phases, two chambers were created, the investigative and the indictment chambers (the second of which was an appeal bench for all issues arising during the investigation), both of which eventually consisted of four judges. For the trial phase, the trial and appeals chambers were created, each of them eventually consisting of three judges a piece, including one foreign judge on each bench.

[1] Offical legal documents of the court are available on EAC website in French: http://www.chambresafricaines.org/; An English translation of the Statute is available at: https://www.hrw.org/news/2013/09/02/statute-extraordinary-african-chambers.

Organization of the Extraordinary African Chambers

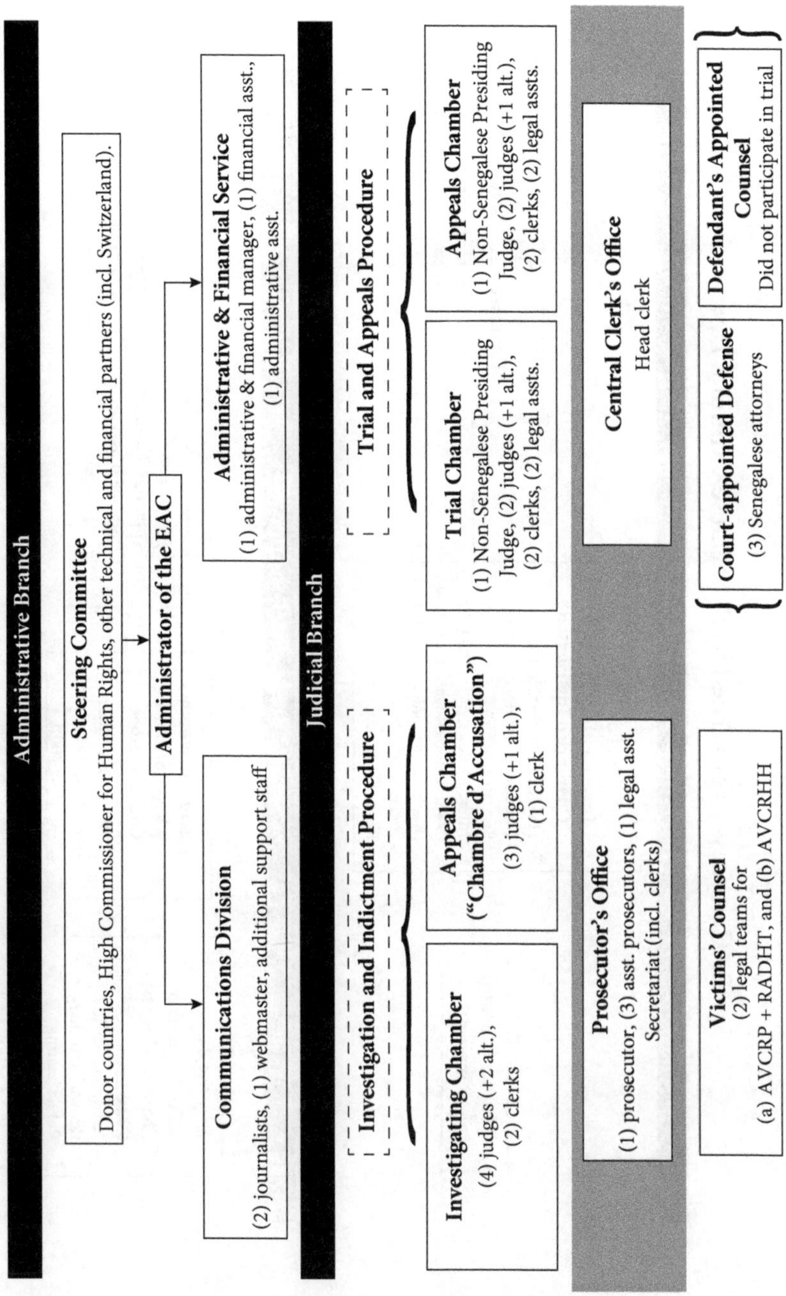

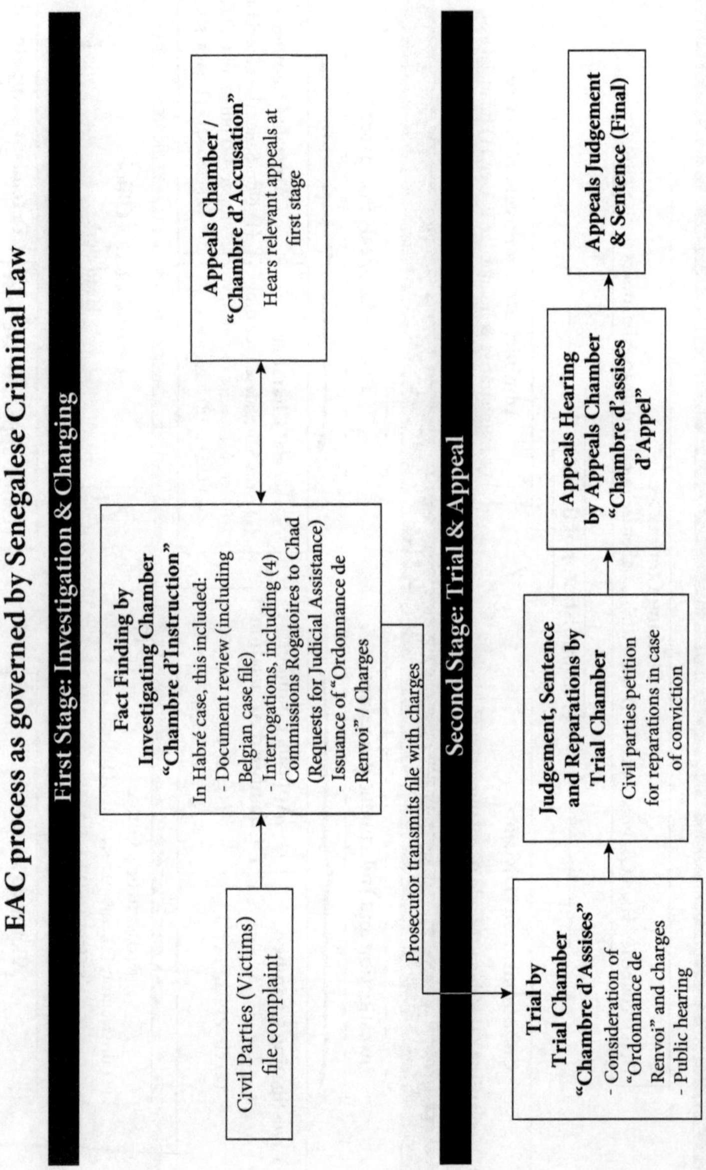
EAC process as governed by Senegalese Criminal Law
First Stage: Investigation & Charging
Civil Parties (Victims) file complaint
Fact Finding by Investigating Chamber "Chambre d'Instruction"
In Habré case, this included:
- Document review (including Belgian case file)
- Interrogations, including (4) Commissions Rogatoires to Chad (Requests for Judicial Assistance)
- Issuance of "Ordonnance de Renvoi" / Charges
Appeals Chamber / "Chambre d'Accusation"
Hears relevant appeals at first stage
Prosecutor transmits file with charges
Second Stage: Trial & Appeal
Trial by Trial Chamber "Chambre d'Assises"
- Consideration of "Ordonnance de Renvoi" and charges
- Public hearing
Judgement, Sentence and Reparations by Trial Chamber
Civil parties petition for reparations in case of conviction
Appeals Hearing by Appeals Chamber "Chambre d'assises d'Appel"
Appeals Judgement & Sentence (Final)

Chad during the Hissène Habré Presidency: 1982–1990

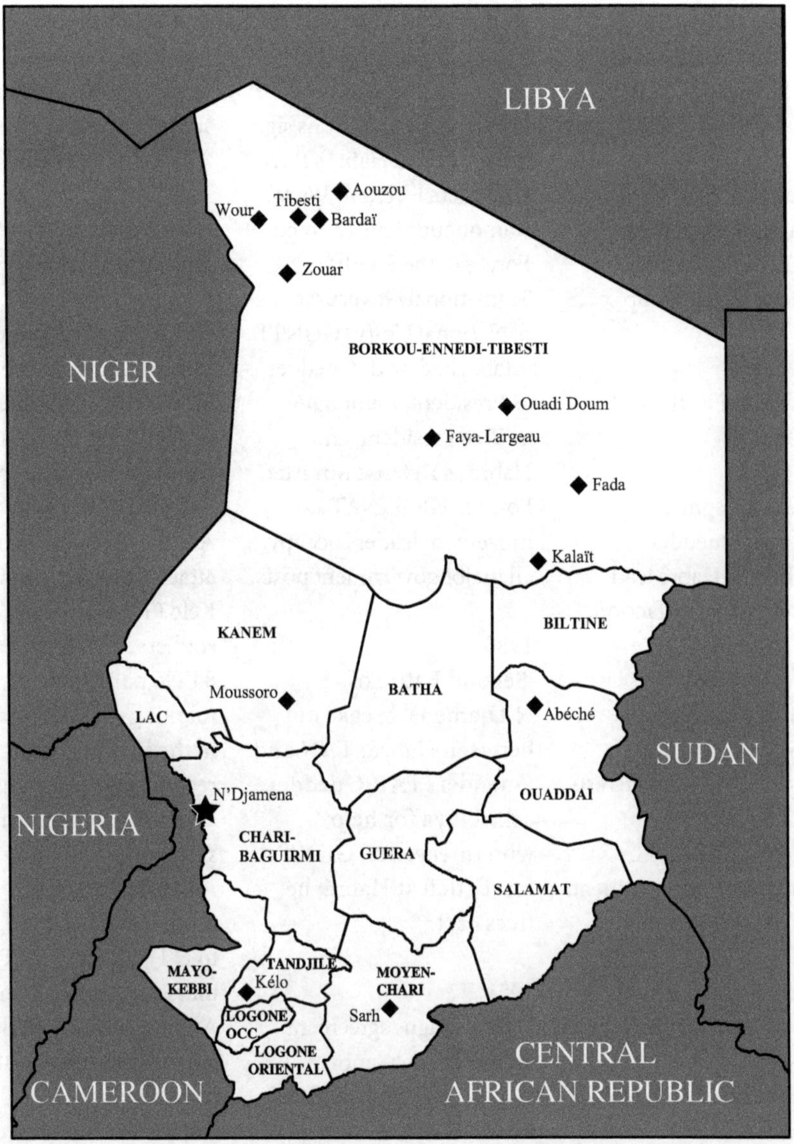

The Rise and Reign of Hissène Habré in Chad (1971–1990)

1942
Hissène Habré born in Faya-Largeau to family of Daza ethnicity.

1960
Chad gains independence from France.

1966
Center, east, and north groups establish FROLINAT to oppose southern ruling group.

1971
Habré joins FROLINAT.

1972
FROLINAT splits. Goukouni Oueddeï and Hissène Habré lead northern CCFAN faction.

1975
Military coup d'état puts CSM in power, which represents southern interests but makes overtures to the north and east. Félix Malloum becomes president.

1976
Oueddeï and Habré split. Habré creates FAN (Armed Forces of the North) and opposes alliance with Libya. Oueddeï seeks Libyan assistance to overthrow CSM.

1978
Habré and Malloum negotiate a formal alliance. Habré becomes prime minister and Malloum remains president.

1979
Habré's and Malloum's factions start fighting. They eventually disarm; Malloum exiled to Nigeria. Other warring factions sign peace accord: Habré's FAN, Oueddeï's FAP, and Wadel Kamougué's FAT (Armed Forces of the South). Transitional Government of National Unity (GUNT) established, with Oueddeï as President, Kamougué as Vice President, and Habré as Defense Minister. Former FROLINAT movement leaders occupy all major government posts.

1980
'Second Battle of N'Djamena' breaks out between Habré's FAN and Oueddeï's FAP. Oueddeï asks Libya for help, who intervenes. GUNT forces defeat Habré; he flees east.

1981
Oueddeï signs agreement with Libya's Muammar Gaddafi merging Chad and Libya. Kamougué leaves GUNT in protest and returns to south, which he controls.

1982
Habré launches offensive with US support, seizes N'Djamena. Oueddeï flees to Cameroon. Kamougué's control falls. Habré takes Sarh and other southern regions and becomes president. Oueddeï creates GUNT army (ANT) with Libyan support in the Tibesti.

1983
Habré establishes state security service (DDS). FAN becomes FANT, official Chadian army. Habré announces amnesty for exiled opponents. GUNT takes Faya-Largeau with Libyan assistance, followed by Kalaït and Abéché. Rebels in south attack CotonTchad in Kélo (Tandjile). FANT soldiers summarily execute 8 Kélo police officers, marking start of repression in the south. Habré reconquers Faya-Largeau; several GUNT ministers summarily executed. A thousand GUNT prisoners transferred to N'Djamena; FANT massacres 150 of them in Ambing. GUNT retakes Faya-Largeau and Habré narrowly escapes. FANT stops GUNT offensive in Battle of Kalaït-Oum-Chalouba, then captures and shoots 53 prisoners of war. US and France give Habré military support throughout.

1984
Foreign Minister Idriss Miskine of Hadjaraï ethnicity dies mysteriously. Habré announces reconciliation with opposition and a new coalition of Habré supporters, UNIR, forms. Southern 'Codos' rebels attack Habré's military outposts; violent reprisals by FANT ensue, known as 'Black September'. Repression of Sara ethnicity peaks. Amnesty International blames Habré's presidential guard for massacre in the south.

1985
Over 100 killed in 'Ngalo massacre'. DDS and FANT authorize transfer of women prisoners to Kalaït military camp; they endure domestic servitude and sexual violence.

1986
Habré's government releases 122 political prisoners and signs peace accord with the 'Codos'. Libyan-supported GUNT forces launch offensive in North. GUNT's vice president Kamougué resigns, announces readiness to join Habré. GUNT and Libyan forces clash. Libyan soldiers bring GUNT leader Oueddeï to Tripoli. He states openness to negotiating with Habré. FANT and Oueddeï's GUNT faction form alliance. Imprisoned Hadjaraï leader Maldoum Bada is released; he forms opposition group, MOSANAT. Acheikh Ibn Omar heads GUNT and makes peace overtures to Habré. Libyan forces attack the north; Habré counter-attacks in Zouar.

1987
FANT retakes Fada and Zouar, killing 800 Libyans and beginning reconquest of the north. GUNT attacks FANT training center in Moussoro and FANT forces near Fada. FANT retakes Ouadi Doum, key Libyan base in the north; Libyan forces evacuate Faya-Largeau. Habré's regime violently represses Hadjaraï ethnicity in Guéra and N'Djamena. Chadian forces reconquer Tibesti; Chad and Libya announce cease-fire.

1988
DDS authorizes transfer of 9 women prisoners to Ouadi Doum military camp, where they endure domestic servitude and sexual violence.

1989
Habré denounces supposed plot against him by Idriss Déby and others of Zaghawa ethnicity. Déby flees to Sudan; Habré launches mass violent repression against Zaghawa. Chad and Libya sign peace agreement. Déby's forces attack FANT from Sudan.

1990
Habré accuses Libya of supporting Déby; relations strain. The countries submit border dispute to the ICJ, which decides in Chad's favor in 1994. Déby and Maldoum Bada establish MPS, which continues to attack FANT. Habré is eventually defeated and his regime collapses in November; he flees to Cameroon and then Senegal, taking more than 3 billion francs CFA from Chadian treasury. Déby's forces arrive in N'Djamena in December. He declares himself president and creates national truth commission.

1991
A victims' group, AVCRP, is established with the goal of prosecuting perpetrators of crimes under Habré's regime.

1992
National Commission of Investigation publishes its report accusing the Habré regime of systematically torturing 40,000 victims. Commission recommends prosecution of Habré and his accomplices and reparations for victims.

An International Affair: The Global Path to a Local Trial

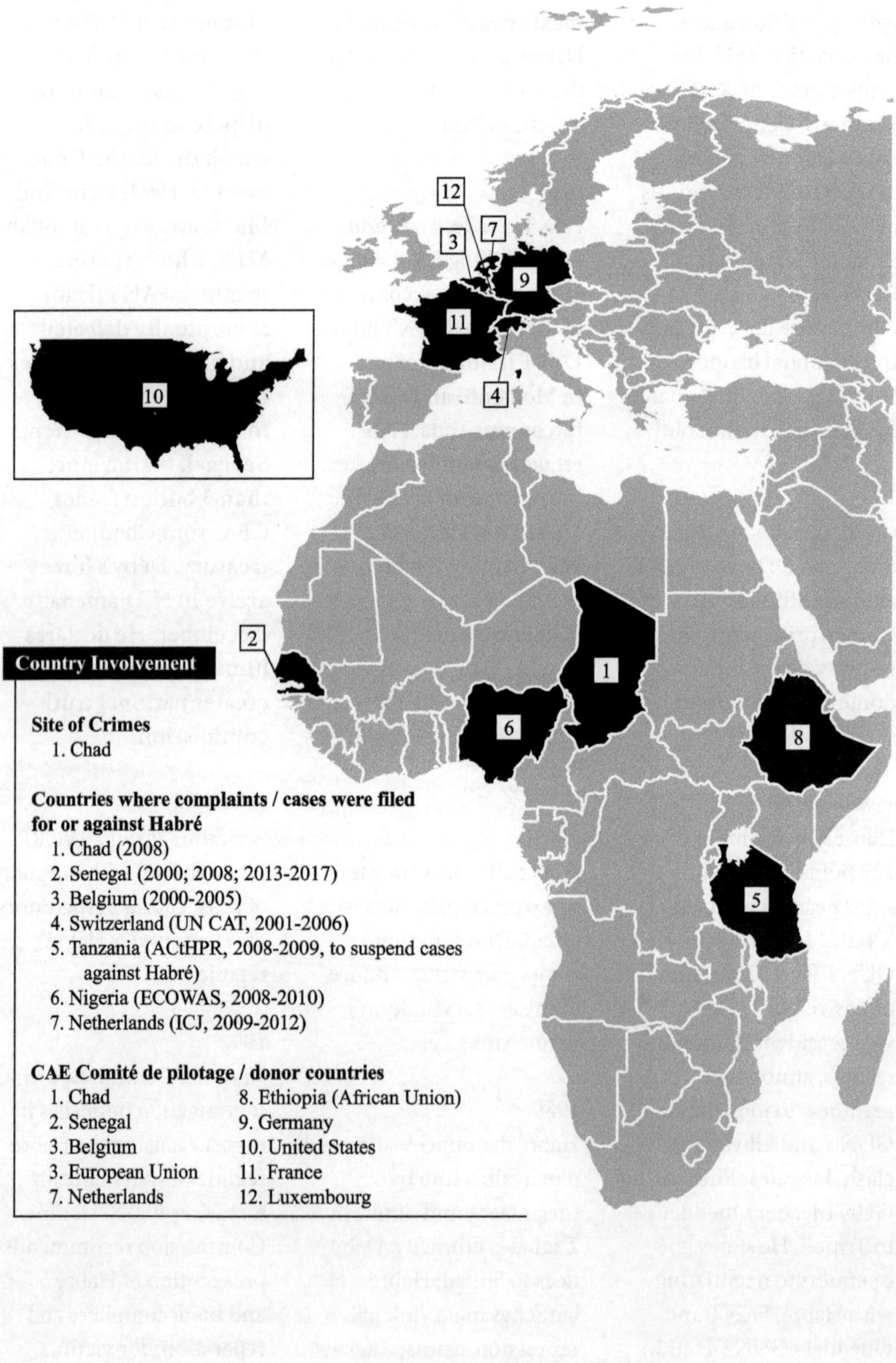

Attempts to Prosecute Habré at Home and Abroad (1990–2017)

1990
Habré flees to Cameroon. Déby's forces arrive in N'Djamena; he declares himself president. Déby authorizes creation of national truth commission (led by Mahamat Hassan Abakar) to investigate human rights violations under Habré. The commission publishes report in 1992.

2000
Chadian victims file a complaint against Habré in the *Tribunal regional hors classe* (regional court) in Dakar, Senegal. Investigating judge Demba Kandji indicts Habré for crimes against humanity and acts of torture and barbarity, placing him under house arrest. Habré appeals at the Dakar Court of Appeal, which eventually rules that Senegal lacks jurisdiction to prosecute him. Ahmed Aganaye, a Belgian national born in Chad, files a complaint against Habré for the commission of international crimes. The Belgian investigating judge Daniel Fransen opens an investigation.

2001
Senegalese Court of Cassation upholds ruling on lack of jurisdiction. President Wade of Senegal announces he has asked Habré to leave Senegal, triggering fear that Habré might flee. Chadian victims and Human Rights Watch (HRW) submit a communication to the UN Committee Against Torture (CAT) to request that Habré not be allowed to leave Senegal except to be extradited. Judge Fransen contacts Senegal requesting cooperation. Following intercessions from the UN, President Wade announces he will keep Habré in Senegal until a country capable of organizing a fair trial claims Habré.

2002
Belgian investigating judge Fransen conduct investigation in Chad regarding complaints against Habré. Chad issues letter to Judge Fransen waiving Habré's immunity.

2005
Judge Fransen issues international arrest warrant for Habré, triggering request for extradition to Belgium. Senegalese authorities arrest Habré, but Dakar Appeals Court rules it has no jurisdiction to rule on extradition request. Habré is released. Senegal's Minister of Interior issues order placing Habré at the disposal of African Union (AU).

2006
AU establishes 'Committee of Eminent African Jurists' to consider prosecution options. UN CAT rules that Senegal violated Convention Against Torture by failing to extradite or prosecute Habré. AU asks Senegal to prosecute Habré 'on behalf of Africa'.

2007
The Senegalese National Assembly adopts legislation giving its Courts retroactive jurisdiction over genocide, crimes against humanity, war crimes, and torture committed outside of Senegal. The European Union, France, and Switzerland announce they will support Senegal for Habré's prosecution. The Senegalese Minister of Justice announces that a trial of Habré will take place but provides no timeline.

2008
Jan.–Sep.: Chadian citizen files an application with the African Court on Human and Peoples' Rights (ACtHPR) seeking to suspend all Senegalese proceedings against Habré.

A Chadian court trying Habré *in absentia* sentences him and eleven rebel leaders to death for attempting to overturn the constitutional order. Fourteen victims file criminal complaints in Senegal against Habré alleging torture and crimes against humanity.
Oct.: Habré files a complaint with the Court of the Economic Community of West African States (ECOWAS) against Senegal, claiming it violated the principle of non-retroactivity. President Wade threatens to expel Habré unless Senegal receives funds from the international community for a trial.

2009
Belgium files application with International Court of Justice (ICJ) requesting ruling that Senegal must prosecute or extradite Habré. Separately, ACtHPR declines to exercise jurisdiction over application to suspend Senegal's proceedings against Habré.

2010
The ECOWAS court rules that Senegal must prosecute Habré before an extraordinary ad hoc international tribunal. The EU, AU, and other sponsors agree to provide Senegal with €8.6 million for proceedings.

2011
Jan.–Feb.: UN CAT reaffirms Senegal's obligation to prosecute or extradite Habré. AU calls on Senegal to begin the trial in accordance with ECOWAS decision, but President Wade refuses to create court mandated by ECOWAS.
Mar.–Sep.: Belgium issues a second extradition request and the AU asks Senegal to prosecute or extradite Habré. The Dakar Court of Appeals rules the extradition request inadmissible on procedural grounds, so Belgium issues a third extradition request.

2012
Jan.: The Dakar Court of Appeals rules the third Belgian extradition request inadmissible on procedural grounds, and Belgium issues a fourth extradition request one week later.
Mar.–Jul.: Macky Sall wins the Senegalese presidential election in March and declares in July that Senegal will try Habré. Five days later the ICJ issues its ruling on Belgium's application, requiring Senegal to prosecute or extradite Habré without further delay. Senegal and the AU agree on the structure for trying Habré.
Aug.–Dec.: On 22 Aug., Senegal and AU sign agreement creating the Extraordinary African Chambers (EAC) within Senegalese judiciary; agreement contains the EAC Statute. Senegalese parliament passes legislation establishing EAC on 19 Dec.

2013
The EAC is inaugurated in Dakar on 8 Feb. Habré taken into police custody on 30 Jun. On 2 Jul., investigating judges charge him with crimes against humanity, torture, and war crimes.

2014
Prosecutions of 29 of Habré's associates (some deceased) commence hastily in Chad in November. Domestic trial precludes their extradition to Senegal. Decision is rendered in March 2015: Twenty are convicted of regime-era crimes.

2016
30 May: Habré is convicted of crimes against humanity, war crimes, and torture, including sexual violence and rape.

2017
27 Apr.: The EAC renders appeals judgment. It largely dismisses arguments focused on procedure and reparations decision but acquits Habré of personally raping Khadidja Hassan Zidane. Other convictions, including for sexual violence committed by Habré's subordinates, are upheld, along with sentence of life imprisonment.

PART I
THE TRIAL AS TOLD BY ITS ACTORS

Part I consists of twenty-six first-person accounts from actors involved in or around the pursuit of Hissène Habré and his trial before the EAC. Motivated by the editors' desire to 'bring the EAC to the world', this portion of the book is designed as an empirical presentation of key actors' roles and experiences. It is divided into four parts, from the first efforts to document and prosecute Habré's crimes (section A), through the establishment of the EAC (section B), to the trial and its workings (section C), and closing with contextualizing voices from outside the court (section D). In all chapters, authors are introduced with the affiliation they held at the time of their involvement in the case.

SECTION A
EARLY PROSECUTION ATTEMPTS (1982–2012)

This section includes seven chapters. We begin with the unlikely discovery of the abandoned archives documenting crimes of Habré and his regime by members of a Human Rights Watch (HRW) team. Olivier Bercault was a HRW researcher in the 1990s when his team stumbled upon the records of Habré's secret service in an unused office in Chad's capital. In this chapter, Bercault discusses how they came to find these documents, what they showed about Habré and his regime, and the significance of the discovered secret police ('DDS') archives in pushing forward Habré's prosecution. Chapter 2 continues on the documentation of Habré's criminal regime. As Habré's successor, Idriss Déby began his rule in 1990 by empaneling a truth commission to document Habré's crimes in Chad. The president of this truth commission, Judge Abakar Mahamat Hassan, writes about the challenges of working for the new regime to discredit the old, as well the Commission's findings and their impact on the future prosecutions for Habré-era crimes in Chad and Senegal.

Chapter 3 then takes us into prisons where Habré's victims themselves had started their own process of documentation. Souleymane Guengueng had been detained and tortured by the DDS. While imprisoned, he began quietly documenting the torture and death of his fellow prisoners in order to build a dossier for later prosecution. In his chapter, Guengueng discusses how he emerged from Habré's jails to organize a victim movement that ultimately led to the conviction of his jailor. Guengueng was aided in the pursuit of justice by Reed Brody of HRW. Brody was the public face of the Habré trial in the Anglophone world. Working with Chadian victims' groups, Brody used the power of HRW's international brand to galvanize international awareness of Habré's victims. In Chapter 4, Brody discusses HRW's strategy, challenges, the role played by civil society, and the strokes of fate that accompanied the twenty-year effort to bring Hissène Habré to trial.

Those legal efforts initiated fledgling prosecutions in Dakar and Belgium along the way. Chapter 5 explores the first cases in Dakar. Hélène Cissé, Habré's defense attorney in 2001, discusses her role as a positivist defense lawyer operating in a politicized prosecutorial environment, giving a singular account of the little-known early cases against Habré. Chapter 6 then takes us to Belgium, which initiated pursuit of Habré under universal jurisdiction laws, with a glimpse of Belgian investigative judge Daniel Fransen's testimony before the EAC.

Finally, the section ends with Habré himself. Chapter 7 presents Habré's own thoughts on his regime and his threatened extradition, excerpted from his 2011 interview with Senegalese reporters from *La Gazette*. It is the last—and perhaps only—interview Habré gave on these matters.

SECTION I

EARLY PROSECUTION ATTEMPTS (1999–2012)

1

The 'Archives of Terror'

Olivier Bercault, Human Rights Watch[1]

Olivier Bercault was a researcher for Human Rights Watch when, in 2001, the archives of Hissène Habré's political police, the 'DDS', were recovered in N'Djamena. This was one year after the filing of the first criminal complaints against the former dictator of Chad by his victims. Hundreds of documents which were used by the 1992 Chadian Truth Commission and lost for almost a decade were accidentally retrieved. This chapter is based on these archives and aims at taking a closer look at their content.

N'Djamena, Chad, May 2001: A crew of Swiss documentarians[2] is filming former political prisoners of Hissène Habré's regime, who are recounting the horrific conditions they suffered in 'La Piscine' (the swimming pool), a prison set up by Habré. This pool, formerly used by families of French soldiers during the colonial period, had been covered by a concrete slab and turned into a jail. For many Chadians, 'La Piscine' had come to symbolize the terror of the Habré era.[3] Two HRW researchers, Reed Brody and the author of this chapter, were helping the filmmakers navigate through N'Djamena and its maze of bureaucratic bodies. In this context, a visit to 'La Piscine', which was next to the abandoned headquarters of Hissène Habré's former political police, the dreaded Documentation and Security Directorate (DDS), was organized. While there, the researchers decided to explore the abandoned building as well.

No one had entered the building in years and to their astonishment, the HRW researchers discovered thousands and thousands of documents, scattered on the floor across several rooms and covered with a thick layer of dust. These were the lost archives of the DDS: hundreds of interrogation reports of opponents or mere citizens suspected of illegal activities, death certificates, intelligence reports, surveillance reports, notes and briefs addressed to the president, propaganda posters, International Committee for the Red Cross (ICRC) memos,[4] thousands of Amnesty International postcards and lists, so many lists. These were lists of political prisoners, prisoners of war, deaths in detention, DDS agents, promotions or nominations within the DDS. Working together, a team of HRW researchers and Habré's victims copied—with an old and heavy photocopier—hundreds of DDS documents in the

1 The author wishes to thank Tristan Burger at USF for her precious comments on earlier drafts.
2 Pierre Hazan, author of Chapter 40 in this book, was one of the documentarians.
3 Olivier Bercault, *The Plain of the Dead* (Human Rights Watch, 2013).
4 The ICRC visits prisons and provides confidential reports on their conditions to national authorities; these reports were useful later at trial to demonstrate that Habré was informed about the deplorable conditions in his prisons.

Olivier Bercaul, *The 'Archives of Terror'* In: *The President on Trial*. First edition. Edited by: Sharon Weill, Kim Thuy Seelinger, and Kerstin Bree Carlson, Oxford University Press (2020). © Olivier Bercault. DOI: 10.1093/oso/9780198858621.003.0002

dusty and dark basement of the DDS headquarters. The conditions were difficult, power on and off, and the heat hardly bearable in May and June. The author of this chapter then carried the photocopies out of Chad in two big bags. It was a few days after 11 September 2001, and airport security was heightened. Former DDS officials still working for the Chadian administration were not particularly pleased with HRW's work on the Habré case in general and our scrutiny of the DDS archives in particular.

It was a trove of evidence that would prove critical in Habré's eventual prosecution. Once the documents reached HRW New York headquarter, Reed Brody's team, with the assistance of the Human Rights Data Analysis Group meticulously analysed the content of the DDS archives.[5] These documents helped to establish the crimes described by hundreds of witnesses and victims of Habré's government through lengthy interviews and the responsibility of Hissène Habré.

The DDS: Habré's instrument of terror

A few months after coming to power, through a presidential order,[6] Hissène Habré set up the DDS. According to the order, the DDS is 'directly subordinated to the Presidency of the Republic due to the confidential nature of its activities', bypassing traditional governmental security ministries and agencies in Chad. Throughout his regime, the DDS was almost exclusively run by members of Habré's family or inner circle or his own ethnic group, the Anakaza.[7]

While originally created to gather information on threats to national security,[8] in particular activities related to Libya, the DDS soon became an extensive network of local cells for monitoring and suppressing any opposition. A sophisticated reporting system kept Habré directly informed on a daily basis.[9] As early as 1983, the DDS opened sub-offices all over Chadian territory. These branches worked independently from one another and reported directly to the DDS headquarters in N'Djamena. A DDS document dated 16 December 1985 entitled '*Listed names of staff serving in the provinces*'[10] mentions the names of 127 DDS agents spread out in all twenty-two Chadian provinces. Another document dated 20 July 1987 cites twenty-five local DDS cells in the same twenty-two Chadian provinces.

[5] See Reed Brody, this volume, Chapter 4.

[6] Order 005/PR dated 26 January 1983—DDS Archives.

[7] Hissène Habré belongs to the Anakaza, part of the Daza ethnic group, sub-group of the larger Toubou group. The Daza are called pejoratively 'Gorane' by the Arab population in Chad. Hissène Habré was almost exclusively referred as a Gorane Anakaza over the years. See Samuel Decalo, *Historical Dictionary of Chad* (1997).

[8] The Order gives the aims as: 'the collection and centralization of all the information [...] likely to compromise the national interest' and 'the cooperation in suppression by creating files of certain individuals, groups and communities suspected of activities contrary or only detrimental to the national interest'. Order 005/PR dated 26 January 1983—DDS Archives.

[9] A directive from the DDS director dated 26 August 1987 explained that 'thanks to the web of information that connected the entire national territory' the DDS became 'the eyes and ears of the President' and the 'nervous system of the state'. Directive 502/PR/DDS/87—DDS Archives. Furthermore, a chart retrieved in the DDS archives shows that Habré was at the helm of the DDS organigram.

[10] Some DDS documents on file with the author do not have a reference or the reference is erased or unreadable. In this case, the footnote will mention: 'DDS Document on file with the author; reference missing, erased, or unreadable—DDS Archives.'

Arbitrary arrests of suspected political opponents were widespread. They were brought immediately to the DDS office for interrogation, where a file was created for each suspect.[11] An 11 January 1986 report related to the arrest and death of a political opponent mentions that Habré himself ordered the arrest: 'The suspect was not heard and was arrested on the orders of the President of the Republic.'[12]

Membership of an ethnic group was also sufficient grounds for arrest. For example, many documents found in the DDS archives established the fact that in 1989 the Zaghawa[13] were targeted and arrested based on their ethnicity.[14]

Systematic use of torture

The DDS had an armed wing, the Special Rapid Action Brigade ('BSIR'),[15] which carried out arrests, torture, and executions and monitored DDS detention centres. Interviews of former political prisoners and DDS documents showed that prisoners were, in the vast majority of cases, systematically tortured. For example, a memo relating to an interrogation mentions in the last paragraph: 'In forcing him to reveal certain truths, he died on October 14, 1984 at 8 am.'[16] Another interrogation report notes that the prisoner 'admitted the facts alleged against him only after a physical beating'.[17] Nearing the fall of his regime, a 1989 report addressed to Habré exposed the frustration of the DDS torturers: 'In the tough interrogations they faced, the detainees unanimously showed unwillingness and dishonesty.'[18]

Inhuman detention conditions

DDS prisoners were subjected to horrendous conditions of detention. Dozens were jammed into cells measuring just a few square metres, including during the unbearable heat of summer. Prisoners suffered from severe dietary deficiencies, lack of medical service and physical activity, as well as insects. Jailers would often wait until several people had died before clearing the decaying corpses out of the cells. Due to these conditions, the daily deaths of detainees were considerable.[19]

[11] A DDS internal memo dated 6 January 1989 instructed that 'Anyone arrested or even called to testify must be identified and have an individual information record.' DDS document on file with the author; reference missing, erased, or unreadable—DDS Archives.

[12] Report 110/PR/DDS/86—DDS Archives.

[13] Sometimes spelled Zakawa in DDS documents.

[14] For instance, memo 114/PR/DDS/SP/89 titled 'Current situation of Zakawa suspects arrested in N'Djamena . . .', dated 26 April 1989—DDS Archives. For instance, memo titled 'Current situation of Zakawa traitors arrested for complicity detained on our premises . . .', dated 26 May 1989—DDS Document on file with the author; reference missing, erased, or unreadable—DDS Archives.

[15] BSIR, French acronym for Brigade Spéciale d'Intervention Rapide.

[16] Memo 84/DDS/BSIR/84 addressed to the DDS director by the BSIR commanding officer, dated 15 October 1984—DDS Archives.

[17] Interrogation report dated 30 August 1986 of Al Hadj Issa Mahamat Youssouf—DDS Document on file with the author; reference missing, erased, or unreadable—DDS Archives. Similarly, a DDS intelligence report dated 9 May 1984 addressed to Habré relates the death of an employee of an international public institution who 'met death as a result of torture in a village called Petit Kordo . . . on April 11, 1984. The attack was perpetrated by a military group of FANT soldiers . . .' Intelligence Report 275/INT-SEC/SUR/RG/84—DDS Archives.

[18] Memo 9 April 1989—DDS Archives.

[19] Olivier Bercault, *The Plain of the Dead* (HRW 2013).

One such incident occurred in 1985, when twenty-four prisoners suffocated to death in an overcrowded cell at the Military Police Brigade in Doba:

> the day of their transfer, they were crammed into a cell measuring 2.38m by 1.87m (with a surface area of 4,4506 m2) with other prisoners. With a headcount of 32 prisoners altogether, the living space for each prisoner measures at 4.4506/32 = 0.14 m2. Consequently, the collective cause of death recorded on June 21, around midnight is suffocation.[20]

Similarly, in his monthly June 1987 report 'regarding the situation of political detainees and prisoners of war on our various premises', the director of DDS penitentiaries wrote: 'Our inmates suffer from conditions [. . .] such as paralysis of the limbs [. . .] amoebic and bacillary dysentery. All of the aforementioned diseases are due to the prisoners' lack of balanced diets.'[21] In his January 1988 report, he states that fourteen out of the 209 registered political prisoners 'died as a result of illness'.[22] Medical doctors working with the DDS scrupulously registered the deaths in detention and the DDS kept the records. The DDS archives contained death certificates for hundreds of prisoners.[23]

The treatment of captured combatants

The treatment of prisoners of war (POWs) was no different. Habré's war with armed northern Chadian opposition groups started in 1983. This included war against Goukouni's GUNT, who were allied with Libyan forces. Over the months, Habré's forces captured hundreds of opposition combatants in Northern Chad and transferred these POWs to DDS-controlled detention centres in N'Djamena.[24] The conditions were as horrendous as for political prisoners.

In March 1984, Habré reluctantly authorized a rare visit of the ICRC to the DDS-run prison of N'Djamena where POWs were detained. The ICRC addressed the overpopulation in the cells, where 660 POWs each had only half a square metre, in a prison that could only accommodate 180 inmates. The ICRC described how conditions in the prison were 'alarming', that malnutrition was widespread, medical care absent, and hygiene nonexistent. 'The toilets are out of order and human excrement contaminates the main courtyard. Prisoners do not have soap.'[25] The ICRC conclusions were unambiguous:

[20] Report from a governmental mission on the political-military situation in the southern administrative regions of Oriental Logone and Tandjilé, 003/DG/PLOR/85, dated 21 July 1985—DDS Archives.

[21] Report 006/PR/DDS/S.P./87—DDS Archives.

[22] DDS Document on file with the author; reference missing, erased, or unreadable—DDS Archives.

[23] A DDS list of Zaghawa prisoners' 'current situation of April 1st fighters who died as a result of illness on our premises', dated 20 December 1989, shows that fourteen prisoners arrested in April 1989 died the very same month. Memo 324/PR/DDS/SP/89—DDS Archives. Another striking report dated 17 June 1985 from the DDS supervisor informed that 'From 1 May to 16 June 1985, 19 detainees died on the premises of the Special Rapid Intervention Brigade' and that 'no treatment was given to the detainees because, for three months, the service station of the BSIR was without medicine'. Report 36/PR/DDS/85—DDS Archives.

[24] A 15 August 1984 DDS document, for instance, 'List of Chadian prisoners of war in detention at the N'Djamena Prison' mentions 530 numbered POWs. DDS Document on file with the author; reference missing, erased, or unreadable—DDS Archives.

[25] ICRC findings and assessments following the visit were reported in a working paper dated 31 March 1984 and addressed to the Director of the DDS as an attachment in a 6 April 1984 ICRC official letter. These materials were retrieved in the DDS archives. ICRC Working Paper—31 March 1984—DDS Archives.

> The combination of these factors has caused a serious situation with regard to the health of prisoners. More than half of them must be classified as gravely ill; 160 prisoners are in very serious condition, 22 have been pulled aside and left for dead and 28 deaths have been reported for the previous two months.[26]

The ICRC's mission had impact. For example, the DDS archives revealed two October 1984 letters written by the Minister of National Defense, one to Hissène Habré directly and the second one copied to him authorizing the transfer of sick POWs to the hospital in response to the ICRC. In both cases, added handwritten notes contested the transfer. On one, the note read: 'From now on no prisoner of war will leave the prison, except in case of death. Because, the ICRC has caused many prisoners of war to flee.'[27] On the second letter, the handwritten note read: 'No, there is no question that due to the Red Cross, many prisoners of war have already fled.'[28] As was established by testimony during Hissène Habré's trial, these handwritten notes were penned by Hissène Habré.

Crimes and massacres in Southern Chad

A few months after Habré came to power, he decided to regain control of the south of Chad. As early as 1983, Habré's forces began committing numerous atrocities. These included targeting the civilian population indiscriminately as well as members of urban elites suspected of complicity with armed opposition groups called 'Codos' that had emerged to counter the violence.[29]

A classified secret administrative memo addressed to Habré informed him of the destruction of the Southern Chad village of Bekor by Chadian armed forces: 'On August 29, 1983, the security forces arrived in Bekor and killed six villagers, including the village chief. Panicked, the civilians dispersed. Many have tried to cross the Logone and drowned. The village would be burned by security forces.'[30]

A 1985 document regarding '... the list of the dead and wounded villagers from DJOLA II and III massacred on Sunday, July 28, 1985 by the Government Forces coming towards the direction of Koumra' gives the names of sixty-eight civilians killed and ten civilians injured.[31] An earlier report from the DDS director to Habré dated 16 February 1985[32] informs that:

> On January 18, 1985, in the northern part of Doba, members of the Mobile Platoon based in Koutoutou, Kara County, kidnapped and killed 14 (fourteen) adolescents in Bedjal in Nassian County and wounded 1 (one) on the head... On January 22, 1985 in Koutoutou in

[26] ibid.

[27] Letter from the Minister of National Defense of Chad to the President of the Republic of Chad, dated 29 October 1984. Letter 312/MDPR/DNACVG/CAB/84—DDS Archives.

[28] Letter from the Minister of National Defense of Chad to the Minister of Foreign Affairs of Chad, copied to the President of the Republic of Chad, dated 29 October 1984. Letter 311/MDPR/DNACVG/CAB/84—DDS Archives.

[29] Olivier Bercault, *The Plain of the Dead* (HRW 2013).

[30] Memo 405/INT/SEC/SUR/RG/83, dated 29 August 1983 from the Director of the Sûreté Nationale—DDS Archives.

[31] Document joined to memo 271/SPMLA/85, dated 10 August 1985.

[32] Report 141/PR/DDS/85—DDS Archives.

> the Kara region where the cotton markets were taking place, 2 (two) ONDR staff including 1 (one) Director of Markets and 1 (one) Productivity Collector were abducted and killed by FANT members in collusion with the Kara County Chief.

Another June 1985 BSIR report notes 'Some members of the BSIR patrolling through the night, apprehended six (6) Codos ... These Codos were killed about 3 kilometres from the village.' The same document bluntly recounts another incident: 'The patrol brought back a person to take information, but he says he did not know anything about the Codos situation. He was executed.'[33]

The United States' support of Hissène Habré

From the years prior to his access to power, the United States considered Habré a bulwark against Gaddafi's growing influence and expansionism and it provided support to Habré in training DDS agents and officers. For example, one document refers to 'The DDS American Counsel Mr. Maurice.'[34] Another document references the 'very special' training of twelve Chadian government security officers, including four DDS agents and two Presidential Security officers in the United States. The participants arrived in Washington, DC, on 6 February 1985 and said that 'After four days in this city, we were taken to a training centre about 400 kilometres southwest of Washington, where we received very special training.' According to the document, the training lasted until 15 March 1985 and focused on matters related to bombs and explosives used by 'terrorists'.[35]

The DDS archives and the case against Hissène Habré

The victims of Hissène Habré's regime started a criminal case against their former dictator in 1999–2000 based on hundreds of detailed testimonies, data gathered by the victims' organizations and the conclusions of the 1992 Chadian Truth Commission. Over the years, more than 300 interviews with victims, witnesses, and former DDS agents were conducted by HRW, together with Chadian nongovernmental and victims' organizations.

The recovery of the DDS archives proved to be decisive for the case. Copies of hundreds of files from the DDS archives were entered into a database and analysed by the Human Rights Data Analysis Group, a California-based organization that applies statistics to the analysis of human rights violations. These files alone contain the names of 1,208 persons who were killed or died in detention, and 12,321 victims of torture, arbitrary detention, or other human rights violations.[36] Later, these archives corroborated the statements made in

[33] Report 90/DDS/BSIR/DTOPS/85, dated 27 June 1985—DDS Archives.

[34] Letter 069/PR/DDS/86, dated 10 September 1986 from the Head of the DDS airport security service to the DDS Director—DDS Archives.

[35] Memo 001/4./DDS/85, dated 25 March 1985—DDS Archives.

[36] Human Rights Data Analysis Group, Benetech, *State Violence in Chad: A Statistical Analysis of Reported Prison Mortality in Chad's DDS Prisons and Command Responsibility of Hissène Habré, 1982–1990* (2010). See: https://www.hrdag.org/content/chad/State-Violence-in-Chad.pdf

court and shed new light on the scale, pattern, and systematic organization of Habré's political police and 'machine of repression'.

The archives also helped to establish Hissène Habré's personal criminal responsibility. The DDS was directly subordinated to Habré who was in total control over its structure and agents.[37] The DDS became 'the eyes and ears of the President'.[38] Hundreds of DDS documents show that Habré was constantly kept informed of what was happening throughout Chad. In certain cases, the DDS appears to have informed Habré of the capture of particular combatants and the circumstances of their detention.[39]

In addition to being decisive in condemning Habré, the DDS archives also combat the silence and anonymity that too often are the hallmarks of authoritarian regimes. The memory of Rose Lokissim, an exceptional woman who was an elite soldier, as well as a political opponent and later prisoner of Hissène Habré, exemplifies this combat. Imprisoned in 1984 and knowing the risks, Rose arranged for information about detainees to be transmitted to the outside world. One day in 1986, she was denounced and interrogated one final time by the DDS. In the written report of Rose's interrogation, DDS agents transcribed this following statement: 'She affirms that, even if she has to die in the dungeon she has no regret because Chad will thank her one day and history will speak of her.'[40] Rose was executed the same day.

The logic of authoritarian violence holds that no-one should ever have heard from Rose again. The recovery of the DDS archives defeated this tragic outcome and fulfilled Rose's prophecy.

[37] Order 005/PR dated 26 January 1983—DDS Archives.
[38] Directive 502/PR/DDS/87, dated 26 August 1987—DDS Archives.
[39] Olivier Bercault, *The Plain of the Dead* (HRW 2013).
[40] Interrogation Report 162/PR/DDS/86 dated 15 May 1986—DDS Archives.

2
The Making of Chad's Truth Commission

Judge Mahamat Hassan Abakar, President of the Chadian Truth Commission

---

Mahamat Hassan Abakar was president of the commission of inquiry into the crimes committed by the regime of the former president Hissène Habré. His role was to direct, coordinate, and supervise the investigations through to the conclusions of the commission. In order to master the investigations and the facts, he was also directly involved in the research work and the collection of evidence. For instance, he personally directed the exhumations of mass graves and the localization of sites of summary executions, in addition to holding hearings judged by the commission to be of particular importance, such as those of Habré's former ministers, of torturers and executioners, and also of the survivors of mass killings.

After studying private law at Damascus University in Syria (1975–1980), he continued his higher education in France. Mr Abakar served as public prosecutor, president of the N'Djamena Court, counsel at the Court of Appeals, and finally as First Deputy General Prosecutor. His qualification as a magistrate led him to be mandated to the commission of inquiry.

The commission of inquiry into the crimes committed by the ex-president, his collaborators, and/or accomplices was established in Chad by decree number 014 on 29 December 1990, barely a month after the new authorities, led by President Idriss Déby, had taken power. This was a primary objective for the governing team; to shine a light on Habré's crimes was also the wish of all Chadians. Déby sought to take advantage of the creation of the commission during the 1996 presidential elections, when he announced to the various populations: 'I saved you from a dictatorship that had 40,000 victims, Habré's dictatorship.' That was his preferred leitmotiv during the campaign.

The mandate of the commission was to execute two essential but distinct missions. The first concerned crimes committed against persons. The mandate indicated to investigate allegations of kidnappings, detentions, assassinations, disappearances, torture and barbarous acts, inhuman treatment, other violations of physical or moral integrity, and all human rights violations and trafficking in illegal substances. The second mission concerned crimes against property. In order to wage war against Gaddafi of Libya, Habré's sworn enemy, Habré had required that all Chadians contribute to the war effort, either in cash or in kind (cattle, camels, etc.). The amount was set arbitrarily according to the mood of the collector. Afterwards it was necessary to verify the financial operations and bank accounts of the ex-president, his collaborators, and/or his accomplices.

The first team of the commission was comprised of twelve people: two magistrates, five police officers, a representative of the Ministry of Finance, two archivists, and two

Mahamat Hassan Abakar, *The Making of Chad's Truth Commission* In: *The President on Trial*. First edition. Edited by: Sharon Weill, Kim Thuy Seelinger, and Kerstin Bree Carlson, Oxford University Press (2020).
DOI: 10.1093/oso/9780198858621.003.0003

administrative clerks. We had six months in total to complete the report and to submit it to the authorities. It was practically impossible, however, to produce a reliable report in that short a period, for several reasons.

First, we searched in vain for a building to house the commission of inquiry, and we had to install the commission in the former headquarters of the political police (DDS). We were well aware of how unpleasant this could be for the victims or their immediate families, but we had no choice. Still, the building in question was a complete ruin. It had been pillaged and vandalized like all the public buildings of the period. No doors, no windows, no desks, no chairs. Files and papers littered the floor. More documentation was outside in the courtyard of the building. So, it took more than two months to refurbish and furnish the police headquarters that had become the seat of the commission.

When the commission began the hearings, I quickly noticed that my investigators, especially the police, were dragging their heels, and were unmotivated by either the importance of the work or by its scope. They would only spend two to three hours at the commission and then they would return to their own regular services. My remarks on their behaviour went unheard. They did not obey. I had to wait patiently until the six months authorized were up. I did, however, take advantage of this time to choose my future colleagues, both police officers and magistrates, most scrupulously.

After the first six-month period, then, I had reinforced and reconfigured almost the totality of my team with more motivated and devoted members. The Minister of Justice at the time, who is also a judicial colleague from my own graduating class, gave his full support to my attempt to revitalize the commission. Thus the commission's mandate was extended for four months as of 29 July 1991. The new team went from twelve to sixteen people: three magistrates, six police officers, three representatives of the Ministry of Finance, two archivists, and two administrative clerks. It is thanks to this second team, more motivated and devoted, that the work could be finally accomplished.

The course of the investigation and the collection of testimony

During the course of its work, the commission had to meet, and overcome, many obstacles and challenges. Yet the immensity of the task and the size of the national territory, 1,284,000 square kilometres, left me perplexed. How was I to undertake this work? Should I start with the provinces or N'Djamena, the capital? Were there particular methods to use in the case of mass crimes? In all humility and despite my judicial experience, I felt the need for a reference, a model to inspire me. My friends from Amnesty International, Michael Dottridge and Jamal Ben Oumar, who were then visiting N'Djamena, convinced me that there simply were no references at the time that they could put at my disposal. And so I had to rely on the sum of my personal and professional experience to conduct the work.

Hearings with the victims and their families began, but people were not lining up to be heard by the commission. They were afraid. That was understandable for a number of reasons. It was the first time in Chad, in fact in Africa, that a national commission of inquiry had been created to shed light on the crimes of an overthrown head of state. This act was very unusual. Chadians, and in fact Africans, are used to the total impunity of those who govern them. Thus people were suspicious. Some victims and their families thought that the goal of the commission was to identify victims and escapees just so that they could be eliminated. In addition, Chad in the 1980s and 1990s was marked by a period of chronic political instability. Who could guarantee that Habré wouldn't rise to power again as he had in 1982? In 1991, just one year after Habré's fall, his armed supporters who had taken refuge in the region of Lake Chad very nearly took power in N'Djamena. These were therefore perfectly legitimate fears.

Nonetheless, the first victims to face up to their fears and doubts who met with members of the commission left reassured and confident. They in turn encouraged and reassured their entourage and their former prison comrades. Even more, they very efficiently brought attention to the commission by word of mouth.

The physical and emotional state of those former political prisoners haunted me. They had lost everything after their arrest. The government of Chad hadn't thought to provide them with either a maintenance allowance or even medical care; they were simply left to their own devices. I feverishly looked for some organization that might help them and relieve some of their suffering. At the suggestion of my Amnesty International friends, we got in touch with a French association called AVRE, headed by Dr Hélène Jaffe, a specialist in the care of former political prisoners. Dr Jaffe responded immediately, and returned regularly with her teams to consult, treat, and provide medicines. Our victims hadn't expected this manna that fell from heaven. Not one had to spend as much as a penny on health care. With this satisfaction, prior suspicions and doubts about the commission melted away, and confidence and admiration took their place. Thanks to this initiative, victims streamed forward and were lining up in the streets.

The executioners, torturers, and informers were heard last. In the beginning, they refused to respond to our summons. Most of them had been rehired by the new authorities in the security apparatus. Having thought themselves definitively rehabilitated, they could not understand on what grounds the commission had asked them to come and answer for their actions. I myself couldn't imagine writing a report that didn't include a chapter on the role of those who had committed the acts. Therefore, I had to see the head of state, Idriss Déby, directly. I explained to him that the former executioners, whom he had so precipitously rehabilitated, were now refusing to come forward to the commission to be questioned—yet, the commission would not be able to conclude its investigations without hearing their statements.

I met Déby several times during the commission's investigation. Each time that I had problems with the commission's functioning that the general administration struggled to resolve, I would go to see him to have the situation unblocked. This was the case when we needed all-terrain transportation to crisscross the country; he unblocked a small budget for me, 4,800,000 CFA, for the commission's overheads. He also made the executioners come to give statements.

President Déby was impatient to receive my report. He thought that the commission had fallen behind on the filing of its report and that the power struggle with the former executioners could only slow things down. Déby reassured me that he would order their director to have them give testimony. And that is how we forced the former executioners to testify. We even attempted at one point to have the victims confront their torturers, but we quickly abandoned that: the power relationship between the two swung heavily to the side of the rehabilitated executioners and we were dangerously exposing victims, whom we did not have the means to protect.

Reuse of 'La Piscine' as a prison

On 13 October 1991, a bloody wave of persecution was unleashed against the members of the Hadjaraye community in N'Djamena by the clan of the sitting president, Déby. The Hadjaraye were hunted, arrested, and tortured; some were killed while others fled. The Hadjaraye had been accused of wanting to overthrow President Déby and take power. The truth was however quite different. The Hadjaraye and the Zaghawa had been allies in the resistance to Habré and had joined forces to eject him. Once they were in control, the cake was cut into two pieces: Déby, as representative of the Zaghawa, was given the presidency of the Republic and Maldoum Bada Abbas, representative of the Hadjaraye, became vice president. Even if this division seems reasonable, the Zaghawa were not satisfied. They wanted all the power for themselves. And that is what motivated the repression of the Hadjaraye that removed them from power.

This situation forced the members of the commission, and in fact the administration itself, to stop work for a week. When we resumed work on 21 October 1991, we discovered that 'La Piscine', which had seen so many tortured or killed under Habré, had been put to that use once again during the repression. The members of the commission immediately decided to suspend their work until that horrible prison had been emptied of its occupants. To that end I wrote a long letter to President Déby in which I expressed our indignation and our determination not to resume work until after the space had been evacuated. Fortunately our demands were met; otherwise, I personally would have thrown in the towel.

Results

The commission worked fifteen months and our harvest was more than satisfying: in addition to N'Djamena, we crisscrossed the major cities of the provinces like Ati, Abéché in the centre, Am Timan, Sarh, Moundou, Doba, and the Tandjile region in the south. We lacked, however, the time to visit the far north of the country, which suffered atrociously.

The commission heard a total of 1,726 people: 662 former political prisoners or prisoners of conscience, 786 close relatives of victims who died in detention or were executed, 236 former prisoners of war, thirty former agents of the DDS, and twelve former senior government officials in the Habré regime, including the former Minister of the Interior Djimet Togou.

In addition, we collected exceptional documentation, exceptional both in quantity and quality, that had been abandoned by the fallen regime and that was used effectively by the commission. Because of all that data we were able to affirm to both national and international opinion that the crimes committed by the Habré regime were not fabrications but had actually taken place.

The number of detainees recorded, dead or freed, totalled 54,000 people. The number of dead recorded by name was 3,780. However, the committee estimated that there were more than 40,000 dead. This is how we reached that number. If we have a quick and macabre calculation of five dead per day per prison (for the six prisons reviewed), that gives a total of thirty deaths per day. The commission found that number excessive and arbitrarily brought it down to thirteen per day for the six prisons. Habré ruled for 2,920 days (eight years), times the number retained per day of thirteen, which gives 37,960 victims. The commission rounded that figure up to 40,000 to take into account deaths by physical exhaustion and summary executions perpetrated in the provinces.[1]

We located and exhumed mass graves as well as sites of open-air executions; arrests had been made arbitrarily every day, for no reason at all or for reasons that had nothing to do with state security. Torture was systematic, whether the person confessed or not. Thanks to victim testimony, the commission depicted through drawings the different forms and scenes of torture practiced in the various detention centres. The social consequences of this repression were equally disastrous. The commission estimated that more than 80,000 children were orphaned, 30,000 women widowed, and 200,000 people deprived of emotional and physical support. Add to that the goods and buildings pillaged and confiscated from peaceful citizens, estimated at a billion francs CFA each year.

Recommendations in the report

As our concern was to protect the population from a second apocalypse, we sought to formulate pertinent recommendations for present and future Chadian leaders. We therefore developed a list of recommendations to keep Chad from falling again into appalling catastrophe, but especially to create an insurmountable barrier against dictatorship and against all forms of barbarity.

Our list had fourteen recommendations, but I will mention just the principal ones here:

1. The establishment of a true democracy and an independent and sovereign judiciary;
2. The immediate creation of a National Commission on Human Rights that would have as its mission to protect and promote fundamental rights;
3. That the authorities should without further delay engage criminal proceeding against those who committed those horrible crimes against humanity;
4. The creation of a monument to the victims;
5. The transformation of the former headquarters of the DDS and its underground prison into a museum to prevent the somber reign of Habré from being forgotten;
6. That upon publication of the report, all former agents of the DDS (political police) who had been rehabilitated by the new security apparatus be removed from their functions;
7. The suppression of detention centers not established by the law;
8. The introduction and teaching of human rights in high schools, universities, and in police and military academies.

Unfortunately, Habré's successors acted on none of these recommendations, which were simply filed away. Déby is a disciple of Habré's. He took power not for the good of the Chadian people, but to be able to enjoy the privileges and abuses of power along the lines of Bokassa of the Central African Republic or Idi Amin of Uganda.

[1] Mahamat Abakar, *Chronique d'une enquête criminelle nationale. Le cas du régime de Habré 1982–1990* (l'Harmattan 2006).

Publication of the report and its impact

Once the report was written and completed, we were preparing to submit it to our mandator, the government. However, my friend Jamal Ben Oumar, formerly a researcher for Amnesty International before he became director of the Carter Center for Human Rights in Atlanta, was following the advancement of our work. One evening he asked how far along we were, and I told him that the report was done and that all that was left was to hand it in to the authorities. Jamal was surprised by my answer. He thought that turning it over to the Chadian authorities without it first being published and circulated would be highly prejudicial to the victims and to the people. As he pointed out, there was no guarantee that the government would release it. I answered that the commission's mandate was entirely silent on the subject. Jamal's remark did nonetheless shake me out of my torpor and underline the importance of taking such steps. I decided that, if publishing and circulating the report was in the best interest of the public, then I would do it. At that instance, I resolved to publish and circulate it widely. I shared this resolution with no one, not the other members of the commission or the Minister of Justice, under whom we worked. I simply acted as if doing so was a part of our mandate.

I was afraid that if I shared my decision to publish with senior officials, there was a real risk that they would object to its publication and circulation. African officials are changeable. Today I have no regrets for my action and in fact am rather proud of it. And time has proven me right. The report was published along with the lists of all the personnel of the DDS, officials, agents, and simple informers. Among the agents were two journalists who were quite well-known in N'Djamena. They were humiliated and brought down.

For the people, the publication and circulation of the report was an exceptional event that marked them profoundly. We had quite simply transformed the headquarters of the commission into a museum of horror and barbarity. All the photos we had taken during the investigation were presented on the walls of our building: the exhuming of the mass graves, the scars from torture on the bodies of some detainees, the drawings showing how certain forms of torture were carried out, the lists of officials and agents of the political police, etc., and of course the commission's film. Not only did we photograph our every act, but we ended up with a forty-five-minute film.

The significance of the commission of enquiry

For myself, I feel that I accomplished my mission freely and with integrity. I think that it would be difficult to condemn Habré without the commission's report. All of the indictments connected with this affair, be they in Dakar, Brussels, or N'Djamena, were based on the commission's report and its victim testimony.

In Chad, the lawyers for the victims had requested my intervention as the president of the commission as a witness in the case. I asked the president of the criminal court to show the commission's film before my deposition, which the court accepted. Reed Brody, who was present at the trial, told me after the hearing that the film and my testimony had completely turned things around.[2]

During the trial of Habré in Dakar, the coordinator of Habré's legal team, Mr Mounir Ballal, said in his closing statement that 'the report produced by Mr Mahamat Hassan Abakar is the cornerstone of all these accusations', and then went on to use that statement to try and discredit it, calling it a tissue of lies. He was unsuccessful.[3]

President Déby, who had ordered the report of the commission and who supported the prosecution of Habré, suddenly refused all cooperation with the EAC. He was frightened because he had continued to use Habré's brutal and deadly methods. Many observers attribute the 1984 massacres perpetrated in the south of the country to him, when he was the commander-in-chief of the national armed forces under Habré's regime. If Habré was being judged for his crimes, then Déby himself would be caught up with one day. Déby could loudly say that he supported trying Habré and even paid for the EAC, but in reality, he never wanted the trial to happen. Déby dreams of a world of complete impunity, like Habré, where the dictator can slit the throat of his opponents without the slightest fear or worry.

Conclusion

The favourable responses to the Habré trial go far beyond the two countries of Chad and Senegal. The trial is a huge victory over impunity not only in Africa. This unprecedented trial destroyed forever the myth of the untouchable head of state.

Without a doubt, the report of the commission of inquiry brought recognition and respect, both nationally and internationally, to its members. For Chad, I am delighted to have been able to bring this difficult and unprecedented mission to its conclusion. All honour and merit go to the team that supported me, that was up to the task, and that worked in such loyalty. They withstood the psychological and material obstacles strewn in our path. I take as my motto the saying 'when you want, you can'. All we needed was to be moved by the spirit of goodwill, a little courage, and a good dose of perseverance to achieve the goals that we set ourselves.

With the publication of the report, I believed that the new Chadian authorities would usher in a new era of democracy, a state of law, the scrupulous respect of their fellow citizens, and good governance. But alas, nothing has changed. The new authorities have espoused without remorse Habré's odious methods. They didn't believe that the trial would ever happen. But it did. And the same causes produce the same effects. Henceforth our hope is immense, for no Habré, either past or future, will escape justice.

On a personal level, this experience has brought me neither benefits nor privileges—only a very heavy responsibility and a national duty that, I recognize, was an honour. Someone else might continue working with the new regime in the hopes of some form of recompense. I chose instead to distance myself by resigning from the court and opening my own law offices.

[2] For a discussion about the trials in Chad, see Chapter 25 'Prosecutions in Chad' by Henri Thulliez.

[3] See also Mounir Ballal, in this volume, Chapter 14.

3

Documenting Crimes and Organizing Victims in Chad

Souleymane Guengueng, Chadian Victim's Representative and Trial Participant

---

Souleymane Guengueng was born in 1951 in Chad to Christian parents. In 1978, he began working as Executive Secretary of the Lake Chad Basin Commission (CBLT), an interstate organization created to manage the water and natural resources of the Lake Chad Basin. He continued to work for the CBLT until 1988, when he was arrested by the Documentation and Security Directorate (DDS) and detained for two and a half years. In 1991, after his release from prison, Souleymane created the Association for Victims of Crimes and Political Repression in Chad (AVCRP). He returned to work at the CBLT but was dismissed in 2002 due to political pressure related to his activities within the victims' association.

Souleymane, together with other torture survivors and assisted by international NGOs, began filing complaints against Habré in Dakar in 2000. Souleymane and his colleagues worked for decades to bring Habré to justice, eventually participating in the EAC both as a civil party and testifying as a witness.

Now Souleymane lives in New York and is the author of the book 'Prisonnier de Hissène Habré' (Prisoner of Hissène Habré).

Historical background

Civil war broke out in N'Djamena in February 1979 between the Armed Forces of the North (FAN) of Hissène Habré, appointed Prime Minister a few months earlier, and the forces of the President of the Republic, General Félix Malloum. Despite a few moments of peace, the fighting around N'Djamena only truly came to an end with a Libyan intervention against Habré in 1980. The FAN and Habré fled to Sudan but returned to power in N'Djamena in June 1982.

Due to this instability, the management of the Lake Chad Basin Commission (CBLT), where I worked, decided in May 1979 to reduce the number of staff and projects. I was the only Chadian Executive Secretary to remain at CBLT headquarters in N'Djamena until the CBLT made the decision, for security reasons, to move its offices and staff to Maroua, Cameroon. So, from 1980 to 1987 I lived in Maroua.

Souleymane Guengueng, *Documenting Crimes and Organizing Victims in Chad* In: *The President on Trial*. First edition. Edited by: Sharon Weill, Kim Thuy Seelinger, and Kerstin Bree Carlson, Oxford University Press (2020). © Souleymane Guengueng.
DOI: 10.1093/oso/9780198858621.003.0004

In 1982, Hissène Habré's FAN succeeded in defeating the opposition forces of the Government of the National Transitional Union (GUNT). For Chad, this was the beginning of a long period in which war continued throughout the country and the population was subjected to a reign of generalized terror. The ethnic groups that suffered most from the repression were the Saras in the south, the Arabs in the east and centre, the Hajarai in the centre, and the Zagawas in the north-east. But Habré's regime affected all ethnic groups in Chad, including his own, the Goran.

In Cameroon, I was registered as a GUNT supporter and Habré's enemy. The Chadian Documentation and Security Directorate (DDS) asked the President of the Republic of Cameroon to arrest and extradite me for arms trafficking and for supporting the Chadian opposition against Habré. The Cameroonian police conducted investigations for several months and concluded that I was innocent. It was at that moment that I realized I was already threatened by the regime. Nevertheless, my family and I returned to Chad following Habré's announcement of amnesty for CBLT members, thinking that I would not be arrested.

But a year later, in August 1988, I was falsely accused and arrested by the DDS. According to the authorities, my cousin in the military had fled to Cameroon with money from the company Coton Tchad, which he allegedly gave me to recruit people to fight the Habré regime. I told them that I did not recognize these facts. The director of the prison service called me a liar and informed me that I was accused of being the first representative of the opposition in Cameroon.

I was held in several prisons for two and a half years. Huddled together, we prisoners were forced to take turns sleeping, sometimes on the bodies of those who were dying. But the worst thing was the psychological torture. We were forbidden to pray to our God. Our families never knew if we were still alive. Every night, the political police would abduct detainees who never returned. I saw the other prisoners die from starvation, torture, or from other inhuman and degrading treatments. I was released from prison on 1 December 1990, when Idriss Déby's forces arrived and overthrew Habré's regime. When the prison doors opened one after the other, we came out like walking skeletons.

I am convinced that my life was preserved by God to obtain justice in memory of the dead and missing. Together with some of my colleagues, themselves survivors and victims of the former dictator Habré's regime, we decided resolutely on the importance of publicly testifying in court about the cruel acts and injustice perpetrated against us.

Creation of a victims' association

On 4 December 1990, Déby declared to the Chadian nation, 'I bring you neither gold nor silver, but only freedom.' His government immediately established a commission of inquiry to investigate Habré's crimes and appointed Magistrate Mahamat Hassan Abakar as its head.[1] Six months after recovering, when I was better able to walk, the Commission of Inquiry went on the radio in June 1991 to call the victims to a convening so they could receive medical care. As I listened to this communiqué on the radio, I thought it presented an

[1] See also Mahamat Hassan Abakar, in this volume, Chapter 2.

excellent opportunity to meet the other torture survivors and make them aware of my plan to organize in defence of our interests.

The next morning, I took advantage of everyone's presence at the former DDS headquarters to convene an informational meeting and suggest to the victims that we organize ourselves. However, the majority's reaction to this proposal was very violent and accompanied by insults. I was called all sorts of names. But this was undoubtedly due to fear and the fact that some victims thought they would end up back in prison. Many torture survivors were afraid to talk about what they had endured, as they did not know what the future had in store for them. Chad's history has been marked by a succession of brutal despots. Despite all this, a courageous few embraced my idea and we began by setting up a committee, of which I was elected Secretary General.

Mr Abakar informed me at the end of the meeting that for a few days now, the commission of inquiry had not been able to begin its work because the victims refused to sign up on the commission's register, which would allow them to be heard. So, I was the very first to sign up, under number 00001. This broke the fear and allowed other colleagues—all of them former DDS prisoners—to register as well. In order to form a national association, the committee of our association decided to join together with a group of widows and orphans that was still in formation. This alliance led to the creation of a national association called the Association for Victims of Crimes and Political Repression in Chad (AVCRP).

A few weeks later, the statutory texts were adopted and the members of the AVCRP National Office were elected. According to my colleagues, no one would have had the courage to hold the position of President of the association. However, during the deliberations, I had kept silent to avoid making people believe that I wanted to take over the association, simply because I was its main initiator. Nevertheless, when the meeting resumed, I was unanimously appointed President.

The AVCRP was thus created in 1991. Our association had six main objectives:

1. Identify victims of political crimes and repression in Chad;
2. Identify property that has been looted or unfairly confiscated;
3. Initiate national and/or international legal proceedings against the perpetrators of these crimes and political repressions;
4. Demand compensation for victims who were physically or mentally harmed, or whose property had been unjustly expropriated;
5. To inform national and international opinion on the methods and means used to commit crimes and political repression; and
6. To prevent, denounce, and combat by all possible means all forms of political crimes and repression.

Before starting legal proceedings, however, it was essential to identify victims and achieve the first two points on our list, at the very least. Ultimately, we managed to collect more than a thousand individual information sheets on each victim.

For nine years the association had no contact with international human rights organizations. Reed Brody, Human Right Watch's (HRW) 'dictator hunter', learned of our work in

1999. At the time, Brody was looking for 'the next Pinochet', that is, former dictators who could be prosecuted. Thus, from July to December 1999, HRW carried out three missions to Chad. The purpose of these missions was to bring back evidence of the AVCRP's work and to prepare victims to file complaints.[2]

In July 1999, the first mission was led by two students from the Human Rights Program at Harvard Law School, Nicholas Seutin and Geneviève Hernandez. These students were conducting research of interest to HRW under the supervision of Peter Rosenblum. Their purpose, as a result of our meeting, was to bring evidence of the victims' existence back to HRW. The two students assured me that HRW was legitimately interested and that it had the financial means to take legal action. For this reason, I decided to provide photocopies of the individual information sheets of each victim, despite the risk of information being leaked or documents lost. My decision was clear.

The second mission took place in November 1999. HRW had seen the individual files and was convinced that further action was well-founded. HRW sent lawyer Pascal Kambale to determine the witnesses and plaintiffs for the future trial. This mission was conducted in an absolutely discreet and even secret manner.

When Councillor Kambale returned in December for HRW's third mission, an information leak threatened to completely end our work. A pause was therefore needed to avoid the secret police, and Councillor Kambale returned to the United States. We met again the following month in Dakar, where we the victims went to file the first complaint on 25 January 2000 before the Senegalese courts and to officially accuse Habré of torture and crimes against humanity.

The prosecutor's office, which had been consulted in advance by the victims' lawyers, was in favour of prosecution. The evidence and documents submitted to the investigating judge contained detailed information on ninety-seven political killings, 142 cases of torture, 100 'disappearances', and 736 arbitrary arrests; most of these crimes were committed by the DDS. A report on the practice of torture during Habré's time in power, written in 1992 by a French medical team, and the report of the Chadian Commission of Inquiry were also submitted. After hearing the victims, the senior investigating judge in Dakar, Demba Kandji, charged Habré on 3 February 2000 with acts of torture and barbarism and crimes against humanity, and placed him under house arrest.

In January 2000, Abdou Diouf and Abdoulaye Wade, both in the presidential election campaign, promised the victims that they would try Hissène Habré once elected or re-elected President of the Republic of Senegal. But once Abdoulaye Wade was elected President, the opposite ensued. Habré filed an application for annulment that was supported by the Prosecutor's Office.

On 4 July 2000, the Indicting Chamber declared that the Senegalese courts did not have jurisdiction to try crimes committed abroad. The proceedings were cancelled and Habré was released. For political reasons related to the election of the new president, our attempts to prosecute in Senegal failed. In parallel, however, some victims had filed a complaint in Belgium by applying universal jurisdiction. Under international pressure, Senegal agreed to keep Habré on its soil until a fair trial could take place abroad.

[2] See also Reed Brody, in this volume, Chapter 4 and Olivier Bercault, Chapter 1.

After four years of investigation, Habré was indicted in September 2005 by Belgian judge Daniel Fransen, who requested his extradition from Senegal. Belgium had to submit three other extradition requests, each met with inaction.[3] It should be noted that, without Belgium's intervention, Habré would have escaped justice entirely when the Senegalese courts cancelled the proceedings against him in 2001. In this case, Belgium, more than any other State involved, acted in accordance with the objective of the Convention Against Torture, which is 'to make more effective the struggle against torture'.

Met with continued inertia, Belgium ultimately filed a motion against Senegal with the International Court of Justice (ICJ) in February 2009. Belgium asked the Court to rule that Senegal had violated the Convention Against Torture and other rules of international law by refraining from prosecuting or extraditing Hissène Habré. Belgium asked the ICJ to order Senegal to submit the Habré case 'without delay' to its competent judicial authorities for criminal proceedings or, failing that, to extradite Habré to Belgium 'without further delay'.

The ICJ ruled in favour of the victims. Finally, in July 2013, Habré was charged in Dakar before the EAC, a hybrid court set up to prosecute Habré and his accomplices. On 30 May 2016, Hissène Habré was definitively sentenced to life imprisonment by the EAC Trial Chamber in Dakar—a sentence upheld by the President of the EAC Appeals Chamber in Dakar on Thursday, 27 April 2017.

Challenges

During this twenty-seven-year struggle for justice, which I helped launch, I endured all kinds of threats and challenges, a few of which I cite below. My fellow prisoners who survived torture and whom I consulted to create the association treated me like a madman. Within our AVCRP executive board, some colleagues who supported the new regime chose to constantly intimidate me, sometimes by using the name of President Idriss Déby, or sometimes by pointing their guns at me, saying things like, 'How many of them did we kill? One bullet is enough for you ... ' and 'President Déby wants to know why you don't want to do his politics. Did he release you for nothing?' My response: 'Go and remind President Déby of 4 December 1990, when he told the Chadian people, "I bring you neither gold nor silver, but only freedom." ' So I am free and I have chosen to fight for human rights. I do not get mixed up with politics.'

Worse still, the regime used a cousin of mine, a general of the Chadian army, to 'sensitize' (that is, scare) my mother, in order to convince me to abandon attempts to prosecute Habré. My cousin said that this struggle I was undertaking was very dangerous. It would provoke the Zagawa to come and kill my entire family, or even destroy our native village, because of me. Through her Christian faith, my elderly mother did nothing but entrust me to God in her daily prayers until her death in April 2010 in Ere. Finally, though, my resistance supported by my Christian faith led fear to change sides. Some of my attackers ended up calling me a secret American agent, saying, 'You're a CIA agent, that's why you're so hardheaded.'

[3] See also excerpts of Judge Fransen's testimony before the EAC in this volume, Chapter 6.

Gaining victims' trust

For us, the main organizers of the victims, the task of gaining the trust of some victims, torture survivors, and relatives of victims was not easy. The victims were afraid—they worried they may be brought back to prison. Moreover, as president and founder of the association, the path was full of obstacles for me personally. This was because some of my direct collaborators were close to the new regime and were pursuing an agenda that seemingly aimed to co-opt the victims' association and use it for political purposes. The Chadians therefore thought that we, the victims, were trying to hurt them. The fear was so great that no one could step forward to assist us. This fear was due in part to the fact that the former torturers held positions in the government. It was not until the creation of the EAC that the victims began to believe in it and agreed to testify.

Initially, the victims' organizational work was carried out in two stages. The first consisted in getting the victims, their relatives, and their supporters to join the association. The second step involved the most challenging work—the investigative work. For this, we used an 'identification form' instead of an investigation form, because the word 'investigation' was very badly received and considered the work of the police and gendarmerie. So we used the word 'identify' or 'understand the problem' to try to assuage people's fear. Some families were able to understand, but most were very reluctant. Sometimes we would go through intermediaries to obtain certain information, since most only trusted people they knew well.

Hostility of the Chadian Government, personal threats, and fear during the trial

Habré's co-authors held positions of power under Déby's regime, which itself refused to prosecute Déby's predecessor. As a result, our complaint was rejected by the Chadian courts on 26 October 2000. And prior to that, the Presidency had asked us to change the statutes of the AVCRP, in particular the provisions relating to the initiation of legal proceedings against the perpetrators of the crimes under Habré.

In addition to the difficulty of conducting investigations with the victims themselves, I was personally targeted for my activities within the AVCRP because of the fear that prevailed under the new regime. Indeed, my car was confiscated and I was the victim of an attempted kidnapping in November 2004. There was pressure placed on my employer until I was dismissed from the CBLT. The CBLT sent me a letter signed by its Executive Secretary at the time. In the letter, he urged me to abandon my desire to prosecute Habré or else to resign from my position at the CBLT. And since I refused to comply with one or the other of his requests, I was dismissed from my position.

For us victims, filing the initial complaint in Senegal was not easy. From N'Djamena to Dakar, and via the United States of America and France, precautions and discretion were the rule. In Chad, the site where we worked to select the victims and prepare the complaints was carefully chosen. Everything was done in total vigilance. Once a victim's statement of declaration was completed, he or she had to leave the site without contacting the other victims scheduled to appear. Thanks to this vigilance, we managed to avert the detectives from the National Security Agency (NSA) of Chad. All of HRW's missions were a success vis à vis the victims. In Dakar, we adopted this same discretion.

After the first complaint was filed on 25 January 2000 in Dakar and our struggle was finally made public, even at the international level, our supporters began to worry about our safety in Chad. This first complaint also led several diplomats to worry about the fate of the victims once they returned to Chad. The French ambassador was the first diplomat to offer us asylum in France for our security. On behalf of all the victims I represented, I declined the ambassador's offer, saying, 'Your Excellency, thank you but I had already accepted death before filing a complaint against Hissène Habré in Dakar; if Déby chops off my head in Chad once I return, I will die a hero.'

Organizational challenges

In addition to the pressures we endured from the new regime, our work was also complicated by logistical and organizational issues. For example, survivors had difficulty confirming the identity of dead and missing persons from the DDS prisons, even if they had seen them in detention before their death or disappearance. During our investigations, we had to differentiate the false victims from the real ones, and cross out their names from our identification forms. However, we kept their statements and indicated that they were supporting members on the membership form. I therefore prepared two different forms: one for the identification of direct and indirect victims, and one for membership.

We also had the idea of translating the membership form from French to Arabic so that victims who were literate in Arabic could fully understand the information before committing to participate. The information on these forms translated word for word the objectives we had set for ourselves. We had to identify the real victims: on the one hand, direct victims who were survivors of torture and, on the other hand, indirect victims who were the beneficiaries of the dead and missing from the DDS prisons.

Conclusion

As far as I am concerned, the outcome of this trial is of paramount importance. Habré's condemnation means the rejection of impunity and the celebration of the value of man created in God's image. It also means that men are born equal and no man has the right to abuse his neighbour, regardless of his class or rank in society. I also decided to put into practice what my father told me: 'My child, if you are right, don't give in and don't be afraid to die. Those who are afraid to die will all die before you.' My confidence rested in my Christian faith, shared with that of some of my colleagues, and which was our unfailing refuge during this twenty-seven-year struggle. Thus, our everyday motto was from Romans 8:31: 'If God is for us who will be against us?'

In light of the above, my colleagues and I were motivated to take the initiative to organize ourselves into an Association so as to fight for justice. My honour, my dignity, and my worth were restored when I testified before the EAC. No one could imagine that ordinary citizens, like us, could put a former President in jail. The satisfaction was absolute. For me, being able to express myself and testify before Habré was the best remedy, what I needed to heal and be definitively cured of all the harm that the DDS had inflicted on me for two and a half years. My testimony was very moving, to the point of prompting Reed Brody to exclaim: 'It was the happiest day of my life to hear Souleymane's testimony.' The women victims were also very courageous. They defied the taboos of our societies and dared to denounce the sexual violence to which they were subjected. Those who have never lived an experience similar to ours will never understand this feeling—the feeling of regaining one's respect and dignity.

Habré's trial is a precedent that should serve as a lesson for all African heads of state in power. Let them know that they are not above the law and sooner or later they must be held accountable for their actions once they leave power. To the citizens of countries where dictatorship reigns: these peoples must also understand that they were the ones who chose their leaders so that they may serve them, and not destroy them.

Finally, some thoughts about the role of external actors in victims' struggle for justice. I have attended many conferences and seminars where I have had the opportunity to meet several victims from different contexts and their organizations. I noticed at these conferences that certain people were trying to marshal victims for political aims. There was more talk of truth and reconciliation, whereas what the victims really wanted was justice like ours. Even if truth and reconciliation are favoured, this should not prevent victims from bringing a civil party action before a tribunal. I could see that the victims were not spearheading these initiatives, but it is of utmost importance that the victims express themselves. The role of external actors must simply be to advise and inform victims of the merits of their struggle for justice, so that they may recover their dignity and claim their rights. When victims are aware of their situation and are committed to truly fighting for their own cause, it changes everything.

4

Tenacity, Perseverance, and Imagination in the 'Private International Prosecution' of Hissène Habré

Reed Brody, Human Rights Watch

Reed Brody and the international human rights advocacy organization Human Rights Watch (HRW) became the public face of the Habré trial in the Anglophone world. Brody shepherded the case against Habré from the initial complaints in Senegal and Belgium and the discovery of the security force documents in Chad through to Habré's final conviction, advocating for prosecution of Habré in Senegal as a means to bring justice to victims and universal jurisdiction to African courts. Working with Chadian victims' groups, HRW's international platform galvanized international awareness of Habré's victims.

The Hissène Habré trial was the fruit of what has been called 'one of the world's most patient and tenacious campaigns for justice'.[1] This campaign was waged over two decades by Habré's victims and their supporters, who improbably succeeded in creating the political conditions to bring a former African president to justice in Africa, with the support of the African Union. The victims' coalition 'essentially serv[ed] the case to the EAC on a silver platter',[2] determining the contours of the prosecution and dictating the nature of the trial itself, thereby contributing to its emancipatory impact. The Habré case shows how a 'private international prosecution' can allow victims to achieve criminal justice on their own terms.

The advent of Hissène Habré's trial, twenty-five years after Habré was overthrown and fled to Senegal, was almost entirely due to the perseverance and creativity of Habré's victims and their activist allies. The victims and their coalition of NGOs spent fifteen years building the factual and legal case against Habré, creating international and forum state support for the trial, and winning victories in the courts of Senegal, Belgium, and Chad, the UN Committee Against Torture, the African Union, and even the International Court of Justice. Living what Bishop Desmond Tutu called an 'interminable political and legal soap opera', the victims made it clear that they were just never going away until they saw Habré in court.

[1] Geoffrey York, 'Former Dictator of Chad Arrested on Allegations of 40,000 Murders' (*Toronto Globe and Mail*, 30 June 2013) <https://www.theglobeandmail.com/news/world/former-dictator-of-chad-arrested-in-senegal-on-allegations-of-40000-murders/article12901175/> accessed 2 July 2019.

[2] Christoph Sperfeldt, 'The Trial against Hissène Habré: Networked Justice and Reparations at the EAC' (2017) 21(9) The International Journal of Human Rights 1243. See also Sperfeldt, this volume, chapter 36.

Reed Brody, *Tenacity, Perseverance, and Imagination in the 'Private International Prosecution' of Hissène Habré* In: *The President on Trial*. First edition. Edited by: Sharon Weill, Kim Thuy Seelinger, and Kerstin Bree Carlson, Oxford University Press (2020). © Reed Brody.
DOI: 10.1093/oso/9780198858621.003.0005

The victims make it happen

In the wake of the 1998 London arrest of Augusto Pinochet, NGOs began looking at ways to build on the Pinochet precedent. Discussions at HRW put forward criteria for choosing the 'next Pinochet case' including: a request from national NGOs; the availability of evidence; the absence of legal barriers such as immunity; the independence of the judiciary and respect for human rights in the forum country; and most importantly the likelihood of success. When Delphine Djiraibe of the Chadian Association for the Promotion and Defense of Human Rights (ATPDH) came to our office to ask the help of HRW, which had intervened in the British courts to oppose Pinochet's immunity, to help Habré's victims bring him to justice in his Senegalese exile, all these criteria seemed to be fulfilled. Senegal's democratic tradition and its leadership role on international rights issues made a successful prosecution conceivable. Senegal was the first country in the world to ratify the treaty establishing the International Criminal Court, and had, like the UK, ratified the UN Convention Against Torture obliging it to 'prosecute or extradite' Habré. In addition, the case was appealing because it presented the possibility that a country in the global South would exercise universal jurisdiction, overcoming what many complained was a paradigm of European courts prosecuting defendants from formerly colonized countries.

We put together a coalition—the International Committee for the Fair Trial of Hissène Habré (the 'coalition')—to assist the victims to file the first case against Habré in Dakar in 2000, where he was indicted by a Senegalese judge. But for the next twelve years, the Senegalese government of former President Abdoulaye Wade gave the victims the runaround, forcing them to take their battle elsewhere, including Belgium, where a judge also indicted Habré. It was only in 2012, over twelve years after that first indictment, when Macky Sall became president of Senegal and the International Court of Justice ordered Senegal to prosecute Habré or extradite him, that the trial was finally set in motion.

The coalition's coordinator was Jacqueline Moudeïna, the victims' Chadian lawyer, and I was its strategist and administrator, but all major decisions were discussed with the victims' leadership. These included Souleymane Guengueng, who almost died from dengue fever during two and a half years in Habré's jails, and who, as he watched dozens of cellmates die, took an oath that if he got out alive, he would fight for justice.[3] When the prison doors flung open, Guengueng rallied wary survivors and widows into an association. When threats from Habré's henchmen finally forced Guengueng into exile, he was replaced by Clement Abaifouta—the 'gravedigger' whose prison job was to bury other detainees in mass graves. Both Guengueng and Abaifouta, as well as the Senegalese activist Alioune Tine and the Chadian activist Dobian Assingar, were members of the coalition's steering committee which fixed the coalition's political, diplomatic, and legal orientations and was in charge of the victims' legal team (also led by Moudeïna, and including Chadian, Senegalese, and international lawyers).

Working as a team across borders, with the victims in the forefront, was a perpetual challenge given the gulf between international activists with access to the media and financial resources and national activists without the same possibilities. To build such a team meant developing a partnership between Chadians and Senegalese, whose realities are very

[3] See also Moudeïna, this volume, Chapter 15; Guengueng, Chapter 3.

different (the Chadians often viewed the Senegalese with suspicion and resentment). It also meant bridging the very real divide between Chadian NGOs, with some advocacy background, and often unsophisticated and illiterate Chadian victims. It meant giving equal weight to Chadians' interest in achieving justice at home in Chad while involving them as protagonists in the campaign abroad. It meant accessing rehabilitative victims' services. It meant training the victims' leadership to be effective advocates (as suggested by the title of one coalition workshop 'From Victims to Human Rights Activists').

Because the initiative was in the hands of the coalition, at each step of the way, each time a new obstacle seemed to doom the case, the coalition found a way to keep their hopes for justice alive and often to win over a new constituency in the process:

- When the complaint was thrown out in Senegal following political interference by Senegalese President Abdoulaye Wade, the coalition filed a new case in Belgium under its universal jurisdiction law to set up a possible extradition. Although it wasn't jurisdictionally necessary, we recruited plaintiffs from Belgium's small Chadian refugee population;
- When Wade announced that he was expelling Habré, potentially placing him out of the reach of an extradition request, the coalition filed a petition before the CAT and then lobbied the committee which called on Senegal not to allow Habré to leave except through a proper extradition;
- When Wade suggested he might let Habré leave anyway, we appealed to Kofi Annan who re-iterated CAT's request directly with Wade who agreed to comply;
- When the ICJ in the Arrest Warrant case (DRC v Belgium) held that Belgium could not pursue the sitting Congolese foreign minister, and suggested that former rulers (such as Habré) enjoyed immunity from the jurisdiction of foreign courts for all acts committed during their period of office other than for acts committed 'in a private capacity,' and the Belgian authorities were ready to drop the investigation of Habré, the Chadian NGOs in the coalition convinced the Chadian government formally to waive Habré's immunity, a move which put the case on a totally different diplomatic footing and the stage for a Belgian judge to carry out a groundbreaking investigative mission to Chad;
- When the Belgian universal jurisdiction law was being repealed under US pressure, we brought the victims to Belgium to plead their case. Looking Belgian officials in the eyes, Souleymane Guengueng recalled the importance of the Belgian judge's visit to Chad: 'you sent us a judge. There were victims who exposed themselves for the first time, who actually filed past their torturers to tell their story to your judge. You can't simply abandon us now!' With his constant references to his time in prison, to his religious faith, and to his hopes in Belgium, he had the politicians eating out of his hands, and brought some of them to tears. As a result, we not only secured a 'grandfather' clause to keep the case there alive, but also created enduring support for the case in Belgium;
- When Senegal rejected Belgium's extradition request and 'referred' the case to the African Union heads of state—many of whom have grounds to fear prosecution one day—the coalition in repeated visits to Addis Ababa improbably turned the AU into an ally to press Senegal to move forward;

- When Senegal first requested \$100 million in international aid to carry out the trial, we visited capitals around the world to help broker an international funding agreement for a \$10 million trial and to raise the \$10 million;
- When a 'bizarre'[4] November 2010 ruling of the ECOWAS Court of Justice barred Habré's prosecution before the regular Senegalese courts, and both Habré's lawyers and president Wade declared the case 'over,' we worked with the AU to devise a streamlined 'EAC' to prosecute the case for \$10 million;
- When Wade cut a deal with Rwanda to send Habré there for trial, a trial which likely would not have been independent nor allowed the needed civil society activism, Moudeïna and Abaifouta went to Rwanda and successfully persuaded the authorities to drop the idea;
- When Senegal continued to stall, the coalition drew on its support in Belgium, where it had created a multi-party (and cross linguistic) support committee to press Belgium to take the case to the ICJ, an idealistic move which had widespread public support.

The personal obsessions of a handful of people like Guengueng, Abaifouta, and Moudeïna made all the difference in keeping the case moving. *The New York Times* would write that '[n]umerous brutal leaders have taken power and mass killings have unfolded on the African continent since Mr. Habré's ouster. But his case has proved unusual for the tenacity of his victims, and of HRW, in seeking to bring him to justice.'[5]

There were, of course, many unsung heroes who added their 'grain of sand'—in particular allies within the system whose personal commitment was critical in helping the victims across the finish line. Gérard Dive, head of the Belgian Task Force for International Criminal Justice, drafted the legislation which allowed the Habré case to survive the repeal of the universal jurisdiction law, and then pushed for Belgium to bring the case before the ICJ. AU Legal Counsel Ben Kioko and his Deputy Fafre Camara saw the importance of being able to prosecute African crimes in Africa. They engineered the AU's mandate to Senegal to prosecute Habré, and held Senegal's feet to the fire for ten years. The commitment and determination of Aminata Touré, Macky Sall's first minister of justice, overcame stiff opposition within the government to get the case back on track in a matter of months. Although the U.S. under Ronald Reagan brought Habré to power and supported him during his brutal rule, the Obama administration supported our quest and Stephen J Rapp, US ambassador-at-large for war crimes issues, made several trips to Senegal as well as to Chad to press for progress.

All the while, the coalition developed political alliances in Senegal. A Senegalese coalition with a paid part-time coordinator organized activities there, including regular visits to Senegal by groups of victims from Chad, who gave interviews, held news conferences and met with opinion-makers. The Senegalese survivor of Habré's jails, Abdourahman Guèye, was a constant presence alongside the survivors who came from Chad; The coalition hired a well-respected journalist as a part-time communications consultant and was able to secure

[4] William Schabas, *Bizarre Ruling on Non-Retroactivity from the ECOWAS Court* (PhD Studies in Human Rights 4 December 2010) http://humanrightsdoctorate.blogspot.com/2010/12/bizarre-ruling-on-non-retroactivity.html.

[5] A Nossiter, 'Senegal Detains Ex-President of Chad, Accused in the Deaths of Opponents' (*New York Times*, 30 June 2013), www.nytimes.com/2013/07/01/world/africa/senegal-detains-ex-president-of-chad.html accessed 14 February 2020

the airing on Senegalese TV stations of international documentaries on the Habré case. It also sent fifteen Senegalese journalists over the years to Chad to allow the Senegalese public better to understand the case, hear about Habré's crimes and see Chadian support for Habré's trial.

Among the many policy-makers influenced by the coalition was Macky Sall, whom the victims, including the Senegalese survivor, had visited in 2009, when he was in the opposition (as it had visited almost all leading politicians in Senegal) Sall said then that he was embarrassed by Senegal's handling of the case, and when he became president in 2012, he moved quickly to change course.

The victims' hegemony over the trial

Sitting in court on 30 May 2016 as Judge Kam read out a summary of the trial court's final verdict, I was struck at how closely it hewed to the narrative which we had been developing with the victims for fifteen years. Indeed, if we had written a model decision back in 2002, it probably would not have looked much different, except for the important chapter on sexual violence.

Key to the coalition's hegemony over the trial process was its marshalling of the factual dossier. By the time the chambers were established, the coalition had spent thirteen years building the factual case against Habré. After the first charges were filed, HRW and the FIDH in 2001–2002 sent a team of researchers to Chad to interview victims. This was followed up by repeated missions by HRW which interviewed over 300 victims and witnesses, including former officials of Habré's government. Bandjim Bandoum, a former high-ranking DDS official now living in Paris, was deposed over several days in 2006, and provided HRW with a fifty-page statement. The key moment in the investigation, however, came in 2001 when Olivier Bercault and I stumbled on tens of thousands of DDS documents in its abandoned N'Djamena headquarters.[6] Among the papers were daily lists of prisoners and deaths in detention, interrogation reports, surveillance reports, and death certificates. The files detailed how Habré placed the DDS under his direct control and kept tight control over DDS operations. HRW entered the documents into a database and analysis by the Human Rights Data Analysis Group revealed the names of 1,208 people who were killed or died in detention and 12,321 victims of torture and detention. In these files alone, Habré received 1,265 direct communications from the DDS about the status of 898 detainees.

Given the widespread and systematic nature of the crimes of Habré's regime over eight years, there was a risk of a never-ending Milosevic-style trial which would ruin the EAC's tight calendar and break its small budget. When the EAC was established, however, HRW presented the minister of justice and then the EAC prosecutor with a seventy-three-page memorandum, with 252 annexes, outlining the background to the case, the main criminal episodes of Habré's government, Habré's control over the state apparatus of repression, the previous investigations (Chadian Truth Commission, Belgium, HRW), as well as suggestions of which particular incidents to investigate within each episode and which witnesses ('insiders', context witnesses, and survivors) to call. While in many respects the investigative

[6] See Bercault, this volume, Chapter 1.

judges naturally followed their own lines of inquiry, the memorandum, the fruit of thirteen years of collaborative investigation with the victims themselves, served to frame the issues and highlight the main events, allowing the court's investigators to avoid wasting time and dispersing their energies.

Thierry Cruvellier has written in the context of the Cambodian court that:

> In the end, [international criminal courts] almost invariably disappoint those who have invested their heart and soul to bringing the truth to light' because of the conflict between the NGOs who 'have dedicated their lives to pursuing justice' and 'the international lawyers who swarm to the court in order to dispense justice in a matter about which they know nothing.[7]

This was not the case here. The investigative judges conducted four missions to Chad, gathered statements from 2,500 direct and indirect victims and key witnesses, including former officials of the Habré government. They appointed experts on data analysis, forensic anthropology, handwriting, the historical context of Habré's government, and the functioning and command structure of Habré's military. But the EAC investigators simply did not have the resources or the time to start from scratch and were forced to begin with the evidence the coalition had developed (particularly of course the DDS documents), as well as its theory of the case.

The chief prosecutor Mbacké Fall deserves an enormous amount of credit in this regard as he was able, while maintaining his independence, to listen to and work with the victims, the NGOs, and Chadian civil society, and to take advantage of their knowledge.[8] During the EAC's pre-trial investigation, it was the Chadian associations which brought the victims to see the investigators, and during the trial it was often the associations who acted as logistical intermediaries, especially for victims outside the capital. The *partie civile*-system also ensured that the victims were parties at the trial and could officially press at every stage their view of the case and the evidence they had collected. The civil parties, of course, were the only Chadians (other than Habré) at the trial.

At trial, HRW prepared, for each witness and victim who would testify, a file containing all their previous statements (to the HRW/FIDH, to the Belgian investigators, and during the pre-trial proceedings) and all the DDS documents in which their name figured or which related to their story, as well as suggested lines of questioning.

Most importantly, the coalition's hegemony over the trial meant that there were no shortcuts. The victims and the coalition always insisted that any trial for Habré include crimes committed against each of Chad's victimized ethnic groups—northern Muslims, southern Christians, Sara, Hadjerai, Zaghawa etc. In contrast, a distant prosecutor, disconnected from national narratives and inherently not accountable to the victims or civil society, can be tempted to narrowly tailor prosecutions in the hopes of securing a conviction or avoiding political resistance. Even the choice among the many survivors of who would testify at the trial was made by Prosecutor Fall in informal consultation with the victims' associations.

7 Thierry Cruvellier, *The Master of Confessions: The Making of a Khmer Rouge Torturer* (Ecco 2015).
8 See Fall, this volume, Chapter 15.

Cruvellier, a frequent critic of international courts, remarked in *The New York Times*, '[n]ever in a trial for mass crimes have the victims' voices been so dominant'.[9]

Sexual violence

The verdict has rightly been hailed as a breakthrough for sex crimes prosecutions. The irony, though, was that sexual violence almost wasn't part of the case at all. In HRW's early interviews with women prison survivors (interviews conducted in private by women), the women never mentioned rape, a taboo in traditional Chadian society. The 714-page HRW study on Habré's rule[10] hardly refers to rape, and the charge was not included in the indictment. It was only as the campaign picked up steam and Habré's trial appeared likely, that the survivors began, hesitantly, to give their full stories to their Chadian lawyer and trusted advisor, Jacqueline Moudeïna, who coaxed them through their concern about coming forward. Moudeïna even returned to Chad during the trial to persuade some of the reluctant survivors to come testify, and she was there in the court, putting them at ease and giving them the courage and the confidence to testify.

In retrospect, it is clear that the coalition, which was not in a position to offer any form of assistance or reparation to survivors of sexual violence, did not initially elicit their real experiences. Once the EAC were formed, however, a targeted effort should have been made in view of the trial to go back to all women survivors using appropriate methodology to get their full stories. The case of Khadidja Hassan Zidane was different. She was active in the victims' association for many years and was happy to repeatedly provide most of her story: how she had been suspected of helping Habré's Libyan enemies, tortured, imprisoned in Habré's presidential palace, and sent to a military camp in the desert north. But she always said that if she ever came face-to-face with Habré, she would have something else to tell. While we all guessed what that secret was, no one saw the necessity of forcing her to reveal it before she was ready, an omission which ultimately excluded the charge she raised at trial.

Private international prosecution

The Habré case stands explicitly on the back of the campaign to bring Augusto Pinochet to justice and alongside other victim and NGO-driven cases like the genocide prosecution in Guatemala of the former dictator Efraín Ríos Montt, and the prosecutions in Haiti of 'president for life', Jean-Claude 'Baby Doc' Duvalier, and before that of the Raboteau massacre.

In each of these cases the protagonists (1) built an advocacy coalition of victims and activists which (2) placed the victims and their stories at the centre of the justice struggle, to (3) help create the political will in the forum state. In each case, the breakthrough was achieved in large part thanks to the courage and perseverance of victims who never gave up

[9] Thierry Cruvellier, 'The Trial of Hissène Habré' *New York Times* (New York, 15 February 2016) <https://www.nytimes.com/2016/02/16/opinion/the-landmark-trial-of-hissene-habre.html> accessed 2 February 2020.

[10] HRW, *La Plaine des Morts* (HRW December 2013) <www.hrw.org/sites/default/files/reports/chad1013frwebwcover_0.pdf, 21.2.2017> accessed 2 July 2019.

hope. And critically, in each case, it was the victims and activists who marshalled the factual evidence.

The most exciting things about these victories is that, because they are the work of civil society actors like activists and victims they are, at least to some degree, replicable. In preparing the Habré trial, we watched a documentary about the Raboteau trial and the wonderful 23-episode short film series of the Rios Montt trial by Pamela Yates and Paco de Onis.[11] After the trial, we prepared a short video[12] and are working on a longer documentary specifically to inspire others to do what we did in the Habré case.

Indeed, three days before the final verdict in the Habré case in April 2017, I went with Guengueng, Abaifouta, Moudeïna and the Senegalese survivor Abdourahmane Gueye to The Gambia to meet a group of victims seeking to bring their exiled former dictator, Yahya Jammeh, to book. The Habré team described their long campaign and tried to draw lessons for their partners. The meeting inspired the Gambians who saw in the Chadians' struggle proof that justice can be achieved, despite the obvious obstacles. Fatoumatta Sandeng, daughter of an assassinated Gambian opposition activist, took away the conviction that 'victims voices mattered'.[13] Baba Hydara, the son of a slain journalist, said that the Chadians explained that it was a 'long, long, long battle, but we are ready. We have hope'.[14]

As a result of that meeting, the Gambians decided to create a Gambian-led 'Campaign to Bring Yahya Jammeh and his Accomplices to Justice' (#Jammeh2Justice) based on the model of the International Committee for the Fair Trial of Hissène Habré. That campaign launched in October 2017 and seeks to ensure that Yahya Jammeh, as well as those who bear the greatest responsibility in the crimes of his government, are brought to trial with all due process guarantees.

The Habré case can be seen, like the Rios Montt, Duvalier and Raboteau cases, as a sort of 'private prosecution'[15] before national courts, using civil party mechanisms. Other groups bringing such cases currently include Civitas Maxima and TRIAL International in Switzerland, the Center for Justice and Accountability, Guernica 37 and the FIDH's Legal Action Group. These 'private prosecutions' are carried out at a fraction of the cost of other international trials. In addition to using existing national judicial institutions, one reason for this economy is that the evidence has been collected and marshalled by the activists themselves. Over the years, HRW was able to access some $6 million from donors to support the work of the coalition. The vast majority of that funding went directly from donors to the Chadian and Senegalese groups involved in the campaign. The main advantage of these cases, however, is that they put the agency in the hands of the victims and activists.

[11] Dictator in the Dock, Genocide on Trial in Guatemala https://skylight.is/films/dictator-in-the-dock/.

[12] *The Trial of Hissène Habré* (HRW, 6 December 2017) <https://www.youtube.com/watch?v=KV18LCTolek&t=> accessed 14 February 2020.

[13] Jaime Yaya Barry and Dionne Searcey, 'Hissène Habré, Ex-Ruler of Chad, Loses War Crimes Appeal' (*New York Times*, 27 April 2017) https://www.nytimes.com/2017/04/27/world/africa/court-habre-chad.html?searchResultPosition=1 accessed 14 February 2020.

[14] *Gambie: partage d'expérience entre les victimes de Jammeh et de Hissène Habré (Radio France International*, 25 April 2017) http://www.rfi.fr/fr/afrique/20170425-gambie-partage-experience-entre-victimes-jammeh-hissene-habre accessed 14 February 2020.

[15] See Dustin Sharp, 'Prosecutions, Development, and Justice: The Trial of Hissein Habré' (2003) 16 *Harvard Human Rights Journal* 147, 148–49. According to Sharp. 'The term "private international prosecution" refers to prosecutions of former heads of state and government officials that stem from the private efforts of NGOs or the victims' families. This term stands in contrast to "international tribunals" or "international prosecutions", which often have the backing of the United Nations or nation states. The actions against Pinochet and Habré are two examples of [private] international prosecutions.'

As such, they can go beyond the much-vaunted 'fight against impunity' to be genuinely transformative of the power dynamic between abusive rulers and the people they have oppressed. During the trial, which was televised each day, thousands of Chadians watched their former president in the dock—put there not by the current Chadian government, which is the way things usually happen in Chad, but because a group of brave Chadians had fought to get him there.

Kaltouma Deffalah, one of the survivors of sexual slavery, testified defiantly that she felt 'strong, very courageous because I am before the man who was strong before in Chad, who ... doesn't even speak now. I am really happy to be here today, facing him, to express my pain, I am truly proud'. It was a sentiment expressed, in one way or another, by many of the survivors who testified. The transitional justice expert Pierre Hazan reflected that 'the case demonstrates the impact of justice at its best: its capacity to transform people who have been damaged to their very cores, and to liberate them'.[16]

[16] Pierre Hazan, 'The Trial of Hissène Habré: A Pivotal Case for International Justice in Africa' (*News 24*, 6 June 2016) https://www.news24.com/Africa/News/the-trial-of-hissene-habre-a-pivotal-case-for-international-justice-in-africa-20160617-3 accessed 2 February 2020. See Hazan, this volume, Chapter 40.

5

Defending Hissène Habré in Senegal During the Early Years

Hélène Cissé, Habré's Defence Lawyer from 2000 to 2004

Hélène Cissé was born in Vietnam and studied in France, where she grew up. She holds a Master's degree in Private International Law and Jurisprudence from the University of Paris. She moved to Senegal with her Senegalese husband in 1981. Since then, she has practiced as a lawyer with the Senegalese Bar Association. She is accredited to appear before the International Criminal Court, where most of her work now focuses.

Hissène Habré was charged with complicity in torture and crimes against humanity by an investigation judge in Dakar following a complaint brought by a group of Chadian victims in 2000. She participated in his defence from May 2000 to March 2001 before the criminal court in Dakar and the Court of Cassation (the highest Senegalese criminal court).

On 25 January 2000, Souleymane Guengueng and seven other Chadian victims, as civil parties, lodged a complaint against Habré in Dakar for acts of torture and other inhumane and degrading treatment, in application of the United Nations Convention against Torture. The victims were represented by Mr Boukounta Diallo, Mr Sidiki Kaba (who later became the Minister of Justice in Senegal), Mr Yerim Thiam from the Senegalese Bar, and Ms. Jacqueline Moudeïna from the Bar Association of N'djamena in Chad.[1] Following the complaint, on 3 February 2000, the investigating judges charged Mr Habré with knowingly aiding and abetting in the commission of crimes against humanity, acts of torture and barbarity against the plaintiffs between June 1982 and December 1990: the period during which he served as President of the Republic of Chad.[2]

Senegalese public opinion was and would remain divided throughout the criminal proceedings. Some of the public was critical of the prosecutions, considering that Senegal had granted asylum to Mr Hissène Habré, who, in their view, had demonstrated exemplary and pious conduct and helped many Senegalese people. He had integrated well into Senegalese society and married a Senegalese woman. For these reasons, a portion of Senegalese public

[1] See also Moudeïna, in this volume, Chapter 15 and Guengueng, Chapter 3.

[2] The accusation was based upon Articles 288 and 294 of the Senegalese Criminal Code (which address battery and torture, respectively), introduced in 1976, before the adoption of the UN Convention against torture that entered into force in 1987.

Hélène Cissé, *Defending Hissène Habré in Senegal During the Early Years* In: *The President on Trial.* First edition. Edited by: Sharon Weill, Kim Thuy Seelinger, and Kerstin Bree Carlson, Oxford University Press (2020).
DOI: 10.1093/oso/9780198858621.003.0006

opinion was dubious of the charges being brought against him. On the other hand, human rights NGOs and part of the public approved of the initiative to prosecute acts of torture and crimes against humanity in the framework of the fight against impunity: in particular those committed by former political and military leaders. Through a strong media campaign, there were NGOs that welcomed the initiation of criminal prosecution by the Senegalese courts, asserting that this represented a significant advancement for democracy and the promotion of human rights.

Habré and his wife were shocked and indignant at the initiation of these criminal proceedings; they believed that the State of Senegal was responsible for a grave violation of the international right to asylum.

Representing Habré

A collective of lawyers was formed to defend Mr Habré and I was invited to join by the president of this collective, Mr Madicke Niang, in May 2000.[3] Mr Niang, president of the Collectif des Avocats de la Défense, had the green light from Habré to choose the members of his team. I believe it was because of my profile as a specialist in international law that I was contacted to join the defence team. As a defence lawyer committed to the principle of the presumption of innocence and due process, I became, like all of the defence team, more and more involved in the media. The purely legal and judicial debate seemed to give way to a communications battle essentially aimed at public opinion, due to the enormous media pressure that NGOs brought to this affair.

During my work with the defence team, I focused primarily on the question of the jurisdictional incompetence of the Senegalese courts to hear the complaint filed by the civil parties. I conducted considerable case law research, particularly concerning the Pinochet cases brought before the English courts (in particular before the House of Lords), the Duvallier cases brought before the French courts, as well as the decisions rendered by the Belgian courts concerning universal jurisdiction.

My contribution took the form of developing arguments based on the theory of dualism, which necessitates the incorporation of international conventions into domestic laws before they can be applied; this relied in particular on the judgments of the House of Lords, and on Belgian and French case-law as the starting point for the applicability of international conventions in domestic law, from the point of view of both jurisdictional and legislative competence.

Together with colleagues from the defence team, I had the opportunity to meet Mr Habré and his wife Mrs Fatima Habré, at their home. Mr Habré and his wife were very calm, ready to discuss and support us on defence strategies, and to shed light on the political and historical context specific to Chad.

Over several work sessions at their home, Mrs Habré was very helpful with my research, particularly concerning the judicial initiatives related to Mr Habré in Chad since 1990. I was thus able to access Chadian legislation from 1990/1991 that created (at least

[3] The group of lawyers who participated in the defence of Hissène Habré before the investigative chamber included Mr Madické Niang (President of the Collective of Lawyers in charge of the defence of Hissène Habré), Mr Abdou Dialy Kane, Mr El Hadji Diouf, Mr Souleymane Ndéné Ndiaye, and myself.

on paper) a special jurisdiction to try all the crimes committed during Habré's regime, as well as related press articles and articles concerning the report by the commission of inquiry—established by the new regime of Idriss Déby in 1990—which were already widely disseminated by media outlets.[4] Mrs. Habré was also helpful in identifying sites and other sources providing access to jurisprudence, as well as the history of Chad since its independence.

At first, Mr Habré and his wife demonstrated their willingness to cooperate and expressed their faith in the Senegalese judicial system, despite the fact that the prosecution constituted a violation of the right of asylum that Senegal had granted them. However, as time passed, in the face of the massive media campaign against him, as well as with the election of Macky Sall (constituting a change of the highest political authorities in Senegal after a decade of peaceful asylum), Habré increasingly felt that the judicial process was a pretext for a personal political elimination enterprise: a feeling reinforced by the fact that he was the only one charged with crimes among a number of Chadian leaders also involved. This sense of judicial masquerade would gradually grow inside the former president of Chad and overcome him. Thus, motivated at the beginning of the procedure by the desire to collaborate with the Senegalese justice system, Habré went on to lose all confidence in it and its capacity to insure that he would receive a fair and impartial trial.

Judicial proceedings (2000–2001)

In a motion dated 18 February 2000, the counsel for the accused, Mr Niang, requested the annulment of the indictment for the following reasons: (1) *Incompetence of the Senegalese courts*, because no provision in Senegal in 2000 allowed Senegal to establish universal jurisdiction over crimes committed abroad by a foreigner and upon foreigners; (2) *Lack of jurisdiction ratione materiae*, because in 2000 no provision in Senegalese domestic law provided for the criminalization of crimes against humanity. In addition, Habré could not be tried for events that took place in the years 1982–1990 on the basis of the provisions of the Convention against Torture, which came into force in 1987 and was incorporated into Senegalese domestic law only in 1996; (3) *Time limitations regarding the incriminating facts*, because the statute of limitations, as provided by Senegalese laws, applied over the acts of torture. They did not contain any provision providing for their non-applicability in case of international crimes.[5]

In its judgment of 4 July 2000, the Court drew a distinction between acts of complicity in crimes against humanity on the one hand, and acts of complicity in acts of torture and other acts of barbarity on the other. Regarding acts of complicity in crimes against humanity, the Court considered that the Senegalese Criminal Code at the time did not contain any relevant legislation. Therefore, the Senegalese courts could not materially review such

[4] See also Akabar, in this volume, Chapter 2.

[5] The accusations of torture were based on Articles 288 and 294 of the Senegalese Criminal Code of 1976, which were in force while the allegations were committed (unlike the later domestic incorporation of the Convention Against Torture adopted only in 1996, and after the relevant facts). Physical assaults covered by Article 294 of the Criminal Code is an offence punishable by imprisonment of up to three years. Autonomous acts of torture set in Article 288 are governed by the statute of limitations for the crime (ten years) or the punishment (three years) as the case may be. Thus, according to Senegalese law, these allegations should have been prescribed.

facts against Mr Habré by virtue of the principle of legality set in Article 4 of the Senegalese Criminal Code.

Regarding the acts of complicity in torture, the Court affirmed the distinction between the substantive rules, which define the offences and fix the penalties, and the jurisdictional rules that determine the competence of the Senegalese courts. The Court thus held that the Senegalese legislator should have—in parallel with the incorporation of autonomous offence of acts of torture as enshrined in the UN Convention Against Torture into the Senegalese Criminal Code in 1996—made amendments to Article 669 of the Code of Criminal Procedure to provide for universal jurisdiction over the crime of torture, in order to give jurisdiction to the Senegalese courts in such situations.

The Court therefore decided that in light of the existing positive criminal law, Senegalese courts could not exercise competence over allegations of torture committed by a foreigner outside the Senegalese territory, regardless of the nationality of the victims because of the wording of Article 669 of the Code of Criminal Procedure which did not recognized such a competence.

Applying the defence team's legal argument, the Court ruled that the question of whether Senegalese courts had jurisdiction to hear the complaint submitted to them by the Chadian victims was a preliminary question that needed to be answered before moving on to any consideration of substantive legislative provisions. The Court held that the Senegalese legislature had not adopted the provisions ensuring it jurisdiction as required by Article 5 of the UN Convention against Torture. If the Senegalese courts did not have jurisdiction, the procedure could not go further and there was no need to examine the relevant substantive legislative provisions. The Court therefore annulled the indictment and subsequent proceedings, reasoning that annulment of the indictment was a matter of public order.

The civil parties filed an appeal against the judgment of the Indictment Chamber before the Court of Cassation, the final court of criminal instance. On 20 March 2001, the Court of Cassation ruled against the civil parties and dismissed the appeal. Referring to the concept of universal jurisdiction, the Court of Cassation stated that no procedural text recognized the universal jurisdiction of Senegalese courts to prosecute when the alleged acts were committed outside of Senegal by foreigners. Consequently, Habré's presence in Senegal alone could not justify the proceedings against him.

Final reflections

To be sure, the arguments raised by the defence—regarding the conditions of implementation of the jurisdictional competence of the Senegalese courts, the necessity of legal adaptation in order to apply international conventions within the internal legal order of Senegal, the application of the principle of the legality to offenses and crimes as well as penalties, and on the non-retroactivity of criminal laws—did not leave the Senegalese legislature indifferent. Following the case, a number of legislative reforms were instituted, including through amendments to the Senegalese Constitution, which seemed to respond to the objections raised by the defence team in the context of the Hissène Habré case. These reforms allowed for the possibility of new proceedings against Mr Habré, but they also allowed Senegalese legislation to comply with Senegal's new international commitments at the national level, among which were, inter alia, the ratification of the Rome Statute creating the ICC.

The February 2007 law which amended the Senegalese Criminal Code and adapted Senegalese legislation to the Rome Statute introduced the criminalization of genocide, crimes against humanity, and war crimes in Articles 431–433. It further modified the jurisdiction of Senegalese courts and introduced universal jurisdiction for crimes of genocide, crimes against humanity, and war crimes, as well as acts of torture and terrorism in cases where the foreign perpetrator is present in Senegal, if the victim resides on the territory of the Republic of Senegal, or if the government obtains extradition. These crimes have also been declared imprescriptible by this new law, ie there is no statute of limitations for those crimes, and the law established exemptions from the principle of legality of sentencing for those international crimes.

Similarly, the new Article 9 of the amended Constitution dismisses the principle of legality regarding crimes and misdemeanors in relation to these new crimes. This means that acts committed before the entry into force of the legislative reforms introducing the crimes of genocide, crimes against humanity, and war crimes into the criminal code may be prosecuted and convicted under this classification, if these facts were already qualified as such by jus cogens, treaties or international custom, despite the fact that at the time of offence these crimes were not yet included in the criminal code.

With regard to acts of torture, the new legislation makes a distinction between acts of torture as autonomous offences and acts of torture underlying crimes against humanity. Acts of torture are qualified by Senegalese criminal law as offences (*délis*), and are punishable by five to ten years' imprisonment along with a fine of between 100,000 and 500,000 francs. However, if torture underlies a crime against humanity, it constitutes a crime and incurs a higher punishment.

The obstacles related to the non-retroactivity of criminal law and the jurisdiction of the Senegalese courts to try Hissène Habré were dealt with through the specific provisions of the 2012 Statute of the EAC and the new Senegalese legislation that was adopted in 2007, mentioned above.

The African Union and the Senegalese government signed an agreement to create a hybrid international criminal institution to try Habré. Article 3 of the Statute of the EAC empowered this institution to try those principally responsible for crimes and serious violations of international law (crimes against humanity, war crimes, and torture) committed in Chad from 7 January 1982 to 1 December 1990, and Article 9 declared that these crimes are imprescriptible, ie fall outside any statute of limitations, thus allowing the institution to settle the questions of non-retroactivity and competence which might challenge the Habré case.

In addition, the legislative reforms introduced in 2007 laid foundations beyond the Hissène Habré affaire and the EAC. It could provide universal jurisdiction for crimes of genocide, crimes against humanity, and war crimes if the victim were residing in Senegal, if the suspects were under the jurisdiction of Senegal, or if Senegal requested extradition.

There is nothing to prevent these provisions from being used as a basis for the prosecution of the perpetrators and/or accomplices of these crimes committed by foreigners outside Senegalese territory, including on victims who are not Senegalese nationals.

My interviews with Mrs. Fatima Habré and the documentation research we undertook helped me to understand the historical and socio-political context of Chad between its independence and the 2000s. This was a situation marked by instability, conflicts and crises of political-military armies, as well as by the apparent and less apparent external interventions of Libya, France, and even the United States. This gave me a taste of the extreme complexity of the political and judicial context in which judicial cases involving the implementation of international criminal law take place.

My subsequent experience in the International Criminal Court, beginning in 2009, in one of the cases relating to the situation in Darfur and Uganda, as well as the continuation of other cases before the ICC, the EAC, and other ad hoc hybrid tribunals, particularly regarding the African continent, have further reinforced my belief that the multifaceted, entangled issues and procedures that are included in international criminal cases contribute to their great judicial complexity and political sensitivity.

The cross-fertilization of international criminal law and international human rights law by an African judicial system, ie that of Senegal, is a huge and exciting challenge. The practical application of a dualist national system requires innovative thinking about many legal issues. But there is a particular challenge that I have had to face regarding the partisan nature of NGOs that tend to strip the defence of any right to fair treatment and of the right to the presumption of innocence, which right is nonetheless strongly asserted by the Convention Against Torture of 10 December 1984 and all international human rights legal instruments. The enormous and unbalanced media pressure gave Mr Hissène Habré and his family the impression that NGOs gave themselves the ability to judge in place of courts. This ignored the need for calmness and objectivity as well as respect for the rights of the defence, which must accompany any work of justice.

6

The Belgian Investigation of the Habré Regime

Excerpt of Trial Testimony by Daniel Fransen, Belgian Investigating Judge

---

Judge Fransen led the investigation under Belgium's universal jurisdiction statute into crimes committed by Habré's regime. In connection with this investigation, he spent 10–12 days in Chad in 2004 and testified about this experience before the EAC. These investigative materials were transmitted to the EAC Prosecutor in April 2013. In the excerpted testimony below, Judge Fransen answers questions of Habré's court-appointed lawyer, Mounir Ballal.

Dakar, Senegal, EAC Trial Chambers 17 September 2015—Minute 13:47'–51'[1]

MAÎTRE MOUNIR BALLAL: In June 2003 complaints were submitted by victims to the Belgium prosecutor against high US and Israeli officials, no need to mention their names, based on universal jurisdiction. Do you know what happened to these complaints? Because four months later, there was a new law that annulled that competence. Do you know what happened to these complaints?

DANIEL FRANSEN, BELGIAN INVESTIGATIVE JUDGE: As a jurist, one needs to see if the case falls within exceptions to the law of August 2003. That would include an ongoing open investigation, and if the complaint is made by a Belgium victim ... if it is not the case, and the case has not been opened, then the file is closed.

BALLAL: Yes, this is what happened.

FRANSEN: Thank you for informing me, I did not know. But I am not sure that this change in law is relevant in the cases you mentioned. Following the ICJ decision of 2012,[2] the case of Yerodia, they would have benefited from immunity in any case.

BALLAL: In the case we are concerned with today, you received the first complaints in November 2000 and then you received successively around 20 complaints. You mentioned 22-23 complaints, something like this. Did you close the file? Did you conclude the judicial investigation opened within the framework of these complaints? Or was it done by another of your colleagues? I am referring to the case Public prosecutor v. Habré.

FRANSEN: I am not certain ... one would have to check with the Belgian judicial authorities, but I am not sure whether the file is closed in Belgium. If it closed in Belgium, then it would be by my colleague who took over after me, because I left in 2009 for the

[1] Transcription and English translation by Sarah Cattin. The original expressions in French are sometimes mentioned in brackets to ensure the exact meaning is not lost with the translation. The passages were slightly edited in some places to ensure fluency. The judge's live testimony is available at: <https://www.youtube.com/watch?v=EtrR7Tr5tGw> accessed 10 February 2020. See also Mounir Ballal, in this volume, Chapter 14.

[2] See also Ventura and Baiesu, in this volume, Chapter 33.

Daniel Fransen, *The Belgian Investigation of the Habré Regime* In: *The President on Trial*. First edition. Edited by: Sharon Weill, Kim Thuy Seelinger, and Kerstin Bree Carlson, Oxford University Press (2020). © Daniel Fransen.
DOI: 10.1093/oso/9780198858621.003.0007

Special Tribunal for Lebanon, so my colleague took over the investigation office, and the Habré case.'

BALLAL: As soon as you arrived in N'Djamena, starting the next day, you began the investigation. Did you have a specific schedule?

FRANSEN: We had sent, beforehand, a schedule to the Chadian investigative judge and Chadian judicial authorities. This schedule, like for the EAC, sometimes needed to be a bit modified to accommodate everyone—for example, if a witness did not appear, we tried to place another one. All this was going on in 'good agreement', so it was not a problem. But in general, we tried to follow the planning. All of this is detailed in the 'procès verbal de descente' which accounts for—maybe not hour by hour but at least day by day—what we did in Chad, the investigative officers, the prosecutor and myself.

BALLAL: Were you accompanied by an investigative magistrate? Or just a representative from the prosecutor's office? And how about investigative officers?

FRANSEN: The Belgian delegation was made up of a member of the federal prosecutor's office, four Belgian investigating officers ('*officiers de police judiciaire*'), my clerk and myself. On the Chadian side, I was not territorially competent to accomplish investigative acts, so there was an investigative judge, his clerk, and four Chadian investigating officers who assisted us. So I did not do anything without being 'covered' by the Chadian investigative judge or an investigative officer. All investigative acts were carried out by the Chadian investigative judge or Chadian investigating officers, with the presence and assistance of the Belgian staff.

BALLAL: Thank you Mr. Fransen for these precisions. Once you were in the field, did you already have an idea about the direction, or directions, in which you wanted to investigate? Not you directly, but with substitution of your Chadian colleagues? Did you have a precise idea?

FRANSEN: Yes. On the one hand, to hear the plaintiffs that had not been heard in Belgium, so that they could confirm their complaints. Two, to hear witnesses we had identified, including members of the DDS. Three, to visit detention centers, and DDS archives. And four, to travel to Ambing and Hamral-Goz. Also to collect other elements. For instance, people had been jailed for distributing a leaflet, and we tried to get that leaflet from the Chadian Documentation Center.

BALLAL: Were you able to obtain this leaflet?

FRANSEN: Yes, I think so.

BALLAL: Is it in the file?

FRANSEN: If I obtained it, yes, it's in the file. Everything I collected, I included in the file. I think the leaflet is in, and also videos we collected from Chadian TV, and other elements useful for the investigation.

BALLAL: Very good, Mr. Fransen. And I think, or I understand, in addition to these activities, you also visited detention centers, the famous seven detention centers, in Ndjamena?

FRANSEN: Yes, it's what I said, detention centers.

BALLAL: You also went to the DDS office?

FRANSEN: Yes.

BALLAL: To examine documents relevant to your mission?

FRANSEN: Yes. Examine them, ask for them to be seized.

BALLAL: All this was in 2000, you spoke of February, the end of February?

FRANSEN: If I remember correctly: 26 February 2002 to 6 March 2003.

BALLAL: So about three months after the referral of the case to you?

FRANSEN: No, a year and three months after the referral.

BALLAL: This is just to clarify the chronology.

FRANSEN: The first complaint was in March 2000, and we traveled to Chad in 2002.

BALLAL: Did you also go to Chad with a forensic expert? No?

FRANSEN: No.

BALLAL: So you didn't take a forensic expert? Why not, if you can tell us? Why did you feel it was not necessary, since you planned to visit at least two mass graves? 'Mass graves', or at least a place where one would find bodies?

FRANSEN: As I told you earlier, going with just one forensic expert would not have had much interest. This is because the exhumation of corpses is heavy, in terms of means and time. We had to make choices. The investigation was not closed. Depending on the evolution of the file ('*dossier*'), I had planned new judicial demands. So I did not think, at first, that it was useful for a forensic expert to go, not knowing the results of the rogatory letters, not knowing if there would be effective collaboration with Chadian authorities, if we would have access to the sites of executions and mass graves. This mission was supposed to be as complete as possible, but it was still an exploratory mission.

BALLAL: So, if I understand correctly, when leaving Belgium, you weren't sure you would be able to see, or at least to access, the mass graves. Is that right? You were not certain?

FRANSEN: I had asked to visit them, the international rogatory letter was accepted, so I had no reason to think I would not. But these are the contingencies. So at first I did not think it was necessary to have a forensic expert, I didn't estimate it was important. We would have needed to do excavation work before he could begin his mission. I was hoping that everything I asked for would happen, but one also has to recognize some things sometimes get impeded by time imperatives, or material difficulties. But in any event I repeat, as I said this morning, the cooperation with Chadian authorities was exemplary. Truly, they gave us all the necessary means so that this rogatory letter could be carried out in excellent conditions.

BALLAL: So if I understand correctly, you were skeptical, regarding the welcome—not the welcome regarding a human interaction of host-guest—but based on your mission? You had some doubts on the fact that you could have a full, frank, complete cooperation? While later on, you explained it was the contrary, you said you were well welcomed, by the judicial authorities—again not just on a human dimension of welcoming guests: in Africa, everyone knows, people receive guests well. So, once again, you did not feel that it was necessary to be accompanied, by at least a forensic expert because it was 'heavy'? 'Heavy' how? Heavy financially? Logistically? The Belgian authorities did not have the capacity to assure you additional funds? When you say heavy, how do you mean? Heavy procedurally? Heavy financially? Heavy how?

FRANSEN: Again, as I told you, going with a forensic expert would not have allowed him to make observations.

BALLAL: Why do you say this?

FRANSEN: Again, we would have needed to also carry out excavation works. The means of all justice systems are limited. The first mission was exploratory. I had a responsibility to make sure we used Belgian funds in the best manner. So I preferred not going with a forensic expert on the first trip, but preferred first see where the mass graves were, and then disperse more funds if needed, in following trips, with concrete results.

: You know, I could also have gone for six months, but it was not possible for financial and organizational reasons. When I came back after eight days, it took me months to get back the arrears I had. This is reality, reality is not: 'I'm leaving to investigate in Chad for six months, with unlimited means, and we will figure out the rest later', for national justice systems and international justice systems. There are also questions of means in terms of logistics, human resources, and financial means.

BALLAL: So it would have cost too much money?

FRANSEN: Again, I did not think at this moment, that I should have disbursed this money. And again, it was my opinion.

BALLAL: This response brings a question to my mind, regarding the goal declared by the Court. You could have gone for six months: yes logistics can be expensive, certain operations can be expensive. Very good. Do you think you would have needed six months to excavate the mass graves in Ambing and Hamral-Goz? You would have needed this much time? Did you know beforehand, in the alleged area called Ambing, that there would be approximately so many corpses? And in that area we call Hamral-Goz? Did you think this would be something that would take a lot of time to process excavations? This is something that can be done quite rapidly, I mean in 2-3 days, you could have done it.

FRANSEN: No, I think you are underestimating, if you want to do it scientifically, juridically. It does not take just not just 2–3 days. You're mistaken. It takes professionals, technicians. It's not digging up... we're talking about human bodies, and the position of human bodies. It's doesn't take 1–2 days if we're talking about 50 bodies. I'm not an expert, you would have to ask a forensic police officer. I think that at the ICTY, for instance, it took more than 2–3 days.

: And again,if necessary, I would have done it. But at some point we needed to fix priorities, like in every case. I hear your criticism. But I estimated that the priorities were first we needed to hear witnesses before doing more.

BALLAL: Do you know the dimensions of these two mass graves? Length and width, when it's a rectrangle? Or sides, when it's a square?

FRANSEN: No, not sure, I think it was mentioned, but I do not remember precisely.

BALLAL: But they're not big, it is not like the mass graves in Bosnia, it is not thousands of dead, more like hundreds.

FRANSEN: No no. I cannot remember now, but I believe its in the report. There you have the dimensions.

BALLAL: So, we can say that in terms of forensic elements, you went back to Brussels empty handed? Corpses were shown to you? Or you did not see corpses and went back to Brussels only with testimonies?

FRANSEN: I did not see corpses. I did not ask to see them. I asked to see the sites of Ambing and Amalgore, this is what I was authorized to do. So I saw them. Some witnesses explained to me about them. This is what I estimated that I needed to see and receive on this first mission.

BALLAL: Ok. To shed light on the situation?

FRANSEN: Yes.

BALLAL: So, now, coming to the DDS offices, you worked there, you went there, you examined the offices?

FRANSEN: Yes.

BALLAL: Can you describe the condition of the offices? Generally? What did you get there? Who accompanied you in the visit? With your staff I suppose?

FRANSEN: Yes, along with Chadian investigating officers, there were several, who were carrying out the investigative acts.

BALLAL: Who were doing what?

FRANSEN: The work of the investigation. I explained to you. And I think, there were members of Human Rights Watch (HRW).

BALLAL: Who from HRW was there? Can you remember names? Do you remember who from Human Rights Watch accompanied you?

FRANSEN: Ms. Koulouris, who did a lot of missions, and maybe Mr. Brody was here as well, I do not remember exactly. You can check the field mission record from December.

BALLAL: And for you it was normal that these persons were here? These NGOs?

FRANSEN: The NGOs showed us the work they carried out.

BALLAL: Very good, very good, the NGOs showed you the work that you needed to carry out.

FRANSEN: No, the work that *they* carried out themselves.

BALLAL: That they did, ok. And do you think their presence was indispensable? Were you not already informed of this by the NGOs? I'm asking the question, I don't know. In the framework of your investigation, of your office?

FRANSEN: Indispensable I don't know, it's all relative, but they were present, they showed us …

BALLAL: So at least two people? A man and a woman? Was there anybody else?

FRANSEN: Some plaintiffs were here.

BALLAL: Chadian residents? Or people who came with you from Belgium?

FRANSEN: No no, people who resided in Chad, we didn't bring Chadians with us.

BALLAL: Who else? From what you can recall?

FRANSEN: There were Chadian judicial authorities. Not sure if the Chadian investigative judge was here or not, I can't remember. And there were the people from Human Rights Watch, and some plaintiffs here to indicate to us… because then we went on the Ambing and Hamral-Goz sites. Those were the people who could show us.

BALLAL: In what conditions were the archives? In two or three words. Well organized?

FRANSEN: One part was well organized, and another part was not organized at all, all covered in dust. Some pictures were taken, you can see. It was all covered in dust, in a deplorable condition …

BALLAL: Chaotic? Is that ok? I do not want to suggest the term to you.

FRANSEN: Yes, chaotic. There were the DDS archives, the archives from the Chadian Truth Commission, and some documents that had been collected by HRW.

BALLAL: OK. Was a member of the Commision of Inquiry present?

FRANSEN: I think not, but I really don't remember.

BALLAL: Before going to Chad, had you read the report of the Commision of Inquiry?

FRANSEN: Yes.

BALLAL: Yes? You'd read it before? I won't ask you what you thought of it …

FRANSEN: I think I explained this just now.

BALLAL: That's very nice, Mr. Fransen. Did you have the impression that people other than you, in the capacity of that international Rogatory investigation, had seen the documents?

FRANSEN: Excuse me, I don't follow. Which documents are you speaking about?

BALLAL: The DDS. We're in the DDS offices. The ones that were well organized.

FRANSEN: Yes, clearly. The report of the Commision of Inquiry said this, actually. They had used the DDS documents. Or at least some of them. There was a whole series of documents that hadn't been used, because they were in a chaotic condition. But for the rest, they were used. For example, there was a box with passports, photos, nationality cards.

BALLAL: So effectively, the Commision of Inquiry had access. Afar as you know, could other people have had access to those docuemnts? As far as you know? Could be yes, could be no. NGOs, for example, did they have accesss to these documents? Apart from you?

JUDGE: What are you asking him?

BALLAL: If he knew . . .

JUDGE: This is speculation. He hasn't seen it.

BALLAL: I withdraw the question, Mr. President. Excuse me. While you were investigating the case in Belgium, did HRW give you documents of this type, from the DDS documents? Any documents?

FRANSEN: Going back to the earlier discussion, if anyone submitted documents to me, it was not HRW. If anyone gave me documents, it was the civil parties. In their capacity of participating in the judicial debate, which HRW does not have. I think that some documents by HRW are among the documents that were submitted, but was it them, HRW, that submitted the DDS documents, we would have to check who submitted them. Honestly, we'd need to verify this.

7
In His Own Words
An Interview with Hissène Habré
Excerpted Interview from La Gazette, Dakar, 2011

Hissène Habré moved to Dakar, Senegal following his expulsion from Chad in 1990, where he lived as a private citizen in an upscale residential neighborhood. Although he left public politics, he participated in local Muslim political life in Senegal, and was protected by Senegal's President Wade. Waves of international attention put pressure on Senegal to extradite or prosecute Habré.

On July 25, 2011, a film crew and reporters from La Gazette interviewed Hisséne Habré in his home in Almadies. It was rumored that President Wade was preparing to extradite Habré to Chad, where he had already been sentenced to death, in absentia, under Deby's regime. In response, Habré broke his typical media silence and agreed to an interview. In this chapter, we present a translation of excerpts of the interview, with headings and footnotes added for clarity.[1]

The Gazette: *We have learned ... (that) the President of the Republic, has just taken an important decision that could have serious consequences in terms of extraditing you to your home in Chad. Are you surprised by this measure?*

First of all, I would like to say a word about Senegal and the Senegalese people. It's exactly twenty years since I came to Senegal. This is the first time I have spoken to a media outlet. On this occasion, I would therefore like to express my deep gratitude to Senegal and the Senegalese people. I, together with my family, feel pride and a deep sense of gratitude for our friendship, our brotherhood, with the Senegalese people. This country welcomed us, these marvelous, wonderful people treated us as their own sons. We feel at home here. We are really at home here. This is an opportunity for me to say thank you to the valiant Senegalese people, thank you to Senegal. And at all times, the Senegalese people have shown us their friendship, their support during all the vicissitudes that we have known, all the problems that I find profoundly unfair that have been done to us. The Senegalese people have been

[1] Abdou Latif Coulibaly, Pape Amadou Fall, and Hamidou Sagna, 'Exclusive interview - Hissène Habré tells all: Wade, Diouf, Senegal ... ' *La Gazette* (Dakar 25 July 2011) (editor's translation). It is available in French here: xalimasn.com/entretien-exclusif-hissene-habre-dit-tout-wade-diouf-le-senegal/ accessed 15 February 2020.

Abdou Latif Coulibaly, Pape Amadou Fall, and Hamidou Sagna, *In His Own Words* In: *The President on Trial*. First edition. Edited by: Sharon Weill, Kim Thuy Seelinger, and Kerstin Bree Carlson, Oxford University Press (2020). DOI: 10.1093/oso/9780198858621.003.0008

next to us, near us ... They're planning a kidnapping to hand me over to their friend Idriss Déby. That is the situation. The Senegalese government, in proceeding in this way, finds itself in the utter unlawfulness.

Neither my lawyers, my friends, nor I will sit by idly. We will all act. If you're asking me what I'm going to do, let me say this: when someone or multiple someones break down your door, enter your home and try to attack you, what do you do? Some people are taken by panic and lower their heads, drop their arms and let themselves be caught like rabbits. Others lean in, brace their legs and face it. In legal jargon, this is called the right of self-defense. And this is the choice I will make in such a situation. Whoever violates my space, my house, to attack me, I will have a right of self-defense ... We are in a situation where the law of the jungle prevails ... In the jungle, when animals attack you, what do you do? These people behave like hyenas towards Hissène Habré. The red line has been crossed. This is inadmissible and unacceptable.

Sometimes we talk about extradition, sometimes we talk about expulsion. What is the rationale behind this logic? For me, there is no doubt about it, it is the execution of a plot to eliminate me physically. Let's say a political plot to assassinate me.

Habré on his enemies, colonialism, and neo-colonialism

I would say, this whole 'Hissène Habré affair'—what is it in its foundations, and at its margins? It is a conspiracy with political and financial dimensions, draped in the cloak of a judicial affair, literally and figuratively. Who is behind this? You have Colonel Gaddafi. He has never hidden his position regarding the dossier. He has officially said so on a number of occasions. You know what Colonel Gaddafi holds against me? The Aouzou Strip and the Bornou Tibesti region. Although everyone focuses on the Aouzou Strip, Gaddafi actually wanted a little less than half of Chad. He failed in his policy of annexation and hegemony. So this is his revenge. Of course, this is directed by French leaders, yesterday Mitterrand and Chirac, and today Sarkozy.

Colonialists and neo-colonialists have persistent hatred. They are not like Africans, they don't forget quickly. This is connected to my political fortunes. At the end of my studies, I returned to the National Liberation Front (Frolinat). I had my reasons. You know, at the time of independence, the French felt that it was necessary to pass power to a region where there was a small elite formed in the Western school, Christians and followers of traditional religions. The French thought that they were the best allies, so it was necessary to pass the power to this small elite. Unfortunately, those Chadians who were handed the reins of power at the time of independence under the presidency of Tombalbaye went on to conduct a disastrous policy of oppression, repression and abuse of all kinds. Instead of unifying and developing the country, they did everything to divide the country, and even dragged some of Chad into revolt. To end this injustice, this disastrous situation, I joined, almost at the end of my studies, the Frolinat. I have a background in law and economics. I then put myself at the disposal of Frolinat to overthrow this regime, to lead a new policy, with an ideal of a truly independent Chad, which would not obey orders from Paris: a free country, deciding its own destiny, with policy defending its national interests. In 1982, when I took power, it was this policy that I put in place. It did not please Paris. Nor did it please Mitterrand, or Chirac, or what is called Françafrique.

…

What France needs from Africa, mainly in francophone Africa, is a 'yes man'. France does not want free men, real partners, people who defend the interests of their country. This is not part of the plan for Françafrique. And I had frankly bad relations with Mitterrand and Chirac, Sarkozy obviously I do not know, but whatever, he is their successor. So as regards this case, France is involved. When Sarkozy came here to Dakar, he insulted all of Africa, all Africans, at Cheikh Anta Diop University. He said that a trial for Hissène Habré would be a good thing. France is therefore fully involved in this business. Let me be understood: I am speaking about the French political elite.

The Gazette: *Are you saying that under the guise of human rights, it is France that is fighting against you?*
Exactly! Exactly! And not only France, but also Libya. Colonel Gaddafi, who was once all powerful, dictated his wants to a number of heads of state who spent their time going to Tripoli as if it was their Mecca. Even though he very publicly despised those African Heads of State; he considered them l'Elysée's[2] trained zoo monkeys. This expression came from Gaddafi himself, not from anyone else.

Habré on NGOs' involvement with the case against him

Senegal is an independent country. Senegal has traditions. Senegal is a country of great saints. Senegal is the country of Sheikh Anta Diop. Still … In Senegal some NGOs are having fun. Only in Senegal do some NGOs have fun.… Do you think it's normal what the NGOs are saying? They sentenced me before the trial. They call me a criminal, is that normal? Doesn't Hissène Habré have any rights? There's no such thing as a presumption of innocence? I condemn this kind of abuse. Hissène Habré has never done anything against Senegal. There is nothing wrong with Hissène Habré.

The Gazette: *Did you detect any warning signs in Wade's behaviour of this sudden extradition?*
First, on what basis, in the name of what, like an object, like a sheep, do we decide to take a former president in exile to Senegal to bring him back to his country? Without even informing him. Is this an abduction? Is this a kidnapping?

Everyone knows my relationship with Déby. In Chad, everyone knows that Déby has been working to condemn Hissène Habré to death. Everyone must know that my former commander-in-chief (Déby) betrayed Hissène Habré, his boss. And that Déby was returned by the French intelligence services after an internship in France, having received from France and Sudan a turnkey army? There are countries—Sudan and France– whose dream it is to see Hissène Habré die. And this is the man to whom they would hand me over. And in the most immediate way. Here we act exactly as the mafia does, in violation of all legal rules, all values, and all principles.

[2] This is a reference to the French seat of government, the presidential palace.

The Gazette:*How do you explain that in Chad there is no dissenting voice with regard to Wade's action? Do you no longer have any friends in the country?*
Contrary to what you say, I would like you to know that Chad is a large open-air prison. People today cannot publicly defend their point of view. It's a matter of life and death.

Habré on his regime

First of all, first you say that 'your regime was very harsh', 'very severe'; that's what they say, that's what everyone says. But the question you should ask is, 'is this true?' Is it? What elements are necessary to say that a regime was a dictatorial or criminal regime? But let me say this: Chad has had a very extraordinary history. I did not come to power like most African heads of state. I am a fighter. I went to war, together with all that that entails. We waged war against a regime that killed women and children, shaved womens' heads,[3] and confined a large part of the country to total misery. So, we took up arms to replace this regime with a truly patriotic regime, which had a vision for Chad. And war is not a festival of joy. We didn't behave like the French army that dumped toxic products on poor populations, raped women, poisoned rare water wells in the desert. In Chad, we were fighting against Libyans who wanted to annex just under half of Chad. We sacrificed ourselves, shed our blood, suffered from cold and from hunger to the point that we could not even stand to pray. But we had faith and noble goals: to liberate our country and its enormous potential. And we had very few means compared to the Libyans and the French, who were playing geopolitics.

…

I do not deny that under my regime, there were deviations or blemishes. Chad is 1,284,000 square kilometers. When I came to power, the country was divided into eleven regions ('*tendances*'). Each region had its territory, its government, its army, its administration. Who suffered from this? It was the population. Consider this: eleven states in one state! We made every imaginable effort to bring peace and to establish, in a short time, a functioning state. In a country in the grip of war, obviously not everyone in the army or the police is a saint. In a country like Chad that has gone through war after war, in every sense, it is incontestable that there were settlings of accounts, I do not deny it. In fact, there have even been cases where the Chadian judiciary has sentenced people to death for abuses.

… I am not against justice or the prosecution of people who might have committed criminal acts. What I denounce is the conspiracy that aims not to shed light but rather to eliminate someone, in place of doing justice. I tried to find out about the people who filed complaints in Dakar. You know, I still have links with my country of origin. I did not find anyone I knew. There is no former minister, no former politician, no former CEO, no former director general, no former general, no former colonel, no former well-known businessman, nor a former director of administration among them. It's as if they want to make people believe that Hissène Habré picked up people in the street and killed them, and then some other people came to file a complaint. But we kill a person for a specific reason.

… Why did Hissène Habré kill a poor citizen who wasn't politically active, or a member of the military, someone who was doing nothing at all? Why would I do it? But finally, the

[3] This appears to be a reference to the French post-second world war practice of humiliating women who had collaborated with Germans during the war. [editors]

case started in 2000, a Senegalese came out of I do not know which hole to make a complaint saying he had been tortured by Hissène Habré. Some Senegalese guy who makes a lot of noise, travels to Paris, talks to RFI, travels everywhere.

... How do you explain that someone who was tortured, when the case began in 2000, gets up one morning in 2006 to file a complaint? Let's assume that this man was tortured as he says himself. He says he was a jeweler, and sometimes he says that he came in a French military plane; he gives three versions. He says that he was stopped at the market or at the French military base. He says he came to sell gems and the police arrested him, tortured him and released him. But how is Hissène Habré responsible for this kind of thing? A president who spends his time chasing chicken thieves, drug dealers or jewel traffickers. All over the world, traffickers and dealers are arrested, some are tortured. Did we prosecute and arrest the Senegalese president because they took traffickers? Never! How does this have anything to do with me? Why didn't he go to Ndjamena to lodge a complaint against his alleged torturers? Certainly someone tortured him if his version is true.

The Gazette: *The report that your 'enemy' produced following your departure, according to which there were 40,000 Chadian deaths under your regime—How do you view the credibility of this report?*
Even you say that this report was cooked up by the person who deposed me.[4] This report was prepared by Dèby's special services, the so-called political police. This report has no value. This report has no value. How can someone who overthrew the government through a coup d'état make a credible report against his predecessor?

... In the voluminous file assembled by the Belgian judge, you will not find anyone, anywhere saying that Hissène Habré tortured him.[5] Nobody, I tell you, nobody. Everyone accuses the regime of Hissène Habré's, the Directorate of Documentation and Security (DDS), the police, and so on. No-one mentioned me by name. ...Even the Senegalese Attorney General, in reviewing the extradition file, said that most of the complaints seemed motivated by political reasons.

A lot has happened in Chad. Libyans have massacred thousands of Chadians, deported young Chadians to Libya and enslaved them. They sent young Chadians to the theaters or war in Lebanon and Iran. They took thousands and thousands of Chadian wild animals: elephants, giraffes, gazelles. Chad has an extremely rich fauna. Libyans even destroyed Chad using napalm gas. The palm groves were burned, the livestock destroyed. Shouldn't we investigate Libya if we want to do justice? Chad has been through a period of endless war. I myself suffered through it during eight years of my stay in power and ten years of guerilla warfare. The French killed, raped, massacred, poisoned our wells, bombarded our cattle and killed Chadians by the hundreds. Why don't they have to answer for their crimes before a court? In Chad, there have been eleven politico-military '*tendances*', and no one looks into them. During the Tombalbaye era, there was nothing that didn't happen in Chad. Under Dèby there are the worst regimes that Chad has known. But what does Déby do? He rules through terror.

We want to do justice for Chad and Chadians, right? I completely consent. I totally agree that independent international justice should be organized according to the norms of

[4] See also Abakar Mahamat Hassan, in this volume, Chapter 2.
[5] See also extracts of Judge Frazen's testimony before the EAC, this volume, Chapter 6.

law and that all Chadians who are criticized for something come to this court. Including Hissène Habré, including the former presidents of Chad. But to choose a man on absolutely political bases, for economic and financial interests, to try to eliminate him and to use legal cover, is not serious.

***The Gazette:** You mean that the history of Chad and that of its main actors must be judged with no exceptions.*
Absolutely. Why must I be the only one to be judged. This is all ridiculous.

Habré on the African Union and its relation to the EAC

What is the African Union? It followed from the Organization of African Unity (OAU). I know the organization from the inside. It's a crab bucket.[6] You meet in corridors where you arrange things and then you organize a plenary to applaud each resolution. That's how it works. The Hissène Habré case followed the same pattern as all important cases. Someone solved the problem in camera somewhere and took it to the African Union summit. Secondly, in the OAU as in the AU, who directs these organizations? It's three or four countries, no more. That's the reality. The African Union is not a court of law. That's what ECOWAS says. Have you seen a similar case in the history of the OAU or the AU? Is there a single case similar to that of Hissène Habré? There are none. But ask yourself the question: why is the African Union, instead of solving the great problems of Africa, focusing on Hissène Habré? You don't find that strange?

In fact, this decision to bring Hissène Habré's case to the African Union is driven by Abdoulaye Wade and Muammar Gaddafi. It's Wade and Gaddafi. This is using justice to solve a problem. They thought about this and reflected over what they could do. Habré won on the judicial level; he was cleared by the highest Senegalese court.[7] The case was definitely dead. But they tried to bring the case back to life and that's why they went to the African Union. What is the AU's position regarding the case of Omar al-Bashir? What is its position with regard to Gaddafi? You can see that there is a double standard. . . .

***The Gazette:** Now, you have swallowed so many bitter insults in Senegal that you are disgusted. Do you want to go elsewhere?*
People have a habit of judging past situations with glasses from the present. When I was seeking political asylum in Senegal, there were at least three other states that were ready to receive me. But I had reasons to come to Senegal, because it was a very good decision. I don't regret doing it. Maybe, if I had chosen another destination, it would have been worse. I have never had any problems with the Senegalese people. On the contrary. They are still my friends, brothers and sisters. That is what is important. If some politicians in the name of sordid interests are trying to destroy Hissène Habré, that is their problem. And there are Senegalese people who suffer from this. That's right, yes! Many Senegalese suffer from this abuse. So I do not regret choosing Senegal, quite the contrary.

[6] 'Panier à crabes'. This expression describes an organization where no one is allowed to succeed because everyone is pulling everyone else down, like crabs in a pail.
[7] See also Hélène Cissé, in this volume, Chapter 5.

***The Gazette:** What can we learn from your time as head of state?*
I am a human being like all of you. Humans are capable of good things as well as bad things. I have devoted most of my youth to my country to serving my people. I fought with weapons in my hands, and I almost died several times, as evidenced by my three war wounds. As a politician I have principles, values and objectives. I have worked for national unity. I have also, with very few resources, worked for economic and social progress. I set up the Chadian administration. I have initiated a number of projects, including the oil project, which largely explains France's position. For me, oil must serve the people. Chad had a 51% share in the operation. In addition, there was a management training programme and another investment programme with donors, fully in line with standards, for the construction of the Chad refinery. All this was to be completed in 1992. And it was going to really benefit the Chadian people. But the people on the other side did not want it.

***The Gazette:** Don't you regret not being able to finish this work?*
I do not regret anything. Objectively, I had exposed myself too much. I could have done as others did, been a servant. This is the problem of our relationship with France. France wants servants and not partners. So I took the risk of being free and independent, and that I will never regret. Power in itself was frankly contrary to my objective. I saw it as a means, not an asset that I had to keep. I could continue war in order to hold on to power, but I said no. What I built, I did not have to destroy.

SECTION B
ESTABLISHING THE EXTRAORDINARY AFRICAN CHAMBER (EAC)

Section B explores the construction of the Extraordinary African Chamber (EAC) and the capture of its only defendant. In 2007, the African Union stepped in to resolve a growing crisis between its member states—Senegal and Chad—and Belgium regarding the prosecution of Habré and its wider implications for both Africa and international legal norms. Senegal had a constitutional obstacle, Chad had a political challenge and African legal institutions (ECOWAS) were staring down international institutions (ICJ). The African Union, itself a new power player, took a definitive step onto the international stage in backing and organizing the EAC. Judge Ben Kioko, former Director of the Legal Department of the Commission of the African Union, led the AU's early efforts to construct a court to try those responsible for atrocities committed in Chad from 1982 to 1990. Chapter 8 describes this process, providing insights in the political drama surrounding the court's creation.

With the court structure in place, a central question became: could the EAC take custody of any defendants? Hissène Habré was a public figure in Senegal, known as a devout Muslim who gave generously to local charities and lived a quiet life as father and husband in Dakar's upscale Ouakam neighbourhood. He lived under the political protection of Senegal's former president, Abdoulaye Wade, for years. The political winds changed with Macky Sall's election in 2012, however. Suddenly, Habré's arrest and trial appeared possible. In Chapter 9, Marcel Mendy, head of Communications for the EAC, discusses the work of his office during Habré's arrest, the most politically sensitive moment of the process. With Habré apprehended, the EAC's work of investigating the case against him and others officially began. Judge Jean Kandé was one of the Senegalese investigative judges for the EAC. Their investigation resulted in the indictment of Habré and five of his subordinates. In Chapter 10, Judge Kandé discusses the investigation phase, the challenges of securing Chad's cooperation with *in situ* fact-finding, and the benefits of working across international borders with other local actors.

There were also administrative challenges for the EAC. Donor countries had insisted on a strict budget and timeline and the court eventually won acclaim for adhering to both. This success is often credited to the efficient functioning of the tiny administrative office, run by Ciré Aly Ba and his two-person staff. In Chapter 11, Amadou Mokhtar Seck discusses his work in the EAC administrator's office, detailing how they organized the budget and how they met their responsibilities despite multiple constraints. Certain administrative functions of the EAC were assigned to a team of seasoned Senegalese clerks, who were seconded from their regular administrative posts to support this novel judicial experiment. In Chapter 12, Abouly Ba notes ways in which the EAC clerking experience compared to that of other Senegalese courts; he also describes the value he took from participating in Senegal's first ad hoc tribunal.

8
Creating the EAC in Senegal
Perspectives from the African Union

Ben Kioko, Legal Counsel to the Commission of the African Union[1]

Ben Kioko was the Legal Counsel and Director of the Legal Department of the Commission of the African Union in November 2005, when President President Wade declared publicly that he would hand over Mr Hissène Habré to the African Union (AU). Kioko was in charge of managing the docket at the AU Commission and reported directly to the Chairperson. This entailed preparing and introducing reports and draft decisions to the AU policy organs, engaging with Senegalese authorities, partner organisations, governments and other stakeholders, and undertaking communications with the media and the outside world. He was involved in all aspects of the establishment of the EAC on the AU side. From this vantage point, he has intimate knowledge of the twists and turns faced in dealing with Senegal on this issue. In August 2012, he was elected Judge and Vice President of the African Court on Human and Peoples' Rights.

The creation of the EAC in Senegal to try those alleged to be most responsible for war crimes and crimes against humanity allegedly committed in Chad during the reign of President Hissène Habré from 1982 to 1990 (Hissène Habré trial), was an important milestone for the African Union (AU). It gave a real meaning to the principles contained in the Constitutive Act that affirm the Union's commitment to fighting impunity and protecting human rights. The process encountered many twists and turns, and obvious machinations and shenanigans meant to delay if not scuttle the trial.

Early stages: The African Union and Senegal

On 19 September 2005, Belgium issued an international warrant, seeking Mr Habré's arrest. Upon on the recommendation of the Senegalese Prosecutor, the Court of Appeal of Dakar declared itself incompetent to rule upon the warrant.[2] Then, former President Abdouleye Wade declared publicly in November 2005 that he would hand over Mr Hissène Habré to the AU, which was seen at the African Union Commission as a politically expedient statement

[1] Observations in this chapter relating to the African Union are based largely, where a source is not indicated, on personal observations and notes of the author as The Legal Counsel/Director Legal Department of the AU. The views expressed in this chapter are strictly personal to the author and are not binding on the AU or the African Court.

[2] The Dakar Appeals Court ruling of 25 November 2005, following which Mr Habré was released.

Ben Kioko, *Creating the EAC in Senegal* In: *The President on Trial*. First edition. Edited by: Sharon Weill, Kim Thuy Seelinger, and Kerstin Bree Carlson, Oxford University Press (2020). © Ben Kioko. DOI: 10.1093/oso/9780198858621.003.0009

intended to ensure that Hissène Habré was never put on trial. As an international lawyer, President Wade was no doubt aware that the AU did not have in place any mechanism with competence to try Mr Habré. President Wade had argued that Senegal would never agree that a former African head of state could be tried in a European Country. However, he did not explain why Senegal did not wish to put Mr Habré on trial despite having jurisdiction over the alleged crimes; similarly, he did not discuss Habré's potential extradition to Chad.

President Wade's declaration, made without any prior consultation with the AU, was followed by a communiqué calling on the African Union Summit to 'indicate the jurisdiction which is competent to try this matter'.[3]

Following consultations with then-Chairperson of the AU Commission, President Alpha Ouma Konare, and other officials, we concluded that Senegal was hoping the AU Assembly of Heads of State and Government (AU Assembly) would declare that Mr Habré should not be extradited to face trial outside the continent without specifying an alternative mechanism. To his credit, President Alpha Oumar Konare saw through Wade's attempts to avoid trying Mr Habré. He insisted that the AU would not be party to such a conspiracy under his watch.[4] With this understanding, my office prepared a response that would direct the forthcoming debate at the AU Assembly towards a legal solution and away from a politically expedient approach.

In the light of these considerations, I recommended setting up a Committee of Eminent African Jurists to propose options for the trial of Mr Habré, and prepared a Progress Report together with the Terms of Reference (TOR) for the Committee and a Draft Decision containing principles and benchmarks.[5] This would be submitted for consideration during the AU Assembly session in Khartoum, Sudan, from 16–24 January 2006. I introduced the Report and the draft TOR and Decision to the AU Assembly then. After a few interventions, these documents were adopted without amendment.[6]

Pursuant to the Assembly decision, I convened the Committee of Eminent African Jurists (CEAJ) in Addis Ababa in April 2006 and a follow up meeting on 30 June 2006, just before the Seventh Ordinary session of the Assembly, held from 1 to 2 July 2006 in Banjul, The Gambia. The Committee's report analysed a number of options for trying Mr Habré, including in Senegal, Chad, and other locations. We also considered trial by ad hoc and regional tribunals. Citing the Convention Against Torture Committee ruling of 19 May 2006,[7] the Committee concluded that 'Senegal is the country best suited to try Habré as it is

[3] 27 November 2005, the Foreign Minister of Senegal, Cheikh Tidiane Gadio, issued a communiqué to the AU.

[4] His successor from 2008 to 2012, Mr Jean Ping, maintained the same stance.

[5] These benchmarks included 'Adherence to the principles of total rejection of impunity and international fair trial standards, including the independence of the judiciary and impartiality of proceedings, jurisdiction over the alleged crimes for which Habré should be tried, efficiency in terms of cost and time of trial, accessibility to the trial by alleged victims as well as witnesses, concrete recommendations on ways and means of dealing with issues of a similar nature in the future, and principally, priority for an African mechanism.' African Union, 'Decision on the Hissène Habré Case and the African Union' (2006) Doc.Assembly/AU/8(VI) Add. 9, <https://au.int/sites/default/files/decisions/9554-assembly_en_23_24_january_2006_auc_sixth_ordinary_session_decisions_declarations.pdf>.

[6] The 'Decision on the Hissène Habré Case and the African Union', among other documents, reiterated 'the AU's commitment to fighting impunity in line with the relevant provisions of the Constitutive Act' and decided to 'set up a Committee of Eminent African Jurists to be appointed by the Chairperson of the African Union in consultation with the Chairperson of the Commission of the African Union' and that the Committee 'shall be assisted in its work by the AU Commission (Office of The Legal Counsel)'. Further, the Committee was mandated 'to consider all aspects and implications of the Hissène Habré case as well as the options available for his trial', taking into account identified benchmarks (see (n 5) above).

[7] UN Committee Against Torture, 36th Session, Communication No. 181/2001: Senegal (19 May 2006) CAT/C/36/D/181/2001.

bound by International law to perform its obligations'[8] and to submit the present case to its competent authorities for the purpose of prosecution or to extradite him.[9]

The Report and its recommendations, together with an accompanying draft decision which my office prepared, were considered by the AU Assembly and adopted by virtue of decision Assembly/AU/ Dec.127(VII). The decision took note of the Report, observed that the African Union did not presently have a legal organ competent to try Hissène Habré, and mandated 'the Republic of Senegal to prosecute and ensure that Mr Habré is tried, on behalf of Africa, by a competent Senegalese court with guarantees for fair trial'.[10] President Wade accepted and undertook to implement the decision.

In implementation of that decision, we engaged Senegal with a view to jointly determine the nature and structure of the tribunal, the applicable law, required funding, etc. Subsequently in January 2007, Senegal enacted a new law, which allowed the domestic courts to prosecute cases of genocide, crimes against humanity, war crimes and torture, even when committed outside of Senegal, followed by an amendment of the Senegalese Constitution.[11] In this regard, Senegal submitted a progress report to the AU which the Assembly considered and adopted on 30 January 2007, by virtue of decision Assembly/AU/ Dec.157 (VIII). The decision took note of 'the interim Report presented by Senegal' and commended 'Senegal for the efforts it has already deployed to speed up the implementation of the Banjul Decision.'[12]

My Office then prepared several key documents: a Draft Agreement between the AU and Senegal, the Draft Statutes for the Special Court that would be set up within the Senegalese judicial system, the Draft amended Senegalese law, and the Rules of Procedure of the Court. The documents were submitted to Senegal for comments in advance of the first review meeting which I had called for.

The ECOWAS decision and tribunal options

While discussion was ongoing, Mr Habré's lawyers moved to the Court of Justice of the Economic Community of West African States (ECOWAS Court of Justice), which curiously decided on 18 November 2010, that Senegal must try Habré through a 'special or ad hoc procedure of an international character', as trial by a Senegalese Court would 'violate the prohibition of non-retroactive penal law'.[13] There was no discernible legal basis for this decision.

Senegal latched to this and insisted that the only way to proceed was by setting up an ad hoc international tribunal. Although we did not agree with the ECOWAS decision, it was final and could not be challenged anywhere. We had to accept it and go back to the drawing board. Mr Habré's lawyer also tried to put pressure on the AU Commission and to persuade

[8] Ibid para 28.

[9] African Union, *Report of the Committee of Eminent African Jurists on the Case of Hissène Habré* (2006) para 18.

[10] See the principles and benchmarks, (n 5) and (n 6) above.

[11] See also, Cissé, in this volume, Chapter 5.

[12] African Union, 'Decision on the Trial of M Hissène Habré and the African Union' (2007) Assembly/AU/ Dec.157 (VIII), <https://au.int/sites/default/files/decisions/9556-assembly_en_29_30_january_2007_auc_the_african_union_eighth_ordinary_session.pdf>. The decision also encouraged Senegal to pursue its initiatives to accomplish the mandate entrusted to it.

[13] See *Hissène Habré v Senegal*, Judgment No ECW/CCJ/JUD/06/10, 18 November 2010.

me personally to advise the AU Assembly that trying Mr Habré in any court would amount to double jeopardy. However, this argument did not hold water since the previous attempts to put Habré on trial in Senegal had been aborted for lack of jurisdiction, thus no trial or acquittal had taken place.

At around this time, President Wade insisted on full international funding for all the costs of the trial, which he estimated at $40 million dollars. He insisted that funds must be deposited with Senegal before the trial could start. This included a substantial amount for reconstruction of the old colonial courthouse as the venue for the trial. This resulted in a stalemate of several years, with no progress report submitted to the Assembly from January 2007 to February 2009. In the meantime, the International Court of Justice (ICJ) of February 2009,[14] on the application of Belgium, accepted Senegal's formal pledge not to allow Habré to leave Senegal pending its final decision. This also put additional pressure on Senegal.

With the view to addressing the new developments, we recommended to Senegal the establishment of the 'African Extraordinary Chambers', modelled on the Extraordinary Chambers in the Courts of Cambodia, commonly known as the Cambodia Tribunal or Khmer Rouge Tribunal, which applied national law and were composed of three Cambodian judges and two foreign judges.[15] In our view the proposed chambers could be considered to be of an international character and thus consistent with the ECOWAS decision. Senegal endorsed this proposal.

With that understanding, we prepared the Draft Agreement between AU and Senegal, the Draft amended Senegalese law and the Statutes of the EAC with inputs from interested parties, notably Mr Reed Brody of Human Rights Watch.[16] We also received inputs from Mr Adama Dieng, then Registrar at the International Criminal Tribunal for Rwanda and Mr Chile Eboe-Osuji of the Office of the UN High Commissioner for Human Rights. These documents were dispatched to Senegal for comments and observations. I also held regular briefing sessions with ambassadors and representatives of Senegal, Belgium, France, Germany, USA, UK, Switzerland, and the Netherlands, European Union Commission Representatives to the AU and in Brussels, other Senegalese authorities, senior Belgian Foreign Ministry officials, as well as with USA authorities including the US Ambassador-at-Large for War Crimes Stephen Rapp and then-Legal Counsel at the State Department, Professor Harold Koh. The proposed trial also featured in the agenda of the annual meetings between the AU Commission and the EU Commission.

Funding and follow-up negotiations with Senegal

Next, at the request of the AU Commission, the EU Commission assigned a team of experts led by Herman von Hebel, then Registrar at the Special Tribunal for Lebanon, to work with the AU team comprising legal, financial and other experts led by Mr Fafre Camara. The 'Joint Mission' team would engage the Senegalese authorities in finalising outstanding

[14] *Questions relating to the Obligation to Prosecute or Extradite (Belgium v Senegal)*, Provisional Measures, Order of 28 May 2009, ICJ Reports 2009, 139, para 72. See also Ventura and Baiesu, in this volume, Chapter.

[15] See Law on the Establishment of the EAC, with inclusion of amendments as promulgated on 27 October 2004 (NS/RKM/1004/006), Article 9.

[16] See also Brody, in this volume, Chapter 4.

issues such as the venue for the trial, provision of local staff, the budget resource mobilisation strategies and mechanisms for management of the funds. They would also propose a module of training for Senegalese judges and other staff as well as a media outreach strategy. The Joint Mission held a series of meetings with Senegalese authorities in Dakar.

The Joint Mission ruled out the disused old colonial house as the venue for the trial since renovation would have required substantial resources. The Team also came up with a budget of about USD$11 Million with provision for the hiring, if necessary, of international staff or staff seconded from the AU Commission to manage the funds in accordance with the AU Financial Rules and Regulations. The Joint Mission also made concrete proposals on the organisation of a Resource Mobilization Round Table, which was ultimately hosted by the AU in Dakar on 24 November 2010. At the Round Table, donors pledged €8.6 million, falling slightly short of the proposed budget. The Round Table established an International Multi-Donor Trust Fund to support the trial of Hissène Habré and adopted the modalities for the administration of the Trust Fund. On the governance and operational arrangements for the Trust Fund, it established a Management Committee and Fund Manager, with the management of the fund being undertaken by the United Nations Office for Project Support (UNOPS).[17] The AU pledged an amount of US$ one (1) million as its contribution to the budget of the trial, which was subsequently authorized by the AU Assembly.[18]

Taking into account my other engagements, Mr Jean Ping, AU Commission Chairperson appointed Mr Robert Dossou as his Special Envoy for the Hissène Habré trial. Mr Dossou undertook many missions mostly in Africa and in Europe accompanied by Mr Camara, who served as Legal Officer and my designated focal point in the Office of the Legal Counsel. In that capacity, he met EU officials, Heads of State of Senegal and Chad, EU Commission officials, and foreign ministry officials in Belgium, France, and the Netherlands.

Then, unexpectedly on 10 December 2010, President Wade announced that 'the African Union must take its case back . . . I've had enough of it at this point . . . I am going to get rid of him, full stop'.

On 13 January 2011, President Wade publicly announced rejection of an AU plan to try Habré before a court composed of Senegalese and African judges. This demand recalled Senegal's earlier position that Mr Habré should be tried by an ad hoc international tribunal that did not involve Senegalese judges. At the AU Assembly session held a few weeks later on 31 January 2011, the African Union expressed its frustration diplomatically by reiterating its position that Hissène Habré had to be put on trial by Senegal on behalf of Africa and called for the 'expeditious' commencement of such a trial.[19]

The first Consultative Meeting between the AU Commission and the Government of the Republic of Senegal took place at the AU Headquarters in Addis Ababa, Ethiopia, on 23–24 March 2011 to finalize the modalities for the expeditious trial of Hissène Habré through a special tribunal with an international character consistent with the 2010 ECOWAS decision.[20] At the end of the consultations, Senegal and the AU Commission agreed to establish

[17] The Donors Round Table took place in Dakar, Senegal on 24 November 2010 and was attended by some AU Member States, Partner countries and institutions, namely: African Union, Chad, Senegal, European Union, Belgium, Canada, France, Germany, Luxembourg, The Netherlands, Spain, Switzerland, the United Kingdom, the United States of America (USA), the Office of the United Nations High Commissioner for Human Rights (OHCHR), and the United Nations Office for Project Support (UNOPS).

[18] African Union, 'Decision on the Hissène Habré Case' (31 January 2011) Assembly/AU/Dec.340 (XVI), adopted by the 16th Ordinary Session of the Assembly.

[19] ibid.

[20] The Senegalese Minister of Justice led a twelve-man delegation while I led a five-person AU delegation.

an ad hoc international court in Senegal using the resources mobilized at the Round Table. The relevant legal documents (statute, agreement, etc) were also considered and it was agreed that a follow up meeting would be held in Dakar to finalise consideration of the documents.

The second consultative meeting was organized in Dakar, Senegal, 30 May 2011. I led the two-person AU delegation and the Senegalese Minister of Justice led a delegation of about twenty-five persons. However, at the opening of the meeting, the Head of the Senegalese delegation indicated that the Government of Senegal wished to move for the suspension *sine die* of the ongoing consultations.[21] As would be expected, I expressed my surprise and disappointment at the turn of events and requested an explanation. The response was that it was a government decision that had just been communicated to the delegation. I then requested a formal written notification as to what necessitated the adjournment *sine die* to enable an appropriate report to the AU Assembly. No response has ever been received to date.

In July 2011, we submitted a progress report to the AU Assembly, highlighting the latest developments. Upon review of this report, the AU Assembly urged Senegal to 'expeditiously put Hissène Habré on trial in accordance with the United Nations Convention against Torture or to extradite him to any country willing to put him on trial'.[22] Additionally, it called upon all AU Member States party to the UN Convention against Torture to notify the AU Commission of their willingness to put Hissène Habré on trial on behalf of Africa.[23] This decision was a diplomatic way of highlighting the growing frustration with the delay and back and forth on the trial. The only country that came forward with an offer to try Mr Habré was the Republic of Rwanda which, in its communication, indicated its motivation to provide home grown solutions to different challenges on the continent, based on Rwanda's unique experience with response to matters of gross human rights violations.[24]

On 11 July 2011, Belgium requested the extradition of Mr Hissène Habré. However, the Appeals Court of Dakar ruled the request invalid for non-compliance with the procedural and substantive provisions of the Law of Senegal on extradition. On 21 July 2011, a communication from the President of the Republic of Chad was delivered to AU Commission, notifying that the Government of Chad had decided to support the extradition of Mr Habré to Belgium as requested by the Association of victims of the Habré regime as well as human rights groups. On 5 September 2011, Belgium issued a new request for the extradition of Mr Habré to Belgium together with the arrest warrant issued against Hissène Habré and its annexes.

The January 2012 report of the AU Commission submitted to the AU Assembly candidly highlighted the marginal progress made in the organization of the Hissène Habré trial since 2006 and recommended two options, either organization of the trial in Rwanda or extradition to Belgium. In the end, the AU Assembly took note of the willingness of the Republic of Rwanda to put Mr Habré on trial and the fact that the Court of Appeal of Senegal had not responded to the renewed request for Habré's extradition to Belgium. Further, it requested

[21] Commission on the Implementation of Assembly Decisions on the Hissene Habré Case, 'Progress Report of the AU Commission on the Hissène Habré case', submitted to the AU Assembly at its 17th Ordinary Session (Malabo, Equatorial Guinea, 1 July 2011) para 11.

[22] African Union, 'Decision on the Hissène Habré Case' (1 July 2011) Assembly/AU/Dec.371(XVII) adopted by the 17th Ordinary Session of the Assembly.

[23] ibid.

[24] Letter from Republic of Rwanda National Public Prosecution Authority to the African Union Commission Legal Counsel, Ref No. I/1566911/14/ON/PJ (27 July 2001).

that the AU Commission consider the practical modalities, as well as legal and financial implications of the trial while continuing to consult with the relevant states and institutions to expedite the trial.[25]

A turning point in 2012

Immediately following Senegal's Presidential elections on 25 March 2012, Senegal's stance changed from non-cooperation to cooperation. President Wade was replaced by the newly elected President Macky Sall. Sall's Minister of Justice reached out to the AU Commission within a month or so of taking office to indicate her government's willingness to move forward with the trial.

With this newfound political will from Senegal, the stage was set for resolving all the outstanding issues in a spirit of cooperation including the venue of the trial, the nomination and appointment of Senegalese and other African judges, the establishment of the Registry, issues around privileges and immunities of the officials and staff, management of funds, contribution of Senegal to the trial, outreach strategy that would allow dissemination of information to Chad and other countries, facilitation and protection of witnesses, etc. The Statute and other documents were agreed upon in early 2013 and the Chambers inaugurated in February 2013. Mr Habré was then charged with crimes against humanity and war crimes and placed in pre-trial detention.

Conclusion

There is no doubt that the trial of Hissène Habré was ultimately made possible thanks to the commitment of President Sall's administration, as well as the efforts of other African leaders and the Chairpersons of the AU and AU Commission, who had not hesitated to put pressure on Senegal. Needless to say, the individual victims (some of whom later appeared as witnesses at trial), the victims' associations, victims' lawyers, other NGOs such as HRW, individuals within the Government of Senegal, and other governments and institutions such as the EU and the OHCHR, also played an invaluable role. With regard to European actors, it should be noted that Belgian officials consistently expressed openness as to the location of a trial, so long as Mr Habré had his day in court. Their flexibility and support helped ensure that the trial took place.

At the local level, the trial of Hissène Habré no doubt enriched the Senegalese judiciary through exchange of experiences and the entrenchment of international standards, particularly relating to fair trial rights. The Outreach Strategy also ensured that information about the trial was relayed throughout West Africa and was accessible to all around the world, thanks to the EAC's statute, which permitted filming and recording of the proceedings for broadcast purposes. The Republic Chad was also obligated under the Judicial Cooperation Agreement to broadcast the proceedings on public radio and television and to allow private

[25] African Union, 'Decision on the Hissène Habré Case' (30 January 2012) Assembly/AU/Dec.401(XVIII), adopted by the 18th Ordinary Session of the Assembly held in Addis Ababa, Ethiopia.

media entities to do the same. A consortium of NGOs was also retained by the EAC to undertake outreach in Senegal and Chad.

Was the trial truly an 'African Solution to African Problems'? Being the first time that Africa has taken such an initiative in favour of fighting impunity, it is no doubt a milestone for the AU and a success that Africa should be proud of. It was also quite cost effective compared with the United Nations ad hoc Tribunals and the International Criminal Court. The hybrid court model also seems to have been replicated in the establishment of a Special Court for crimes in the Central African Republic as well as the proposed Hybrid Court for South Sudan. However, one must remain mindful of the important contribution of many other players, as already indicated. There would have been no trial without the relentless efforts of the victims, their lawyers, the victims' associations, human rights groups, and various other individuals. Africans must continue to interrogate how international crimes committed on our continent can be prosecuted on African soil while ensuring that the interests of the victim are at the centre of all these efforts.

9
Arresting Habré

Marcel Mendy, EAC Head of Communications[1]

Marcel Mendy was the head of the Communications Unit of the EAC. Prior to the establishment of the EAC, he had worked as communications advisor at the Ministry of Justice, where he was part of a working group led by Mme Aminata Touré. She was then the head of the department and later Minister of Justice, advising on the organization of the trial of Hissène Habré. Mendy took an active part in developing both the statute and rules of procedure for the EAC as well as the accord between the African Union and Senegal and the road map for putting the EAC into place.

At the EAC, his unit reported on the activities of the EAC, represented the EAC as spokesperson, and organized media events for the public prosecutor. The Unit was the first point of contact for press, researchers, and others, and it performed public relations tasks, such as greeting visitors and managing the EAC's image. A central task of the Unit was to organize media coverage of the trial by the national and international press through accreditation and streaming the trial on the EAC's website. The Communications Unit was in charge of keeping Habré's arrest confidential until the operation occurred.

At around 1pm GMT on 30 June 2013, by a masterstroke, for that is what it was, Hissène Habré was arrested by police officers who came for him at his home. It is easy to imagine the stir that this arrest caused. The news spread like a wildfire across the city, the main topic of discussion from the neighbourhoods to the main squares. The incredulous supporters in the Ouakam district refused to believe that the man who passed for a 'good Muslim' and a 'generous patron' had been arrested. And yet there was no denying the evidence: after more than twenty years in Senegal, Hissène Habré had been arrested and taken into custody, like any other citizen, and would shortly face the Investigative Chamber to answer charges of 'war crimes, crimes against humanity and torture'.

Preparing the arrest

On the basis of information obtained from investigation reports established in both Brussels and N'Djamena about detention centres and suspected locations of mass graves,

[1] Author of *Affaire Habré: entre ombres, silences et non-dits* ['The Habré Affair: Between shadows, silences and the unspoken'] (editor's translation).

Marcel Mendy, *Arresting Habré* In: *The President on Trial*. First edition. Edited by: Sharon Weill, Kim Thuy Seelinger, and Kerstin Bree Carlson, Oxford University Press (2020). © Marcel Mendy. DOI: 10.1093/oso/9780198858621.003.0010

the Prosecutor's office had sufficient serious and concordant evidence for an arrest. Based on this evidence and after consulting with his team, the Prosecutor M'Backé Fall decided to proceed with the arrest of Hissène Habré a few days after his return from a mission in Chad.

On Thursday, 27 June 2013, Prosecutor M'Backé Fall instructed the Criminal Investigations Division (CID) to that end. Information had to be locked down to keep the opposing camp from being alerted, even if it was difficult to imagine that Habré could escape: his passport had by then already been confiscated and then what country would have been willing to accept him? M'Backé Fall had nonetheless ensured that I was kept in the loop. He told me to speak to no one under any pretext, and that I would have to communicate with the press afterwards. There were no public disturbances of any kind.

The CID did not just charge in. These professionals of this sensitive, critical service thought out and planned every step, taking all aspects of the problem into account: should they go in on a working day, given the threats made in the press by staunch supporters of Habré to act as a human shield to protect their 'benefactor' should anyone try to arrest him? How far would the most diehard be willing to go in affronting the police, how would the neighbourhood react to a police presence, etc.

From the outset the domicile of his second wife, Fatimé Raymonne, was the obvious choice. As it was located in the Almadies, a chic neighbourhood of Dakar, there would be less risk of popular resistance or demonstrations compared with the residence of his first wife in Ouakam, the working-class neighbourhood where Habré was an admired figure who made generous gifts to people in the community.

This preliminary work enabled the CID to determine the best moment—a Sunday—and the best location so that the arrest could go off without a hitch. They worked in conjunction with the gendarme units, who were responsible for guarding the Habré home and without whom the plan would have failed. This was especially true as the gendarmes had jurisdiction in the residential neighbourhood.

D-Day: 30 June 2013. At exactly 1pm, after one final consultation, the police and gendarmerie moved in. Having been localized at the home of his second wife in the Almadies where he was relaxing, Habré had no idea what was coming. The first step: infiltrate the dwelling to learn his exact location in the building. Second step: the order was given to the Polyvalent Intervention Brigade to take the house while sharpshooters waited outside. Instructions were given that Habré was not to be able to use any object that might allow him to harm himself or take his own life. The fear was that, if he felt the game was up, his pride might push him to a desperate act.

Once inside the building, Habré was escorted to the living room by, among others, his head of security, who had of course been briefed. He read the charges to Habré, who stood and started to become agitated. Habré asked to be allowed to go upstairs to fetch something. The security forces left no possible course of action that he could take advantage of, and he was immediately restrained.

One member of the security force that arrested Habré felt that this was the best solution. The risk was, had they allowed him to go back upstairs, his family might have witnessed a bloodbath. Military weapons were assumed to be present in the house, and that was immediately confirmed when the home was searched. The weapons were seized and submitted to the Clerk of the EAC. Habré himself had warned *The Gazette* in July 2011 in an exclusive interview:

> ... If you ask me what I'm going to do if a person or people break down the door, come into your house and try to attack you, what would you do? There are people who would panic and lower their heads, give up, and let themselves be taken like so many rabbits. Others are going to stick out their chests, plant themselves firmly on their legs and face their attackers. That's what is called legitimate defense in legal jargon. And that's the choice I'd make.' He concluded: 'Whoever violates my space, my house, to attack me, I have a legitimate right to defend myself.'[2]

In the execution of the operation to arrest Hissène Habré, it must be noted that the members of the CID kept cool heads. Habré was arrested and taken quietly and without violence or harm, into custody, and into the vehicle that was waiting outside. The public only learned of the arrest the following day.

From simple citizen to defendant before the EAC

Direction rue Carde, and the headquarters of the CID. Hissène was immediately received by the head of the service, the young and dashing Police Commissioner Idrissa Cissé. With all the respect to which he was due, Habré was informed by Commissioner Cissé of the mission that the prosecutor had given him. Habré's only response, given in a firm tone, was that he had nothing to say, and that the EAC had no legal basis in his eyes. Consequently, he would answer no questions, refusing even to state his name. This declaration was taken down as a statement which he did agree to sign. Habré remained in custody for forty-eight hours, in a cell arranged for him in the Special Commissariat of the Port of Dakar.

The following day, 1 July 2013, the Prosecutor M'Backé Fall, in charge of the proceedings, spoke at a press conference that we organized in the offices of the EAC and to which we invited all the national and international press, with many journalists.

On 2 July 2013, Hissène Habré was taken to the offices of the EAC, on the basis of the arrest warrant issued by the head of the CID at the request of the prosecutor, to hear the charges against him, and to confirm his pre-trial detention. He was then transferred to the special pavilion at the Aristide le Dantec Hospital. A team of lawyers was assembled to prepare his defense, which included François Serres, a specialist in international law and member of the Paris Bar, El Hadji Moustapha Diouf, and Ibrahima Diawara of the Dakar Bar, and Mamadou Ismaïla Konaté, of the Bamako Bar.

The arrest of Hissène Habré aroused no particular reaction among the Senegalese population beyond his usual supporters. There are some two dozen daily newspapers in Senegal; four or five of them were expressly in favour of Hissène Habré right through the end of the trial. The African Collective to Support Hissène Habré (CAS-HABRÉ), produced an incendiary communiqué against what it called the 'Extra-judicial African Chambers'. Friends of the former Chadian head of state belched out:

[2] Exclusive interview with Hissène Habré: Abdou Latif Coulibaly, Pape Amadou Fall, and Hamidou Sagna, 'Exclusive Interview—Hissène Habré Tells All: Wade, Diouf, Senegal ...' *La Gazette* (Dakar, 27 July 2011) (editor's translation). It is available in French here: xalimasn.com/entretien-exclusif-hissene-habre-dit-tout-wade-diouf-le-senegal/. See extracts are excerpted in this volume, Chapter 7.

> This Tuesday July 2, 2013, after 48 hours of sequestration, President Hissein Habré was charged and held under detention, in disregard of all legal rules and procedures . . . He was kidnapped on Sunday, 30 June 2013 at around 11 a.m. from his home by his own security guard, without arrest warrant or even official notification, worthy of mafia practices.[3]

Then the collective denounced and condemned in the strongest language 'these unrelenting attacks to which President Habré has been perpetually subjected for more than a decade, despite all the decisions of the highest national and international jurisdictions'. Finally, they cautioned the Senegalese government that national and international public opinion would witness 'everything that might happen to President Habré', and called again for 'respect for decisions handed down', to conclude with a demand for 'his immediate and unconditional release'.[4]

Reflection on the political context

It must be recalled that the arrest took place shortly after the visit of the American President Barack Hussein Obama to Dakar, so much so that clever minds did not fail to make the correlation between the two events. Did Senegalese justice wish to make a gift of Habré to Obama? Yes, some answered. Habré's lawyer El Hadji Diouf was unequivocal saying that by arresting Hissène Habré only two days after the American president's speech, Prosecutor M'Backé Fall had upset Senegal because he projected an image of a docile state under the thumb of an all-powerful America. In reality, that had nothing to do with it. The decision to arrest Habré was made well before Obama arrived in the Senegalese capital. It had of course raised concerns, and some suggested that the operation be put on 'standby'. But finally, the majority opinion opted to move forward, despite any comments that might be made. There was no connection. Speculation and wild rantings are free, and nothing can be done about them.

[3] Press release published 2 July 2013, by the CAS-HABRÉ. It was reported on in Marianne Ndiaye, 'Collectif africain de soutien à Habré rue dans les brancards' *Seneplus* (Dakar, 3 July 2013) <https://www.seneplus.com/article/collectif-africain-de-soutien-%C3%A0-habr%C3%A9-rue-dans-les-brancards> accessed 2 July 2019.

[4] ibid.

10

Investigations in Senegal and Chad

Cooperation and Challenges

Judge Jean Kandé, EAC Investigative Chamber

Kandé was one of the six investigating judges nominated to the EAC by the President of the African Union Commission based on a proposition by the Senegalese Minister of Justice. He was officially installed in Dakar on 8 February 2013. Following a Senegalese rule whereby the priority of rank was given to the eldest member, the title of coordinator of the chamber fell to him. On the administrative level, Kandé became the interlocutor for the court vis-à-vis the Administration of the EAC and all the parties connected to the case. On the judicial level, Kandé oversaw hearings where the accused was interrogated and depositions of civil parties and witnesses. He directed four international rogatory missions in Chad and one in France.

In the common law system, the Prosecutor intervenes to gather evidence required for the preparation of a possible trial. In a civil law system like the one created by the Statute of the EAC, however, this role is taken on by the investigating judge. The role of the Investigative Chamber was to undertake pre-trial preparation by performing whatever acts are necessary to uncover the truth and by looking for both incriminating and exonerating evidence to determine whether the trial should occur. Initially planned to take fifteen months, the investigating phase ended up taking nearly two years, from July 2013 through February 2015. At the end of the investigation, the investigating judges drafted the indictment that the Prosecutor then proceeded to present to the court.

The investigating judges received no particular training for the management of this procedure, except for a five-day seminar in Dakar on international criminal and humanitarian law, initiated by the African Union and organized and financed by the International Committee of the Red Cross (ICRC). Additionally, in September 2014 and at the invitation of the International Nuremberg Principles Academy, the investigating judges and the prosecutors went to Germany to participate in an experience-sharing seminar with judges, including Judge Daniel Fransen, serving on other international or internationalized criminal courts.[1]

During the investigation phase, members of the Chamber, humbly aware of their abilities to carry out such a mission, and out of the need for credibility, politely declined all

[1] Judge Daniel Fransen was at that time a judge at the Special Tribunal for Lebanon. He was previously the Belgian investigating judge on the Habré case and a witness at the trial. See extracts of Fransen's testimony, in this volume, Chapter 6.

Jean Kandé, *Investigations in Senegal and Chad* In: *The President on Trial.* First edition. Edited by: Sharon Weill, Kim Thuy Seelinger, and Kerstin Bree Carlson, Oxford University Press (2020). © Jean Kandé. DOI: 10.1093/oso/9780198858621.003.0011

offers of external help of experts or assistants to be attached permanently to the Chamber to assist them.

The discussion that follows will examine the traditional role of the investigating judges, the Chamber's work, its international rogatory missions in Chad, and the process of drafting the indictment closing the investigation.

The investigation in Senegal

In July 2013, investigations related to international crimes presumed to have been committed in Chad between 7 June 1982, and 1 December 1990, by Hissène Habré and others were referred to the Investigative Chamber.

Hissène Habré was arrested at his home on 30 June 2013 by the Commissioner of the Directorate of Criminal Investigations (CID), at the request of the prosecutor of the EAC, and a few days later, on 2 July 2013, the Investigative Chamber put Hissène Habré under pre-trial detention.[2] On 5 July and 11 October 2013, it issued international arrest warrants for his co-defendants, warrants that were all returned unexecuted on 11 December 2014.

Habré's interrogations

The first appearance before the investigating judge went forward in a spirit of cooperation. The defendant, who came to this appearance from detention, was accompanied by his counsel of choice. Subsequently, however, there were two incidents. First, instead of replying to the judges in response to the charges, the defendant wanted to read a document of several pages. Confronted with the firm opposition of the Court, his response was, 'First, I'm here completely illegally. I was the victim of an abduction, a kidnapping. Second, the question of the legality of the EAC is at stake and the question is before the Economic Community of West African States Court of Justice. Consequently, I refuse to answer your questions as I do not recognize the jurisdiction of the EAC, which I consider to be an administrative service.'[3]

The second incident happened when the defendant was about to be notified of his pre-trial detention. Despite the vain efforts of his counsel to resist this by attempting to impose contradictory arguments on the question of detention, which was not permitted under Senegalese law, he was detained, but threatened that he would no longer respond to summons to appear before the judges. A goodwill mission that went to see him in his place of detention was able to make him see reason. From then on until 22 December 2014, the date of our last meeting, our work with the defendant went ahead normally. The defendant typically sat in total silence, refusing to answer a single question—this after entering the audience chamber completely relaxed and then greeting us. We of course responded to his greeting. We even occasionally chatted briefly on matters not related to the case. Otherwise, true to his line of defence, the defendant never responded to questions or comments by the judges, and systematically refused to reread the records of the questioning and confrontation of

[2] See also Mendy, in this volume, Chapter 9.

[3] Evidence List D 33 in the case file.

witnesses and of the opening of sealed evidence, expert witness reports, or other documents. He also refused to sign documents presented to him for that purpose.

Hearings of the civil parties

The hearings of the civil parties began in Dakar on 17 July 2013, when four Chadians from N'Djamena and one Senegalese, all presumed victims of the Habré regime and accompanied by counsel, gave depositions at the headquarters of the EAC. They continued until the day before the investigation ended. On 3 August 2014, two of them, accompanied by council, were confronted with the defendant, who had been personally implicated in their prior declarations. Not only did the defendant not answer any of the questions of the judges concerning these repeated allegations, he ignored the witnesses completely. Not once did he so much as look at them.

The Republic of Chad made a request to be included as a civil party in the case on 25 February 2014, estimating that the State had been harmed by Habré's pillaging of the public property that he took with him when he fled the country. It was contested by both the civil parties and the prosecutor's Office, and the Investigative Chamber refused the request, arguing that the pillaging had nothing to do with the allegations for which Habré was being tried; Chad could not therefore be constituted as a civil party. This sudden desire of the Republic of Chad to be included in the trial, seven months after the start of the investigation already marked by two international rogatory missions on Chadian territory, can most certainly be explained, I believe, by an unacknowledged objective. If Chad had been accepted as a civil party, it would have had access to all the documents in the case file and would thus have been aware of all of the statements on file, including statements that were highly embarrassing for some authorities who were already in power during the regime of Hissène Habré. The Republic of Chad would have thus been in a position to put pressure on the authors of those statements and to block their planned or possible appearance in court. Nevertheless, one cannot be certain that this attempt to keep a constant eye the case and to exercise some control over the proceedings was a complete failure. Given that one of Habré's former lawyers was later seen with colleagues representing one of the victims' associations, it is perfectly legitimate to believe that the goal was achieved by this underhanded way.

Witness hearings

There were two principal sources of primary witness testimony. The first was during the Belgian investigating hearings. The Belgian judiciary opened a case against Hissène Habré on 30 November 2000. An international rogatory mission led by the Belgian investigating judge Daniel Fransen enabled many people to make their depositions during the first trimester of 2002. We were able to go through those depositions to select those individuals we wanted to hear ourselves, if they were still alive. That was a legitimate question, as by the time the EAC was created, eleven years had already passed and some of the witnesses had in fact died.

The reports from missions led by a doctor[4] who interviewed victims tortured by the Documentation and Security Directorate (the DDS, Habré's political police) was a second source. The reports were useful for the dossier and for the descriptions of events it contained. Witnesses provided the profile of an individual serving in military intelligence in Southern Chad during the repressions committed there, as well as of an individual who had been a frontline actor and witness to the creation of the Transitional Government of National Unity (GUNT) and its subsequent mutation into an armed political-military opposition movement against the regime in power. They also contained the declaration of a former GUNT military leader, a long-time member of this rebel movement who later became President Habré's military advisor. The option of giving testimony in Senegal allowed them a measure of protection from government pressure, enabling them to express themselves freely and amply.

A rogatory mission to France was also carried out in January 2014 at the French war crimes investigation unit, in order to investigate an 'insider'. As there was an international arrest order issued by a Chadian judge in the context of the trials in Chad dealing with the Habré period, the 'insider' was afraid of being arrested should he go abroad. As a former head of the DDS, he provided extensive details of the structures, internal functioning, unit staff heads, ad hoc commissions created to eliminated selected ethnic groups, missions to eliminate local elites, and atrocities committed particularly against southern civil populations by the regular army, as well as of the emergence of the 'Codos'—guerrilla opposition-groups.

Rogatory missions in Chad and France

The rogatory missions in Chad had two legal foundations: Article 3.1 of the Statute and Article 16 of the Judicial Cooperation Agreement of May 2013.

The four rogatory missions were carried out by the senior investigating judge of N'Djamena, with the constant presence of members of the Chamber.[5] At the beginning of the mission, a small delegation composed of the prosecutor of the EAC, the prosecutor of the N'Djamena Appeals Court, the senior N'Djamena judge and myself met the Chadian Minister of Justice to discuss the measures taken to facilitate our mission, as per the Cooperation Agreement, and to express our concerns. At that period, the cooperation with our Chadian colleagues was exemplary.

Leading rogatory missions in Chad was no easy task given the distance between where the events took place and the headquarters of the EAC in Senegal; the extent of the geographical area in Chad where the events took place; the sheer number of purported civil parties to hear; the huge mass of documents from the DDS to consult and exploit; and the short time allotted by the AU for the investigating phase.

The strategy for executing the international rogatory missions was structured around places of detention, sites presumed to contain mass graves, the archives of the DDS, and the hearing of civil parties and witnesses.

[4] This was Hélène Jaffre, a French doctor belonging to a socio-medical-legal structure called AVRE (Association for Victims of Repression in Exile), who brought medical aid to some 700 victims in Chad freed after Habré's fall (Evidence List D 1215 of the case file).

[5] The dates were 19 August to 3 September 2013; 1 to 23 December 2013; 15 to 31 March 2014; 24 May to 9 June 2014.

Visiting detention centres and exploiting the archives

The principal places of detention in N'Djamena from the period that were still extant were visited, photographed, and topographically measured, particularly to have a sense of the size of the cells in order to verify the credibility of a number of declarations that repeatedly referred to their overpopulation, largely superior to their intended capacity. Along with experts from the Equipo Argentino de Antropologia Forense (EAAF), we also visited sites situated near N'Djamena presumed to contain mass graves.

After evaluation, only those sites indicated by witnesses and civil parties that were intact, accessible, and appearing to be representative of the killings committed in Chad during the period in question were visited. Then, and with only one exception, experts meticulously examined their contents in our presence, contents which included personal belongings of a variety of types and human remains, occasionally with bullet holes. DNA samples were taken to be compared with samples from family members of presumed victims. The report the experts submitted provided scientific confirmation of the allegations.

As per the Cooperation Agreement, certified copies of the DDS archives were transferred to Senegal for examination under calmer, less hurried conditions. Despite their often deplorable condition, the archives were a precious mine of information on how the Habré regime functioned.[6] Other documents included in it were press clippings from the period, added by the expert brought in to illuminate the historical context of the Habré period and to illustrate his affirmations.

Hearing of the civil parties and the witnesses

Hearings and depositions involved the civil parties, direct and indirect victims, and witnesses. Their testimony was bolstered by the documentation provided by the expert who drafted the report on the historical context and by the DDS documents that had been saved from destruction, making it even more credible. The archives made the Habré case probably one of the best-documented international trials.

As the number of the civil parties was particularly impressive, the strategy was to have the Chadians and their Senegalese colleagues work from a precise questionnaire. Based on statistics provided by the Chadian judicial police, the total of all civil parties heard by its service during the first international rogatory mission was already 2,386. Credit for the success of this method also goes to the victims' associations that accompanied and organized their members.

All witnesses, including expert witnesses, made depositions before Chadian judges in our presence. It was thus that we heard some former DDS agents from the period who were then detained in N'Djamena, explain the organization and functioning of their former service, occasionally with a certain reticence. Some of them told us confidentially that they would very much like to be heard in Senegal, where they would be more ready to talk. They were no doubt intimidated by being before judges who were their compatriots and towards whom their distrust was palpable.

[6] See also Bercault, in this volum, Chapter 1, and Brody, in Chapter 4.

It should be specified that some of those giving testimony were heard directly by Chadian judges: as we had already read their depositions from the dossier on which the decision to proceed to investigation was based and knew that their testimony was of particular interest.

The limits of judicial cooperation

There were, however, limits to our judicial cooperation, including refusal to serve international arrest warrants or to charge individuals named in those warrants, but also simply not keeping promises that had been made.

Former military and political leaders' refusal to cooperate

Some important political and military leaders, including ex-President of Chad Goukouni Oueddei and Commander-in-Chief of the Armed Forces Wari Koni, simply refused to give statements as they were asked to. Oddly, the legal means to constraint them, as outlined in Article 10.3 of the Judicial Cooperation Agreement between Senegal and Chad of 3 May 2013, were not employed. The surprising official reason given to us by the senior judge was that they did not wish to be heard in the context of this case.

Among the individuals refusing to be heard was the President of Chad, Idriss Déby Itno. Our various attempts to obtain his cooperation, via the magistrate who served as liaison with the EAC to set up the appropriate conditions, all failed. It became clear that this question had become a red line for N'Djamena, too irritating and embarrassing for the Investigative Chamber to be allowed to cross. And yet it was the president himself who had said in a broadcast on a private radio station in Dakar in September 2013, one month after the arrest and detention of Habré. 'Let me say this clearly. I worked with Habré. If the judges want to hear me, I am available. I am a Chadian citizen … We have not excluded the possibility of testifying if it is deemed necessary and of the judges request it.'[7]

Another individual we did not hear was an important former leader of the 'Codos' rebels. He was in the middle of his deposition and had promised to provide documents to support his declarations, when the hearing had to be suspended because of a call he had received telling him that a close family member had died. Yet he never returned, despite his promises to do so. Unofficial but reliable sources indicated that he had been put under pressure not to testify; that pressure was ultimately effective.

Promises not kept and obstacles raised

Based on several incidents, one could, correctly or incorrectly, assume a hidden desire to limit the scope of the investigation, not on the part of the Chadian colleagues with whom were worked regularly, but rather on the part of administrative authorities whose contribution was essential as they supplied the vehicles requisitioned to be at our disposition for

[7] See 'Procès de Habré: Idriss Déby prêt à témoigner' *Seneweb News* (Dakar, 17 September 2013) <www.seneweb.com/news/Justice/proces-de-Habré-idriss-Déby-pret-a-temoigner_n_106007.html> accessed 2 July 2019.

travelling around N'Djamena. In December 2013, visits to sites situated in various regions were planned to begin in the south. Our transportation was to be vehicles provided by the Public Administration. In the end we used private vehicles rented by the EAC and paid for out of the budget for the international rogatory missions. We had no alternative when at the last minute we were informed that the state of dilapidation of the administration's automobile fleet meant that our transportation would be unreliable. Based on that experience, we always preferred the option of renting vehicles from private individuals for all our subsequent travel to zones at some distance but still accessible after several hours of driving.

Also, the welcome given to the final EAC rogatory mission was rather different from that for the preceding ones: with the exception of the senior judge, the local judicial authorities were conspicuous by their absence. We then had to come up with our own accommodation: after several hours spent tracking down hotel rooms throughout the city, we finally found lodging in several hotels quite distant from each other, where no particular security measures were taken for us. But this state of affairs in no way hindered us from accomplishing our mission.

Refusal to serve arrest warrants

Arrest warrants issued for two ranking leaders of the ex-DDS, Saleh Younous and Mahamat 'El Djonto' Djibrine, remained unserved. They were being held in N'Djamena in the context of a pending legal procedure in Chad that had been in hibernation for more than ten years, then curiously reactivated three days after Habré was charged. It then went into overdrive, in stark contrast with the extreme slowness that had hitherto prevailed, so that that case actually went to trial in the first instance before the case pending before the EAC.

To bypass this difficulty, a final request was sent to the N'Djamena senior judge: a final international rogatory mission in order to hear the individuals concerned. The response was a scathing rejection on the grounds that they had already been charged by the Chadian investigating judge responsible for trying Habré and his accomplices. While initially we had worked cooperatively, the change in attitude to one of non-cooperation began following the decision on appeal of the Trial Chamber to reject Chad's request to be included as a civil party by the Investigative Chamber—a sound legal decision, but one that was poorly received in Chad.

The closure of the investigation

The preparatory step: building a database

The complexity of the case and the impressive amount of evidence required from the outset procedures that were radically different from those usually employed on our jurisdictions. The strategic decision to construct a database, an unquestionably excellent one, was enacted through a series of steps. The first was to list documents in chronological order as they were produced, to classify them and to scan them, making the dossier available in a digital version. To make this flow of information easily accessible and following a model suggested by us members of the court, an information technologist designed a database expressly for us with rubrics that included the document listing number, the name of the victim, the name of the perpetrator and his profession, the date and place of the event and the type of infraction committed. Then, for the judges, the work was divided by infraction type, and the data collected was inserted progressively into the constituent elements, allowing each charge to be accompanied by any scientific evidence, documents or testimony. Finally, mutual exchange and cross-referencing of our individual work, accompanied by any observations, preceded the final validation of the collective work. This step intervened to prepare the final phase of the investigation, confirmed by the issuance of the closing order.

The indictment

At the end, when the Investigative Chamber deemed that it had concluded its work, it respected the formality of placing the dossier at the disposition of council for the defendant and the civil parties. Then it transmitted the dossier to the prosecutor by order of referral for final on 5 January 2015, allowing him to hand down the final indictment, which he was required to submit to us to close the investigation. At that time, we were thirty-six days from the end of the investigation phase set by the AU.

The prosecutor took one month to establish its final indictment, which was prejudicial to us due to time pressure, as I explain below. As the days passed without the dossier coming back to us, the Chamber requested of the AU, as a precaution should the prosecutor experience a lengthy delay (which it did), that it grant one final, exceptional extension of a further ten days. This was not well-received. The AU was apparently more attentive to the extremely parsimonious management of its financial resources than to the objective examination of the merits of the request.

On 6 February, the day after the request for an extension of the mission and nine days before the final deadline of 15 February the dossier was returned to us with a definitive indictment and order of referral to the EAC Indicting Chamber, a document of 176 pages. The time remaining to complete the mission was objectively very short when compared to the period of reflection that jurisdictions are usually accorded between the opening of deliberations and the date retained for the announcement of the verdict, particularly for an international trial of this scale. Any failure on our part, in this brief period accorded to us, would have seriously compromised going to trial. But, thanks to our anticipating this situation, we already had a working draft of our orders and the effects of the AU's refusal to grant an extension were thus attenuated. As soon as the dossier with the prosecutor's final indictment reached us, we made multiple close readings of the lengthy document, carefully examining and analysing the arguments of the Ministry, not all of which we found fully convincing, and made our final modifications. Well aware of the responsibilities that rested on my shoulders as coordinator of the Chamber, I made the commitment to my colleagues to reread our over 100-page document entirely and thoroughly. Some typos did escape my attention during my long night of labour; quite honestly, the quality of the document could have been higher had the AU not been so intransigent.

It was thus on 13 February 2015, under constant pressure, after validation and having met so many challenges, that the Investigative Chamber concluded its mission by issuing an order to refer (ie indictment) Hissène Habré to the Trial Chamber of the EAC for crimes against humanity, war crimes, and torture. The order contained no references to sexual violence as the presumed victims either refused to speak out, or spoke in vague or allusive terms, or refused to provide enough detail to enable evidence from the case to corroborate their accusations. That is why during the investigation phase we were unable to substantiate those charges sufficiently in their constituent elements to be able to retain them.

Conclusion

Preparing this process entrusted to Senegal gave rise to important legislative modifications. Introducing the notion of universal jurisdiction into the Code of Penal Procedure and integrating international crimes into the Senegalese Penal Code allowed crimes subject to international law to be incorporated into national law. Additionally, the Constitution was amended to accord a special derogation to the rule of non-retroactivity of criminal law, thus allowing the fight against the impunity of those suspected of committing mass crimes.

Ultimately, despite the noble intentions justifying it, and despite perceptions of its being a critical step and a turning point in the fight against impunity, the trial leaves a sense of unfinished business in that Hissène Habré was alone in the indictment. Everything that could possibly be done was done so that all the principal suspects of the international crimes committed in Chad during the period in question, individuals identified and, in some cases, detained in N'Djamena, could be transferred to Senegal to be tried. But then Chadian officials, whose initial collaboration had been so appreciated, decided to cease to cooperate.

What I myself learned from participating in this unprecedented trial in Africa is that how much chance a rogatory mission for international crimes has of succeeding depends, first, on open and loyal cooperation between all the actors involved. Second, it relies on the quality of the applicable laws. In the Statute of the EAC, the rule of primacy of the international criminal law, usually present in international statutes, was sadly lacking. Similarly, in the ad hoc Judicial Cooperation Agreement signed by Senegal and Chad on 3 May 2013, requiring the consent of both the individual and the Republic of Chad before that individual could be temporarily transferred to Senegal to appear as a witness, was, in practice, particularly harmful for the proceedings. These obstacles seriously compromised the trial organized by the EAC, a criminal jurisdiction marked by its mixed nature. This mixed nature was indicated by the duality of applicable law. It was also mixed in that its judges were mostly Senegalese with only two judges of other nationalities, one of whom was President of the Trial Chamber and the other of the Appeals Chamber. This near-homogeneity in the Investigative Chamber certainly allowed it to avoid the kind of misunderstandings that can lead to blockages, such as those described in the Extraordinary Chambers within the Cambodian Courts, a source of inspiration for the EAC.

11
Managing the EAC

Amadou Mokhtar Seck, EAC Administration and Finance Office

The mission of the Administrator's Office was to ensure the smooth functioning of the EAC, managing its budget, accounting, logistics, and personnel. The Office was directed by Mr Ciré Aly Bâ, a magistrate by training who had acquired significant experience in international justice from having been seconded to the International Criminal Tribunal for Rwanda for six years. Mr Bâ had also been Chief of Staff to the Prime Minister of Senegal for three years. Mr Amadou Mokhtar Seck, Administration and Finance Manager and the author of this contribution, had more than a dozen years' experience in administration and management in both public and private structures in Senegal and a mastery of the procedures of several funding organizations, including the European Union.

As of 10 September 2017, the EAC budget was adopted at 5,527,399,330 CFA francs, equivalent to 8,426,466 euros or 10,086,495 dollars. The budget came from contributions received from financial partners including the Netherlands, Belgium, Chad, the African Union, the European Union, Germany, France, Luxemburg, and the United States. Senegal, the host country, made magistrates, legal aids, and some legal and penal infrastructures available to the EAC, which it continued to finance. It also exempted from duties and taxes all acquisitions made by the EAC in the context of their operations.

Given the prior experiences of similar tribunals as well as the slowness and delays inherent in this type of procedure, it was possible that an extension of the trial's original timeframe would be required. Thus, rather than limiting itself to executing the budget as initially planned, the Administrator's Office worked to identify areas for potential savings over the course of the EAC so as to finance any eventual delays.

EAC structure and personnel

The EAC was installed within Senegalese jurisdictions and included both administrative and legal personnel:

- an Investigative Chamber with six Senegalese investigating judges (four judges, two substitutes) and two clerks;
- an Indicting Chamber, acting as an appeals chamber over the investigative judges, with four Senegalese judges and a clerk;
- a Trial Chamber with four judges—three of Senegalese nationality (two judges, one substitute) and the President of another nationality—two clerks and two legal aides;

Amadou Mokhtar Seck, *Managing the EAC* In: *The President on Trial.* First edition. Edited by: Sharon Weill, Kim Thuy Seelinger, and Kerstin Bree Carlson, Oxford University Press (2020). © Amadou Mokhtar Seck. DOI: 10.1093/oso/9780198858621.003.0012

- an Appeals Court with the same configuration as the Trial Chamber;
- A Prosecutor's Office with a Prosecutor and three deputy prosecutors, two clerks, and a jurist;
- an Administrator's Office that, in addition to the Administrator who led, supervised, and coordinated activities, included personnel with varied backgrounds: an administration and finance manager; two assistants (administrative and accounting); two journalists; a webmaster; a head of the central registry; support staff including four secretaries (spread out across the judicial chambers), two record-keeping staff, and six chauffeurs; and a police security detail assigned to the presidents of the Chambers, the Prosecutor, and also responsible for overseeing security on the premises.

The Administrator's Office was responsible for overseeing the personnel, managing the budget, and providing necessary logistical support for the smooth functioning of activities at the EAC. In addition to supporting the above-mentioned courts, this diverse team was charged with assisting the Prosecutor, the civil parties, and the defence, all while managing personnel, budgets and financing, general services, security, and communications for the court. In the context of fulfilling its mission, the Administration of the EAC confronted several challenges that it met through the development and implementation of an array of strategies.

Controlling the budget and working with the Steering Committee

Given the specificities of the EAC, a number of political, judicial, financial, and time-related challenges needed to be met. As budgetary items related to legal activities (such as rogatory missions, expert consultations, jurisdictional assistance, etc) were difficult to control and depended entirely on the decisions of the judges, the Administrator's Office focused instead on finding opportunities for reducing costs related to equipment and operating expenses.

The strategy for equipment (furniture, rolling stock, office and computer equipment), consisted of dividing the contracts into homogeneous lots and retaining basic, standard technical specifications when developing documentation for calls for tender. This strategy enabled us to attract the largest possible number of bids and thus benefit from the best cost-price ratio. In the end, the office saved 125 million CFA francs, equivalent to 190,00 euros or 228,00 US dollars on equipment purchases relative to the amount budgeted.

Concerning operating expenses, rigorous supply management and better monitoring of the pace of consumption allowed us to generate significant savings. These savings, which accumulated month after month, can be estimated at 156,000 CFA francs (237,820 euros or 285,000 US dollars).

Together, the savings generated allowed not only for financing extensions, but also for occasioning a remaining balance of 300,000 CFA francs (500,000 euros or 550,000 US dollars) after the closure of the EAC. This balance was transferred to the African Union, constituting the first contribution to the victims' reparations fund being put into place.[1]

[1] See also Sperfeldt, in this volume, Chapter 35.

The Steering Committee

A financial Steering Committee was created for the EAC as per Article 7 of the Joint Financial Accord of the Chambers. It was composed of representatives from Senegal, the African Union, Germany, Belgium, the United States, France, Luxemburg, the Netherlands, and Chad. Switzerland and the High Commissioner for Human Rights also attended Steering Committee meetings as observers.

The representative of the African Union or, in his absence, the representative of the Government of the Republic of Senegal presided over the Steering Committee, which met quarterly. Upon request of the Administrator, the President of the Steering Committee can convoke an extraordinary session to discuss a predetermined agenda, when needed.

The Steering Committee's mission included overseeing the securing of resources for the Fund, assisting in setting up programs for outreach, media information, and trial monitoring, receiving and examining periodic reports from the Administrator of the Chambers, and providing advice and directives concerning all the non-judicial aspects of the Chambers' operations and their efficiency.

In this context, the Prosecutor and the President of the Trial Chamber were invited to the Steering Committee to support their request for extensions.

The reports prepared by the consultant charged with implementing the outreach program were also submitted to the Steering Committee for validation.

Rogatory missions

Proper functioning of the rogatory missions in Chad required making office supplies and logistical support available on site (for example, vehicle rental for the judges' transportation within Chad).[2] The duration of these missions meant significant funds were needed that could not be managed from Dakar, given challenges related to communication and banking cooperation between Senegal and Chad. For obvious security reasons, it was out of the question to directly provide mission leaders with sufficient sums. We thus used a system of temporary accounts with debit cards to transfer the necessary funds.

Management of witnesses

Nearly all the witnesses called to testify lived in remote areas of Chad very far from N'Djamena, the capital. Moreover, most of them did not have travel documents allowing them to go to Dakar.

We thus needed to develop a strategy to contact them with enough time to:

- Identify those who did not have travel documents and arrange to have them issued;
- Plan their trip to Dakar according to the schedule for court appearances set out by the Prosecutor's Office;
- Organize their lodging, security, and their return to Chad.

[2] See also Kande, in this volume, Chapter 10.

More than ninety witnesses and experts made the trip to Dakar, primarily from Chad. Travel documents were successfully arranged for fifty-seven of them.

To attain this result, since we could not station personnel from the EAC in Chad, we had to put together a multidisciplinary team that could work with the Administrator's Office to coordinate locating witnesses across the various regions and ensuring their security. Once in Dakar, the witnesses were greeted and accompanied by two social workers whom the EAC Administrator recruited to ensure the witnesses received adequate care. Since the original budget had not accounted for hiring these social workers, the Administrator's Office took the initiative of reducing the number of additional security personnel assigned to the courtroom (reduced to fifteen instead of twenty) and applied the savings to the two additional salaries.

The social workers were of tremendous help for the wellbeing of the witnesses, most of whom had never travelled outside their home country, much less testified before a tribunal of this kind. In fact, it became necessary for the administrative and financial manager and his assistant to provide the social workers with additional support in responding to panic attacks and other symptoms of distress, which were not uncommon. They were at times called upon in the middle of the night to come to the aid of a witness who was unwell, or to contact emergency services if necessary.

The witnesses were housed in a local hotel, whose management had signed a contract agreeing to rent out an entire floor for three months. The witnesses stayed there while awaiting their turn to testify during the initial trial. One room on the floor was reserved for the security agents assigned to their protection.

Similarly, each of the three primary victims associations designated a representative for whom the EAC arranged transportation, food, and lodging.

Arrangements for broadcasting the trial

On the basis of an initial communication plan drawn up by the EAC with the assistance of a Swiss development cooperation, a memorandum was signed with Radiodiffusion Télévision Sénégalaise (RTS). The RTS agreed as part of its public service mission to take on half of the broadcasting expenses, as the EAC could only contribute the amount budgeted for that purpose (50 million CFA francs or 91,240 US dollars).

Key moments of the trial could thus be seen from the four corners of the earth. The hearings were also streamed via the EAC website thanks to measures put in place by the RTS. Chadian television also benefited from all necessary support thanks to the terms of the memorandum.

Other challenges were also satisfactorily overcome, such as the installation of a video conferencing system that allowed witnesses who could not make the journey to testify nonetheless.

The EAC's financial steering committee played a decisive role in implementing these strategies, as its mediation allowed for reaching agreed solutions to conflicting demands and pressures.

As a trial is not the sort of event whose broadcasting can simply be left to any willing contender, it was necessary to limit private operators' access to the debates. Moreover, Chad

had at first also wished that broadcasting be entrusted to an official structure capable of distributing the signal to organizations that requested it.

Swiss development cooperation provided the EAC with an archiving expert, who made various proposals and assisted the EAC and its Trial Chamber with the development and organization of both electronic and hard copy archives.

Conclusion

The EAC emerged as a decisive step for the construction of an equitable justice. Nationally, the court strengthened both the judicial system and its actors. Until Dakar become 'The Hague of Africa', however, it is important for Africa as a whole to reflect on how to make this step permanent, particularly by resolving the nagging question of financing. Even though a fund to compensate the victims has been created, ensuring that reparations are in fact made also remains a critical issue.

12
Professionalizing a Political Trial
A Clerk's Perspective

Aboubacry Ba, Clerk to the EAC

Upon leaving school Abouly Ba was assigned to the Magistrate's Court in Guédiawaye, where he served for six years before being transferred to the High Court of Kaolack. At the EAC, he worked as a court clerk and participated in all the trial phases, from the preliminary investigation all the way through to archiving documents before the Trial Chamber and the Court of Appeal.

In any trial, the clerk is a critical link as the guarantor of the proceedings. The EAC under Senegalese jurisdiction had qualified clerks to accompany the Administration, the different courts, and the Prosecutor's Office in the preparation, investigation, and judgment of the Hissène Habré case.

According to Article 13(5) of the Statute of the EAC, the Minister of Justice put out a call for applications for the six clerks who would be appointed to the above-mentioned courts. The candidates selected from the fifty-six applicants were seconded from their posts to dedicate themselves exclusively to the Chambers; each had at least eight years of professional experience.[1]

It should be noted that the Habré trial, which was a first for Senegal, was almost a leap in the dark for us clerks as we had had no experience with or training on the international courts which usually dealt with the types of crimes being brought before the EAC. The clerks nonetheless executed their work quite satisfactorily at the various posts to which they were assigned.

During the investigation phase where there were two of us, adopting an assembly-line type of process made the work much easier. To make the extremely voluminous case file as easy to read as possible, each document had to be listed, as with any investigation report. Administrative documents such as summonses and judges' orders went into List A and were numbered according to their order of reception or emission. This was also the

[1] Madame Ndeye Macoura Cissé, previously attached to the Senegalese Supreme Court, served as coordinator of the central clerk's office. When she retired before the end of the trial, she was replaced by Madame Ndeye Ndiaré Ndaw, previously of both the Court in Dakar. Mr Cheikhou Oumar Sall, the only head clerk among us, was seconded to the Prosecutor's Office, where he served with Madame Marie Rose Touré. Madame Touré was previously attached to the Court in Dakar, notably in the Investigative Chamber for over ten years before being appointed to the clerk's office. Mr Abdoul Abass Sy served at the Appeals Court of Dakar; for the EAC, he managed the clerk's office of the Indicting Chamber during the investigation phase before being transferred to the Trial Chamber and then to the Court of Appeal. Mr Boucounta Mendy served successively at the High Court in Saint-Louis and as Technical Advisor to the clerk's office at the Ministry of Justice.

Aboubacry Ba, *Professionalizing a Political Trial* In: *The President on Trial*. First edition. Edited by: Sharon Weill, Kim Thuy Seelinger, and Kerstin Bree Carlson, Oxford University Press (2020). © Aboubacry Ba. DOI: 10.1093/oso/9780198858621.003.0013

case for documents pertaining to the identity of the accused (such as identification records and character investigations), which went onto List B. Documents concerning detention (such as detention orders, arrest warrants, or records of unsuccessful searches) went into List C. Finally, evidence went onto List D and was numbered in the same manner. Once this initial work had been completed, the judges could begin their investigation, still with our continued organizational assistance.

The Habré trial was a rich experience in all manner of ways. On a professional level, it allowed some of us to complete or participate in procedures that we had previously known only in theory. It was also a rich human experience that gave us an inside view into a whole section of the history of an African country in which we had never previously set foot and of which we knew neither the languages nor the culture.

The trial is of immense pedagogical interest as it was the first time that a former president was tried on African soil. To evoke the professionalization of political trials in Africa leads us first to review the responsibilities of the Senegalese clerk and then to discuss in detail the role of the clerk within the hybrid character of the EAC.

Responsibilities of the Senegalese clerk

In the organization of Senegalese courts, there are always three distinct entities: the Prosecutor, the Judge and the Registry. The Registry is both the entrance and exit door to any legal proceeding, hence its importance in the proper administration of justice. Thus whether for common law courts or courts of special jurisdiction, there is always a Registry whose mission, with a few exceptions, is more or less the same.

Traditional role in Senegalese courts

The Registry, in the lexical sense of the legal term, is the court secretariat, in particular where cases are opened and closed. Clerks work with judges and prosecutors as well as with investigations judges. Every day they perform specific but varied tasks which collectively are known as the work of the registry.

In each court, there is a registry headed by a clerk administrator (formerly the head clerk), who is aided in his work by clerks, secretaries, and administrative staff. The actual work of a clerk depends on the court to which it is attached.

Prosecutor's clerk

The clerk receives the charges and transmits them to the Prosecutor, who then decides on the appropriate course of action. The clerk is also responsible for receiving and sending the Prosecutor's correspondence. He transmits cases opened by the Prosecutor to the appropriate judges. Under the supervision of the Prosecutor, the clerk oversees the enforcement of sentences and issues visiting permits. He is the natural buffer between the litigant and the Prosecutor who, by virtue of his status, is sometimes inaccessible.

Investigative Chamber clerk

During the investigation phase, the clerk assists the examining investigating judge in all steps of the legal proceedings. He participates in hearings by taking down the minutes of the proceedings as dictated by the judge. When a judge opens an investigation, the clerk organizes the case file starting with the listing of documents and maintains a summary table to oversee the regularity of the procedures and, especially, to keep an eye on the expiry dates for detention orders and other procedures. Under the authority of the investigating judge, the clerk delivers visiting permits and sends and receives correspondence for the chamber. He transmits the judge's orders and the indictment to the lawyers and civil parties once the case is over.

Court clerk

The clerk works closely with the judges in all the audiences and court's procedures. In the courts, the clerk serves with judges for civil cases, felony cases, police court, and summary judgments. The clerk writes parts of the judgment, reviews it, and sometimes even writes judgments in whole. He is responsible for keeping minutes and delivering copies of judgments. For the High Court, the clerk produces and delivers extracts of criminal records under the supervision of the public prosecutor. He also maintains the Trade and Personal Property Credit Register, and redirects litigants and provides information concerning their cases. In the magistrate's Court, the clerk fulfils his traditional function and in addition provides certificates of nationality.

These are the principal functions of a clerk in a traditional jurisdiction. The role of the clerk in a jurisdiction like the EAC is roughly the same.

The role of the clerk in the EAC

The central registry of the EAC had a clerk at its head who was assisted in her work by a secretary and three transcribers. She was in charge of centralizing appeals, preparing the formal documents, and transmitting them as appropriate. She supervised the work of the transcribers and transmitted transcriptions of proceedings to judges, prosecutors, and other parties.

In the Prosecutor's Office, there were two clerks whose tasks were fairly limited: reception and transmission of dossiers, documents, and correspondence between the Prosecutor and the various courts as well as the Chancery and the prison administration.

Two clerks were assigned to the investigation phase. Their work load was fairly heavy as they played an important role from the opening of the investigation to its conclusion. Upon referral to the Investigative Chamber, the clerks had to track and label all elements in the dossier so as to facilitate its usage for all parties. After this preliminary work, the clerks prepared summons orders for the various parties as per the judges' orders. The everyday work of the clerks of the Investigative Chamber was to aid judges during court sessions by serving notices and by drawing up notices of orders issued for all parties whenever the judges issued orders. It was also their role to inform expert witnesses of their designation, to receive any reports from them, and to provide copies of such reports to all parties.

The clerks were also responsible for the transmission of judges' orders of referral to the Prosecutor should one party so require. When one party contested an order, clerks ensured that the dossier was complete and up-to-date before transmitting it to the Trial Chamber.

Furthermore, clerks handled incoming and outgoing correspondence for the Investigative Chamber. They received all documents from the different parties and transmitted them to the investigating judges. They also participated in all the international rogatory missions to Chad, during which they assisted the judges at the hearings and participated in the visits to the detention centres and mass graves in various Chadian villages.

At the end of the investigation phase, the clerks informed the parties, inventoried the completed dossier, and transmitted it to the Prosecutor's Office. In addition, the clerks were responsible for establishing visiting permits for those wishing to visit the accused.

In the Trial Chamber, the clerk assisted the judges during the sessions, established and issued summonses, and handled the correspondence of the chamber. The clerk was also responsible for transmitting any decisions handed down to the concerned parties.

In the Trial Chamber and the Court of Appeal, the work of the clerks was primarily to aid judges in the everyday functioning of the court. Clerks established and issued summonses, served beside judges during hearings to keep records of statements made by the parties, and were also responsible for receiving and transmitting all documents submitted by the parties. Those individuals wishing to be included as civil parties addressed their applications to the clerks, who would then transmit these requests to the judges. Clerks took care to notify interested parties of all of the judges' decisions. Clerks also had to track down missing documents, and recorded all documents and materials supplied by the parties. Clerks from the Trial Chamber were retained at the end of the trial to serve at the Court of Appeal.

During the appeal phase, clerks were required after every session to visit the accused in detention (as his presence was not required in court) and read him the complete account of the hearing. The court-appointed lawyers acting for the defence had requested that their client not be compelled to attend the sessions, a request that the President of the Trial Chamber had granted. To ensure that he was nonetheless as informed of the day's events as the other parties, the attending clerk wrote up minutes at the end of every session to be presented to him. It should be noted that every time we went to the detention house to meet with Mr Hissène Habré, he refused to see us either to hear the minutes read to him or to receive a written copy, a fact which was noted in the visiting logs by the Director of the prison where the accused was being held.

At the end of the appeals trial, the clerks made and distributed copies of the final judgments to all parties.

Once the appeal had been judged, two clerks were designated by the Administrator to ensure that the dossier was correct and complete and to proceed with archiving it with the Dakar Court of Appeals. This included putting all files and registers, as well as any sealed evidence that was not being returned, into archive boxes. The boxes were numbered in chronological order and their contents noted on the exterior of the box. The mission of the clerks ended with the transmission of the complete dossier to the Dakar Court of Appeals, which the Statutes of the EAC, in Article 37, line 2, had designated for their conservation.

It should be noted that clerks with the EAC benefited from immunity in accordance with Article 29, line 2 of its Statutes.

The Senegalese clerk and the hybrid character of the EAC

Once staffing was complete, the Administrator of the EAC assigned clerks to the various services, including two to the Prosecutor's Office, one to the Central Registry, one to the Indicting Chamber, and two to the Investigative Chamber. I myself was assigned initially to the investigation phase, then to the Trial Chamber, and then to the Court of Appeal. At the end of the entire trial, the Administrator designated me and my colleague at the Central Registry for the archiving and transmission of the entire dossier to the Dakar Court of Appeals.

If the work of a clerk is essentially the same in all jurisdictions, the EAC nevertheless had their own specificities, given that they were a hybrid instance that functioned under their own statutes while also resorting to the Senegalese Code of Criminal Procedure in instances where the statutes were silent, as provided for in Article 16, lines 1 and 2 of the Statutes. This required a certain level of self-sacrifice on the part of us clerks, to be up to the task. For instance, during the trial in the first instance, we spent several weekends in the office to sort through lists of victims that included over 6,000 names, and to organize them both in terms of their status as either a direct or indirect victim but also according to the associations with which they were affiliated.

It must nevertheless be recognized that the clerks had no difficulty in shouldering their responsibilities as, over the course of their careers, their hierarchical superiors had found their work to be of the highest standard. Even with this track record, however, achieving a similar outcome was not a foregone conclusion as we started our work at the EAC with no specific training in its functioning. We had to remain highly adaptable so as not to inhibit the smooth functioning of the courts, particularly as we had very tight deadlines to respect.

The Hissène Habré trial was a unique experience for the clerks as we had never before worked in an international jurisdiction and doing so enabled us to collaborate with experienced judges from other countries. In the future, Senegal could incorporate a tribunal for international crimes in its legal system: this experience demonstrated that is has the necessary human resources, both in quality and quantity, to carry out this type of work.

It would require, however, a more direct collaboration between actors in order to avoid in the future certain stumbling blocks that cropped up during the trial. One that struck me was the voluntary omission by the trial judges of the clerks' signatures even though the clerks had participated in all aspects of the case. The signature of the clerk is a legal formality, and its omission demonstrates the extent to which judges undervalued the clerks. Indeed, the President of the Trial Chamber, who had previously served on international courts, judged it necessary to import to this jurisdiction the practice of having only judges sign decisions. However, the EAC was bound by Senegalese legal procedure when there was no specific procedure mentioned in the Statutes, and Article 304 of the Senegalese criminal code requires that judgements handed down by the Criminal Court be signed by both the president and the clerk. (The Criminal Court replaced the Assize Court, which is the equivalent of the Trial Chamber of the EAC.)

It would also have been useful to have more adequate working conditions for clerks, for a higher productivity. Outside of their salary and some training materials left at their disposal, no other measures were taken to facilitate the work of the clerks. To go to court to take part in a hearing, clerks first had to go to the headquarters of the EAC and from there a car shuttle service took us to the court. All the others who served on the court, however, were provided with vehicles by the Administration of the EAC, which informed us that the steering committee had only planned for transportation for clerks departing from headquarters. Given the traffic jams, it was better to go to court directly on our own dime rather than run the risk of arriving late.

From the organizing of the dossier to its archiving via all the other steps involved, the clerks were at the heart of this trial and played a role which enabled all the actors (judges, prosecutors, lawyers, legal aids, and the parties) to have a clear, easy access to all the elements of the case.

Additional complications arose in this case because one single man was tried before an international tribunal for a great many crimes. This explains why the Chadian government only provided support when doing so corresponded with its own interests. This was abundantly clear during certain missions in Chad. Having participated in all the rogatory missions in Chad, I witnessed with my own eyes the reticence and resistance of the Chadian authorities. During the final mission, members of the delegation were obliged to find their own accommodation, and the very cold welcome of the legal authorities dampened the mood during our entire stay. The Chadian government also refused to release to the EAC individuals who were being detained in N'Djamena but who were subject to international arrest warrants. And when an international rogatory mission was sent to charge and interrogate them, Chadian legal authorities refused to allow access.

This trial leaves a sense of unfinished business and even a sense of a double standard of justice, in the sense that important figures in the period under scrutiny (1982–1990) were spared or protected from being tried by the EAC.

SECTION C
THE TRIAL

Section C focuses on the trial itself, and it begins with its prosecutor. Mbacké Fall led the prosecution of Hissène Habré from the creation of the EAC through the final appeal. In Chapter 13, Fall explains how he took on the role of prosecuting a dictator, as well as how he balanced the legal elements of that prosecution with the political. For example, he notes his decision to proceed with the case against Habré even in the absence of Habré's co-defendants and despite limited cooperation from the Chadian authorities. Fall also discusses the trial and appeal process, particularly as regards the management of oral, sometimes unexpected, testimony. Moving from the prosecution to the defence, Chapter 14 brings us to the 'commis d'office', the court-appointed attorneys installed by the EAC when Habré ordered his own attorneys not to participate in the trial. Mounir Ballal, part of this court-appointed team, describes the process of his nomination and his experience defending a client with whom he had no contact. He discusses the defence strategy his team developed and how defending Hissène Habré before the EAC differed from his previous professional experience. Ballal also critiques the praise the EAC has received for being efficient and economical, explaining how time and financial constraints violated the rights of the accused.

Based on the civil law tradition in Senegal, the EAC also allowed civil parties to join the proceedings. Chapter 15 is written by Jacqueline Moudeïna, the first woman to practice law in Chad, who nearly lost her life in 2000 from a hand grenade thrown because of her work representing victims in the Habré case. In her chapter, Moudeïna details how she became connected to Habré's victims, as well as how she organized and prepared them for trial. She also discusses the development of the role of the civil parties before the EAC and lessons learned with respect to enabling disclosure of sexual testimony, which became central to the trial. The international-national collaboration regarding the civil parties team is the subject of Chapter 16, contributed by attorneys Alain Werner and Emmanuelle Marchand. They discuss how victim representation worked at the EAC and how it differed from other international tribunals such as the Extraordinary Chambers in the Courts of Cambodia.

Chapter 17 presents an attempted intervention from beyond the case parties: the *amicus curiae* brief offered by over a dozen experts on the prosecution of sexual violence under international law may have been a game changer for the trial, both in terms of its relevance as a mechanism of international criminal justice, as well as in highlighting the EAC's power to address crimes of sexual violence despite their omission from original charges. In this chapter, Kim Thuy Seelinger, Naomi Fenwick, and Khaled Alrabe, who drafted on behalf of intended *amici*, discuss how they became involved in late 2015 and how they prepared and submitted the brief on short notice, despite the absence of formal submission procedures.

Chapters 18 and 19 summarize the trial judgment and appeals decision, which the EAC only published in French, provided by Elise LeGall, a French attorney who worked in the

EAC prosecutor's office as an international criminal law expert. Detached from the process that created them, both judgments have become international criminal jurisprudence, ie actors in themselves. Chapter 20 then offers reflections of EAC Appeals Judge Ouagadeye Wafi, who discusses producing the highly anticipated appeals decision. Specifically, he comments on the challenge of ruling on multiple procedural challenges raised by the defence, as well as the reasoning behind maintaining the conviction in its entirety save for acquitting Habré of personally raping Khadidja Hassan Zidane.

Finishing the trial section, NGO advocates Gaëlle Carayon and Jeanne Sulzer reflect in Chapter 21 on the ongoing battle to deliver victims' reparations. Courts in Chad, as well as the EAC, have ruled that reparations must be distributed. Securing the funds remains elusive, however.

13

Prosecuting International Crimes in Senegal

Mbacké Fall, EAC Prosecutor

Mbacké Fall was the Public Prosecutor of the EAC, in the case of The Public Ministry vs Hissène Habré, Saleh Younous, Mahamat Djibrine El Jonto, Akbar Torbo Ralma, and Guihini Koreï Zakaria Berdeï. *The Senegalese Minister of Justice nominated him for the position to the African Union. Before assuming his function on February 2013, Mbacké Fall had been a Supreme Court judge from 2011 to 2012, advocate general to the Court of Appeals of Dakar from 2006 to 2011, public prosecutor in Saint-Louis from 2003 to 2006, prosecutor in Kolda from 2000 to 2003, a civil, commercial, and correctional judge from 1992 to 2000, and an examining magistrate from 1989 to 1992. He is currently a judge on Senegal's Supreme Court.*

The case against Hissène Habré was the first time in Senegal that a prosecutor applied the principle of universal jurisdiction in a case of criminal repression and serious violations of international law. This meant that the proceedings would depend on judicial cooperation between Chad, where the events had taken place and where the witnesses and victims lived, and Senegal, where Hissène Habré had taken refuge.

It is obvious that the success of such an enterprise required a great depth of knowledge concerning the facts surrounding the crimes and serious violations of international law as well as the jurisprudence of international criminal tribunals and their relation to infractions that were outside the nation judicial jargon. To that end, prosecutors and examining judges attended three-day-long seminars on international human rights law, organized by the Red Cross in Dakar in May 2014, and on international criminal law, organized by the Wayamo Foundationat the International Nuremberg Principles Academy from 11 to 13 November 2014. Two countries offered technical assistance. Switzerland seconded magistrates Louis Peila and Laurent Kaspar Ansmetto to provide their expertise. Canada organized a teleconference as part of a training session led by Fannie Lafontaine of the University of Laval on 22 May and 23, 2013,[1] and assisted the Prosecutor's Office by a training session in March 2013 on international criminal law that was led by Robert Petit, Joint Prosecutor of the Extraordinary Chambers in the Courts of Cambodia. In addition, the Prosecutor's Office had the services of jurists including intern Marie Lugaz, a student at Aix-Marseille University, and French lawyers Elise Le Gall,[2] Emmanuel Guematcha, and Chloé Gaden-Gistucci. Together, this team assisted me in integrating evidentiary practices from other international, hybrid, and national jurisdictions.

[1] See Érick Sullivan and Fannie Lafontaine, in this volume, Chapter 26.
[2] See Le Gall, in this volume, Chapters 18 and 19.

Mbacké Fall, *Prosecuting International Crimes in Senegal* In: *The President on Trial.* First edition. Edited by: Sharon Weill, Kim Thuy Seelinger, and Kerstin Bree Carlson, Oxford University Press (2020). © Mbacké Fall. DOI: 10.1093/oso/9780198858621.003.0014

The Prosecutor's role in *Public Ministry vs Hissène Habré and others*

In civil law systems, the preliminary investigation led by the prosecutor is followed by submissions to the investigating judge. The file is transferred to the investigating judges, who carry out the investigation independently and draft the indictment.

Here, the case was governed by the statute of the EAC, that provided that the prosecutor is competent to pursue those responsible for international crimes committed in Chad between 8 June 1982, and 1 December 1990 (Art 3). The EAC statute also provided that proceedings follow the statute and the dispositions of the code of Senegal criminal procedure (Art 12.3).

The statute remained silent, however, on how these two distinct investigation phases (of the prosecutor and the investigating judges) should be conducted. It appears to require the prosecutor to open judicial proceedings without delay. While the statute set the overall length of investigation at seventeen months, beginning with the nomination of the members of the prosecutor's office in March 2013, the timeframe outlined in the EAC's provisional budget did not set aside a period for the prosecutor's preliminary investigation.

As we felt it important to analyse the different sources of evidence and the report of the initial criminal investigation of Habré instituted in Belgium was not yet available, we decided to allow a period of reflection of five months for the preliminary investigation. This explains in part why the mandate was prolonged for a period of six months.

With the accusation of Hissène Habré by the Prosecutor's office on 2 July 2013, the investigative judges took over the investigation. The Prosecutor's office, however, joined the execution of the different international rogatory missions in Chad, carried out with some difficulty. In Senegal, the Prosecutor's office participated in Hissène Habré's interrogation sessions and ensured the regularity of procedure for interlocutory appeals before the Accusation Chamber.

The preliminary investigation phase (March to June 2013)

The strategy of the prosecutor began with an in-depth analysis of the reports above, which allowed us to evaluate the body of evidence through the lens of the infractions falling under the competence of the EAC. Evidence included reports from NGOs such as Human Rights Watch and Amnesty International, from the Chadian National Commission of Enquiry,[3] and victim statements. We then constructed an initial database to help with the development of a prosecutorial strategy. Analysis of evidence in this database revealed serious indications of the commission of fundamental crimes. In April 2013, we received the Belgian investigation reports through international cooperation with the Belgian legal authorities.

These Belgian files were especially useful. Following the filing of a complaint in Belgium by eight Chadians, judge Daniel Fransen had begun legal proceedings against Hissène Habré on 6 December 2001 for crimes against humanity, act of torture, and barbarous acts. After the execution of rogatory missions in Chad, the judge had found sufficient charges to issue a warrant *in absentia* for the arrest of Hissène Habré and to demand his extradition on

[3] See Abakar, in this volume, Chapter 2.

22 September 2005, 15 March 2011, 5 September 2015, and 17 January 2012. The repeated refusal of Senegal to extradite Habré triggered the politico-judicial process that became known as the Habré Affair.

After an initial analysis, we met the Belgian federal prosecutor in Brussels to compare notes. The Belgian investigators had examined archive material found in the headquarters of the Direction de la Documentation et de la Sécurité (DDS) and had heard victim testimony, the substance of which directed their investigations towards Habré insiders).[4] This included major collaborators identified in our introductory submission, whose names had come up time and again in both the archive material and the victim statements.

First trip to N'Djamena (8–16 June 2013)

An impressive list of possible defendants had been assembled from the various statements collected from the archives and from NGO interviews with victims and witnesses. The next step was to go to the 'scene of the crime', which is why we undertook a mission to N'Djamena, with the authorization of the Chadian authorities, who had just signed an international legal cooperation agreement with Senegal.

This was the beginning of some relief for the victims, exasperated by the long wait for a trial to be held someday. Meetings were held with victims' associations to ensure that all were aware of their right to participate in the legal proceedings and of the need to find representation who could keep an eye on their common interests, as per Article 14 of the EAC Statutes.

We also visited the building that had been the headquarters of the DDS, where the archives had been stored and where a prison had been constructed in an empty swimming pool. We finished up our mission by visiting Amral-Goz and Ambing, suspected locations of mass graves.

This initial visit of the 'crime scene' reinforced our conviction of the existence of serious presumption of the commission of crimes against humanity and war crimes.

Naming the accused

The final phase of the preliminary investigation was to establish a framework of prosecution in terms of the crimes and the persons suspected of committing them. We found that given the serious and concordant evidence of the crimes indicated above, Hissène Habré should be arrested and indicted, and that warrants of arrest should be issued for his collaborators. We also demanded his detention to preserve public order and calm during the proceedings. Care had to be taken during his arrest: his personality and the depth of public sympathy he inspired among the local Senegalese population could have been used to shield him from arrest.[5]

While mandating Habré's arrest posed no particular difficulty given the charges of crimes against humanity, war crimes, and torture, the decision had to be made whether to try him

[4] The Belgian judge provided testimony before the EAC. For an excerpt, see in this volume, Chapter 6.
[5] See also Mendy, in this volume, Chapter 9.

alone as having primary responsibility, or to try him with his closest collaborators as the authors of specific crimes. The latter seemed to us to be more in conformity with the statute that authorized the EAC to prosecute and judge crimes and serious violations of international law committed in Chad from 8 June 1982 to 1 December 1990. It was therefore decided to prosecute five of Habré's close collaborators: Saleh Younous, Mahamat Djibrine El Jonto, Abakar Torbo Rahma, Guihini Koreï, and Zakaria Berdeï, whose names had been regularly cited by victims. The charges thus highlighted a repressive machinery, set up by Habré and operationalized by appointed torturers dedicated to his cause.

The investigation phase (July 2013–February 2015)

Hissène Habré's interrogation sessions in Dakar

The investigating magistrates organized six interrogation sessions with Habré and two confrontations with witnesses. As per the Senegalese Code of Criminal Procedure, the prosecutor was permitted to attend (Art 107).

The sessions with Habré were calm but punctuated by heated exchanges with my office: the investigating judges seemed to continuously highlight Habré's status as a former head of state and to forget that this was also someone who had been charged for serious crimes and violations of international law. In response to the gentle tones of the judges, in my capacity as prosecutor, I raised my voice to ask questions that annoyed the defendant but which directly addressed the atrocities committed. But the procedure went forward. The questions were always included in the hearing records, which Habré refused to sign. His lawyers, Ibrahima Diawara, El Hadji Moustapha Diouf, and Cheikh Amadou Diop were present and assisted their client.

My office formulated several requests to the investigating judges concerning appraisals of and conservatory measures for Habré's assets. Only two requests were rejected: the prohibition against Habré's wearing a turban as per dispositions concerning maintenance of order,[6] and the extension of the financial investigations in the tracing of Habré's assets.[7] In the first matter, the indicting chamber had considered Habré's wearing of a turban to be 'contemptuous and disrespectful of justice', but the Investigative Chamber now found that the turban was a form of traditional clothing. For the second matter, the prosecutor had asked to hear the testimony of the former prime minister, who had declared to the press that he had opened a bank account in Habré's name upon Habré's arrival in Dakar. It made sense to learn how much had been received and to help trace his assets so as to be able to award compensation to his victims at some point. However, the investigating judges deemed that the investigations that had enabled them to order temporary seizure of an apartment building belonging to Habré were sufficient.

[6] Orders of 13 February 2014, denied by decision of the Indicting Chamber of 29 April 2014.

[7] Orders of 7 November 2014, rejecting the demand for a hearing of former Prime Minister Abdoul Mbaye and the demand for an additional investigation into Hissène Habré's assets.

International rogatory missions in Chad and transfer of witnesses

There were five international rogatory missions, four in Chad and one in France.[8] My office (myself and my three deputies) participated in the missions in Chad, which was facilitated by a good working relationship with Chadian colleagues. For the mission in France, a deputy prosecutor and an examining magistrate travelled to hear the testimony of insider Bandoum Bandjim, former torturer and head of operations for the DDS.

The principle obstacle that the opposition struggled with was the refusal of the Chadian authorities to cooperate in transferring individuals detained in N'Djamena who were named in the indictment as well as detainees who were requested to appear as witnesses. Essentially, there were two categories of detainees for whom transfers were requested:

1) Saleh Younous and Mahatmat Djibrine 'El Jonto' had been detained by a senior investigating judge of N'Djemena in the context of legal proceedings opened in Chad for murder and torture connected to events relevant to the competence of the EAC. These two individuals were names in the indictment and were to be indicted by the EAC Investigative Chamber for crimes against humanity and torture.
2) Thirteen other detainees who were not named in the submission but the EAC requested appearance in court as witnesses was requested by the court, including five torturers who served in Habré's political police force and who were included in the group of twenty defendants condemned to life in prison or to hard labor by the N'Djamena Criminal Court in session on 25 March 2015.[9] Even though they had been heard in N'Djamena in the context of the execution of the International Rogatory Missions, these individuals did not appear in public audience because they were never transferred to Dakar.

The arrest warrants for Saleh Younous and Mahatma Djibrine El Jonto (detained in Chad) and for Guihini Korei, Zakaria Berdeï, and Abkar Tobo Rahma (at large) were never executed or even presented to those named and therefore they were never even charged. It was thus impossible to bring them with Habré before the court.

Statements released to the press by the prosecutor to denounce this situation had no impact, despite the Chadian authorities' repeated promises to accede to our demands for prosecution. It was only when the investigation in Dakar was being concluded that a separate trial was organized in N'Djamena to try these individuals. The Chadian people contested the haste with which the Chadian dossier had been concluded and welcomed statements denouncing the stalling of international judicial cooperation with enthusiasm.

Apart from this failure, the international rogatory commissions concerning the archives, the visits to the mass graves and the hearing of 2,500 victims and witnesses were executed to satisfaction in the presence of magistrates from the Prosecutor's Office, who ensured that the law was fairly applied.

[8] Chad IRM 1: 19 August–2 September 2013; Chad IRM 2: 1–20 December, 2013; Chad IRM 3: 15–31 March 2014, Chad IRM 4: 24 May–9 June2014; and France IRM: 12–19 January 2014.

[9] See Thulliez, in this volume, Chapter 25.

The Prosecutor's Office before the Trial Chamber

The Office of the Prosecutor of the EAC continued its work up to the final decision of the Court of Appeal. Its role during the trial was to bring proof of the accusations brought against Habré in the indictment and to ensure compliance with the Statutes and the rules of procedure.

Before the Trial Chamber of the EAC

The arraignment and bringing to trial of Hissène Habré before the Trial Chamber allowed the prosecutor to speak before the court and to deliver oral arguments as to his guilt and his punishment. We occasionally had to remind the President, the only foreign judge in the bench, that the trial was to be governed by the Senegalese Code of Criminal Procedure, even though we came close to creating an incident by doing so. As the judge had experience with the procedures of the ICTR, his tendency was to allow adversarial procedure to slip into the proceedings.

It was necessary to distinguish between the witness and the victims for their swearing in, even if the civil parties were both victim and witnesses of particular atrocities. After interrogating and establishing their identities, those appearing had to give their status as either victim or witness so that the Tribunal could decide whether or not to swear them in.

This brings to mind an unprecedented situation, to which a legal response had to be found to save the case. Hissène Habré, who had regularly appeared before judges of the Investigative Chamber, refused to appear in public audience before the Trial Court. In criminal matters, the Code of Procedure allows the possibility of obliging a defendant to appear before the court, a possibility left to the discretion of the President. We therefore requested orally that Habré's resistance be certified by a bailiff and that Habré be forced to appear, as allowed under Senegalese criminal procedure. As the order was being executed, Habré's own lawyers decided to boycott the audience, their unstated objective being to keep the order from being executed: Senegalese law prohibits a defendant from being judged without the presence of a lawyer. Faced with this unprecedented situation, the President of the Trial Chamber ordered that three lawyers be appointed to ensure Habré's defence.[10] In order to respect the defendant's rights, the trial was adjourned, which had repercussions on the provisional calendar that had been established before the opening of the trial. Even though arrangements were made, they were insufficient to curb the absences and delays in the appearances of victims and witnesses.

For the rest, the trial unfolded smoothly through the closing of debates, marked by closing arguments made by the prosecution that were mostly followed by the judges.

[10] See Ballal, in this volume, Chapter 14.

Before the Appeals Court of the EAC

The prosecutor filed his submissions and defended the decision to condemn Hissène Habré for crimes against humanity, war crimes, and torture. Under Article 25 of the Statute, an appeal can be based only on three grounds: error in the procedure, error under law, and factual error leading to a denial of justice. The appeals procedure is essentially written. The presence of the defendant not being obligatory, the prosecutor did not deem it necessary to compel his attendance. His defence was nonetheless undertaken by the three court-appointed lawyers from the first instance. They found several bases of appeal, including the composition of the Trial Chamber, the absence of a clerk's signature and Hissène Habré's conviction for rape.[11]

Regarding the supposed irregularity of the court's composition, they claimed that one of the sitting magistrates had spent his entire career in the Prosecutor's Office although the statute required that members of the court be designated from among persons having held the function of judge for at least ten years. We replied that the notion of judge in international law was a broad one and could include lawyers, law professors, and magistrates chosen on the basis of their moral integrity and their experience in a particular field. The international character of the EAC and the statute (which drew on the jurisprudence of international criminal tribunals) largely justified this interpretation, especially as the magistrate in question had more than twenty years of professional experience.

Concerning the absence of a signature on the court's ruling, we noted that in practice in international criminal courts, rulings were only ever signed by the judges. The office of clerk in national law is not the same as in international jurisdiction where the clerk has no judicial function but instead has administrative ones, like those attributed to the administrator of the EAC. But we opined that to ensure compliance with internal procedures, the omission could be corrected to avoid problems in the ruling's execution in Senegal or abroad. The court followed our recommendations by ordering the clerks to add their signatures to the initial judgement.

The only amendment of the ruling of the first instance was Habré's acquittal on appeal for the rape of Khadija Zidane. The court concurred with the defence that the criminal responsibility for rape had been raised for the first time during the trial and that the charge of rape did not appear on the indictment. It is true that evidence of rape was not sufficiently documented in the investigation file as the victims wished to speak for the first time and in detail only in the court's audience. By the way, during the preparation of the introductory submission, the prosecutorial team had debated whether to include rape among the charges levelled against Habré and others. The decision taken was to note it on the charge sheet but not to target it to avoid having the charge dismissed in the Investigative Chamber. The door thus remained open for the court to rule on the qualifications given by the investigative chamber. That is why the judge, inspired by international jurisprudence in terms of qualification of charges, had requested the observations of the parties, with respect to the rights of the defence, on his decision to give the evidence all legal qualification including the allegations of rape and sexual violence presented by the victims. As no objection was raised, the trial chamber retained the guilt of the defendant for the rape of Khadija Zidane. We

[11] See Abouly Ba, in this volume, Chapter 12.

reiterated the reasoning of the first judge during the appeal but the Court of Appeal applied the rules of national law more strictly.

Conclusion

By judging Hissène Habré, Senegal fulfilled its obligations as defined by the United Nations Convention Against Torture Other Cruel, Inhuman, or Degrading Treatment or Punishment. It also fulfilled the mandate given by the African Union via the accord that created the EAC within its proper jurisdictions.

The organization of this trial allowed for the on-the-job training of Senegalese magistrates who followed seminars in international criminal law and international humanitarian law through international cooperation and technical assistance. The collaboration with legal assistants, which is commonplace in international criminal courts, was an important contribution to the working methods and deepened understanding of international criminal justice.

Today Senegal has the legal tools to investigate and judge fundamental crimes wherever they are committed, provided that the author or authors are arrested in Senegal or that the victims reside on national territory. It is not impossible that, in the struggle against impunity, victims could organize to take up temporary residence in Senegal. A dossier like that of Hissène Habré could be conducted in the same way by the Prosecutor's Office while following the rules of procedure that apply under Senegalese criminal law. It would be necessary, however, to resolve the problem of financing the trial and the cooperation of the states linked to the crimes prosecuted.

14
Defending Habré

Mounir Ballal, Habré's Court-Appointed Lawyer

President Habré appointed his own lawyers, whom he instructed not to participate in the proceedings because he contested the EAC's legitimacy. Under Senegalese criminal procedure rules, it is not possible for a defendant to appear unrepresented before a court and thus the EAC decided to appoint defence counsel, called 'commis d'office' in French. Mounir Ballal, together with colleagues of the Dakar Bar Ma Sene, and Abdul Nging, were appointed by the EAC to assure Habré's defence during the trial and his appeal, although Habré never cooperated with them.

Mounir Ballal was born and grew up in Senegal, with family of Lebanese origin. He completed all of his studies in Senegal, where he has also led his professional life. His experience is primarily in criminal law but he also has significant experience in private law.

Let me begin by offering a brief consideration of the circumstances in which the defence counsel was assigned to the case as '*commis d'office*' (designated counsel). In the first half of July 2015, I was contacted by telephone by an associate of the president of the Dakar Bar to see if I was available to serve as defence counsel to President Hissène Habré. My answer was spontaneously to tell him, basically, that I had no objection, imagining that for me it was an opportunity to practice my profession as counsel for the defence.

After hanging up, I wondered what I had gotten myself into. I'd heard about the case, like everyone. At this moment, I began to measure the complexity and the weight of the task which awaited me.

Two or three days later, I learned that the members of the Trial Chamber of the EAC had paid a visit to the Bar Association, to ask the president of the Bar to propose a list of attorneys who could possibly serve as defence to Hissène Habré, in case Habré's own attorneys continued to refuse to participate. The president of the Bar told the EAC judges that he didn't see any reason why not, and asked the EAC to put the demand in writing officially. The President of the Bar then made a list of about ten attorneys who would be able to serve.

When the trial opened 20 July 2015, and the case was called, neither the accused nor his chosen attorneys were present.

I was at the courthouse that day, in room 5, on another matter. A colleague called from room 4, saying that I was appointed. So I went towards room 4, and could see that Habré's hearing was suspended, and then I was informed that the Trial Chamber had retired and

Mounir Ballal, *Defending Habré* In: *The President on Trial.* First edition. Edited by: Sharon Weill, Kim Thuy Seelinger, and Kerstin Bree Carlson, Oxford University Press (2020). © Mounir Ballal. DOI: 10.1093/oso/9780198858621.003.0015

asked me to come forward as soon as possible. That's where I could see that members of the EAC were there: members of the prosecutor's office, the attorneys of the civil parties, and my two colleagues Nging and Sene. Everyone was there. I was the last because I'd just been at the court for other business.

The next day, 21 July 2015, the EAC decided to call the accused by force, applying the Senegalese code of criminal procedure. The same day, the EAC pronounced an order that appointed us as counsel, *commis d'office*.

A few days after our appointment in July 2015, we *commis d'office* went to visit Habré in prison and interview him. It was our ethical obligation to try to visit him. Of course, we didn't expect him to receive us. We arrived, told the director that we were there, and were asked to wait in the lawyers' waiting room. Ten minutes later, the director returned and said he was sorry, he couldn't welcome us. The prison director said that Habré had called the EAC an administrative not a criminal court, and that therefore Habré didn't recognize us in the role of *commis d'office*.

All the actors in the trial knew Habré's strategy: he had retrenched behind total silence. Habré refused to respond to any question that was asked of him by the EAC or his accusers. He never spoke to us either. The only time Habré spoke a word to the defence was at the re-opening of the trial in September. He turned, and nose to nose with us, said 'You! You band of mercenaries! What are you doing here? You don't belong here!'

As an aside, I would note that things could have been different. Everyone knew that Habré's two attorneys would never plead before the trial chamber. Over five *commission rogatoires* during the investigation phase Hissène Habré's private counsel had refused to collaborate because their position was that the EAC was an illegitimate body. There was no reason to imagine anything would be different once the case moved to the trial phase. Those attorneys had skipped the investigation part of the procedure, so everyone knew long before the trial that there would be problems. This is an area where things should have been better organized.

We *commis d'office* were not in contact with the other defence lawyers, Habré's private counsel, at all. They looked at us like we were traitors. They did not agree with our participation in the trial, which is understandable. But, before we accepted the appointment by the court, we had *séance de travail*, all three lawyers met together and looked at the proceedings from all angles. Our conclusion was that the law obliged Habré's private lawyers to accept our appointment. After all, if we had not been engaged, the proceeding could not have gone forward.

Time and resource constraints

The EAC announced a forty-five-day delay to let us get to know the case. Typically it's three months, so this was rather short. And at the moment they announced the forty-five-day delay, I had no idea of the amount of material we'd have to review. The EAC must have known how much material there was to review—25,000 pages. We hadn't been part of the process up to this moment in any way. Had they told me all of this when offering the appointment, I would have said no. I asked for three months; they said no. Ironic, given how international tribunals elsewhere have all the time they need but we Africans were told to hurry and stick to schedule

The day we left the EAC with the forty-five-day delay, we three '*commis d'office*' defence counsel got together and took over the conference room on the third floor of the Maison des Avocats in downtown Dakar. That was when I realized the colossal, herculean nature of the task before us.

The EAC gave us the case dossier on a USB key, something I've never seen. They called it 'a digital dossier'. I can barely use the internet, and I had to keep asking our IT assistant to pull out all the elements of the dossier that we found important, to have them printed. Even so, most of the material we just couldn't digest. The Belgian investigation dossier, for example: we skimmed this. There was no time. The calendar controlled everything. It was a huge handicap.

We did have the monetary means to run the defence the way we wanted. That said, we still had a large feeling of frustration. The whole *instruction* and investigation had already been carried out before we came onboard and without us being able to be a part of it. In such a trial, we didn't get on the train after it left the station: we basically got on the train as it was arriving at its destination.

So this was the first obstacle, that there was an imperative time schedule, imposed by the African Union and other international organizations. Everything was in a fixed window: judgment by 30 May 2016 and 30 April 2017 for the appeal. The schedule dictated when the trial should finish and the Trial Chamber intended to honour it. Judge Kam told us, 'me, I'm done the 30th of May! My contract is up'. Everyone had obligations elsewhere. This constraint seriously prejudiced the defence. And it was the same with the appeal decision.

Lack of familiarity with international crimes

The second obstacle was that it wasn't just that the material was new for us, but also this kind of trial. Of course, we never hid this; the EAC asked us about our experience and expertise in the topic, and I told them it was the first time I had ever defended anyone for violations of human rights, crimes against humanity, war crimes. It was the same for my co-counsel.

Everyone else received support apart from the defence lawyers—the bench, the civil parties. We did not get any training. There should be training in international penal law also for the defence lawyers

Investigation: Inculpatory and exculpatory obligations

Working within the statute of the EAC was quite different professionally. There is nothing wrong with hybrid procedure per se. And the EAC was clearly written on the model of ad hoc tribunals. But very little thought was given to the rights of the accused. We in the defence had the sense that every time the law was more favourable for the accused in international law, then national law was applied.

For example, Article 21 of the Statute outlines the rights of the accused before the EAC. It does not provide for the right to remain silent. This is not random, in my opinion. It's strange. Given that the drafters already knew Hissène Habré wouldn't collaborate, this seemed very subjective. Another problem had to do with how the prosecution investigated and developed the case. At the EAC, the prosecutor only raised incriminating evidence, what we call '*à charge*'. The fact that Habré remained silent did not relieve the prosecutor and the investigating judges from their duty to seek exculpatory evidence. Unlike in common law systems, the prosecution and the investigating judge have the same investigative duty—to seek both incriminating and exculpatory evidence. But this did not happen here. So it was a trial exclusively '*à charge*' and not '*à decharge*'. Guilt was foreordained.

Take the example of Mgallo, a village in Chad, where there was a massacre. When Habré learned about the massacre, he had the guilty soldiers publicly executed in the village square. This instance of Hissène Habré exercising discipline could have been construed as exculpatory. However, it was instead brought as an element against the defence, as an example of one more war crime for which Hissène Habré was guilty.

All in all, the defence didn't have a single witness, not even one! There were none from the investigation phase. During the trial, we had only one day of pleading. The sole person the EAC called as a 'defense witness' was Reza Gisa, a superior officer of FANT, the Chadian army—and he was only used to clarify military hierarchy.

Of course, it's not impossible to have a trial comprised entirely of incriminating evidence. But in this case, we are talking about an eight-year time span, across the whole of Chad. Given the sort of crimes alleged, and the repetitive character of these crimes that were committed nearly everywhere in Chad, we can't imagine that only incriminating elements could be established. There must have been certain moments that would be exculpatory.

All this is to say, the dossier was already made. From a purely procedural point of view, the defence counsel *commis d'office* was completely deprived of any initiative regarding facts. We couldn't even appeal anything from the investigation phase, because the appeals period had run.[1]

Habré's criminal responsibility

The prosecution argued for Habré's complete responsibility, saying that he ordered crimes, or that he didn't sanction those that did. But it can't have been that this one man acted alone. There, the absence of Habré's co-accused before the EAC was a big problem. And why were the co-accused absent? There was an agreement signed between Senegal and Chad specifically for this trial, yet Chad decided to try some of Habré's co-accused itself, citing reasons of sovereignty. We the *commis d'office* never negated that crimes happened. Rather, our point was that the circumstances surrounding the crimes never became clear. If you listened to the prosecution, there wasn't a fly in Chad that Hissène Habré didn't know about. They presented him as a superman who knew everything and was in charge of everything. But it's just not possible that this one man, as a super technocrat, good administrator, and hard worker, never slept, wrote everything that was sent to everyone, and gave all instructions. He's just human.

[1] See background on civil law procedure in page xxx.

Hybrid treatment of parties civiles and witnesses

Another difficulty was the statements of the *partie civile* at the beginning of the proceedings. The witnesses were considered as *partie civile*, which is a hybrid structure. The issue is that if someone is considered as *partie civile* the objective is that they should tell what they know about the proceedings. However, if someone is a witness, they should tell what they know about specific facts, and they should be in a separate room during the trial and should only come when they are called upon. The witnesses during the trial sat in on the proceedings from the very beginning, and they also participated in meetings with Human Rights Watch etc. In order words, they followed the entire proceedings, and the judges permitted that.

Witness credibility

Another problem was the credibility of the witnesses. This is again related to the imposition by the EAC of a schedule and a certain order that locked the defence in place in a foreordained result. At trial, rather curiously and at the prosecutor's request, the EAC decided to let background witness, so-called 'context witnesses' testify at the opening of trial. Although it is normal and reasonable to begin with historical facts, I don't believe that it was normal or judicious to let the other contextual witnesses come first. These guys, the psychologist who investigated Habré's personality, medical anthropologists, handwriting experts—these guys were expensive, and the EAC brought them in, had them testify, and then let them go. When it was time for the defence to counter, it wasn't possible, they were already gone!

Or take another example, a witness who said he was the sole survivor of a massacre in a village where 149 were killed. He said he was hit by seven bullets. We asked, 'were you bleeding a lot?' 'Yes' was the answer. He told us he walked from village to village. 'How did you stop the bleeding?' we asked. 'I recited the Quran,' was the answer. 'Credible,' said the EAC. But did this massacre even happen? If we'd had the context witnesses following the fact witnesses, had they simply come later in the trial, we could have asked them to evaluate the fact witnesses.

There was another witness who said he was wounded so badly his intestines were outside his body. We asked him how he managed, with intestines outside his body and no bandages: he said he used a bird's nest. We asked him how he kept himself alive, and he claimed he fed himself on a certain kind of tree fruit. However, the incident he was describing should have happened in August, but the fruits he named only ripen in December.

Moreover, the judges did not properly identify the witnesses when they were called. We had difficulties in identifying witnesses and we did not know where they came from. Several times, if the defence read out witness statements from Chad to the witnesses, they stated that they had not said it. There were contradictions in witness statements, and they were here from the beginning.

Massacres like the ones these witnesses described were two big examples of war crimes that were used as evidence against Habré. The contextual witnesses could have helped sort it out, but those big guys had left and couldn't be brought back because budgetary constraints didn't permit it. Also, since Idriss Déby is still head of Chad, controlling the flow of information on that side, there was no real possibility of investigating authority.

Judicial impartiality

Then there was the question of the rape of Khadija Zidane, for which Habré was convicted by the trial chamber but which was overturned by the appeals chamber. This violation of procedure was so flagrant that the appeals chamber couldn't do otherwise than acquit Habré of this charge. And this is what I mean by evidentiary inconsistency: in the case of this rape, no one had ever spoken of it. There was no mention to the investigating Belgian judge Fransen, or to any of the investigating commissions in Chad, or at any point in time before the trial chamber. And yet Judge Kam said in court, 'Tell this woman that she can't leave until she's said everything. She has to say everything before she leaves.' This to me is incredible, it constitutes instigation on the part of the judge. The trial chamber should be neutral. I might have expected such a thing from the prosecution, but not from a judge. We were all shocked: I remember this as if it was yesterday. Judge Kam poked the air with his finger and told the interpreter to tell the witness that 'she would not be allowed to go until she told everything.' The witness asked the interpreter, 'What does he want me to say?' The interpreter told the tribunal that the witness had said all she had to say. Kam insisted. And then the rape testimony emerged.[2]

But it wasn't just the testimony that was tortured, it was also the way the tribunal used the testimony. First, the credibility of the witness Zidane was established by another witness, who testified that the witness had recounted this in confidence while they were both in Ouadi Doum prison.[3] But then, after establishing that Habré had committed the rape in this way, this became a way to prove that Habré must have known that his men were doing the same, or that he couldn't ignore that his men were doing the same thing in the prison. The argument was presented in this way, as if, by being a rapist, Habré was encouraging others, setting an example.

So that leaves the question, why did Judge Kam interfere in this way? In my opinion, this was due to a relationship between the prosecution and the court that was too close. I'm not sure how this works at other international tribunals. And of course, it's not a problem that the prosecution meets with Kam, that's not forbidden. But I understand that the judges travelled, went to external seminars regarding the case, and in my opinion, this is not correct; the judges should stay more sequestered. In all these respects, I would not compare the Habré trial to trials before the International Criminal Court (ICC). At the ICC, defendants' rights are much better protected.

[2] Video of Khadija Zidane's testimony in French and Arabic is available here: https://www.youtube.com/watch?v=2dNhGNx7Rg4

[3] See Moudeïna, in this volume, Chapter 15. TrustAfrica provided English language summaries of each day of testimony before the EAC here: http://www.trustafrica.org/en/component/k2/item/3212-the-public-prosecution-versus-habre

Judgment and appeal

On the day of the judgment, 30 May 2015, only an eighteen-page document was presented. The appeal needed to be handed in fifteen days later and had to include specific points of argument motivating it. However, the 600-page final judgment was only delivered two months after the appeal deadline. We had no way to know how to formulate the appeal. This was not fixed by the statute. It is a shame.

And then there is the drafting of the judgment. The judgment was not written by the judges on the bench, but by international staff. This is important because it means that the judgment was written by people who were not in the trial and who were not present to evaluate the evidence.

It is of course normal that the judges are helped by clerks. But in the trial court judgment, you could see that it had been drafted by people outside of our system, and not edited correctly by the judges. For example, the judgment spoke of 'division' not 'direction' of investigations. This demonstrates that the drafters are not magistrates or experienced with the Senegalese system. They clearly weren't even African: for example, in the judgment, we see a reference to 'springtime in Chad', even though there is only a rainy season and a dry season there. When you put this together with other moments in the judgment, you see the external influence.

Also, the trial court bench was composed of two judges and a prosecutor. However, according to Article 11 of the statute, it was supposed to be three judges each with ten years of experience. I believe that part of what explains certain facets of the trial judgment, even the life sentence, which isn't part of the Senegalese Criminal Code, can be explained by a desire to humiliate Habré. Habré didn't recognize the EAC. This got under the judges' skin. My brother Africans are very sensitive. Judges in other places, they don't care. They can be cold and bring the most just sentence. But in this case, the judges felt Hissène Habré had insulted the tribunal, by not recognizing it, by hiding his face under a turban and sunglasses, by not rising for the judges when they entered the chamber. You could hear the judges' frustration with him in the summary they read out in May 2016, where they noted that though he refused to stand when they entered, he never refused to be applauded by his supporters every time he left the chamber, and never showed any compassion for the victims. In my view, this was ego talking, not the judges in their professional capacity, which is very dangerous.

But even in all this, I did not honestly expect such a harsh punishment, a life sentence. I expected that Habré would be sentenced to ten to twenty years. So really, we appealed against the punishment. There's always hope in the defence team, we keep it in the bottom of our hearts and spirits. We hope that certain elements of proof will come out and will switch the balance from one side to the other. When you consider all that came before the trial, the fact that since 1991 there had been so much publicity surrounding the question of trying Habré, and the way that this trial was supported by NGOs and several foreign governments, we knew that it would be very difficult, if not impossible, to see the trial chamber come to an acquittal. It was clear that many different groups supported, in one way or another, a trial organized to judge Hissène Habré. It took fifteen years to get to the EAC, and all of that ruled against an acquittal.

I really wished it would have been done in a better way. Everything around the trial could have been done much better, in a way that did not violate the rights of the defence.

15

From Victim to Witness and the Challenges of Sexual Violence Testimony

Jaqueline Moudeïna, Chadian Victims' Lawyer

Jaqueline Moudeïna is a Chadian lawyer. She coordinated the team of lawyers who represented nearly 4,000 victims in the trial of the former Chadian President Hissène Habré before the EAC. Moudeïna was born on 17 April 1957 in southern Chad. Her mother was a nurse and her father was the first Chadian doctor. She lost both parents at a very young age. In February of 1979, when the war broke out, she was forced to flee to the south of Chad. In 1982, she and her husband fled to Brazzaville, because he was threatened as a journalist who was very critical of the regime. There, she began her legal studies and obtained a law degree and a master's degree in private law. She was one of the first women to be admitted to the Chadian Bar. Moudeïna wanted to become a lawyer in order to defend the voiceless people whom she believed needed to be heard. Her struggle for human rights began early on. In Brazzaville, in 1993 she joined the Congolese branch of the Chadian Association for the Promotion of Human Rights (ATPDH), where she served as secretary of legal affairs. When she returned to Chad, she joined the headquarters of the association and kept her position as secretary of legal affairs. Today, she is the president of the ATPDH.

There was once a flagrant example of impunity in Chad: the reign of Hissène Habré. When Idris Déby came to power, his government ordered an investigation on the crimes committed under Habré, led by a magistrate Mahamat Hassan Abakar. It emerged from this investigation that there were nearly 40,000 deaths, thousands of missing persons, widows, and orphans. The report was published and brought to the attention of the president of the republic.[1] But nothing was done. Habré was living in exile in Senegal and all his accomplices had been reintegrated into the security apparatus of the new regime. We absolutely had to fight against this impunity. Thus, many organizations, the ATPDH, the Chadian League of Human Rights (LTDH), the African Meeting for The Defense of Human Rights (RADDHO) in Senegal, and the Inter-African Union of Human Rights (UIDH) in Burkina Faso decided to lead a reflection, following which it was decided to pursue Hissène Habré.

We had an idea as to how to proceed. In 1998, we had learned of Pinochet's trial and sought to contact Reed Brody of Human Rights Watch (HRW). In 1999, Mrs Delphine Djiraibe, who at that time chaired the ATPDH, was in the United States. She was referred to Reed Brody at HRW, to whom she explained our intentions to pursue Habré. Brody was

[1] See Abakar, in this volume, Chapter 2.

Jaqueline Moudeïna, *From Victim to Witness and the Challenges of Sexual Violence Testimony* In: *The President on Trial*. First edition. Edited by: Sharon Weill, Kim Thuy Seelinger, and Kerstin Bree Carlson, Oxford University Press (2020). © Jaqueline Moudeïna.
DOI: 10.1093/oso/9780198858621.003.0016

immediately seduced by the idea and joined us for the trial preparations which lasted about two years.

In 2000, we felt ready. We had to constitute a team of lawyers. The two human rights associations, namely the Chadian Association for the Promotion of Human Rights and the Chadian League of Human Rights, chose me as their representative. But even before I was appointed, I had always told myself that I would be the victims' lawyer if one day Habré were to be tried. I had always had this thought in mind. That's how I officially became the lawyer of the civil parties.

The trial and its many challenges

Meeting with the victims' association

I met Souleymane Guengueng, the president of the Association of Victims of Crimes and Political Repression (Association des Victimes de Crimes et Répression Politique or AVCRP), for the first time in 1998. At that time the association did not exist as such. Souleymane had compiled files of victims, which he hid carefully. Within the ATPDH, it was Delphine who had the first contact with Souleymane. She told me of his experience in prison before I met him. His story was similar to that of others we had heard from survivors of prisons operated by the Direction of Documentation and Security (DDS).

We began to seriously work with the victims' association after the filing of the first complaint in February 2000. I advised them to restructure the association so that we could work more efficiently. The association experienced difficulties and divisions at its beginnings. Originally there was only one group, the AVCRP, founded by Souleymane Guengueng.[2] Unfortunately, our detractors did everything to create a split within the group. The other two associations that formed as a result of the split were supported both by the government and our detractors, who did not want the trial to take place. But the divisions within the association never prevented me from doing my job. The victims' association that I defended included northerners, southerners and even people of Hissène Habré's ethnic group.

When I returned to Chad, after filing a complaint in Dakar in 2000, I began to travel to northern and southern villages in search of evidence. I took statements from victims, who had experienced different forms of torture in prison. The survivors still bore the stigma and wounds of the violence inflicted by the DDS.

Most importantly, I had to identify the places where the large scale massacres occurred. I went to the Deli farm in southern Chad, where the Codos (anti-Habré army coalition) and civilians were massacred in 1984. The farm's security guard showed me all the mass graves. This evidence later allowed the investigating judges of the EAC to appoint Argentine experts to exhume the site. In Koumra and Sarh, there were mass graves as well. We were able to locate them with the help of victims and villagers, who would tell us about specific massacre sites. We were later able to show these places to the judges who conducted their own investigations in the field.

[2] See Guengueng, in this Volume, Chapter 3.

The preparation of the victims

I was the coordinator of the team of lawyers representing the civil parties, which was not really my decision. The fact is, I was the only lawyer who had worked with victims from the very beginning for almost a decade. So it seemed natural that I should coordinate the team's work, based on my relationship with victims. Furthermore, my job was not that of a regular lawyer, it had many aspects. For example, since the trial was very political, Reed Brody and I were doing a lot of advocacy work all over the world, in search of allies to our cause. We were human rights defenders and politicians.

The preparation of the victims was a long term undertaking and a day-to-day effort. I am the one who helped the prosecutor select the victims who had to testify; I knew their stories very well and they had to be told during the instruction phase. Then once the victims were on the list of witnesses to appear in Dakar, I had to explain everything to them: the reasons for their presence, the purpose of their testimony, the configuration of the room and the role of each person in a trial, the place where they would stay. Most came from remote villages in Chad. Some had never even been to the capital N'djamena. Others had never seen such large halls or a city as big as Dakar or even lived in a house (like the hotel they were in). There was really a fear of the unknown, of an environment that was not theirs, seeing these judges and lawyers in their robes. This fear was normal. The judges noticed it and understood.

Of course, we had some surprises during the testimonies. Some trembled and others could not accurately give an account of everything they had suffered. Some were frightened and intimidated by the questions of the defence, which tried to ridicule them. It was very difficult for the victims but the majority stood their ground.

About sexual violence

I always knew that rape was practiced systematically. All the victims had told me it happened, except the women themselves who were the actual victims. No woman dared to admit it to me explicitly. They were unable to say 'I was raped'.

I want to explain this. Rape remains an absolute taboo in a society as traditional and conservative as the Chadian society. Women who reveal their rape run the risk of being rejected by their community. A raped woman is not a victim but a source of contempt for her community: she brings shame and disgrace to her family. So I encountered many difficulties in getting information from these women. It took ten years for one of the women, Ginette Ngarbaye, to finally confess to me even in vague terms that she had been raped. She told me, '*When a woman finds herself in a situation with men, you can imagine the rest*.' But for the trial, I wanted them to admit it explicitly and say that they had been raped. Some women had even been deported to a military base in northern Chad in the desert to serve as sexual slaves.

I must admit that this job was far from easy. Many people, including my fellow lawyers, threw stones at me. Some tried to dissuade the victims by telling them I was deceiving them and that the case would never succeed. But I was able to establish a climate of trust between these women and myself. It was only when the EAC was created that the women began to realize that this case was real.

When the trial began, I was forced to leave my colleagues in Dakar and return to Chad for a week in order to talk to these women and explain to them the importance of talking about sexual violence. I summoned them all and tried to convince them to testify in Dakar. I told them that most women are at risk of rape in our lifetimes and that it was absolutely necessary to fight for it to stop. I added that if they did not speak, their daughters and granddaughters would be potentially exposed to rape. Putting an end to this crime began with their admission. They would reply that the trial was broadcasted live and that their children would be in front of the screen every day hearing their testimonies. These women feared that everyone around them would know that they had been raped. I understood but reminded them to think about their daughters.

When the women arrived in Dakar to testify, I still had to work with them before they appeared in front of the judges. Until the day before their testimonies, I worked with them at their hotel until midnight. When I left, I was not reassured; they kept telling me how hard it was to admit in public that they had been raped. Until the last minute, I wasn't sure what they would do.

But when the day came, I was relieved. All the women spoke out. The presence of the judges and Hissène Habré played a part. In fact, Khadija, one of the women, had often told me that she had a lot to say but that she would say it only when the right time came. The right time was the day she appeared in front of the judges and Hissène Habré. That day, she admitted to having been raped four times by the former president. Khatoulma Deffalah clearly said that several women, including herself, had been deported to serve as sexual slaves for the military. At the end of the day, after their testimony, I went to see them and they all told me, '*We have been liberated.*' And even today when I see them in Chad, I feel they are more fulfilled, I see a certain pride in their eyes.

I should note that the *amicus curiae* brief on crimes of sexual violence was of great importance as background information. It helped clarify rape as an international crime in itself. It was a notable element.[3]

Victory and the persistent fight for reparations

The verdict was handed down on 30 May 2016. That day, I cried a lot. The fight had not been easy: seventeen years of persistent hard work. It took all these years to prosecute Habré but we did it. If I had given up or had listened to that little voice in my mind that kept saying '*I'm tired of it all, I cannot go on any longer, I've suffered enough*', it would never have happened. For me it was the trial of my life, the result of a long fight, which was worth it.

I did not give up mainly because of all the people—widows, orphans—who relied on me. There was no way for me to disappoint them. Abandoning them before the finish line would have been a real betrayal. It was the constant presence of these widows and orphans, who sometimes came to my house, that gave me the courage to continue the struggle. They still come to my home today.

There was also great joy among the victims, who had long waited for this judgment. But they all expressed different feelings to me. Some told me that the fact that Hissène Habré

[3] See Seelinger and others, in this volume, Chapter 17.

was found guilty was enough. A victim told me, '*Appearing in front of the judges, explaining what my family and I have experienced is enough for me. Your efforts made my wish come true*.' Others told me that the conviction was not enough and that they had to be compensated. Today, my impression is that some victims have been restored in their dignity, especially the women. But for most of them, the work is incomplete because they have not been compensated yet.

With respect to reparations, the victims expressed their wishes before we filed our request to the court. We obviously had to obtain their consent for everything. We explained that there were different forms of reparations: collective, pecuniary and individual. In this regard, we were assisted by an organization called Redress, which is experienced in the field.[4] The victims' preferred choice was pecuniary or monetary reparations. This is, in my opinion, due to the fact that their lives in Chad are very precarious and that only money can help them overcome the extreme poverty and misery in which they live. But the victims are aware that money can never fully restore their suffering.

Regarding collective reparations, we focused on the swimming pool that Hissène Habré had transformed into a prison, and where masses had died from heat. With the victims' consent, we requested that 'la Piscine' be turned into a museum. We explained the importance of building memorials on sites of massacres. They gave their consent to that idea as well. But when spoke of building schools and hospitals, they refused. They wanted money. I was a little surprised. I had even suggested income-generating projects that could help them in the long run, but their choice had clearly been focused on financial compensation. So I passed on their wishes.

The court ordered Habré to pay a total of $97 million to his victims, with amounts ranging from $36,000 for victims of sexual violence to $27,440 for victims of torture, arbitrary detention, and prisoners of war or survivors and $18,290 for each indirect victim. As the plaintiffs' lawyers, we had initially claimed $324 million in reparations. But I was personally satisfied with the amounts awarded by the EAC, especially in comparison with other experiences, such as the ICC or hybrid tribunals. But it is difficult to explain to victims who suffered unimaginable harms that they are privileged compared to others. They expected higher amounts.

The amounts awarded were based on the categorizations we had made in our compensation claims: direct, indirect victims, prisoners of war, deported and raped women. All the women who were among the victims had been raped because rape had been systematic. The rape of men had also been practiced but it was completely silenced.

The judges simply considered our categorization and referred to other international tribunals to strike a balance. The judges had very little time to spend on the reparations determination; even the clerk admitted it to me. This is partly due to the fact that the court had a fixed term which was about to end. This was very inconvenient.

One villa and two bank accounts belonging to Hissène Habré were seized for a total amount of $ 900,000. These seizures were validated by the EAC, so we can claim these assets. But they are clearly not enough.

Even today, we continue in our efforts to obtain the reparations ordered by the EAC, but we are not the decision-makers. We eventually turned to the United Nations to express our

[4] See Carayon and Sulzer, in this volume, Chaper 21.

discontent with the non-execution of the judgment. As a result, a working group has prepared a report and pressed Chad to act. We went to the African Court of Human Rights to have Chad execute the court decision. We organize outings and press conferences to denounce the failures to respect the judgment with respect to reparation claims. We wanted to march but peaceful demonstrations are forbidden in Chad.

In Addis Ababa, we met with African Union officials to express our wish that the reparations fund be quickly put in place at the African Union level. A fund was legally created by African Union heads of states in July 2016 but it remains empty. There are people at the African Union commission who are in charge of working on it but nothing has been done so far. We can only go to those people and remind them of their obligations. We have no other means.

Experiences and lessons

The first lesson, I would say, is preparation—especially in relation to a procedure as complex as this one. We had to provide many explanations. The judges of the EAC did not know the story of the eight-year reign of Hissène Habré in Chad. It was necessary to explain the entire history and to place the atrocities in the context of the regime so that the judges could understand how, where and by whom the massacres were committed. We made sure not to forget anything. We categorized the most important historical periods and incidents: the massacres of the Sarra, the Hadjarais, the Zaghawas, the prisoners of war, and deportations of women.

It was also very important to seek allies to our cause. Our allies were the human rights organizations, Chadian, African, and European: The Chadian League of Human Rights, the International Federation of Human Rights (FIDH), (HRW), Redress, and RADDHO. The press was an important ally because it kept the case alive in the media and made sure it was not forgotten. And when it came to writing petitions—at the time when Senegal did not want to extradite Hissène Habré at all—we had personalities like Desmond Tutu who signed our petition and referred to the case as an endless politico-legal soap opera.

We stayed close to Belgium and pleaded until it ended up pursuing Senegal to the International Court of Justice.[5] The court condemned Senegal to try Habré without delay, failing to extradite him.

The last and most important lesson in my opinion is perseverance. Anyone who wants justice can obtain it; one just has to work hard. Initially we think it is impossible to pursue people as powerful as Habré. But what this trial has shown us is that it is possible for ordinary people to sue powerful heads of state. It is not the African Union but the victims themselves who were the initiators of this trial.

Everyone, including myself, persevered. This type of work was very difficult from a personal point of view. Indeed my fight and my activities were not undertaken without risks. A human rights organization is always targeted by authoritarian regimes. In 1998, the police broke into my house and subjected me to a very intimidating interrogation that lasted over an hour. Then on 11 June 2001, the main torturer under the Habré regime attempted

[5] See Ventura and Baiesu, in this volume, Chapter 33.

to assassinate me with a grenade during a peaceful demonstration organized by Chadian women to denounce electoral fraud during the May 2001 presidential election. I was severely injured. I was hospitalized in Paris for fifteen months. I had four surgeries and it took 500 sessions of physical therapy before I was able to walk again. In fact, as we speak, I just came back from Paris for my medical care. This attack and these intimidations never deterred me. On the contrary, they only stimulated and comforted me in my commitment. I did not understand why people were attacking me when I was simply trying to put an end to impunity by prosecuting a person who had completely destroyed Chad. I absolutely had to take on the challenge and lead the victims to victory, which I did. It was seventeen long years of struggle. I dropped all my cases to focus on the Habré case because it was no longer possible to represent the victims and at the same time continue my regular clients. I decided to devote myself to the Habré case, which was pro bono.

Areas for improvement: Political will and compensation for victims

The political will needs to be improved. Political leaders in Chad and elsewhere must take on the fight against impunity and ensure that victims of political repression are compensated. Impunity, in my opinion, is the cancer that plagues our countries and the main cause of human rights violations in Africa and in the world. Compensation is crucial, a guilty verdict is not enough. It is necessary to compensate the victims to restore them in their dignity. Money cannot buy that dignity back, but it's still an acknowledgment of one's victimhood. Reparation is an obligation incumbent upon any state in which massacres have been perpetrated. It would be unfortunate to conclude that pursuing Habré was worthless. The African Union needs to consider several means to make these funds available to victims. These are international crimes, so all of humanity is concerned, especially the fifty-four states of the African Union.

We were disappointed with some things, including the fact that the EAC did not characterize certain facts as war crimes. The protection of the victims and other actors of the trial was also lacking. I was personally assaulted by Mrs Habré outside the courtroom.

Otherwise everything we presented before the EAC was taken into account. I have nothing to reproach the EAC with. This is a first in Africa. Not everything could be perfect. But if you take the trial as a whole, I cannot complain. No one thought it would happen one day. Yet, we did it.

16
Supporting Victims at Trial
Civil Parties' Perspective

Alain Werner and Emmanuelle Marchand, Civil Parties Legal Team

---

Alain Werner is the director of Civitas Maxima, an NGO specialized in the documentation of international crimes and in the legal representation of victims of such crimes.[1] *He has been involved with Human Rights Watch (HRW) in the Habré case since 2008 and was one of the civil parties lawyers during the court case in Dakar. He was involved inter alia in the pleading of the case in front of the EAC and served as expert in international criminal law for the team.*

Emmanuelle Marchand is a senior legal counsel for Civitas Maxima. Since 2013, Emmanuelle has been conducting investigations in international crimes committed in West Africa. She also provides trainings on the documentation of international crimes including sexual and gender-based violence. She was involved as a legal consultant for the civil parties in the Habré case from May 2016 and assisted the civil parties' lawyers by drafting the legal briefs and preparing examination of witnesses.

The Extraordinary Chambers in the Courts of Cambodia (ECCC) and the EAC are the only ad hoc tribunals that have allowed victims participation. The reason for this is that both hybrid tribunals are rooted in the French civil law system, which awards civil party status to the victims. This status recognizes victims as a legal party to the proceedings. The procedure of the International Criminal Tribunal for the Former Yugoslavia (ICTY) and the International Criminal Tribunal for the Rwanda (ICTR) was inspired by the common law system where the participation of victims is generally restricted to the role of mere witnesses. The International Criminal Court (ICC) is based on a mixed system inspired by both common law and civil law. Indeed, one of the particular aspects of this system is that victims are allowed to participate and request reparation. Nonetheless, they are not considered as parties, but rather participants to the proceedings, which restricts their participation.[2]

1 For more information see: https://www.civitas-maxima.org/en.
2 Hakan Friman, 'The International Criminal Court and Participation of Victims: A Third Party to the Proceedings?' (2009) 22(3) Leiden Journal of International Law 485, available at https://www.cambridge.org/core/journals/leiden-journal-of-international-law/article/the-international-criminal-court-and-participation-of-victims-a-third-party-to-the-proceedings/878006EC2818CD01AC3075493AADC2D3

Alain Werner and Emmanuelle Marchand, *Supporting Victims at Trial* In: *The President on Trial*. First edition. Edited by: Sharon Weill, Kim Thuy Seelinger, and Kerstin Bree Carlson, Oxford University Press (2020).
DOI: 10.1093/oso/9780198858621.003.0017

Overall, in the Habré case, the different roles amongst the national and international lawyers representing the victims were better defined than in the first trial in front of the ECCC. Similarly, the collaboration between the civil parties' lawyers and the prosecution was better organized in the Habré trial than before of the ECCC. In the following chapter, we consider some of the particularities, challenges, successes, and lessons learned from our work on the Habré case.

Representing victims before the EAC

In total, more than 8,000 victims participated in the proceedings against Hissène Habré. This figure is a reflection of the high casualties suffered by the Chadian population during Habré's reign. It is estimated that at least 40,000 people were killed by the regime.[3] The Documentation and Security Directorate (DDS)—the political police force created by Hissène Habré—targeted political opponents, as well as certain ethnic groups, who were perceived by the government as hostile to the regime, during several waves of repression. Perceived opponents were systematically detained in inhumane conditions, tortured and/or killed. Some detainees were also victims of rape and sexual slavery.

The EAC pioneered in the field of victims' participation, where rights accorded to the victims were much broader than the ones awarded by the ECCC.[4] All civil parties' lawyers were able to question every witness who took the stand and enjoyed the full rights of participation as stipulated by the Senegalese Code of Criminal Procedure. When defence tried to limit the scope of the final pleadings of one of the lawyers of the civil parties during the appellate proceedings, the presiding judge made clear that no restriction would be imposed. Compare this to the ECCC, where the *Duch* chamber prevented civil parties from questioning the accused and witnesses on the defendant's character and from making submissions on sentencing,[5] and where victims were required to exercise their rights not individually but rather as a consolidated group.[6] Moreover, the EAC is the first ad hoc

[3] See *Chad: Report of the Commission of Inquiry into the crimes and misappropriations committed by ex-President Habré, his accomplices and/or accessories* (Chad Commission of Inquiry 7 May 1992). The report is available at https://www.usip.org/sites/default/files/file/resources/collections/commissions/Chad-Report.pdf.

[4] *Victims Participation before the Extraordinary Chambers in the Courts of Cambodia* (ECCC, ADHOC, and Harvard Humanitarian Initiative January 2013) available at https://www.eccc.gov.kh/sites/default/files/Victims-participation-before-ECCC-Baseline-Study-Jan-2013.pdf; see also David S Sokol, 'Reduced Victim Participation: A Misstep by the Extraordinary Chambers in the Courts of Cambodia' (2011) 10 Washington University Global Studies Law Review 167, available at http://openscholarship.wustl.edu/cgi/viewcontent.cgi?article=1016&context=law_globalstudies; *Victim's Rights: Before the Extraordinary Chambers in the Courts of Cambodia (ECCC), a Mixed Record for Civil Parties* (FIDH, 20 November 2011) available at https://www.fidh.org/IMG/pdf/eccc_victrights_rep_nov2012_en_web.pdf; ECCC, case 001, general information, available at https://www.eccc.gov.kh/en/case/topic/1.

[5] See ECCC, *Prosecutor vs Kaing Guek Eav alias Duch*, *Decision on Civil Party Co-lawyers* joint request for a ruling on the standing of Civil Party lawyers to make submissions on sentencing and directions concerning the questioning of the accused, experts and witnesses testifying on character, 9 October 2009. See also Michelle Staggs Kelsall et al., *Lessons Learned from the Duch's Trial: A Comprehensive Review of the First Case before the ECCC* (The Asian International Justice Initiative's KRT Trial Monitoring Group 28 December 2009); Eric Stover, 'Confronting Duch: Civil party participation in Case 001 at the Extraordinary Chambers in the Courts of Cambodia' (2011) 93(882) International Review of the Red Cross 503, available at https://www.researchgate.net/publication/259419919_Confronting_Duch_Civil_party_participation_in_Case_001_at_the_Extraordinary_Chambers_in_the_Courts_of_Cambodia

[6] Ignaz Stegmiller, 'Legal Developments in Civil Party Participation at the Extraordinary Chambers in the Courts of Cambodia' (2014) 27(2) Leiden Journal of International Law 465, available at https://www.cambridge.org/core/journals/leiden-journal-of-international-law/article/legal-developments-in-civil-

jurisdiction to award individual reparation to the victims.[7] The ECCC only recognized the right of victims to collective and moral reparation.[8]

The EAC statute recognized the victims' right to participate in the proceeding and victims' right to reparation (Articles 14 and 27 of the Statute). Article 14 of the statute providing the principle of victims' participation as civil parties, indicated in paragraph 5 that their participation is regulated by the Senegalese Code of Criminal Procedure. This includes *inter alia* the right for the civil parties to be heard at the investigation stage; the right to question the accused, witnesses or all persons brought to the stand during trial; as well as the right to appeal decisions related to the civil action.

During the trial, two teams of lawyers represented the victims. In the first group, a team of Chadians and Senegalese lawyers represented a total of 3850 victims grouped under the umbrella of the associations AVCRP (*L'Association des Victimes des Crimes de Répression Politique*) and RADHT (*Le Réseau des Associations des Droits de l'Homme du Tchad*).[9] In the second group, our team represented the victims grouped under the AVCRHH (*L'Association des Victimes des Crimes du Régime de Hissein Habré*). The AVCRHH represented the largest group of victims during the proceedings, including 4,733 direct and indirect victims.[10]

The AVCRP was founded by Souleymane Guengueng in September 1991. The aim of the organization was to prosecute perpetrators of crimes and repressive acts committed under the Habré regime, and to demand reparation for the victims. The AVCRHH was created in 2008 by Clement Abaifouta, one of the victims of Habré's regime, as a result of an internal crisis within the AVCRP.[11] Most of the victims of the AVCRP, including its founder Souleymane Guengueng, joined the AVCRHH before the creation of the EAC.

The RADHT was created during the proceedings. Some considered that the creation of the RADHT was an attempt by the Chadian government to get involved in the proceedings, its Chadian lawyer having represented the President of Chad in the past.[12]

The victims represented by the AVCRP and the RADHT benefited from the legal assistance provided by the statute of the EAC. In fact, the EAC administrator appointed two Senegalese lawyers,[13] who were joined by two Chadians lawyers to represent them. The AVCRHH civil parties legal team was composed of lawyers from different backgrounds and origins: One Senegalese national (Assane Dioma Ndiaye), three Chadian lawyers

party-participation-at-the-extraordinary-chambers-in-the-courts-of-cambodia/F1F0AAEBCF86E9A2308B7D0D9291559D

[7] EAC, Article 28-2 of the Statute.

[8] ECCC, rule 23 of the Rules of Procedure and Evidence; *see* ECCC, *Moral and Collective Reparation*, general information, available at https://www.eccc.gov.kh/en/topic/477.

[9] EAC, Judicial Documents, Brief on compensation filed by the RADHT-AVCRP victims group, (*Mémoire aux fins d'indemnisation déposé par le groupe de victimes RADHT-AVCRP*) (10.06.2016), p 14, available at http://forumchambresafricaines.org/wp-content/uploads/2015/08/160610_Conclusions_PC_AVCRP_RADHT_demandes_r-°parations.pdf

[10] EAC Judicial Documents, Claims for reparation by the civil parties Abaïfouta and others (AVCRHH) (*Demandes en réparation des parties civiles Abaïfouta et consorts (AVCRHH)*) (10.06.2016), p 13, para 35, available at http://forumchambresafricaines.org/wp-content/uploads/2015/08/160610_Conclusions_PC_Aba-»fouta_et_autres_demandes_r-°parations.pdf.

[11] Clément Abaïfouta, 'Du prisonnier fossoyeur au président de l'association des victimes' (*Le monde Afrique* 2015) available at http://www.lemonde.fr/afrique/article/2015/09/08/clement-abaifouta-du-prisonnier-fossoyeur-au-president-de-l-association-des-victimes_4749150_3212.html

[12] See also Kandé, in this volume, Chapter 10.

[13] RCN Justice and Démocratie, 'Sensibiliser sur les Chambre africaines extraordinaires: Le Bulletin numéro 46' (December 2014) p 14, http://rcn-ong.be/IMG/pdf/bulletin_46.pdf.

(Jacqueline Moudeïna,[14] Delphine Djiraibe, and Soulgan Lambi) and three European lawyers: Georges-Henri Beauthier from Belgium, William Bourdon from France, and Alain Werner from Switzerland. These three individuals were the only non-Africans participating directly in the proceedings.

All these lawyers had been involved in the case for many years when the trial started in Dakar. Moudeïna, Djiraibe, and Lambi were the original lawyers representing the victims in Chad and early on in the case, Ndiaye became the Senegalese lawyer for the victims in Dakar in coordination with his Chadian colleagues. Beauthier was the lawyer representing Chadian victims when the case was litigated in Belgium and Bourdon was defending Jacqueline Moudeïna in N'djamena in a criminal case brought against her and had been involved in the first complaint filed against Habré in 2000. Alain Werner worked on the case from 2008 onwards, to advise as a consultant on some legal issues.

While both teams were involved with defending the victims' interests, no common strategy was defined between them. While the coordination between victims groups is not an obligation, lessons learned from the ECCC case 001 indicate that the absence of collaboration can lead to the restriction of civil parties' rights. This lack of coordination sometimes resulted in different views on strategic decisions. For example, at the appeal stage, the AVCRP and RADHT teams appealed the amount of reparations awarded at the trial stage stating that this amount should be increased.[15] Conversely, the AVCRHH decided not to challenge this amount based on several reasons. One of them was that they were concerned that a revision of the Trial Chamber's decision could lead to a reduction of the reparations.

Both local and international lawyers worked with victims on the case. The Chadian lawyers had the historical knowledge of the case. Since 2000, Ms Moudeïna, Ms Lambi, and Ms Djiraibe led the effort of bringing Habré to trial and fought to achieve justice for the victims of his regime for over fifteen years. Their in-depth knowledge of the facts of the case was vital during both witnesses' examinations and the drafting of our final conclusions. Their years of work, hand in hand with those who suffered from the crimes committed by Hissène Habré, gave them unique insights and access to the victims. For example, their hearing preparation work with the victims empowered many of the survivors to testify about sexual violence they had suffered. This would have been absolutely impossible without the trust and rapport that the Chadians lawyers had built with the victims over the years. They were also the ones who conducted the meticulous census of all the victims and their prejudice in order for them to be recognized as civil parties. This painstaking work was also essential during the reparation and appeal stages, as it became the basis of the Trial and Appeals Chambers' analysis regarding the attribution of individual reparations.

The value added by the Europeans lawyers was their knowledge and experience of international law and procedure. The European lawyers were able to advise the team in terms of legal filings, examination of witnesses as well as on international criminal law including modes of liability and legal qualifications of crimes. For example, our civil party team was at the origin of the request for requalification of the facts prompting the Trial Chamber to include *inter alia* sexual crimes in the charges against Habré.[16] We also called for the

[14] See Moudeïna, in this volume, Chapter 15.

[15] EAC, 'Habré case, Appeal brief of the lawyers representing RADHT and AVCRP—Civil interests' *Mémoire en appel des avocats représentant le RADHT et l'AVCRP—Intérêts civils* (7 December 2016).

[16] EAC, 'Habré case, Civil Parties Lawyers, Request relating to the legal qualification of the facts' *Requête relative à la qualification juridique des faits* (14 October 2015); *see also* EAC, Habré case, Trial Chamber Judgment, 30 May 2016, para 150.

assistance of an *Amicus Curiae* to support this point.[17] The request led to the condemnation of Habré for rape and sexual slavery, charges that had not been included by the prosecutor or the investigating judges.

Particularities of representing victims before the EAC

The EAC was established on an ad hoc basis and therefore had limited jurisdiction. Under Article 3 of the Statute, it was only authorised to prosecute crimes committed in Chad between 7 June 1982 and 1 December 1990. The EAC was destined to disappear after the appeal judgment in the Habré case.

This ephemeral aspect of the jurisdiction has created a risk related to the implementation of the judgments issued. For example, the Trial Chamber granted individual reparations to the victims but did not indicate precisely in its judgment how the reparations would be administered and by which organ.[18] By failing to indicate the modalities for the implementation of reparations, the Trial Chamber created the risk that reparations would never actually be granted once the EAC disappeared. This would render Article 27 and Article 28 of the statute, which recognises victims' rights to compensation, meaningless. It was thus important for the civil parties' lawyers to request the Appeals Chamber to identify the organs competent with the implementation of the decision.[19] This ground of appeal was granted by the Appeals Chamber. In its judgment, it identified the Trust Fund created by the African Union and the 'Tribunal de Grande Instance hors classe de Dakar' as being in charge of the implementation of the decision on reparation.[20]

The EAC does not have its own set of rules of procedure and evidence and therefore applied the Senegalese Code of Criminal Procedure, putting it in a unique situation where it had to conduct an international trial by applying a national tool, which was not really adapted to the exercise. This particular situation was highlighted at the appeal stage. Indeed, the nature of appeal provided by the EAC is international, ie it is limited to errors of law or of facts which occurred in the trial judgment. Thus, it does not allow the case to be reopened on the merits (Article 25 of the Statute), whereas the appeal procedure, as defined by the Senegalese Code of Criminal Procedure Code, tends to reformulate the judgment of first instance and has a devolutive effect (ie: the appeal brings about a retrial of the merits of the case, Articles 367-6 to 367-10 of the Senegalese Code of Criminal Procedure). As noted by the Appeals Chamber, neither the agreement with the African Union, nor the Statute gives any indication of the practical functioning of the appeal system within the EAC.[21] We found ourselves in the unprecedented situation where the question of the nature and functioning of the appeal within the EAC was discussed and settled only a few weeks

[17] Amicus Curiae brief of the Human Rights Center at the University of California, Berkeley, school of law and international experts on sexual violence under International criminal law, 'Rape and other forms of sexual violence as crimes against humanity, war crimes, and torture under customary international law', 8 December 2015. See also Seelinger and others, in this volume, Chapter 17.

[18] EAC, Habré case, Trial Chamber Judgment, 30 May 2016, paras 575–681.

[19] EAC, Habré case, Civil Parties' Lawyers, 'Appeal brief of the lawyers representing the civil parties Abaifouta et al (AVCRHH) - Civil interests', *Mémoire en appel des avocats représentant les parties civiles Abaifouta et consorts (AVCRHH)—Intérêts civils* (5 December 2016), paras 59–68.

[20] EAC, Habré case, Appeal Chamber Judgment, 27 April 2017, paras 899–900, available online at: https://assets.budh.nl/tijdschriften/aj/hissein_habre_02.pdf.

[21] EAC, Habré case, Appeal Chamber Judgment, 27 April 2017, para 65.

before the actual appeal proceedings started.[22] On one hand, the defence asserted that the appeal procedure should be a national one as the procedure within the EAC relied on the Senegalese Procedural Code. This option would have led to a *de novo* trial with the possibility to call witnesses and induce new evidence. On the other hand, the prosecution and civil parties' lawyers referred to the international nature of the proceedings as mentioned in the Statute.[23] We provided the appeals judges, who had a more limited international law experience, with detailed observations regarding the implication of the proceedings of the international nature of the appeal. This includes *inter alia* important restrictions on the admissibility of new evidence at the appeal stage.[24] In its judgment, the Appeals Chamber followed the reasoning of the civil parties by consecrating the international nature of the appeal proceedings.[25]

Another important issue related to victim participation was the standard of proof applied by the EAC regarding the recognition of civil party status. Both the EAC Statute and Senegalese law were silent regarding the standard of proof related to the identity of victims.[26] Moreover, during the proceedings, the Trial Chamber never clearly indicated which documents it would accept as proof of identity. It was only in its judgment that the chamber dismissed hundreds of civil party applications on the ground that they did not bring sufficient proof of identity.[27] As civil parties' lawyers, we appealed this decision and argued that the Supreme Court of the ECCC, in a similar situation, held that the failure to inform the victims of the applicable standards prior to the judgment creates a lack of clarity that causes civil parties a prejudice.[28] We indicated that the ECCC Supreme Court considered that this damage could be remedied by allowing the civil parties to submit additional evidence in order to convince the court that their civil party's applications were admissible.[29] We submitted a request to the Appeals Chamber to be granted a similar remedy.[30] The Appeals Chamber rejected our submission before the start of the appeal proceedings because it interpreted it as being a request to admit new evidence, which is very restricted at the appeal stage.[31] However, our argument was not lost. Indeed, in its judgment, the Appeals Chamber, even if it considered that no prejudice was caused by the Trial Chamber, allowed the rejected

[22] *See also* EAC, Habré case, Appeal Chamber Judgment, 27 April 2017, paras 63–82.

[23] EAC, 'Habré case, Civil Parties' Lawyers, Comments of the lawyers of the civil parties concerning the appeal procedure in the African Extraordinary Chambers' *Observations des avocats des parties civiles concernant la procédure d'appel au sein des chambres africaines extraordinaires* (17 November 2017).

[24] EAC, 'Habré case, Civil Parties' Lawyers, Comments of the lawyers of the civil parties concerning the appeal procedure in the African Extraordinary Chambers' *Observations des avocats des parties civiles concernant la procédure d'appel au sein des chambres africaines extraordinaires* (17 November 2017), paras 5–18.

[25] EAC, Habré case, Appeal Chamber Judgment, 27 April 2017, paras 63–82.

[26] EAC Habré case, Appeal Chamber Judgment, 27 April 2017, paras 686–87, 727.

[27] EAC Habré case, Trial Chamber Judgment, 30 May 2016, paras 51–52. *See also*: EAC Habré case, Civil Parties' Lawyers, 'Appeal brief of the lawyers representing the civil parties Abaifouta et al (AVCRHH) - Civil interests', (*Mémoire en appel des avocats représentant les parties civiles Abaifouta et consorts (AVCRHH)—Intérêts civils*), 5 December 2016, para 24.

[28] ECCC, *Prosecutor vs Kaing Guek Eav alias Duch*, Supreme Court Judgment, 3 February 2012, para 534.

[29] ECCC, *Prosecutor vs Kaing Guek Eav alias Duch*, Supreme Court Judgment, 3 February 2012, para 534. *See also*: EAC Habré case, Civil Parties' Lawyers, 'Appeal brief of the lawyers representing the civil parties Abaifouta et al (AVCRHH)—Civil interests' (*Mémoire en appel des avocats représentant les parties civiles Abaifouta et consorts (AVCRHH)—Intérêts civils*); 5 December 2016, paras 25–26.

[30] EAC Habré case, Civil Parties' Lawyers, Appeal brief of the lawyers representing the civil parties Abaifouta et al (AVCRHH) - Civil interests', (*Mémoire en appel des avocats représentant les parties civiles Abaifouta et consorts (AVCRHH)—Intérêts civils*); 5 December 2016, paras 25–26.

[31] EAC, Habré case, Preliminary decision, 29 December 2016, paras 44–47; EAC, Habré case, Appeal Chamber Judgment, 27 April 2017, para 766.

civil parties to present new elements of proof to the trust fund. It also tasked the latter with re-evaluating their applications accordingly and to award them reparations.[32]

Another challenge faced during the proceedings was the politics that surrounded the Habré case. The day after the Trial Chamber rendered its verdict, the Senegalese minister of justice mentioned the possibility of a presidential pardon to be granted to Hissène Habré in the event of final guilty verdict.[33] As civil parties' lawyers we had to react immediately and we issued a press release reminding Senegal of its obligations under international law, including the ones arising from the agreement signed with the African Union for setting up the EAC.[34]

We also had to raise the issue of sentencing during the appeal stage, which is traditionally not the role of civil parties *in the civil law system.*[35] Indeed, during the appeal hearing, the Prosecution stated that it deferred to the Chambers' assessment regarding the question of the existence of mitigating circumstances and the possibility of adjusting Habré's sentence.[36] This position was at odds with the prosecutor's final pleading at the trial stage requesting life sentence for Habré.[37] We considered that it was our responsibility for the victims, to safeguard the sentence handed down by the Trial Chamber. We had to amend our original oral pleading to include the sentencing issue. In response, we emphasized the correct evaluation of aggravating factors done by the Trial Chamber when it sentenced Habré for life imprisonment. We also reminded the state that Senegal was bound by its obligation to implement the sentence pronounced by the EAC.[38] The Appeals Chamber followed our observations and confirmed the sentence pronounced by the Trial Chamber, also referring to Senegal's obligations to implement the sentence in full as requested by Article 26(3) of the statute.[39]

Lessons learned

External expertise

Throughout the trial, the civil parties' lawyers called for external expertise to strengthen its assistance to the victims. First, we relied on an *amicus curiae* brief to deal with particular issues. As previously mentioned, we called for the assistance of international experts on sexual and gender-based violence (SGBV) to support our request for the inclusion of sexual crimes in the charges against Habré. Similarly, we called upon the assistance of 'Redress[40] the leading organization in terms of reparation to provide an *amicus curiae* on

[32] EAC, Habré case, Appeal Chamber Judgment, 27 April 2017, para 608 and 769.
[33] EAC Habré case, Appeal Chamber Judgment, 27 April 2017, paras 552–53.
[34] EAC Habré case, Appeal Chamber Judgment, 27 April 2017, paras 552–53.
[35] EAC Habré case, Appeal Chamber Judgment, 27 April 2017, paras 552–53.
[36] EAC Habré case, Appeal Chamber Judgment, 27 April 2017, para 551.
[37] EAC Habré case, Trial Chamber Judgment, 30 May 2016, para 2294.
[38] EAC Habré case, Appeal Chamber Judgment, 27 April 2017, para 552–53.
[39] EAC Habré case, Appeal Chamber Judgment, 27 April 2017, paras 560, 566; Article 6-3 of the Statute provides 'All detention conditions, whether in Senegal or in another African Union Member State, shall be governed by the laws of the State of enforcement, in conformity with international standards. The State of enforcement shall be bound to comply with length of the sentence.'
[40] For more information see: https://redress.org/.

the establishment of a trust fund.[41] Even if the EAC rejected the *amicus curiae* in both instances,[42] there is no doubt that they played an important role in highlighting crucial issues to the court.[43] Secondly, we consulted external experts to assist us with the drafting of our brief related to the civil claim. Legal advisers from both Redress and Amnesty International, who have previous experience in mass reparation claims, led the work on this important issue. Additionally, Reed Brody and HRW, who initiated and spearheaded the whole case, worked extremely closely with the civil parties' lawyers throughout the trial. Their assistance was invaluable due to their unparalleled knowledge of the facts of the case.

The complexity of victim legal representation in international proceedings calls for the use of partnership and external expertise. The possibility to file *amicus curiae* offers infinite resources that should be used whenever possible.

Role of rules of procedure and evidence

Some argued that the use of the Senegalese Procedural Code by the EAC was time saving as all lawyers from civil law countries applied more or less the same rules, and thus, all the lawyers engaged in the proceedings were familiar with the procedural system adopted by the court. The experience at the EAC also demonstrates that the sole reliance on national procedural rules by hybrid courts is not adapted to their mandate, however. Indeed, as explained earlier in relation to the question of the nature of the appeal within the EAC, the rules developed in a national context can be ill-fitted to international procedures.

In addition, the standards developed in the framework of human rights procedure are different from the ones developed at a national level. For example, the burden of proof required for compensation eligibility has been eased in the cases of reparation claims linked to human rights violations. Indeed, courts have considered that claimants often have difficulty proving eligibility for compensation due to a lack of evidence 'related to the circumstances that led to the losses and violations that are being addressed through the program'[44] and have thus accepted in the absence of official documents a whole series of private documents, directly or indirectly supporting the claim.[45] Despite the international standard being clear, we had to raise the question of the standard of proof related to the identity of victims before the Appeals Chamber due to the lack of specific procedural rules related to this issue.[46]

Legal certainty could be preserved, and time consuming debates on which criteria to apply could be avoided, by the development and adoption of specific procedural rules by the court.

41 See: 'Establishing a Trust Fund for Victims in the case of Hissène Habré: options for the way forward', Redress and the Association Tchadienne pour la Paix et les Droits de l'Homme (ATPDH), April 2017, available here https://redress.org/wp-content/uploads/2017/12/April-Establishing-a-Trust-Fund-for-Victims-in-the-case-of-Hissene-Habre-options-for-the-way-forward.pdf

42 EAC Habré case, Appeal Chamber Judgment, 27 April 2017, paras 600 and 601.

43 EAC Habré case, Appeal Chamber Judgment, 27 April 2017, para 602.

44 Heike Niebergall 'Overcoming Evidentiary Weaknesses in Reparation Claims Programmes' in Carla Ferstman et al (eds), *Reparations for Victims of Genocide, War Crimes and Crimes against Humanity* (Brill 2009) (« Niebergall ») 150. *See also*: CPI, Chambre préliminaire II, situation en Ouganda, *Décision relative aux demandes de participation des victimes a/0010/06, a/0064/06 to a/0070/06, a/0081/06 to a/0104/06 and a/0111/06 to a/0127/06, ICC-02/04-101*, 10 août 2007, para 15.

45 ECCC, *Prosecutor vs Kaing Guek Eav alias Duch*, Supreme Court Judgment, 3 February 2012, para 523.

46 EAC Habré case, Appeal Chamber Judgment, 27 April 2017, paras 686–87, 727.

Conclusion

The EAC, the first international tribunal created by Africans to try African people accused of the most serious crimes, is seen as a model for fighting impunity on the continent. Its emergence raises hope for the establishment in Africa of other similar structures in order to judge the atrocities committed on the continent and, especially, in situations where the ICC would not have jurisdiction.[47] The Habré trial also demonstrated that extending victims' participation rights is not an obstacle to a speedy and fair conduct of the proceedings. On the contrary, the EAC showed that civil parties can be a real asset in raising issues that have been disregarded by other parties. As previously mentioned, thanks to the victims, the important issue of sexual violence committed during conflict has been dealt with by the EAC. This legacy is important at a time when other international courts try to limit the role of victims during the proceedings.

47 Alain Werner and Emmanuelle Marchand, *Chambres Africaines Extraordinaires* Dictionnaire encyclopédique de la justice pénale international (Berger-Levrault 2017).

17

Can We Be Friends? Offering an *Amicus Curiae* Brief on Sexual Violence to the EAC

Kim Thuy Seelinger, Naomi Fenwick, and Khaled Alrabe,
Human Rights Center—University of California, Berkeley

At the time of the Habré trial, the authors were all affiliated with the Sexual Violence Program at the Human Rights Center, based at the University of California, Berkeley, School of Law. Kim Thuy Seelinger, JD, served as the Sexual Violence Program's founding director from 2010 to 2019; she was also a Lecturer in Law at Berkeley. She is an expert on conflict-related sexual violence, having represented survivors for many years and consulting in war crimes trials around the world. Seelinger currently works at Washington University in St. Louis as Visiting Professor of Law and Research Associate Professor of Social Work. Naomi Fenwick, LLM, was a researcher at the Sexual Violence Program from 2014–2016 and now works on capital defence cases at the Texas Defender Service in Houston, Texas. Khaled Alrabe, JD, served as a researcher at the Sexual Violence Program from 2015–2017 and is now a Staff Attorney at the National Immigration Project.

On 27 April 2017, the appeals panel of the EAC upheld Hissène Habré's conviction for war crimes, crimes against humanity, and acts of torture.[1] In doing so, Judge Wafi Ougadeye reaffirmed a trial judgment that had, since its rendering in May 2016, become famous for its heightened treatment of sexual violence.[2] Among other international crimes, Habré had been convicted of forms of sexual violence as a crime against humanity and as a form of torture. The affirmation of Habré's life sentence for massive sexual violence committed by his secret police (DDS) agents was hailed as a tremendous victory for international criminal justice and the rights of sexual violence survivors. However, the conviction for sexual crimes was not complete and its path was not linear.

In this chapter, we review the unexpected emergence of rape and sexual slavery in the trial as well as how and why we, as outside observers, attempted to weigh in on this evidence mid-trial by submitting an *amicus curiae* brief on sexual violence under customary international law.[3] We will summarize the legal and practical challenges encountered in our

[1] *The Prosecutor v Habré*, EAC Appeals Chamber, 27 April 2017. See Le Gall, in this volume, Chapter 19.

[2] *Public prosecutor v. Habré*, EAC, 30 May 2016. See also Le Gall, in this volume, Chapter 18, and Wafi, Chapter 20.

[3] 'Rape and other forms of sexual violence as crimes against humanity, war crimes, and torture under customary international law', Available at https://humanrights.berkeley.edu/sites/default/files/publications/micus-curiae-brief-of-the-human-rights-center-at-the-university-of-california-berkeley-school-of-law-and-international-experts-on-sexual-violence-under-international-criminal-law-eng.pdf.

Kim Thuy Seelinger, Naomi Fenwick, and Khaled Alrabe, *Can We Be Friends? Offering an Amicus Curiae Brief on Sexual Violence to the EAC* In: *The President on Trial.* First edition. Edited by: Sharon Weill, Kim Thuy Seelinger, and Kerstin Bree Carlson, Oxford University Press (2020). © Kim Thuy Seelinger, Naomi Fenwick, and Khaled Alrabe. DOI: 10.1093/oso/9780198858621.003.0018

briefing process, including attempts to articulate the state of customary international law at the time of Habré's regime (1982–1990) and actually submit the brief to the Dakar court. Finally, we will note the apparent impact of the brief and reflect on lessons learned from the drafting and filing effort.

The emergence of sexual violence testimony

Amongst the many forms of violence alleged in the record against Hissène Habré, witness testimony before the EAC between September and November 2015 revealed that persons detained by the DDS[4] had suffered multiple forms of sexual violence. Detainees were raped and gang raped by prison guards and high-level officials,[5] forced to have sexual relations in exchange for necessities of survival,[6] and subjected to sexualized forms of torture such as electric shocks to the breasts and genitalia.[7] At least two groups of female detainees were also transferred to military camps in the desert, where they were forced to serve Chadian soldiers.[8] The harrowing testimony of survivors even included an account of sexual violence committed by Habré himself.

For example, a former prisoner had witnessed the repeated rape and gang rape of women at the prison Les Locaux, by security guards and high-level officials. This testimony echoed Human Rights Watch (HRW) reports already in the underlying record, which had referenced rape committed against prisoners by male guards working at Habré's prisons. This included forcible sex with female detainees in exchange for necessities of survival, like food and medicine. Evidence also indicated that even children were raped: one former detainee testified about soldiers raping and killing a girl of seven or eight years of age.

Some witnesses spoke of slavery. Their testimony elaborated on earlier HRW documentation, which had indicated that women were detained and exploited by Habré's agents in military camps in the desert. For example, a witness testified that she was part of a group of

[4] The *Direction de la documentation et de la sécurité* was created in 1983 and operated under the direct orders of Habré. Initially tasked with preventing pro-Libyan activities, the DDS conducted thousands of arbitrary arrests. *La Plaine des Morts: Le Tchad de Hissène Habré* (HRW 2013) 84 <https://www.hrw.org/sites/default/files/reports/chad1013frwebwcover_0.pdf> accessed 30 November 2015 [hereinafter HRW].

[5] Testimony of Khadidja Hassan Zidane, Monday, 19 October 2015, Trust Africa, 'The Public Prosecution v. Hissène Habré—Summary of the Twenty-Eighth Hearing Held on 19 October 2015' (2015) <http://www.trustafrica.org/en/component/k2/item/3212-the-public-prosecution-versus-Habré> accessed 30 November 2015; Testimony of Bandjim Bandoum, Thursday, 22 October 2015; Testimony of Clément Abaifouta, Tuesday, 9 November 2015, Trust Africa, 'The Public Prosecution v. Hissène Habré—Summary of the Thirty-Sixth Hearing Held on 9 November 2015' (2015) <http://www.trustafrica.org/en/component/k2/item/3212-the-public-prosecution-versus-Habré> accessed 30 November 2015.

[6] (n 4) 234.

[7] Testimony of Fatimé Sakine, Thursday, 22 October 2015, Trust Africa, 'The Public Prosecution v. Hissène Habré—Summary of the Thirty-First Hearing Held on 22 October 2015' (2015) <http://www.trustafrica.org/en/component/k2/item/3212-the-public-prosecution-versus-Habré> accessed 30 November 2015; Testimony of Garba Akhaye, Monday, 28 September 2015, Trust Africa, 'The Public Prosecution v. Hissène Habré—Summary of the Sixteenth Hearing Held on 28 September 2015' (2015) <http://www.trustafrica.org/en/component/k2/item/3212-the-public-prosecution-versus-Habré> accessed 30 November 2015; Id. Testimony of Ahmat Maki, Monday, 28 September 2015.

[8] Testimony of Katouma Deffalah, Tuesday 20 October 2015, Trust Africa, 'The Public Prosecution v. Hissène Habré—Summary of the Twenty-Ninth Hearing Held on 20 October 2015' (2015) <http://www.trustafrica.org/en/component/k2/item/3212-the-public-prosecution-versus-Habré> accessed 30 November 2015; HRW, *La Plaine des Morts: Le Tchad de Hissène Habré* (2013), <https://www.hrw.org/sites/default/files/reports/chad1013frwebwcover_0.pdf> accessed 30 November 2015 [hereinafter HRW], at 239.

women that was transferred to a camp in Ouadi Doum, where they were used as domestic servants and sexual slaves for a year.

Oral testimonies also reflected earlier reference to torture, confirming that men and women detained in Habré's prisons were routinely subjected to torture in the form of rape and intentional injury to the genitals. One victim was pregnant in detention; her child did not survive. Another cellmate reportedly received electric shocks to her breasts and genitals, which left her unable to walk. Similarly, one witness said he had observed DDS agents inserting pieces of wood into his cellmates' penises.

Finally, some testimony built out earlier indications of other forms of grave sexual violence. For example, Dr Hélène Jaffe, who had treated hundreds of survivors of Habré's prisons, testified that many of the men bore injuries consistent with sexual violence. Other forms of sexual violence that emerged from witness testimony included forced nudity in detention and the forced intake of oral contraception.

Not all the testimony described sexual crimes committed by Habré's DDS agents. On Monday, 19 October 2015, the Court was stunned by the testimony of one former detainee in particular, Khadidja Hassan Zidane. Zidane testified that Hissène Habré had summoned her to the presidential palace and violated her on four separate occasions. In a particularly stunning moment, she offered to show the judges her scars, from when Habré had stabbed her with a pen as she resisted him. Zidane paid dearly for her accusation. Habré's media team immediately attacked her on its website, challenging her character, and accusing her of being a 'nymphomaniac' and a drug-user.

A call for intervention

It should be noted that, prior to survivors' testimony of multiple forms of sexual violence, little of the case record before the EAC focused on these crimes. Despite allusion to sexual torture in the underlying record (including the insertion of chili peppers into a detainee's penis), the investigating judges of the EAC had not specifically charged crimes of sexual violence in the 'ordonnance de renvoi' (the indictment) they forwarded to the Trial Chamber.[9] It seemed, rather, that various sexual abuses committed by the Habré's agents were characterized more broadly as torture in the initial charges.

Concerned by the accounts of sexual violence articulated by so many victims at trial, civil society organizations quickly organized to emphasize the importance of addressing these crimes. In October 2015, seventeen groups from across Senegal, eastern Democratic Republic of the Congo, the Netherlands and the United States issued an open letter to Judge Gberdao Gustave Kam, president of the EAC Trial Chamber, and Prosecutor Mbacke Fall, calling for greater consideration of sexual crimes. The letter specifically urged the EAC to heed the lessons of the *Akayesu* case before the International Criminal Tribunal for Rwanda two decades earlier, in which witness testimony about rape prompted an amendment of charges to include sexual crimes. This ultimately led to the landmark 1998 judgment establishing rape as an act of genocide. The letter's signatories closed by requesting that the

[9] *Ordre de renvoi,* 13 February 2015. See Kandé, in this volume, Chapter 10.

judge and prosecutor allow more victims and witnesses to offer relevant testimony before the end of the trial stage.

Around the same time, groups observing the trial contacted the Human Rights Center's Sexual Violence Program, based at University of California, Berkeley, School of Law. They requested that we draft and submit an *amicus curiae*, or 'friend of the court', brief on international crimes of sexual violence as quickly as possible. Ideally, this advisory brief could assist the trial judges by mapping out how existing evidence might fit within both the court's statute and customary international law in effect at the time of Habré's regime. This would, in turn, assist the judges in their determination as to whether and how to amend the charges to more specifically address crimes of sexual violence. However, it was already late September. Trial would like close by early December 2015, so any *amicus curiae* brief would need to be coordinated, drafted, translated, and filed in Dakar within two months.

At first, we simply agreed to coordinate a broad drafting effort. However, when it became clear that time was limited and no volunteers had come forward to do the actual research and writing, our team found ourselves responsible for generating a draft brief for review. We recruited local human rights lawyer Natasha Fain to put a fourth shoulder to the wheel. Our work would be guided and reviewed by a select group of the world's eminent experts on the prosecution of sexual violence and international crimes, including Justice Richard Goldstone, Patricia Viseur Sellers, Kelly Askin, Christine Chinkin, and George Kegoro.[10] Our hope was to assemble a cross-section of respected *amici* from the African continent and beyond, to impress upon the Trial Chamber judges the consensus that many of the acts of sexual violence surfacing in the evidence could be legitimately charged, should they so choose.

[10] Intended *amici* were drawn from leading practitioners and academics from African and beyond. Their names and affiliations at the time: Dr Kelly Askin, Former Legal Advisor to ICTR / ICTY, United States of America; Professor Olympia Bekou, Professor of Public International Law, University of Nottingham; Head, International Criminal Justice Unit, Human Rights Law Centre, United Kingdom; Dr Anne-Marie de Brouwer, Associate Professor of International Criminal Law, Tilburg University, Netherlands; Professor Christine Chinkin, Emerita Professor of International Law and Director, Centre for Women, Peace, and Security, London School of Economics, United Kingdom; Cllr Felicia Coleman, Counsellor-at-Law, Former Chief Prosecutor, Sexual and Gender-Based Crimes Unit, Ministry of Justice, Liberia; Ms Natasha Fain, International Human Rights Attorney, United States of America; Justice Richard Goldstone, Supreme Court of South Africa, Constitutional Court of South Africa, and first Chief Prosecutor to ICTR / ICTY, South Africa; Cllr Deweh Gray, Counsellor-at-Law, Board Chair, Association of Female Lawyers of Liberia, Liberia; Mr George Kegoro, Executive Director, Kenya Human Rights Commission, Kenya; Ms Magali Maystre, Legal Officer, Appeals Chamber of the UN International Criminal Tribunal for the former Yugoslavia (ICTY) and UN International Criminal Tribunal for Rwanda (ICTR); and Senior Adviser, Case Matrix Network; Professor Noah Novogrodsky, Professor of Law and Co-Director of the Center for International Human Rights Law and Advocacy, University of Wyoming, United States of America; Ms Elvina Pothelet, University of Geneva, Switzerland; Ms Madeleine Rees, OBE, Secretary General, Women's International League for Peace and Freedom, Switzerland; former gender expert and Head of Office in Bosnia and Herzegovina, Office of the United Nations High Commissioner for Human Rights; Ms Kim Thuy Seelinger, Director, Sexual Violence Program, Human Rights Center, University of California, Berkeley, School of Law, United States of America; Prof. Beth Van Schaack, Leah Kaplan Visiting Professor in Human Rights at Stanford Law School and former Deputy to the United States Ambassador-at-Large for War Crimes Issues, United States of America; Dr. Patricia Viseur Sellers, Special Advisor for Prosecution Strategies to the Prosecutor of the International Criminal Court; Visiting Fellow, Oxford University; Acting Senior Trial Attorney and Legal Advisor for Gender Crimes at the ICTY / ICTR, United States of America.

The brief

As noted earlier, the charges brought against Habré did not explicitly address sexual violence despite the indication and discussion of such crimes in the *ordonnance de renvoi* narrative emanating from the Investigative Chamber.

This was a remediable omission, given the ample options available to the EAC in its statute, which granted the EAC jurisdiction to prosecute crimes of sexual and gender-based violence under multiple legal characterizations. Amongst other crimes, the statute provided for the prosecution of rape as a crime against humanity,[11] or as the war crimes of torture or inhuman treatment,[12] and of outrages upon personal dignity,[13] or as the independent crime of torture.[14] Facts of sexual slavery could be prosecuted under the statute as the crime against humanity of sexual slavery,[15] or as the war crime of outrages upon personal dignity.[16] The statute further supported the prosecution of other forms of 'sexual violence of comparable gravity' as crimes against humanity.[17]

However, for each of these potential charges, the EAC judges would first have to satisfy the principle of legality, which requires that a charged offense entailed criminal liability under international customary or conventional law at the time of its commission.[18] *When* an act occurs can be the most important factor in this determination; the legality analysis is in essence a historical one. To assess whether an act was in fact a crime under customary or conventional law at the time of alleged commission, jurists have examined not only the jurisprudence of past tribunals, but also military manuals, national legislation, national cases, and Security Council resolutions existing at the time in question.

Prosecution of sexual violence under international criminal law is particularly complicated where, as in the Habré case, the crimes are alleged to have occurred prior to the events considered by the International Criminal Tribunal for the Former Yugoslavia (ICTY) and the International Criminal Tribunal for Rwanda (ICTR). The tribunals' combined jurisprudence clarified rape and other forms of sexual violence to be war crimes, crimes against humanity, and even potential acts of genocide under customary international law in effect by the mid-1990s.

But Habré was in power from 1982 to 1990. What could be said about the customary law status of these acts then?

To assist the tribunal in assessing the legality of potential charges permitted by the EAC statute, the *amicus curiae* brief opened by noting the judges' authority to charge and

[11] Statute of the EAC, article 6(a).
[12] ibid, article 7(1)(b).
[13] ibid, article 7(2)(c).
[14] ibid, article 8.
[15] ibid, article 6(f).
[16] ibid, article 7(2)(e).
[17] ibid, article 6(a).
[18] In fact, the legality question was at the heart of Habré's challenge before the Court of the Economic Community of West African States (ECOWAS). Although that challenge was eventually answered by ECOWAS, it nevertheless highlighted the fact that legality constituted a potential obstacle to the prosecution of Habré for crimes committed from June 1982 to December 1990. In 2008, ECOWAS agreed that pursuits on the basis of retroactively enacted amendments to Senegal's criminal and constitutional law would violate the principle of legality. Instead, the ECOWAS Court suggested that the legality challenge could be obviated by the creation of a special ad hoc judicial chamber within the Senegalese judiciary before which to try Habré. *See* Cour de Justice de la Communauté économique des Etats de l'Afrique de l'Ouest, 18 novembre 2010, Hissein Habré c. République du Sénégal, Arrêt n° ECW/CCJ/JUD/06/10. See also Kioko, in this volume, Chapter 8.

prosecute acts of sexual violence committed by the Habré regime under customary international law developed even before the jurisprudence of the ICTY and ICTR. It outlined the evidence of sexual violence that had emerged from documentary and trial testimony, much of which was publicly available due to hearing broadcasts online. It then summarized the potentially relevant provisions of the EAC statute. Finally, in the heart of the brief, we presented the historical jurisprudence of sexual crimes under customary international law prior to 1990, in order to map out the legality of potential charges related to actions taken in the 1980s. In this section, we traced the lineage of the major sexual crimes listed as war crimes in the EAC statute as far back as the 1907 Hague Convention on the Laws and Customs of War and war crimes trials in the 1940s, including before the International Military Tribunal for the Far East (IMFTE) and even several domestic trials of rape as a war crime, guided by the UN War Crimes Commission. We also traced the emergence of sexual violence as a crime against humanity through the twentieth century and the ways rape and other forms of sexual violence meet the longstanding definition of torture. In this way, the *amicus curiae* brief offered an efficient review of the customary international law framework through which charges of crimes of sexual violence could be brought against Habré under the EAC statute, without infringing the principle of legality.

After feedback from intended *amici*, we finalized the brief for translation into French. *Amici* hoped the brief would assist the EAC judges as they considered exercising their authority to revise the charges to reflect the full scope and gravity of the sexual violence described by the victims.

Friends or acquaintances?

Now that the brief was written, we had to find a way to file it. *Amicus curiae* briefs are not common practice in civil law systems and there was no formal mechanism in Senegalese procedural law for filing such a submission before the EAC or any other chamber in the Senegalese judiciary. To address this awkward posture, we prepared an introductory memorandum,[19] requesting leave to file the brief in light of (a) EAC judges' uncontested power to 'requalify' or 'recharacterize' established facts in the record and revise charges accordingly and (b) examples of receptivity to *amicus curiae* briefing by other courts based in civil law systems, where such interventions are not traditionally common.

While waiting for the everything to be translated, we consulted with Senegalese lawyers about general filing advice: type and format of submissions, number of copies, etc. To determine our latest possible deadline, we checked with trial observers and others close to the case about the hearing schedule—we wanted to make sure that the brief was received while court was still in session so that all parties could access it immediately. Then, we looked up the physical address of the EAC administrative office and called DHL for shipment on 8 December 2015. We had also tracked down email addresses for contacts at the EAC and notified them that a shipment of documents was on its way; our email was acknowledged as

[19] 'Demande d'autorisation de presenter un mémoire d'amicus curiae concernant la question de la qualification juridique des crimes sexuels en droit international coutumier,' available at https://humanrights.berkeley.edu/sites/default/files/publications/habre_demande-memoire-damicus-curiae_violence-sexuelle_151208.pdf

received. A few days later on 14 December 2015, we received another email from the EAC confirming receipt of the actual box of hardcopy documents.

A journalist from The Guardian contacted us that same week. Celeste Hicks had been covering aspects of the Habré trial and was intrigued by the international call for increased attention to sexual crimes. She wanted to know what we, as a specialized research unit, thought about amending the charges to include sexual violence. In speaking with Ms Hicks, we mentioned our attempt to map out potential charges by submission of an *amicus curiae* brief and informed her that while the fate of the brief itself was unclear, we were confident that the survivors' testimony at trial was powerful enough to move the judges to reconsider amendment of charges. If this was their wish, we believed the brief would provide a helpful mapping of options.

On 16 December 2015, we received an email from the EAC, advising that the brief could not be formally admitted into the trial record as such but that, as the Chamber could avail itself of any and all pertinent background documents, it might yet prove useful. We were disappointed that the *amicus curiae* brief would not be formally included as a court submission, since this would have enabled all parties to consider and debate the value and legitimacy of sexual violence-related charges. However, we had understood from the beginning that the filing was a longshot. We were simply encouraged by the possibility of the brief serving as background material for the judges, if not a formal brief.

On 22 December 2015, Ms Hicks' article came out online in The Guardian.[20] We were pleased to see she not only mentioned the *amicus curiae* brief, but she had included a link to it through the Human Rights Center website. In this way, the brief entered the public domain—it was now technically accessible to all parties to the Habré trial: the prosecutors, the defence, and victims' counsel. We had renewed hope that our work might prove useful.

Reflections on a relationship

As a drafting team, we have mixed feelings about our attempt to engage the EAC as *amici*. On one hand, it was clear that sexual crimes had been overlooked despite their acknowledgement by the investigative chamber's report and the extensive testimony from individual victims and witnesses in late 2015. In light of the recurrent side-lining of gender-based crimes in indictments before international criminal tribunals, it felt important to at least highlight the omission in case judges were inclined to reconsider and revise charges.

With the amendment of charges to include sexual crimes in January 2016, we felt encouraged that our efforts had helped illuminate a troubling void in the case. We were not sure who or what had convinced the judges to revise charges—presumably the powerful testimony of witnesses and victims in court had prompted them to reconsider. Perhaps the increasing international attention to the case and demands for charge amendment had also had impact. All we knew was that the brief had, even informally, provided a helpful roadmap if they decided to go down that route.

[20] C Hicks, 'Lawyers Press for Chad's Hissène Habré to Face Sexual Slavery and Rape Charges' *The Guardian* (London, 22 December 2015) <https://www.theguardian.com/global-development/2015/dec/22/chad-hissene-habre-lawyers-sexual-slavery-rape-charges-trial>.

Then, on 30 May 2016, we sat in court behind a row of Habré's victims—several of whom had testified about sexual violence—as Judge Kam read a summary of the trial judgment. Once Kam uttered the words 'guilty' and 'life imprisonment', the dozen women stood up and started singing. It was a song they had held silent for nearly thirty years. In that moment of Habré's conviction for rape and sexual slavery as crimes of humanity and acts of torture, we felt moved beyond words.

In reviewing the final decision, as well as the submissions of the parties to the case, it seems clear that the brief had informed the trial. Though on appeal, Habré was acquitted of the specific charges related to direct commission of rape against Khadidja Hassan Zidane, his conviction for several counts of rape and sexual slavery committed by his subordinates remained intact. These were crimes against humanity and acts of torture, as we had argued in the brief. While we were unclear at first as to why they were not also accepted as war crimes, we felt satisfied that at least the survivors of sexual violence had been acknowledged in the final judgement. Parties close to the case confirmed that the brief had provided invaluable clarification of possible charges for sexual crimes.

On the other hand, we understand that this attempt to join as *amici* was more creative than conventional. Unlike *amicus curiae* briefs we have worked on in the United States and elsewhere, this one was not officially accepted by chambers. Ideally, the EAC would have permitted its admission, giving all parties a chance to review and debate its contents. However, without a formal mechanism through which an *amicus curiae* brief could be admitted, the trial chamber judges were constrained in their official reception of our submission. Were it not for an article in The Guardian, it is unclear if the brief's analysis would have reached the parties and worked its way into their final positions.

To avoid this sideways influence of *amicus curiae* briefing, it would be helpful if the statutes underlying chambers such as the EAC—even in civil law systems—clearly provided for the acceptance of *amicus curiae* briefs or other external interventions deemed useful by chambers. Access to outside *amici* can be particularly important for national level courts trying international crimes cases for the first time. External input on complex matters of international criminal law, especially the complicated evolution of sexual crimes over time, is useful in most chambers—and especially in contexts where local expertise is still new and where alleged crimes took place in less common ways or time periods.

All in all, we were grateful to have had the opportunity to offer the trial chamber *amici*'s insights on the evolution of sexual crimes under customary international law. While *amici* did not become close friends of the court, it seems that our brief interaction had proven valuable.

18

The Habré Trial Judgment

A Summary of the First Instance Judgment of the EAC

Élise Le Gall, International Criminal Law Expert with the EAC Office of the Prosecutor

---

After several months of trial, the judges retired to deliberate. On 30 May 2016, the deadline imposed by the donors, the president of the trial chamber read out a twenty-five-page summary of the judgment. The 536-page judgment was issued one month later, after the appeals deadline had passed, meaning appeals were filed based on the summary alone. Detached from the process that created it, the judgment has become a jurisprudence in international criminal law, an actor in itself.

The following two chapters offer a summary of the judgment and appeal written by Élise Le Gall, a French lawyer and member of the Paris Bar, who served as an expert in international criminal law within the EAC, working closely with Prosecutor Mbacké Fall.

The EAC Trial Court ruling of 30 May 2016 found Hissène Habré guilty of crimes against humanity, war crimes, and the autonomous crime of torture. He was acquitted on several counts of war crimes, namely: unlawful transfer, deprivation of a prisoner of war or any other person of the right to a fair and impartial trial by a court, destruction and appropriation of property not justified by military necessity, and pillage. For the crimes of which he was found guilty, the judges of the EAC upheld Hissène Habré's individual criminal liability, as well as his liability pursuant to joint criminal enterprise and command responsibility. As punishment, the judges of the Trial Chamber sentenced Hissène Habré to life imprisonment but did not impose the penalty of confiscation of the seized property. The Chamber also rendered a second decision on 29 July 2016 as to civil interests granting individual reparations to the victims. This chapter summarizes the key points of the Trial Chamber's judgments.

I. Findings on crimes committed in Chad from 7 June 1982 to 1 December 1990

Crimes against humanity and autonomous crimes of torture

Hissène Habré seized power on 7 June 1982. Mass arrests of Chadian citizens ensued. At first, arrests targeted Habré's political opponents, including members of the various GUNT

Elise Le Gall, *The Habré Trial Judgment* In: *The President on Trial*. First edition. Edited by: Sharon Weill, Kim Thuy Seelinger, and Kerstin Bree Carlson, Oxford University Press (2020). © Elise Le Gall. DOI: 10.1093/oso/9780198858621.003.0019

(Gouvernment d'Union National de Transition) factions and suspected allies of Libya.[1] In a second phase, however, any Chadian or foreign citizen suspected of being in opposition or perceived as such because of their family, social and/or ethnic ties was likely to be arrested, including women and children.

In its factual conclusions, the Trial Chamber notes that these arrests were carried out by members of the Documentation and Security Directorate (DDS) and the Special Rapid Action Brigade (BSIR) outside of any judicial process. After arrest, people were generally interrogated at DDS or BSIR headquarters, and then nearly systematically incarcerated in one of the DDS detention network prisons in N'Djamena ('The Premises', 'Swimming Pool', 'Martyrs' Camp', 'Prison of the Presidency', 'Gendarmerie', 'BSIR', and 'Moursal').[2]

Torture was systematic during large-scale interrogations by DDS and BSIR agents. The EAC Trial Chamber expounded that the means of torture included notably a form of binding called the *arbatachar*,[3] torture with sticks,[4] torture using an exhaust pipe,[5] forced intake of water,[6] sexual violence against both women and men,[7] insufficient nourishment, and appalling detention conditions: overcrowded cells, unclean conditions, and heat.[8]

At the same time, the Hissène Habré regime embarked on the reconquest of southern Chad by using brutal repression against the Codos' commando groups, as well as against the civilian population of the South, considered as an ally of the Codos.[9]

Beginning in 1987, the Hadjarai community also suffered large-scale repression. A specialized commission composed of DDS or BSIR officials were tasked with systematically arresting, torturing, and disappearing them, in addition to subjecting them to inhumane detention conditions.[10]

The final major wave of repression then targeted the Zaghawa community, where again a special commission composed of DDS and BSIR officers was created to carry out the repression.[11]

The Trial Chamber also concluded in its factual determinations that Hissène Habré, using his position of authority and with full intention, ordered the execution of two men in response to the Ngalo massacre of 27 July 1985.[12] There was no doubt for the Trial Chamber that the order Habré gave contributed directly and substantially to the commission of the

[1] Judgment, *Ministère Public c. Hissein Habré* (EAC Trial Chamber) 30 May 2016 §481–700.
[2] ibid §492–536.
[3] ibid §557–62.
[4] ibid §574–76.
[5] ibid §567–68.
[6] ibid §563–66.
[7] ibid §610–24.
[8] ibid §649–80.
[9] ibid §912–1114.
[10] ibid §1115–1211.
[11] ibid §1212–289.
[12] ibid §1040.

crime. He was thus found guilty, pursuant to Article 10(2) of the Statute, of having ordered intentional homicide as an underlying act to crimes against humanity. Notably, the Trial Chamber argued that this crime could not have been considered a legitimate punishment—so Habré was not relieved of liability per command responsibility.[13]

Furthermore, analysis of the factual determinations and testimonies given at the Trial Chamber enable measurement of the prevalence and extent of sexual violence within the regime's repressive system. According to the Trial Chamber, the evidence demonstrated that between 1984 and 1989, several women and girls detained and/or interrogated in several DDS prisons in N'Djamena were subjected to forced sexual relations by DDS agents, members of the authorities in charge of the prison facilities, and BSIR soldiers.[14]

These include reports of events that took place between 1985 and 1986, when eleven women were confined in the Kalaït military camp, kept as domestic workers, and subjected to forced sexual relations by Chadian soldiers in the Kalaït camp.[15] The Trial Chamber also drew on the events that took place between 1988 and 1989, when nine women and young girls were confined in the Ouadi-Doum military camp, held as domestic workers, and subjected to forced sexual relations by the commander and Chadian soldiers.[16]

Finally, in its factual determinations, the Trial Chamber focused in particular on the treatment of Ms Khadija Hassan Zidane in the presidential palace, concluding that she was:

> (…) a victim of physical abuse—including sexual violence—during her detention in the presidential palace by DDS officials including Mahamat Djibrine, known as El Djonto. In addition, the Chamber concludes that during his presence in the presidential palace, Khadija Hassan Zidane suffered sexual violence committed by Hissein Habré on four occasions.[17]

From its conclusions and by virtue of its power of reclassification, the Trial Chamber then concluded that these facts constitute the autonomous crime of torture, referred to in Article 8 of the Statute, and the crimes against humanity of torture and rape, referred to in Articles 6(a) and (g) of the EAC Statute. With regard to the acts committed in the Kalaït and Ouadi-Doum camps, the Trial Chamber concluded that they also constitute the crime against humanity of sexual slavery, referred to in Article 6(a) of the Statute.

On the basis of all the evidence presented before it, the Trial Chamber concluded pursuant to Article 10(2) of the EAC Statute that there was a systematic and widespread attack against the civilian population of Chad in addition to the autonomous crime of torture referred to in Article 8 of the Statute and the crimes against humanity of wilful killing,[18] rape and enslavement,[19] the widespread and systematic practice of summary executions,[20]

[13] ibid §1864.

[14] ibid §700–822: 'Beyond the specific factual conclusions detailed above, the Chamber considers that in the context of the generalized repression of opponents—those persons considered as enemies of the regime and those of Arab, Hadjeraï, and Zaghawa ethnicities—the treatment of women was particularly cruel. The Chamber highlights the particularly intimate nature of the violence committed against women detained in a situation of acute vulnerability in the DDS prisons in N'Djamena and in the military camps of Kalaït and Ouadi-Doum, and considers that this contributed to the particularly grave and cruel character of these abuses' [editors' translation].

[15] ibid §811–20.

[16] ibid §778–810.

[17] ibid §736. On the case of the treatment of Khadija Hassan Zidane at the presidential palace, see §719–36. Translation by editor.

[18] ibid §1446.

[19] ibid §§1480–1538.

[20] ibid §§1446–449.

abduction of persons followed by their disappearance,[21] torture,[22] and inhumane acts,[23] as referred to in Articles 6(a), (b), (f), and (g) of the EAC Statute.

In contrast, the Chamber found insufficient evidence that Arabs and foreigners were targeted because of their ethnicity or ethnic group, but rather because of their alleged opposition to the Hissène Habré regime. Although the Chamber maintains that Arabs suffered repression in Chad, it nevertheless stated that:

> (. . .) these repressions did not target Arabs as an ethnic group or defined racial entity. The repression was carried out only against Arabs for their likeness to Libyans, for the supposed support they provided to Libyans, but also for their supposed or real membership of the CDR, a political opposition group.[24]

War crimes and the autonomous crime of torture

From 1983 to 1987, conflict broke out in southern Chad between governmental armed forces—(including the FANT) and the Codos. However, after determining the applicable law and the constituent elements of war crimes, the Trial Chamber concluded that the Codos did not constitute an 'organized armed group' as required in the context of a non-international armed conflict.[25] Given that a non-international armed conflict must meet criteria related to both 'intensity of violence' and 'organized armed groups', the Trial Chamber considered it unnecessary to examine whether the 'intensity of violence' criteria were met. The Trial Chamber therefore concluded that there was no non-international armed conflict in southern Chad between 1983 and 1987. This is why the Chamber did not find the commission of war crimes in southern Chad during that period.

On 30 July 1983, the FANT took over Faya-Largeau. Evidence before the Trial Chamber demonstrated that the FANT subsequently arrested 150 civilians and soldiers of the GUNT, took them out of combat, and executed them. During this battle, the FANT arrested at least 1,000 GUNT fighters and Libyan soldiers and then detained them in the Faya-Largeau remand centre for six days. The conditions of detention were particularly terrible, with little food or water, the wounded dying for lack of care, and FANT soldiers perpetrating physical violence against those in their custody. These prisoners of war were then transferred to N'Djamena and kept in difficult conditions: little food and of poor quality, crowded cells, disease, death, and abuse during interrogations. They were detained in a section of the prison that was under the responsibility of the DDS, who assigned day-to-day management to the COPO-FANT (FANT People's Committees). In August 1983, 150 prisoners were selected and removed from the prison by DDS agents. Escorted by soldiers, the prisoners were taken to Ambing for execution. Only one survived. Similarly, following the Battle of Kalaït-Oum-Chalouba in August 1983, fifty-three prisoners of war who had been captured by the FANT were shot. There was only one survivor.

[21] ibid §§1450–479.
[22] ibid §§1539–589.
[23] ibid §§1590–1607.
[24] ibid §911.
[25] *Habré* (n 5) §§1656–666.

The Trial Chamber found that at the time of these events, there was both a non-international armed conflict in northern Chad between the FANT and the GUNT and an international conflict between Libya—allied to the GUNT—and Chad, supported by France and the United States.[26]

Thus, pursuant to Article 10(4) of the Statute, the Trial Chamber found Hissène Habré guilty of the war crimes of wilful killing and murder,[27] torture,[28] inhumane treatment,[29] and unlawful detention,[30] per Articles 7(1)(a), (b), and (f) of the Statute. Additionally, in accordance with Article 7(2)(a) of the Statute, the Chamber found him guilty of the war crimes of murder, torture, and cruel treatment.

In contrast, the Trial Chamber judges concluded that the elements of the case file were not sufficient to establish the war crime of unlawful deportation or transfer, referred to in Article 7(1)(h) of the Statute.[31] The judges also did not uphold the war crimes of depriving a prisoner of war or any other person of the right to a fair and regular trial, nor of carrying out executions without previous judgment, referred to in Articles 7(1)(e) and 7(2)(g) of the Statute. The investigating judges found that these crimes could not be proven due to lack of sufficient evidence. In the absence of appeal by the Parties, this decision became final on these points.[32] Then, finding insufficient evidence, the Trial Chamber did not convict Habré of the war crimes of destruction and appropriation of property not justified by military necessity, nor the war crime of pillage, referred to in Articles 7(1)(e) and 7(2)(f) of the Statute.[33]

Finally, given that the constituent elements of the autonomous crime of torture are identical to the constituent elements of torture as both a war crime and a crime against humanity, the Trial Chamber concluded that the facts presented also amounted to torture in and of itself.[34]

II. Conclusions on Hissène Habré's individual criminal responsibility

Individual criminal responsibility for rape

In addition to Hissène Habré's individual criminal responsibility for the wilful killing of two persons suspected of having committed the Ngalo massacre, the Trial Chamber also concluded that Hissène Habré was individually criminally responsible for forcing sexual relations upon a woman prisoner. This allegation was not initially included in the referral

[26] ibid §1691: 'Thus, in a simultaneous and interwoven manner, there existed on Chadian territory a non-international armed conflict from May 1983 to 14 November 1988 between the Hissène Habré regime and the FANT, on one side, and the GUNT and its armed group the ANL, supported by Libya, on the other side; and an international armed conflict from 31 July 1983 to 31 August 1989 between Libya and Chad, which was supported by France, the United States and Zaïre' [editors' translation].

[27] ibid §§1699–1722.

[28] ibid §§1723–736.

[29] ibid §§1737–762.

[30] ibid §§1783–1800.

[31] ibid §§1778–782.

[32] ibid §174.

[33] ibid.

[34] ibid §§1805–808.

decision of 13 February 2015 rendered by the Investigating Chamber—the victim, Khadija Hassan Zidane, had only made this allegation during her hearing at trial.

In its reasoning, the Trial Chamber first stated that the testimony of a victim of sexual violence does not require corroboration. The Trial Chamber then confirmed it had meticulously analysed Ms Zidane's testimony in light of the parties' arguments.

The Trial Chamber found Ms Zidane's testimony implicating Hissène Habré consistent in and of itself; it was also supported by the testimony of another credible detainee. The judges argued that Ms Zidane clearly explained the reasons for her initial silence, namely that in addition to modesty, she was afraid and ashamed. She was waiting to face Hissène Habré before recounting everything. The Trial Chamber explained that it was thus convinced that she spoke truthfully.[35]

The Trial Chamber was further convinced that Hissène Habré forced Khadija Hassan Zidane to have non-consensual sexual intercourse three times and non-consensual oral sex after it emerged that he violently stuck a pen in her lower abdomen and legs. Under these circumstances, the Trial Chamber had no question that Hissène Habré knew that his victim did not consent. Instead, he took advantage of his position as President of Chad to subject Khadija Hassan Zidane to these rapes and abuses.[36]

Consequently, the Trial Chamber concluded that pursuant to Article 10(2) of the Statute, Hissène Habré committed the crime of rape as an underlying act of crimes against humanity referred to in Article 6(a) of the Statute. He also committed the crime of torture as an underlying act of crimes against humanity referred to in Article 6(g) of the Statute and committed the autonomous crime of torture referred to in Article 8 of the Statute.[37]

Joint criminal enterprise

Joint Criminal Enterprise (JCE) is a form of responsibility based on participation in a common criminal purpose. Although Article 10§2 of the EAC Statute did not explicitly provide for this mode of liability, the Trial Chamber noted that other international criminal jurisdictions (ICTY, ICTR, SCSL) considered participation in a JCE as a form of 'commission' to be a mode of individual responsibility recognized by customary international law and included this mode of liability in their respective statutes.[38]

Customary international law recognizes three forms of JCE. The first is characterized by cases where participants share the same criminal intention to achieve a common purpose.[39] The second form is characterized by the existence of an organized criminal system of ill-treatment, such as concentration or detention camps.[40] The third form allows one member of the JCE to be held liable for certain crimes committed by other members even if these

[35] ibid §§1826–840.

[36] ibid.

[37] ibid §1840.

[38] Appeal Judgment, *Ntakirutimana* (ICTR-96-10-A and ICTR-96-17-A), ICTR Appeals Chamber, 13 December 2004, para 468.

[39] Appeal Judgment, *Kvocka et al* (IT-98-30/1-A), ICTY Appeals Chamber, 28 February 2005, para 82; Judgment vol 2, *Popovic et al.* (IT-05-88-T), ICTY Trial Chamber II, 10 June 2010, para 1021.

[40] *Kvocka et al* Appeal Judgment, para 82; Appeal Judgment, *Vasiljevic* (IT-98-32-A), ICTY Appeals Chamber, 24 February 2004, para 98.

crimes go beyond the common purpose, provided that they are a natural and foreseeable consequence of the execution of this purpose.[41]

In its reasoning, the Trial Chamber sought to demonstrate the existence of: (1) a material element, namely a common criminal purpose consisting in or involving the commission of one of the crimes referred to in the Statute; and (2) a moral element, namely the intention to commit the crimes and contribute to the achievement of the common criminal purpose.

The existence of a common criminal purpose consisting of the commission of one of the crimes covered by the Statute or involving the commission of such crimes

In order to uphold Hissène Habré's criminal responsibility under Joint Criminal Enterprise (JCE), the Trial Chamber referred to similarities between the uninterrupted and large scale waves of repression carried out during the eight years of Habré's regime. These demonstrated the existence of a common purpose: to quell any rebellion or opposition that could, in the regime's view, undermine Chadian unity and sovereignty, and to prevent any attempt at opposition by imposing a regime of terror.

The Trial Chamber noted that to achieve this common purpose, the members of the JCE intentionally resorted to the crimes of intentional homicide, mass and systematic summary executions, abduction of persons followed by their disappearance, torture, and inhumane acts.

Interestingly, the Trial Chamber clarified that the evidence did not demonstrate that all members of the JCE intended to resort to rape and sexual slavery to achieve the common purpose. However, the Trial Chamber was convinced that the rape and sexual enslavement of women prisoners was a natural and foreseeable consequence of the execution of the JCE.[42]

Regarding the contribution of the Accused to this joint criminal enterprise, the Trial Chamber found from the evidence that:

- Hissène Habré controlled most of the security organs involved in the repression and achievement of the common purpose; in particular, he created and controlled the DDS,[43] the BSIR,[44] and the SIP,[45] appointing and dismissing agents, including key actors; he was also involved in the daily management of these organs;[46]
- Hissène Habré authorized the establishment of the DDS prison network and ensured its operation by way of the DDS, BSIR, SIP;[47]
- Hissène Habré was directly involved in interrogations and torture sessions, sometimes by inflicting or ordering abuse himself;[48]
- Hissène Habré was President of the Republic, Commander in Chief of the Armed Forces and, beginning in March 1986, Minister of Defense; he controlled the FANT who were also involved in achieving the common purpose.[49]

41 Appeal Judgment, *Stakic* (IT-97-24-A), ICTY Appeals Chamber, 22 March 2006, para 65.
42 *Habré* §1934.
43 ibid §§1980–985.
44 ibid §§1986–996.
45 ibid §§1997–2000.
46 ibid §§1937–975.
47 ibid §§1976–2027.
48 ibid §§2028–2047.
49 ibid §§2001–2021.

In its findings, the Trial Chamber was convinced that Hissène Habré, acting in conjunction with the members of the JCE, used the security and military bodies under his control to achieve the common purpose and that his contribution to the JCE was not only important but essential and determinative.[50]

Intention to commit the crimes and participate in the achievement of the common criminal purpose

Proving intent is required to establish JCE. In this regard, the Trial Chamber noted that Hissène Habré gave orders and participated in some of the crimes committed by members of the JCE and/or other agents utilized to achieve the common purpose. The Trial Chamber thus held that these acts demonstrate Hissène Habré had the intention of committing these crimes.

In addition, the Trial Chamber held that Hissène Habré was fully aware of the extent and nature of the crimes committed to achieve the common purpose. He received information on a daily basis from multiple sources and he officially took note of and sometimes annotated and responded to correspondence, reports and forms addressed to him.[51] Despite this knowledge, Hissène Habré did not take any action to sanction perpetrators of these crimes, even though they continued uninterrupted for eight years without diminishing in intensity.[52] In addition, the Trial Chamber highlighted that Hissène Habré explicitly stated his criminal intentions in a speech to the UNIR on 19 May 1989, in the midst of the recently launched wave of repression against the Zaghawa. The Trial Chamber thus concluded that Hissène Habré was a member of the joint criminal enterprise.[53]

Command responsibility

Effective control over and knowledge of subordinates' war crimes

From the evidence, the Trial Chamber concluded that Hissène Habré had effective control over the FANT soldiers and DDS agents.[54] The Chamber details several incidents (Faya-Largeau,[55] detainees in the DDS prison,[56] execution of prisoners in Ambing) demonstrating that Hissène Habré himself ordered the hostilities, or that he knew his subordinates had arrested and/or were about to execute GUNT military personnel. Moreover, the Trial Chamber was also convinced that, having failed to sanction the perpetrators of the Ambing massacre, Hissène Habré had reason to know that further executions of prisoners of war, detained at the N'Djamena prison, were about to take place.

50 ibid §§2144–170.
51 ibid §§2068–2135.
52 ibid §§2136–143.
53 ibid §§2144–170.
54 ibid §§2191–2205.
55 ibid §§2222–229, 2230–234.
56 ibid §§2235–256.

Failure to comply with obligations to take necessary and reasonable measures to prevent crimes or punish subordinates

In determining that Hissène Habré did not at any time intervene to prevent and/or punish the crimes committed by his subordinates,[57] the Trial Chamber concluded that, on the basis of command responsibility pursuant to Article 10(4) of the Statute, Hissène Habré was guilty of the war crimes of wilful killing, torture, inhumane treatment and unlawful detention, as referred to in Article 7(1)(a) and (f) of the Statute. He was also found guilty of the war crimes of murder, torture and cruel treatment, as referred to in Article 7(2)(a) of the Statute.[58]

III. The sentence

While the Trial Chamber judges proceeded with the sentencing, they took into account the extreme gravity and scale of the crimes,[59] the personal situation of the accused,[60] the aggravating circumstances,[61] and the mitigating circumstances.[62]

Regarding the aggravating circumstances, the judges considered the uninterrupted nature of these crimes (committed continuously during the entire duration of Hissène Habré's reign), the number of victims, and the degree of involvement in the commission of these crimes. They also considered Hissène Habré's central role—his role as conductor—in the all-out repression of the civilian population and in the rape on multiple occasions of a particularly vulnerable person. Lastly, they considered his attitude at the trial, which they found contemptuous, insulting toward the Chamber and the victims, lacking compassion, and bereft of remorse.

Concerning the mitigating circumstances, the Trial Chamber judges pointed to the age of the accused, as well as the fact that he is a good family man who supports his relatives. Nevertheless, the Trial Chamber concluded that, 'after assessing the seriousness of the crimes committed and in light of Hissène Habré's personal situation, […] no mitigation of the sentence is justified and […], in the present case, the aggravating circumstances clearly outweigh the mitigating circumstances.'[63]

In the end, the judges of the Trial Chamber requested a life sentence and the non-confiscation of the seized property.[64]

57 ibid §§2257–259.
58 ibid §§2260–262.
59 ibid §§2297–314.
60 ibid §§2315–316.
61 ibid §§2317–322.
62 ibid §§2323–326.
63 ibid §2328.
64 ibid §2329: 'Furthermore, the Chamber notes that the Investigative Chamber, in effecting the seizure of Hissène Habré's property, founded its order on the necessity of taking provisional measures to protect the interests of the civil parties. The prosecutor does not provide sufficient evidence to determine that the seized property is the fruit of the crimes committed by Hissène Habré and thereby susceptible to being confiscated.'

IV. Reparations

In a subsequent decision rendered on 29 July 2016, the Trial Chamber judges addressed the question of reparations. With respect to civil party applications, the judges declared admissible those victims who had been heard during the proceedings and those who had proven their identity and kin relationship with direct victims.[65]

In its decision, the Trial Chamber granted individual reparations in the amount of CFAF 10 million for each indirect victim,[66] CFAF 15 million for each victim of torture and survivor of massacre and arbitrary detention,[67] and CFAF 20 million for each victim of rape and sexual slavery.[68]

In contrast, the Trial Chamber declared inadmissible the claims of victims not substantiated by identifying information. They also rejected calls for collective and moral reparations.[69] The Trial Chamber additionally ruled inadmissible the call for the Chadian State to be held responsible for financial reparations not paid by Habré[70] and validated the precautionary measures taken by the investigating judges.[71]

Finally, the decision refers to the existence of a Victims Trust Fund to ensure financial reparations for victims. So far, funding comes from one of Hissène Habré's residences located in Dakar. However, voluntary contributions can also be made by States, international institutions or any source wishing to contribute to the compensation of victims.

[65] Jugement sur les intérêts civils [Civil Judgment], *Affaire Ministère Public c. Hissein Habré* (EAC Trial Chamber) 29 July 2016 §§52–53.

[66] ibid §68. 10 million CFAF is approximately 15,270 Euros and $17,200 US dollars at time of editing (July 2019).

[67] ibid §65. 15 million CFAF is approximately 22,900 Euros and $25,800 US dollars at time of editing (July 2019).

[68] ibid §62. 20 million CFAF is approximately 30,540 Euros and $34,400 US dollars at time of editing (July 2019).

[69] ibid §§70–71.

[70] ibid §76.

[71] ibid §§78–80.

19

The Habré Appeals Judgment

A Summary of the Appeals Decision of the EAC

Élise Le Gall, International Criminal Law Expert with the EAC Office of the Prosecutor

The Appeals Chamber of the EAC, composed of President Wafi Ougadeye, a Malian judge, and two Senegalese judges, Matar Ndiaye and Bara Gueye, issued its appeals decision on 27 April 2017. Upon appeal, the judges upheld Hissène Habré's life sentence for crimes against humanity, war crimes and torture. However, Hissène Habré was acquitted of one of the sexual violence-related charges: the direct commission of rape of Khadija Hassan Zidane. With regard to reparations, the judges clarified Hissène Habré's sentence to pay financial compensation to 7,396 victims.

The grounds of appeal that may be invoked before the Appeals Chamber include errors of procedure, errors of fact and/or errors of law. It should be proven that those errors led to a denial of justice and that the error was a decisive factor in the outcome. The chapter summarizes all the grounds of appeals—of the defence and the civil parties—and the Appeals Court's corresponding decisions. It first presents the appeal brought by Habré's appointed defence lawyers, grouped into errors of procedure, errors of law, and error of fact.[1] Then the chapter proceeds to present grounds of appeals of the civil parties on the reparation judgment, as later rendered on 29 July 2016.

The appeal of the defence

Alleged errors of procedure that would result in a denial of justice

The defence raised several procedural error claims which all were rejected by the appeal judges:

(1) The Trial Chamber was irregularly composed, due to the presence of Judge Diouf, who lacked the requisite of ten years of judicial experience required by Art 11.5 of the EAC Statute; further, it had failed make the profiles of the judges of the Chamber available.[2]

[1] The defence lawyers' claims were submitted through two appeals (I) an appeal of the Trial Camber's order that declared the defence's application for the suspension of the proceeding to be inadmissible, (II) an appeal against the Trial Chamber's decision of 30 May 2016 (see the above chapter).

[2] Appeal Judgment, *Le Procurerur Général c. Hissein Habré* [Public Prosecutor v Hissène Habré], Extraordinary African Appeals Chamber, 27 April 2017, §§125–32.

Elise Le Gall, *The Habré Appeals Judgment* In: *The President on Trial*. First edition. Edited by: Sharon Weill, Kim Thuy Seelinger, and Kerstin Bree Carlson, Oxford University Press (2020). © Elise Le Gall. DOI: 10.1093/oso/9780198858621.003.0020

The Appeals Court ruled that the Trial Chamber was correct to dismiss this claim on the grounds of delay, as it had not been presented on the merits and had had no bearing on the existence of the infraction. Further, the appellate judges also relied on the case law of international criminal courts, which provide that in practice not only prosecutors but also law professors and diplomats can be appointed to the bench as long as they have the qualities necessary for the performance of the function.[3] Further the appellate judges noted that there was no text requiring that information about chamber composition be made available.[4] They also agreed with the civil parties' arguments that the profiles had been published on the EAC website prior to the trial and that if the defence wanted more information, it would have been up to them to seek it.[5] The court also rejected the claim that irregular composition of the Trial Chamber rendered it incompetent to rule on Habré's civil claim.[6] The appellate judges deemed that the Trial Chamber had properly responded to the defence's plea concerning the precautionary measures regarding Hissène Habré's property and that it had jurisdiction over them.[7]

(2) The Trial Chamber misrepresented the defence's request for civil interests by using the term 'motion' instead of 'statement'.

The appellate judges rejected this claim, relying on a judgment from the Criminal Chamber of Senegal, which stated that 'the misrepresentation claim is only admissible when the trial judges have failed to understand the clear and precise meaning of a document'—which was not the case here.[8]

(3) Violation of the principle equality of arms and the rights of the defence where the Trial Chamber relied on a prosecutor's submission not communicated to the defence.

The court rejected this claim as the defence did not specify the passages concerned or even the submission in question, nor did it provide any information enabling the appellate judges to assess and verify the allegations on the violation of the rights of the accused.[9]

(4) Failure to declare the indictment void, as it concerned Hissène Habré alone and not his co-defendants, against whom there was sufficient evidence.

The defence asserted that the decision not to indict Hissène Habré's associates made it impossible to assess Hissène Habré's liability under joint criminal enterprise (JCE) in his capacity as a civilian and military commander. The defence added that the arrest warrants issued to his associates by the Investigative Chamber shows that there were enough facts for incrimination.[10] In rejecting this claim, the appellate judges pointed out that an indictment

[3] ibid §§133–43.
[4] ibid §151.
[5] ibid §§152–53.
[6] ibid §309.
[7] ibid §§296–308.
[8] Arrêt n°15, *Affaire Ibrahima Baldé et autres c. Ministère public et Khaoussou Dramé* (Cour suprême du Sénégal, Chambre criminelle), 16 décembre 2008.
[9] ibid §177.
[10] ibid §§182–84.

cannot be appealed at this stage nor before the Trial Chamber, which had no jurisdiction to rule on the acts and decisions of the Investigative Chamber. The investigative Chamber has its own court of appeal.[11]

(5) Reading only a summary judgment and failing to render the entire judgment to all parties during the appeal period, which is essential for the examination and verification of the grounds for the ruling.

The appellate judges considered that on the day the judgment is pronounced, both Senegalese law[12] and international criminal law[13] permit judges to read a summary of the judgment as long as the ruling is then communicated to the parties in its entirety as soon as possible.[14] The appellate judges subsequently found that the trial judgment was communicated in its entirety to the parties at the earliest opportunity.[15] The appellate judges also considered the rights of the accused. On this point, the appellate judges deduced from the jurisprudence of the European Court of Human Rights (ECHR) and the practice of international criminal tribunals that it is the impact of these rights that matters, meaning that it is not necessary for the full verdict to be available before the deadline as long as the accused has sufficient information to lodge an appeal.[16] The appellate judges found that the summary made available by the Trial Chamber contained the indictment, the factual findings according to which the Trial Chamber established the criminal responsibility of Hissène Habré and the corresponding sentence—sufficient information to make an appeal.[17]

(6) Failure to clearly identify the witness and the civil parties (as through the use identity cards), whose testimony provided the evidence upon which the accused was convicted.[18]

The appellate judges recalled that, while the establishment of a civil party is subject to the clear substantiation of the identity of the persons concerned, this need should not deprive victims of their opportunity to participate in the proceedings for reasons beyond their control, such as material difficulties in obtaining official papers. In addition, the appellate judges mentioned that the applications of persons whose identity could not be proven by any means were rejected but that, conversely, the applications of those whose identity was corroborated by other documents were retained.[19] The appellate judges further ruled that in any event the defence should have raises this argument during the trial phase and not on appeal.[20]

[11] ibid §§192–206. (Editors' comment: It should be noted, that the appointed defence lawyer were not in office at that stage; they started to work on Habré's defence at the trial stage, once the investigation was over and the indictment final.)
[12] ibid §§215–18.
[13] ibid §§219–27.
[14] ibid §§228–29.
[15] ibid §229.
[16] ibid §§276–83.
[17] ibid §§287–90.
[18] ibid §230.
[19] ibid §§235–45.
[20] ibid §245.

(7) Absence of the Registry's signature on the appealed judgment as required by Senegalese rule of procedure.

In rejecting this ground of appeal[21], the appellate judges noted that according to Senegalese rules of procedure the non-fulfilment of this requirement does not result in a nullity of the judgment in question.[22] In addition, drawing on the practice of international criminal tribunals, rulings and judgments are only signed by the judges of the relevant Chamber.[23] The appellate judges remedied the situation by ordering the Trial Chamber clerks to sign the verdict.[24]

Alleged errors of fact that would result in a denial of justice

The appeals court judgment addressed the following grounds of appeal based on error of fact.

(1) Prosecution witnesses followed the proceedings up until the time of their hearing, thus tainting their testimony.

In declaring this ground inadmissible, the appellate judges found that the defence did not file objections before the Trial Chamber and that it was therefore inappropriate to invoke them before the Appeals Chamber.[25]

(2) Public broadcasting of the hearings contaminated testimony.

In declaring this ground inadmissible, the appellate judges concluded that the delayed public broadcasting of the hearings did not constitute an error of fact leading to a denial of justice.[26]

(3) Testimony of Belgian investigating judge Daniel Fransen should have been prohibited.

In deciding that this ground for appeal was inadmissible, the appellate judges examined Senegalese, French, and international law. The appellate judges noted that the Senegalese Code Criminal Procedure and the Criminal Code provide for a list of persons who cannot testify—a list that does not include the investigating judge.[27] In addition, the jurisprudence of the French Court of Cassation has frequently recognized that there is no incompatibility between the status of witness and that of investigating judge, given that the latter cannot be considered to have contributed to the judgment of the case.[28] Finally, the appellate judges

21 ibid §§269–70.
22 ibid §§265–66.
23 ibid §264.
24 ibid §§267–70.
25 ibid §§318–28.
26 ibid §§333–38.
27 ibid §§346–56.
28 ibid §§357–60.

specified that under international law, it is irrelevant whether the witness was an investigating judge in the same case. Once sworn in, that person becomes a witness for the purpose of establishing the truth and the trial judges have a sovereign right to weigh the probative value of the testimony given.[29]

(4) Conviction of Hissène Habré for war crimes in Ambing and Kalait Oum Chalouba was based on conflicting and insufficient testimony.

Regarding this ground of appeal, the appellate judges recalled that the Trial Chamber had acknowledged the existence of these inconsistencies but had determined that the testimony was nevertheless credible in that it had subsequently been corroborated.[30] The appellate judges considered that the conclusions of the Trial Chamber were reasonable.[31]

(5) Failure to take into account Article 2 of the decree establishing the DDS, which placed it under the supervision of the Ministry of the Interior and not Habré, precluded the accused's liability under command responsibility.

The defence emphasized that the accused was absent at the time of the events and that effective control of the military troops was exercised by Idriss Déby. In ruling this claim inadmissible, the appellate judges first considered that the Trial Chamber had effectively established Hissène Habré's de facto control over the DDS despite the existence of such an article granting de jure authority to the Ministry of the Interior.[32] Then, on Hissène Habré's liability under command responsibility, the appellate judges noted a contradiction in the appeal filed by the defence, as it was in the context of joint criminal enterprise that Hissène Habré was found guilty for the events in question.[33] The appellate judges clarified, based on international jurisprudence, that in order to hold an accused person liable for joint criminal enterprise and/or command responsibility, it is by no means necessary for the other members or subordinates to be so held. According to the appellate judges, Idriss Déby's liability therefore has no impact on that of Hissène Habré.[34]

Alleged errors of law that would invalidate the decision

Finally, the appeals judgment addressed the following arguments alleging errors of law.

(1) Ms Zidane's rape allegations were made for the first time before the Trial Chamber and at the instigation of its President.

With respect to this appeal, the Prosecutor's Office replied that under international criminal law, a single witness can establish the legal existence of a fact and that, in addition, it

[29] ibid §§361–68.
[30] ibid §§380–92.
[31] ibid §§392–93.
[32] ibid §§408–14.
[33] ibid pp 92–95.
[34] ibid §§415–16.

is not necessary to corroborate testimony of sexual violence.[35] The Prosecutor's Office also recalled the Senegalese Code of Criminal Procedure, whose dual condition with regard to requalification it considered met: namely, a.) restoring the seriousness of the offences and b.) not violating the rights of the accused.[36] In addition, the prosecution pointed out that the Trial Chamber, having a sovereign power of requalification and having notified the parties of the possibility that it would reconsider the facts during its deliberations, had respected the rights of the defence.[37]

The appellate judges first recalled the procedure under Senegalese, French, and international law.[38] They then ruled that while the Trial Chamber did have the power of requalification, it was not authorized to consider new facts as a basis for its decision. The Trial Chamber had to limit itself to the facts which appeared in the indictment, which irrevocably established its competence and scope.[39] The appellate judges considered that the facts of the rapes of Khadija Hassan Zidane were neither submitted to the investigating judges nor to the accused and that they did not appear in the indictment.[40] Consequently, the Trial Chamber had exceeded its jurisdiction on this particular charge and Hissène Habré was acquitted of the direct (personal) commission of the rape of Khadija Hassan Zidane.[41]

(2) Failure to take into account the judgment of the Court of N'Djamena (25 March 2015) that was rich of evidence in favour of the defendant, leading to a violation of the rights of the defence and his right to a fair trial.[42]

The Prosecutor's Office responding position was that the judgment of the N'Djamena Court convicted the accused's former collaborators for offences different from those provided for in the EAC Statute, and that taking this judgment into account had no impact on the actual decision of the Trial Chamber.[43] In rejecting this claim, the appellate judges noted that the defence had not provided said judgment as evidence to be put on the record and, as a result, the Trial Chamber was not required to refer to it.[44]

Appeal against the reparations judgment issued on 29 July 2016

In addition to appealing aspects of the core Trial Chamber decision, various appeals were lodged against the later decision regarding reparations (rendered 29 July 2016). They are summarized as follows.

35 ibid §423.
36 ibid §424.
37 ibid §425.
38 ibid §§432–41.
39 ibid §§498–513.
40 ibid §514.
41 ibid §§515–31. (Editors' comment: It should be noted that Habré's convictions for the rape and sexual slavery committed by his subordinates had not been appealed, so these remained intact, and his sentence remained unchanged.
42 ibid §§532–33.
43 ibid §§534–35.
44 ibid §§541–46.

I. Errors of law that would invalidate the decision

(1) Absence of a substantiated decision concerning the inadmissibility of the applications by direct and indirect victims to join the proceedings as civil parties, despite previous confirmation by the Investigative Chamber.

In rejecting the appeal brought by the civil parties, the appellate judges considered that the Trial Chamber had justified its decision to dismiss certain applications on the ground of insufficient evidence of the identity of the direct victims and, for the indirect victims, of the kin relationship between them and the direct victims.[45] The appellate judges noted that the investigating court was limited to automatically registering the applications to join the proceedings as civil parties, without having made any assessment as to admissibility. The appellate judges also noted that it was incorrect to consider the Trial Chamber's conclusion on this admissibility issue as a re-examination since the defendant's Referral Order does not bind the trial court, which remains free to assess both the admissibility of criminal and civil actions as well as the qualification of the facts and the culpability of the accused.[46] The appellate judges then carried out an in-depth analysis of national and international law to establish that the civil party lawyers must have known that the examination of the admissibility of claims would necessarily take place before the Trial Chamber and that the registration of claims at the investigation phase was in no way binding on the Investigative Chamber.[47]

(2) Incorrect legal standard concerning the admissibility of applications to join the proceedings as a civil party.

After analysing national and international law relating to this ground, the appellate judges recognized that the standard of proof to be applied to the reparations phase is indeed that of the balance of probabilities.[48] However, the appellate judges considered that the Trial Chamber had applied this standard well and that it was particularly flexible in only requiring proof 'by any means' of the identity of the direct victims and of the relationship of kinship for indirect victims.[49] Partially upholding this plea, the appellate judges reassessed the admissibility of the applications and corrected the material errors committed by the Trial Chamber by ultimately increasing the number of direct and indirect victims and the number of admissible civil parties.[50]

(3) Error of law regarding the lack of criteria for assessing claims for collective and moral reparations and regarding the application of an inadequate standard.

The civil parties considered that the Trial Chamber had not sufficiently substantiated its ruling and that it had used criteria for assessing damages that did not exist prior to the

[45] ibid §§659–66.
[46] ibid §§623–31.
[47] ibid §§632–58.
[48] ibid §§738–69, 829–30.
[49] ibid §§678–79.
[50] ibid §§770–825.

aforementioned ruling.[51] The Prosecutor's Office stressed the essential nature of collective and moral reparations for victims of mass crimes, considering it unlikely that the full amount of the financial penalties would be recovered.[52] However, the Prosecutor's Office noted that for such reparations to be granted, it was necessary to obtain the approval of the Chadian authorities and, to that end, the Prosecutor's Office suggested to the appellate judges that such reparations measures should be put in place.[53]

Regarding this ground, the appellate judges supported the decision of the Trial Chamber in that it could not have favourably accepted the request to reserve 30% of the funds for purposes of moral and collective reparations without impinging on the sovereignty of the Chadian State, thus making its application hypothetical and uncertain. In this regard, the appellate judges indicated that in accordance with Article 27 of the EAC Statute, they had requested submissions from the Government of Chad, which did not respond favourably to the remedies requested by the civil parties. Nevertheless, the appellate judges stressed the crucial importance of these remedies and called on the Fund, civil parties' groups and interested States to implement such programmes.[54]

As to the applicable standard, the appellate judges found that the civil parties' requests for collective reparations were too imprecise to be granted.[55]

Errors of fact that would result in a denial of justice

1) Erroneous identification of certain victims as belonging to certain groups of civil parties, leading to a risk of incorrect payment of reparations.

Declaring this ground for appeal admissible,[56] the appellate judges verified the alleged errors and corrected the material omissions in the first-instance ruling on reparations.[57] The appellate judges therefore declared admissible the victims who appeared at the investigative hearing who had been omitted by the Trial Chamber and corrected, where possible, errors in membership of victims' associations.[58]

2) Lack of precision in the procedures for carrying out individual reparations, the absence of an estimate of the overall amount of the reparations, and the procedure for recovering Hissène Habré's property.

With this ground for appeal, the civil parties of the group 'Clément Abaïfouta and others' requested that the entity responsible for the implementation of financial reparations for victims be identified.[59] The appellate judges considered that this ground of appeal had become moot in the context of the appeals judgment since it had already provided the information

51 ibid §§831–34.
52 ibid §836.
53 ibid §§835–37.
54 ibid §§838–47.
55 ibid §§874–75, 848–49.
56 ibid §§876–79.
57 ibid §§881–87.
58 ibid §888.
59 ibid §§889–93.

requested.[60] It was concluded that the Trust Fund for Victims has the jurisdiction to determine the modalities for the execution of reparations. In the event of a judicial issue during the execution of reparations, then the Tribunal de grande instance de Dakar will have jurisdiction.[61]

3) Failure to take certain victims into account as a result of Chadian judicial custom according to which a representative is designated by the family council to represent the beneficiaries, making him (the representative) the sole beneficiary.

With regard to this ground for appeal, the appellate judges pointed out that the civil parties' counsel did not provide precise reference as to the victims who could have been harmed by this custom. Therefore, actual injury could not be verified.[62] However, unlike the Trial Chamber, the appellate judges considered that, in accordance with the principle of equality before the law, all indirect victims who provided the required evidence were admissible, not just the representative.[63]

4) Amount of reparations awarded, deemed insufficient in view of the suffering endured.

In rejecting this ground for appeal, the appellate judges first recalled that the assessment of damages falls within the sole discretion of the trial judges, and that this principle is rooted both in national law and in international criminal jurisprudence.[64] Second, the appellate judges considered that the amount allocated was reasonable or even significantly higher than that normally allocated by some international criminal tribunals.[65] Finally, the appellate judges noted that the appellant civil parties did not demonstrate the type of error that would justify the Court's intervention in this matter.[66]

[60] ibid §§897–901, 607–16.
[61] ibid §§667–68.
[62] ibid §§905–17.
[63] ibid §§918–19.
[64] ibid §§929–32.
[65] ibid §§934–42.
[66] ibid §§926.

20
Reflections on the Habré Appeals Decision

Judge Ouagadeye Wafi, EAC Appeals Judge[1]

Judge Ouagadey Wafi was named president of the Court of Appeal of the EAC on 28 September 2016, by the president of the African Union Commission, alongside Senegalese presiding judges Mr Matar Ndiaye and Mr Bara Gueye, and deputy judge, Mr Amadou Tidiane Sy. The judges' term at the Appeals Court began on 1 October 2016 and ran until 30 April 2017, allowing seven months to face the enormous challenge of completely concluding the examination of the appeal made in the historic trial of Hissène Habré. To do so, Judge Wafi brought to Dakar all of the experience acquired throughout his career, and in particular his thirty-eight years as a magistrate.

Judge Wafi began his career in Mali as a magistrate in 1978. He worked as an investigating judge, a justice of the peace, a sitting judge, an attorney general, president and advisor in courts such as those of first instance, Appeals Courts, the Special Court of State Security and the Supreme Court. On a national level, he served Mali as the Consul General in Paris and as legal advisor to the Presidency, as a member of the National Commission for the drafting of penal codes and criminal procedures and as a legal expert to ECOWAS. Active on both a regional and international level, he is a member of the International Association of Prosecutors and the International Association of Judges. He also served on the United Nations' Special Committee on Jurisdictional States and their Properties and has taught at OHADA's Regional Superior School of Magistrates.

My role consisted of presiding over the Appeals Court, with all of the various functions this entails. I began by acquainting myself with the existing case file, featuring the investigation, the judgment, and the appeal submissions of the different parties. The next task was to coordinate the team work, defining a course of action and establishing a legal timeframe encompassing the various stages of the appeal process in light of the time constraints we found ourselves under, pressed as we were to produce a verdict by the end of April 2017. After analysing the case file in detail, the main problems quickly emerged first with respect to the conviction of the accused by the Trial Camber for the direct perpetration of rape, not referred to in either the initial submission nor in an additional submission by the prosecutor

[1] I wish to thank Margaux Lenormand for her assistance in the writing of this text, as well as for her invaluable collaboration during the appeal process to the EAC.

Ouagadeye Wafi, *Reflections on the Habré Appeals Decision* In: *The President on Trial*. First edition. Edited by: Sharon Weill, Kim Thuy Seelinger, and Kerstin Bree Carlson, Oxford University Press (2020). © Ouagadeye Wafi.
DOI: 10.1093/oso/9780198858621.003.0021

and not upheld in the indictment presented by the Investigative Chamber and second, respecting the formation of the civil parties and the thorny issue of compensation. We thus embarked on months of work punctuated by weekly meetings in which the members of the team from the Appeals Court came together to share the fruit of their research and reflections. Although heated legal debate and certain differences of opinion ensued, I was always keen to listen to everyone's individual points of view and to promote constructive dialogue both with the judges in theAppeals Court and my legal assistants.

Taking care to ensure the proper flow of the hearing and in order to allow each of the parties to express themselves freely before the commencement of the process—particularly in light of the difficulties raised by the court-appointed lawyers following the trial—I quickly organized a pre-hearing conference with all parties to set the procedural calendar. Hearings were to begin in early January 2017, with the filing of appeal submissions set for 7 December 2016 for the defence and 27 December 2016 for the prosecutor's responses and those of the civil parties.

Within three months of taking office, the Appeals Court had reviewed the submissions from the various parties and issued a preliminary ruling on the defence's request for new witnesses to be heard at the appeal stage ('Preliminary Ruling').[2] The week for appeal hearings in the Hissène Habré case thus began on 9 January 2017 at the Lat Dior Courthouse in Dakar.

The EAC's tradition of civil law and the role of judges in the Appeals Court

The EAC was a court that is hybrid in nature, with internationalized criminal jurisdiction founded by an international agreement between the African Union and the Republic of Senegal.[3] This means that although the statute[4] is applied alongside Senegalese law and international criminal law,[5] the EAC was integrated into the Senegalese legal system based on the civil law model[6] derived from the tradition of Romano-Germanic law.

Such a juxtaposition of the statute, Senegalese national law and the law of international criminal jurisprudence has on occasions served as a source of appreciable relief and on others as a source of difficulty, with the application of the various laws not always leading to the same practical conclusion. Moreover, this multiplicity of sources generated a bit of legal uncertainty for parties who did not share the same vision of the primacy of national or international law under the EAC system. Thus, the delimitation of the competence of the appeal before the EAC was the first source of disagreement among the parties at the

[2] EAC, Appeals Court, *Preliminary Ruling on witnesses and new evidence*, 29 December 2016: http://www.chambresafricaines.org/index.php/le-coin-des-medias/communiqu%C3%A9-de-presse/650-d%C3%A9cision-pr%C3%A9liminaire-de-la-chambre-d-assises-d-appel.html ('Preliminary Ruling').

[3] EAC, *Agreement between the Government of the Republic of Senegal and the African Union on the creation of EAC within the Senegalese Courts*, 22 August 2012 ('Agreement').

[4] EAC, *Statute of the EAC within the Senegalese Courts for the prosecution of crimes committed in Chad in the period from 7 June 1982 to 1 December 1990*, signed on 22 August 2012 in Dakar and in force as of 28 December 2012: http://www.chambresafricaines.org/pdf/Accord%20UA-Senegal%20Chambres%20africaines%20extra%20Aout%202012.pdf ('Statute').

[5] EAC, Agreement, art 1, para 4.

[6] Senegal incorporated the EAC into its legal system on 28 December 2012 with the adoption of law no 2012-29.

conference. While the defence argued for a 'nationalist' approach to the appeal procedure in reviewing both the law and the facts, the civil parties and the prosecution defended an 'international' appeal procedure in which only certain errors fell within the jurisdiction of the Court of Appeal. Thus, from the outset, the Court of Appeal had to define the framework and the contours of the legal regime under which the appeal would be heard. Such a task was primarily addressed in the Preliminary Ruling to refuse the hearing of witnesses and the production of new evidence, and then in the ruling given on 27 April 2017 ('the Appeals Judgment'), which devotes an entire section to it.[7]

The Statute allows the Court of Appeal to consider appeals 'as a last resort' by the prosecutor, the defence or the civil parties on three grounds: procedural error, an error on the question of substantive law that invalidates the ruling (including an error of jurisdiction), or any factual error that led to a miscarriage of justice.[8] The clarity of the statute in this respect, the international nature of the jurisdiction and the time restrictions assigned to the appeal phase all tipped the debate, with the Court of Appeal finding that its role was limited, just like other international criminal court to an examination of procedural errors, legal errors invalidating a ruling, and factual errors leading to a miscarriage of justice.[9]

The result was a hybrid appeal system in which the role assigned to the Court of Appeal encompassed a number of functions devolved from, in criminal cases, the jurisdiction of the Appellate and Supreme Court in the Senegalese legal system. Indeed, in Senegalese criminal procedure, two courts may decide on an appeal against a ruling delivered in a court of first instance, with the criminal Court of Appeal re-examining the merits of the case on the basis of the evidence produced in the first instance, or, according to the case, on appeal.[10] The Senegalese Supreme Court serves as a second appellate court only for questions of law. The framework for appeals made to the EAC therefore combines the existing avenues available within the Senegalese penal system with the Appeals Court's own system. The practical functioning of this appeal system was never defined, however, whether by the agreement or the statute. Unlike similar courts, the EAC has no rules governing evidence and procedure. According to the agreement,[11] the Appeals Court is inspired by the procedural rules in force on an international level, especially as its grounds for appeal are very similar to those employed by other international or ad hoc courts,[12] and therefore already well established in international criminal law.[13] The Court of Appeal only exerted remedial jurisdiction and was not meant to examine the case in its entirety *de novo*.[14]

Instead of serving as a '*second court of the first instance*',[15] the role of the Appeals Court was limited to examining procedural errors, legal errors invalidating a ruling or factual

[7] EAC, Appeals Court, *Judgment*, 27 April 2017, p 14, paras 63–82: http://www.chambresafricaines.org/pdf/Arr%C3%AAt_int%C3%A9gral.pdf ('Judgment').

[8] EAC, *Statute*, art 25.

[9] ICTY, *Anto Furundžija c. The Prosecutor*, case no. IT-95-17/1-A, Judgment, 21 July 2000, para 40.

[10] Senegalese Code of Criminal Procedure (CPP), art 319 issued by law no 2016-30 of 8 November 2016.

[11] EAC, Agreement, art 1er, para 4.

[12] ICTY, Statute, art 25; ECCC, Act establishing the ECCC, art 36; ECCC, Internal regulations, regulations 104 and 105; ICTR, Statute, art 24.

[13] ICTY, *The Prosecutor Case c. Stanislav Galić*, no IT-98-29-A, Judgment, 30 November 2006, para 6.

[14] ICTY, *Milorad Krnojelac c. The Prosecutor*, case no IT-95-14/2-A, Judgment, 17 September 2003, para 5; ICTY, *The Prosecutor Case c. Stanislav Galić*, no IT-98-29-A, Judgment, 30 November 2006, para 8; ICTY, *Zoran Kupreškić, Mirjan Kupreškić, Vlatko Kupreškić, Drago Josipović, Dragan Papić, Vladimir Šantić, aka 'Vlado'. c. The Prosecutor*, case no IT-95-16-A, Judgment, 23 October 2001, para 22.

[15] ICTY, *Anto Furundžija c. The Prosecutor*, case no IT-95-17/1-A, Judgment, 21 July 2000, para 40.

errors which contributed to a miscarriage of justice. As the final court of law of the EAC, the Court of Appeal was required to determine whether an error had effectively been committed on a substantive or procedural issue when a party raised such a claim.[16] Firmly anchored in civil law, the role of the appeals judges, like that of their peers in the trial courts, was the same as that performed by the criminal magistrates in countries under a system of civil law such as Senegal where judges act *in rem* and must judge cases according to their *intime conviction*[17] with respect to the rights of the accused. The internationalized nature of the jurisdiction, did, however, lead the Appeals Court to adopt a dual hybrid appeal regime: first, by borrowing from national and international traditions, and second, by borrowing from the traditions of appeal and civil law cassation. As Malian and Senegalese judges of the civil law tradition, we were required to adapt to this new regime.

The work of the Court of Appeal

In practical terms, when not conducting a hearing, the Appeals Court was located on the top floor of the building housing the EAC, with these premises serving as the main place of work, offering excellent conditions in complete confidentiality. The Appeals Court was also provided with IT, administrative, and legal support.

In terms of resources, the Appeals Court had nine full-time staff members. Apart from my administrative assistant and me, the team was formed of three assessor magistrates and one deputy magistrate, Matar Ndiaye, Bara Gueye, Amadou Tidiane Sy, all with ample experience of the Senegalese criminal justice system, and with the four of us combining over ninety-three years' experience of judging. Two legal assistants, Margaux Lenormand and Mamadou Falilou Diop,[18] with highly complementary profiles, proved to be of great assistance to the Court of Appeal both in terms of research and in terms of report writing. Final acknowledgement must be paid to clerks Abouly Ba[19] and Abdoul Abass Sy, whose knowledge of the case and procedure was of great help in the handling of such a large file, both electronically and in paper format.

The appeal judgment

After analysing the case file, our work naturally consisted of studying the grounds of the appeal. First, the defence appealed the court order declaring unfounded their request for the suspension of the proceedings. The defence arguments were the following: first, the irregular composition of the Trial Chamber as well as the fact that the information on the profile of the judges in the court was not made available, invalidated the judgment. Second, they claimed that the principle of equality of the arms and the rights of the defence were violated by the Trial Chamber which was '*influenced by arguments raised by the prosecution*

[16] ICTY, *Milorad Krnojelac c. The Prosecutor*, case no IT-95-14/2-A, Judgment, 17 September 2003, para 10.

[17] The standard of guilt under civil law.

[18] Margaux Lenormand is a lawyer (French bar). She previously worked at the Extraordinary Chambers in the Cambodian; Mamadou Falilou Diop holds a PhD in public international law and teaches at the Faculty of Law at Cheikh Anta Diop University in Dakar, Senegal.

[19] See Ba, in this volume, Chapter 12.

and included them in the reasons for its decision without having communicated them to the defense'.[20] All those grounds were rejected: as the Appeals Court prevailed an international definition of the term 'judge' on the internal one, there was no irregularity in the constitution of the Trial Chamber;[21] further, the publicity around the appointment of the Trial Chamber judges was done on the EAC website, and the fact that no request was made in this sense, invalidated the argument developed by the Defence;[22] lastly, also the final argument was rejected because it did not meet the criteria of the grounds of appeal as defined by international jurisprudence.[23]

Secondly, the defence presented twelve grounds of appeal related to the public prosecution: six procedural errors,[24] five factual errors,[25] and finally, two legal errors.[26] All of these errors were subsequently rejected, except those related to allegations of rape directly perpetrated by Hissène Habré. Although the Court of Appeal did not accept the defence's reasoning that these allegations would have occurred 'at the request' of the chief justice, it found that the indictment did not deem Hissène Habré directly liable for rape. The Appeals Court ruled that in such a case, the legal requalification of the facts (ie accusation) could not be made during the trial without further procedural steps in order not to violate the rights of the defence and the principle of referral *in rem*. It therefore reversed Hissène Habré's conviction for the direct perpetration of rape.[27]

Finally, while the defence did not issue any observations on civil interests, the various victims' associations articulated eight grounds: four legal errors[28] and four factual errors.[29] The grounds of appeal over civil interests, and in particular in terms of compensation, posed a tremendous amount of work for the Court of Appeal. Compensation has served as a thorny issue in all respects, primarily in terms of the beneficiaries. The Trial Chamber upheld the individual compensation measures (without, however, naming the beneficiaries as a whole) and rejected the collective and moral compensation measures due to a lack of evidence. The Appeals Court therefore found itself in a situation where it had to decide on the status of thousands of applicants (and certainly many more to come in light of the Statute entitling those not taking part in the proceedings to obtain compensation!), with those to have been

[20] EAC, *Appeal no 04*, 12 July 2016.
[21] EAC, *Judgment*, pp 22–38.
[22] EAC, *Judgment*, pp 38–40.
[23] EAC, *Judgment*, pp 41–44.
[24] The defence argued that the Trial Chamber failed (i) to rule on the plea of nullity against the ordinance that was considered to be contradictory, (vi) to respond to the conclusions, (ii) to read the judgment out properly at the hearing and (iii) to adequately identify the witnesses and the civil plaintiffs. The Defence further argued that (iv) the judgment was invalidated by the lack of the Registry's signature, (v) and that the latter was not available during the period for the appeal.
[25] The Defence challenged: (i) the presence of witnesses during the proceedings and (ii) the public identification of the witnesses, which would have influenced the testimonies, (iii) the fact that former Belgian examining magistrate Daniel Fransen was heard as a witness, (iv) Hissène Habré's conviction for certain war crimes, and finally (v) the failure to consider an official decree in the assessment of his superior status.
[26] The Defence claimed that (i) the allegations of rape made against Hissène Habré were obtained at a public hearing on the insistence of the President of the Trial Chamber and that (ii) the latter would not have taken into account the judgment made in the N'Djaména Court, which attributed the responsibility for the acts (for which allegations were presented against Hissène Habré in the EAC) to one of his co-accused.
[27] EAC, *Judgment*, pp 95–124.
[28] The Trial Chamber had applied a wrong legal standard and did not justify its decision not to recognize the status of certain persons as civil parties. As for the requests for collective and moral compensation, the Trial Chamber did not indicate the assessment criteria and applied an unsuitable standard.
[29] Certain civil parties were wrongly identified, individual compensation was not stipulated in exact terms and some victims would not have been taken into account due to Chad's legal customs, with the amount of compensation awarded insufficient.

successful in the request but considering their compensation imprecise, and those to have had their civil party status declared unfounded by the Trial Chamber. In spite of the lack of debate on this question in court and the highly restrictive timeframe, how could all of the requests presented be treated in a fair, just and individual manner? In terms of the compensation itself, how could collective indemnity be ordered and executed in a territory of a sovereign state to have hardly shown any cooperation during the trial? As for individual compensation, the amounts awarded in the court of first instance (to have become definitive for one of the victims' associations that had not appealed against the amount), could not be reduced without implications for the other associations. However, the amounts allocated—even in light of the suffering endured—represent an astronomical sum for a fund which, at the time of writing, is still not operational. Finally, in terms of the execution of the Appeal Judgment—which remains the very essence of the EAC enterprise—questions remain on its implementation and the feasibility of the compensation ordered. These are all dilemmas to which the Appeals Chamber has attempted to provide the most just response possible.

Conclusion

In hindsight, it seems to me that the main challenge presented by the appeal was to satisfactorily deal with the recognition of the civil parties and the question of compensation with only twenty-eight working weeks to do so. Although I did not observe any political influence or pressure, I feel that the time limit, albeit understandable and intrinsically linked to the budget, served to hinder the work of justice, which in itself should not be so strictly regulated. As a result, the Appeals Court was forced to encumber the Trust Fund for Victims with tasks that it could have undertaken itself had it had the necessary human, financial and time resources. Particularly in terms of eligibility, this would have allowed the victims to definitely be in the know at the time of the verdict was announced, and which would also have prevented new actors from the need to delve into such a sprawling file, saving precious time.

The Habré trial will forever serve as the first international criminal trial implementing universal jurisdiction on African soil, conducted within a timeframe and with exemplary financial means compared to other international tribunals. I feel that such an undertaking, to which I had the privilege of contributing, has been a great success. It is all the more important in such a time of crisis for international criminal justice, with distrust of the International Criminal Court and the establishment of neighbouring ad hoc jurisdictions such as the Special Criminal Court in the Central African Republic. Nevertheless, both the legacy and the credibility of the EAC rest upon the African Union and the Trust Fund for Victims, whose operations are crucial for the thousands of victims of Hissène Habré, ensuring that the judgment delivered won't remain a dead letter.

21
The Real Fight Begins
Victims Struggle for an Effective Right to Reparation

Gaëlle Carayon, Redress and Jeanne Sulzer,
International Federation of Human Rights / FIDH

Gaëlle Carayon is an expert on victims' rights including reparation for international crimes. She assisted one team of victims in the Habré case as Redress' Post Conflict policy advisor in the lead up to and following the victims' reparation filing. She assisted with the drafting of the reparation filing in coordination with Chadian, Senegalese, and international lawyers and then advocated for the implementation of the reparations decision. She now works as a Senior Manager for the New South Wales Commissioner of Victims' Rights in Australia.

Jeanne Sulzer has been involved in the struggle for justice of the Chadian victims of Habre and the NGOs supporting them from 1999 to 2006 as Head of the International Justice Desk of the FIDH and consequently coordinator of its Litigation Action Group. In this capacity, she worked on the first Senegalese case in 1999 and the Belgium case in 2000 and contributed to the research and drafting of the communication before the UN Committee against Torture. After five years working at the ECCC in Cambodia, in 2016, she participated in a Redress/ATPDH workshop in N'Djamena with victims' focal points and lawyers to discuss comparative best practices on the reparation process. After the verdict in May 2016, she assisted, in her own capacity, in the formulation of the reparations filing.

In November 1999, the FIDH organized a Regional Conference on International Justice in Dakar gathering civil society organizations from the African continent to call for the ratification of the Statute for the International Criminal Court (ICC). Senegal had been the first country to ratify the Rome Statute and was leading the way.

A few months before this meeting, on 17 July 1998 in Rome, 134 states had agreed to create the first permanent international tribunal to investigate and prosecute war crimes, crimes against humanity, and genocide. However, the ICC would have no jurisdiction over crimes committed before the entry into force of its statute. Nevertheless, a couple of weeks later, on 16 October 1998, former Chilean general, Augusto Pinochet was arrested in London. Following an indictment by Spanish magistrate Baltasar Garzón, the arrest was based on the principle of extra-territorial jurisdiction contained in the 1984 United Nations Convention Against Torture. For the first time, the impunity of a former head of state was

Gaëlle Carayon and Jeanne Sulzer, *The Real Fight Begins* In: *The President on Trial*. First edition. Edited by: Sharon Weill, Kim Thuy Seelinger, and Kerstin Bree Carlson, Oxford University Press (2020).
DOI: 10.1093/oso/9780198858621.003.0022

challenged before a domestic court, outside of the traditional territorial state. These remarkable events set the context within which the Dakar meeting took place.

An informal side meeting was convened around the pool of the international hotel hosting the event. Sitting around the table: Sidiki Kaba, the current Senegalese minister of foreign affairs and former president of the ICC Assembly of States Parties, who was at that time president of the *Organisation Nationale des droits de l'Homme* in Senegal and prominent human rights lawyer; Reed Brody and Olivier Bercault of HRW; FIDH former Executive Director Antoine Bernard, Jeanne Sulzer (co-author of this article) then ICC FIDH program officer and President Patrick Baudouin; Dobian Assingar President of the Ligue tchadienne des droits de l'Homme; and Chadian lawyer Jacqueline Moudeina, lawyer and President of the Association Tchadienne de protection des droits de l'Homme. The gathering had a clear objective: design a strategy to bring Hissène Habré to justice outside of Chad, given that all attempts to achieve justice domestically had failed. With these started decades of what would later be described as the diplomatic and judicial 'soap opera' that brought former dictator Habré to justice.

On 30 May 2016, some of these protagonists met again in Dakar, this time to listen to the EAC convict Hissène Habré for crimes against humanity, war crimes, and torture, including sexual violence and rape, for which he was sentenced to life in prison. Sitting in the courtroom was Spanish judge Baltasar Garzón. The arrest of Pinochet in London in December 1998 had inspired Chadian victims in their efforts against impunity and Judge Garzon's presence for the verdict against Hissène Habré acted as a symbol of solidarity.

The judgment against Hissène Habré was hailed as an « *immense victory for the victims and the 4733 civil parties* that we represent» by one of the Chadian lead victim's lawyer, Jacqueline Moudeina, who represented one of the groups of victims. The celebration that ensued did not last long, however: the CAE President called all parties the next morning and ordered that submissions on reparation be filed within two weeks. When concerns were raised at the short timeframe given for such an important filing, the reply was swift: considering the number of years it had taken to bring Habré to justice, victims should have been ready!

'*The real fight begins* now', Moudeina added.

This chapter considers some of the challenges and lessons learnt from that phase and the developments that ensued during and following the appeal.

Reparation before the EAC: a slow awakening

As per the civil law applicable in Senegal, Chadian and Senegalese victims before the EAC were not 'invited' in the criminal proceedings. Contrary to common law jurisdictions, they were full rights parties in the proceedings and held recognized rights, including legal representation, access to the case file, right to question the accused and the witnesses and specifically the right to request reparation. However, in the context of the EAC, the reparation procedure was indeed 'extraordinary': it differed from domestic Senegalese procedure and was also distinct and went beyond what would be possible before the ICC, for example. It was yet another *sui generis* process.

Victims participation versus reparation: building priorities

Arguably, reparation was always important to victims of Habré. Nevertheless, it did not have a central place in the advocacy and efforts during the years leading to his trial by the EAC.

The Statute of the EAC refers to the chambers' ability to award reparations and provides that reparations can be awarded to victims 'individually or collectively, whether they have participated or not in the proceedings before the EAC'.[1] By the end of 2015, with the hearings in the case coming to an end, there was still no clarity as to how victims who had not participated in the case would be able to access reparation, what link they would need to show to Habré's crimes nor what the reparations phase of the case would look like. The judges of the Trial Chamber had not released directions on the types of documentation that would later be required to be entitled to reparation. In fact, this issue was only resolved by the Court reparation order which rejected thousands of applications because of the victims' failure to provide sufficient proof of identity or family link to a direct victim. At the time, there was also limited comparative practice the EAC could draw upon: the *Lubanga* case, the first case that had reached the reparation phase at the ICC, provided more examples of what *not* to do than best practices.

In addition, victims' associations, which had been working tirelessly to bring Habré to justice, only had partial data on the thousands of victims they represented. (three victims' associations were represented in the case: the association of victims of crime and political repression 'AVCRP', the association of victims of crimes the Habré regime 'AVCRHH', and the network of human rights associations in Chad 'RADHT'). There had been no systematic record of the specific harm suffered by each victim. Data was also missing with regards to the financial loss sustained as a result of the torture or of the loss of a family member. Decades had passed since the commission of the crimes.

In December 2015, Redress, a UK based NGO assisting victims of torture and mass atrocity crimes to obtain justice and reparation, undertook a mission to Dakar. Having engaged in extensive work on reparation both before the ICC and other regional and domestic jurisdictions, the organization sought to assess the state of play in relation to reparation in the Habré case and, as appropriate, contribute expertise in that regard. Discussions with victims' representatives together with high level court officials and members of the EAC's Steering Committee ('Comité de pilotage') revealed that while consensus existed on the importance of reparation, little had been done to plan for that phase of the proceedings. Stakeholders had various views about who should set up and administer the Trust Fund central to the reparations process. For some, such a function fell under the remit of the EAC's administrator. Others felt the Steering Committee / Comité de pilotage ought to be in charge. Still others suggested that the African Union, as the body which created the EAC, would be the appropriate administrator of the Trust Fund.

With regards to the procedure that would apply to the reparation phase, interlocutors were similarly hesitant. The reasons advanced varied between the need to focus first on obtaining a conviction, the lack of time to prepare for reparation considering the fast pace

[1] Art 27(2) states that 'The EAC may order that a reparations award for compensation be made by the intermediary of the Trust Fund as provided for in Article 28 of this Statute'. Art 28(1) states that 'A Trust Fund shall be established for the benefit of victims of crimes within the jurisdiction of the EAC, and of the beneficiaries of such victims. The Trust Fund shall be financed by voluntary contributions from foreign governments, international institutions, non-governmental organizations and other entities wishing to support the victims'.

of the trial, and the alleged need to guarantee the presumption of innocence. This argument had also been made in the context of ICC proceedings in the *Lubanga* case where some court officials were reluctant to discuss what reparation proceedings would look like prior to a conviction. Many at the EAC feared that any substantive discussion around reparation would open the EAC to accusations of bias against the accused. The issue of funding was also of concern: few of Habré's alleged assets had been tracked down; donors which had supported the EAC were reluctant to spend more on the court, including on reparation. Some states also questioned whether it was appropriate for them to fund reparation when the financial responsibility for reparation clearly fell on Habré.

Once the closing hearings concluded, in January 2016, there was no choice but to finally consider the issue. A verdict was expected within a few months and it was essential to utilize that time to advance, as much as possible, what would ultimately form the basis of the victims' reparation claim. The first challenge to arise was to consult victims, as we will now discuss.

Building a strategy: the challenge of consulting the victims

In order for lawyers to come to agreement about a final reparations request, it was first essential to consult the victims themselves. While informal systems had been put in place to facilitate the flow of information between victims and their lawyers, gathering the views and concerns of victims was still a titanic task and an immense challenge. Many of the thousands of victims lived in remote areas of Chad with little communication means. Any consultation thus required a complex organization.

The EAC did not possess a Victims Support Section similar to what existed before the Extraordinary Chambers in the Courts of Cambodia (ECCC) or the ICC. There was no electronic filing or communication system in place nor court administered database where victims' information would be recorded. Contrary to the procedure before the ECCC or before the ICC, which requires the victims to file a pre-established application form with the registry, there was no such formality before the EAC. The lack of formalism and absence of application form provided by the EAC facilitated the filing of simplified civil party applications at the earlier stages of the case. The victims represented by the team led by Jacqueline Moudeina had provided information on the kind of reparation they wished to claim during focus groups organized by the lawyers or the victims' intermediaries but the information collected was not very specific. Now, for the reparations phase, the EAC's bare bones application record was proving a serious hindrance. Without clear, accurate and up to date data on the situation of their clients, victims' lawyers were limited in what they could put forward in the reparation claim.

Chadian victims' organization ATPDH was guided by the experience of the participation of victims before the ECCC and that of the *Association for the Defense of Human Rights in Cambodia* (ADHOC). ADHOC, which assisted 1,800 of the 4,000 civil parties in case 002 against the main Khmer Rouge leaders, had indeed set up a network of intermediaries amongst victims to facilitate communication. The ATPDH set up a network of twenty-three focal points, themselves civil parties, to each serve as intermediary for another fifty civil parties. They were chosen based on geographical criteria, in light of the presence of civil parties in both N'Djamena and across all of Chad's provinces. These focal points were to facilitate civil parties' access to their lawyers, keep them notified of important decisions concerning them (in the absence of an effective postal service), and collect information to assist in their effective representation.

The established network made it possible to identify and systematize the collection of information on victims, to document their injuries and to organize consultations on their specific requests for reparation to which all victims' associations in Chad could participate.

As the verdict loomed, preparations for the reparation phase started and the scale of the work required became apparent. Two weeks before the 30 May 2016 verdict, one of the victims' organizations, ATPDH, together with Redress, organized a workshop in Ndjamena to discuss best practices and lessons learnt from other international justice cases regarding reparation issues. With much of the attention so far focused on bringing Hissène Habré to justice, little was known amongst victims about what reparation could look like and what could or should be requested. The need to be realistic as to what to request also had to be combined with the equally important need to reflect the scale of the harm suffered by victims and the impacts the crimes had had on their and their relatives' lives. Participants discussed a strategy for the reparation phase. They also agreed on some key elements of the reparation claim, including the need to divide victims into subcategories, for whom different amounts of compensation would be requested.

Challenges in the drafting of the reparation request

In the two weeks that were granted by the Chamber to file the reparation request, each of the three civil party teams proceeded to put forward their clients' reparation claim. While the possibility of a joint filing between all civil parties' teams was considered, it was not pursued due to several factors (including the limited time to consult all parties, the need to reconcile differing views and a level of mistrust between the organizations representing victims).

For the victims represented by ATPDH, international lawyers worked hand in hand with Senegalese and Chadian lawyers[2] to ensure that the ultimate reparation filing echoed the concerns and preferences expressed by victims. They also strategized on how best to address the shortcomings of the legal framework and the practical challenges faced to give their claim the best chance of success.

Grouping the victims to facilitate the reparation process

Following the consultation with the focal points, the lawyers decided to group victims in categories based on the crimes that they had suffered. Such grouping is in conformity with the practice of domestic reparation proceedings[3] and mass claim processes for large number of victims.[4] It was decided to split victims into two main categories: direct victims and indirect

[2] The team was composed of Me Delphine Djiraibé, Me Soulgan Lambi, Me Assane Ndiaye, Me Alain Werner (and his team from Civitas Maxima), Me William Bourdon, and Me Georges-Henri Beauthier.

[3] See for example Report of the Kenya Truth, Justice and Reconciliation Commission, 2013, Volume IV, pp 102ff,

[4] See for example the United Nations Compensation Commission (UNCC), http://www.uncc.ch/.

victims with a further sub categorization of the direct victim category. Ultimately the following classification was adopted for the ATPDH supported 4,733 victims, represented by the team led by Jacqueline Moudeina:

Category 1—Direct Victims (1,049 victims)

- Subcategory 1: Victims of arbitrary detention and torture in detention
- Subcategory 2: Victims of rape in detention
- Subcategory 3: Victims of sexual slavery in the military camps of Wadi Doum and Kalait
- Subcategory 4: Victims of massacres (survivors)
- Subcategory 5: Victims of Prisoners of War

Category 2—Indirect Victims Family Members of disappeared, murdered or victims of torture (3,684 victims)

Formulating victims' expectations into requests for reparation
The following step was to articulate what, concretely, would be requested as reparation.

Victims that were consulted were eager to see Habré convicted. The consultations indeed brought out the fact that for many victims, their participation in the criminal proceedings was a form of rehabilitation. They saw a potential guilty verdict as a form of reparation. Most victims also felt that this would not be sufficient and that other forms of reparation were also warranted, however. The EAC indeed had the ability to order 'restitution, compensation and rehabilitation' (Article 27 of the EAC Statute) all of which were needed by the many victims who were still suffering from the trauma (physical and psychological) of what they endured or who had lost everything under Habré's rule.

At the time, a number of discussions were taking place at the international level with regards to what forms of reparation was appropriate in cases where limited funds were available to repair large numbers of victims. In the ICC's first reparation order, the chamber had indeed ruled that collective reparation was more appropriate in such cases. Some experts consulted also expressed concerns an unrealistic award would raise expectations unduly and ultimately lead to further victimization if not implemented. However, and also drawing on lessons learnt from the *Lubanga* case—where many victims had been disappointed that only collective reparation had been ordered when they had expressed a clear preference for individualized awards—the victims' lawyers and their teams were keen to understand what victims themselves perceived as reparative. Victims consulted expressed their overwhelming preference for individual compensation. Victims consulted also recognized the need for some collective reparations given that some groups had been targeted, especially the southern populations, ie the Hadjar and the Zaghawa. They also acknowledged that crimes had an impact not only on the individuals and families directly concerned but also on all their communities.

These findings had a direct impact on the drafting of the reparation request. It became clear that both individual compensation and collective reparation had to be requested. It was also clear that one should not come to replace the other and that collective reparation should not be considered an 'easy way out' of ordering significant amounts of compensation.

Determination of the reparation request

When it came to deciding how much compensation to request, one of the main difficulties faced was to quantify the harm suffered. The task was in and of itself impossible: ultimately no amount would ever repair the harm that had been done. In addition, few victims had in their possession documents accurately detailing the extent of the financial harm they had suffered. It was also impossible to calculate the loss of income suffered by victims as a result of the torture or the death of a relative. Habré's regime targeted a wide range of individuals with different financial situations. Family units varied greatly with the majority of victims having at least two wives and five children. The age of victims ranged from children to elderly. There was no single profile of victims as far as the harm they suffered was concerned and it was thus impossible to assess the exact amount corresponding to their harm. The jurisprudence from other courts, while informative, also provided limited guidance: there is no universal scale of what amounts are appropriate to repair victims of specific crimes and amounts vary greatly both across and within jurisdictions.

Given the high number of civil parties, the limited time available to draft the filing, the lack of material evidence and the challenge of assessing the exact prejudice suffered by victims, the use of presumptions was deemed most appropriate. This technique had been used successfully by many other claims processes[5] and by the Inter American Court for Human Rights.[6] It involves judges using circumstantial evidence, presumptions of fact, and drawing inferences to remedy gaps in the information available 'when they lead to consistent conclusions as regards the facts of the case'.[7] In the circumstances of the Habré case, the use of presumptions was facilitated by the fact that the findings of the verdict could be used to support the lawyer's arguments. For instance, the lawyers referred to findings according to which it could be inferred that victims who had been detained had also suffered from torture and ill treatment. They thus argued that a presumption of acute physical and psychological prejudice should be applied. Similarly, it was presumed that all the persons that disappeared were deceased based on evidence collected during the trial that persons arrested by the DDS were later killed.

Individual compensation and collective reparation requests

Despite the use of presumptions, it was still impossible to arrive at an exact amount corresponding to the harm suffered by victims. Data was missing in relation to key indicators necessary to undertake an accurate assessment of the harm. For example, while it could be assumed that most of those tortured had been unable to fully resume work, it was not possible to precisely calculate the resulting loss of income. The only certainty, based on the average life expectancy and salary in Chad at the time, was that victims had suffered an

[5] For example, the International Commission on Holocaust Era Insurance Claims. See also Heike Niebergall, 'Overcoming Evidentiary Weaknesses in Reparation Claims Programmes' in C Ferstman, M Goetz, and A Stephens (eds), *Reparations for Victims of Genocide, War Crimes and Crimes Against Humanity* (Brill/Nijhoff 2009) 145–66.

[6] Inter-American Court for Human Rights, *Castillo-Petruzzi et al*, Judgment (30 May 1999) para 62.

[7] Inter-American Court for Human Rights, *Gangaram Panday v Suriname*, Merits, reparations and costs, Judgment of 21 January 1994, Series C No 16, para 49.

important financial loss as a result. The lawyers thus suggested that the court apply the principle of equity. In this context, it meant arriving at an estimation of the harm in financial terms that would reflect «*an objective consideration of what is fair, equitable and reasonable in the circumstances of the case*»[8] considering for example the challenges faced by victims to establish in exact terms the extent of their loss but also the «*general context in which the violence took place.*».[9] A set amount would be requested for each category of victims rather than a specific amount for each individual victim.[10] This also had the benefit of facilitating a swift decision on compensation: the chamber had a limited time to rule on reparation and would likely have been unable to undertake an individual assessment of the situation of each victim within that time frame. The civil party lawyers thus requested that the chamber allocate, on the basis of equity, individual compensation ranging from 35 to 75,000,000 CFA (from 61,000 to 130,900 USD) in damages for each of the victims who personally suffered harm.[11] The reparation request also submitted that a gendered approach should be followed; it asked that rape and sexual slavery be considered as torture and set out some of the specific harm suffered by victims of rape or sexual slavery. These included the fact that rape was culturally taboo in Chad, that some victims had born children out of rape, some of whom died at birth or suffered from developmental issues, and that rape attracted a strong sense of shame and humiliation in Chadian society.

With regard to the families of victims of massacres, executions, disappearances and deceased victims, the civil parties asked the court to order the sum of 30,000,000 CFA of compensation to each of the 3,684 indirect victims. The amounts are somewhat arbitrary—the line had to be drawn somewhere—but were arrived at through consideration of: what amounts some victims themselves had advanced, what amounts had been awarded for similar harm by other courts/reparation bodies and the circumstances such bodies had considered in reaching their conclusions, what victims' lawyers expected the judges to consider appropriate as well as the need to ensure that victims would not feel let down by their lawyer should amounts deemed too low be requested. The team's lawyers provided examples of what other courts had ordered in similar cases, particularly the IACtHR which had rendered a number of judgments in relation to reparation for massacres, mass scale crimes and sexual violence. With regards to indirect victims, they also highlighted the fact that many of those executed or disappeared were male under twenty-five and likely the main source of income for their families and thus be estimated to be around thirty years of income. Noting the annual average salary in Chad and life expectancy at the time the loss of income alone could be estimated between 4.5 million CFA and 150 million CFA depending a person's activity.[12]

The team was also conscious that the Chamber was under pressure to wind down the EAC's activity and thus would spend limited time considering the reparation requests; if

[8] ECtHR, *Al-Jedda v the United Kingdom*, application no 27021/08, Decision of 7 July 2011, para 114.

[9] ibid; *Ahmadou Sadio Diallo (Guinea v DRC)*, Compensation, Judgment, ICJ Reports 2012, 324.

[10] In contrast, before the ICC, the Trial Chamber in Katanga requested that detailed individual assessment of harm be submitted for each claimant.

[11] Reparations requests for categories of direct victims were as follows: victims of arbitrary detention and torture in detention: 50,000,000 CFA francs; victims of sexual slavery in the military camps of Oadi-Doum and Kalaït: 75,000,000 CFA francs; victims of rape in detention: 60,000,000 CFA; victims of massacre: 35,000,000 CFA; victims who were prisoners of war: 50,000,000 CFA.

[12] Equivalent to thirty years of income with average annual income ranging from 150.000 CFA for cattle raisers and farmer to 5.000.000 CFA for civil servants and managers.

the amounts requested were considered exorbitant, there was a chance the claim would be quickly dismissed or delegated to the Trust Fund, which was yet to be set up at that stage.

Additionally, victims indicated the wish to see the following collective reparations ordered by the Chamber:[13] the development of community income generating projects, building memorials on the sites of important massacres, teaching this period of Chadian history in school, commemorating 30 May as a day of the fight against impunity and building professional training centres for the children of Habré's victims.

The Chamber's ruling

The Trial Chamber[14] considered that the amounts requested were not justified and were even in some cases 'exorbitant' or 'unreasonable' and would be 'contrary to the interest of the victims' given that the effectivity of the reparation could not be guaranteed.[15] It concluded that all the direct victims should receive the same amount of 15,000,000 CFA with the exception of the victims of rape and sexual slavery who would receive 20,000,000 CFA.[16] Similarly, the Chamber decided that each of the indirect victims would be granted 10,000,000 CFA as a compensation. While the ruling is not surprising—many expected the Court to order less than what had been requested—it is worth noting that other courts had ordered amounts similar to the ones originally requested, as was stressed in the reparation request. The Appeals Chamber confirmed the amount ordered by the Trial Chamber and stated that these reparations were 'reasonable'.[17]

In addition, the Trial Chamber rejected the requests for collective reparations. It ruled that the victims' lawyers had failed to provide 'any precise data' enabling it to assess their feasibility 'in particular data relating to the costs and precise location of the monuments, the type and cost of development'.[18] The Appeals Chamber confirmed that interpretation.[19] This came somewhat as a surprise. At no time during the proceedings did the chamber instruct the parties as to the formulation or requirements of the claims for reparations The ruling was thus perceived as unfair: victims were sanctioned for failing to comply with requirements that had never been set out.

Ensuring implementation of reparation: the Trust Fund

With the prospect of reparation now real, the focus quickly shifted to how reparation ordered would be operationalized.

The EAC statute provisions creating the Trust Fund in some ways reflected the ICC Trust Fund for Victims, with a similar mandate to act as an intermediary to distribute reparation

13 EAC, Memo by civil party attorneys regarding reparations §§ 147–52.

14 EAC, Décision sur les réparations, 29 July 2016, § 62.

15 EAC, Chambre africaine d'assises d'appel, *Le Procureur général c. Hissène Habré,* 27 April 2017, § 936.

16 The reparation request had sought higher amounts for victims of rape and sexual slavery of 60,000,000 CFA and 75,000,000 CFA respectively.

17 EAC, Chambre africaine d'assises d'appel, *Le Procureur général c. Hissène Habré,* 27 April 2017, § 934 and 941.

18 EAC, Ministère Public c. Hissein Habré, *Jugement sur les intérêts civils, 29 juillet 2016,* §§ 69–70.

19 EAC, Chambre africaine d'assises d'appel, *Le Procureur général c. Hissène Habré,* 27 April 2017, §874.

awards made by the chamber and to provide support to victims of crimes within the jurisdiction of the EAC (Art 27(2) and 28(1) of the EAC Statute). The Statute was vague, however. For example, there was no indication of who was to create the Trust Fund or under whose authority it would operate. Significant disagreements existed on basic aspects of the future fund: Where should it sit? What structure should it have? How would it ensure that funds would really reach victims?

With the end of the trial looming, some victims' and civil society representatives grew anxious that unless victims put forward a clear proposal on how any awarded reparations could be implemented, reparations would never concretize. These fears were not unfounded: a court in Chad had ordered significant reparation to victims of the Habré regime in March 2015 that have still not been implemented. Victims filed a complaint before the ACHPR in 2017 against Chad on this issue. In addition, it had always been clear that the EAC were to be temporary: they would shut down following the appeals judgment. At the same time, the Trust Fund was yet to be set up. Without clear indication as to what would happen once the EAC closed down in April 2017, there was a real risk that any reparation ordered would be no more than a paper promise.

The Trial Chamber's decision on reparations fell short of providing the much-needed clarifications that victims expected. It did not set out how reparation would be implemented. It did not specify Habré's total financial liability either, raising questions as to how the judgment might be enforced to recoup some of his assets. Victims raised the lack of specificity in that regard as a ground for appeal, highlighting that the chamber's failure to rule on implementation was a breach of their right to an effective remedy.[20] They also stressed the need for the Appeals Chamber to clearly identify the body that would oversee implementing reparation and to consider how disputes that may arise during the implementation stage would be resolved. Since the EAC would close a few months after rendering its appeals judgment, any monitoring of the implementation of reparations would need to be undertaken by a separate entity.[21]

The Appeals Chamber heeded victims' concerns in this regard. It set out that the Trust Fund would be the implementing body for reparation and urged the African Union to set it up speedily. The Appeals Chamber confirmed that before the EAC the right to compensation was not conditioned on a victim being formally recognized as a civil party in the trial proceedings. It thus found that it would be up to the Trust Fund to examine new elements brought by victims who had been declared inadmissible as civil parties. The Fund is also to decide on claims for compensation from victims who did not participate in the proceedings. The Appeals Chamber ruled that any dispute relating to the implementation of reparation would be settled by a Senegalese tribunal.[22]

The Chamber also called that any funds, including proceeds of property or fines, be used solely for the benefit of the victims and not for the core operation of the Fund structure.

The ruling was welcomed by victims' lawyers. It became clear at that point that the advocacy had to shift to the setting up of the Trust Fund. Following the verdict in May 2016, and around the same time the reparation judgment was issued (July 2016), the African

[20] *Appeals Submission of Abaifouta Clément et al. against the Reparations Verdict*, Public Prosecutor v Hissein Habré, EAC, 5 December 2016, §§ 46–49.

[21] In contrast, at the ICC, the Trial Chamber retains oversight when the Trust Fund is tasked with implementing reparation.

[22] EAC, Chambre africaine d'assises d'appel, *Le Procureur général c. Hissène Habré*, 27 April 2017, § 900.

Union had issued a decision formally creating the Trust Fund.[23] However, by the time the Appeals Judgment came out (April 2017) little progress had been made on getting the fund set up. At the time of writing, the African Union has been working on a draft statute for the Trust Fund, but it is yet to be adopted. It is also unclear where resources for the fund will come from.

The struggle is therefore not over in particular for the victims' lawyers who have the extremely difficult task to explain and manage the expectations of Chadian victims who have put some hope and endless efforts in this case. The 'soap opera' continues.

Lessons learned

(At least) two lessons learnt have emerged from that process.

First, despite legitimate fears with regards to raising victims' expectations, it is important to consider and gather information that will assist in the establishment of victims' claims for participation and reparation at the outset. This is true both for victims and for the court. In the case against Habré, neither civil parties' lawyers nor the EAC sought to clarify what information would be needed to justify victims' reparations claims. This was only clarified in the Trial Chamber's ruling, which excluded some victims for failing to provide sufficient proof of identification. While victims declared inadmissible at the EAC may be able to submit additional data to the Trust Fund and could still obtain reparation, greater clarity and preparedness on both sides would have ensured a smoother process. It was clear that the EAC expected victims' lawyers to be ready at the time of the judgment. While this may seem reasonable, it is also risky: why spend precious time and resources gathering information relevant for the reparation claim when a conviction is not yet certain? Donors may be reluctant to fund such initiatives until it is clear that reparation will be awarded. However, in light of recent experience, we argue that the stakes are too high to wait until a verdict. Chambers could give additional time following a guilty verdict for the reparation requests to be prepared, although this would only partly mitigate the challenge and lead to new ones. As seen in the *Katanga* case, where the chamber sought specific information and harm assessments for each victim, there is significant effort and time requirements necessary for compiling reparation requests. In cases such as the *Habré* case, where the number of claimants reaches multiple thousands, it is unlikely that the addition of a few weeks (or even months) would make much of a difference. At the same time, any delay risks jeopardizing victims' ability to receive reparation in a timely manner. A clear direction by the chambers, at the outset of the case, as to what information they are likely to require or what minimum requirements will apply for the demonstration of harm could enable victims' lawyers to prepare earlier on. This is particularly true when cases span multiple years and also has the benefit of preventing the loss of information (for example if victims are displaced, or documents get lost).

[23] African Union, Twenty-Seventh Ordinary Session, 'Decision on the Hissène Habré Case', Assembly/AU/Dec.615(XXVII), Doc EX.CL/986(XXIX) (18 July 2016) http://www.au.int/en/sites/default/files/decisions/31274-assembly_au_dec_605_-620_xxvi_f.pdf

Second, there is also a need to consider early on how reparation will be implemented. In the Habré case, it was understandably difficult to know exactly what type of structure ought to exist to implement yet to be decided reparation. The failure to set up an implementation structure in time has meant that even years after the appeals ruling, victims are yet to receive reparation, and we do not have a clear path for when this will change.

As an additional consequence of this slow awakening to the issue of reparation, the 'reparation phase of the case' has also somewhat failed to benefit from the momentum that had been gathered prior to and during the trial. For many, both within the NGO and diplomatic sphere, the trial of Habré was a success and it was now time to turn our attention to other matters. This is not the view of many of his victims. One should hope that the same efforts and dedication that led to the successful conviction of Hissène Habré will be applied to ensuring that Habrés victims receive reparation.

SECTION D
BEYOND THE COURTROOM

This Section brings us to those who influenced and contributed to the court from the outside. The EAC benefitted from significant donor support from several countries, most notably Chad, Senegal, Belgium, the Netherlands, Germany, the United States, France, Luxembourg, and the European and African Unions. While the most obvious elements of such support were financial, other more discrete 'in kind' support, consisting of training and the secondment of personnel, were also provided. Sarah Valentina Fall's Chapter 22 discusses the challenges of providing necessary, but politically sensitive, Western support to a tribunal overtly designed to be an African mechanism.

Another seminal element of the EAC is that it is the first international tribunal to include a significant outreach budget within the overall budget of the court. In Chapter 23, Franck Petit details how the EAC communications team structured public debates and other outreach activities during and after the trial in Chad and Senegal. He also notes the challenges and opportunities of working across countries, cultures, and politics in seeking to publicize the work of the EAC. Like Petit, Senegalese journalist Ndieng Gorgoi learned the difference between reporting in Senegal and reporting in Chad, where freedom of press is relatively limited. In Chapter 24, Ndieng, who covered the Habré tribunal for the Dakar daily *Le Quotidien*, discusses the process of reporting on Habré, including her travels to Chad to observe fact-finding efforts there. Chapter 25 continues the focus on Chad, with Henri Thulliez's discussion of recent trials and convictions of Habré-era collaborators there in 2015. Among those convicted were defendants named with Habré in the EAC's indictment. By trying Habré-era collaborators in Chad, current President Déby ensured that these collaborators of Habré could not participate in the EAC. Moreover, many of those convicted in 2015 have already been freed, making the trials in Chad a pyrrhic victory for justice.

In the last chapter of this section, Érick Sullivan and Fannie Lafontaine from Canada's Laval University describe how their clinical work with law students supported both the trial as well as student engagement with international criminal justice.

22
A Donor's Perspective

Sarah Valentina Fall, Swiss Embassy in Dakar

The EAC benefited from significant donor support from several countries. While the most obvious elements of such support were financial, other more discrete 'in kind' support, consisting of training and the secondment of personnel, was also provided. This chapter discusses the challenges of providing necessary, but politically sensitive, Western support to a tribunal overtly designed to be African.

Two principal elements motivated Switzerland's actions in Senegal: Switzerland's commitment to promoting international criminal justice and its longstanding engagement with Chad.[1]

Switzerland has maintained a longstanding relationship with Chad, most notably through its development program first established in Chad in 1965. For the last ten years, the Human Security Division of the Federal Department of Foreign Affairs (DFAE) has complemented this engagement in development cooperation through four main themes: reinforcing dialogue between political actors and between political and civil society actors, supporting work to address the past, strengthening capacities in the area of human rights, and supporting the reconciliation of communities.

It is therefore within this context of strong and active engagement in Chad, along with the direct repercussions for the people of Chad of the trial of Hissène Habré, that it became apparent that Switzerland should actively engage with the EAC. Concretely, this engagement entailed making a range of technical assistance available and facilitating relations and communications among the various stakeholders, rather than financing the EAC as a donor. This choice was made in light of the ongoing concern of ensuring that actions in Senegal could also have a positive impact for Chad. Switzerland additionally participated in the Steering Committee for the financing of the EAC as an observer.

[1] Switzerland has supported peace policies for some fifteen years. In this context, it collaborates with national and international experts. Having developed extensive expertise, it has considerably reinforced its engagement in support of peace. Different actions have thus been carried out in five principal areas: programs promoting peace; mediation and support for peace processes for parties in conflict and states in a transitional period; dealing with the past; the provision of specialists and diplomats from our pool of experts; and diplomatic initiatives and interventions within international organizations.

Sarah Valentina Fall, *A Donor's Perspective* In: *The President on Trial*. First edition. Edited by: Sharon Weill, Kim Thuy Seelinger, and Kerstin Bree Carlson, Oxford University Press (2020). © Sarah Valentina Fall. DOI: 10.1093/oso/9780198858621.003.0023

Switzerland's engagement

Since 2013, Switzerland has launched several initiatives in conjunction with the EAC, notably with the prosecutor, the Communications Unit, and the Trial Chamber. Switzerland contributed in different ways to the EAC and, more globally, to its surrounding processes. Switzerland's support was consistent and continuous, incorporating multifaceted actions, which gave it an overarching understanding of the challenges and stakes. This understanding was particularly enhanced thanks to close collaboration with colleagues in Dakar, N'Djamena, and Berne.

This was especially important as Switzerland was not a funder, a position which allowed for ease of contact with both Chadian and Senegalese actors (including authorities, civil society, and the EAC). Switzerland had no political or economic interest in its engagement, working solely in the interest of peace. It did not seek success for itself but rather sought to work in the service of others. This discrete mode of functioning based on partnership was appreciated, as it was driven by a desire for effective engagement rather than obtaining results at any price. This role of facilitator gave Switzerland means not generally available to other countries and allowed it to advance and accompany important processes in a robust yet straightforward manner.

This unique position allowed for facilitating a clearer mutual understanding among each of the stakeholders in the context of their shared experience. This was the case, for example, with the national trial of former DDS agents held in N'Djemena in 2014/2015: Switzerland shared its insights on the conduct of the case, the excited reaction of the public, and the case's political and social impact on the country with the prosecutor of the EAC. Being able to understand and have a sense of the local context allowed all the stakeholders to have a better grasp on the trial proceedings. In a similar vein, simpler forms of assistance also occurred, such as sharing the Chadian criminal code (as part of the demand to extradite indicted individuals such as Mahatma Djibrine, known as 'El Djonto', and Saleh Younous) or furnishing a topographical map of Chad from the period.

In addition to missions to identify needs and make experts available, Switzerland was committed to questions of how to deal with the past. Through the DFAE's 'Task Force for Dealing with the Past' and its operational partner, the Swisspeace Foundation, Switzerland organized training sessions on dealing with the past (transitional justice) in which key members of the EAC and the Chadian government participated. Chadians and Senegalese had the opportunity to interact in a neutral space and to become familiar with the stakes and realities pertinent to each, thus initiating a constructive dialogue.

At the same time, Switzerland's involvement focused on the high stakes of communication about the trial. Broadcasting and communication were particularly important as images of the trial and how they were used would have significant repercussions on Chadian as well as Senegalese and international audiences. These same images would also constitute an important archival source for this page of Chadian history. Switzerland therefore mounted communication workshops on international criminal trials, as much for the members of the EAC and the Chadian legal pool (in charge of the Habré trial) as for representatives of Senegalese Radiotelevision (RTS) in charge of covering the trial. The aim was to emphasize the importance of images (particularly of high quality images) for undertaking fundamental historical work, and to raise the issue of dealing with the past and, especially, the work of memory.

Even though the EAC is now closed, Senegal still has important work to do for which Switzerland is ready to offer its expertise: the archiving of the dossier. The archive is the memory of the EAC and of the trial. It is the public's access to paper and audiovisual documentation of the proceedings (at least, to non-confidential documentation), and it is the guarantor of history. This work of great importance is now underway. Additionally, Switzerland wishes to undertake substantive work with the relevant authorities in Chad on archives relating to this period in history, so as to guarantee that Chadians have access to these records essential to national memory.

Perspectives on the EAC

Positive elements

In Chad

The work of the EAC seems to have had little impact on the Senegalese population. In contrast, Chad experienced a rare openness, particularly in terms of the press and the media, which published articles and documentaries that presented both facts and opinions. The process begun by the EAC served as a sort of outlet for the population. Despite restrictions on discussion of this still burning issue in Chad, this difficult period in history was openly discussed and people were able to express their lived experiences.

While at times criticized for both its form and its functioning, the trial in Dakar and the extradition requests for certain former DDS agents (Saleh Younous and Mahamat Djibrine) dovetailed with the national trial in Chad of former agents for acts of torture, assassination, sequestration, arbitrary detention, assault and battery, and acts of barbarism. This trial, which only lasted a few months (from 14 November 2014 to 25 March 2015, when a verdict was issued), found twenty-eight individuals guilty, of whom seven were ultimately condemned to life in prison.[2]

Finally, despite occasionally strained and complicated relations between Chadian and Senegalese authorities, it is nevertheless important to emphasize that even if the EAC was unable to complete all the work as initially intended—such as being able to hear from key witnesses during the trial, including former DDS agents detained in Chad—the essential was accomplished.

In Senegal

The commitment of the magistrates was widely appreciated. They demonstrated professionalism and dedication to getting the job done properly, despite the difficulties of transposing national law into international law and the very real pressures that accompany this type of trial.

Senegal emerged from the trial a pioneer. It had not only welcomed this special tribunal but shouldered a unique and important responsibility and met it fully. Globally, the EAC was a groundbreaking expression of international justice and marked a crucial moment in African history.

[2] See also Thulliez, in this volume, Chapter 25.

Difficulties and disappointments

Within the EAC

From the beginning, the EAC encountered challenges that inhibited its smooth functioning. Indeed, the various steps and timing of the process were established without fully taking into account how long each step would really require. For example, the prosecutor's Office worked for three months to prepare its introductory submission, even though this phase did not figure in the initial budget. Additionally, no residual mechanism was planned for after the EAC shut its doors.

Furthermore, the work of the EAC was not always understood and supported. There was a gap between the reality on the ground, the work of the magistrates, and the funders: some of the funders on the Steering Committee for the financing of the EAC, while understandably concerned with sound financial management, were largely unaware of the activities of the magistrates and the prosecutor. This gap and its ensuing misunderstandings inhibited the committee's ability to provide optimal support to the EAC.

The internal structure also had certain weaknesses. Beyond the usual practices of clerks and administrations, no archival system for the dossiers had been foreseen.[3] In addition, document security was piecemeal at best, given that employees used their personal email and messaging services for correspondence, even for highly confidential communications.

Beyond the EAC

Initially, the African Union (AU) was closely involved with the EAC, having signed the accord with Senegal that created it in August 2012.[4] Over time, however, the AU seemed to lose interest in the case, responding slowly to requests and demonstrating little enthusiasm despite presiding over the Steering Committee. No AU representatives were present when the trial opened on 20 July 2015, giving rise to a certain number of questions as to the AU's genuine interest in and ambitions for proposing an alternative form of international criminal justice.

Moreover, and on a different note, there was enormous potential to leverage in terms of communication and awareness-raising. The Consortium for Awareness-Raising did a commendable job in Senegal and especially in Chad, but the visibility of the EAC remained limited.

The issue of archives, which are fundamental to memory, seemed to interest very few people. Despite the insistence of Switzerland and its willingness to accompany the various countries in this endeavour, advances have been slow and political decision-making remains vague. The AU also seems to be losing interest in this question.

As for a fund for victims' reparations, which is provided for in the Statutes and long awaited by the victims themselves, implementation has been difficult.[5] After the closing of the EAC, only the AU had the power to set up an appropriate structure. But without the insistence of the victims' associations, the various partners, and certain members of the Steering Committee, this fund would not have come to fruition. The Statutes and rules of procedure were written and voted on by the partners during the final sessions of the Steering Committee. Following the simultaneous closing of the EAC and the Steering Committee, the AU was responsible for the creation and management of the reparations fund. Despite

[3] See Ba, in this volume, Chapter 12.
[4] See Kioko, in this volume, Chapter 8.
[5] See Carayon and Sulzer, in this volume, Chapter 21.

reaching an agreement in principle during the summit of Heads of State in July 2017, the actual creation of the fund still awaits ratification, as required in accordance with the AU's internal processes.

Lastly, some victims and witnesses no longer feel safe in their countries, and a number of them wish to seek asylum in Europe or elsewhere to protect their families and their children.

International criminal justice and the hybrid nature of the EAC

Switzerland has advocated for the International Criminal Court (ICC) since its creation and has supported international criminal justice more generally. The ICC is not the only avenue for justice, and Switzerland promotes all mechanisms working to advance peace and the struggle against impunity writ large. In the specific case of the EAC, the trial brought to life behind its doors marks a turning point in the history of justice in Africa. It is the first time that the courts of one State have tried the former leader of another State for international crimes (war crimes and crimes against humanity).

While some African states are critical of the ICC, it is nonetheless useful to underline the complementarity of this instance with national or regional jurisdictions, which are first and foremost responsible for trying international crimes. The hybrid formula of the EAC has quite clearly proven its worth. But should the process carried out in Dakar, under an AU mandate, serve as a model for future tribunals dedicated to fighting against impunity on African soil? Is its duplication for other cases possible? For Senegal, the effects of this trial were not all positive. Political pressure and strained relations with other African countries were not always easy to manage, especially with Senegal's Minister of Justice, Sidiki Kaba, presiding over the Assembly of States Parties of the ICC.

Conclusion

The process that led to the trial and eventual conviction of the former President of Chad, Hissène Habré, is the result of unwavering commitment and perseverance on the part of the victims, despite intimidations, challenges, and refusals to collaborate, both in Chad and in Senegal. The unprecedented character and success of the EAC is theirs to claim. It was not states that brought this trial but the civil parties—with, of course, the eventual participation of States, particularly as regards the financing of this special tribunal.

Despite criticisms that justice singled out Hissène Habré alone, despite the deafening silence of the defendant during the trial, and despite the fact that only certain periods of his regime were covered, the trial—equitable and impartial—was held. The magistrates did their work and justice was rendered.

Switzerland works to promote peace and human rights throughout the world. International justice, and more specifically international criminal justice, as Switzerland envisions and perceives it, responds to these challenges and to the demand for justice: an essential component for building the rule of law.

23

Outreach for the EAC

An Extraordinary Experience

Franck Petit, Team leader of the EAC Outreach Consortium[1]

Franck Petit was part of a three-body consortium managing outreach for the EAC across Senegal, Chad and internationally. The EAC was the first court to provide for outreach in its budget and to make outreach activities an official element of court's structure and output. Petit is a journalist by training who works in the field of human rights and communications; he has been covering international criminal justice for decades.

November 2013. When the telephone rang to offer me the position of expert on outreach for the EAC, I had already been covering international tribunals for fourteen years. First was the International Criminal Court for Rwanda (ICTR), which made nearly no attempt whatsoever to reach out to Rwandans, who responded with comparable contempt. On the phone was Ms Martien Schotsmans, director of RCN Justice & Démocratie, the Belgian NGO that was putting together a bid for the future outreach consortium. She was offering me the chance to participate in the adventure of 'an African court run by Africans for Africans'. It was tempting. The winds were unfavourable for big international tribunals, but this little court seemed modest, realistic, and of human scale: all conditions necessary for a better acceptance of awareness. I accepted her offer.

A well-known aphorism illustrates the fundamental principle, too often neglected by international tribunals, of holding open court hearings: 'not only must justice be done; it must also be seen to be done.'[2] The trust of the public depends on it, emphasized the European Court of Human Rights,[3] as 'this public character protects litigants against the administration of justice in secret with no public scrutiny', furthermore considering that when members of the tribunal engage in illicit activities the general interest may require that the public be informed about an act that affects the functioning of the judiciary. This general principle is at the heart of the outreach work, justifying its conception as part and parcel of the work of justice, not at the service of an institution but of the common good.

[1] The views, thoughts, and opinions expressed in the text belong solely to the author.

[2] Lord Chief Justice Gordon Hewart (*R v Sussex Justices, ex parte McCarthy* ([1924] 1 KB 256, [1923] All ER Rep 233).

[3] ECtHR, *Werner v Austria,* judgment of 24 November 1997, *Reports of Judgements and Decisions* 1997-VII. *Rizos and Daskas v Greece*, No 65545/01, judgment of 27 May 2004.

Franck Petit, *Outreach for the EAC* In: *The President on Trial*. First edition. Edited by: Sharon Weill, Kim Thuy Seelinger, and Kerstin Bree Carlson, Oxford University Press (2020). © Franck Petit. DOI: 10.1093/oso/9780198858621.003.0024

Show, don't tell

The chambers were extraordinary on many levels, beginning with a dramatic image that is now part of the Chadian collective memory: that of the old lion draped in white carried by black-hooded guards to the opening of his trial on 20 July 2015. In the rather formal annals of international justice, it's an unusual image.

From my perspective, that of a specialized journalist, professional satisfaction can come at the beginning or the end of a trial, but even more so during its course. Working on outreach allows a similar follow up on the development and the detailed accounts of the long course of a trial. On the other hand, it is impossible from my perspective to play the part of a militant who demands to 'believe' blindly in justice and who only expects a conviction. Besides, experience has shown that when international courts malfunction or violate the rights of the accused, the NGOS that support them turn a blind eye. Such were my thoughts as I prepared to 'go over to the other side' and to work for an NGO under contract with a court, even though the principle of neutrality of our program had been affirmed. I understood it as a way of informing people, with the sole intention of giving those most closely concerned, those in Chad who had experienced crimes and those in Senegal who would see the trial, the means to 'see' justice. As we kept repeating to our publics, we were there to allow justice to be seen, not to be believed.

A mantra: reduce the distance

In terms of outreach, the EAC offered both challenges (physical and temporal distance) and means to meet those challenges. The authors of its statutes had clearly learned from the lessons of the past. Annexed to the agreement creating the EAC, the statutes called for the 'setting up of outreach activities'. Even better: 10% of the court's budget was dedicated to outreach, an unprecedented ratio in the history of international justice. Even if the EAC budget was incredibly realistic and modest, the dedicated amount went far beyond a symbolic engagement: right from the start, the EAC very clearly and deliberately gave itself the means to give the extra effort deemed necessary to, as we repeated like a mantra, 'reduce the distance' between the court and Chad.

The image might seem ludicrous: how can one 'reduce' the 4,000 kilometres as the crow flies that separate Dakar from N'Djamena? Even the EAC's call for bids at the end of 2013 to select the organization that would carry out this outreach work seemed to slightly underestimate the difficulty: 'Holding the trial on African soil will have the incontestable advantage of allowing all the victims and all the witnesses to follow all the steps of the trial, or at least to have ready access to all the information concerning it.' But opening the selection to competition was at the same time innovative and pragmatic: for the first time an international tribunal called for public bids and thus made the deliberate choice to externalize awareness of its activities.

Birth of the outreach 'consortium'

Our proposal, whose three member organizations would guarantee territorial coverage in both Senegal and Chad (via two local organizations) as well as an international dimensions (through the Belgian organization and its experts), was selected by the EAC at the end of December 2013. This partnership would be the strength of the 'outreach consortium' where three entities would strive to do what none of them would be able to do separately. Internationally, RCN Justice & Démocratie, an NGO with experience in supporting the reconstruction of state under the rule of law, brought the experts in international law—through the work of the jurist Hugo Moudiki Jombwe and in communication through my own work; and coordinated the financial and technical management of the project. In Chad, Magi Communications, a communication cabinet directed by a respected figure of civil society, Gilbert Maoundonodji, would work in the capital and the regions. In Dakar, Primum Africa Consulting, a dynamic firm directed by Abdou Khadre-Lô, would work in connection with the seat of the EAC and would develop the Senegalese part of the program. Trimestral reports and steady exchanges with the EAC administration and communications unit ensured effective management of the project and coordination with the court.

The many activities suggested by the EAC were quickly instituted to follow a twenty-one-month calendar, which was the length of the initial contract with the EAC, to reach out to the public in Senegal, Chad, and internationally. First was a workshop designed to involve members of the court, its communications unit, the Chadian judicial pool, and the Senegalese minister of justice. In all, some twenty-five activities incorporating 478 outreach actions were set up during this period: exchange workshops for the defence and for the victims lawyers;[4] radio and television programs, radio spots; an interactive platform, Forumchambresafricaines.org, in three languages; public debates in Senegal and Chad, in the capital cities and the provinces; academic exchanges with professors, researchers, and students; workshops for journalists and for artists; dialogue sessions with the victims; speaking at universities in Chad, Senegal, Africa, and Europe; publication of a special edition of the RCN Justice & Démocratie bulletin;[5] as well as comic books, posters, filmed summaries of the trial, etc.

Benefits of outsourcing

The service contract between the consortium and the EAC gave us a supervised operational autonomy in the context of a detailed, structured program that imposed rigorous administrative and financial reporting procedures. Outsourcing was in that context certainly a more flexible, more efficient, and less expensive solution than an institutionalized model. But its even deeper interest was that it impacted how the work was perceived. It was not the court that spoke to the public from on high, but a more neutral relay physically and culturally closer to it, one that popularized the court's work and made sure that its debates were publicized. In Senegal, Senegalese were in charge of the program. In Chad, Chadians were.

[4] Despite our invitations, the defence lawyers declined to participate.

[5] RCN Justice & Démocratie, 'Sensibiliser sur les Chambre africaines extraordinaires: Le Bulletin numéro 46' (December 2014) 46, http://rcn-ong.be/IMG/pdf/bulletin_46.pdf.

When the EAC was unknown, these relays initiated exchanges on their respective territories, drawing on existing legitimacies. With this model, the program could be launched a couple of weeks after the contract was signed.

The principal effects of outsourcing: as noted above, no lag time between the signature of the contract and the launching of activities as each one of the three organizations had its networks and local knowledge available to it. There was no rivalry between those working on outreach and those on communication: the Communications Unit spoke for the institution, while the Outreach Consortium explained the work of the court on the ground and created conditions for concrete dialogue. These complementary functions (communication and outreach) were coordinated but still autonomous on a day-to-day basis. Concretely, communiques from the Communications Unit, directed by Marcel Mendy, were relayed by the outreach on the ground and, in the other direction, outreach passed on the public's preoccupations to the members of the EAC via its publications, the Communications Unit, or the administrator of the chambers.[6]

This crystal clear distinction between public relations and outreach is a specificity of the EAC. In international tribunals, outreach is generally subordinate to, or intertwined with, public relations. This most often damages the effectiveness and spontaneity of the outreach while at the same time complicating the public relations work. If there is no universal definition of outreach, one of its distinctive characteristic is that it seeks 'consistent and interactive dialogue between the court and the public',[7] while many international courts define outreach as an objective under public information. This theoretical distinction between unidirectional communication and interactive outreach was probably never so clearly applied as at the EAC.

Initial scepticism in Chad

Two scenes spring to mind to illustrate both the state of mind of the Chadian people at the beginning and the need to create a trusting relationship with the public.

The first took place in September 2014 in Sarh, Southern Chad, on the border with the Central African Republic, in the governor's office. The Chadian team was crisscrossing the provinces to explain the work of the court. We encountered mostly scepticism. Fourteen years earlier, the first complaints had been filed in Dakar. The investigation of the case, then underway, was confidential and invisible. The victims no longer believed in the possibility of a trial and were still afraid of the former agents of the DDS.[8] Journalists stumbled over the meaning of the acronym 'EAC' and were telling us about the general lack of enthusiasm for the subject. Local representatives of civil society organizations were also wondering about the value of mobilizing victims for a case that some of them described as 'old and buried'.

When we arrived in Sarh, just as when we arrived anywhere, we went to introduce ourselves to the local authorities. The governor listened patiently to my presentation before he spoke: 'I'm going to tell you what everybody here is thinking. That story about trying Mr

[6] See also Mendy, in this volume, Chapter 9.

[7] Research Unit, International Center for Transitional Justice, *Outreach Strategies in International and Hybrid Courts: Report of the ICTJ-ECCC Workshop, Phnom Penh, March 3–5, 2000* (April 2010) https://www.ictj.org/sites/default/files/ICTJ-Outreach-ECCCWorkshop-Report-2010-English.pdf.

[8] Direction de la Documentation et de la Sécurité, Hissène Habré's security apparatus.

Hissène Habré is all very pretty, but nobody here really believes that he'll ever be judged. Here's what is going to happen. Some morning, we're going to hear on the radio that he died in his cell. End of story. And we won't see the likes of people like you again.' He said it with a smile, but his words really touched us. Anything could happen, and we weren't there to tell people whose dreams of justice had already been disappointed a hundred times that they should believe that a trial would happen this time. All we could do was to explain modestly what was happening, the procedures, the facts, and the history and functioning of the EAC, and to point victims towards associations that could help them participate. Perhaps to compensate for his frankness, the governor of Sarh elegantly helped us organize a public debate in the afternoon by providing a generator and fuel.

The following day an open dialogue session was organized with the victims. At a third meeting, with local associations, we explained what legal steps had already been taken, such as the detention of Mr Habré and the investigative missions from Chad. The representatives of the local associations quickly became more hopeful and in seven cities of Chad they formed coalitions that would pass on information to the local population. That same evening in Sarh, Arnaud Djimounoum, a journalist from the Lotiko community radio station, organized a live broadcast. This Sarh mission was a typical one, based on three pillars: local civil society partners,[9] local community radio stations,[10] and face-to-face meetings with both the public and victims.

At this stage, the inhabitants of Sarh had many questions: 'What have the EAC planned in terms of compensation for victims?' 'Why has it taken so long? Since the EAC was created, it's really dragged on!' 'What sort of broadcasting has been planned? During the Bokassa trial,[11] we had our ears glued to the radio, which broadcast the trial live. Will that happen with the EAC?' 'How can we give statements if we haven't done it yet?' 'Who's going to represent the victims and can we be certain that a minimum quota of victims will be able to attend the trial?' 'Many abuses have been attributed to the current president, Idriss Déby Itno, who headed up the army during the Habré regime—why isn't he being prosecuted? 'And if Mr. Habré dies—then what happens?'

With a rhythm of two to three round trips in the regions per year, the outreach team repeated these sessions, during which we engaged in a close relationship with the people.[12] With the local civil society coalitions and the community radios, some of which sent journalists to Dakar, in a lot of places Chadians had a number of trained interlocutors to help them understand, to inform them, and to express their concerns. But it wasn't until the release of the first images of the trial that perceptions really began to change. After that, interest grew exponentially, although the public never took anything for granted! Still in Sarh, at the height of public interest, a few days before the verdict, a showing of a filmed summary of the trial drew 2,000 captivated people one May evening at dusk in 2016, in the courtyard of the Don Bosco Center.

9 With a network of seventy organizations regrouped in coalitions in seven major cities.

10 Twelve community radio stations, chosen for the trust that local communities placed in them, passed on news on the EAC.

11 In 1987, in neighbouring Central African Republic.

12 In Sarh, but also in Moundou, Bongor, Mongo, Abéché and in N'Djamena, the capital. The consortium visited Massakory, Biltine, Ati, Pala, Doba, Moissala, Bedjondo, Koumra, Mataya, Guelendeng, and other cities, but less regularly.

Acceptance and disappointment

The second scene that demonstrated a 'qualitative' impact of the outreach program took place in May 2017, again in Sarh, in a crowded classroom in the same Don Bosco Center. The definitive judgement on appeal had been pronounced on 27 April 2017, in Dakar. It upheld a life sentence for Hissène Habré, who was also condemned to pay heavy individual compensations totalling 124 million euros.[13] More than 300 victims were at our meeting, all with the same question on their lips: am I on the list of 7,396 victims recognized by the EAC to receive financial reparations? After the satisfaction of the conviction came another period of waiting in Chad. People were polite, and thanked the outreach consortium for enabling them to follow the trial, but then followed the questions: 'Why are there so few recognized victims when the conclusions of the Chadian commission of enquiry[14] talked about 40,000 victims?' And the criteria retained by the EAC—to bring proof of identity or of affiliation—seemed inappropriate in a country whose administration was not particularly helpful and where papers were therefore difficult to obtain.

Emmanuel was there, leaning against a wall. He was a regular at the outreach sessions. A painter, he had survived the jails of the DDS. His narrow, pock-marked face evoked suffering and the passage of time. He was beside himself: 'I have only one question: when will I, Emmanuel, victim of arbitrary detention, receive my indemnity?' In a period of economic crisis in Chad, any unkept promise would be untenable. The outreach team explained that yes, there had been a ruling which at least had the benefit of being clear as to the amounts and as to the individuals beneficiaries. Yes, the decision attributed financial reparations, but to only some victims, and the total amount exceed the value of assets that Mr Habré was known to own. Yes, a trust fund for the victims was planned, but as yet it was neither created nor provided with funds. We answered directly without sugar-coating: 'I would love to be able to tell you otherwise, but I'm not going to lie to you Emmanuel. The money isn't there. There can be no reparations for the moment.' Emmanuel was disappointed—but oddly, he smiled, though anger and reproach weren't far off. An ability to accept born, no doubt, of the number of encounters we'd had and the trust we'd developed. Contrastingly, the following day in Bedjondo, a smaller, more isolated town where we had not been before, anger and frustration boiled over.

In a context of mass crimes, the expectations of the population can only vastly exceed the capacity of courts to judge (not all of the criminals will ever be judged) and to repair (not all of the victims will ever receive reparations). It's commonplace to present outreach as a means of 'managing' these expectations. The term is inelegant as it embraces expectations and memories that are the most painful for the victims. However, Emmanuel's temperate reaction, as compared with those of the inhabitants of Bedjondo, demonstrate the utility, both for the population and for the impact these trials can have on society, of ensuring long-term trusting relationships that make it possible for people to accept the court's decisions, especially as we know, from the start, that those decisions will never be able to fully meet people's expectations.

13 82,290 billion francs CFA.

14 Report of the National Commission of Enquiry. Chadian Ministry of Justice, *Les crimes et détournements de l'ex-président Habré et de ses complices* (L'Harmattan 1993). See also Abakar, in this volume, Chapter 2.

Favourable winds

For victims, the wait for a trial, a decision, and reparations will always be too long. Outreach can also 'manage' that wait by accompanying the population through the steps, thus providing meaning to what happens between mediatized moments. There it must be acknowledged that several factors facilitated our task. First, the fact that the trial followed a well-oiled civil law procedure over a duration that was humanly comprehensible: four months of trial with nearly 100 court witnesses and experts is astonishingly expeditious for international justice. Second, the fact that the trial was filmed by a Senegalese TV crew and transmitted via Internet and Chadian public television. Third, the fact that the trial was entirely public, without any in camera hearing even for the testimonials on sexual violence. Fourth, the fact that nearly a dozen Chadian and Senegalese journalists attended every day, each court session. All these elements contributed to the success of the outreach work and made the trial feel closer, more real, and more popular in people's eyes.

For the rest of Africa and the world, thanks as well to the powerful lobbying effort of Human Rights Watch, the Habré trial was much more visible than many others had been. In addition to our regular activities in Chad, Senegal, and Europe, our outreach experts travelled throughout Africa to answer questions from jurists, the media, and civil society[15] at meetings organized in nearly a dozen African countries.

In Chad, interest in the trial only grew after the first hearing. In Senegal, interest was already marked before, having been stirred up through a harsh public controversy: should anyone even try this elderly gentleman, appreciated in his neighbourhood, generous to religious organizations, integrated into the life of a country renowned for its *teranga* (hospitality), and who had caused no trouble whatsoever since his December 1990 exile? From the initial indictment, the media were giving the floor to his vituperative lawyer, El Hadji Diouf, once standing on top of a yellow taxi dressed in black robes, more often on television shows, hammering a self-styled 'pan African' argument: the West, led by France and the United States, who had long supported Habré before he distanced himself from them, were now financing this 'retaliatory' trial. Furthermore, he claimed, Chad's current strongman, who had overthrown Habré in December 1990, supported the trial by financing it. In Senegalese public opinion, however, that message was countered by an otherwise strong and significant social demand for political leaders to be held accountable for their actions. In the end, when discussion heated up over Friday fish and rice, most Senegalese concurred that at least the trial would give Habré the chance to defend himself.

Obstacles?

Unfortunately, Habré's defence team did not permit us to relay as fully as we wished their perspective in the case. Although we systematically invited them to participate to the outreach program on the same basis as the other parties to the trial, the defence equally systematically declined our invitations, without publicly saying why. We had to rely on statements made to the press to try and explain their positions to the public. Unfortunately, too, we had

[15] In Cotonou, Bangui, Tunis, Kampala, Kinshasa, Lubumbashi, Bujumbura, Johannesburg, Abidjan, and Yaoundé.

virtually no contact with the African Union which, while funding and being at the origin of the creation of the EAC, was remarkably discrete in its public support to the EAC. However, the fact that the EAC birth certificate was signed by AU raised the court legitimacy in the eyes of the African public, as the outreach could genuinely assess that this tribunal was not a creation of the West. Still on cooperation issues, in Chad or Senegal, we encountered no obstacles from authorities as we conducted out program and also none in any other African country.

Noted above was the importance given to outreach by the EAC at their creation in both budget and Statutes. Our only substantial obstacle to continuing our mission was, nonetheless, financial and administrative. At the end of the term of the contract signed with the outreach consortium, a term of twenty-one months (January 2014 to October 2015), the administration of the EAC did not renew it, which led to a one month suspension of the program in the middle of the trial. Our weekly syntheses that supplied information to the local associations and radio partners in the regions of Chad were suddenly cut off. Our staff was no longer paid and our international law expert had to leave for another project. The beautiful ideal of an outreach program conceived as an integral part of justice work drew the short straw. Despite their praise for the outreach outcomes, none of the EAC funders was able to intervene except for The Netherlands, which un-blocked an emergency grant that allowed us to resume and fulfil our mission for the duration of the trial and beyond, to explain the decision on reparations through the end of 2017, with the final year being funded by Belgium.

Conclusion

The points raised in the chapter were chosen to enlighten some of the lessons learned from this extraordinary experience of running an outreach program on an internationalized tribunal that has worked, a program partly inspired from previous ones but that was mostly quite innovative. Most interesting is the utility of an outsourced outreach model, dissociated from yet coordinating with public relations, delegated to local organizations with solid legitimacy and able to develop a program both close to people and rigorous in its ethics and management.

The trial of a former president on African soil within a reasonable time framework and the popularity of the intense struggle of Chadian victims fueled this successful and invigorating outreach program. In Chad, Senegal, elsewhere in Africa and Europe, the three members organizations of the consortium—RCN Justice & Démocratie, Primum Africa Consulting, and Magi Communications—and their local partners joined forces to ensure that this first inter-African tribunal was understood, explained, and debated, neutrally and transparently, and as close to the public as possible. Thus, even beyond its context, this experience supports the idea of outreach programs run by professionals outside heavy institutional structures, programs therefore more efficient, less expensive, and more able to come close to a public without fear or deference to provide information and facilitate a dialogue based on hard facts and not false hope, programs modestly and worthily aware that 'it will be long before the justice of men joins with true justice'.[16]

[16] Victor Hugo, *The Man Who Laughs* (1869) .

24

Covering Habré

The Diary of a Local Journalist

Ngoundji Dieng, Senegalese Journalist for The Quotidien

Ngoundji Dieng is a reporter with the newspaper Le Quotidien, an independent Senegalese newspaper. She began to follow the Hissène Habré case when the lawyers of the victims came to Dakar and organized press conferences with elements of Senegalese civil society—notably, the Rencontre Africaine pour la Défense des Droits de l'Homme (RADDHO)—to demand justice. At the time, the Senegalese weren't interested in the case, but she continued to cover on a regular basis, challenging a narrative that this was a case driven by international activists.

I was responsible for monitoring and covering all the news of the trial. I produced daily reports on the hearings. These reports were accompanied with analysis papers to allow our readers to better understand the decisions and operations taken by the EAC. For this purpose, interviews were made with experts, lawyers of the various partie, the prosecutor and specialists in international criminal law, who commented the hearing.

Hissène Habré had become Senegalese by adoption and was living holed up in his splendid villas in Ouakam and in Almadies. His neighbors said he was well-behaved, going to the mosque and participating discreetly in the life of the neighbourhood, far from the media. In general, the Senegalese only heard about Habré when the victims' lawyers came to Dakar to demand justice. This continued until the creation of the EAC, an ad hoc court within the Senegalese courts created by the African Union and mandated to try the former Chadian head of state. Shortly after its creation, the EAC detained and indicted him for war crimes and crimes against humanity. Not particularly interested in the Habré case until then, the Senegalese began to form opinions about the case. For some, Habré was a guest in Senegal and as such he should be left alone, especially as his behaviour was that of a very pious man acting in solidarity with his community. For others, particularly the pan-Africanists, the trial was inappropriate because they saw the hand of the West behind it. Others thought he should be held responsible for his acts. The debates were heated and passionate for months.

Just after he was detained and charged, the preliminary investigation began in N'djamena. As a journalist, my role was to inform the public. You'll agree that in such a climate handling information wasn't easy. Opinion was already deeply divided, and the allegations against Habré concerned events dating from 1982. Add to that the fact that the theatre of operations was thousands of kilometers away from Senegal, where the trial was to be held. But our editors had chosen to remain neutral, as always, and to remain as objective as possible, even if challenging.

Ngoundji Dieng, *Covering Habré* In: *The President on Trial*. First edition. Edited by: Sharon Weill, Kim Thuy Seelinger, and Kerstin Bree Carlson, Oxford University Press (2020). © Ngoundji Dieng. DOI: 10.1093/oso/9780198858621.003.0025

Covering the rogatory missions in N'djamena

It was necessary to look for information, to go into the field, to be the eyes and ears of our readers. This decision allowed us to go to N'djamena twice. I went to the capital of Chad during the first international rogatory mission with the judges, the prosecutor, and the whole EAC team. I was the only Senegalese journalist who made the trip—a privilege. My newspaper got it all first. For ten days, I passed on everything that happened in N'djamena. I shared with my readers the work of the judges and the prosecutors on the ground with my readers.

I was able to observe the investigating judges at work in the judicial pool in N'djamena. Even though I did not have access to the judges, the prosecutor was available and—without betraying the confidentiality of the investigations—he allowed me to obtain information for my reports. I learned what the victims expected from the trial, what their hopes were, etc. My trip also enabled me to show our readers sites that had been prisons during the Habré regime. I was even allowed to see the infamous prison, the 'Swimming Pool,' of the Documentation and Security Directorate (DDS). Photos showed that the Swimming Pool was the only place that remained untouched.

At the central commissariat, officers of the Chadian judicial police aided by members of the Criminal Investigation Division of Dakar began witness hearings. That was one of the moments that marked me the most during my stay in the capital. Victims came from all over the provinces, often having travelled hundreds of kilometers, to bear witness to what they had experienced; people whom I referred to in one article as 'the nation of victims.' I did stories, I described scenes, I relayed emotions.

I gave a voice to the victims. I also reported in an article entitled 'War of Associations' on the tensions between the different victims' groups. They had all demanded that Habré be tried, but their interests diverged. For some victims it was important to bring justice and to fight against the passivity of the state towards this case. For others, it was important to hold the trial and compensate the victims. I interviewed the prosecutor, Mbacké Fall, who spoke directly to our readers to explain the legal procedures and the charges against Hissène Habré. He also explained the status of the EAC and the different chambers that comprised the court. I also interviewed the Chadian Minister of Justice at the time, Jean Bernard Padaré, who explained the judicial cooperation accord between Senegal and Chad.

It was important for me to explain to the Senegalese, who were not involved in this case, how the judges had worked on Chadian soil. I had to explain, to analyse the procedure, clarify the challenges of cooperation between Senegal and Chad—the challenges and the limits of this cooperation.

During the third international rogatory commission, I remarked that, unlike during the first rogatory mission, the Chadians no longer seemed to believe in the trial. I was surprised to see that the Habré case did not spark political mobilization, even among the opposition. I learned during an interview I conducted with Saléh Kebzabo, one of the opposition leaders, that the opposition had taken no action. The press was not interested, either. I realized that the Habré Case was of more interest to Senegalese journalists than to Chadian ones. That surprised me enough that I commented on it in one of my articles.

Covering the trial

The coverage of the trial exposed us to criticism from the Habré camp. The lawyers for the defence who had made the decision not to collaborate with the EAC had also decided to declare war on us, refusing to talk to our paper despite multiple requests on our part. They rejected all the requests for interviews that we sent them. But we did not become discouraged. We maintained our neutrality during the hearings, of which I wrote accounts. I tried to reflect accurately what was happening in the courtroom. I gave a voice to the civil parties as well as the defence—a defence appointed by the court because Habré's own lawyers had chosen to boycott the trial.

I did not attend all the sessions because the trial endured over many months. But I arranged to cover the important moments, such as when a key witness was scheduled to testify. In addition to the reports on the proceedings, it was sometimes necessary to let an expert have his say, to take a moment to explain what was happening. For example, during the trial, several persons, including the Chairman of the Bar Association, expressed their regret at the absence of Idris Déby from the trial. I felt it useful to take a moment to allow experts to discuss the Déby case. Sometimes my articles explored a particular angle. I had noticed that all the witnesses before the bar were witnesses for the prosecution—every single one.[1] Not one witness failed to give testimony against the former Chadian president. I found that rather unusual and thought that the point deserved to be underlined. Only one witness was to be called by the defence and everyone was looking forward to hearing him. He'd really aroused my curiosity and attracted my interest. As a journalist, I thought 'phew, finally a witness in Habré's defence'. How great was my surprise, then, when this man started to tear into Hissène Habré. He said that Habré knew everything that was happening in the country, that he was at the heart of the killing machine. The next day, his testimony was on the front page of all the papers.

Everybody who was following the case knows what happened next as that man was one of the final witnesses before the judgment in the first instance.

[1] See also Ballal, in this volume, Chapter 14.

25
Prosecutions in Chad

Henri Thulliez, Human Rights Watch

Between August 2011 and March 2016, Henri Thulliez worked at Human Rights Watch (HRW) as Senior Coordinator for the Hissène Habré case. Working under the supervision of Counsel and Spokesperson Reed Brody, he did not belong to any usual department of HRW, such as the 'Africa' or 'International Justice' department. Within HRW's internal database, where the name of Thulliez's department should have appeared, it simply read 'Hissène Habré'. Thulliez was the only one to have the name of a former African dictator on his HRW badge, under his own name. This was representative of his work at HRW during that time, as he had to deal with every aspect of a human rights activist's job: documenting and investigating abuses, advocating, fundraising, communicating, liaising with local civil society groups, advising, travelling, etc. He became the behind-the-scenes man of the Habré case.

The EAC was created in 2012 and launched in 2013; the Senegalese prosecutors and judges were investigating between 2013 and 2014; the trials in Chad of Habré's accomplices began in December 2014; Habré's trial finally began in Senegal in July 2015. During those years, I travelled regularly to Chad to work with the victims and their lawyers. I was helping to consolidate the casefile, finding new evidence, and evaluating the testimony of victims who had not been interviewed in years. I was also helping the victims' associations get organized during the four investigatory missions carried out by the magistrates of the EAC in Chad. To our surprise, it was also during that time that the Chadian authorities decided to properly trigger the prosecutions against Habré's former henchmen.

The ripple effects of the EAC

The arrest in Dakar on 30 June 2013 of Hissène Habré and his indictment on 2 July created an electroshock back in Chad. On that day, the Chadian President Idriss Déby Itno appeared on Chadian national television to congratulate his 'brother', Senegalese President Macky Sall, the victims, and the NGOs. In one of his rare television appearances, Déby actually seemed weak, scared, and shaky as he finally declared and promised what the victims had been awaiting for years:

> *I ask Chadian Justice to prosecute everyone who participated to this macabre action. The moment will come when, the living and the dead will be indemnified by the Chadian Government. [. . .] The Chadian Justice and the Government will make themselves available for the magistrates who are appointed to prosecute Habré. No one should remain unpunished.*

Henri Thulliez, *Prosecutions in Chad* In: *The President on Trial*. First edition. Edited by: Sharon Weill, Kim Thuy Seelinger, and Kerstin Bree Carlson, Oxford University Press (2020). © Henri Thulliez. DOI: 10.1093/oso/9780198858621.003.0026

I do say no one. [. . .] Everyone who participated to this macabre work, the Chadian justice will come to you.[1]

Anyone who has followed recent Chadian history cannot help but grin at Idriss Déby Itno's hypocrisy and cynicism while reading or hearing these words. Déby helped Habré take power in 1982. He was then appointed as Chief of the Forces armées nationales tchadiennes (FANT) from 1983 to 1985. At a minimum, these forces committed atrocities in Southern Chad between June and September 1984 during a deadly period nicknamed 'Black September'. Déby, as Chief of the army, was regularly going to the South throughout that period. In 1985, after studying in France, he was replaced as Chief and became Habré's Defence and Security Adviser. In April 1989, during a repression conducted by the regime against his ethnic group, Déby fled to Sudan and launched a new rebellion to fight Habré, who was overthrown on 1 December 1990. Simply put, Déby could only be intimidated by the prospect of a trial of Habré and of his henchmen. Not only was he one of these henchmen, but he could be scared that information about his role—and perhaps his crimes—would come out of these proceedings.

While Déby and his government cooperated with the EAC by financing them and by letting EAC magistrates investigate in Chad, things became more complicated when the EAC started to look at prosecuting a few of Habré's henchmen who were living in Chad: Mahamat Djibrine 'El Djonto', Saleh Younous, and Zakaria Berdei.

Faced with this development, Déby and his government had three options. First, they could extradite these three people to Senegal and let them say whatever they wanted in open court—in which case, what would stop them from targeting Déby? Second, they could refuse to extradite them and do nothing—marginalizing Chad within the Habré case and with regard to international justice. Finally, they could organize the trial of Habré's accomplices in Chad, thereby controlling the narrative while also finally responding to the longstanding request of the victims. The authorities decided to pursue the third option, which we labelled the 'ripple effect' of the EAC.

Justice starts in Chad

As important as a foreign tribunal's trial of Habré would be, it was clear that it would not guarantee full justice to the victims of his regime nor would it permit Chadian society to confront its past before finally moving on. For over two decades, the victims had also struggled for justice back home—daring to file numerous criminal complaints, demanding reparations from the Chadian government, and speaking out against their many former oppressors.

In 1992, the National Truth Commission recommended the prosecution in Chad of those who participated in crimes during Habré's rule.[2] It also called for the officers of Habré's political police, the Documentation and Security Directorate (DDS), to be relieved of their state security duties, and for measures to be taken to honour the memory of the victims.

[1] 'Tchad: déclaration de Déby sur l'arrestation de Habré' (*Tchadinfos*, 1 July 2013) <https://www.youtube.com/watch?v=di9ZX5m8rKw> accessed 7 March 2018.

[2] See also Abakar, in this volume, Chapter 2.

In October 2000, seventeen victims lodged criminal complaints against named members of the DDS for a range of alleged crimes committed under Habré's rule, including assault and battery, torture, mass arrests, illegal and arbitrary detention, and cruel, inhuman and degrading punishment. The victims and their counsel had rushed to file this complaint to avoid the expiry of the ten-year statute of limitations provided for in Chadian legislation for such crimes. Even though most of the crimes committed during Habré's regime could be characterized as crimes against humanity, the Chadian authorities had not included the relevant provisions in national law.

The investigative judge initially found he did not have jurisdiction over the case,[3] but following appeal by the victims, Chad's Constitutional Court held in a landmark ruling that the cases could go forward.[4]

Investigations finally began in May 2001, after which dozens of other victims came forward to file their complaints against their direct torturers. As a precaution, the complaints were filed against *all* former members of the DDS, thereby allowing for any of them to be tried on indictment by the Chadian investigative judge.

The investigating judge then began hearing victims and seeking the testimony of the defendants, some of whom refused to appear before the judge. One of the defendants, Mahamat Wakaye, who was deputy director of national security under Habré, reportedly tore up his summons in front of the judge.[5] On the basis of these preliminary investigations, the Chadian courts indicted at least twenty-seven former DDS agents for 'premeditated murder, murder, arbitrary arrests and assault and battery'.[6]

All activities then stagnated and remained at a standstill for over a decade. During this period, the Chadian investigating judge repeatedly requested additional funding and personal protection in order to carry out the investigation. In May 2003, the Council of Ministers declared that it was 'ready to implement any action so as not to impede the path of justice',[7] but then did nothing to follow up on its commitment.[8]

In 2005, HRW published a report in which it found that the Truth Commission's recommendations remained largely ignored. HRW identified a priority list of 41 former mid-level and high-level DDS agents still holding key leadership or security positions in Chad. The Chadian government responded to the report by dismissing six of Habré's alleged accomplices from state security positions and wrote a letter to HRW committing to remove all alleged accomplices from government positions, to quickly consider a draft law to compensate Habré's victims, and to construct a monument in honour of the victims as soon as funding became available. Progress stalled there, however.

Then in 2013, promising developments in Chad followed in the wake of the launch of the EAC. On 14 May 2013, three months after the establishment of the EAC and forty-five days before Habré's arrest, one of his most notorious henchmen was arrested in Chad and

[3] Ordinance N° 135 of 23 November 2000 (First Investigative Chamber, Court of First Instance of N'Djamena, Chad)

[4] Decision N°002/PCC/SG/001 of 6 April 2001 (Constitutional Court, Chad)

[5] 'Chad: Submission to the Universal Periodic Review March 2013' (*HRW*, 17 October 2013) <http://www.hrw.org/news/2013/10/17/chad-submission-universal-periodic-review-march-2013> accessed 7 March 2018.

[6] HRW interview with Massingarel Kagah, Chief Prosecutor of N'Djamena, N'Djamena, 17 December 2013.

[7] 'Engagé à tout mettre en œuvre pour ne pas entraver le cours de la justice' 'Chad: The Victims of Hissène Habré Still Awaiting Justice' (2005) 17(10a) HRW <https://www.hrw.org/reports/2005/chad0705/chad0705.pdf> accessed 7 March 2018.

[8] See also: 'Chad: Government Promises Justice for Victims of ex-Dictator' (*HRW*, 25 August 2005) <http://www.hrw.org/news/2005/08/24/chad-government-promises-justice-victims-ex-dictator> accessed 7 March 2018.

placed in pretrial detention.[9] Nicknamed 'El-Djonto,' Mahamat Djibrine was chief of internal security and Coordinator of Documentation of the DDS and was listed by the Truth Commission as among Habré's 'most feared torturers.'[10] His arrest made the headlines of the national and international press.[11] After El Djonto's arrests, many more arrests ensued. The investigative judge Amir Abdoulaye Issa reopened the file, and on 4 September 2014 issued an order retaining twenty-one Habré-era officers for trial. After appeals by the Prosecutor, victims, and the Accused, twenty-nine former agents were indicted by the Indicting Chamber on 23 October 2014.[12]

The victims' lawyers and HRW feared that the Chadian government was trying to rush the case through without the attention and preparation it deserved, in order to justify the non-transfer of Younous and Djibrine to Dakar. Many of the complainants were not interviewed by the investigating judge, who also did not arrange for the standard meetings between the complainants and the defendants.

A hasty trial

The trial date was announced by the Prosecutor on 30 October 2014, just one week after the Indicting Chamber decision, giving all sides only two weeks to prepare for this important trial. The Indicting Chamber's decision referred twenty-nine persons for trial, but three had been listed by the investigating judge as deceased, another apparent sign of haste. A fourth accused could not be located. The name of another alleged torturer charged by the Investigating Judge and referred to the Indicting Chamber disappeared from the list for no apparent reason. The apparent haste and inconsistency suggest that the trial was probably organized solely to prevent the five individuals sought by the EAC from being sent to Senegal for trial. Chadian authorities also refused to let ex-agents who were not convicted travel, however.

The Indicting Chamber accused all twenty-nine persons of murder, torture, kidnapping, arbitrary detention, and assault and battery. The indictment drafted by the prosecutor was only twenty-eight pages long and was not precise, lacking detail and relying mainly on the Truth Commission's conclusions. The prosecutor did not insist on the role of each of the accused with regard to the crimes that were committed, and simply stated the positions of the accused at the time of Habré's regime.

All those accused had held positions within Habré's repressive administration: in the DDS and its armed branch, in the BSIR, in the National Security Agency, in the Army or in the 'Sécurité fluviale,' the organ in charge of surveilling the river Chari which marks

[9] See eg: 'Tchad: Arrestation d'un ancien tortionnaire du régime de Hissène Habré' (*20 minutes*, 15 May 2013) <https://www.20minutes.fr/monde/1156011-20130515-20130515-tchad-arrestation-ancien-tortionnaire-regime-Hissène-Habré> accessed 4 February 2013.
'Tchad: 'El Djonto,' tortionnaire sous le régime d'Hissène Habré, a été arrêté' (*RFI*, 15 May 2013) <http://www.rfi.fr/afrique/20130515-tchad-el-djonto-tortionnaire-sous-le-regime-Hissène-Habré-arrete-mahamat-djibrine-bourreau-torture> accessed 4 February 2014

[10] Chad National Commission of Inquiry, *Chad: Report of the Commission of Inquiry into the Crimes and Misappropriations Committed by Ex-President Habré, his Accomplices and/or Accessories*, 7 May 1992, p 43.

[11] 'Tchad: Arrestation d'un ancien tortionnaire du régime de Hissène Habré' (n 8).
'Tchad: "El Djonto," tortionnaire sous le régime d'Hissène Habré, a été arrêté' (n 8).

[12] 'Chronology of the Habré Case' (*HRW*, 27 April 2015) <https://www.hrw.org/news/2015/04/27/chronology-Habré-case https://www.hrw.org/news/2015/04/27/chronology-Habré-case > accessed 7 March 2018

the border between Chad and Cameroon. The DDS, as the main authority which perpetrated abuses, was the most represented and almost all the accused had spent some time working there.

Besides El Djonto, the most notorious of the accused was Saleh Younouss, former head of the DDS between 1983 and 1987, Nodjigoto Haunan, former director of the National Security Agency implicated in the repression of the Zaghawa ethnic group, and Khalil Djibrine, former department head of the DDS in the south of Chad during the southern repression of 1983–1984.

On 14 November 2014, the trial began with great fanfare—the trial took place in the big hall of the former National Assembly building. Many Chadian journalists showed up and hundreds of victims queued—but also with a certain tension. Some of the accuseds' family members tried to intimidate victims, dozens of security agents and soldiers—some of whom were heavily armed—were present, and people were searched for phones, cameras, pens or pieces of paper. Only State journalists and cameras were allowed to cover the sessions. The Chadian government was in control.

The trial was suspended a few days later on 21 November due to a lawyers' strike, with the Chadian Bar Association demanding $84 million in owed judgments and fees. (It is important to note that Chadians lawyers generally work in very poor conditions with a 'courthouse' located in an abandoned building of N'Djamena and with hearings taking place in the yard.)

When the trial resumed on 23 December hundreds of Chadians attended it daily, and it was summarized each day on the evening news.[13] The defendants for the most part denied any brutality, and the hasty investigation meant that no real record was prepared and new plaintiffs came forward each day—to the loud complaints of the defendants' lawyers. In addition, because the court had strangely called only one outside witness, it was sometimes the survivor's word against the agent's.

On 22 March 2015, the court gave its decision, read out to a completely silent audience of about 400 people by Court President Timothée Yénan. Twenty of the accused agents were convicted, while four were acquitted. The court additionally ordered that the Chadian Government and the convicted persons pay $125 million in reparations to over 7,000 victims. The court ordered that the government erect a monument within a year, in recognition of those who were killed under Habré's regime. Finally, it ordered that the former DDS headquarters be turned into a museum. These were both among the long-standing demands of the victims' associations.

A moment of truth for the victims

While the trial in Chad could be seen as a kind of a warm-up for the main event, that being Habré's own trial which started a few months later, it was also a moment of truth and justice for the victims.

Seeing their torturers in court and standing up for hours listening to the survivors' testimonies had a healing effect according to the victims I interviewed. Habré remained

[13] 'Peines de prison pour les complices du procès de Hissein Hab' (*Tchadinfos*, 26 March 2015) <https://www.youtube.com/watch?v=VriUo3xtDP8> accessed 7 March 2018.

silent during his own trial, but his accomplices did talk during the hearings in Chad. Even if most of them refused to acknowledge the facts or their own responsibility—sometimes even denying that their names were written on the DDS archives that victims' lawyers presented—they did target the former President as the main man in charge and as the most accountable person. Amid the outpouring of heart-wrenching stories, the defendants appeared to be having difficulty defending themselves. Saleh Younouss, former Director of the DDS, claimed to be the victim of 'a genuine set-up' and placed all responsibility on Habré's shoulders: 'We received orders directly from the head of state,' he testified. Nodjigoto Haunan accused human rights organizations of paying the victims to lodge complaints, provoking a wave of laughter in the courtroom.

Their testimonies, however, did serve to clarify the structure of the political police, the use of fear that prevailed as a governing method, and links to foreign secret services that existed. As Younouss explained, 'we had a strong relationship with the Direction Générale de la sécurité intérieure (DGSE), the CIA, the Mossad and the Sudanese services.'

The audience was largely composed of the victims themselves, whereas the audience for the trial in Dakar was mostly made of Senegalese people and other foreigners. When the Presiding Judge would order Mahamat Djibrine El Djonto to stand up very straight as if he was a kid, all the victims would laugh. The survivors could freely express their anger. 'They appear to be men, but really they are devils who created a hell,' roared torture survivor Robert Hissein Gambier in court, proclaiming, 'The dead must have justice.' Dozens of victims like Gambier could speak up during the trial to describe their suffering.

I remember the first victim who took the floor. His name was Oumar Goudja. He was a wealthy businessman from the Zaghawas ethnic group. In April 1989, as Hissène Habré's government was conducting a campaign of repression against Zaghawas, he was arrested in front of his family by the DDS. Goujda's pregnant wife was seized with panic and rushed to the hospital where she lost her child that very night. She would not see her husband again until his release from prison twenty months later.

At trial, looking straight at Nodjigoto Haunan, Goudia shouted: 'they owe me a child, they're going to pay for what happened to my child!' Following his arrest, Goudia was bound to a chair for five days and subjected to electric shocks before being locked up in inhumane conditions for months afterward. 'I watched Nodjigoto Haunan order his staff to torture me,' he said. 'He was smoking a cigarette and asking me questions. I saw the viciousness in his eyes.' But Haunan refused to admit that he even knew Oumar Goudja.

One of the only witnesses to be called to testify was Mahamat Hassan Abakar, the president of Chad's 1992 National Truth Commission. He told the court that 'torture was systematic' in the DDS: 'the DDS agents were supermen because they enjoyed total impunity. Once you were arrested by the DDS you had no recourse.'[14] Just an hour prior to the presentation of this testimony, many in the courtroom had wept at the screening of the video produced by the Commission, showing a series of mass graves, the inside of Habré's jails, drawings of the main forms of torture, and footage of emaciated prisoners released after Habré's fall, some of whom were present in the courtroom that day. In the courtroom, the deterrent effects of justice were soon apparent: security forces watched carefully as, one after another, their former bosses attempted to clear themselves. Nearly all the defendants were policemen by

[14] See also Abakar, in this volume, Chapter 2.

training who, after their time with Habré, had been recycled by the current administration of President Déby into the roles they knew best: director of public security, head of counter-intelligence, chief police commissioner, head of police investigations, and the like.

Conclusion

More than two and a half years after this trial, what I remember the most is the joy of the victims on the day of the verdict. When the presiding judge stopped reading the decision, some remained seated quietly, not believing what they had just heard. Others just stood up, shouting in happiness, clapping their hands and embracing each other.

A few minutes later, all the victims gathered with their three courageous Chadian lawyers, Jacqueline Moudeïna, Delphine Djiraibé, and Soulgan Lambi. All these people from different ethnic groups, different ages, and different religions were singing and dancing. All had been waiting for this moment for twenty-five years. Here, in that particular moment, I could really witness and understand the true power of justice, its healing effect.

Weeks later though, everyone who had fought for this transitional justice effort became disillusioned. The Chadian government never paid the reparations to the victims, nor did it help to erect a monument or turn the DDS Headquarters into a museum. For Habré's trial in Senegal, Chadian authorities continually refused to send DDS accomplices, convicted or not, to testify before the EAC. Also, they never responded to the EAC's request to have them testify via video conference, although this latter system was put in place for victims who could not travel to Senegal.

This refusal by Chadian authorities and the hasty way in which the national trial was dealt with can be interpreted as suggesting the trial was a tactic meant to prevent these insiders from telling their stories, and perhaps targeting Déby, in open court. That said, the Chadian trial was a positive step towards justice for the victims who finally managed to knock these torturers off their pedestals. After years of intimidation and being forced to watch them walk freely in the streets and work in police stations, the victims finally succeeded in seeing these torturers condemned.

A few months after the end of the trial, victims reported that some of the accused had been freed and were back in N'Djaména. The Chadian authorities denied this allegation. One of them, Mahamat Wakaye, against whom Jacqueline Moudeïna had filed a suit for torture in 2000, had been Habré's former deputy director of national security. In 2001, Jacqueline Moudeïna was the victim of a hand-grenade attack while she was participating in a non-violent women's demonstration in the streets of N'Djaména to protest the results of the Chadian presidential election. The police squad responsible for the attack was commended by Mahamat Wakaye, who, at that time, was the Director of the Judicial Police.[15] During the trial, when Moudeïna was defending victims who were targeting Wakaye, she remained calm and strong. For this icon of dignity, the proceedings were 'a necessary step toward reconciliation in Chad, for an end to impunity, and above all else, so that the crimes of the past will never be repeated'.[16]

[15] See also Moudeïna, in this volume, Chapter 15.

[16] Henri Thulliez, 'Chad: Torture Survivors Finally Get Their Day in Court' *The Huffington Post* (4 December 2014) <https://www.huffingtonpost.com/henri-thulliez/chad-torture-survivors-fi_b_6269698.html> accessed 7 March 2018.

26

Academia as Partner in the Habré Trial

Érick Sullivan and Fannie Lafontaine, Université Laval, Faculty of Law[1]

Université Laval's students and researchers have been involved in different ways in the strategic litigation of the Habré case. Training was providedto the EAC's prosecution team by professors of the Laval University Faculty of Law in Canada. A partnership was established between the International Criminal and Humanitarian Law Clinic (the 'Clinic') and HRW, which was supporting the victims. Students published blogposts and papers on the Habré case, including (for a time) the only available written version of the Trial Chamber's judgment, typed live as it was rendered orally. Conferences were organized and were largely discussed in mainstream media, raising awareness of the case with broad audiences, etc. Through all these activities, academics and students supported practitioners involved in the Habré case, who in turn provided research insight to academics as well as learning opportunities to students, which often also helped them get their first professional activity in the international law arena.

The *Habré* case is a landmark prosecution of a former African head of state by an institution based in Africa, created and administered by Africans, that offered justice to African victims. It lasted many years and was debated in five different jurisdictions. It mobilized a large number of stakeholders and cost billions of dollars. This case is mainly considered as a great achievement for international criminal justice and for Africa. It is also a good example of a promising trend in strategic litigation: engaged partnership between academia and practitioners to contribute to strengthening access to justice for victims of international crimes. This chapter offers a perspective on these promising directions in legal academia and strategic litigation in light of Université Laval's multifaceted involvement in the *Habré* trial.

Changing law and society with strategic litigation

According to many, the *Habré* case was strategic litigation.[2] It was debated in two national jurisdictions (Senegal and Belgium), at the Committee against Torture, and at the International Court of Justice. All these procedures were engaged to prosecute Hissène Habré and to provide justice and reparation to his victims. It was also done to fight against

[1] This chapter was partially supported by the Canadian Partnership for International Justice and the Social Sciences and Humanities Research Council of Canada.

[2] Annemie Schaus et al, *Strategic Litigation: Using Courts Achieve Social Change? Fighting Poverty and Impunity in Judicial Arenas* (Projet avancé 2014–2019) 9 <http://arc-strategic-litigation.ulb.ac.be/wp-content/uploads/2016/11/ARC_Descriptif_complet-1.pdf> accessed 1 May 2019.

Érick Sullivan and Fannie Lafontaine, *Academia as Partner in the Habré Trial* In: *The President on Trial*. First edition. Edited by: Sharon Weill, Kim Thuy Seelinger, and Kerstin Bree Carlson, Oxford University Press (2020). © Érick Sullivan and Fannie Lafontaine.
DOI: 10.1093/oso/9780198858621.003.0027

impunity of international crimes and to encourage Africans to prosecute their own wrongful leaders. These strategic litigations led to the creation of the EAC where Habré was prosecuted and convicted. But what is a strategic litigation?

This '(mainly) US-originated practice',[3] also known as public interest litigation, 'human rights litigation, […] test case litigation, impact litigation, social action litigation, and social change litigation',[4] is not a new legal and social phenomenon. Indeed, for example, 'both England and Scotland have a long history going back at least to the late 18th century of litigation by pressure groups for a political goal. Slavery was successfully challenged in both jurisdictions by cases taken as part of the anti-slavery movement'.[5] Similarly, '[i]n the American struggle for social justice, public interest litigation has [also] played an indisputably important role'.[6] In that country, '[t]he public interest law movement that emerged in the 1960s and 1970s advanced this vision of court-centered social change, drawing on models from civil rights and civil liberties groups'.[7]

Generally led by civil society organizations or human rights lawyers[8] in the human rights field, it is presented as 'part of exercising the right of access to justice'[9] in order to ask for 'the effective fulfillment of human rights, ordered by national or international courts of justice'.[10] Strategic litigation is also described as the 'practice of taking an emblematic case to court to provoke broader changes in law and society in line with certain collective ideals or values',[11] but also to contribute to the fight against impunity for human rights through the criminal sanction or through other legal actions of another nature.[12] Such litigation aims at producing a social impact through law by challenging the existing legal framework, reinforcing judicial institutions, supporting the development and implementation of laws and interpretations that favour the full respect of human rights while provoking a public debate and a civic education.

The implementation of a strategic litigation with broad legal and social objectives notably requires the development of partnerships and strategic alliances.[13] These improve the capacity of litigators to face the numerous issues that will arise in the course of their litigation (funding, evidence collection, knowledge of the applicable law, human resources, threats

[3] Ana Milena Coral-Díaz, Beatriz Londoño-Toro, and Lina Marcela Muñoz-Ávila, 'El concepto de litigio estratégico en América Latina: 1990–2010' (2010) 121 Vniversitas Bogotá (Colombia) 49, 53; see also Charles J Ogletree and Randy Hertz, 'The Ethical Dilemmas of Public Defenders in Impact Litigation Colloquium' (1986) 14(1) New York University Review of Law and Social Change 23.

[4] James A Goldston, 'Public Interest Litigation in Central and Eastern Europe: Roots, Prospects, and Challenges' (2006) 28(2) Human Rights Quarterly 492 at 496.

[5] Roger Smith, 'Experience in England and Wales: Test Case Strategies, Public Interest Litigation, the Human Rights Act, and Legal NGOs' (2003) 1 <http://www.essex.ac.uk/armedcon/story_id/000696.pdf> accessed 6 February 2020.

[6] Scott L Cummings and Deborah L Rhode, 'Public Interest Litigation: Insights from Theory and Practice' (2009) 36(4) Fordham Urban Law Journal 603 at 604.

[7] ibid.

[8] Schaus (n 2) at 3.

[9] R Yrigoyen, *El litigio estratégico en derechos humanos*, 4 (Informe para la Fundación Soros sobre litigio estratégico en Guatemala, Guatemala, 2007), cited in Coral-Díaz, Londoño-Toro, and Muñoz-Ávila, (n 4) at 53.

[10] Yrigoyen, *El litigio estratégico en derechos humanos*, cited in Coral-Díaz, Londoño-Toro, and Muñoz-Ávila, (n 47) at 53.

[11] Schaus(n 4).

[12] Avocats sans frontières Canada, *Le litige stratégique : un outil de défense et de promotion des droits humains* (Bamako 2018) 5.

[13] Catherine Corey Barber, 'Tackling the Evaluation Challenge in Human Rights: Assessing the Impact of Strategic Litigation Organisations' (2012) 16(3) International Journal of Human Rights 411 at 417; Helen Duffy, *Strategic Human Rights Litigation: Understanding and Maximising Impact* (Hart Publishing 2018) 248–49.

to personal, etc.). Building on their network, the strategic litigators will be in a position to implement an integrated plan of strategic litigation which may include strategies to protect stakeholders, to communicate and advocate, to develop stakeholders' capacity, to empower affected victims and communities, etc.

As in many other strategic litigation launched around the world,[14] partnerships and alliances were developed in the *Habré* case, for instance: HRW and the International Federation for Human Rights (FIDH) with its affiliated networks (in Senegal: the *Organisation nationale des droits de l'Homme*; in Chad: the *Ligue tchadienne des droits de l'Homme*) merged their efforts to support the *Association des victimes des crimes et répressions politiques* (AVCRP). In this case, it was necessary to rely on a large number of organizations whose resources were complementary. For example, the FIDH had a large network in Africa, but less funding, while HRW had never worked before in the *Habré* case in Chad nor in Senegal, but had important financial resources. They were also looking for help to provide information on law and case law which they found notably at the Harvard's Human Rights Law School and at Université Laval.[15]

Clinical Education and Researchers as Partners in Strategic Litigation

In contexts such as the *Habré* litigation, strategic litigators can turn to many potential partners. Among them are law faculties offering clinical legal education. Clinical legal education 'is a legal teaching method based on experiential learning'.[16] In general, 'students are confronted with problem situations of the sort that lawyers confront in practice'.[17] They are linking, on the one hand, members of the communities, their lawyers and supporting civil society organizations and, on the other hand, students and their supervisors, who are often professors and researchers at their law faculties. Through such a structure, both practitioners and academics can co-create innovative solutions and practical tools that directly serve the practice of community or legal actors while providing a highly valuable education to law students. In this way, research is informed by practice and practice is informed by research.

Université Laval's researchers and students' involvement in the *Habré* case

Since 2013, Université Laval's students and researchers have been involved in different ways in the strategic litigation of the *Habré* case. Training was provided to the EAC's prosecution

[14] See, for example, the emblematic cases of Lawyers Without Borders Canada (https://www.asfcanada.ca/projet/resultats-emblematiques/), accessed 6 February 2020.

[15] Julien Seroussi, 'L'affaire Hissène Habré. Une justice transitionnelle internationalisée' (2008) 53(1) Mouvements 131 at 134; Julien Seroussi, 'L'internationalisation de la justice transitionnelle : l'affaire Hissène Habré' (2006) 30(1) Critical International 83 at 86, 98, and 134

[16] European Network for Clinical Legal Education (ENCLE), 'Definition of a Legal Clinic' (*ENCLE*) <http://encle.org/about-encle/definition-of-a-legal-clinic>. accessed on 6 February 2020.

[17] Robert Dinerstein, 'Report of the Committee on the Future of the In-House Clinic' (1992) 42 Journal of Legal Education 508 at 511.

team by professors of the Faculty of Law; a partnership was established between Laval's Clinic and HRW, which was supporting the victims; students published blogposts and papers on the *Habré* case, including (for a time) the only available written version of the Trial Chamber's judgment, typed live as it was rendered orally; conferences were organized and were largely discussed in mainstream media, raising awareness of the case with broad audiences, etc. Through all these activities, academics and students supported practitioners involved in the *Habré* case, who in turn provided valuable research insight to academics as well as highly effective and interesting learning opportunities to students, which often also helped them get their first job or internship in the international law arena.

This section presents these implications, notably the innovative mobilization of its Faculty of Law's Clinic.

Training course

In 2013, the then Counsel-Team Leader of the *Crimes Against Humanity and War Crimes Section* at Justice Canada, Mr Robert Petit, was sent by Canada to the EAC's *Parquet général* to provide support during the investigation, considering his previous experience as prosecutor at the Extraordinary Chambers in the Courts of Cambodia. At that time, the needs of the five talented prosecutors of the *Parquet* were numerous, as they had not been involved in such international criminal law case before.[18]

In this context, one of Petit's terms of reference was to look out for (unexpensive) potential sources that can offer technical assistance and training in French.[19] As of 2013, he and Professor Fannie Lafontaine exchanged numerous correspondence to concretize this project. The possibility to organize on-site training sessions and to draft legal memoranda,[20] which are classical examples of the implementation of universities' community engagement mission, were discussed, but considering the limited budget of the EAC, it was difficult to bring experts in Dakar (Senegal) for an extensive training session. Therefore, with the technical assistance of the Canadian Embassy in Dakar, which accepted to provide their technical capacities,[21] the training session took place on 21–22 May 2013 by videoconference linking Québec City (Lafontaine and Professor Julia Grignon), Ottawa (Petit), and Dakar (the EAC' Prosecutors team composed of the General Prosecutor Fall and three of his Deputies: Youssoupha Diallo, Ante Ndiaye Diop, and Moustapha Ka).[22]

The topics were decided in full collaboration with the General Prosecutor, who expressed his main interests and principal needs. The Prosecutor initially wished the training to address three points: the chapeau elements of crimes against humanity (attack; widespread or systematic; civilian population) and the applicable *mens rea*; the constitutive elements of war crimes, especially the distinction between internal and international armed conflicts,

[18] Reed Brody, *L'affaire Hissène Habré : Le combat des victimes pour traduire leur dictateur en justice* (Brot für die Welt 2017) at 36.

[19] Robert Petit, *Correspondence between Robert Petit and Fannie Lafontaine—11 March 2013.*

[20] Robert Petit and Fannie Lafontaine, *Correspondence between Robert Petit and Fannie Lafontaine—11–22 March 2013.*

[21] Robert Petit, *Correspondence between Robert Petit and Fannie Lafontaine—22 March 2013.*

[22] Mbacké Fall, *Correspondence between Mbacké Fall and Fannie Lafontaine—21 May 2013.*

the violations of Additional Protocols to the Geneva Conventions, as well as the concept of 'protected population'; and command responsibility.[23]

The training team raised the opportunity to address other topics such as sexual and gender based violence, the sources of international law, and the evidence of international crimes.[24] The Prosecutor confirmed his interest for the format and subjects, including his specific interest in command responsibility for sexual crimes and in how to go up the chain of command.[25] The official training program also included a new segment on the crime of torture as a specific crime in international law, as well as a much more detailed analysis of few additional modes of criminal liability in international law (perpetrator liability, joint criminal enterprise, co-perpetration, indirect perpetration, and complicity).[26]

The clinic's mobilization

The Clinic at Université Laval started its activities in 2008 and became more formalised in 2010. It recruits students every semester, all year long, who have a background in law or in international studies and who are enrolled in bachelors, masters or doctorate programs. The Clinic then selects the candidates and matches them to a professional partner based on their interests, their training and language skills. Professionals are free to give students any mandate they wish within the general mandate of the Clinic. The Clinic's *leitmotiv* is to adapt its activities to the specific needs of its partners, and students execute the mandate according to the practitioner's indications and under the supervision of the Clinic's supervision, at Université Laval. Since its creation, the Clinic has trained over 400 students and has partnered with more than thirty partners in international institutions, NGOs and lawyers working on strategic litigation.

At the early stage of the ad hoc collaboration between Université Laval and the EAC's *Parquet général*, Lafontaine also suggested using the services of the Clinic and Petit accepted to include it in its recommendation to the *Parquet* in 2013.[27]

Lafontaine raised this possibility with Prosecutor Fall in April 2013 while discussions were ongoing on the possibility to organize the course.[28] 'Through this structure', she explained to the Prosecutor, 'qualified students would perform tasks the Prosecutors would entrust them, like researching, participating in the drafting of legal documents or reports, and analysing facts, under the close supervision of the Clinic's directors'.[29]

Fall considered the idea, but expressed the need for longer and full-time involvement, and invited Lafontaine to recommend very good volunteering students that can be deployed for a short stay to his office as interns within the international technical assistance program supporting the EAC.[30] A student from Université Laval performed a six-month

[23] Robert Petit, *Correspondence between Robert Petit and Fannie Lafontaine—25 March 2013.*

[24] Fannie Lafontaine, *Correspondence between Mbacké Fall and Fannie Lafontaine—7 April 2013.*

[25] Mbacké Fall, *Correspondence between Mbacké Fall and Fannie Lafontaine—16 April 2013.*

[26] Fannie Lafontaine, *Plan de formation—V2* (2013); Fannie Lafontaine, Julia Grignon, and Robert Petit, *Formation en droit international pénal : Plan de cours* (unofficial document, 2013).

[27] Robert Petit, *Correspondence between Robert Petit and Fannie Lafontaine—19 March 2013.*

[28] Lafontaine (n 24).

[29] ibid.

[30] Mbacké Fall, *Correspondence between Mbacké Fall and Fannie Lafontaine—8 April 2013*; Mbacké Fall, *Correspondence between Mbacké Fall and Fannie Lafontaine—10 April 2013.*

independent internship with the *Parquet* in 2014.[31] This is another way to engage in the community, as student placements is one of many 'sophisticated tools for fostering third mission activities and knowledge and dissemination and transfer'.[32]

Two months after the course, Reed Brody, the legal counsel and spokesperson for HRW, heavily involved in the *Habré* case since its beginning, asked whether the Clinic would support the Civil Parties through his organization. There was 'an enormous amount of legal work to do' in French to improve the capacity of the Civil Parties to argue Habré's challenges, help put together the victims' case, and support their lawyers in Dakar. Obviously, this potential collaboration was impossible if the Clinic or its directors were to further their collaboration with the *Parquet* or to develop additional training courses for the judges. However, all collaboration with the *Parquet* was over and there was no other collaboration envisaged with, for instance, the EAC's instruction judges. The Clinic, HRW and the Civil Parties thus started collaborating in September 2013.

During the five years that lasted this collaboration in the framework of the *Habré* case (2013–2017), twenty-eight undergraduate and graduate students in Law and International Studies were recruited, trained and supervised. For the most part, they had to research the law and case law in various legal systems to draft research memoranda that were then sent to HRW's team, who verified their content, provided feedback and processed the documents through their own channels to the Civil Parties and their lawyers.

Overall, fifteen legal memoranda were produced by the students. They provided information on many topics depending on the legal challenges that were ongoing at this period. Students researched on Senegal's international obligations, including towards ECOWAS's Court of Justice and the African Union. They looked at the procedural law of the ECOWAS's Court of Justice as well as of the EAC. They also conducted research on some of the substantial crimes contained in the EAC's Statute. Their research also focused on other topics such as '*grâce*', disjunction, *in absential* trial, prescription, legal representation of victims, interlocutory appeals, court-appointed counsels, and reparations, for example.

In 2016, students were also mobilized to produce a written transcription of the judgement the EAC's Trial Chamber was partially reading at loud during an online broadcasted audience. Until the release of the official written decision by the EAC, this unofficial summary was the only available document reporting quite extensively the Chamber's decision. It was especially important for the Civil Parties, as it helped disseminate this important precedent for international criminal justice when nothing else was available.

Other relevant activities

In addition to these two main projects, other activities were undertaken at Université Laval as part of its community engagement mission.

[31] International Criminal and Humanitarian Law Clinic, 'La Clinique: une porte ouverte sur le monde!' (*Clinique de droit international pénal et humanitaire* (*CDIPH*, 19 March 2014) <https://www.cdiph.ulaval.ca/fr/actualites-de-la-clinique/la-clinique-une-porte-ouverte-sur-le-monde> accessed the 31 May 2019. A second former member of the Clinic, Élise Le Gall, followed Marie Lugaz and became a legal collaborator of the *Parquet* in January 2015. See also, Le Gall, in this volume, Chapters 18–19.

[32] Patricio Montesinos et al, 'Third Mission Ranking for World Class Universities: Beyond Teaching and Research' (2008) 33(2) Higher Education in Europe 259 at 270.

In April 2016, a conference was organized at Université Laval[33] by the Clinic in partnership with the Canada Research Chair on International Criminal Justice and Human Rights, HRW, Avocats sans frontières Canada ('ASFC'), and the project *Droit et cinéma*. At this occasion, Reed Brody presented to a broad audience a lecture on the *Habré* trial after the screening of Pierre Hazan's film, *Chasseur de dictateurs*.

At this moment, an exclusive meeting with the press was also organized.[34] It was opened by the *Batonnière de Québec*, Ms Catherine Claveau, and titled *Au coeur de la chasse aux dictateurs et criminels de guerre*. During this meeting, Reed Brody (HRW), Pascal Paradis (president of ASFC) and Lafontaine were interviewed by many local and national media. The speakers talked about the *Habré* case as well as of other strategic litigations such as the *Duvalier, Pinochet* and *Ríos Montt* cases, in which HRW and ASFC worked, often with the support of the Clinic.

The *Habré* case was discussed in blogposts written by students on *Quid Justitiae*, formerly known as the *International Criminal and Humanitarian Law Clinic's Blog*.[35] These posts addressed the trial of Hissène Habré, the jurisdiction of the EAC, and the victims' perspectives. They were interesting and appreciated sources of information for the *Quid Justitiae*'s readers and had the advantage of providing free access legal analysis to a broad francophone audience worldwide.

Through all these activities, academia supported practitioners involved in the *Habré* case, who in turn provided highly effective and interesting learning opportunities to students, which often also helped them get their first job or internship in the international law arena, including in the *Habré* case itself.

Conclusion

During the five years that lasted Université Laval's involvement in the *Habré* case, academics and students alongside practitioners undertook numerous activities. All of them are examples of how academia can provide education and high quality scientific research outputs while developing exchange relationships with practitioners, generating knowledge of mutual benefit based on a shared assumption that some learning or discovery outcomes require access to external entities with distinctive knowledge and expertise.

33 International Criminal and Humanitarian Law Clinic, 'Reed Brody: l'affaire Habré', (*Clinique de droit international pénal et humanitaire (CDIPH)*, 6 April 2016) <https://www.cdiph.ulaval.ca/fr/activites-a-venir/reed-brody-laffaire-habre>.

34 Ian Bussières, 'Bush ciblé par le "chasseur de dictateurs"', *Soleil Qué* (6 April 2016) <https://www.lesoleil.com/actualite/bush-cible-par-le-chasseur-de-dictateurs-2fd202e3020f91a048ef7d98ef32c8a4>.

35 Hugo Moudiki Jombwe, 'Chronique juridique: Affaire Hissein Habré devant les Chambres africaines extraordinaires. Quelques questionnements soulevés à l'ouverture du procès' (*Quid Justitiae*, 23 September 2015) <https://www.quidjustitiae.ca/blogue/chronique-juridique-affaire-hissein-habre-devant-les-chambres-africaines-extraordinaires> accessed 1 May 2019; Raymond Ouigou Savadogo, 'Les Chambres africaines extraordinaires: compétence, définition des crimes, modes de responsabilité et participation des victimes' (*Quid Justitiae*, 23 April 2013) https://www.quidjustitiae.ca/blogue/les-chambres-africaines-extraordinaires-competence-definition-des-crimes-modes-de accessed 1 May 2019; Marie Lugaz, 'Une perspective de justice pour les victimes de Hissène Habré après plus d'une décennie de procrastination sénégalaise' (*Quid Justitiae*, 15 November 2012) <https://www.quidjustitiae.ca/blogue/une-perspective-de-justice-pour-les-victimes-de-hissene-habre-apres-plus-dune-decennie>; Pascale Langlais, 'Une journée dans l'univers d'Hissène Habré - Récit d'une journée d'audience aux Chambres Africaines Extraordinaires' (*Quid Justitiae*, 4 December 2015) https://www.quidjustitiae.ca/blogue/une-journee-dans-lunivers-dhissene-habre-recit-dune-journee-daudience-aux-chambres-africaines accessed 1 May 2019.

This collaboration demonstrated how legal clinics can be used as a hub bridging academia and community in the context of strategic litigation. Through them, researchers' outputs are feeding strategic litigators, and practitioners' applied knowledge is feeding the researchers' agenda, thus allowing both to co-create innovative arguments that will be used in strategic litigation to achieve the expected long-lasting impact on law and society.

Université Laval's clinical activities with community partners nurtured the creation, in 2016, of a vast partnership between twenty-four academics and practitioners and twelve universities and NGOs.[36] This novel partnership structure hosted at Université Laval links academic researchers, legal clinics and NGO partners across Canada to work on an interdisciplinary research program that has both international and Canadian dimensions comprised of three main axes that pertain to different and complementary routes that victims of international crimes can take in Canada, in other states and before international institutions, to seek criminal, civil, and administrative or other remedies.

The *Habré* case is a landmark in international justice and in the exercise of national criminal jurisdiction to fight impunity for atrocity crimes. It also is a prime example of how true partnerships between academia and civil society actors can bring about real change and contribute to strengthening access to justice for victims. This modern interpretation of the community engagement mission of universities is, we think, the only way forward.

[36] Canadian Partnership for International Justice, 'About the Canadian Partnership for International Justice' <https://cpij-pcji.ca/> accessed 1 May 2019.

PART II

REFLECTIONS ON THE SIGNIFICANCE OF THE HABRÉ CASE AND BEYOND

For this part of the book, we asked academics in the field of international criminal law to consider the importance of the Hissène Habré case. We have grouped the expert contributions according to their particular positionalities towards international criminal law. As discussed in the introduction of the book, by positionality we mean how the authors stand in relation to international criminal law. We have identified four themes. First, we have collected those authors who consider international criminal law organically and who conduct structural inquiries on the field, its institutions and actors (section A). Next, we have gathered those contributions that take international criminal law as their focus, but which make normative or practice-based assessments (section B). The next section gathers authors who question what should be included in international criminal law, by (re)imagining it to include excluded voices, norms, or practices (section C). The final section looks at how politics interact with the doctrine and institutions of international criminal law in terms of how the field is influenced by, and itself acts as a driver of, politics (section D). This grouping is designed to add another layer for the reader, who can, of course, read the chapters individually or by topic.

SECTION A
PORTRAITS, POSITIONALITY, PARADIGMS

International criminal law is a highly defined field of study, approached via legal doctrine, historical significance, political relevance, and actor trajectories. Each of these categories maps broadly onto a wider discipline of study (ie law, history, political science, sociology). Section A consists of chapters which are *portraits* of international criminal justice. They offer perspectives positioned in relation to international criminal law while also describing and theorizing significant elements of its practice. We begin with Sara Dezalay, who challenges current debates in global justice and the fight against impunity. Starting with the case against Habré, she demonstrates that no debate in isolation can meaningfully capture what is central to the field. Instead, she suggests a framework of several 'boxes' as a more useful method for addressing the field. This consideration would focus on the structural conditions regarding institutionalization as well as the trajectories of the actors involved and political linkages and networks. Following Dezalay's chapter is Ndeye Amy Ndiaye, a Senegalese academic who worked at the EAC in the trial chambers as a judicial clerk. Ndiaye situates the EAC among wider Senegalese and African justice initiatives in her chapter, examining the EAC as a reappropriation of international criminal justice by African actors. Ndiaye's chapter further regards the dynamics of an emerging regional criminal justice system across Africa.

The final two chapters in this section bring their organic focus to the structural constraints inherent in adjudication of international crime. Julien Serroussi worked for several years as a social science expert at an ICC trial chamber and in the French war crimes investigation unit. His chapter draws from these experiences to discuss how contextualizing facts can alter judicial outcomes. He shows the necessity of developing a sociological theory about the facts of a case in order to ascribe responsibility in a court. Similarly Dov Jacobs, an academic who also practices before the ICC as a defence lawyer, offers a consideration of the (non)possibility of a fair defence before considering examples of structural challenges relevant to the defence of Hissène Habré.

27

Africa Against Global Justice? Stakes for Building a Political Sociology on the Future of International Criminal Justice

Sara Dezalay[1]

'This is our continent, not yours!'[2] The conviction of Hissène Habré by the Extraordinary African Chambers (EAC) on 30 May 2016 in the Senegalese court system happened in a context of growing contest against the International Criminal Court (ICC). At the Addis Ababa Summit of January 2016, AU member states endorsed a so-called 'ICC withdrawal strategy',[3] through which they denounced the African bias of the ICC. The balance sheet of the Court undoubtedly lends credence to this perception. Ten out of the eleven situations under investigation at the ICC target African states. Specifically, it is the indictment of two African sitting heads of state—Omar Al-Bashir in 2009 and Uhuru Kenyatta in 2011—which exacerbated what commentators widely staged as a 'divorce' between Africa and the ICC.[4]

The contrast with the trial that was unfolding in parallel against Hissène Habré, an African head of state, albeit deposed, in a *foreign* court, yet endowed with this task by the AU 'in the name of Africa' is staggering. Commentators have heralded the decision of the Extraordinary African Chambers, confirmed on appeal on 27 April 2017, as a historical trial. Yet, they have also been quick to assert that this success story was not replicable because the 'tide had turned' against global justice.[5] Certainly, the success of this 'interminable legal and political soap-opera' to quote the words of Bishop Desmund Tutu, which unfolded over the course of fifteen years across multiple geographical sites and forums, was the result of a unique set of factors, of a legal but also political nature. It is undoubtedly testament to the key *strategic* role played by the individuals who built up the case against Habré—all of whom recount their stories in this volume—that they keenly grasped, mobilized and took advantage of these factors to build the case against Habré. What Reed Brody, in particular,

[1] This chapter is partly based on Sara Dezalay, *L'Afrique contre la Cour pénale internationale? Éléments de sociogenèse sur les possibles de la justice internationale* (Politique africaine 2017) 165.

[2] Susanne Koelbl and Jan Puhl, *This is our continent, not yours, interview with Ugandan President Museveni* (Der Spiegel, 2016), http://www.spiegel.de/international/world/interview-with-ugandan-president-yoweri-museveni-a-1096932.html (accessed 1 July 2019).

[3] Addis Ababa, *Withdrawal Strategy Document, Draft 2*, (*African Union*, 2017), https://www.hrw.org/sites/default/files/supporting_resources/icc_withdrawal_strategy_jan._2017.pdf (accessed 1 July 2019).

[4] See S Allison, *African revolt threatens International Criminal Court's legitimacy* (*The Guardian*, 2016), https://www.theguardian.com/law/2016/oct/27/african-revolt-international-criminal-court-gambia accessed 1 July 2019.

[5] See Christophe Châtelot, '*La condamnation de Hissène Habré : un précédent sans lendemain?*' (*Le Monde*, 24 May 2016) https://www.lemonde.fr/afrique/article/2016/05/31/la-condamnation-de-hissene-habre-un-precedent-sans-lendemain_4929547_3212.html accessed 1 July 2019. My translation from French.

Sara Dezalay, *Africa Against Global Justice? Stakes for Building a Political Sociology on the Future of International Criminal Justice*
In: *The President on Trial*. First edition. Edited by: Sharon Weill, Kim Thuy Seelinger, and Kerstin Bree Carlson, Oxford University Press (2020). © Sara Dezalay. DOI: 10.1093/oso/9780198858621.003.0028

describes as a dynamic of 'private international prosecution' hinged foremost on creating strategic opportunities—notably by allying the *know-how* and media savviness of critically positioned international NGOs such as Human Rights Watch and the FIDH, and a Coalition of Chadian victims who by bringing their voice to the frontstage of the process also endowed it with legitimacy.[6] These strategies also included making compromises limiting the purview of the EAC's focus, notably to ascertain Chad's support for the process.[7] It is not this chapter's task to revisit these dynamics and how they made the Habré case feasible; nor is it to assess and question the *strategic* opportunities that may lead to the emergence of a new 'Pinochet of Africa' in the future. Rather, this chapter questions the position of the Habré 'success story' as an *anomaly* in the context of a wider backlash of Africa against the ICC, and with it, against global justice.

With Burundi to date the only African state to have effectively pulled out of the Rome Statute, commentators have asserted that the demurely termed 'fraught' relationship between the AU and the ICC was nurtured by misperceptions and misunderstandings. While some call for a reform of the ICC, starting with the role played by permanent members of the Security Council,[8] others continue to underline that there is no working alternative for an African version of global justice as the 2014 Malabo Protocol instituting a criminal chamber within the African Court of Justice and Human Rights is still unlikely to enter into force.[9] Yet others point to the distance[10] —geographic, philosophic, procedural—of the Court as a detrimental factor, one seen by contrast has having enhanced the legitimacy of the EAC.

Yet, these responses continue to reproduce the lines of an ideological war of position between a neo-colonial form of global justice and the wheels (albeit rusty) of universalism. Sidiki Kaba's comment that 'when we think of African justice, we think of justice on the cheap'[11] encapsulates the overwhelming tendency, in scholarship and policy circles alike, to think of judicial institutions across the African continent as both a *solution* to the failure of political elites—and a *problem* shaped by the legacy of colonialism. This perception underlines that the explanation of a backlash of Africa against global justice is itself a projection: one that is embedded in an ideological turf battle.

This chapter seeks to move beyond these political and ideological representations by examining the structural conditions that help explain the conflicted relationship between African states and global justice. It suggests a roadmap to interrogate the socio-genesis of the present, and with it of the futures of global justice. Specifically, this requires moving away from the symbolic politics of global justice towards the structural conditions of its institutionalization and authority over time. Using the tools of a structural sociology attentive to the resources and strategies deployed by agents to invest in international criminal

[6] See Brody, in this volume, Chapter 4.

[7] See Hazan, in this volume, Chapter 40.

[8] See Mark Kersten, *How three words could change the ICC-Africa relationship* (*Justice in Conflict*, 2017) https://justiceinconflict.org/2017/05/09/how-three-words-could-change-the-icc-africa-relationship/#more-7344 accessed 1 July 2019.

[9] Fifteen member-states need to ratify the protocol. As of 1 July 2019, fifteen states had signed it but none had ratified it.

[10] See Phil Clark, *Distant Justice. The Impact of the International Criminal Court on African Politics* (Cambridge University Press 2018).

[11] Christophe Châtelot, '*Quand on pense justice africaine, on pense justice au rabais*' (*Le Monde*, 6 November 2015) <https://www.lemonde.fr/afrique/article/2015/11/06/sidiki-kaba-quand-on-pense-justice-africaine-on-pense-justice-au-rabais_4804648_3212.html > accessed 1 July 2019. Author's translation from French.

justice institutions as much as to push back against them, this chapter opens up three series of 'black boxes' which form part and parcel of the way the ICC has been institutionalized, in particular in its relationship with Africa.

The first section recalls that international criminal justice is first and foremost a symbolic market that remains exceptionally contested. As the first permanent Court with jurisdiction over egregious crimes, the ICC constitutes the most prominent institutionalized dimension of a diffuse 'reforming common sense'[12] on the criminalization of state and armed violence worldwide. But it operates in a global space where the judicial response to such crimes remains questioned, fragmented and uneven. Looking at global justice as a symbolic market opens the necessity to consider together these competing markets for the production, circulation and reception of norms, values and practices about the criminalization of global crimes. This leads to opening a second black box: the representation of the 'African bias' of the ICC as a driver of erosion of the authority of this institution as a global court. Tracing the historical forces that led to the adoption of the Rome Statute in 1998 and the global context of the first years of the ICC at the turn of the 2000s highlights that the Court's predilection for African situations does not merely reflect its weakness as an institution. It underscores the structural embeddedness in politics of international criminal justice as a 'weak field', that is, a space that is weak as regards its internal autonomy but not weak in its wider social effects.[13] Beyond the contingency of these factors, this chapter opens a third black box: African lawyers themselves. In mainstream scholarship on law and legal institutions in the African South, lawyers in the (post-)colonial realms continue to remain the suppressed underside of the North, when not marginalized to the point of oblivion. This chapter argues that looking at their trajectories and strategies can be a powerful entry-point to trace the uneven and unequal connection between Africa and the world over time, and that this provides a much more complex story than a divorce between Africa and the ICC.[14] This chapter may admittedly raise more questions than answers. Its ambition, however, by channelling the tools of a structural sociology attentive to the trajectories, resources and strategies of agents invested in these dynamics, is to look beyond the specific conjuncture of the Habré case, or that of an apparent backlash against the ICC, so as to reposition the relationship between African states and international criminal justice institutions within fields of practices that are also shaping the future of global justice.

[12] Christian Topalov (ed), *Laboratoires du nouveau siècle. La nébuleuse réformatrice et ses réseaux en France (1880–1914)* (Editions de l'EHESS, Paris, 1999).

[13] ibid.

[14] This chapter is based on over two hundred interviews carried out in the past ten years in the framework of a research strategy that has sought to embrace the diversity of the markets for the production and reception of international dynamics for the criminalization of societal and state violence—in the global North as much as the African South, including: the growth and transformation of non-profit sectors of intervention in the African South since the 1990s; professionalization dynamics within the ICC; the social and professional structure of the field of international justice; the roles played by African lawyers in the trajectory of the state across Africa, and that of globalization.

Shifting the focus from symbolic politics to the *market* for global justice

Contests against the imperial politics of the ICC come on a par with a now long-boiled discussion over the global ambition of international criminal justice. A number of recent studies are pushing back against the monopolistic claims made by the ICC as a first response to war, and with them the 'tribunalization' of political conflict, deemed to come at the cost of competing alternative forms of justice, if not peace.[15] These debates pinpoint the contradictory symbolism conveyed by global justice.[16] These symbolic politics derive as much from the competition of a diverse range of stakeholders (to invest in, or contest the Court), as they reflect the conflicting interests of 'shareholders'[17] in the material conditions of the Court's operations—not only its budget, but also its capacity to yield the policing support of states and the collaboration of other actors on the ground to arrest individuals indicted by the Court, and gather evidence.

Symbolic politics about Africa itself are also deeply entrenched in the very operations of the ICC, not least because they partake in a projection of justice onto the imaginaries of the White saviour mission. The image of the child soldier as the epitome of the victim fuelled the fast-food advocacy of the 'Kony 2012' campaign all the while legitimating US military operations in the Great Lakes region.[18] Within the Court itself, the trial against Ongwen, both an author of crimes but victim himself as a child soldier grown commander of North Uganda's Lord Resistance Army, is feeding into conflicting imaginaries of victimhood that build into the competition between the Office of the Prosecutor (OTP) and other stakeholders within the Court.[19] These representations of Africa run both ways. The ambiguous project for an 'African Renaissance' championed by former South African president Mbeki in the context of the transition of the Organization of African Unity into the AU in 2002 has been mooted for contradictory positions, lending itself, so to speak, to games of 'double language'[20] between a rhetoric of opposition to global justice as a form of neo-imperialism and fluctuating practices of alignments with international interests.

These symbolic politics underscore that the authority itself of global justice is contested.[21] They are also a reminder that global justice is a symbolic market, that is, to use Pierre Bourdieu's reflections,[22] a space in which the belief in global justice as a symbolic good is a condition for the authority of global justice institutions. As such, it is also, crucially, a space that is made up of the dynamic relationship between restricted markets of

[15] See Sarah MH Nouwen and Werner G Werner, 'Monopolizing Global Justice. International Criminal Law as Challenge to Human Diversity' (2015) 13 Journal of International Criminal Justice 157.

[16] See Kamari Maxine Clarke, *Fictions of Justice. The International Criminal Court and the Challenge of Legal Pluralism in Sub-Saharan Africa* (Cambridge University Press 2009).

[17] See Sarah Kendall, 'Commodifying Global Justice. Economies of Accountability at the International Criminal Court' (2015) 13 Journal of International Criminal Justice 113.

[18] See Adam Branch, '*Dangerous ignorance: the hysteria of Kony 2012*' (*Al Jazeera*, 12 March 2012) <https://www.aljazeera.com/indepth/opinion/2012/03/201231284336601364.html > accessed 31 January 2019.

[19] Barrie Sanders, '*We need to talk about Ongwen: the plight of victim-perpetrators at the ICC*' (*Justice in Conflict*, 19 April 2016) <https://justiceinconflict.org/2016/04/19/we-need-to-talk-about-ongwen-the-plight-of-victim-perpetrators-at-the-icc/ > accessed 1 July 2019.

[20] See Ivan Crouzel, 'La "renaissance africaine": un discours sud-africain?' (2000) 77(1) Politique Africaine 171.

[21] Ron Levi, Sara Dezalay, and Michael Amiraslani, 'Prosecutorial Strategies and Opening Statements: Justifying International Prosecutions from the International Military Tribunal at Nuremberg through to the International Criminal Court' (2017) 26 Comparativ: Journal for Global History and Comparative Social Science 58.

[22] Pierre Bourdieu, 'Le marché des biens symboliques' (1971) 22 L'année Sociologique 49.

producers and wider markets of buyers of global justice. Looking only at one end of this space—be it the discourse produced by and for the ICC, discourses of contenders of the Court, or mobilizations targeting specific individuals such as Hissène Habré on the basis of universal jurisdiction—can at best shed a partial light on how this space functions. This means that it is necessary to understand at once the structure of positions, over time, within the ICC, within competing international spaces for the criminalization of certain practices, and within national fields of state power in the Global North and the Global South, and the dynamic relationship between these different spaces.

This is by no means a simple task. Not only because it requires tracing the interplay between competing fields of expertise and national fields of state power, notably between diplomacy, development, security and law. But also because of the very fragility of the ICC's position within this wider context. The Court certainly epitomizes the institutional culmination of a 'reforming common sense' on the criminalization of state and societal violence.[23] But it suffers from a protracted weakness. Seventeen years after inception it remains constrained by a logic of the 'constant coup',[24] as it needs to continuously adapt to and deflect political, economic and other external constraints, from waning state support to outright shunning. Commentators increasingly wonder whether the 1990s represented a high-water mark for the broad institutionalization of global justice that is unlikely to be sustained. The limited and contested record of the ICC continuously underscores that international criminal justice is still struggling with its ultimate goals, a tension capped most vocally in the 'peace versus justice' trade-off.[25]

Thus, despite the strength of international criminal justice as an overall frame, there is an acute competition for professional authority over global justice. Concurrent experts of the international, including diplomats, international organizations but also militaries and non-profits find themselves in competition with lawyers for handling crises globally. This competition seems to foreclose routinization, that is, the actions of 'repeat players'[26] amenable to streamline the operations of international criminal justice and to contribute to the stability of the field.

The effects of this competition particularly impact the structure of the restricted academic-judicial market of producers of international criminal legal doctrine that has constituted itself around the ICC. The 'role of academics is to provide an accurate fiction about the Court'[27] explained a prominent law professor at one of the core centres which produce scholarly knowledge about the Court, the Grotius Centre for International Legal Studies at the law faculty of the University of Leiden. Combining a double position as a scholar and a counsel at the Court, a multi-positionality that is characteristic of this space, this insider indicated that scholarly discourses were part and parcel of the struggles about the ICC. But he also signalled a strategy of fencing performed by the very restricted market

[23] Christian Topalov, *Laboratoires du nouveau siècle,* (La nébuleuse réformatrice et ses réseaux en France 1880–1914) (n 12).

[24] Sara Dezalay, 'Weakness as routine in the operations of the International Criminal Court' (2016) 17 International Criminal Law Review 281.

[25] See Leslie Vinjamuri, 'Deterrence, democracy, and the pursuit of international justice during conflict' (2010) 24(2) Ethics International Affairs 191.

[26] Mark Galanter, 'Why the "haves" come out ahead: speculations on the limits of legal change' (1974) 9(1) Law and Society Review 95.

[27] Author's interview with CS, The Hague, 5 June 2012.

of producers of an authoritative discourse about the Court, one that could be described as a bunker position.[28]

This fencing strategy stands in stark contrast with the massive expansion of the specializing streams in international criminal law within North-American and European universities since the 1990s. Ongoing research tends to highlight that career options within this space as a professional market remain extremely limited. In particular, the distribution of positions within the ICC itself is characterized by a closed-up and impermeable dual structure.

On the one hand, 'high judges,' or lawyer-diplomats among the elected members of the Court[29] overwhelmingly display a personalized set of capital of legal and social authority and are multi-positioned across national and international forums and diverse social and professional networks—legal practice, academia, diplomacy, politics and human rights advocacy. On the other hand, the two dozen legal counsels operating in the ICC's Chambers display a judicial form of capital, more technical and exercised collectively. They play a core role in the constitution of a technical form of expertise on international criminal procedures. This expertise is validated via an entry-cost into the professional market of international criminal justice sanctioned by the very scholarly centres—like the Grotius Centre, or the University of Amsterdam—that are clustered around the ICC, and by scholarly productions that reflect and consolidate the internal cleavages of this small community of insiders.[30]

There is not yet any systematic data that has traced the career options of this small community of insiders. Lateral movement within the Court, that is, between the Chambers and the OTP, is rare and usually discouraged. Beyond, and particularly with the closing down of the two ad hoc international criminal tribunals for the former Yugoslavia (ICTY) and Rwanda (ICTR), the stake would be to trace the possibilities of valorization and conversion of this judicial capital at the international and domestic levels.

This fencing strategy is visible in the grammar itself that has been used by the Prosecutor, and by the Chambers in their decisions to date. Between 2002 and 2016, the grammar used to justify prosecutions has gradually been channelled towards a narrow set of justification, focused on the 'pure law' of criminal procedure, specifically the rights of the defence.[31] This stands in stark contrast with the justificatory model of 'organizational hedging'[32] that was deployed during the Nuremberg trials after World War II. The Gbagbo case is emblematic. Commenting on the decision to acquit Gbagbo and Blé Goudé, Morten Bergsmo, a legal practitioner and academic, whose career closely followed the trajectory of international criminal justice as a field from the early 1990s,[33] underlined that the ICC Prosecutor 'should *exclusively* use the language of the

[28] Since Ocampo's tenure, this has rendered research on the Court and the production of knowledge departing from authorized discourses extremely difficult, as access to academics is tightly controlled.

[29] The eighteen judges and the Prosecutor elected by the Assembly of state parties to the Rome Statute.

[30] Dezalay 'Weakness as routine' (n 24).

[31] Levi, Dezalay, and Amiraslani (n 21).

[32] David Stark, *The Sense of Dissonance: Accounts of Worth in Economic Life* (Princeton University Press 2011).

[33] Morten Bergsmo was a Legal Adviser at the UN Commission of Experts for the Former Yugoslavia established pursuant to Security Council resolution 780 (1992) (1993–94). He represented the ICTY to the UN negotiation process to establish the ICC (1996–2002). He coordinated the establishment of the ICC Office of the Prosecutor in 2002–2003 and acted as Senior Legal Adviser and Chief of the legal Advisory Section of the ICC Office of the Prosecutor until 2005.

law'.[34]

This vision of a clear-cut division between law and politics raises significant difficulties as it obscures more than it reveals—as I will outline below. It also masks the fluidity of the frontiers themselves of the field of international criminal law, beyond the microcosm of the Court. Ongoing research by Mikkel Christensen and Ron Levi is underscoring the relevance of shifting the focus away from the ICC as an institution, towards the diverse and competing networks of experts that contribute precisely to defining the frontiers of global justice as a field. They underline in particular the competition between two dynamics of criminalization of transnational practices that are generally conceived as distinct: state and armed violence on the one hand, and on the other crimes of corruption, drug trafficking and crimes of multinationals.[35]

Yet, the social and professional structure of these two apparently segmented spaces of practice signals overlaps, if not a continuous reconfiguration of their relationship. The trajectory of Luis Moreno Ocampo, the first Prosecutor of the ICC between 2003 and 2012, illustrates this dynamic. Vice-prosecutor in the trials of the Junta during the Argentinian transition in the 1980s, Ocampo then directed the Latin American office of Transparency international before his election to the ICC. He now practices within a New York based law firm, Getnick & Getnick LLP to open new ground in universal jurisdiction cases, focusing not on the international crimes under the purview of the ICC, but on the defence of whistleblowers of corporate crimes. Thus, rather than accepting the category itself of 'international criminal justice' as a given, this underscores the relevance of examining the frontiers and the social and professional structure of the transnational spaces of expertise and practice of criminalization. But to lay out this agenda of research and to trace the interplay between these networks and the African continent, it is necessary to start by opening a second black box.

The 'African bias' of the ICC: A structural weakness of the field of international criminal justice

Recent studies have underscored how the judicial interventions of the ICC play into domestic politics in recipient states—notably by contributing to re-apportioning ethnic and political lines along a dichotomy between 'friends' and 'foes' of the Court. But it is not enough, simply, to 'do justice to the political'.[36] It is the articulation between law and politics itself that needs to be fed back into the debate: both as a core driver in the constitution and legitimation of national state power—as traced by Pierre Bourdieu in his posthumous *Sur l'État*[37] —but also in the structure of the international as an arena of projection of national interests and of institutionalization of the legalization of politics. 'International law

[34] Morten Bergsmo, '*La CPI, l'affaire Gbagbo et le rôle de la France*' (*Le Monde*, 18 January 2019) <https://www.lemonde.fr/afrique/article/2019/01/18/la-cpi-l-affaire-gbagbo-et-le-role-de-la-france_5410996_3212.html > accessed 1 July 2019. My translation from French; emphasis added.

[35] Mikkel Christensen, '*Crafting and promoting international crimes: a controversy among legal professionals of core crimes and anti-corruption*' (2017) 30(2) Leiden Journal of International Law 501; Mikkel Christensen and Ron Levi (eds), *International Practices of Criminal Justice. Social and Legal Perspectives* (Routledge 2018).

[36] Sarah MH Nouwen and Wouter G Werner, 'Doing Justice to the Political: The International Criminal Court in Uganda and Sudan' (2011) 21(4) European Journal of International Law 941.

[37] Pierre Bourdieu, *Sur l'État. Cours au Collège de France (1989-1992)* (Le Seuil 2012).

is so primitive, that for us it is law, but for others it is just one option among others.'[38] This lapidary comment of Luis Moreno Ocampo reflects the overwhelming tendency to adopt a narrow, functionalist focus on international criminal courts *qua* judicial institutions. Thus, 'justice often remains a kind of background, an institution taken as a given, static in its (legal) forms and equal in its effects (of legitimation)'.[39] The very mandate of the ICC, which enables it to perform 'real time' justice, not only *ex post*, but also *ex ante*, by launching prosecutions in the context of on-going conflicts, has exacerbated this perceived cleavage between justice and politics as two antithetic goals.

Interrogating precisely these oppositions, ongoing research is highlighting how the ICC, just like other international criminal tribunals, needs to stave off constraints that are born out of the specific features of the 'atypical political environments' in which they are embedded, that is: 'highly contentious environments in which surrounding political conditions lead to a departure from routinized criminal justice, so that courts must develop organizational models to cope with, mobilize, and at times deflect, the political landscape in which they operate.'[40] In this sense, the structure itself of the OTP of the ICC reflects the double strategy of survival adopted by international criminal tribunals since the 1990s, through accretion[41] and institutional conversion.[42] In particular, Luis Moreno Ocampo set up a Jurisdiction, Complementarity and Cooperation Division designed specifically to act as an interface with diplomatic *milieux* and the international non-governmental organizations (INGOs) that gravitate around the Court.[43]

This wider context matters not only to trace the paths of institutionalization of global justice, but also to explore how the field of international criminal justice is structured. This socio-historical perspective is critical to understand both the specific juncture that led to the adoption of the Rome Statute in 1998 and the geopolitical context in which it is now operating. A number of studies have underlined how the un-tapping of the 'Nuremberg legacy' from the 1980s was shaped by the aligned interests of great power politics and the international human rights movement. The dis-alignment of these coalitions following the NATO intervention in Kosovo in 1999[44] and foremost the 9/11 attacks and the US-led coalition in Iraq account in turn for the less than favourable early years of development of the ICC. This changing geopolitical context helps explain the structure of the field of global justice itself as a 'weak field' that is, a space at once permeable to external shocks but also dependent on adjacent fields for its survival.

38 Author's interview (with Ron Levi) with Luis Moreno Ocampo, Toronto, 8 November 2012.

39 Antoine Vauchez, 'La justice comme "institution politique": retour sur un objet (longtemps) perdu de la science politique' (2006) 63–64 Droit et société 493. Author's translation from French.

40 Ron Levi, John Hagan, and Sara Dezalay, 'International Courts in Atypical Political Environments: The Interplay of Prosecutorial Strategy, Evidence, and Court Authority in International Criminal Law' (2016) 78(4) Law and Contemporary Problems 289.

41 Thus, beyond a case-law built in reference to the experience of previous international criminal tribunals, the prosecution strategies of the ICC relied in great part on these antecedents (with about 1/3 of the personnel coming from the ad hoc tribunals).

42 See Heather Schoenfeld, Ron Levi, and John Hagan, 'Crises extrêmes et institutionnalisation du droit pénal international' (2007) 36 Critique Internationale 37.

43 See Jens Meierenrich, '*The evolution of the Office of the Prosecutor at the International Criminal Court: insights from institutional theory*' in Martha Minow, C Cora True-Frost, and Alex Whiting (eds), *The first global prosecutor. Promises and constraints* (The University of Michigan Press 2015).

44 Yves Dezalay and Bryant G Garth, 'From the Cold War to Kosovo: The Rise and Renewal of the Field of International Human Rights' (2006) 2 Annual Review of Law and Social Science 231.

The early interest of the ICC in African situations could be construed in part as a default strategy, one indeed that was aligned in the early 2000s with African states' interests. African states constituted a core driver of the 'like-minded' group that lobbied for the adoption of the Rome Statute in 1998. But it also foremost befitted the interests of great powers.[45] It notably served to appease the hostility of the US against the Court during its first years of operation.[46] The African bias of the Court was also embedded in the parallel transformation from the early 1990s of the international political economy of interventionism on the African continent. The strong policy pull towards a recalibration of sovereignty as 'responsibility'[47] targeted specifically the African state and its 'failures.' From the early 1990s, the redefinition of conflict as a disease of underdevelopment and poor governance fostered the massive expansion of competing international networks and markets for the production of expertise and practice on the resolution of conflict and rule of law reforms, involving public and private actors, security, development and human rights sectors. These transformations have enabled and justified the growth of criminalization as a legitimate form of external intervention into the African continent.[48]

Staking weakness as a strategy, the OTP has heavily relied on these networks of intervention to gather evidence.[49] During his tenure, Luis Moreno Ocampo deployed a strategy of investigation through teams constituted nearly exclusively of former agents of NGOs, contrarily to the experience of the ad hoc international criminal tribunals, where investigation was carried out foremost by police investigators. Ocampo also prided himself in his capacity to investigate situations at a distance, by relying on pre-positioned networks of NGOs already operating in the situations under investigation. This strategy certainly aimed at responding to the weakness of the means of the prosecutorial teams, including their actual impossibility to investigate on-site in particular in the Democratic Republic of the Congo in the first years of operation of the ICC due to the active hostility of the US.

The case-law of the Court, from its first decision regarding Thomas Lubanga, through to the Laurent Gbagbo and Charles Blé Goudé cases, has consistently denounced the fallibility of the evidence gathered by the Prosecutor. Not only because of the reliance on secondary sources of information, but also because the OTP has vested its prosecutorial strategies on the media-oriented grammar of victimhood of human rights NGOs ill-befitted to the rights of the defence.

To complete these insights, it would be necessary to trace systematically the structure of positions within sites of reception of global justice across national legal and political fields on the African continent. The detailed analysis of Mills on the relationship between the

[45] A journalist of *Mediapart*, Fanny Pigeaud thus uncovered how the French diplomacy collaborated with the OTP in 2011 so that Laurent Gbagbo be arrested and imprisoned before an investigation had been opened by the Court. See the series of articles, Fanny Pigeaud, 'Retour sur l'histoire du dossier de Laurent Gbagbo à la CPI' (*Mediapart*, 16 January 2019) <https://blogs.mediapart.fr/fanny-pigeaud/blog/160119/retour-sur-lhistoire-du-dossier-de-laurent-gbagbo-la-cpi > accessed 1 July 2019.

[46] See David Bosco, *Rough Justice: The International Criminal Court in a World of Power Politics* (Oxford University Press 2014).

[47] Francis M Deng, Sadikiel Kimaro, Terrence Lyons, Donald Rothchild, and I William Zartman. *Sovereignty as responsibility. Sovereignty in Africa* (The Brookings Institute 1996).

[48] See Sara Dezalay, *Revamping Law by Circumventing the State. Non-governmental organizations in the international management of social violence on the African continent* (PhD of Laws, European University Institute, Florence 2011).

[49] Sara Dezalay, 'Weakness as Routine in the Operations of the Intentional Criminal Court' (2017) 17(2) International Criminal Law Review 281–301

AU and the ICC opens up a number of paths by underlining that the AU itself is straddling fluctuating African political spaces.[50] The prosecutions launched by the ICC against two sitting African heads of state certainly exacerbated the hostility of the organization against the ICC, but they did not foster a consensus among state members of the AU. On the contrary, alignments (and dis-alignments) about global justice are reflected in conflicting national positions and the relative influence of member states within the organization. One of the dynamics of contest against global justice has been heralded by Rwanda's President Kagame not so much against the ICC itself, but against universal jurisdiction and the opening of investigations since 2006 in Spain and in France against high level members of the Rwandan Patriotic Front.[51] This points to the embeddedness of Kagame's position in the microcosm of ambiguous relations between France and Rwanda.

What this opens, therefore, is a research agenda amenable to document over time the structure of the 'weak field' of global justice and its articulations not with 'Africa' but with differentiated national and regional dynamics across the continent, by retracing the composition of the networks located at the interface between the ICC and the domestic level—be they the African delegations to the Assembly of state parties to the ICC and their relationships with national fields of state power, or the roles played by lawyers themselves within national legal fields on the African continent. This requires opening a third black box.

Africa's lawyers: State builders and interstitial elite on the (inter) national markets for global justice

The election in 2012 of Fatou Bensouda as Prosecutor of the ICC galvanized hopes to revamp the fragile legitimacy of the Court. The implicit (and at times explicit) imaginaries[52] projected on her own stature as an African and as a woman crystallize the ideological, when not racist, images that are vested in the figures of lawyers on the African continent. Contrary to other regions in the world, there is a dearth of knowledge on legal professions in the African South and the roles they have played from the colonial eras through to contemporary African politics. What George Steinmetz termed 'imperial entanglements'[53] has served to uncover how the history of the disciplines of anthropology and of sociology was deeply entrenched in the colonial enterprise. To date, studies of law and legal institutions in the African South have not undergone such an *aggiornamento*. Lawyers on the African continent continue to be predominantly studied within the lens of the contemporary hegemon, under the purview of the US sociology of legal professions, with two self-opposed images.[54]

[50] Kurt Mills, '"Bashir is dividing us": Africa and the International Criminal Court' (2012) 34(2) Human Rights Quarterly 404.

[51] Nine investigations and forty others have been launched respectively in France and in Spain between 2006 and 2008. The Rwandan justice minister Tharcisse Karugarama evoked a 'neo-colonial judicial *coup d'État*' (see Julia Geneuss, 'Fostering a better understanding of universal jurisdiction: a comment on the AU-EU Expert Report on the principle of universal jurisdiction' (2009) 7(5) Journal of International Criminal Justice 946).

[52] See this article stating in 2011: 'She's black and she's African, which helps.' adding as an afterthought 'But she's also very good'. Simon Allison, *'Fatou Bensouda: the woman who might save the ICC in Africa'* (*Daily Maverick*, 11 December 2011) <https://www.dailymaverick.co.za/article/2011-12-11-fatou-bensouda-the-woman-who-might-save-the-icc-in-africa/> accessed 1 July 2019.

[53] George Steinmetz (ed), *Sociology and Empire. The imperial entanglements of a discipline* (Duke University Press 2013).

[54] See Mitra Shafari, 'A new history of colonial lawyering: Likhovski and legal identities in the British Empire' (2007) 32(4) Law and Soceity Inquiry 1059.

Lawyers are either construed in heroic terms as missionaries of the rule of law[55] or they are subsumed under the drive of the market,[56] including as mercenaries of neo-colonial interests.[57]

Contrary to these representations, ongoing research is laying out the hypothesis, precisely, that lawyers, their trajectories, their resources and their professional strategies can constitute a powerful entry-point to trace in the *longue durée* the unequal and uneven relationship between Africa and the world. This reflects on the one hand the research path opened by Ernst Kantorowicz[58] and others in his wake, who have shown that lawyers are structurally positioned to play 'double games'.[59] While at the service of power holders—and thus playing a central role of legitimation of state power—lawyers also need to distance themselves from politics, as a condition to protect the autonomy of the law, and with it their professional practices. It also takes in the specificity of the interstitial position of African legal elites, across time and space, in the trajectory of the state and as intermediaries of the successive phases of globalization on the African continent.[60]

The trajectory of Fatou Bensouda herself provides an emblematic illustration. Born in 1961, Bensouda belongs to the very small legal elite of the Gambia. After graduating in law at the University of Ife in Nigeria,[61] she was called to the Bar of the Gambia in 1987. She rose very quickly through the ranks of the judiciary and was promoted deputy director of public prosecutions in 1994. After Jammeh's *coup d'état* in 1994, she remained deputy director, before being appointed director of public prosecutions in 1996. The transition was smooth: 'we even provided advice to the militaries and the new government so that they re-establish as soon as possible a democratic system.'[62] She was appointed attorney general and minister of justice at the age of thirty-seven, before being dismissed by Jammeh in 2000.[63] She thereafter set up a law firm and took the direction of a leading commercial bank in the Gambia before being appointed in 2002 Legal Adviser and Trial Attorney at the ICTR, rising to the position of Senior Legal Advisor and Head of The Legal Advisory Unit. She joined the ICC in 2004 as vice-prosecutor and was elected Prosecutor of the Court in December 2012, with the support of the AU, after an intense lobbying by the Gambia at the Malabo Summit of the AU in 2011.

In Bensouda's trajectory, the international certainly played the role of an extraverted resource, to use Jean-François Bayart's notion[64] that is, the rent derived from material and symbolic links with the international and deployed at the domestic level. It enabled her to

[55] Terry Halliday, Lucien Karpik, and Malcolm M Feeley (eds), *Fates of political liberalism in the British post-colony. The politics of the legal complex* (Cambridge University Press 2012).

[56] Richard Abel and Philip Lewis, *Lawyers in Society* (three vols) (University of California Press 1988–89).

[57] See Thomas Burgis, *The Looting Machine. Warlords, tycoons, smugglers and the systematic theft of Africa's wealth* (Harper Collins Publishers 2015).

[58] Ernst Kantorowicz, *Les deux corps du Roi* (Gallimard 1989).

[59] See Yves Dezalay and Bryant G Garth, 'State politics and legal markets' (2011) 10 Comparative Sociology 38.

[60] See Sara Dezalay, 'Les juristes en Afrique: entre trajectoires d'Etat, sillons d'empire et mondialisation' (2015) 138 Politique africaine 5.

[61] The university of Gambia was created only in 1998 (the first cohort of lawyers obtained their diploma in 2013). Until then, the government had instituted a program of fellowships to sponsor the studies abroad of the best students.

[62] Pascal Hairault, '*Fatou Bensouda: "Non, la CPI n'est pas à la solde des Blancs"*' (Jeune Afrique, 2 January 2012) <https://www.jeuneafrique.com/188943/politique/fatou-bensouda-non-la-cpi-n-est-pas-la-solde-des-blancs/> accessed 1 July 2019.

[63] Esther Addley, '*Fatou Bensouda, the woman who hunts tyrants*' (*The Guardian*, 5 June 2016) <https://www.theguardian.com/law/2016/jun/05/fatou-bensouda-international-criminal-court-tyrants> accessed 1 July 2019.

[64] Jean-François Bayart, 'Africa in the world: a history of extraversion' (2000) 99 African Affairs 217.

take her distances with the Jammeh regime, while her very position at the international level was mooted as an influence strategy of the Gambia within the AU and in relation to the ICC. Her trajectory also highlights how her 'Africanness' obscures the symbolic and material forces that have shaped her career.

This example underscores how uncovering the layered *habitus* of African lawyers, across time and space, can provide a powerful way to tackle the question of the representativeness of the ICC as a global court, which constitutes one of the drivers of the discord between the AU and the ICC. Recent scholarship has emphasized the relevance of looking at the social and professional characteristics of the lawyers involved in international dispute settlement mechanisms.[65] Studies on the genesis of international justice institutions at the turn of the twentieth century have underscored that the multi-positioning of lawyers invested in these early endeavours—across scholarly positions, legal practice, service to state diplomacy and at times political positions at the national level—was a key condition for the inception of international justice precisely because these agents could at once reflect national political and economic interests and deflect them by constructing the doctrine of international law as universal.[66] These studies have also shed light on the specific role played by legal elites from the Global South in these early institutionalization processes.

Dubbed 'gentlemen politicians of law' these legal elites played a crucial role of legitimation of international institutions, both because they were co-opted into a belief of the universal crafted at core scholarly centres in Europe and the US, but also because they could convert new generations of lawyers to the efficiency of international justice, that is, in other words, build markets of users of international justice at the national level.[67] Though there is not yet any systematic study of the agents invested in the ICC, an initial survey of the profiles of the judges elected to date to the Court[68] underscores the remarkable continuity of these characteristics of the genesis. The forty-one judges elected to the Court since 2003 have all held, successively or cumulatively, positions typical of the genesis in legal practice, civil service, or academia. Not only is there a continuity with judicial profiles at other international courts, but there is no apparent specificity of the eight African judges elected to the Court since 2003—the only, though remarkable, caveat being the number of women—five out of eight, who have all occupied prominent positions within the Court, and who all hold prominent positions as women's and children's rights activists. The trajectory of one of these female judges, the Malian Fatoumata Diarra,[69] elected to the Court in 2003, helps shed some light on the possible roles played by these women from the African South in the legitimation of the ICC.

[65] See D Terris, C PR Romano, and L Swigart (eds), *The International Judge: An Introduction to the Men and Women Who Decide the World's Cases* (Oxford University Press 2007); Sara Dezalay (with the contribution of Yves Dezalay), 'Professionals of international justice. From the shadow of state diplomacy to the pull of the market of arbitration' in Jean d'Aspremont, Tarcisio Gazzini, André Nollkaemper, and Wouter Werner (eds), *International Law as a Profession* (Cambridge University Press 2017).

[66] Guillaume Sacriste and Antoine Vauchez, 'The Force of International Law: Lawyers' Diplomacy on the International Scene in the 1920s' (2007) 32(1) Law and Society Inquiry 83.

[67] ibid.

[68] Based on the official profiles of ICC judges, on the Court's website <https://www.icc-cpi.int/about/judicial-divisions/biographies/Pages/current-judges.aspx> accessed 1 July 2019.

[69] Sara Dezalay, 'Fatoumata Dembélé Diarra: trajectory of a Malian magistrate and civil society advocate to the International Criminal Court' in Josephine Jarpa Dawuni and Akua Kuenyehia (eds), *International Courts and the African woman judge. Unveiled narratives* (Routledge 2018).

Diarra was born in 1948 in Koulikouro, a military port city in what was then a French colony, the *Soudan Français* (current Mali). This geographic position—her father worked for the colonial administration—partly explains a strong family investment in education. Handpicked by the Catholic mission's primary and education system to pursue a higher education, Diarra followed a legal trajectory typical of the first generation of the immediate post-independence lawyers in former West African French colonies: studies in Dakar, followed by the *École nationale de la magistrature* in Paris, with a fellowship from the French *Coopération* in 1975–1977—and this despite the political break of Mali first President Keïta with France, in a country where there were only two Malian lawyers at Independence. She then combined a career to the higher tiers of the judiciary and justice administration in Mali with activism. She created several NGOs for the defence of women's and children's rights from the early 1990s. These militant activities, reinforced by international resources (through support and funding from INGOs), also enabled her to maintain a degree of independence under Traoré's dictatorship.

It is out of this national platform—combining activism, a high judicial position, and international resources—that she acceded first to the ICTY as *ad litem* judge in 2001-2003, and then to the ICC in 2003. Much like her counterparts from British colonies trained at Inns of Courts in England, the *imperial* realm, fashioned as it was on highly selective *meritocratic* criteria of access, defined the stratification of Mali's legal professions at Independence, with a higher tier modelled on social ties and resources drawn from internationalization within the ambit of the former empire. In turn, her selection by Mali to be elected to the ICC's bench in 2003 may have been a strategic choice, echoing her country's alignment with international development organisations' *engouement* for gender from the early 2000s. But it also befitted precisely the structure of international criminal justice as a weak field, as it tapped on, specifically, her straddling position across judicial practice and civil society advocacy for the rights of children and women. Far from a simple biographical anecdote, this trajectory uncovers a *layered* habitus, fashioned by multiple historical strata of globalization of law on the African continent, from the colonial era to the present. This individual trajectory also points to the inter-connectedness—between the local, the national, the global, but also across law, economics and politics—that have shaped and are shaping local politics as much as the position of Africa in the world.

Conclusion

Shifting the lens from the symbolism of global justice towards the structural conditions that have shaped international criminal justice as a field over time can help reposition the Habré success story not simply as an anomaly in a context of wider backlash against the ICC, but rather as a reflection of the structure of global justice as a weak field. It is interesting to note that the long-winded road of the Habré prosecution and trial, between N'Djamena, Brussels and Dakar, over fifteen years itself mapped onto the life-span of the ICC. Alignments and dis-alignments around the 'cause of universal jurisdiction' from the Pinochet case through the 2010s have echoed closely the alignments and dis-alignments around a world court with jurisdiction over the most egregious crimes.[70] Certainly, the setting up of the EAC

[70] See Julien Seroussi, 'La cause de la compétence universelle. Note de recherche sur l'implosion d'une

in Dakar benefited from the strategies and combination of political alliances developed by the victims' Coalition in Senegal along with the conjunctural political factor of the election of Macky Sall as president of Senegal in 2012.[71] But looking at those only would obfuscate wider, structural, transformations at play. Uncovering those, indeed, can help underline that more than a divorce between the continent and global justice it is the unevenness and unequal character of Africa's relationship with the global that is undergoing profound changes.

To make sense of these transformations, it is urgent to study systematically the evolution of legal markets on the African continent. In this, the project to institute a criminal chamber within the African Court of Justice and Human Rights has perhaps been too promptly dismissed as overly ambitious due to the lack of resources and state support within the AU. Interestingly, this project includes not only the crimes under the purview of the ICC, but also various other trans-border crimes such as trafficking, corruption, and the illicit exploitation of resources. The prominence taken in recent years by Africa as a new 'mining frontier'—and with it, as a new haven for US and UK multinational corporate firms—underscores the timeliness of opening research paths on these ongoing transformations across the continent.

South Africa certainly looms large in these evolutions. The dynamism of its corporate legal hemisphere makes it one of the drivers of corporate legal globalization across Africa since the turn of the 2000s. One of the vocal voices against the ICC, the country is also at the forefront of a growing backlash by emerging countries against international investment arbitration as a modality to solve disputes between multinationals—including the extractive industry—and states. The former president of the AU Commission, the South African Nkosazana Diamini-Zuma, mandated an NGO, the African Court Research Initiative, to study the practical modalities of implementing the Malabo Protocol. Yet, the recently appointed National Director of Public Prosecutions, Shamila Batohi, tasked with combatting grand corruption in South Africa, also pursued a great part of her career ... at the OTP. These complexities not only highlight the urgency of departing from an objectified understanding of global justice so as to trace the networks that are shaping and transforming global justice institutions. They also underscore that South Africa just like other parts of the African South may well become a new frontier in the transformation of the position of Africa in world politics, and with it of the field of global justice.

mobilisation internationale' (2008) 173 Actes de la recherche en sciences sociales 98.

[71] See Brody, Part II, Section A.3, this volume.

28

The Habré Trial and the Malabo Protocol

An Emerging African Criminal Justice?

Ndeye Amy Ndiaye

Introduction

On 22 August 2012, after a long struggle by the victims,[1] Senegal decided to sign an accord with the African Union (AU) creating the Extraordinary African Chambers (EAC) within the Senegalese courts.[2] The objective of this institution was an innovative one in that its goal was to judge, on Senegalese territory, a Chadian president for crimes committed in Chad between 1982 and 1990. The task was thus doubly symbolic for Senegal, which needed to adopt legislative measures to allow the accord to be put into effect, as well as to transpose it into its internal legal framework. It was also symbolic for the continent since the primary goal of the legal founding text of the EAC was to meet a continental requirement. This is made clear in Article 1 of the Statute, which emphasizes that 'The purpose of this Statute is to implement the decision of the AU concerning the Republic of Senegal's prosecution of international crimes committed in Chad between 7 June 1982 and 1 December 1990, in accordance with Senegal's international commitments'.[3]

On 27 April 2017, after twenty months of trial, the former President of Chad Hissène Habré was definitively sentenced to life imprisonment by an extraordinary African court. In addition to its penal function, this innovative trial seems both symbolic and dissuasive. It needs to be seen in the context of the uncomfortable relationship between Africa and the International Criminal Court (ICC): one could almost view it as a trial pitting Africa against international criminal justice. But what did the Hissène Habré trial actually bring to international and regional criminal justice? It's in light of the various responses to this question that the impact of this unprecedented trial will come to be measured.

It is obvious that the trial of the former dictator took place in the context of conflictual relations between Africa and the ICC. Since the arrest warrant issued for Omar Al Bashir, relations between the ICC and the states forming the AU have gone steadily downhill,[4] to such

[1] Presumptive victims of the exactions carried out by the regime of Hissène Habré organized around Souleymane Guégueng first brought their case to the senior investigative judge of the Dakar Regional Special Court in 2000.

[2] Accord between the Government of Senegal and the AU on the creation of the EAC within the Courts of Senegal, 22 August 2012.

[3] Statute of the Extraordinary African Chambers within the courts of Senegal created to prosecute international crimes committed in Chad between 7 June 1982 and 1 December 1990, available at https://www.hrw.org/news/2013/09/02/statute-extraordinary-african-chambers. Accessed 16 August 2018.

[4] African Union press statement of 4 February 2010 on the decision of the Appeals Court of the International Criminal Court on Darfur, http://www.operationspaix.net/DATA/DOCUMENT/407~v~Communique_de_la_Chambre_d_Appel_de_la_Cour_Penale_Internationale_sur_le_Darfour.pdf. accessed 16 October 2015;'Decision on the Report of the Commission on the Meeting of African States Parties to the Rome Statute of the International Criminal Tribunal (ICC)—Doc Assembly/AU/13 (XIII), https://au.int/sites/default/files/

Ndeye Amy Ndiaye, *The Habré Trial and the Malabo Protocol* In: *The President on Trial.* First edition. Edited by: Sharon Weill, Kim Thuy Seelinger, and Kerstin Bree Carlson, Oxford University Press (2020). © Ndeye Amy Ndiaye.
DOI: 10.1093/oso/9780198858621.003.0029

an extent that the AU came to envisage creating its own court through the Malabo Protocol. What we appear to be increasingly witnessing is the determination to regionalize African criminal justice, as may be concluded from the recent adoption of the Malabo Protocol and the call to withdraw from the ICC.

The EAC was created by the AU to shed light on a situation that took place in Chad. It is important to note that the innovative aspect of the trial that has had the most positive impact was its demonstration of an African determination first to fight against impunity, and second to participate in the progressive development of international criminal justice. The following will attempt to address these two points as a means of estimating what the EAC has contributed to criminal justice.

Firstly, we will examine the clear desire of the continent to fight against impunity. This determination was made concrete by the creation of the EAC, according to a process that highlighted the AU's desire to judge a former African leader accused of committing serious human rights violations. The second part of the chapter will attempt to clarify how visible this desire was at all levels and, through the trial judgement and then the final, dissuasive judgement after appeal, how it falls with the gradual development of international and African criminal justice. Particular attention will be paid to perspectives raised by the jurisprudence of the Habré case, which could become a model for future hybrid (mixed or Africanized) courts, but also on the future African Criminal Court envisioned by the Malabo Protocol.

The Habre Trial as an expression of African determination to fight impunity

'International justice varies according to circumstance. It only attacks leaders of weak countries. While we are against impunity, we object to the double standard in the implementation of the principle of universal competence.'[5] This statement made by the AU illustrates that, despite their reticence towards the ICC, African countries opposed the commission of international crimes and advocated for the struggle against impunity in Africa. The AU made this position concrete through creation of the EAC and, with it, a symbol of a new birth of international criminal justice.

The engagement of the African States in establishing the EAC

The trial of Hissène Habré took place at a moment where the future relationship between the ICC and the AU was uncertain. The disaffection between the continental organization and the ICC arose from the issuing of an arrest warrant for Al Bashir in the Darfur situation and subsequently worsened with the prosecutor's *motu proprio* court referral in the Kenya

decisions/9560-assembly_en_1_3_july_2009_auc_thirteenth_ordinary_session_decisions_declarations_message_congratulations_motion_0.pdf. See also Chapters 3 and 15 in this book.

[5] Dossier 'Justice internationale jusqu'où ira la CPI?' *Jeune Afrique*, week of July 19, 2008.

situation.[6] Faced with what it considered to be the ICC's judicial 'persecution' of 'Africa' and in particular of African heads of state, the AU adopted a radical position in relation to the ICC, marked by two major resolutions. It decided 'that in view of the fact that the request by the AU has never been acted upon, the AU Member States shall not cooperate pursuant to the provisions of Article 98 of the Rome Statute of the ICC relating to immunities, for the arrest and surrender of President Omar El Bashir of The Sudan'.[7] Thus the AU demanded that the Member States of the 13th session cease all cooperation with the ICC. It also reserved for itself the right to take any decision or step that it judged necessary to preserve and safeguard the dignity, sovereignty and integrity of the continent.[8]

In that same logic, the AU envisaged the creation of an African mechanism to deal with African crimes. It therefore decided to create a Regional Criminal Court by merging the African Commission on Human and People's Rights (ACHPR) and another court in the planning stages.[9]

All these initiatives taken by the AU demonstrate the determination of the organization, not to renounce international criminal justice, but rather to have its own regional mechanisms of achieving it. This firm commitment to provide justice to victims of atrocities, by no means isolated, was evident in the Hissène Habré case. The AU was actively implicated in the establishment of the EAC and in the launching of the trial on African soil.

The creation of the EAC

As the commission report notes, the repression of the most serious crimes falls fully under the competence of the AU, as its Constitutive Act indicates.[10] Thus in accordance with Assembly Decision AU/Dec.103 (VI), adopted in January 2006 in Khartoum (Sudan), the AU Conference decided to put into place a Committee of Eminent African Jurists (CEAJ) mandated with examining all aspects and all implications of the Hissène Habré case as well as options for trying him.[11] On the basis of the CEAJ report,[12] the AU asked Senegal to prosecute Hissène Habré in the name of Africa, at its seventh summit, 1–2 July 2006, in Senegal.[13]

In addition, Decision 127 (VII) on 'the Hissène Habré case and the AU', adopted by the AU Heads of State and of Government Summit, in Banjul (The Gambia), considered the Hissène Habré Case to 'fall within the competence of the African Union'. The implication of the AU is unreserved, mandating 'the Republic of Senegal to prosecute and ensure that

[6] Ndeye Amy Ndiaye, *Le Statut de Rome créant la CPI et ses défis de mise en œuvre*, doctoral thesis, Gaston Berger University of Saint-Louis, 2016, pp 323–33.

[7] Assembly/AU/Dec.245(XIII)Rev.1, p 3. https://au.int/sites/default/files/decisions/9560-assembly_en_1_3_july_2009_auc_thirteenth_ordinary_session_decisions_declarations_message_congratulations_motion_0.pdf

[8] ibid.

[9] Draft Protocol on Amendments to the Protocol on the Statute of the African Court of Justice and Human Rights, EX.CL/846(XXV), 27 June 2014.

[10] Article 4 grants 'the right of the Union to intervene in a Member State pursuant to a decision of the Assembly in respect of grave circumstances, namely: war crimes, genocide and crimes against humanity'.

[11] Report of the Commission on the Hissène Habré Case, Executive council 29th Ordinary Session 10–15 July 2016 Kigali (Rwanda), para 1.

[12] Report of the Committee of Eminent African Jurists on the Case of Hissène Habré, https://www.peacepalacelibrary.nl/ebooks/files/habreCEJA_Repor0506.pdf (accessed 2 August 2018).

[13] Decision on the Hissène Habré Case and the AU Doc Assembly/AU/Dec. 127 (VII) (2006).

Hissène Habré is tried, on behalf of Africa, by a competent Senegalese court with guarantees for fair trial'.[14] Thus the AU came to name Robert Dossou[15] as its special envoy to the case.

Given a number of options, the AU decided to explore an African mechanism. This decision is significant on several levels. It demonstrates Africa's commitment to punish the most serious of crimes and violations of international human rights law committed in Chad, despite the time and distance (as the trial was to be held in Senegal). Twenty-five years after the fact, the victims would obtain justice, and African heads of state demonstrated their collective commitment not to allow any individual, including a former president, to escape the reach of the law. To do this, a group of experts mandated by the AU called on Senegal to take the necessary legislative steps to expand the jurisdiction of its courts to enable it to prosecute the crimes of which Habré was accused. To do this, Senegal established a commission to supervise the legislative reforms and, with the active participation of the AU, to raise funds for the trial.[16] Chad announced that it would contribute three million euros.[17]

In order to enable the Habré trial to be organized rapidly before a special international court, the President of the AU Commission had to appoint prosecutors and judges for the chambers, following recommendations from the Senegalese Minister of Justice. Although the other judges were Senegalese, the Presidents of the different chambers had to be from a third country.[18] The Presidents of the Trial and Appeals Chambers were therefore from Burkina Faso and Mali, respectively.

The AU and the government of the Republic of Senegal thus signed the Accord creating the EAC, an ad hoc international court within the courts of Senegal, to prosecute those persons having committed international crimes in Chad between 7 June 1982, and 1 December 1990. The Statute of the EAC is an integral part of the Accord and the focus of its Article 1, which summarizes the strong, foundational role of the AU, demonstrates that the AU occupied a central place in the implementation and functioning of the EAC.[19]

The AU and the financing of the EAC

In addition to its involvement on the legal and political process, the AU also focused on operationalizing the EAC by becoming a key player in its financing and a partner in the search for and monitoring of its funding. Article 32, paragraph 1 of the accord creating the EAC stipulates that the 'creation and functioning of the EAC are financed by the budget approved by the Round Table of 24 November 2010.[20]

14 Doc Assembly/AU/Dec 127 (VII) (2006).

15 Robert Dossou, Member of the Bar of Cotonou (Benin) and former professor at the University of Paris I Sorbonne-Panthéon? Robert Dossou presided over the Constitutional Court of Benin and is today Honorary President of the Conference of Constitutional Jurisdictions of Africa.

16 Legislatively, on 23 July 2008, the Senegalese Congress adopted a constitutional amendment that confirmed the competence of Senegalese courts to judge crimes against humanity perpetrated in the past. The amendment, which came into force on 7 August 2008, paraphrases the International Covenant on Civil and Political Rights, Article 15(2).

17 See Chapter 8 in this book.

18 Article 11 of the EAC Statute: Composition of the EAC and Nomination of Judges.

19 'The purpose of this Statute is to implement the decision of the AU concerning the Republic of Senegal's prosecution of international crimes committed in Chad between 7 June 1982 and 1 December 1990, in accordance with Senegal's international commitments.'

20 Human Rights Watch, Table ronde des donateurs pour le financement du procès de Monsieur Hissène Habré, 24 November 2010. https://www.hrw.org/sites/default/files/related_material/Table%20ronde%20donateurs%20document%20final.pdf accessed 16 June 2014.

A Round Table of donors financing the Habré trial was held on November 24, 2010, in Dakar (Senegal). It brought together members of the AU and partner countries and institutions: the AU, Chad, Senegal, the European Union, Belgium, Canada, France, Germany, Luxemburg, the Netherlands, Spain, Switzerland, the United Kingdom, the United States, the Office of the United Nations High Commissioner for Human Rights (OHCHR), and the United Nations Office for Project Services (UNOPS).[21]

Even better, the AU was also a member of the Steering Committee created by Article 7 of the Joint Financial Accord on financing the trial, signed on 15 January 2013, by the AU, Chad, Senegal, and the various partners. The Steering Committee sessions were presided by the AU. During the different sessions, the Steering Committee recommended and adopted the following decisions, among others: the financial reports and the progress reports of the Administrator of the EAC, validated and approved by the Audit Division and by auditors external to the AU.[22]

The engagement of African States united by the AU clearly shows their commitment to end impunity. By judging Hissène Habré, they made a strong symbolic gesture of their desire to dissuade any future leader from committing international criminal infractions.

The symbolic character of the EAC

The creation of the EAC was a symbolic moment in the history of the fight against impunity, not only for Africa but also for the entire world. According to Schabas, 'It provides for the establishment of something that must be without precedent in the annals of international criminal law and, indeed, in the annals of law: a national tribunal created by one State with exclusive jurisdiction over acts perpetrated in another State.'[23] Its symbolic character can be seen from two angles: historic and dissuasive.

The creation of the EAC was indeed historic, innovative, and symbolic on many levels. It was the first time that a former African head of state was judged in Africa, and it was the first time ever that the courts of one country judged the head of state of another country for crimes against humanity, citing universal jurisdiction by an internationalized tribunal.

Similarly, the conviction of the former President of Chad by an African mechanism created by Africans with a verdict pronounced by African judges transcends Black/White and African/Western divisions. It was a major turning point in international criminal justice. Through it, Senegal was able to send a clear message that it refused henceforth to give refuge to those accused of committing international crimes, allowing them impunity, even if the individual in question was an African head of state or government.

Senegal is emerging as a model for Africa in the field of international criminal justice. The experience of the EAC established that European and North American countries were not alone in having the determination and the ability to exercise universal jurisdiction,

21 AU, Report of the Commission on the Hissène Habré Trial, Executive Council Twenty-ninth Ordinary Session, 10–15 July, Kigali (Rwanda), SC17394-38/2/15, para 15.

22 https://archive.au.int/collect/oaucounc/.../EX%20CL%20986%20(XXIX)%20_F.pdf accessed 16 June 2018.

23 William Schabas, 2013, 'Senegal's Chambres africaines extraordinaires to judge Habré', 5 February. Available at: <http://humanrightsdoctorate.blogspot.com/2013/02/senegals-chambres-africaines.html> accessed 20 February 2020.

especially when dealing with former heads of state. Senegal should thus be a source of pride for Africa, and Africa should be a source of pride for the rest of the world.

The AU became aware that it could not legitimately criticize the transfer of certain of its leaders to The Hague if it was not able to demonstrate that they could be properly tried in Africa. The International Human Rights Federation was congratulatory, noting: 'We would like to acknowledge the survivors, the States and the AU, who participated, organised and supported this trial, demonstrating not only that Africa can judge those responsible for the gravest crimes, including former heads of State, but also that attempts to allow impunity will always be countered by the determination of victims, and the NGOs who support them, to see that justice is done.'[24]

The Hissène Habré case rang alarm bells for all presidents, heads of government, political leaders, or warlords that someday they would be called to account. The most serious crimes, even when committed by the highest leaders, remain imprescriptible: those who commit such crimes can be prosecuted an any moment of their lives. From that angle, the Habré trial was a critical step forward for African countries taking responsibility for prosecuting the most serious international crimes. By deciding to intervene concretely and to support the creation of the EAC, the AU committed itself not only to the fight against impunity, but also to dissuading present and future African leaders from committing international crimes.

Consequently, in addition to compensation for damages for the victims, Habré's conviction and life imprisonment pave the way for very dissuasive jurisprudence. In the context of African dissent and fierce attacks on the ICC, the EAC has opened the door to the application of universal jurisdiction in Africa.[25]

The Habre trial as a catalyst for the development of a regional criminal justice system

Beyond its symbolic character, the Hissène Habré case has contributed in a number of ways to the progressive development of international law. Africans were among the first to support the creation of the International Criminal Court, massively ratifying the Statute of Rome and leading the implementation of its rules. Even when it became disenchanted with the ICC, Africa never called into question the principle of fighting impunity. At the Kampala Conference, the African States highlighted the need for a better usage of the principle of complementarity, noting that the efforts of the international community tended to provide greater support for the reinforcement of the national judicial capacity of signatory states to the Rome Statute when dealing with cases relating to international crimes.[26]

The objective was in no way to pull out of the ICC in order to entrench impunity; on the contrary, Africans placed more emphasis on sovereignty in the fight against impunity and

[24] https://www.fidh.org/en/region/Africa/chad/hissene-habre-case-a-historic-and-long-awaited-verdict-19999.

[25] Ibrahima Bayo, 'Condamnation de Hissene Habre : le verdict qui fait trembler certains présidents africains', 28 June 2017, https://afrique.latribune.fr/politique/2017-04-28/condamnation-d-hissene-habre-le-verdict-qui-fait-trembler-certains-presidents-africains.html accessed 10 January 2019.

[26] Mutoy Mubiala, 'Chronique de droit pénal de l'Union Africaine. L'élargissement du mandat de la Cour africaine de Justice et des droits de l'homme aux affaires de droit international pénal' (2014) 85.3 Revue internationale de droit pénal 749–58.

wanted the system of deterrence to be more orientated toward the national or even regional. It is because of this that the EAC, the most recent iteration of hybrid jurisdictions, is considered as 'the most national of international tribunals'.[27]

The affirmation of African sovereignty over its legal cases

In the context of 'priority for an African solution', as the Conference prescribes,[28] the Committee of Jurists of the AU formulated concrete recommendations for trying Hissène Habré as well as for means of dealing with similar problems that might appear in the future, which they then presented in their report to the Ordinary Session of the Conference in July 2016 in Banjul (Gambia).[29]

With the opening of the EAC in August 2013, the continent affirmed its sovereignty over its judicial dossiers. The courts of one State (Senegal) would, for the first time, judge the former leader of another State (Chad) for alleged human rights violations. The EAC was not the first criminal institution created in Africa or for Africa.[30] However, the United Nations was involved in the creation of previous international or internationalized courts. The EAC was entirely African.

Because of the experiences of South Africa and Rwanda, Africa had already made its mark on a particular kind of international criminal justice, with the Truth and Reconciliation Commissions and the *Gacaca*.[31] The Habré case was an extension of these. It met an African imperative to reconcile African preoccupations with the exigencies of international criminal justice in the fight against impunity in the commission of international crimes. Africa has now proven that it is capable of reconciling the two with the creation of the EAC within the Senegalese courts for the trial of the former Chadian President Hissène Habré, a singular example of regionalized international justice. Even better, Africa is creating the means to equip itself with a regional jurisdiction on the continent charged with fighting and punishing serious crimes committed by African leaders.

The Malabo Protocol: The regionalization of international criminal justice

A series of collectively organized actions demonstrates the African will to work towards the regionalization of internal criminal justice. That is what emerges from the conclusions of various AU summits.

The Extraordinary AU Summit of October 2013 was organized around the threat of collective withdrawal from the Treaty of Rome by AU member states. At the Addis Ababa

[27] Raymond Savadogo, 'Les Chambres africaines extraordinaires au sein des tribunaux sénégalais: Quoi de si extraordinaire?' (2014) 45.1 Études internationales 105–27.

[28] AU, Report of the Commission on the Hissène Habré Trial, Executive Council Twenty-ninth Ordinary Session, 10–15 July, Kigali (Rwanda), SC17394-38/2/15, para 15.

[29] Report of the Commission on the Hissène Habré Trial, para 2.

[30] An International Criminal Tribunal was created for Rwanda (ICTR) and a Special Court for Sierra Leone (SCSL).

[31] The term *gacaca* denotes popular tribunals in Rwanda, http://www.un.org/fr/preventgenocide/rwanda/about/bgjustice.shtml, accessed 10 January 2019.

summit of January 2016, these same states adopted a 'withdrawal strategy' from the International Criminal Court.[32] In between, in June 2014 in Malabo (Equatorial Guinea), the AU adopted the Protocol to the African Charter on Human and Peoples' Rights on the Establishment of the African Court on Human and Peoples' Rights (ACHPR) (Malabo Protocol) to bring its regional competence in line with its desire to regionalize jurisdiction for international crimes committed in Africa.[33] The Protocol created an international criminal law section in addition to the two previously existing sections, a general law section and a human rights section.[34]

The Malabo Protocol is a key element in the move towards a more regionalized international criminal justice. If many of the crimes that come under its jurisdiction are defined by specific universal or African regional treaties (terrorism, corruption, money laundering, human trafficking, and drug trafficking), others are specific to Africa. These include unconstitutional change of government (UA Constitution; African Charter on Democracy, Elections, and Governance of 2007); mercenary activities (OAU Convention of 1977 on the elimination of mercenary activity in Africa); trafficking in hazardous waste (Bamako Convention of 1991 banning the importation of hazardous waste and controlling their cross-border movements in Africa); and the illegal exploitation of natural resources (International Conference on the Great Lakes Region Protocol against the Illegal Exploitation of Natural Resources, 2006). What emerges from these precedents of the Malabo Protocol is a regional codification of universal norms of international criminal law that ensures the progressive development of a certain number of regional rules in that domain.

Even though this protocol could address a number of challenges, it should be noted that the African Court of Human Rights and Justice (ACHRJ) could, with an expanded mandate, also play a very positive role on a continent chronically faced with armed conflicts and where crimes of international laws are frequent, and frequently committed with impunity.

By attributing jurisdiction over international crimes to this new African means of fighting impunity, the states of the AU wanted to express their collective determination to prevent such crimes from being perpetrated and to repress them according to African values.[35] Even though in practice many elements must be put into place first before this protocol can come into force,[36] its effectiveness would offer the continent another mechanism that would ally international criminal justice and legal judicial sovereignty.

Additionally, the desire to regionalize international criminal justice through the Malabo Accord must be relativized. With a long, ambitious list of crimes, genocides,

[32] AU, 'Withdrawal Strategy Document, Draft 2' Addis Ababa, African Union, 12 January 2017 https://www.hrw.org/sites/default/files/supporting_resources/icc_withdrawal_ strategy_jan._2017.pdf, accessed 19 May 2017.

[33] Mutoy Mubiala, 'L'Afrique et la justice pénale internationale, note d'analyse' (January 2014) Revue internationale de droit pénal.

[34] The African Court on Human and People's Rights is the product of the merging of the African Court on Human and People's Rights (established in 1998 by the Protocol of Ouagadougou (Burkina Faso) and coming into force in 2004) and the Court of Justice of the African Union (the statute o which was adopted by the Protocol of Maputo (Mozambique) of 2003). The Protocol that created the ACHPR was adopted in Sharm El-Sheik (Egypt) in July 2008.

[35] See Pacifique Manirakiza, 'L'Afrique et le système de justice pénale internationale' (2009) 3 African Journal of Legal Studies 21–52.

[36] See Margaret M deGuzman (2017), 'Complementarity at the African Court', Temple University Legal Studies Research Paper No 2018-01, pp 1–43, Social Science Research Network. https://papers.ssrn.com/sol3/papers.cfm?abstract_id=3078119.

unconstitutional changes of government, terrorism, corruption, piracy, immunity questions for heads of state and other senior officials, the protocol remains problematic.[37]

Regional justice must meet international norms and guarantees for the accused but must especially ensure the rights of victims. Fundamentally, it should be executed with independence, basing itself on international law and distancing itself from political questions. In all cases, regional criminal justice must go hand-in-hand with the principle of universal jurisdiction as was used for the Hissène Habré trial.

Implementation of universal jurisdiction

The rule of universal jurisdiction derogates from the principle of territoriality of criminal law, by which an individual is tried and judged by the authorities of the State where the infraction was committed, according to the law in force in that State. It is also distinguished from traditional criteria for extraterritorial competence (active personality, passive personality, and meaningful jurisdiction) by the diminution or even suppression of any connection to the country of the forum.[38] To implement universal competence, Senegalese law had to be amended[39] to give national tribunals extraterritorial jurisdiction over international crimes.[40]

According to the doctrine, the principle of universal competence has multiple definitions. It can be defined according to the degree of authority of the judge and of conditionality.[41] In Africa, the trial of Hissène Habré in Dakar is the first case where a former head of state was judged by another State on the basis of universal jurisdiction exercised by a special tribunal set up with the accord of a regional organization. For the first time in international criminal justice, a special court was created to exercise universal jurisdiction, normally the prerogative of a state. The EAC was nonetheless not created to exercise universal jurisdiction in Senegal on a permanent basis, but rather on an ad hoc one.

It must be recognized that the principle of universal jurisdiction is a double-edged sword. Used wisely, it can positively reinforce criminal justice and ensure the effectiveness of the rights and duties of several regional African instruments, including the African Charter of Human and People's Rights. Politically instrumentalized, notably to protect African leaders

[37] This was reflected in the discussions in the regional seminar entitled 'Understanding the Malabo Protocol: opportunities, challenges, and next steps towards an international justice in Africa', organized by Amnesty International in Dakar in December 2017.

[38] D Vandermeersch, 'La compétence universelle en droit belge', in *Poursuites pénales et extraterritorialité = Stra fprocesrech en extraterritorialiteit*, Dossier de la Rev. dr. pén., n°8, 2002, p 41.

[39] On 31 January 2007, The Senegalese National Assembly adopted a law allowing cases of genocide, crimes against humanity, war crimes, and torture to be brought before the court even if they were not committed on Senegalese territory.

[40] Youssoupha Diallo, 'L'Interaction normative entre les Chambres Africaines Extraordinaires (CAE) et le Système Juridique National Sénégalais' (2017) African Journal of International Criminal Justice 1–2.

[41] The level of accreditation of the national judge allows to designate absolute universal jurisdiction, according to which the national judge sets himself up as spokesperson for the international community by directly referring to international law. This is how the Senegalese investigative judge decided to charge Hissène Habré for crimes committed in Chad without being able to refer to Senegalese national law. In contrast, there is a delegated universal competence which required the judge to have a statutory basis in national law voted by Parliament to be able to avail themselves of the interest of humanity. Thus the Belgian investigative judge charged Hissène Habré on the basis of the Belgian law of universal jurisdiction voted a few years earlier. (Julien Seroussi, 'La cause de la compétence universelle. Note de recherche sur l'implosion d'une mobilisation internationale' (2008) 3 173 Actes de la recherche en sciences sociales 98–109.)

currently or about to be prosecuted by the ICC or non-African courts, the principle of 'regional competence' would contribute to reinforcing the culture of impunity in Africa.[42]

Conclusion

In summary, the example of the most sophisticated international criminal trial on African territory is that of Hissène Habré, which can be likened to a 'trial pitting Africa against international criminal justice'. The positive impact of the Hissène Habré trial can be seen through the angles of the fight against impunity and its participation in the progressive development of international and/or regional criminal law.

What emerges from this analysis is that, contrary to what Christophe Châtelot predicted when he considered 'the condemnation of Hissène Habré [to be] a precedent with no future',[43] this trial has a concrete impact on the future of Africa. The EAC seems to embody the project of empowerment of the AU, which is clear in its desire to withdraw from the ICC. The uneasiness of certain African governments faced with a selective international justice, oriented towards Africa and which, in their eyes, freely violates the principle of national sovereignty, has incited them to create a regional criminal justice. The Habré jurisprudence can be applied in other situations, as in the case of the former Ethiopian dictator Haile Mengistu, who lives in Zimbabwe today. The victims of Gambian Yahya Jammeh are also organizing to prosecute their former president. Lastly, it has to be seen how the process that started in Malabo will progress.

[42] Mutoy Mubiala, 'Chronique de droit pénal de l'Union africaine. Vers une justice pénale régionale en Afrique' (2012) 83 Revue internationale de droit pénal 547–57.

[43] Christophe Châtelot, 'La condamnation de Hissène Habré : un précédent sans lendemain?' (*Le Monde*, 24 May 2016).

29

Expertise in the Bench? The Dis-embeddedness of International Criminal Justice

Julien Seroussi

Introduction

It is no secret within international courts that international lawyers are facing very sparse access to information when they have to judge foreign situations from abroad. Thus, the judges elaborate what I call 'folk sociological theories' (FST), which are sociological narratives, that can provide them with a grasp of the situation as well as a guide for the selection of facts that can demonstrate responsibility or guilt in the accomplishment of crimes.

Looking at how international lawyers handle facts, I stress that international lawyers select FSTs which present strong elective affinities with recognized legal theories rather than elaborate on the complex sociological realities in which the actions under investigation take place. These FSTs are meant to solve problems and limit evidentiary requirements to the level of the reasonable and manageable, even if they bear little relation with the sociological reality experienced by the social actors on the ground.

This chapter explores the origins and ramifications of the Katanga and Ngudjolo cases, suggesting that it raises important conceptual implications for understanding the epistemological limitations of international criminal proceedings. In December 2012, Mathieu Ngudjolo was acquitted of all charges against him for lack of evidence. In March 2014, Germain Katanga who had been prosecuted as a perpetrator was sentenced to twelve years in prison as an accessory to war crimes and crimes against humanity.

I will examine the production of FSTs through a pragmatic approach showing when such folk theories successfully produce the irrelevance of facts in fact-finding processes, and when they fail the reality tests of legal procedure. These FSTs tell investigators which empirical and contextual aspects they can disregard and wilfully ignore. In so doing, FSTs offer both advantages and present risks: in the short term they can propose shortcuts for prosecutors to demonstrate the liability of the incriminated parties. However, as I will show, they also may reduce complex realities too much, leading the judges to reject claims of criminal responsibility.

Folk sociological theories in international criminal proceedings

Several anthropologists of international criminal law have pointed out that some of the legal theories entertained by international judges are at odds with the cultural settings of the affected communities. This debate broke out especially regarding the judgments of crimes

Julien Seroussi, *Expertise in the Bench? The Dis-embeddedness of International Criminal Justice* In: *The President on Trial*. First edition. Edited by: Sharon Weill, Kim Thuy Seelinger, and Kerstin Bree Carlson, Oxford University Press (2020). © Julien Seroussi. DOI: 10.1093/oso/9780198858621.003.0030

committed in Rwanda and in Sierra Leone. In the footsteps of Danny Hoffman's[1] critical account of his own testimony as an expert witness at the Special Court for Sierra Leone (SCSL), Tim Kelsall[2] asked whether international criminal law does not represent a new form of cultural imperialism.[3] Through a review of different legal decisions of the SCLS, he found that the facts could have been adjudicated better through a more culturally informed looking-glass. For instance, Kelsall criticized the prosecutor's choice to look at the militia as a hierarchical military organization (characterized by the concept of 'command responsibility') rather than the militarization of a social network. For him, the court's lack of contextual familiarity ultimately jeopardized its ability to understand the real chain of command within a society dominated by fragmented patronage networks. While shedding an important light on the cultural challenges of international justice, Kelsall reduces the question of the ascertainment of truth to a clash between Western and non-Western cultures.

Understanding the establishment of facts in an international tribunal requires more than a binary juxtaposition of Western and non-Western systems. In her eloquently titled book *Fact-Finding without Facts*,[4] Nancy Combs also admits that trials are plagued with cultural clashes between the international legal staff and the witnesses and concerns over translation problems. Although some of her conclusions are more extreme than Kelsall's—since she goes so far as to cast doubt on the possibility of establishing facts in international justice—her critical analysis relies on a deeper understanding of the legal practices. Drawing a comparison between the work of several international tribunals (mostly the SCLS, the International Criminal Tribunal for Rwanda [ICTR] and the East Timor Special Panels), she concludes that because international justice usually rests on a narrow factual basis—as the judges are not able to argue beyond reasonable doubt that the accused is guilty—they tend to lower the evidentiary threshold to fit their intimate conviction and charge the defendants as guilty. For her, many of the witnesses who appear before international tribunals lie and international judges often cover up their lies. Indeed, many external reasons push in this direction: the high cost of trials, which does not allow the luxury of too many acquittals, as well as the pressures of donor states, which would be less willing to invest in the field of international justice if a large number of the trials ended up in acquittals. Combs' study has the merit to say out loud what most of the international legal establishment refuses to say publicly to protect the legitimacy of international tribunals. Although she casts an insightful eye on how criminal law practices are disrupted by investigations, Combs is nevertheless too focused on the failings of the international tribunals.

The genealogy of a new legal mode of liability

In the case against Germain Katanga and Mathieu Ngudjolo case the Pre-trial Chamber adopted a theory of liability called 'indirect co-perpetration'. This theory innovatively

[1] Danny Hoffman 'The Meaning of a Militia: Understanding the Civil Defence Forces of Sierra Leone' (2007) 106 (425) African Affairs, 639–662.

[2] *Culture Under Cross-Examination: International Justice and the Special Court for Sierra Leone* (Cambridge University Press 2009).

[3] This chapter is based on a longer article: Julien Seroussi, 'The role of folk sociological theories at the International Criminal Court' (2018) 69(4) British Journal of Sociology 962.

[4] *Fact-Finding without Facts: The Uncertain Evidentiary Foundations of International Criminal Convictions* (Cambridge University Press 2010).

combines different ways to hold someone responsible for mass crimes outlined in Article 25(3)(a) of the Rome Statute. The objective elements of this new legal characterization are displayed in the 'Decision on the confirmation of charges' as follows: (i) control over the organization; (ii) organized and hierarchical apparatus of power; (iii) the execution of the crimes secured by almost automatic compliance with orders; (iv) the existence of a common plan or agreement; (v) the coordinated essential contribution by each co-perpetrator resulting in the realization of the objective elements of the crime.[5]

The 'automatic compliance with orders', which is the cornerstone of this new approach to liability, was not self-evident, as it had not been previously used in international criminal law, and it is not found in the Rome Statute; rather, it emerged from jurisprudence mostly in Germany and Latin America. Laying down the legal foundation of their definition of indirect co-perpetration, the principal preliminary judge quoted Claus Roxin, a German legal scholar, who published a theory of perpetration by means of a subordinate after the trial against Adolf Eichmann held by Israel in 1961[6]. Claus Roxin intended to undercut Eichmann's defence strategy, which described him as a simple cog in an organization with no knowledge of the final purpose of his work.[7] Turning the argument against Eichmann, this legal approach holds that the Nazi leaders could be considered the author of the crimes committed by their subordinates, as each member of the organizational apparatus is reduced to a mere interchangeable and disposable tool.

If we look at the judicial precedent supporting indirect co-perpetration, the first important legal recognition of this concept was asserted by the German Federal Court of Appeals when it adjudicated the human rights violations committed by the border police of the German Democratic Republic. Besides Germany, the preliminary judges also claimed that national courts from Argentina, Chile, Germany, Peru, and Spain had all accepted the legal theory of indirect co-perpetration.[8] Unsurprisingly, the composition of the legal staff who played a key role in the debate on the confirmation of charges against Katanga and Ngudjolo was dominated by lawyers from Latin America: specifically Argentina and Brazil. The elected Prosecutor of the ICC, Luis Moreno Ocampo, as well as the director of the trial division, Fabrizio Guariglia, were Argentinian; the president of the Preliminary Chambers, Sylvia Steiner, was Brazilian, and its most senior legal officers, Hector Olasolo and Alessandro Kiss, were from Spain and Argentina respectively; while the legal officer of the President of the ICC, and ex-officio member of the Appeals Chamber, Volker Nerlich, was German. As indirect co-perpetration had been at the heart of legal cross-citation between Germany and Latin America, this configuration of the ICC offered fertile ground to create a passageway for this concept to be introduced into international case law.

[5] Pre Trial Chamber I, The Prosecutor against Germain Katanga and Mathieu Ngudjolo, Decision on the confirmation of charges, 30 September 2008, paras 487–526.

[6] 'A concept has developed in legal doctrine that acknowledges the possibility that a person who acts through another may be individually criminally responsible, regardless of whether the executor (the direct perpetrator) is also responsible. This doctrine is [...] identified by the term: 'perpetrator behind the perpetrator' (Täter hinter dem Täter). (Pre-Trial Chamber I, Decision on the confirmation of charges, 2008, para 496).

[7] See Isabelle Delpla, *Le mal en procès. Eichmann et les théodicées modernes*. Paris: Hermann 2011; Mark Osiel, *Making Sense of Mass Atrocity* (Cambridge University Press 2009).

[8] 'The Federal Appeals Chamber of Argentina, The Juntas Trial, Case No 13/84, chapter 7/5. Judgment of the Supreme Court of Justice of Peru, Case No 5385-200, 14 December 2007. Supreme Court of Chile (investigating magistrate), Fallos de Mes, ano XXXV, novembre de 1993, 12 November 1993; Supreme Tribunal of Spain, penal chamber, Case No 12966/1994, 2 July 1994 (Judge Bacigalupo). National Court of Spain, Central investigating tribunal No 5, 29 March 2006 (Pre-Trial Chamber I, Decision on the confirmation of charges, 2008, note 666, p 169).

Other epistemic communities in the field of international criminal justice reject the grounds of such a theory of responsibility. For instance, historians of Nazi Germany have established that local troops acted with a great deal of creativity while carrying out orders formulated by their superiors. To a certain extent, the destruction of European Jewish communities was also the result of the benchmarking of the most efficient killing methods invented by subordinates in the field. Thus, from a sociological point of view, the notion of 'compliance with orders' appears to be highly dubious, and seems hard to understand why such a distinguished crowd of international judges as those sitting at the ICC would have privileged it among all possible alternative legal theories of liability. However, such criticisms are met with a relative indifference by the lawyers, who do not consider that legal concepts are descriptive. Indeed, the Pre-Trial Chambers' choice to invent a whole new mode of liability by introducing 'indirect co-perpetration' should be rather analysed as a legal means to deal with a higher level of uncertainty in the field rather than for its descriptive ability.

The problem of investigative capacities

Beyond the existence of a network of German and Latin American lawyers for whom indirect co-perpetration was part of their 'tool kit'[9] of prosecutorial strategies, a more pragmatic reason played a role in the establishment of this legal doctrine. The Pre-Trial Judges' approach to responsibility took into account the very limited investigative capacity of the prosecutor. From the point of view of the sociology of knowledge, the writing of the legal narrative in the case against Germain Katanga and Mathieu Ngudjolo is not a historical account of the events, but an attempt to overcome the numerous challenges raised by the difficulty of collecting material in the field and the very high probative threshold required by criminal proceedings.

To understand the conflict under examination, the prosecutor gathered open source documentation and contacted expert witnesses to understand the general dynamic of the conflict. In the case of the crisis in Congo, this first step turned out to be already very challenging. As one of the most senior experts of the Great Lakes Region testified in Court, trustworthy open source information was hard to find. The chaos generated by the splintering and reversal of alliances between different armed groups made it impossible to assess which militias had attacked which villages. The attempt of the UN reports to account for the different attacks reflected more their efforts to foster peace building than the course of the events. Reports by the UN described better what the UN was doing than what military groups on the ground were doing[10].

In the midst of such uncertainty, the prosecutor had trouble elaborating his criminal policy; that is, choosing a certain number of incidents he wished to investigate among the many dramatic events in the given situation, and targeting a few persons of interest to stand trial. He had to limit his investigations to the best-documented attacks instead of focusing on the most lethal ones. The attack against Bogoro on 24 February 2003 was neither a significant battle for the war in Congo, nor among the attacks with the heaviest death toll. It

[9] Ann Swidler, 'Culture in Action: Symbols and Strategies,' (1986) 51(2) American Sociological Review, 273–286.

[10] Trial Chamber I, Gerard Prunier, Expert Witness, 27 March 2009, pp 12–23.

seems that the ICC prosecutor simply focused his efforts on this ordinary attack because Bogoro was one of the rare villages that the UN had been able to visit shortly after the assault. As a matter of fact, the UN human rights officer who had led this human rights fact-finding mission became one of the prosecutor's key witnesses at the trial against Katanga and Ngudjolo.

Thus, as far as investigative capacities are concerned, the investigators of the ICC faced a difficult situation. As the war was still ongoing, they had to sort out the factual truth in a very complex, changing and unfamiliar environment. Even if violence had significantly abated since the end of the Congolese war in 2003, several militias were still active in the region when the prosecutor started his investigation in Congo. Moreover, the Congolese suspects were not part of an elaborate bureaucratic machinery leaving a trail of written reports that the prosecutor could use to convict the accused. The investigators of the ICC largely depended on oral testimonies, a very fragile type of evidence, which can easily be shattered by cross-examination.

Fortunately, the theory of legal responsibility that the Pre-Trial Chamber adopted provided guidelines to help the investigators find their way through the Congolese mist. On the legal side, the choice of combining the two different modes of liability—'co-perpetration' and 'indirect perpetration'—into the new concept of 'indirect co-perpetration' allowed the investigators to take a certain number of shortcuts in the field. As an 'indirect co-perpetrator', Germain Katanga is not only responsible for the acts committed by his own foot soldiers, but can also be convicted for the crimes committed by the soldiers loyal to Mathieu Ngudjolo despite the fact that Katanga never gave them any orders.[11] Generated by the concept of indirect co-perpetration, this mutual attribution of the crimes committed by subordinates spared the investigators from significant fact-finding issues. As both accused could be held responsible for any crimes committed during the attack, the prosecutor did not have to sort out which militia committed which crime.

Similarly, the Pre-trial Chamber also tried to take into account the limited capacity of the prosecutor when elaborating on the facts of the case by resting its reasoning on what seemed to be the most easily collectible type of evidence. Drawing on an FST to prove when 'automatic compliance with orders' could be observed on the ground, the 'Decision on the Confirmation of Charges' (DCC) asserted that the automatic control of the commanders over their subordinates required mainly to show that the militia was composed of numerous child soldiers of the same ethnicity as their officers:

> 547. [...] because the soldiers were young, were subjected to a brutal military training regime and had allegiance to the military leaders of their ethnic groups, they were likely to comply with the orders of those leaders almost automatically, without asking any questions. For instance, there is sufficient evidence to establish substantial grounds to believe that in the FNI and FRPI camps:

[11] 'An individual who has no control over the person through whom the crime would be committed cannot be said to commit the crime by means of that other person. However, if he acts jointly with another individual—one who controls the person used as an instrument—these crimes can be attributed to him on the basis of mutual attribution. Although the importance of this notion to the present case will be further clarified below, it must be kept in mind that, due to ethnical loyalties within the respective organisations led by Germain Katanga (FRPI) and Mathieu Ngudjolo Chui (FNI), some members of these organisations accepted orders only from leaders of their own ethnicity'. (Pre-Trial Chamber I, Decision on the confirmation of charges, 2008, paragraph 493).

i. Child soldiers were trained using violent methods, they learned how to handle weapons, and at the end of their training received machetes, spears and guns;
ii. Soldiers were militarily trained under the orders of Germain Katanga and Mathieu Ngudjolo Chui and were often paraded in their presence;
iii. Germain Katanga was the key decision-maker regarding the transfer of children to, from, and within FRPI camps;
iv. Germain Katanga also used child soldiers in his personal escort because 'he preferred to be escorted by soldiers who were less than 15 years-old as the latter executed his orders without opposition';
v. Mathieu Ngudjolo Chui also used child soldiers in his personal escort. According to Witness 280, in the FNI camps, a significant number of children were in the Military Police; the Military Police was in charge of arresting soldiers who caused trouble in the camp or in the village (every camp had a Military Police whose size depended on the size of the camp).[12]

In a bid to consider the prosecutor's limited resources, the Pre-Trial Chamber proposed to kill two birds with one stone by using the evidence collected to prove the 'use of child soldiers' as the backbone for the assessment of the 'automatic compliance with orders'. Since the fact that the majority of soldiers recruited in their militia were children can be considered a sufficient evidence of obedience, the prosecutor could limit its investigations in the field to finding evidence that most soldiers were under fifteen years old, the threshold retained by the Rome Statute to distinguish a child from an adult. The prosecutor was not compelled to provide a complete picture of the workings of the militia's organization to prove the authority of each suspect over their soldiers.

From my discussions with different legal officers who had to weigh whether this biological approach to authority was convincing or not, it appeared that the backdrop of the reasoning was a consistent finding in case law across a wide variety of national contexts that parents are held responsible for the deeds of their children up to a certain age. As the soldiers of the militia were underage, their commanders could bear the responsibility of their actions 'as if' they were their parents. Hence, the intellectual core of the FST, developed to characterize the facts of the case, was yet another legal reasoning that could appeal to judges—who would have encountered it in their national courtrooms before becoming members of the ICC—rather than a sociological reading of the Congolese context characterizing the operations of militias.

Naturally, this process raises the question of whether international lawyers need sociology at all. It could be argued that their FST may well be adapted to the legal needs despite its lack of sociological validity. To a certain extent, the Pre-Trial Chamber was right to follow purely pragmatic reasons related to the relative ease with which the specific case would be litigated. However, if one leaves aside the principled question of whether historical truth should be sacrificed on the altar of bureaucratic efficiency, the conduct of the trial against Katanga and Ngudjolo shows how dangerous it can be to ignore social sciences, even to fulfil the narrowest judicial goals.

[12] Pre-Trial Chamber I, The Prosecutor against Germain Katanga and Mathieu Ngudjolo, Decision on the confirmation of charges, 30 September 2008, para 547.

Folk sociological theories under cross-examination

Once the 'Decision on the Confirmation of Charges' (CDC) is issued, the case is transferred from the Pre-Trial Chamber to Trial Judges who will have to adjudicate on the guilt of the accused person. The judges of the Trial Chamber do not have access to the record of the Pre-Trial Chamber, and discover the facts of the case during the hearings as the prosecutor and the defence call witnesses and present new exhibits in court. In order to follow the debates, the Trial Judges rely on the FST put forward in the DCC by their colleagues of the Pre-Trial Chamber.

During his investigations, the Prosecutor had cast three child soldiers to testify on the ability of Germain Katanga and Mathieu Ngudjolo to elicit obedience from their soldiers. In accordance with the FSTs developed by the prosecution's brief, all three witnesses only needed to prove that they were less than fifteen years old at the time. Beyond the words of the witnesses, the prosecutor was able to show the court the passport issued by the Congolese authorities. However, the cross-examination of the defence team quickly proved the weak probative value of these elements by confronting the witness with alternative official documents—such as school records, voting registration, or employment contracts—which all gave different birth dates.[13]

According to the defence team, these contradictions on birth dates demonstrated that the witness had deliberately lied to the court in order to benefit from protective measures granted by the Witness Protection Unit Section, which can extend to a total re-localization of the witness in a different country. The defence argued that the witnesses did not come forward to tell the truth but to benefit from material gain and to get a second chance in life. As the witness showed signs of confusion and prostration towards the imperative demand to choose one birth date over another, the judges tried to resort to other means to assess their ages. However, the request for more documentary evidence only increased the level of uncertainty. The judges did not have sufficient knowledge on administrative practices in the DRC to decide whether they should prioritize the passport over the voting cards or vice versa.

President of the Trial Chamber, Judge Bruno Cotte, feared that he would not be able to understand the case, especially as the alleged crimes occurred in a country he had never set foot in during a war he had only heard about in the media. To address this issue, he took the decision to hire social scientists onto his team. This decision seemed in line with the existing practices in France where special task forces of judges and special assistants have been assembled in order to address complex cases. However, it was not the case at the ICC, where not a single social scientist had been working in the judges' chambers. Academics can be called as expert witnesses on specific questions, but judges cannot call upon them to help with assessing evidence in the deliberation room. During the hearing, judges can

[13] 'With regard to P-279's age, the Chamber recalls that the Prosecution did not challenge the authenticity of documents [...] which show that the witness was over the age of 18 years when the attack on Bogoro occurred. The situation with regard to this Witness is quite different from that of P-280 and P-28. Indeed, P-280 stated in court that he was unsure of his precise age and that he wished to have an identity document issued stating his true date of birth. P-28 admitted to having forged school reports in order to continue his studies and to having provided false information regarding his age in order to be accepted into the demobilisation programme for adults. P-279 also admitted to attempting to appear older when giving his date of birth as 30 August 1984 for the issuance of his voter's card. He claimed that this card would guarantee his security if FARDC forces were to conduct an identity check'. (Trial Chamber II, 7 March 2014, 'Judgement pursuant to article 74 of the Statute', para 280.)

sometimes collect new intelligence on a situation, but they do not have the opportunity to put the social scientists' skills to use to analyse the file for them. As a matter of fact, the expert witness do not have access to the file and are only asked very narrow questions.

In the context of the ICC, the hiring of a sociologist turned out to be very controversial. A number of lawyers thought that the presence of social scientists in the chambers would put the fairness of the trial in jeopardy: they believed that the social scientists would be able to whisper in the ears of the judges evidence that wasn't discussed in the courtroom by the parties. Judge Cotte bypassed the latter obstacle by recruiting a sociologist that had no experience whatsoever in Congo, and who could thus not be suspected of bringing evidence through the back door. Although one might get the impression that this choice defeats the purpose, Judge Cotte was not looking for facts that the parties would have ignored, but for skills that enabled him to ask the right question to the witness to grasp the facts of the case and ascertain the truth.

Despite this frustration, some sociological insights convinced the judges to dismiss the claim of the defence team that all three witnesses should be excluded because of their multiple birth dates. The judges reckoned that the manipulation of birth dates in the DRC could be easily explained by the collapse of state administration during the war, rather than by malicious individual conduct fuelled by greed. They admitted that most people in the DRC had learned to take advantage of the administrative deficiencies of the state and to adapt their official identities to the different government services, as to secure their civil rights or to benefit from development programmes. As all witnesses brought by the prosecutor both in the *Katanga* case and the *Lubanga* case were impacted by the same problem, the judges realized that they were not facing individual lies but a collective practice.

Nevertheless, it remains that the factual basis supporting the FST put forward by the Pre-Trial Chamber in the 'Decision on the confirmation of charges' brief, had disintegrated during the course of the trial. Considering whether there was still a case to answer, the Trial Chamber decided to take matters into its own hands by trying to understand the organization of the militia. Shouldered by the presence of a sociologist in his team, Judge Bruno Cotte posed his own questions to the witnesses, which went beyond the examination in chief and cross-examination by the parties. Attempting to grasp the militia's complex chain of command, they drew attention away from the biological approach to obedience, based on the age of the soldiers, to focus on the military role of the 'féticheurs' (medicine men). As the following excerpts shows, they discovered that, far from being simple doctors, the 'féticheurs' had military responsibilities: they decided when the battle should take place, who was fit for combat, and provided the witchcraft required to go to battle.

Q. What kind of techniques were you taught during the military training?
A. We were taught how to use certain types of medication in particular; so that if they sent us off to fight, we wouldn't have any problems.

Q. So that things are perfectly clear, when you refer to medication what exactly are you referring to?
A. When I refer to medication, let me explain in the following way. If you follow the indications that are given for a particular medication, you won't be hit by bullets. (Trial Chamber II, Witness 279, hearing of the 20 May 2010, pp 42–43)

A. When you went to take those fetishes, they would try to assess whether you were 100 per cent fit, you would go to the fighting. And if it was only 99 per cent, you would not go to the battle. And if you were stubborn, you would be killed. (Trial Chamber II, Witness 279, hearing of the 27 May 2010, p 32)

Q. Were you given any particular instructions as to how to use the fetishes?
A. Yes.

Q. What were you told?
A. Well, they said the following: first of all, you mustn't take a woman by force. Secondly, you must not pillage others' property. Those were the two conditions. In addition, there was another condition which was that you must not cross a stream or you must not put your foot in a river. (Trial Chamber II Witness 280, hearing of the 16 June 2010, pp 7–8)

Q. Prior to the attack on the village of Bogoro, the 'féticheurs', did they give you authorization to do what you wanted or did they impose conditions on you such as the conditions we spoke about a few days ago?
A. Having had the fetish to go to Bogoro, they told us that we had the green light. We could do everything that we needed to do. And when they said 'everything that you need to do', you can pillage. You can do everything you want.[14]

The details provided by the witness on witchcraft in the militia enabled the judges to put forward an alternative FST of 'automatic compliance with orders'. Before each battle, the medicine men would perform on the soldiers the magic rituals. Through this ceremony, the soldiers became instruments in the hands of their leaders who had to abide by very strict rules, that evolved from one battle to another, in order to benefit from the protection of the spirits. In other words, the transformation of soldiers into living fetishes ensured the compliance with orders.

The social scientists in the chambers prodded the judges into asking questions regarding the organization of the militia to foster the emergence of a stronger folk sociological theory. Yet, the success of this strategy opened up a legal controversy—legible in the final judgment—on whether endorsing an alternative narrative, more respectful of the witness's words, would jeopardize the impartiality of the bench by favouring the prosecutor. In this context, the judges had to ascertain whether the new FST exceeded the 'facts and circumstances' delimited by the 'Decision on the Confirmation of Charges'. As they agreed that they were not able to assess that the accused had the ability to give orders based on the evidence brought by the prosecutor, and that relying on a new FST would require a whole new trial, Mathieu Ngudjolo was acquitted of all charges while Germain Katanga was convicted as a simple accomplice. This stage of the trial shows that a FST must be sufficiently flexible to allow the judges to adapt it to the course of the trial. If the age of the militiamen had not been the central element to prove the 'automatic compliance with orders', the judges would have had the legal leeway to make the appropriate adaptations to the legal narrative.

[14] Trial Chamber II, Witness 280, hearing of 23 June 2010, p 42.

Conclusion

The presence of a sociologist in the chambers proved to be useful to help the judges ascertain the truth. Although legal arguments forbade relying on a more sophisticated FST to convict the accused, the judgment did rely on all the findings of the judges during the trial to provide—to the best of their knowledge—an elaborate description of what transpired in the eastern part of the DRC. Notwithstanding the question of the guilt of the accused, the judgment presented an extensive interpretation of the determination of the truth and delivered on this commitment. In this regard, one must remember that justice is not only a question of putting people behind bars, but also of reparation for the victims and the establishment of the truth. To a certain extent, it could be argued that the determination of the truth is more important than the conviction of any given individual, as the latter will always be long, risky and rare to achieve at the ICC.

A better understanding of the facts is crucial for the future of international criminal justice. While national judges can rely on tremendous powers to strengthen their interpretation of events, international judges don't have an international police force to provide the required evidence that would enable them to produce the facts in the courtroom. As it does not have the same strength as any domestic tribunal, the ICC can only overcome its difficulties to grasp facts by intellectual investment, especially in the social sciences. Far from pulling away from its core mission, it could rejuvenate the importance of the determination of the truth, which has fallen to the bottom of the agenda of international criminal lawyers, despite the fact that it is considered one of the victim's three fundamental rights, along with justice and reparation.

One can raise the question whether a sociologist would also be needed in a hybrid tribunal which mixes national and international judges. Ideally, the international staff will be able to have all the necessary contextual information to understand the issues at stake and the national one the necessary distance to break free from local political pressures. Leaving aside the fact that this a very idealistic vison of hybrid tribunals, it is also useful to recall that professional sociologist is someone trained to find the proper combination of involvement and detachment, as Norbert Elias as pointed out.[15] Since investigating international crimes requires walking the line between impartiality and truth, the inclusion of social scientists in the teams at all levels of the proceedings is a question of effectiveness.

[15] Norbert Elias, 'Problems of involvement and detachment' (1956) 7(3) British Journal of Sociology 226–52.

30

Hybrid Justice and the Rights of the Defence

Existence at the Periphery

Dov Jacobs[1]

Introduction: a short theoretical reflexion on hybrid tribunals

In the late 1990s, so-called 'Hybrid' tribunals were lauded as a new and viable accountability model. This newfound preference for these tribunals had a number of reasons, both pragmatic (hybrid tribunals are perceived as being more cost-effective) and conceptual (hybrid tribunals are perceived as being more closely embedded in the local realities, allowing for an increased ownership of the process by affected communities). Beyond these specific reasons that militated for some in favour of the development of hybrid solutions, and while it is beyond the scope of this chapter to analyse the position of hybrid tribunals in the general narrative of international justice, it is nonetheless interesting to note that the interest for 'hybrid' solutions can be understood in light of what can be described as a paradigm shift from international justice to transitional justice.

For many years, the narrative of international criminal justice was constructed around a notion of international progress and following a monolithic *rationale*, that of enhancing an international system of accountability for international crimes. However, this story does not take into account a paradigm shift that occurred at the end of the nineties, from the promotion of *international criminal justice* to the promotion of *transitional justice*. It is only if the diversity of paradigms that underlie the project of international criminal law, both from a substantive and institutional point of view, is acknowledged, that the tensions within the field can truly be understood.

What founds these two paradigms? In a nutshell, the international criminal justice paradigm is premised on the protection of an international public order. It allows the international community to prosecute and punish those responsible for crimes that, beyond their immediate victims, affect the international community as a whole. This logic can be seen in international instruments such as the Rome Statute which proclaim that certain crimes affect the well-being of the world and therefore that jurisdiction should be exercised to prosecute persons responsible for the 'most serious crimes of international concern'.[2]

On the other hand, the transitional justice paradigm finds its source, not in some form of international universality, but in the particularities of local situations. The idea is not so

[1] All views expressed here represent solely the views of the author and not the institutions he works for.

[2] The Rome Statute of the International Criminal Court, article 1. One can note that the French version of the Statute appears to be slightly different on this point, by referring to crimes ayant une portée internationale. Therefore, the English version seems to focus on the perception of the crimes by the international community, the French version seems to focus more on the crime itself, the expression portée internationale being able to refer to either the nature of the crime, or its consequences.

Dov Jacobs, *Hybrid Justice and the Rights of the Defence* In: *The President on Trial*. First edition. Edited by: Sharon Weill, Kim Thuy Seelinger, and Kerstin Bree Carlson, Oxford University Press (2020). © Dov Jacobs. DOI: 10.1093/oso/9780198858621.003.0031

much that of ensuring respect of an international public order, but the establishment of the rule of law in post-conflict countries. One primary example of this logic is the 2004 report by the United Nations Secretary General on the 'The rule of law and transitional justice in conflict and post-conflict societies'.[3] This report illustrates how trial mechanisms, both international and national, can be integrated in more general reflections on the needs of societies that emerge from civil conflict.

The identification of these two paradigms does not in itself constitute a major finding. However, taking them into account explains a number of tensions in the practice of international criminal justice, particularly in the context of hybrid tribunals. This tension exists on two different levels.

First of all, it exists in the traditional opposition between the national and the international. In that perspective, international justice efforts are often required to strike a difficult balance between what the international community would require in order to preserve the international public order and what the national community would require to ensure a smooth political transition from civil conflict.

Second of all, and possibly more problematic, it exists *within* the practice of the international community. Indeed, as the examples of Kosovo and East Timor illustrate, the international community, through the UN, increasingly exercises functions in certain States that would traditionally be exercised by national authorities. In this sense, it is the international community itself, in exercising these several functions, that must strike the balance, in a holistic manner, between the national and the international.

These considerations are not simply theoretical, they affect the way we analyse and understand the way these hybrid tribunals function, depending on the paradigm that is put forward. Indeed, legal outcomes or institutional achievements of these tribunals will necessarily not be considered in the same way, depending on whether the focus is on domestic capacity building for example or on the development of universal norms in the fight against impunity.

With this in mind, this chapter will briefly address generally the issue of the position of the Defence in hybrid tribunals, more particularly at the Extraordinary African Chambers before proposing those reflections on the role of the Defence within the international criminal justice project.

An overview of the defence in hybrid tribunals and at the Extraordinary African Chambers

Whatever balance is struck between the two paradigms of international justice identified above, as the realisation of a universalist ambition of fighting impunity or as a means to reconcile societies after a conflict, practice has shown that the rights of the Accused and his Defence often are merely one parameter to be taken into consideration on a policy level, when it is taken into account at all.

On an institutional level, one must acknowledge that punctual efforts seem to have been made in a number of hybrid tribunals to provide a space for the Defence to voice

[3] UN Doc S/2004/616, 23 August 2004.

its concerns. The Special Court for Sierra Leone was one of the first international justice mechanisms to provide for an actual Defence office, as opposed to a mere sub-section of the Registry, even if it was technically under the Registrar's authority.[4] Moving things even further, the Special Tribunal for Lebanon provided for a Defence office that was legally considered as entirely separate organ of the Court, along with the Chambers and the Office of the Prosecutor. This has been presented by many as an improvement and a recognition of the Defence as one of the pillars of international justice, possibly a viable model for the future.[5] However, while it is possibly an improvement on what took place at other international tribunals, it is doubtful whether it is a transposable model: the STL was set up to essentially deal with one case, with no Defendants (the trial is conducted in absentia), which makes it materially possible to centralize Defence activities in one office. This will never be the case at the ICC, which deals with numerous cases in very different situations, where the political context calls for a diversity of approaches. More recently, the Kosovo Specialist Chambers provided for the creation of a Defence office that resembles more the Sierra Leone model than the STL model, in the sense that it is part of the Registry.

When it comes to the Extraordinary African Chambers, it should be noted that the initial agreement and Statute of the Chambers, signed in 2012 did not include any specific provision relating to an institutional representation of the Defence within the institution. However, in 2014, an addendum to the initial agreement was signed between Senegal and the African Union in order to create a Defence office within the Extraordinary African Chambers.[6] The addendum is unclear as to the exact status of the Defence office, ie whether it is to be part of the Registry (as at the ICC) or whether it should be considered as a distinct organ of the Chambers (as at the STL). Either way, the ambition of this addendum was clearly to promote the respect for the rights of the Defence at the African Chambers, as noted in the Preamble to the addendum, where the right to a fair trial and the presumption of innocence are reaffirmed as fundamental principles.[7]

It is also interesting to note that the African Union and Senegal did feel the need to also indicate in the preamble that they were 'strongly convinced that they have a duty to fight against impunity in conformity with the provisions of Article 4(o) of the constitutive act of the African Union'.[8] Because there is no logical reason to include such a statement in this particular addendum, given that it is simply an amendment to the Statute of the Chambers which does not change its purpose, one can only assume that this preambular sentence was included in order to avoid the perception that promoting the rights of the Defence might somehow, in a sort of zero-sum game, deflect from the 'fight against impunity'. Obviously, the accurate way of presenting things would have been to explain that the 'fight against impunity' cannot be legitimate without respect for the rights of the Accused. In other words,

[4] John RWD Jones, Claire Carlton-Hanciles, Haddijatou Kah-Jallow, and Sam Scratch, 'The Special Court for Sierra Leone—A Defence Perspective' (2004) 2 Journal of International Criminal Justice 211

[5] François Roux, *La Parole est à la Défense* (Indigène Editions 2016) 52.

[6] Avenant A L'accord Entre Le Gouvernement De La Republique Du Senegal Et L'union Africaine Relatif Au Statut Des Chambres Africaines Extraordinaires Pour La Poursuite Des Crimes Internationaux Commis Au Tchad Durant La Periode Du 7 Juin 1982 Au 1er Decembre 1990, 24 July 2014.

[7] Avenant A L'accord Entre Le Gouvernement De La Republique Du Senegal Et L'union Africaine Relatif Au Statut Des Chambres Africaines Extraordinaires Pour La Poursuite Des Crimes Internationaux Commis Au Tchad Durant La Periode Du 7 Juin 1982 Au 1er Decembre 1990, 24 July 2014, preamble.

[8] Avenant A L'accord Entre Le Gouvernement De La Republique Du Senegal Et L'union Africaine Relatif Au Statut Des Chambres Africaines Extraordinaires Pour La Poursuite Des Crimes Internationaux Commis Au Tchad Durant La Periode Du 7 Juin 1982 Au 1er Decembre 1990, 24 July 2014, preamble.

respect for the fundamental rights of the Defence is actually part and parcel of the 'fight against impunity', if it is to be anything else that the exercise of popular revenge.

This example might seem anecdotal, but it is symptomatic of a general perception of the Defence in international and hybrid Courts, as discussed in the final section of this Chapter.

More generally, beyond these institutional arrangements, all hybrid tribunals formally recognise basic rights of the Accused in their founding documents, in more or less the same terms. The Accused have always been represented in Court, mostly been able to examine witnesses and submit relevant motions and responses. More particularly in relation to the Extraordinary African Chambers, Article 21 of the Chambers' Statute provides for the usual rights of the Accused, including the Presumption of innocence, the right to be informed of the nature of the charges, the right to benefit from adequate time and facilities to prepare a Defence case and the right against self-incrimination. It is however difficult to evaluate to what extent these rights were indeed respected concretely during the trial. Indeed, there are no public records available, other than the Trial and Appeals Judgments.[9] It is therefore impossible to determine what challenges might have been raised by the Defence in the course of the trial and how it was dealt with by the Judges.

Despite this lack of available information, a few thoughts might be presented on the challenges for the Defence at the Extraordinary African Chambers.

Two examples of challenges for the defence at the Extraordinary African Chambers

As noted previously, in the absence of a public record, it is impossible to exhaustively address legal challenges faced by the Defence during the trial and how they were dealt with by the Trial and Appeals Chamber. Two examples can however be put forward as illustrations.

Beforehand, it is important to note the particular difficulty in this case for the Defence lawyers: the Accused refused to participate actively in the proceedings, which led the Chambers appointing ad hoc counsel to represent the interests of the Accused, without his consent. This obviously made the Court-appointed work hard, because they had to build a theoretical Defence case, with no instructions from their client. It is even doubtful, for example, whether Hissein Habré actually wanted for an appeal to be filed.[10] In this context, it is extremely difficult, from the outside, to make an entirely fair or accurate assessment of the situation.

[9] This goes beyond the scope of the present contribution, but the absence of available public records would merit discussion in and of itself. Indeed, one of the goals of international justice is to act as a pedagogical tool for the affected communities. In that respect, the final Judgment, while important, cannot be deemed sufficient to achieve this pedagogical goals, because it follows a process that also needs to be explained if the outcome is going to be considered credible. Moreover public control of the process is part of the legitimisation process, in order to avoid any perception of opacity and claims of arbitrariness.

[10] Celeste Hicks, *The Trial of Hissène Habré: How the People of Chad Brought a Tyrant to Justice* (Zed Books 2018) 110.

The violation of the principle of legality

First of all, one of the key issues that arose in relation to the Extraordinary African Chambers is whether its creation conformed with the principle of legality. As is well known, the Extraordinary African Chambers were set up following series of domestic and international decisions which led the African Union and Senegal to create the Chambers. This timeline is summarized adequately in the Judgment itself.

In a nutshell the relevant steps for the purposes of our discussion are the following. A procedure initiated by a group of victims before domestic Senegalese Courts in 2010 was rejected on the basis that 1) crimes against humanity were not criminalised in the Senegalese criminal code and 2) that there could be no extraterritorial prosecution for torture allegations. Senegal amended applicable legal texts in 2007 and 2008 to 'correct' these two difficulties, and a new procedure was started against Hissein Habré. However, Hissein Habré obtained a ruling from the ECOWAS Court stating that:[11]

> However, the Court notes that the implementation of the mandate of the African Union should follow international custom which has taken the habit in such circumstances of creating ad hoc or special jurisdictions. The expression '*jurisdiction compétente*' contained in this mandate means nothing other than the establishment of a judicial ad hoc framework and its powers would find their basis in the provisions of Article 15.2 of the International Covenant on Civil and Political Rights and that Senegal is responsible for proposing the principal forms and modalities of implementation of such a structure. Thus, any endeavour from Senegal outside of such a framework would violate, firstly, the principle of non-retroactivity of criminal law, as enshrined in international human rights instruments as an inalienable right and other hand, would obstruct the principle of impunity by the same international texts.

It is on the basis of this decision that the African Union and Senegal created the Extraordinary African Chambers. Article 1 of the Agreement provides that the Chambers have an 'international character'.[12] This 'international character' of the tribunal was confirmed by the subsequent challenged raised by Habré before the ECOWAS Court. For the ECOWAS Judges: 'The African extraordinary Chambers, even if they were created within the Senegalese domestic courts, do not have less of an international character given their mode of creation on the one hand (an international agreement) and their rules of functioning different that those of national Senegalese courts (Statute of the Chambers) on the other: that the existence on a national territory (here Senegal) and the at least partial presence of national judges within these Chambers (in this case Senegalese) does not in any way remove the international character of these Chambers.'[13]

[11] ECOWAS, *Habré v Sénégal*, 18 November 2010, para 58 available in French at : https://www.hrw.org/fr/news/2010/11/18/arret-cedeao/ecowas-ruling-hissein-habre-c-republique-du-senegal.

[12] *L'accord Entre Le Gouvernement De La Republique Du Senegal Et L'union Africaine Relatif Au Statut Des Chambres Africaines Extraordinaires Pour La Poursuite Des Crimes Internationaux Commis Au Tchad Durant La Periode Du 7 Juin 1982 Au 1er Decembre 1990*, 22 Août 2012, Article 1(4).

[13] ECOWAS, *Habré v Republic of Senegal*, 5 November 2013, available in French at http://www.chambresafricaines.org/index.php/l-affaire-habre/552-d%C3%A9cision-de-la-cour-de-justice-de-la-cedeao.html.

There are however three major difficulties with this reliance on the 'international character' of the Extraordinary African Chambers in order to circumvent the prohibition against non-retroactivity of criminal provisions.[14]

First of all, it is doubtful whether the Extraordinary African Chambers are in fact 'international'. While the agreement between the African Union and Senegal is indeed an international treaty, the Extraordinary African Chambers were technically created by domestic implementation law and therefore should actually be legally considered as domestic Courts. In this sense, it is more comparable to the Extraordinary Chambers in the Courts of Cambodia, similarly created through domestic legislation after an agreement between Cambodia and the UN. The facts that these Chambers have their 'own rules of functioning' does not alter this fact in any way, as domestic courts within the same national judicial system might also function according to different rules but still remain domestic.[15]

Second of all, it is doubtful whether, even if the Chambers were to be considered 'international' for the sake of the discussion, such character could in fact cure the problem of non-retroactivity. Indeed, on what logical basis could Senegal and the African Union have the competence to create an ad hoc jurisdiction which could do, according the ECOWAS Judgment, what an individual State (here Senegal) could not ? Simply affixing the term 'international' to the institution or referring to 'international custom'[16] does not magically make disappear all jurisdictional obstacles.[17] In other words, if Senegal cannot prosecute Habré for whatever reason, it cannot transfer such power to prosecute which it does not have to a newly created international tribunal.

Third of all, it could be argued that the principle of legality and its corollary, the non-retroactivity of criminal offenses, requires not only the prohibition to exist prior to the alleged conduct, but also the legal basis for actual prosecution. This would mean that the actual creation of a tribunal after the facts would also violate the principle of legality. Indeed, as argued elsewhere,[18] foreseeability as a necessary aspect of the principle of legality implies not only the existence of an abstract norm prohibiting certain conduct, but the existence of an institution capable of implementing this norm in a particular situation.

As a result, there are serious doubts about the way the Chambers dealt with the problem of the principle of legality.

[14] For a further analysis of the issue see Valentina Spiga, 'Non-retroactivity of Criminal Law : A new Chapter in the Hissène Habré Saga' (2011) 9 Journal of International Criminal Justice 5–23.

[15] For a more holistic analysis of why the Extraordinary African Chambers are not comparable to other examples of international or hybrid courts, see Emanuele Cimiotta, 'The First Steps of the Extraordinary African Chambers : A New Mixed Criminal Tribunal?' (2015) 13 Journal of International Criminal Justice 177–97.

[16] It should be pointed out that the ECOWAS Court does not give much detail on what this international custom to create ad hoc tribunals might be, what is its content or how it is triggered. This would have been particularly useful given that in fact, the practice of so-called hybrid tribunals is very heterogeneous, apparently random, and, interestingly for the present discussion actually never applied to a case similar to the Habré one : extra-territorial prosecution with limited connection to the State where the trial is taking place. Quite the opposite: all other hybrid tribunals were created to deal with crimes committed in the territory where the tribunal was set up (with the exception of the Special Tribunal for Lebanon). As noted by Sarah Williams, the EAC now sets a precedent for the creation of an internationalized criminal tribunal that operates exclusively on the basis of universal jurisdiction (Sarah Williams, 'The Extraordinary African Chambers in the Senegalese Courts: An African Solution to an African Problem?' (2013) 11 Journal of International Criminal Justice 1139–160 at 1140).

[17] See ibid. For a similar discussion in relation to immunities, see Dov Jacobs 'The Frog that Wanted to Be an Ox: The ICCs Approach to Immunities' in Stahn (ed), *The Law and Practice of the ICC: A Critical Account of Challenges and Achievements* (OUP 2015).

[18] Dov Jacobs, 'International Criminal Law' in D'Aspremont and Kammerhofer (eds), *International Legal Positivism in a Post-Modern World* (Cambridge University Press 2014) 451–74.

The absence of a written judgment prior to filing the appeal

A second, possibly less important difficulty faced by the Defence is the fact that it was expected to file its appeal of the Trial Judgment without having actually been notified of the written judgment. Indeed, a summary of the Trial Judgment was read out in Court on 30 May 2016 and the written Judgment was only made available on the 31 July 2016, weeks after the deadline to file an appeal had expired,[19] the Defence having filed its appeal on the 10 June 2016.[20] The Defence raised this issue on Appeal. For the Appeals Chamber, 'the question to be answered is that of knowing if the summary made available to the parties within the period to appeal was sufficiently enlightening as to the reasoning and the reasons of the Trial Chamber so that the parties are put in a position to exercise their right to appeal in a significant manner. In the affirmative, the fact that the parties were not in possession of the entirety of the Judgement but only its summary does not per se violate the rights of the Defence. In the negative, [...] one should conclude that the rights of the Defence were breached'.[21] After analysis of the summary, the Appeals Chamber considered that it contained sufficient information for the parties to be able to appeal, even in the absence of a full written judgment.

This is obviously not very convincing. A twenty-five-page summary of a 536-page judgment cannot reasonably be considered to contain all the relevant information to appeal.[22] Indeed, by definition, the summary essentially contains factual conclusions, with no information on how these conclusions were drawn from the available evidence. In those circumstances, how can a Party claim an error of fact if it does not actually know what evidence was relied on? Moreover, the summary contains no developments on the applicable law, whether in relation to the crimes, the modes of liability or sentencing. It is equally impossible for a Party to determine whether an error of law has been committed. In sum, it is unlikely that the Defence was put in a position to effectively exercise their right to appeal in the absence of a written judgment. It should be noted, for the sake of completeness, that there is no evidence that the Defence initially requested more time to file their Appeal, or that they requested additional time after the issuance of the Judgment to file additional grounds of Appeal,[23] which might have a been a reasonable request, if only to put the situation on the record of the case.

[19] Appeals Judgment, para 276.

[20] It should be noted that several other appeals were filed by the Defence after that date, including after the issuance of the written Judgment, but they related not to the main judgment but to subsequent decisions, particularly in relation to civil matters and reparations (Appeals Judgment, paras 27–37).

[21] Appeals Judgment, para 287.

[22] Setting aside the fact that, even had the full Judgment been available, fifteen days to appeal is vastly unreasonable.

[23] With the caveat, as recalled previously, that there are no available public records of the case.

Taking a step back: the conceptual foundation for the lack of consideration of the defence in international and hybrid tribunals

One could wonder why the rights of the Accused often take a back seat in discussions of international criminal tribunals, and are not as respected as one would expect, despite usual claims to the contrary.[24]

In fact, looking at the particular circumstances in which these tribunals operate, there is nothing really surprising about this state of affairs. Indeed, there are a number of particular features of international criminal trials which explain why considerations related to the rights of the Defence are not a matter of real concern (4.1). It should however be kept in mind that these features are reinforced by the unfavourable context of criminal law generally (4.2).

A theoretical understanding of criminal law generally

Before looking at the features of ICL, it should be noted from the outset that lack of attention to the rights of the Defence is not something that is exclusive to international criminal law. Defence lawyers in a number of national systems face difficulties in ensuring that persons accused of crimes get a fair trial. Moreover, they often get no sympathy from the general public. The most asked question of any Defence lawyer, both domestically and internationally, is probably: 'how can you defend such people?'. There is clearly a misunderstanding by most observers of criminal law of the process by which a person is tried and acquitted or convicted, the length and complexity of the procedure being a source of amazement for most.

In a sense, the heart of the problem is as follows: the whole point of criminal law is to institutionalize private vengeance, by granting the power to punish to the State rather than individuals (and particularly the victims of the alleged crimes). This State monopoly of the exercise of legitimate violence is a traditional feature of the social contract.

The result of this transfer is twofold. First of all, there is a distrust of the State, which leads to the imposition of safeguards to protect people against the arbitrary exercise of power by the State. In the criminal law context, this means protecting the rights of the accused, particularly through *habeas corpus*, the presumption of innocence and the principle of legality. Second of all, there is an inevitable frustration that the natural revenge instinct is delegated to another authority. These two dimensions are perfectly understandable taken separately. But it is when they are combined that we have an explanation as to the current situation: the procedural safeguards of criminal law are seen not as protecting individuals generally against the State, but shielding criminals against the ire of society and more particularly victims.

As a result, one of the hardest things to explain to outsiders—and sometimes even insiders—of criminal law is that procedure is a not some cold bureaucratic framework meant to obscure the conduct of the trial. Procedure is not a technicality. It is a societal

[24] This section relies on part of the author's already published chapter: D Jacobs, 'A tale of four illusions', in G Zyberi and C Rohan, *Defence Perspectives on International Criminal Justice* (Cambridge University Press 2017), reprinted with permission.

normative and moral choice to protect the rights of the Accused through a fair and equitable procedure.

The particular features of international criminal law

The general unfavourable view of the criminally accused in domestic criminal law does not explain entirely the situation in international criminal law. International criminal tribunals operate in a very particular context which creates even more tension with any genuine consideration for the rights of the Defence. This chapter cannot be the place to expand in detail on all possible specificities of ICL, but the main ones will be presented briefly and it should be noted that they are of course inter-related.

The first and most obvious feature of ICL is the nature of the crimes considered. International criminal courts generally only have jurisdiction over those crimes that are considered to be the most egregious crimes, 'unimaginable atrocities that deeply shock the conscience of humanity'.[25] These are crimes which therefore carry a particular moral weight which serves to inversely diminish any consideration for the rights of the Accused. More particularly, the crimes within the jurisdiction of international courts are usually mass crimes which, as a result, have countless victims who are seen as the beneficiaries of these trials. This constitutes a shift in the rationale of criminal law, which is traditionally the response of society in reaction to an offense against its societal values, rather than a direct remedy for victims for their personal suffering. By putting victims at the heart of ICL, the Accused does not face the objective features of the State through the Prosecutor, but instead faces the subjective features of the alleged victims. It is much harder to focus on the rights of accused person in that context because, as noted before, those rights can now be argued not as protecting the individual against the arbitrariness of the exercise of sovereign power by the prosecuting institution, but as a means of shielding the Accused from those who directly claim to have suffered from his acts. In this symbolic confrontation, the Accused—who is in fact entitled to the presumption of innocence—is likely to be denied that right.

The second feature to be considered is the particular nature of international criminality. International crimes share, to a lesser or greater extent, depending on the crime considered, a requirement of some form of collective action, which is usually embodied in the legal requirement of identifying the contextual element of the crime. War crimes require an armed conflict; crimes against humanity require a widespread or systematic attack against any civilian population and—at the ICC at least—a State or organisational policy; genocide requires—at least at the ICC—a manifest pattern of similar conduct. The consequence of this is that in international trials considerable attention is devoted to establishing this context, with consideration of the actual role of the Accused taking a back seat. It suffices to open any Judgment of the ad hoc tribunals to note that hundreds of pages can go by during which the factual findings are made and legal conclusions are drawn on the commission of crimes, with the Accused hardly being mentioned.[26] This is also true of the Habré Judgment,

[25] The Rome Statute for the International Criminal Court preamble.

[26] The structure of most international judgments is an oddity in itself. Indeed, findings on the commission of crimes are usually made with no knowledge of the direct individual perpetrators of the underlying acts, and therefore with no discussion of the intent of those direct perpetrators. While this is common practice in ICL, it is technically impossible to determine the existence of a crime, in a legal sense, without considering both the *actus reus*

where the discussion of his individual criminal responsibility only starts 400 pages into the Judgment.

This leads naturally to the third feature of ICL: the nature of the criminal responsibility. Even when the Accused is considered, it is most of the time not for his direct commission of the crimes, in the traditional sense of the term. International Defendants are usually high up the military ranks or are individuals who held political office. They are not those who actually pulled the trigger—metaphorically speaking. Establishing their responsibility for crimes committed by others often requires adopting modes of liability that connect them to the crimes in some remote way, such as ordering, planning or being a superior in the case of command responsibility. In addition to that, the collective nature of international criminality, as noted previously, means that ICL relies heavily on collective modes of liability, such as Joint Criminal Enterprise at the ad hoc tribunals or indirect co-perpetration at the ICC. These modes of liability further dilute the conduct of the Accused in light of the actions of the group which is claimed to have perpetrated the crimes, which in turn makes it easier to ignore the actual conduct and/or *mens rea* of the Accused. Interestingly, in the *Habré* Judgment, in addition to Hissein Habré's responsibility as a superior and as a member of a joint criminal enterprise, the Chambers also convicted him for his role in two specific incidents, one as a direct perpetrator of sexual violence against a woman detained at the Presidency[27] and one for having ordered the execution of two soldiers of his own army as punishment for having allegedly been involved in the commission of war crimes in the village of Ngalo.[28] These findings linking high-ranking officials directly to the commission of crimes are quite rare in such trials.

A fourth, less legal, but no less important feature of ICL is the political context of international crimes. The label of 'criminality' has the effect of putting a veil over the often very political dimension of the alleged criminal conduct. Indeed, ICL tends to depoliticize what is almost always political violence, irrespective of its legality or illegality under international law. As a result, international judges or prosecutors regularly claim that they are not making political determinations, by only looking at the individual criminal responsibility of the Accused. This is in fact not true. International tribunals cannot avoid making findings that have political implications.

First of all, a stated goal of international justice and the trials conducted in the international criminal courts is to provide an accurate historical record of a given conflict.[29]

and the *mens rea* elements of that crime, which makes a large proportion of legal findings on the commission of crimes in international Judgments inappropriate from a criminal law perspective.

27 Trial Judgment, paras 1819–840. Habré was actually acquitted on appeal for this incident because it was based on allegations which emerged for the first time in Court when the victim testified, and had therefore never been included in any indictment prior to the trial. The Appeals Chamber therefore considered that Habré could not be convicted on the basis of facts and a crime which he had not been notified of at any point prior to the testimony (Appeals Judgment, paras 527–32).

28 Trial Judgment, paras 1841–864. Habré's Defence actually admitted to the facts on the basis that these executions essentially constituted energetic punishment for the commission of massacres by the soldiers. The Trial Chamber considered however that the summary execution constituted a war crime and that ce crime ne saurait s'analyser comme constitutif d'une punition telle que requise au titre de la responsabilité du supérieur hiérarchique. En effet, un supérieur hiérarchique est tenu de prendre des mesures nécessaires et raisonnables pour punir la commission d'un crime par ses subordonnés, pas de commettre un autre crime (Trial Judgment, para 1864). However, one could imagine that a measure might actually constitute both a war crime and an effective measure of punishment in the context of command responsibility, given that the rationale behind such a responsibility to punish is to deter from the future commission of crimes. Arguably, an execution might be considered to satisfy this objective.

29 Whether international tribunals should in fact have such an ambition in the first place is a different debate.

International criminal tribunals will necessarily delve into the political history and context of the crimes; you cannot accurately write about history without describing the extant political situation.

Second of all, and more importantly, a great number of international judgments, especially regarding those accused who were higher up in the hierarchy at the time of the crimes alleged, are naturally required to consider—directly or indirectly—political motives as part of the claimed collective criminal intent. Joint Criminal Entreprise requires proof of a common purpose, just as indirect co-perpetration requires a common plan, both of which will often be alleged as political.

Third of all, even the evaluation of the facts of the case might require some indirect but unavoidable political evaluation. For example, in the *Gbagbo* case, the Prosecutor's opening words of the trial were the following: 'Let me be very clear right from the start, the purpose of this case is not to determine who won the elections in 2010, nor who should have won the elections. The purpose here is to establish individual criminal responsibility of the two accused for crimes committed in the framework of post-electoral violence which took place in 2010'.[30] Yet, the Prosecution also claims that the Defendant elaborated and engaged in a common plan to stay in power by any means. There is an obvious contradiction here because the Prosecutor's case necessarily implies that Gbagbo lost the election, otherwise why would he have to set in motion his common plan to stay in power by any means?

The consequence of this feature is once again a dilution of the actual conduct of the Accused not only in the context of collective criminal conduct, but also as to collective political conduct. Moreover, once this mixed legal/political message leaves the courtroom, there is a natural filter by which only the political dimension reaches the general public, therefore reinforcing the idea that the rights of Accused during the legal proceedings are not that important.

Leaving the courtroom leads us to the fifth feature, that of the media attention on the situations that international criminal courts deal with; attention which usually occurs well in advance of the court processes themselves. This necessarily taints any perception of the Accused, especially when they are high ranking military commanders or well-known political figures. Most international defendants have been thoroughly 'pre-judged' by the media and the general public, based on the role that people understand them to have had in the State apparatus. As a result, the expectation is that there will be a conviction, and the higher the position, the higher that expectation. Who would ever expect Muammar Ghadaffi, Saddam Hussein or tomorrow, Assad or Bashir to be acquitted? For such political figures, international trials are purely symbolic; a formal validation of what everybody thinks they already know about what they did. There is little room for concern about the rights of the Accused in such a context even though no fair, valid legal system can proceed without continued concern for such individual rights.

With this consideration we come back full circle to our initial point: the shift from the rights of the Accused to the symbolic objectives of the international community and more particularly the interests of victims. And with this shift comes another shift, that of the general understanding of justice. The 'justice' of the international criminal trial is not, as in most domestic jurisdictions, measured by the fairness of the proceedings, but by the favourable

[30] ICC, *Prosecutor v Gbagbo and Blé Goudé*, Transcripts of 28 January 2016, ICC-02/11-01/15-T-9-ENG, p 40 lines 4–7.

outcome from the victims' perspective. Proof of that can be found in any reaction to convictions and acquittals. A conviction is traditionally labelled as a 'victory for Justice',[31] whereas you will never hear such claim in the event of an acquittal, despite the fact that an acquittal after a fair process should normally also be considered as a 'victory for Justice'.

The *Habré* trial is a perfect illustration of this victim-oriented trend of international criminal justice. Indeed, arguably more than any other international prosecution in the past twenty years, the *Habré* trial was more or less purely the result of a struggle from a number of victims (described as a 'grassroots movement'[32]) before Senegalese and Belgium courts, under the guidance of Human Rights Watch, among others.[33] Moreover, victims and *Parties civiles* were extremely present throughout the proceedings. As noted by Thierry Cruvelier even before the Judgment was delivered, 'Although the verdict isn't expected until May 30, the *Habré* trial already seems to be a success: Never in a trial for mass crimes have the victims' voices been so dominant'.[34] Generally, as noted by Kerstin Bree Carlson: 'the predominant narrative hails the *Habré* Trial as a success story for human rights advocates and Chadian victims, as three decades of efforts finally resulted in the conviction of the dictator who oversaw Chad's repressive state apparatus'.[35]

What is ultimately worrying is that this view seems to be shared not only outside the tribunals but also *within* these institutions. Indeed, while one can possibly understand the psychological and emotional desire of alleged victims to get a conviction, there is something disturbing about the fact that those who work at these institutions and produce the decisions also think in this way, because it demonstrates a bias against the Accused which puts in the question the fairness of the process in a systemic way. Examples abound of this. A few years ago, an ICTY staff survey was leaked to the press and it transpired that the morale was low because there had been a couple of acquittals in the preceding months.[36] In 2016, the ICTY website and twitter account made every effort not to say that Seselj had been acquitted, while a conviction obviously always makes the front page.[37] And probably the most striking example is the poster that everyone could see in the lobby of the ICTY, which shows two sets of handcuffs, one in stainless steel—to be used on ICTY Defendants –, one in a more rudimentary fabric—used against some victims of the conflict—with the following text: 'bringing perpetrators to justice and justice to victims'. This illustrates perfectly the fact that justice for the Defendant means putting him in handcuffs, while the 'real' justice is for

[31] See for example, in relation the Taylor Judgment : Dov Jacobs, 'Taylor Judgment: 'A Victory for Justice', Spreading the Jam, 26 September 2013, available at https://dovjacobs.com/2013/09/26/taylor-judgment-a-victory-for-justice/ (last visited 30 April 2016).

[32] Celeste Hicks, *The Trial of Hissène Habré: How the People of Chad Brought a Tyrant to Justice*, p 11.

[33] On this, see Reed Brody, 'Bringing a Dictator to Justice The Case of Hissène Habre' (2015) 13 Journal of International Criminal Justice 209–17.

[34] Thierry Cruvelier, 'The Trial of Hissène Habré', *New York Times*, 15 February 2016 (https://www.nytimes.com/2016/02/16/opinion/the-landmark-trial-of-hissene-habre.html).

[35] Kerstin Bree Carlson, 'Trying Hissène Habré "on Behalf of Africa": Remaking Hybrid International Criminal Justice at the *Chambres Africaines Extraordinaires*' in Joanna Nicholson (ed), *Streghtening the Validity of International Criminal Tribunals* (Brill 2019) 342 at 343.

[36] Dov Jacobs, 'Low morale at the ICTY' (*Spreading the Jam*, 23 August 2013) available at https://dovjacobs.com/2013/08/23/low-morale-at-the-icty/ (last visited 30 April 2016).

[37] Dov Jacobs, 'Is the ICTY Ashamed by its own Seselj Judgment ?' (*Spreading the Jam*, 31 March 2016) available at https://dovjacobs.com/2016/03/31/is-the-icty-ashamed-by-its-own-seselj-judgment/ (last visited 14 March 2019).

the victims.[38] Needless to say that there is little room for the rights of the Defence in such a framework of analysis.

Ultimately, for all the above reasons, the Accused at an international/internationalized criminal tribunal can only ever be peripheral to his trial, rather than be at the centre of it as should be the case, because the stakes go far beyond his mere individual criminal responsibility or lack of criminal responsibility. The Accused is but one element of a broader political, historical and societal discussion and this in turn diminishes his role in the courtroom itself and explains why, as a consequence, his individual rights are less of a concern even though they are codified in numerous international instruments.

The *Habré* Trial is an ideal illustration of such a context. It is a perfect case-study for the possibility of victims utilising all possible legal avenues to obtain the indictment not only of one man, but of an entire regime. This process involved domestic courts of several countries (Belgium, Senegal), a number of international courts (ECOWAS, ICJ) and the African Union. When the process culminated in the creation of the Extraordinary African Chambers, it was the result of decades of struggle which could not decently be accepted to fail at this final stage. This is one case where the broader societal objectives of the process outweighed by far any consideration for the Accused himself. For some, this is a model to be emulated in the future.[39] If it were to be the case, then it would be the end of any ambition for international criminal law to adhere to liberal principles of criminal law at the heart of which one finds the presumption of innocence and the rights of the Defence. Whether this constitutes true progress will remain to be seen.

[38] Incidentally, this poster, rather than promote the conduct of fair proceedings, actually seems to promote a more basic eye for an eye logic, which is far removed from an institutional consideration for the rights of the Defence.

[39] Within certain limits, given the specific context which led to the creation of this institution. See Celeste Hicks, *The Trial of Hissène Habré: How the People of Chad Brought a Tyrant to Justice*, page Chapter 5. For a more subtle analysis of the impact of the Extraordinary African Chambers, see Kerstin Bree Carlson, 'Trying Hissène Habré "on Behalf of Africa": Remaking Hybrid International Criminal Justice at the *Chambres Africaines Extraordinaires*' in Joanna Nicholson (ed), *Strengthening the Validity of International Criminal Tribunals* (Brill 2019) 342.

SECTION B
INSTITUTIONS, NORMS, AND PILLARS

The second section regroups the voices of authors writing on the normative and institutional structure of international criminal law, grounded in practice and pragmatism. We begin with Mark Kersten and Kirsten Ainley's consideration of the emerging preference for hybrid judicial institutions; they survey several hybrid courts to illustrate how each institution is tailored to the particular conditions of its environment. Leila Bourguiba offers a comparative consideration of the efficacy of civil versus common law in adjudicating atrocity crimes from the perspective of civil law jurist, using the example of the French war crimes unit prosecution practice. Manuel Ventura and Victor Băieşu step back to examine the wider jurisprudential frameworks established by the International Court of Justice in its decision regarding the extradition of Habré, and what that should mean for the extradition of other leaders, like Sudan's Al-Bashir. Framing the structure of international criminal law from the other end of the spectrum—the victim, and not the leader—Liesbeth Zegveld's chapter examines and challenges the promise of victim participation before the ICC, the most established such practice in all of international criminal law.

31

Hybridization—A Spectrum of Creative Possibilities

Mark Kersten and Kirsten Ainley[1]

Introduction

After a sharp decline in interest, it appeared that the hybrid tribunal had become an 'orphan' of the international criminal justice project.[2] That was not to be. Recent years have seen a spate of hybrids established or proposed, from Syria and South Sudan, to the Central African Republic and Sri Lanka. Perhaps most prominently, a hybrid court was set up in Dakar, Senegal, to prosecute former Chadian President Hissène Habré in 2013, a development that has stood out as the vanguard of a new generation of hybrid tribunals.

The re-emergence of the hybrid has been addressed by numerous scholars.[3] Yet despite its renewed popularity, it remains unclear what, precisely, it means to be a hybrid court and how the latest hybrids might contribute to furthering the project of international criminal justice. The answer to the first question is typically assumed to be simple: hybrid tribunals are 'of mixed composition and jurisdiction, encompassing both national and international aspects, usually operating within the jurisdiction where the crimes occurred'.[4] But hybrids are much more than just middle-ground institutions that marry national and international components. As this chapter demonstrates, they are institutions whose very hybridity creates productive space for creative solutions aimed at responding to some of the most endemic challenges facing international criminal justice.

What makes a hybrid tribunal hybrid?

We rely primarily on knowing a hybrid when we see it—when some 'mix' of the local and the global meet within a juridical forum. Prior and contemporary hybrids have featured

[1] The authors would like to thank Anne Della Guardia, Charles Jalloh, and Mohamed Sesay for their encouraging and generous feedback on the chapter. We would also like to thank the Rockefeller Foundation and the LSE Institute of Global Affairs for funding the Hybrid Justice project which we co-direct and from which this chapter has drawn. See https://hybridjustice.com

[2] Padraig McAuliffe, 'Hybrid Tribunals at Ten—How International Criminal Justice's Golden Child became an Orphan' (2011) 7 Journal of International Law and International Relations 1–65.

[3] See Harry Hobbs, 'Hybrid Tribunals and the Composition of the Court: In Search of Sociological Legitimacy' (2016) 16(2) Chicago Journal of International Law 494; Beth Van Schaack, *The Building Blocks of Hybrid Justice*, Stanford Public Law Working Paper No 2705110 (22 March 2016); Mark Kersten, *As the Pendulum Swings—The Revival of the Hybrid Tribunal*, in Mikkel Jarie Christensen and Ron Levi (eds), *The Institutions of International and Transnational Crime* (Routledge 2017)

[4] United Nations Office of the United Nations High Commission for Human Rights, *Rule-of-Law Tools for Post-Conflict States—Maximizing the Legacy of Hybrid Courts* (Geneva 2008) 1

Mark Kersten and Kirsten Ainley, *Hybridization—A Spectrum of Creative Possibilities* In: *The President on Trial*. First edition. Edited by: Sharon Weill, Kim Thuy Seelinger, and Kerstin Bree Carlson, Oxford University Press (2020). © Mark Kersten and Kirsten Ainley.
DOI: 10.1093/oso/9780198858621.003.0032

varying combinations of international and domestic staff, operative law, structure, financing and rules of procedure.

But the threshold of where a court emerges as a hybrid tribunal rather than a domestic or an international court remains unclear. What are the defining elements that make a court hybrid? How much international law versus domestic law does a court need to use before it is hybrid? Is there a point at which the mix of international and national components tip the scales and make an institution hybrid or, alternatively, international or domestic?[5]

It is, of course, understood that there has to be *some* mix of international and domestic for a hybrid court to be a hybrid court. But it would be a mistake to think of hybrid courts as static, as though they can easily be categorized together as a generation of tribunals which can be replicated in different situations with contextual tweaks here and there. Neha Jain's 2008 observation still resonates: 'There is little clarity on exactly what elements must be present to classify a tribunal as hybrid', and scholars have eschewed 'a definition based on essential elements'.[6] And as Muharremi adds: 'there is no uniform model of how a hybrid court should look like and how the ratio, or blend, between international and national elements should look like.'[7] This lack of consensus as to what exactly a hybrid constitutes is precisely the advantage of this model of tribunal.

Rather than seeking a strict or categorical definition, it is more useful to view hybrids as 'joint ventures'[8] between the international and national actors which reside on a multi-axis *spectrum* with fully internationalized and fully domestic at the extremes, as suggested by Sarah Williams as well as Harry Hobbs.[9] Each axis, then, represents a component that may be hybridized to a greater or lesser extent: substantive law, location, staff, etc. Hybrids can be seen as having different levels of hybridity for each constitutive component.

It is their presence on this spectrum and their concomitant adaptability which permits hybrids to respond creatively to some of the seemingly endemic challenges facing international criminal justice. This chapter examines hybrid creativity through four specific examples, each allocated to a section of the chapter: (i) the outsourcing of outreach efforts at the Extraordinary African Chambers in order to communicate to affected and interested communities of Habré's trial on charges of war crimes and crimes against humanity; (ii) combating victors' justice at the Kosovo Specialist Chambers; (iii) sharing concurrent jurisdiction between the Central African Republic's Special Criminal Court and the International Criminal Court; and (iv) using the premises of previous hybrid courts to host new tribunals and therefore reduce the financial and security costs of international criminal justice.

The analysis that follows is optimistic in many ways. We outline what we believe to be beneficial innovations in the pursuit of international criminal justice. We recognize both

[5] To complicate matters further, some of the institutions commonly categorized as hybrids do not wish to be described as such. The Kosovo Specialist Chambers and the Specialist Prosecutor's Office, for instance, describe themselves as 'internationalised' rather than hybrid as they are embedded in the domestic system. A distinction could be made between mixed and hybrid courts—mixed courts being domestic bodies with some level of international assistance, and hybrid courts being created through partnerships or agreements between international and domestic actors—but for simplicity in this chapter we refer to all of these courts as 'hybrid'.

[6] Neha Jain, 'Conceptualising Internationalisation in Hybrid Criminal Court' (2008) 12 Singapore Year Book of International Law 81

[7] Robert Muharremi, 'The Kosovo Specialist Chambers and Specialist Prosecutor's Office' (2016) 76 Houston Journal of International Law 988

[8] Hobbs (2016) 492.

[9] ibid; Sarah Williams, *Hybrid and Internationalised Criminal Tribunals* (Hart Publishing 2012) 249–50.

the problems inherent in evaluating the success of tribunals and the criticism that has been levelled against hybrids, however.[10] The chapter does not seek to justify hybrid justice *tout court* but rather to highlight creative responses to challenges in the broader practice that have been developed by hybrids.

Outsourcing outreach: The extraordinary African chambers

It has become almost cliché to stress that justice must not only be done, but also needs to be *seen* to be done.[11] Yet public awareness of a tribunal's work and how accountability efforts are perceived remains critically important to the legitimacy of the international criminal justice project.

How affected and interested communities *view* justice is determined by the effectiveness of a tribunal's outreach efforts. In general, war crimes tribunals have had a mixed record in conducting outreach efforts. Some, like the SCSL, are generally regarded as having conducted 'impressive' outreach programming, although the focus of these efforts was very prosecution-heavy.[12] The ECCC is widely praised for the number of Cambodians that were able to visit the tribunal's premises and thus take in some of the proceedings.[13] Efforts to disseminate its work have, according to recent research, had a significant impact on the understanding of crimes committed by the Khmer Rouge among young Cambodians.[14] Others, like the ICTY, have been criticized for their 'poor outreach activities' which produced citizens who 'did not know of or accept the facts established through the ICTY's work' and left them not believing 'that justice has been served through its judgements.'[15] Generally, outreach efforts have improved with time, as the intimate, correlative relationship between communicating justice and realizing it has become clearer.

Outreach, however, is more than just communicating the work of a tribunal. It can take on many forms: radio and television programming; educational activities in schools; public debates and competitions; efforts to bring citizens to watch proceedings; town hall or village

[10] Kirsten Ainley, 'Evaluating the Evaluators' (2017) 11(3) International Journal of Transnational Justice 421–42; Kirsten Ainley, Rebekka Friedman, and Chris Mahony (eds), *Evaluating Transitional Justice: Accountability and Peacebuilding in Post-Conflict Sierra Leone* (Palgrave Macmillan 2015).

[11] See Rachel Kerr, *Procedure: 'Justice Must Not Only be Done, but Must be Seen to be Done'*, in <https://www.hrw.org/reports/2004/sierraleone0904/>

[12] Kerr writes that the SCSL's outreach was 'far more extensive and ambitious than anything that has previously been undertaken'. See Rachel Kerr and Jessica Lincoln, *The Special Court for Sierra Leone Outreach, Legacy and Impact (Final Report)*(Kings College London 2008). A Human Rights Watch Report similarly states that 'Outreach at the Special Court consists of an impressive and diverse set of initiatives that represent a marked improvement over outreach efforts by the ad hoc tribunals'. See Human Rights Watch, Bringing Justice: The Special Court For Sierra Leone—Accomplishments, Shortcomings, and Needed Support, Vol. 16, No. 8(A).

[13] For an interesting discussion of Cambodian citizens attending proceedings at the ECCC, see Thierry Cruvellier, *The Master of Confessions—The Making of a Khmer Rouge Torturer* (Harper Collins 2011) 10–13. As he writes in relation the prosecution of Duch: 'Duch's trial will give thirty-thousand Cambodians the chance to spend at least a day inside the court, unique in their country. No other international trial has had an audience as vast and wide-ranging as this one.' ibid p 13. See also See, for instance, Tom Fawthrop, '*Cambodia's Khmer Rouge Tribunal: Mission Accomplished?*', The Diplomat (17 July 2017) at https://thediplomat.com/2017/07/cambodias-khmer-rouge-tribunal-mission-accomplished/

[14] Caitlin McCaffrie, Somaly Kum, Daniel Mattes, and Lina Tay, *'So We Can Know What Happened': The Educational Potential of the ECCC'*, Report for the WSD HANDA Center for Human Rights and International Justice at Stanford University and the East-West Center (January 2018)

[15] Olivera Banjeglav, 'The Micro Legacy of the ICTY in Croatia—A Case Study of Vukovar' in Martina Fischer and Olivera Simić (eds), *Transitional Justice and Reconciliation—Lessons from the Balkans* (Routledge 2016) 94

meetings and rallies to consult communities, etc. Importantly, effective outreach is not about telling the prosecution's story—but the narrative of the tribunal. This ensures that other actors, including defence lawyers and members from the Registry, Presidency, and other organs, are involved and that their work is (better) understood. Effective outreach also means reaching those in opposition to the tribunal's work, combating misconceptions, confronting falsehoods, and 'shrinking the space of denial'.[16]

Apart from being tailored to the realities of the political violence to which a tribunal is responding, identifying the appropriate target audiences for outreach efforts depends, in significant part, on the location of a hybrid tribunal. Some tribunals, like the SCSL or ECCC, had this task, more or less, easily defined: their outreach efforts were focused on communities in Sierra Leone and Cambodia, respectively (as well as on interested international audiences and, to a lesser extent, members of the diaspora). Tribunals that are located outside of the locus of violence have an altogether more complex challenge in that they have distinct—often unrelated—communities to target with outreach programming. For example, if the proposed Hybrid Court for South Sudan is established, it will likely be located in Arusha, Tanzania. In addition to affected and interested populations in South Sudan, at least some effort will have to be made to communicate and explain the work of the HCSS to Tanzanians as well as internationally.

The situation that faced the Extraordinary African Chambers (EAC) was altogether more complex. The EAC heard a single case: that of Hissène Habré. It was set up in Dakar, Senegal in 2013 in order to prosecute the former President of neighbouring Chad. Habré's victims were Chadian but the former leader had fled to Senegal in 1990. Eventually the demands of victims for justice—and in no small degree, political realities—caught up with Habré.[17] The challenge for the EAC was to design outreach programming that would reach three constituencies: (i) victims, survivors, and interested communities in Chad, an endeavour made only more difficult due to the fact that 'the conditions for a full and open discussion of transitional justice issues do not exist';[18] (ii) citizens in Senegal where the proceedings were taking place and where Habré had spent the preceding twenty-plus years; and (iii) a sceptical international community. According to trial observers, ten percent of the court's budget was allocated to outreach efforts.[19]

In order to address the particular outreach-related challenges it faced, the EAC decided to outsource outreach activities to a consortium of three organizations. Franck Petit, the head of the so-called Outreach Consortium that was contracted to do the EAC's outreach has reflected on this unique arrangement:

The main innovation of the Extraordinary African Chambers was to fully externalise the outreach. This meant delegating outreach work to the many organisations that have credibility on the ground, in Chad, in Senegal and on the international level. There were

[16] Diane F Orentlicher, *Shrinking the Space for Denial—The Impact of the ICTY in Serbia*, Open Society Justice Initiative (May 2008) <https://www.justiceinitiative.org/uploads/a0be82c5-aa8a-4bcd-9d23-bcef4d94f93c/serbia_20080501.pdf>

[17] See an excellent overview of the dynamics that led to Habré's prosecution in Dakar, see, Celeste Hicks, *The Trial of Hissène Habré—How the People of Chad Brought a Tyrant to Justice* (Zed Books 2018) esp Chapters 2 and 3

[18] Reed Brody, 'Bringing a Dictator to Justice: The Case of Hissène Habré' (2015) 13(2) Journla of International Criminal Justice 209–17, 215

[19] Celeste Hicks, *The Trial of Hissène Habré and What it Could Mean for Justice in Africa*, Justice in Conflict (27 March 2018), at https://justiceinconflict.org/2018/03/27/the-trial-of-hissene-habre-and-what-it-could-mean-for-justice-in-africa

three organisations working together as a unit known as the Outreach Consortium. RCN Justice & Démocratie based in Belgium took care of things at the international level while Magi Communication, based in Ndjamena, handled Chad, while the Dakar-based Primum Africa Consulting was responsible for outreach in Senegal.

The consortium of these three organisations was implementing the program with the tribunal organisation in Chad, the Senegalese organisation in Senegal and the international NGO at an international level was also doing the backstopping of projects and everything dealing with financial reports. This guaranteed that the program really went well. So the combination of the three organisations was very effective and I don't think it would be possible for one of the three organisations alone to execute the whole project singlehandedly and have the same results as we did.[20]

In addition to the consortium members contracted to conduct the outreach programming of the court, civil society organizations worked to facilitate the travel of Chadian journalists to cover proceedings in Dakar and Senegalese journalist to travel to Chad.[21] Observers have generally concluded that the outreach efforts of the Consortium were a success.[22]

The lessons from the EAC, and to some extent the ECCC and SCSL, are that the success of outreach is a fundamental determinant of the perception of success of the tribunal as a whole, and that successful outreach relies on smart targeting as well as a significant investment of resources. The diverse nature of the constituencies that the EAC needed to reach and the resource constraints faced by the tribunal created fertile ground to identify a creative solution to outreach efforts. Rather than have one outreach entity, the EAC had three working in conjunction and cooperation with each other. Instead of complicating matters, the shared expertise of the Consortium members made outreach efforts more credible with affected populations, expeditious, and efficient.[23] The Outreach Consortium in turn ensured that the EAC could both better reach its targeted audiences as well as avoid expending resources to replicate expertise which already existed outside of the court. Whether this innovation sets a precedent to be followed by courts facing similar constraints remains to be seen but it is undoubtedly one that could only have been generated by the conditions faced—and met—by a hybrid tribunal.

Combating victors' justice in Kosovo

Since its inception, international criminal justice has been plagued by allegations that it represents the law of the victors imposed upon the vanquished. The Nuremberg and Tokyo International Military Tribunals have been repeatedly criticized for their production of

[20] See comments by Franck Petit in Brian Obara, *Outreach in the Hissène Habré was an Exercise in Winning Hearts and Minds* (Justice Hub, 1 October 2017), at https://justicehub.org/article/outreach-hissene-habre-trial-was-exercise-winning-hearts-and-minds. See also Chapter 23 in this volume.

[21] Human Rights Watch, *Q&A: The Case of Hissène Habré before the Extraordinary African Chambers in Senegal* (3 May 2016), at https://www.hrw.org/news/2016/05/03/qa-case-hissene-habre-extraordinary-african-chambers-senegal

[22] See Hicks (2018) p 138.

[23] See comments by Petit in Hicks (2018) 136.

victors' justice,[24] including by Judges on their benches,[25] although others have defended their record and offered important nuance to the debate.[26] Still, fifty years after the creation of the Nuremberg and Tokyo Tribunals, the International Criminal Tribunal for Rwanda (ICTR) faced the same critique—and not devoid of merit. When it closed its doors in 2015, all of the ninety-three individuals for whom the ICTR had issued arrest warrants were Hutu génocidaires. Despite widespread allegations of atrocities, not a single individual from the Rwandan Patriotic Front was indicted by the Court.[27] The International Criminal Court (ICC) has likewise been criticized for its one-sided prosecutions.[28]

While not always couched in terms of 'victors' justice', allegations that international criminal law is so intimately tethered to power that only the weak are selected for prosecution continue to plague the field. Hybrid tribunals, however, have generally received less criticism relating to allegations of victors' justice and many have fared better in prosecuting the various sides of the conflicts to which they are a judicial response. But no tribunal—hybrid or otherwise—has been established to so directly challenge the notion of victors' justice as the Kosovo Specialist Chambers (KSC).

Legally, the KSC is not a hybrid court, but 'part of the judicial system of Kosovo ... attached to each level of the Kosovo court system'.[29] At the same time, the KSC and SPO not only are informed by international law, they are located in The Hague, are staffed entirely by internationals, and are funded by the European Union.[30] As Aidan Hehir writes: 'the choice of location and personnel was justified as necessary to ensure the court's impartiality and guard against intimidation.'[31] Other 'special' features of the KSC have been elaborated elsewhere and generally point to it fitting neatly within accepted conceptualizations hybrid courts.[32] Thus, even though its staff may be at pains to say it is not a hybrid court, for excellent reasons to do with domestic politics, ownership and legitimacy, the KSC shares both the features and the rationale of a hybrid tribunal. We describe the KSC as a hybrid—even if it does not describe itself as such– because it has the key features of one.

[24] The concept of victors' justice is generally attributed to Victor Minnear's *Victors Justice—The Tokyo War Crimes Trial* (Princeton University Press 1971)

[25] Judge Radhabinod Pal, who sat on the International Military Tribunal for the Far East, famously condemned the Tokyo Tribunal for pursuing victors' justice in post-war Japan. Pal found all defendants facing trial at the Tokyo Tribunal 'not guilty'. See Latha Varadarajan, 'The Trials of Imperialism: Radhabinod Pal's Dissent at the Tokyo Tribunal' (2015) 21(4) European Journal of International Relations 793–815

[26] See, eg, Victor Peskin, 'Beyond Victor's Justice? The Challenge of Prosecuting the Winners at the International Criminal Tribunals for the Former Yugoslavia and Rwanda' (2005) 4(5) Journal of Human Rights 213–31; Kirsten Sellars, 'Imperfect Justice at Nuremberg and Tokyo' (2010) 21(4) European Journal of International Law 1085–1102, Yuki Tanaka, Timothy LH McCormack, and Gerry Simpson (eds), *Beyond Victor's Justice? The Tokyo War Crimes Trial Revisited* (Brill 2011);

[27] United Nations Office of the United Nations High Commission for Human Rights, *Report of the Mapping Exercise documenting the most serious violations of human rights and international humanitarian law committed within the territory of the Democratic Republic of the Congo between March 1993 and June 2003* (August 2010).

[28] See Alana Tiemessen, 'The International Criminal Court and the Politics of Prosecutions' (2014) 18(4)–(5) International Journal of Human Rights 444–61; see also Mark Kersten, *Justice in Conflict—The Effects of the International Criminal Court's Interventions on Ending Wars and Building Peace* (Oxford University Press 2016) 162–84.

[29] That these are the first two sentences one reads on the institution's website is illustrative of just how important and politically sensitive the matter of *not* being a hybrid court is in Kosovo.

[30] As Sarah Williams points out, the KSC is the first hybrid court to exclusively employ international staff. See Sarah Williams, 'The Specialist Chambers of Kosovo: The Limits of Internationalization?' (2016) 14(1) Journal of International Criminal Justice 25–51

[31] Aidan Hehir, 'Step Towards Justice or Potential Timebomb?' (2018) Balkan Investigative Reporting Network 4

[32] Carsten Stahn, *Tribunals are Dead, Long Live Tribunals: MICT, the Kosovo Specialist Chambers and the Turn to New Hybridity*, (EJIL: Talk! 23 September 2016), at https://www.ejiltalk.org/tribunals-are-dead-long-live-tribunals-mict-the-kosovo-specialist-chambers-and-the-turn-to-new-hybridity/

The KSC and SPO were established in 2015 in order to investigate and prosecute the alleged atrocities committed by members of the Kosovo Liberation Army (KLA), or against Kosovo nationals, between 1 January 1998 and 31 December 2000, during and after the Kosovo War.[33] Of particular interest to the KSC are alleged crimes committed by KLA forces against ethnic Serbs and those KLA figures who escaped prosecution at other courts (including the International Criminal Tribunal for the Former Yugoslavia). Many of these are widely seen as war heroes in Kosovo and have, in the meantime, ascended to positions of political power.[34] The challenge of bringing Kosovo's victors to justice was alluded to in a statement by the Dutch government when the creation of the KSC was announced:

Possible suspects may be seen by sections of Kosovan society as freedom fighters, and witnesses may feel threatened in Kosovo. This is why the option of trying cases outside Kosovo was explored.[35]

The Chambers are a direct response to the Council of Europe's 2010 report, named after its author, Dick Marty, and which concluded that members of the KLA were responsible for international crimes as well as transnational organized crimes such as the harvesting and trafficking of human organs.[36] In Marty's crosshairs were the very KLA leaders who are revered by many and have emerged as political leaders since Kosovo's war with Serbia. That includes current President Hashim Thaçi, whom Marty described as a criminal 'boss' and Ramush Haradinaj, the current Prime Minister. Both have been periodically hostile to the court, with Thaçi describing allegations against KLA combatants as 'groundless' and allegedly threatening to release the names of ethnic Albanians who cooperate in Marty's investigation.[37] Thaçi has also insisted that the KSC was imposed upon Kosovo by the European Union, an allegation corroborated by some scholars.[38] According to Thaçi, Kosovo had to decide between a court established by the European Union or a court consecrated by the United Nations Security Council where permanent member Russia is an ally of Serbia.[39] In late 2017 and early 2018, Thaçi and Haradinaj's supporters in parliament pushed forward a vote to abolish the KSC by revoking the law that created it. Following domestic pressure and strongly-worded diplomatic statements by Western leaders, the effort was rebuked.[40] Thaçi retorted that while the KSC 'cannot be revoked and will not be revoked,' the 'establishment of this court is a historic injustice; no other place went through this.'[41]

[33] Republic of Kosovo, Law No.05/L-053, On Specialist Chambers and Specialist Prosecutor's Office (3 August 2015), available at: http://www.kuvendikosoves.org/common/docs/ligjet/05-L-053%20a.pdf

[34] Muhareemi writes that 'the Specialist Chambers were construed as an extension of the ICTY dedicated to prosecuting and indicting former Kosovo Albanian KLA members only.' See Muharremi (2016) 975.

[35] Government of The Netherlands, *Kosovo court to be established in* The Hague (15 January 2016), at https://www.government.nl/latest/news/2016/01/15/kosovo-court-to-be-established-in-the-hague

[36] See Council of Europe, Committee on Legal Affairs and Human Rights, *Inhuman treatment of people and illicit trafficking in human organs in Kosovo*, (12 December 2010)

[37] See Chuck Sudetic, *The Bullies who run Kosovo*, Politico, (21 July 2015), at https://www.politico.eu/article/kosovo-hashim-thaci-un-special-court-tribunal-organ-trafficking-kla-serbia-milosevic-serbia-ramush/

[38] See Muharremi (2016) 968.

[39] Die Morina and Taulant Osmani, *Kosovo President: Special War Court Can't Be Stopped*, Balkan Transitional Justice (1 February 2018), at http://www.balkaninsight.com/en/article/special-court-cannot-be-revoked-kosovo-president-says-02-01-2018

[40] The American Ambassador to Kosovo Greg Delawie issued a harshly worded statement that read: 'This effort, if it succeeds, will have profoundly negative implications for Kosovo's future as part of Europe. It will be considered by the United States as a stab in the back. Kosovo will be choosing isolation instead of cooperation and I have to say we would hate to turn the clock back for Kosovo on progress when it has come so far.' Ambassador Delawie's Statement to the Media about Undoing the Special Court Law, see https://xk.usembassy.gov/ambassador-delawies-statement-media-undoing-special-court-law/

[41] ibid.

Indeed, no country has had a tribunal created with the express purpose of holding the victors of its wars to account for war crimes and crimes against humanity. The Kosovo Specialist Chambers are unique in this regard. It remains to be seen whether the KSC can achieve justice for the KLA's alleged crimes. Many are sceptical. One report found that, due to a combination of the positions of power held by alleged perpetrators, a lack of witnesses willing to testify or still alive, and corruption in the country, few Kosovars have faith that the KSC will be able to fulfil its mandate.[42] Some, like Aidan Hehir, also argue that the alleged responsibility of Western states, NATO, and the United Nations Mission in Kosovo is unlikely to be investigated by the KSC and SPO, undermining their legitimacy and perception in Kosovo.[43]

Whether or not the KSC and SPO successfully prosecute the former senior leadership of the KLA is currently unclear. Given the political and legal sensitivities touched upon above, it will be a tall order. But that does not take away from the fact that a hybrid court was, for the first time in the history of international criminal justice, set up with the express purpose of prosecuting the domestic victors of a conflict.

Shared jurisdiction: The Special Criminal Court in the Central African Republic

Hybrid courts need to be sensitive to the matter of concurrent jurisdiction—whether the tribunal shares jurisdiction over crimes with other judicial institutions. For most hybrid tribunals, this is particularly relevant for their relationship with domestic bodies which may also have jurisdiction over the international or transnational crimes that the hybrid is investigating and prosecuting. An assessment of the domestic criminal code of the state, and therefore any legislation which can be invoked or needs amendment in order to prosecute international crimes, will influence the precise blend of national and international law that the hybrid applies, as well as the appropriate mix of national and international staff that should populate the tribunal. However, there may also be times when a hybrid tribunal is established and has concurrent jurisdiction with an *international* court.

Hybrids should not only be seen as an appropriate judicial response to situations where there is an accountability 'blind spot' and therefore *no* tribunal present. It would be deleterious to present conflict-affected communities with a trade-off whereby a choice would have to be made between exclusively domestic, international, or hybrid justice. On the contrary, hybrid tribunals may be most successful in situations where there is concurrent jurisdiction with both internationalized courts *and* domestic institutions. In a prescient 2003 essay, Laura A Dickinson observed the following:

> ... the ICC will not be equipped to try more than a handful of cases arising from any given post-conflict situation. Yet local courts may not be able to try such cases either ... [I]t is precisely in these circumstances that huge numbers of cases cannot be adequately resolved by local courts—and the number of the cases that cannot be resolved adequately will likely

[42] Hehir (2018) 13–14.

[43] Aidan Hehir, *A New War Crimes Court is born, but who is Responsible in Kosovo?*, Justice in Conflict (10 August 2015), at https://justiceinconflict.org/2015/08/10/a-new-war-crimes-court-is-born-but-who-is-responsible-in-kosovo/

> far outnumber the ones that might come before the ICC. Under these circumstances, hybrid courts can play a useful role in shoring up the capacity and legitimacy of criminal proceedings to try those accused of committing mass atrocities ... These courts hold considerable promise, even in a world after the ICC.[44]

There is an increasing understanding and acknowledgement that the ICC cannot—and should not—be seen as the only or even the ideal response to mass atrocities. The re-emergence of hybrid tribunals is indicative of this reality. As Beth van Schaak writes:

> [T]here is an enduring need for the international community to create, enable, and support additional accountability mechanisms to respond to the commission of international crimes ... Rather than threatening to undermine the ICC, many proposals [to create hybrid courts], if pursued, have the potential to contribute to a more integrated, differentiated, and impactful international justice system that will mount a stronger challenge to impunity by reaching more victims and perpetrators.[45]

Such an integrated approach can be seen most clearly in the Central African Republic (CAR). where the hybrid Special Criminal Court (SCC) and the ICC share concurrent jurisdiction over war crimes, crimes against humanity, and genocide committed since 1 January 2003.[46]

The SCC was created via domestic legislation in response to ongoing political violence in CAR, particularly the atrocities perpetrated by Séléka and anti-Balaka forces between 2012–2014 in which thousands of civilians were killed.[47] It is to be financed by voluntary contributions, primarily from Western donors and supported by the UN mission in the country, MINUSCA, 'in the areas of investigations, arrests, detention, criminal and forensic analysis, evidence collection and storage, recruitment and selection of personnel, court management, prosecution strategy and case development and the establishment of a legal aid system, as appropriate, as well as, to provide security for magistrates, including at the premises and proceedings of the SCC, and take measures for the protection of victims and witnesses, in line with the CAR's international human rights obligations, including with respect to fair trials, and due process;'[48]

44 Laura A Dickinson, 'The Relationship Between Hybrid Courts and International Courts: The Case of Kosovo' (2003) 37(4) New England Law Review 1072

45 Van Schaak (2016) 101–03.

46 For a discussion of the SCC's concurrent jurisdiction with the ICC as well as the ordinary Central African court system, see Patryk I Labuda, 'The Special Criminal Court in the Central African Republic—Failure or Vindication of Complementarity?' (2017) 15 Journal of International Criminal Justice 191–95

47 The United Nations' mandated International Commission of Inquiry on the Central African Republic observed that: 'The Commission considers that in the context of the CAR conflict, it is not in a position to establish with any degree of accuracy the number of people who were killed in the conflict, during the two years covered by the mandate. The difficulties of collecting accurate data in this regard are due to various reasons, including the practice of Muslim communities to bury their dead almost immediately and the difficulty of getting access to mass graves, especially in the countryside and forests, in the midst of continuing conflicts. The various estimates so far available during this period range from 3,000 to 6,000 people killed, but the Commission considers that such estimates fail to capture the full magnitude of the killings that occurred.' See https://reliefweb.int/sites/reliefweb.int/files/resources/N1471229.pdf

48 See United Nations Security Council Resolution 2448, S/RES/2448 (2018), (13 December 2018), available at: https://minusca.unmissions.org/sites/default/files/_resolution_2448_2018.pdf

The SCC's establishment came soon after the ICC opened its second of two investigations in CAR, into the anti-Balaka—Séléka violence. The ICC thus has two active investigations in CAR, although it is notable that it has only prosecuted one individual for atrocities committed in CAR, Jean-Pierre Bemba, a national of the Democratic Republic of Congo, who was initially convicted and later controversially acquitted on appeal.[49] Moreover, as Patryk Labuda explains, the 2015 domestic legislation establishing the SCC gives primacy to the ICC over the SCC which, he argues, may constitute a violation of the ICC's rules on complementarity.[50] Labuda also notes that the SCC may be seen as 'a failure of the ICC's decade-long intervention in the country and epitomizes the shortcomings of the international community's efforts to fight impunity in Africa.'[51]

Still, the SCC is notable for being the first-ever hybrid court to exist concurrently with active ICC investigations (as well as possible activity among domestic courts). Rather than competing over cases or dealing a 'death blow to the ICC's legitimacy',[52] staff at the SCC and ICC have gone to significant lengths to ensure that their mandates complement each other. Letters that could form the basis of a formal Memorandum of Understanding between the institutions have been exchanged.[53] In March 2018, senior staff from the ICC, including the chief Prosecutor, held training sessions with magistrates from CAR, including senior prosecutors from the SCC.[54] The ICC has also offered to train SCC judges and investigators and, as some civil society organizations have pointed out, it may be wise for the two institutions to cooperate on other ventures, including outreach efforts, as well.[55]

The level of violence and atrocity perpetrated in CAR is far beyond what either the SCC or the ICC could effectively respond to alone. Indeed, it is likely beyond what both can do, even taken together with the domestic judiciary.[56] It remains to be seen what direction either tribunal takes; at the time of writing, neither have issued warrants of arrest pertaining to crimes committed by Séléka and anti-Balaka forces. But by striking a cordial and cooperative relationship with the ICC and by using the Court's expertise and knowledge to develop and improve its own, the SCC remains unique among tribunals. It has demonstrated that a hybrid court and the ICC can function in a complementary fashion whilst operating in the same jurisdiction and investigating the same crimes. It is, of course, far too early to cast judgement upon this novel experiment in international criminal justice, but it at least holds the potential of an effective division of labour between hybrids and the ICC that patches the all-too-apparent gaps in the system of international justice. Moreover, forging

49 For instance: Jennifer Trahan, *Bemba Acquittal Rests on Erroneous Application of Appellate Review Standard*, Opinio Juris at http://opiniojuris.org/2018/06/25/bemba-acquittal-rests-on-erroneous-application-of-appellate-review-standard/

50 Patryk Labuda, *The Special Criminal Court in the Central African Republic*, American Society of International Law, https://www.asil.org/insights/volume/22/issue/2/special-criminal-court-central-african-republic

51 Labuda (2017) at p 204.

52 This was suggested as a possibility had the SCC competed for cases with the ICC. See L Luigi Prosperi, 'Is a Hybrid Court for the CAR a Good Idea?' (*Justice Hub*, 15 May 2015), at https://justicehub.org/article/hybrid-court-car-good-idea

53 See Human Rights Watch, 'Looking for Justice' The Special Criminal Court, a New Opportunity for Victims in the Central African Republic (2018) at https://www.hrw.org/sites/default/files/report_pdf/car0518_web.pdf 30

54 See International Criminal Court, *ICC holds training for Magistrates in Central African Republic* (22 March 2018) at https://www.icc-cpi.int/Pages/item.aspx?name=pr1373

55 See Human Rights Watch (2018) 29.

56 See AFP, *Criminal justice a Rare Commodity in Central African Republic* (18 October 2017), at https://www.timeslive.co.za/news/africa/2017-10-18-criminal-justice-a-rare-commodity-in-central-african-republic/

such cooperative arrangements between tribunals may make a useful contribution which resonates beyond the relationship between hybrids and the ICC.

Scholars and observers have become increasingly interested in the African Union's Malabo Protocol and the possibility that the jurisdiction of the African Court on Human and Peoples' Rights would be expanded to include the core international crimes embodied in the Rome Statute.[57] Despite certain problematic caveats in particular around sitting head of state immunity,[58] such an institution would be a welcome development as a means to investigate and prosecute international and transnational crimes in the region—not in competition with the ICC, but in a complementary fashion.[59] Indeed, the Protocol already envisions being complementary to other regional and national judicial bodies. This could—and should—be extended to its relationship with international tribunals such as the ICC. As Margaret M deGuzman maintains:

> [A]s regional and sub-regional criminal courts such as the [African Court] emerge, they should not be viewed as forming a jurisdictional hierarchy, with national courts at the top and the ICC at the bottom, but rather as providing a menu of adjudicative options . . . In this way, national, regional, and international criminal courts can enter into a truly complementary relationship.[60]

The complementary and cooperative experience of the SCC-ICC relationship looks set to make a precedent for how such courts can operate and cooperate together.

Cutting costs, pooling premises

Tribunals generally do not enjoy funding sufficient to meet the demands and expectations of justice and accountability. Funding has been a particularly difficult challenge for hybrid courts. While it is generally accepted that assessed contributions are the preferred means of resourcing a tribunal, many have been funded voluntarily.[61] Voluntary funding poses severe

[57] See, eg, Amnesty International, *Malabo Protocol—Legal and Institutional Implications of the Merged and Expanded African Court* (2016); Gerhard Werle and Moritz Vormbaum (eds), *The African Criminal Court A Commentary on the Malabo Protocol* (Asser Press 2017); Charles Jalloh, Kamari Clarke, and Vincent Nmehielle (eds), *The African Court of Justice and Human and Peoples' Rights in Context* (Cambridge University Press: Forthcoming 2019).

[58] An amendment to the Malabo Protocol provides for immunity for heads of state and senior government officials.

[59] When asked whether the expansion of the African Court's jurisdiction would be a 'slap in the face', ICC chief Prosecutor Fatou Bensouda responded that 'In fact, ICC is a court of last resort. We will be encouraged by national jurisdictions taking up their responsibility to investigate and prosecute these crimes.' See Caroline Schmitt, *13 years, 1 billion dollars, 2 Convictions: Is the International Criminal Court worth it?* (*Deutsche Welle*, 27 January 2016) at https://www.dw.com/en/13-years-1-billion-dollars-2-convictions-is-the-international-criminal-court-worth-it/a-19006069

[60] See Margaret M deGuzman, 'Complementarity at the African Court', in Charles Jalloh, Kamari Clarke, and Vincent Nmehielle (eds), *The African Court of Justice and Human and Peoples' Rights* (Cambridge University Press 2017); Temple University Legal Studies Research Paper No 2018-01, p 1 Available at SSRN: https://ssrn.com/abstract=3078119,

[61] For example, in a report on the SCC, Erica Bussey has written that due to it being '[f]unded solely by voluntary contributions, it is difficult to see how the SCC will avoid ongoing financial crises similar to those that destabilised and undermined the work of the Special Court for Sierra Leone and to this day affect the work of the Extraordinary Chambers in the Courts of Cambodia.' See Erica Bussey, *Progress and Challenges in Establishing the Special Criminal Court in the Central African Republic*

challenges for tribunals. It exposes tribunals to potential intrusions on their independence by donors who can hold resources hostage for particular judicial outcomes. Voluntary contributions can also sap the energy of senior staff who are forced to devote time and energy to fundraising rather than pursuing the core investigatory, prosecutorial, or juridical functions of the Court. Some estimate that senior staff at the SCSL, for example, spent as much as a third of their time on fundraising and related activities.[62]

A tribunal's premises must meet certain standards of functionality, security, and technology. As a result, the creation of a tribunal can be a costly endeavour, particularly in relation to the financial situation of the communities in or for which they are established. For example, the estimated cost of building the premises of the SCSL was $6 million at a time when the GDP per capita of the Sierra Leonean population was under $328.[63] Post-conflict states should not be expected to carry the burden of building modern courts when the very edifices of other public institutions are suffering. Nor should they be solely responsible for maintaining the upkeep of such tribunals during the lifespan of the court or, as importantly, once the tribunal's mandate is completed. However, a sense of dependency is created if external donors must maintain such facilities for years after the tribunal's work is completed, leaving an uneasy choice between a decreased sense of local ownership if internationals maintain facilities, and the possibility of the bricks-and-mortar of tribunals being allowed to fall into disrepair and disuse if the burden falls on a less-developed host state.

At the same time, it is not always feasible for hybrid tribunals to be located within the state in which the alleged atrocities occurred due to security reasons and fears of political destabilization and interference. This may be true for all proceedings before the tribunal, as is the case with the KSC, or may only be partial. The latter scenario was evident when former Liberian President Charles Taylor was prosecuted not on the premises of the SCSL in Freetown but in The Hague, in courtrooms seconded by the ICC and the Special Tribunal for Lebanon to the SCSL.

Previous iterations of international and hybrid tribunals have bequeathed a physical legacy that could help to alleviate the set-up costs and security challenges faced by a new generation of hybrid courts. By pooling tribunals, the unique flexibility of hybrids could help policy- and lawmakers alleviate the cost and insecurity burdens present when setting up tribunals. Consider the examples of South Sudan and Liberia.

The proposed hybrid court for South Sudan

Given the current political context and ongoing instability, it is implausible that the proposed Hybrid Court for South Sudan (HCSS) could be located in the capital of Juba. Indeed, given security concerns and the resources that it would require of an impoverished and

(*Amnesty International*, 2 October 2017), at https://www.amnesty.org/en/latest/campaigns/2017/10/progress-and-challenges-in-establishing-the-special-criminal-court-in-the-central-african-republic/

[62] Conversation with former senior staff member of SCSL.

[63] See Special Court for Sierra Leone Press and Public Affairs Office, Press Release (11 October 2002), available at http://www.rscsl.org/Documents/Press/2002/pressrelease-101103.pdf; World Bank, World Integrated Trade Solution, *Sierra Leone GDP per capita constant 2010 US$ 2000–2006* (accessed 20 July 2018), at https://wits.worldbank.org/CountryProfile/en/Country/SLE/StartYear/2000/EndYear/2006/Indicator/NY-GDP-PCAP-KD

severely conflict-affected state (even with international donor help), such a proposition would be unfair. One can imagine, for example, that rebel attacks on tribunal staff would result in severe criticism of the state. This has inspired some consideration of alternative premises for the HCSS outside of Juba. One possibility is Arusha, Tanzania.

Arusha is a stable and secure city, which some refer to as 'The Hague of Africa' due to its numerous international bodies and courts, including the ICTR. Notably, despite closing down and being replaced by the residual institution the Mechanism for International Criminal Tribunals (MICT), a new and modern headquarters was built for the ICTR just outside of Arusha. Due to the continued existence of some fugitives indicted by the tribunal, these premises may still be used to prosecute Rwandan génocidaires. However, they could also be used as something analogous to a permanent hybrid court, housing proceedings for tribunals established to investigate and prosecute atrocities but which remain too unstable to host tribunals and secure tribunal staff.[64] Indeed, some senior MICT staff have suggested that this should indeed be the case and that they would welcome the use of the building's courtroom for such purposes.[65] Some diplomats have also intimated their preference that proceedings at the HCSS take place in Arusha instead of Juba.[66]

While the premises of the MICT could host proceedings from states in the region, like South Sudan, unless there are no other possibilities, it should not act as a host for prosecutions of perpetrators happening in disparate regions of the continent or world. There are other options.

A potential war crimes court in Liberia

Since the election of George Weah as President of Liberia in December 2017, there has been a strong push from international and domestic civil society to establish a Liberian war crimes tribunal. In all likelihood, such a court would take the form of a hybrid tribunal. In its final report, issued in 2009, the Liberian Truth and Reconciliation Commission recommended that an 'internationalized domestic criminal court' be established with a mandate to investigate and prosecute core international crimes in addition to certain economic and domestic crimes. Since Weah's ascension to power, pressure on the government to set up a tribunal has grown.[67]

As of this writing, it remains unclear whether the government is interested in such a tribunal. Ministers have said it is not a 'priority' for the government.[68] Weah's selection of Jewel Howard Taylor, the former wife of Liberian President Charles Taylor, as Vice President

[64] For a discussion on this proposal, see Kersten (2018) 270–72.

[65] Conversation with ICTR / MICT Staff, 2017.

[66] Conversation with senior African Union staff involved in establishment of the HCSS, 2018.

[67] See, eg, Front Page Africa, Liberia Fails To Disclose Plans for War Crimes Before UN Human Rights Committee (11 July 2018), at https://frontpageafricaonline.com/liberia-war-crimes-trial/liberia-fails-to-disclose-plans-for-war-crimes-before-un-human-rights-committee/; The Center for Justice & Accountability, Liberia (accessed 20 July 2018), at https://cja.org/where-we-work/liberia/ https://www.civitas-maxima.org/en/campaigns/liberian-quest-for-justice-campaign; Human Rights Watch, Liberia: 76 Groups Seek Justice for War Crimes (5 July 2018), at https://www.hrw.org/news/2018/07/05/liberia-76-groups-seek-justice-war-crimes.

[68] See Lennart Dedoo, *Liberian Govt. Not Interested in War Crimes Court For Now* (*Front Page Africa*, 11 May 2018), at https://frontpageafricaonline.com/politics/liberian-govt-not-interested-in-war-crimes-court-for-now-deputy-information-minister/

is reportedly 'seen by many Liberians as a snub to the victims'.[69] Further complicating matters, many individuals allegedly involved in the political violence of Liberia's civil wars are in positions of power and public office.[70] Removing them from office and/or power could be destabilizing to a country that held its first peaceful transition of power since 1944 in 2017.

One means to reduce tensions and the potentially destabilizing effects of prosecutions would be to outsource some of the proceedings to the premises of the SCSL. This would also reduce the start-up costs associated with creating a war crimes tribunal, which would likely be attractive to both the Liberian government as well as international donors. There is, as the saying goes, no need to reinvent the wheel. The SCSL premises would have to be updated, which is a resource-intensive proposition. But this would cost significantly less than the construction of a new tribunal in Monrovia that met international standards.

Of course, hosting proceedings in Freetown would create distance between the locus of the crimes that were committed in Liberia (Monrovia and Freetown are 525 km apart), but with the saved costs, more resources could be allocated to effective outreach programming in both Sierra Leone and Liberia. As a Sierra Leonean scholar astutely observes: 'The conflicts in Sierra Leone and Liberia are intertwined and it is easier to bring Liberians to Freetown to witness the trials live. Future trials (from Liberia or elsewhere) will also remind Sierra Leoneans of the legacy of the [SCSL] that impunity for grave crimes is no longer acceptable.'[71] With time and the continued consolidation of peace and security, prosecutions could be transferred to domestic courts in Liberia, similar to the practice of case transfer from the ICTY and the Bosnian War Crimes Chamber to relevant courts in the former Yugoslavia.[72]

Whatever features a Liberian war crimes tribunal ultimately has and whether or not the HCSS eventually hears cases in Arusha, hybrid courts have the unique and endogenous flexibility in their institutional design to utilize the strategic advantages of their predecessors. It would be a remarkable legacy if the facilities of previous tribunals could become residences of a new generation of hybrids.

Concluding reflections—Problem-solving justice

In her 2003 essay on hybrid tribunals, Laura Dickinson made the following observation:

> [hybrid] courts have developed in an ad hoc way, the result of on-the ground-innovation rather than institutional design ... they hold a good deal of promise and actually offer an approach that may address some of the concerns about purely international justice, on the one hand, and purely local justice, on the other.[73]

[69] See Cristina Krippahl, *Liberians Still Seek Justice for War Crimes* (*Deutsche Welle*, 10 July 2018), at https://www.dw.com/en/liberians-still-seek-justice-for-war-crimes/a-44599243

[70] See Rodney D Sieh, *Liberia: Quiet Pursuit of War Criminals Signals Hope Against Impunity* (*Front Page Africa*, 22 October 2017), at http://frontpageafricaonline.com/liberia-war-crimes-trial/liberia-quiet-pursuit-of-war-criminals-signals-hope-against-impunity/

[71] From a discussion with Mohamed Sesay (31 July 2018).

[72] See Ivanišević Bogdan, *The War Crimes Chamber in Bosnia and Herzegovina: From Hybrid to Domestic Court*, International Center for Transitional Justice (2008).

[73] Dickinson (2003) 1059–60.

It is this ad hoc and flexible nature that animates hybrids. One tribunal need not be the same as the last. Each represents an opportunity to rectify any missteps of the last and improve on the record of its predecessors. This chapter has demonstrated how hybrids can be forums of creative thinking to address the shortcomings of international criminal justice: the EAC's innovative outreach programming which reached its multiple constituencies; the KSC's unprecedented mandate to investigate and prosecute the victors of the war in Kosovo; the SCC's sharing of concurrent jurisdiction and a cooperative relationship with the ICC; and the possibility of future hybrids, including the proposed HCSS and a war crimes court for Liberia, being housed in the premises of their predecessors. Some of these novel efforts may not be exclusive to hybrid courts. But there is something about the very hybridity of these institutions that can inspire innovative solutions which can, in turn, address the pitfalls of prior tribunals.

The analysis offered in this chapter is not an attempt to paint an overly rosy picture of hybrid courts or international criminal justice. With the rise of populism and a growing animosity towards international criminal law among powerful and weak states, tribunals and their proponents face, as perhaps they always have, an uphill battle. While recent years have seen the re-emergence of the hybrid tribunal as a popular mechanism of international criminal justice, with the EAC arguably a prime example, their predecessors—the SCSL, ECCC, STL, etc—had a mixed and contentious record. The latest generation of hybrids will have their own flaws, weaknesses, critics, and mixed records. Their ability to successfully confront the particular challenges they face remains to be seen. But hybrids offer something that other tribunals do not: an opportunity to continuously reimagine and problem-solve international criminal justice.

32

Is the Opposition Between Civil Law and Common Law Criminal Procedure the Lock or Key to International(ized) Tribunals' Success?

Leïla Bourguiba[1]

On 16 October 2017, representatives of international criminal courts and tribunals met in France at the French National School for the Judiciary. Their meeting resulted in the signing of a *Declaration on the effectiveness of international criminal justice* (Paris Declaration). In its preamble, this document states, '*in compliance with their founding texts, specific procedures should be devised and practices developed to cater to the complexity of the crimes these courts and tribunals must adjudicate*'.[2] As regards 'specific procedures,' the declaration makes no mention of 'civil' or 'common' law, or 'inquisitorial' or 'adversarial' systems. Yet in gathering professionals from international courts and tribunals where the need to comply with founding texts and specific procedures can challenge those who, by habit, comfort or conviction, draw on their national practise to interpret and apply the rules of procedure, the question of common versus civil law pr*actice was the implicit focus.*

The Paris Declaration was adopted at a time when disappointment towards the 'efficiency' of international(ized) tribunals and courts is high. They are considered too slow and too costly. In this context, it is not unusual to hear that international trials would be better managed and more efficient if they borrowed more elements of 'civil law' on their 'common law' foundation.[3] This makes it sound like success is a question of correctly measuring the ingredients. Is a good blend possible?

To address this issue, the main characteristics of each procedural system will be described (I), to help identify which procedural model has been favoured before international(ized) tribunals (II) before questioning whether national investigation and prosecution of core international crimes are more efficient. The French experience of the Specialized war crimes and crimes against humanity Unit will serve as an example (III).

[1] The author underlines that this article is submitted in her own capacity and expressed her personal views. Thus, it does not necessarily reflect the views of any of the institutions she worked for or currently works for.

[2] Paris Declaration on the effectiveness of international criminal justice, developed by representatives of international criminal courts and tribunals on 16 October 2017, accessible on the web page of the French Magistrate school, ENM, https://www.enm.justice.fr/sites/Default/files/publications/Declaration_Paris_EN.pdf

[3] See for instance, Le Monde Diplomatique, Cyril LAUCCI, *Deux modèles concurrents à la Cour pénale internationale : Quand le droit anglo-saxon s'impose*, Avril 2014. Libération, François ROUX, *La crise* d'adolescence de la justice pénale internationale, 22 octobre 2013.

Leïla Bourguiba, *Is the Opposition Between Civil Law and Common Law Criminal Procedure the Lock or Key to International(ized) Tribunals' Success?* In: *The President on Trial*. First edition. Edited by: Sharon Weill, Kim Thuy Seelinger, and Kerstin Bree Carlson, Oxford University Press (2020). © Leïla Bourguiba. DOI: 10.1093/oso/9780198858621.003.0033

Civil law and common law systems: from the initiation of the investigation to trial proceedings, who takes the lead?

Traditionally, systems of criminal procedure have been schematically categorized as belonging to 'common law' or 'civil law' systems.[4] Common law systems are called 'adversarial' whilst civil law systems, also called Romano-Germanic system, are referred to as 'inquisitorial'. This schema provides a useful framework, although these categories are also misleading as there exist differences in practise within the same category as well as mutual influence between categories that defy a clean split between them.[5] We will rather delve into what crystallizes most of the disputes before international(ized) tribunals and courts, on elements that are seen as being symptomatic of either systems.

Civil law and common law systems may be distinguished by reference to the goals pursued by the trial. Civil law systems search for truth, while common law systems, though also concerned to know what happened, essentially aim to resolve a dispute between the parties.[6] This distinction can also be represented procedurally as a difference between *party-driven* or *judge-driven* investigations.[7] Other commentators distinguish between the oral (adversary) versus written (inquisitorial) nature of the systems, and how this impacts the trial.

Investigation

Both in inquisitorial and adversarial systems, the initiation of criminal investigation and prosecution is essentially or exclusively vested in the prosecutor, who will usually supervise the initial investigations conducted by police officers. In an adversarial system, prosecutors have discretionary power to decide whether to bring charges or not, despite the existence of sufficient evidence, if s/he finds it is not in the public interest.

The adversarial system embraces a *party-driven approach*. The prosecutor and the defence conduct their own investigations without judicial supervision.[8] The information collected during the investigations becomes 'evidence' once it is admitted at trial. The prosecutor has the obligation to disclose to the defence the information collected ahead of trial but is not under the obligation to disclose it at the time it is collected. The accused, in light

4 Other criminal systems exist, such as the religious-based system of Sharia's law. However, in addition to the fact that they formed the main basis of criminal procedures before international(ized) tribunals, the focus on 'common law' and 'civil law' systems may also be explained by the fact that they 'cover over 70% of the world's population in over 62% of the jurisdictions'. See Alexander Heinze, 'International Criminal Procedure and Disclosure' (2013) Duncker & Humblot 106.

5 See for instance, Kai Ambos, 'International criminal procedure: "adversarial", "inquisitorial" or mixed?' (2003) 3 International Criminal Law Review 1–37; Mireille Delmas-Marty and J Spencer, *European Criminal Procedures* (2002); F Pakes, *Comparative Criminal Justice* (Willan Publishing 2004) ; Mirjan Damaška, 'Evidentiary Barriers to Conviction and Two Models of Criminal Procedure: A Comparative Study' (1973) 121 University of Pennsylvania Law Review 506–89.

6 See for instance Mirjan Damaška (n 5) and Mirjan Damaška, *The Faces of Justice and State Authority: A comparative approach to the legal process* (Yale University Press 1991).

7 See for instance, Craig R Callen, *Cognitive Strategies and Models of Fact-Finding, in Crime, Procedure and Evidence in a Comparative and International Context* (Hart Publishing 2008).

8 There is nonetheless judicial supervision when intrusive measures are required such as phone surveillance or searches. Disagreement regarding party conduct or cooperation can also become the subject of motions made to the court for the judge to resolve.

of their right against self-incrimination, is not under the obligation to disclose all the results of their investigations.

To the contrary, the inquisitorial system is *judge-driven*. The judge leads or supervises the pre-trial investigations. The information is mainly collected by an investigating judge[9] or a prosecutor[10] and must include both incriminating and exculpatory evidence discovered in the course of the investigation. The judge will direct the lines of investigations by deciding which investigative steps need to be undertaken, witnesses heard and information collected. The parties are not completely passive; they may submit documents or request the investigating judge to proceed with specific investigative steps such as identifying witnesses to be heard. The information collected is made accessible to both the prosecutor and the defence as well as the *parties civiles* (victims), in a file known as the *dossier*. The central role played by the *dossier* mitigates the onerous rules of evidence controlling what is admitted before the court in adversarial systems.

The trial and presentation of evidence

In an accusatorial system, the parties decide what evidence to present and which witnesses to call at trial. The judge is an umpire, an observer without any prior knowledge about the facts of the case and with the essential duty to ensure that, during the presentation of their case, the parties respect the rules of procedure, the fairness of the proceedings. As a result, the dynamism of the trial depends on the parties' input and ability to litigate actively, which hinges on the parties' means. Unlike the factually unprepared adjudicator, the judge in an inquisitorial system plays a central and active role in the fact-finding process. The trial judge has the benefit of the *dossier* as well as the investigating judge's decision prior to trial. During the trial, judges play, as a result, an active role, notably in questioning the accused and the witnesses. The judges inquire on the personality of the accused, including his background and path, and the facts.

Victims

Following the movement on victims' rights in the 1970's, interest in victims' participation in criminal proceedings increased both in civil law and common law systems, essentially to mitigate victims' secondary victimization by their treatment during criminal proceedings. In 1985, the United Nations Declaration of Basic Principles of Justice for Victims of Crime and Abuse of Power[11] further called upon States to enhance victims' participation in national criminal proceedings. Despite this UN Declaration, victims still do not enjoy the same role and rights before civil law and common law driven systems. Victims in common law systems have no independent role, they merely appear as witnesses. The bipolarization of the proceedings between the defence and the prosecutor is preserved. However, many

9 See France, Spain, and The Netherlands for instance.

10 See for instance Germany where the investigative judge has disappeared and replaced by a prosecutor who directs the pre-trial investigations.

11 United Nations General Assembly, Resolution 40/34, UN Doc A/RES/40/34 (1985).

common law driven jurisdictions allow victims to make submissions at the sentencing hearing. This impact statement usually contains information on the physical, psychological and financial impact the offense had on the victim.[12] Circumscribing victims' intervention to the sentencing stage does not allow them to provide possible relevant information during the trial, thus impacting on the determination of the guilt or innocence of the accused. The inquisitorial system provides a more active and independent role to victims in criminal proceedings. Victims can often initiate proceedings by filing a civil party complaint (*plainte avec constitution de partie civile*) and/or take active part in the criminal proceedings initiated by the prosecutor by a civil party application (*constitution de partie civile*) to join these proceedings. As participants in the proceedings, these victims enjoy procedural rights, notably: access through their lawyers to the record of the case (dossier); may request specific investigative steps; may question witnesses at trial through their lawyers and submit their views on the guilt or innocence of the accused.

The performative, and potentially unpredictable, nature of the common law trial leads some common law scholars to suggest that only adversarial systems respect the maxim 'innocent until proven guilty'. Civil law scholars reject the contention that their systems prejudice defendants, noting the many judicial professionals who intervene, at various stages of the process, with the duty to find all incriminating and exculpatory evidence as a safeguard for justice, neutrality, and unbiased professionalism. These commentators can also reference the gap between theory and practice at common law, where cases come to trial in as few as 1% of cases. In short, while both systems aim for justice, the distinctions between 'specific procedures' employed to realize justice make each distrustful of the other.

Have international(ized) tribunals clearly adopted a model of criminal procedure?

The statutes of the ad hoc courts drafted in the 1990s do not contain any reference to the type of criminal procedure system to be followed. The judges were entrusted with the task of adopting the rules of procedure and evidence for the conduct of the pre-trial investigation, the trial and appeals.[13] They adopted a largely common law procedure at their commencement, where, for example, the prosecutor enjoyed autonomy in the conduct of investigations without supervision by a judicial body, and the prosecution's duty to disclose materials to the defence started only after the issuance of an indictment committing a person to trial. Over the years, however, judges amended the rules of procedure in a direction many found symbolic of an inquisitorial tradition.[14]

Unlike the experience of the ad hoc tribunals, the drafters of the Rome Statute governing the ICC constrained the judges' capacity to determine their own rules of procedure. They vested the Assembly of State parties with this legislative power.[15] In the drafting of the Rome Statute and of the rules of procedure and evidence, efforts have been made to elude

[12] United Nations Office for Drugs Control and Crime Prevention, Handbook on Justice for Victims: on the use and application of the Declaration of Basic Principles of Justice for Victims of Crime and Abuse of Powers (1999).

[13] ICTY Statute, article 15 and ICTR Statute, article 14.

[14] For a discussion of the procedural evolution of ICTY practice see Kerstin Bree Carlson, *Model(ing) Justice: Perfecting the Promise of International Criminal Law* (Cambridge University Press 2018) chapter 3.

[15] Article 51 of the Rome Statute.

formula clearly coming from either system such as 'examination in chief' or 'cross examination'. On 5 September 2017, the Appeals Chamber recalled in a judgement that the 'Court's legal framework combines elements from the Common Law and Romano-Germanic legal traditions'.[16] However, constructive ambiguity characterized the drafting of these articles and rules, opening the door to interpretation disputes hinging on the distinction between common law and civil law systems. The debates on witness proofing and the extent of victims' participation or the admission of written statements at trial are illustrative of this.

The following sections examine three emblematic examples—plea bargaining, presentation of evidence, and participation of victims—to show how procedural practice rooted in either civil or common law tradition is operating before international tribunals.

Plea bargaining

Generally, in a plea bargain, the suspect agrees to plead guilty, eventually also cooperating with the prosecutor, in exchange for reducing the charges and/or the prosecutor's promise to request a lower sentence. This mechanism is seen as an efficient way to save resources as it allows parties to negotiate an agreement, focus on certain aspects of the case and thus avoid a full trial. It also enables the prosecutor to secure key information in complex criminal cases where the need for insider information appears crucial to unravel the extent of the criminal network.

For a long time, plea bargaining had been considered a purely common law practise, regularly used in the United States, Australia, or South Africa for instance. This mechanism is criticized even before these jurisdictions as it can turn into an incentive for innocent people to plead guilty and does not consider victims' thirst for justice. Procedural safeguards have therefore been set up. In the United States, the judiciary ensures that the guilty plea of the suspect is voluntary, informed and factually based. In the British criminal procedure, the prosecutor has to consult with the victims if s/he wishes to negotiate a plea bargaining.

While originally perceived as antithetical to the quest for truth and the principle of mandatory prosecution, some countries employing civil law systems have begun to accept the possibility of plea bargaining, at least for non-violent offenses.[17]

Plea bargaining before international criminal tribunals is controversial. Entrusted with the investigation and the prosecution of the most heinous crimes, one may wonder whether it is fair for an international tribunal to agree on a lesser sentence when the suspect pleads guilty for war crimes, crimes against humanity, or genocide. Thinking about the 'accurate historical record' and the reconciliation goals that are often perceived as being pursued by these tribunals, there is an additional question about how plea bargaining, which enables some charges, and thus arguably some facts, to be dropped from the indictment, might work towards these goals.

[16] ICC, *The Prosecutor v Bosco Ntaganda*, 5 September 2017, para 52.

[17] France, for example, plea bargaining has been introduced to settle corruption cases, see the so-called Loi Sapin II, Law n°2016-1691 of 9 December 2016 on transparency, fight against corruption and modernization of the economy which introduces the « convention judiciaire d'intérêt public » (see article 22 of the Law).

Originally, neither the ICTY nor the ICTR permitted plea bargains. The practice was even expressly rejected when the United States proposed using plea bargaining as a tool to elicit evidence and get to the top of the chain of command. Judge Antonio Cassese underlined that 'no one should be immune from prosecution of crimes such as these, no matter how useful their testimony may otherwise be'.[18]

The RPE were amended early in ICTY practice, however, to accommodate the guilty plea of Drazen Erdemović in 1996. In this case, the Prosecutor and Erdemović agreed that, in exchange for his guilty plea, he would be prosecuted for lesser war crimes' offenses and that the Prosecutor would request a lower sentence to the judges. While the Appeals Chamber found that this guilty plea was not admissible because Erdemović was not sufficiently informed when entering it, it nonetheless accepted the possibility to negotiate plea bargaining at the ICTY. In total, twenty plea agreements have been entered before the ICTY.[19]

Before the ICC, article 65(5) of the Rome Statute is entitled 'proceedings on an admission of guilt'. It is worth noting that while this proceeding has not been called 'plea bargaining', paragraph 5 nonetheless makes explicit reference to the possible 'discussions between the Prosecutor and the defence regarding modification of the charges, the admission of guilt or the penalty to be imposed'. It however underlines that such discussions shall not be binding on the Court.

All in all, for a guilty plea or an admission of guilt to be valid, it shall be demonstrated that (i) it has been voluntary entered,[20] (ii) the suspect was well informed, i.e. s/he understands the nature of the charges brought against her/him and the consequences of pleading guilty to them;[21] (iii) it is unequivocal[22] and (iv) factually based. In relation to the latter, however, the ICC Statute excludes that the agreement forms the only grounding for the factual basis for the admission of guilt. More specifically, the ICC procedure provides for a more balanced approach to guilty plea or admission of guilt, entrusting the judges with decisive powers. The judiciary determines whether the admission of guilt is supported by the facts of the case as contained in: (i) the charges brought by the Prosecutor and admitted by the accused; (ii) any materials presented by the Prosecutor which supplement the charges and which the accused accepts; and (iii) any other evidence, such as the testimony of witnesses, presented by the Prosecutor or the accused. The judges have the power to request the prosecutor to present additional evidence or to order the trial to be continued under the ordinary trial procedures, if the Trial Chamber 'is of the opinion that a more complete presentation of the facts of the case is required in the interests of justice, in particular the interests of the victims' [emphasis added].[23]

So far, only one case has led to an admission of guilt before the ICC. Ahmad Al Faqi Al Mahdi, member of Ansar Eddine, head of the 'Hisbah' until September 2012. He pled guilty to the destruction of the religious and historic buildings in Timbuktu and was thereafter

[18] Antonio CASSESE, President of the ICTY, Statement made at a briefing to members of Diplomatic Missions, UN Doc IT/29, 11 February 1994.

[19] See ICTY website http://www.icty.org/en/cases/guilty-pleas

[20] ICTY, *The Prosecutor v Drazen Erdemovic*, Case n°IT-96-22-A, Joint separate opinion of Judge McDonald and Judge Vohrah, 7 October 1997. See also article 65(1)(a) of the ICC Rome Statute.

[21] ICTY, *The Prosecutor v Drazen Erdemovic*, Case n°IT-96-22-A, Joint separate opinion of Judge McDonald and Judge Vohrah, 7 October 1997. See also article 65(1)(b) of the ICC Rome Statute.

[22] ICTY, *The Prosecutor v Drazen Erdemovic*, Case n°IT-96-22-A, Joint separate opinion of Judge McDonald and Judge Vohrah, 7 October 1997, paras 28–30.

[23] Articles 61(1)(c) and (4) of the Rome Statute.

sentenced to nine years' imprisonment, a sentence within the range recommended by the Prosecutor in the 'Agreement regarding admission of guilt'.[24] The Al Mahdi trial lasted two days. Interestingly, this agreement, which is essentially an archetypal common law procedurewas signed by Al Mahdi and his counsels, a Tunisian and a Belgium lawyer, the Prosecutor and her Senior Trial Lawyer, a French lawyer.

Considerations on evidence at trial and the role of judges

Traditionally the rules on presentation of evidence before international criminal tribunals have been largely influenced by the common law approach. Witnesses are orally examined and cross-examined by the parties during the trial. Leading questions to the witness by the calling party are forbidden and allowed during cross-examination by the other party or during questioning by the judges.[25] This lengthy procedure has often been seen as contributing to the overall, much criticized, length of trials. In addition, at odds with the civil law approach, the accused can testify at her/his own trial.[26]

Oral presentation of evidence has been favoured rather than documentary evidence. Amendments to the procedure have however introduced 'inquisitorial' elements by, for example, allowing the Chamber to receive the evidence of a witness in written form, when the interests of justice allow;[27] the admission of previous statements in cases where the witness has died, cannot be found anymore, or because s/he can no longer testify orally because of a health condition revealed after s/he gave the statements;[28] the admission, in whole or in part, of the evidence of a witness in the form of a written statement or a transcript of evidence, when it was given in proceedings before the Tribunal, *in lieu* of oral testimony. In this last scenario, it is required that the subject matter of such written statement may not be 'the acts and conduct of the accused as charged in the indictment'.[29]

At the discretion of the ICC trial chamber[30] the parties may submit written evidence instead of oral evidence which may include written statements, transcripts or written reports. In addition, this influence, of civil law system is also perceivable in relation to the role played by trial judges. For instance, Rule 140(2)(b) of the ICC's RPE, entitled 'Directions for the conduct of the proceedings and testimony', classically provides for the prosecution and the defence's right to question witnesses. Paragraph (2)(c) further provides for the Trial Chamber's right to question a witness before or after a witness is questioned by a participant.[31] Furthermore, Rule 120 of the ICTY RPE[32] entitled 'Powers of Chambers to order

[24] ICC, *The Prosecutor v. Ahmad Al Faqi Al Mahdi*, ICC-01/12-01/15, Agreement regarding admission of guilt, 18 February 2016, accessible on https://www.icc-cpi.int/RelatedRecords/CR2016_05666.PDF.

[25] ICC, Trial Chamber, *The Prosecutor v Thomas Lubanga*, Decision on judicial questioning, 18 March 2010.

[26] See rule 144(D) of the STL's RPE. If there is no such specific provision before the other international tribunals, such testimony is allowed as of right.

[27] Rules 89 and 90 of the ICTY RPE (December 2000). See also ICTY, Appeals Chamber, *The Prosecutor v Slobodan Milosevic*, Decision on Interlocutory Appeal on admissibility of evidence in chief in the form of written statement, Case n°IT-02-54-AR, 30 September 2003.

[28] Rule 92*quater* of the ICTY RPE.

[29] Rule 92*bis* of the ICTY RPE.

[30] Before the ICC, the presiding judge of the trial chamber has to power to 'give directions for the conduct of the trial' (article 64(8)(b) of the Statute).

[31] See also r 98 of the ICTY and ICTR's RPE.

[32] Former r 98 of the RPE.

production of additional evidence', provides that a trial chamber may order either party to produce additional evidence and may also *proprio motu* summon witnesses and order their attendance. It thus foresees moments where judges will exit their passivity. It should be noted that the level to which this action is exercised depends on the judges.

Victims' participation

The United Nations Security Council Resolution 827 (1993) establishing the ICTY underscored that the tribunal was created '*for the sole purpose of prosecuting persons responsible for serious violations of international law*' [emphasis added], leaving aside any role to be played by the victims of these heinous crimes. As a result, victims are limited to the role of witnesses, called by one of the parties in support of the presentation of her/his case. For this reason, victims were often referred to as mere 'instruments' in the hands of the party. Permitting voiceless victims is also based on the incorrect assumption that their interests will always be adequately protected by the prosecutor, ignoring the possibility that sometimes the prosecutor may be more concerned with obtaining a conviction than addressing the different interests of the victims.

Conversely, the ICC was inspired by a civil law approach in relation to victims. It provides victims with statutory procedural rights, recognizing an active role in the proceedings for them. At the beginning of the Rome Conference which led to the creation of the ICC, non-governmental organizations opined, 'Punishing criminals is not enough. There will be no justice without justice for victims. And in order to do justice for victims, the ICC must be empowered to address their rights and needs.'[33] The conference resulted in the adoption of a Statute according to which victims have a right to participate at all stages of the proceedings.[34]

Beside this general right, other articles of the Statute provide for more specific victims' procedural rights. According to article 15(3) of the Statute, victims have the right to participate at the earliest stage of the proceedings, the decision of the Pre-Trial Chamber whether to authorize or not a *proprio motu* investigation by the Prosecutor. Victims also enjoy the right to be informed of the closure of that investigation (article 15(6) of the Statute). In addition, article 19(3) provides for a right for victims to participate in proceedings with regard to the specific issues related to jurisdiction or admissibility. A mechanism for awards for reparation (including restitution, compensation and rehabilitation) is introduced with article 75 of the Statute. Nonetheless, the victims cannot be equated to parties in the proceedings. Victims have to apply for participation in the proceedings to the Chamber.[35]

While the Rome Statute provides for an interesting legal and procedural framework, the challenges faced by victims along the way of exercising their right to participate at the different stages of the proceedings oblige us to question the effectiveness of such right.[36] Such

[33] Statement by Fiona McKay, representing Redress, on behalf of *The Victims Rights Working Group* delivered to the Rome Conference on 17 June 1998, reprinted in BITTI, G. and FRIMAN H. (2001), Participation of Victims in the Proceedings, in Roy S Lee, *The International Criminal Court, Elements of Crimes and Rules of Procedure and Evidence* (Transnational Publishers 2001) 456–74.

[34] Article 68(3) of the Rome Statute.

[35] Rule 89(1) of the RPE of the ICC.

[36] See Gilbert Bitti and Leïla Bourguiba, 'Victims Before the International Criminal Court: much remains to be done' in *The Public in Law* (Ashgate Publishing 2012).

challenges include access to proper information in a timely fashion, geographical distance between the court and the affected communities, and physical protection. The length of trials also poses a challenge to victims' rights. When also keeping in mind the goals of the tribunals to satisfy victims of the crimes, one might wonder whether this can be fulfilled with trials that last for several years. This brings into question the visibility of the action of the tribunals, and their capacity in keeping the victims informed of the evolution of the investigations and the prosecution. There are also conflicts between the length of the trial and victims' needs for rapid rehabilitation and trauma care.

As the late Judge Cassese stated in his dissenting opinion in the *Erdemovic* Appeals Judgment, '[i]nternational criminal procedure results from the gradual decanting of national criminal concepts and rules into the international receptacle. [...] International criminal procedures] combine and fuse, in a fairly felicitous manner, the adversarial or accusatorial system (chiefly adopted in common-law countries) with a number of significant features of the inquisitorial approach.'[37] This assertion is being challenged since todays' complaints are founded on the inefficiency of international criminal procedures seen as mostly following a common law approach.

A parallel to the Hissène Habré Trial: French national courts investigating and prosecuting core international crimes

Because critics of international tribunals' effectiveness have often been situated in their common law procedure mostly adopted, it is perhaps relevant to have a look at the experience of a national tribunal when they exercise universal jurisdiction in the prosecution and investigation of core international crimes. In this vein, it is quite interesting to see the evolution of French criminal procedure on this matter as France is often regarded as the quintessential representative of the civil law system. In 2012, France created a Specialized Unit with jurisdiction over the prosecution and investigation of core international crimes.

As of October 2018, the French Specialist Unit (prosecutors and investigating judges) is involved in fifteen different geographical areas, including crimes allegedly committed in Syria, Iraq, Libya, Chad, the Democratic Republic of Congo, Uganda, Afghanistan, Rwanda, or Chechenia,[38] with Syria, Central African Republic, and Rwanda the most important. This represents in total more than 105 files including forty-three preliminary investigations. In less than three years, we have witnessed a 400% growth in the number of ongoing investigations.[39]

After seven years of existence, has the Specialised Unit demonstrated that the civil law system is more efficient in dealing with the investigation and prosecution of core international crimes? So far, three persons have definitively been found guilty and sentenced to

[37] ICTY, Appeals Chamber, *The Prosecutor v Drazen Erdemovic*, Appeals Judgement, Dissenting opinion of Judge Antonio Cassese, 7 October 1997.

[38] See Interview of Prosecutor Aurélia Devos, 17 October 2018, http://www.justice.gouv.fr/justice-penale-11330/crimes-contre-lhumanite-bilan-du-pole-du-tgi-de-paris-31897.html.

[39] This recent exponential growth has an additional explanation: the adoption of Law n° 2015-925 of 29 July 2015 on the asylum law reform. According to its article 10, the director of the French Office for the Protection of Refugees and Stateless Persons transmits to the Public Prosecutor all relevant information linked to its decision to reject an asylum or stateless protection request, when such rejection is motivated by an exclusion clause as defined in article 1 F of the 1951 Geneva Convention on Refugees.

prison at the end of two trials. These figures might appear quite low, especially when one considers that some cases are under investigations for several years if not a decade. However, while it is still perfectible, over the years, the Unit has developed working methods, an important network and expertise. The peculiarity of the cases led the first judges and prosecutors of the Unit to challenge their routine practise and be open to new tools and practises while respecting the coherence of French national criminal law and procedure.

In respect to the overall length of the procedure, in the case against Ngenzi and Barahiera the trial on their alleged involvement in the Tutsi genocide in Rwanda in 1994 lasted two months, including three weeks dedicated to context. A quick overview of the files indicates that in a case marked with constant investigative efforts and no significant cooperation obstacles, pre-trial investigations led by a judge last on average at least five years. This overall optimal length appears similar to the overall length of some cases before international(ized) tribunals. Yet, in this quest for a correct balance, it is important to keep the trial in a reasonable time frame. Excessively lengthy trials are no longer understandable nor followed by the victims or the affected community. Even the staff working on a trial might lose sight of the heart of the case, not to mention possible departure of staff members. Meanwhile, although it appears difficult to gather a jury for several months, a trial held in less than two months leaving little rest to the jury, may not give the jurors enough time to grasp all the peculiarities of the context of commission of crimes, the cultural and sociological dimensions to properly hear the witnesses and to grasp tremendous amount of information. The correct balance still has to be sought, even before civil law driven domestic courts.

The prosecutor of the Specialized Unit enjoys, as usual, autonomy in presenting charges *throughout the pre-trial stage* of the proceedings,[40] under the oversight of an investigating judge who leads the pre-trial investigations having due regard to incriminating and exculpatory materials and hearing the witnesses and the suspects.

In the French system and as well as for the Specialized Unit, it is the indictment order—drafted by the investigating judge—that establishes the parameters of the trial. It is transferred together with the full case record. The record of the case contains the document initiating the proceedings (the prosecutor's initial request or the civil party complaint) and all documents and incriminating and exonerating evidence gathered during the pre-trial investigations (*inter alia* witness' statements; documentary evidence; parties' requests and investigative judges' orders).

The materials, both incriminating and exculpatory, are made available to the parties, well in advance of the start of the trial. The defence counsel can consult the case record and request a copy thereof,[41] subject to confidentially.[42] The defence's access to the case record assisting its preparation before the commencement of the trial. This is fundamental in light of the complexity of the cases and the length of the proceedings. Bearing in mind the different challenges presented by the investigation of core crimes pursuant to universal

[40] On 9 August 2010, the Law 2010-930 adapted the French criminal code to the Statute of the ICC.

[41] Articles 113-3, 114, and 114-1 of the criminal code of procedure.

[42] Pre-trial investigations are confidential. Access to the case record is given to the Defence counsel of the person under judicial examination as well as to the defence counsel of the 'assisted witness' (*témoin assisté*). The assisted witness includes any person mentioned by name in an initial or subsequent prosecutor's submission and who is not under judicial examination. See articles 113 and following in the criminal code of procedure. Aware of the consequences of potential breaches to confidentiality, and in order to maintain the principle of access to the file, the witness and victims' protection scheme has been enhanced in order to adapt our legislation to the specificity of such cases (Law n°2016-731 of 3 June 2016).

jurisdiction,[43] the early defence involvement is key and can be instrumental in identifying and gathering exculpatory evidence as well as in challenging victims' and prosecutor's requests and judicial orders.[44] Indeed, investigations can last for several years and a trial a few months; the case-record may be voluminous. Without financial means, a dynamic involvement of the defence throughout the proceedings can be very challenging, as only few lawyers will have the means and resources to focus their efforts on one case only, to the detriment of the proper functioning of their practice. The legal aid scheme does not provide for any additional means for core international crimes cases, such as expenses for travel costs for site visits. Yet, in most cases, the suspects benefit from the legal aid scheme. It is important to reflect on the need to improve this situation.

The case record is chronologically organized and therefore it is a useful tool in understanding the lines of investigation followed. If the pre-trial stage was conducted efficiently, this *dossier* will provide the trial chamber with a complete account, clearly distinguishing between contextual elements and the heart of the criminal case brought against the accused. An outsider should be able to understand the line of reasoning and the guiding lines of the investigation and the consequent decision committing the person to trial. The indictment order serves as an efficient tool to the presiding judge of the trial chamber[45] to organize the court sessions, the calling of evidence and the questioning of witnesses. Held before a jury, only the presiding trial judge will have access to the case record. Parts of the indictment order will be read at the beginning of the trial and this is how members of the jury will get knowledge of its content.[46] When presenting, concisely, the imputed facts as contained in the indictment order, the presiding judge will also indicate the incriminating and exculpatory elements therein mentioned, as well as the legal characterization of the imputed facts.[47]

Victims' participation before the ICC has often been seen as a French victory. Victims' participation before national courts in criminal proceedings related to core international crimes also raises issues and practical challenges that are similar to those before international(ized) tribunals. It is interesting to see that the scheme in relation to universal jurisdiction over core international crimes differs in some respects from ordinary French criminal procedure. Firstly, the Law 2010-930 adapting the French criminal code to the Statute of the ICC,[48] subjected the exercise of universal jurisdiction to four conditions.[49] It introduced prosecutorial discretion; thus, proceedings can only be initiated at the request of the prosecutor. By introducing this requirement, the French legislator has explicitly restricted the civil party complaint mechanism in relation to the prosecution of core

43 For in instance, access to the field, cooperation challenges and context sensitivity.

44 French Law does not expressly foresee the possibility for the defence to undertake independent investigations. While no provision prevents the defence from doing so, it is nonetheless not generally accepted in practise as it is assumed that the defence should rely on the prosecutors and investigative judges' investigations, duty bound to look for incriminating and exculpatory evidence.

45 The Trial is held before a trial chamber composed of the presiding judge, two assessor-judges and a trial jury composed of six jurors when the court of assizes rules at first instance and nine jurors when it rules on appeal (article 296 of the criminal code of procedure)

46 In addition to the presiding judge, during the trial, the two assessor-judges as well as member of the jury may question the accused or witnesses (article 311 of the criminal code of procedure).

47 Article 327 of the criminal code of procedure.

48 This law notably criminalizes direct and public incitement to commit genocide; amend the definition of crimes against humanity to conform to the definition of article 7 of the Rome Statute; inserts Title IV*bis* in the Criminal Code wherein, for the first time in the criminal code, acts as constitutive of war crimes or offenses are listed.

49 As modified by Law n°2019-222 of 23 March 2019.

international crimes pursuant to universal jurisdiction. This however has a drawback as, in practise, victims are tempted to file a civil party complaint for an alleged crime of torture within the meaning of the New York Convention to circumvent this problem, whilst sometimes the act might—as well—be legally characterized as amounting to a crime against humanity.

In addition, ordinary proceedings involving victims' participation, become more challenging when exercising universal jurisdiction over core international crimes. Interestingly, the difficulties and questions appear, to a certain extent, quite similar to those before international(ized) tribunals. In principle, article 80-3 of the code of criminal procedure obliges the investigating judge to inform, at the beginning of the investigation, the victim of the crime of her/his right to become a *partie civile* in the proceedings. However, by definition, mass crimes involve a large number of potential victims. How to reach out to these victims, how to inform them of their rights, how to maintain contact throughout the proceedings which last several years, how to provide them with the relevant information in a language they understand? These questions are unresolved and show the difficulties, thought not insurmountable, to reach out to victims and keep contact when they are unrepresented.

Conclusion

Is the perfect(ible) blend possible? Throughout the years and cases experience, the balance before the ad hoc tribunals and following international tribunals between a common law and a civil law approach has evolved. While equality of arms remains an important concern, judges now play a more active role and victims, while still striving for legitimacy, are acquiring procedural rights. The hybridization is ongoing but not achieved. This hybridization, as called for by the creation of the ICC seek to define and protect an identity that should not merely be coined as being mostly common law or civil law based.

Recalling the words of the late judge Cassese, since international criminal procedure is an amalgamation of two different legal systems, it is therefore only natural that procedures do not 'uphold the philosophy behind one of the two national criminal systems to the exclusion of the other; nor do they result from the juxtaposition of elements of the two systems'. Thus, international criminal procedure 'begets a legal logic that is qualitatively different from that of each of the two national criminal systems: the philosophy behind international trials is markedly at variance with that underpinning each of those national systems.'[50]

To define such identityrequires an agreement on a common purpose. More than a simple dispute on the procedural scheme to be followed, today's crisis of international criminal justice goes to the roots of international(ized) tribunals' *raison d'être*.

On several occasions, these international criminal tribunals and their progenitors have advanced objectives that are much wider than those sought by national criminal law such as establishing a record of past events which can provide a basis for a long-term reconciliation.[51] This has been upheld by the ICTY itself when submitting its annual reports stating

[50] ICTY, Appeals Chamber, *The Prosecutor v Drazen Erdemovic*, Appeals Judgement, Dissenting opinion of Judge Antonio Cassese, 7 October 1997.

[51] United Nations, Secretary General, *Report of the Secretary-General on the Rule of Law and Transitional Justice in Conflict and Post-Conflict Societies*, UN Doc S/2004/616, 23 August 2004.

that 'through its judicial proceedings the Tribunal establishes a historical record'.[52] These tribunals have also been assigned the goals of satisfying the victims of these heinous crimes as well as restoring peace and security and deterring the commission of further crimes. However, there are voices against such broad goals, calling for a traditional criminal law approach by which such international(ized) tribunals shall only focus on the determination of a person's guilt or innocence.[53] The latest ICC Pre-trial decision refusing to open an investigation into alleged crimes committed in Afghanistan raises, among others, questions as to the judges' understanding of the Court's mandate.[54]

Thus, before seeking improvements in criminal procedure to enhance international tribunals efficiency, clear and agreed goals have to be identified. When there is not a clear understanding of the objectives pursued, it is unlikely to have all stakeholders of a tribunal working in the same direction and to develop a comprehensive and harmonious jurisprudence. Obviously, when a judge feels invested with the task of searching the truth, s/he will exercise its mandate differently. The understanding of the *raison d'être* of the tribunals have consequences for the rules of procedure adopted but also, and most importantly, on the practise developed.

In this respect, while initiatives like the Paris Declaration are to be welcomed, such professional exchanges on practises and challenges faced in the investigation and prosecution of core international crimes should be extended to the national specialized units exercising universal jurisdiction, where the civil law and common law systems are represented. In doing so, one can only notice that these units, while applying their own national criminal procedure, face challenges too.

[52] ICTY, Fifth Annual Report, UN Doc A/53/219, para 202, 10 August 1998; See for instance, ICTR, *The Prosecutor v Karemera et al*, Case No ICTR-98-44-AR73, Decision on Prosecutor's interlocutory Appeal of Decision on Judicial Notice, para 35, 16 June 2006.

[53] United Nations, Security Council, Resolution 827 (1993) underscoring that the ICTY was created 'for the sole purpose of prosecuting persons responsible for serious violations of international law'.

[54] ICC, Pre-trial Chamber, Decision Pursuant to Article 15 of the Rome Statute on the Authorisation of an Investigation into the Situation in the Islamic Republic of Afghanistan, 12 April 2019 accessible on https://www.icc-cpi.int/Pages/record.aspx?docNo=ICC-02/17-33.

33

The ICJ's Senegal v Belgium Judgment and the Obligation to Prosecute or Extradite Alleged Torturers

The Case of Al Bashir and the ICC

Manuel J Ventura and Victor Băieşu[1]

Introduction

The judgment in the *Questions Relating to the Obligation to Prosecute or Extradite (Belgium v Senegal)* was the first judgment in which the International Court of Justice ('ICJ')'s judges authoritatively articulated the material scope and the measures necessary for the implementation of an obligation to prosecute or extradite (*aut dedere aut judicare*). In this case, this obligation arose under the Convention Against Torture and Other Cruel, Inhuman or Degrading Treatment or Punishment ('Torture Convention') (1984). The ICJ's judges also decisively held that the prohibition of torture had attained the status of *jus cogens* and that the existence of a common interest of State Parties to the Torture Convention (1984) in the compliance with *erga omnes* obligations alone suffices for any State Party to have standing to invoke the responsibility of any other State Party for breaching such obligations. These were broad-reaching, novel and significant findings with potential reverberations beyond the Habré case. This chapter analyses the impact of these ICJ pronouncements in the context of the ICC's arrest warrants against Omar Al Bashir who, since being deposed in April 2019, now only enjoys functional immunity *ratione materiae*.

The *Belgium v Senegal* case before the ICJ

In February 2009, Belgium filed an application before the ICJ to institute proceedings against Senegal in relation to Habré. Belgium argued that Senegal had breached its obligations under Article 5(2) of the Torture Convention (1984) by failing to take the necessary measures to establish its jurisdiction over any act of torture. Further, by failing to initiate a preliminary inquiry against Habré, who was present on its territory at the time, Senegal remained in breach of its obligation under Article 6(2) of the Torture Convention (1984). According to Belgium, Senegal was also in continuing breach of its obligation under Article

[1] The views expressed herein are those of the authors.

Manuel J Ventura and Victor Băieşu, *The ICJ's Senegal v Belgium Judgment and the Obligation to Prosecute or Extradite Alleged Torturers* In: *The President on Trial*. First edition. Edited by: Sharon Weill, Kim Thuy Seelinger, and Kerstin Bree Carlson, Oxford University Press (2020). © Manuel J Ventura and Victor Băieşu. DOI: 10.1093/oso/9780198858621.003.0034

7(1), and under other rules of international law, by failing to prosecute Habré, or by failing to comply with an outstanding Belgian extradition request.[2]

Jurisdiction and admissibility

None of Habré's alleged victims were Belgian nationals at the time of the torturous acts, and Senegal therefore argued that Belgium's claim was inadmissible and that the Court could not exercise jurisdiction. Belgium responded that, as the jurisdiction of Belgian courts were based on the complaint filed by a Belgian national of Chadian origin, they were exercising passive personality jurisdiction. Belgium further argued that, besides its status as a Party to the Torture Convention (1984), it relied on the existence of a special interest, namely, that Belgium had availed itself of its right under Article 5 to exercise its jurisdiction and to request Habré's extradition. That distinguished it from other States Parties and entitled it to bring a claim to the ICJ concerning the cessation of an alleged violation by another State Party of its obligations.[3]

A majority of the ICJ found that the obligations of a State Party to conduct a preliminary inquiry into the facts and to prosecute under the Torture Convention (1984) are triggered by the mere presence of the alleged offender on its territory. Relying on the *Case Concerning Barcelona Traction, Light and Power Company, Limited (Belgium v Spain)*, the majority found that all States Parties to the Torture Convention (1984) have a common interest that the State in whose territory the alleged offender is present complies with these obligations. That interest implied that the obligations in question are owed by any State Party to all other States Parties. All States Parties thus 'have a legal interest' in the protection of the rights involved.[4] Furthermore, invoking the similarity between the relevant provisions of the Torture Convention (1984) and those of the Convention on the Prevention and Punishment of the Crime of Genocide (1948), the majority of the ICJ concluded that the dispute before it involved obligations *erga omnes partes* so that each State Party had an interest in the obligations being complied with.[5]

The ICJ finding the case admissible on an *erga omnes* theory—rather than the more problematic passive personality/'injured State' theory—was one of the most progressive moves that the Court has made in recent years.[6] Belgium's reliance on admissibility based on the nationality of the victims—which gave Belgium the status of an 'injured State'—was problematic because the individuals that filed the complaint had only become Belgian nationals years after the alleged torture, while Senegal only recognized Belgium's passive personality jurisdiction in respect of victims that possessed Belgian nationality at the time of the facts. Dissenting Judge ad hoc Sur pointed out that State Parties to the Torture Convention (1984)

[2] *Questions relating to the Obligation to Prosecute or Extradite (Belgium v Senegal)*, Judgment, ICJ Report 2012, 422, 450, para 71 (20 July).

[3] ibid 448–49, paras 64–67.

[4] ibid 449, para 68 (citing *Barcelona Traction, Light and Power Company, Limited (New Application: 1962) (Belgium v Spain)*, Second Phase, Judgment, ICJ Rep 1970, 3, 32, para 33 (5 February)).

[5] *Belgium v Senegal* (n 2) 449, para 68 (citing *Reservations to the Convention on the Prevention and Punishment of the Crime of Genocide*, Advisory Opinion, ICJ Rep 1951 (28 May), p 23).

[6] See M Andenas and T Weatherall, 'International Court of Justice: Questions Relating to the Obligation to Extradite or Prosecute (Belgium v Senegal) Judgment of 20 July 2012' (2013) 62(3) International and Comparative Law Quarterly 753, 765–66.

are not obliged to establish passive personality criminal jurisdiction, meaning that other States Parties to the treaty are not obliged to recognize it, in particular when their own criminal law makes no provision for it. He thus concluded that Belgium's request for extradition from Senegal was inadmissible, as was its right to request Senegal to exercise its own criminal jurisdiction, since Belgium did not have a direct right to invoke an 'injured State' status.[7]

In this respect, one cannot exclude the possibility that one reason for the majority's embrace of its progressive approach to admissibility was prompted by its intention to circumvent the potential problems that could have arisen if it found Belgium to be an 'injured State', as formulated by dissenting Judge ad hoc Sur.[8] Rather, the majority based its findings on Belgium's right to engage Senegal's responsibility resulting from its failure to comply with obligations *erga omnes partes*, such as those arising under Article 6(2) and Article 7(1) of the Torture Convention (1984). Because it did not consider whether Belgium was an 'injured State', the ICJ held that there was no need to further consider whether Belgium also had a special interest with respect to Senegal's compliance with the Convention, namely Senegal's abovementioned failure to comply with Belgium's extradition requests for Habré.[9]

Erga omnes, jus cogens, and customary international law

Until the present case, the ICJ had confined its *erga omnes* jurisprudence—that is, obligations owed to the international community as a whole, in the performance of which all States have a legal interest—by avoiding entering into an examination of peremptory norms (*jus cogens*). Although formulated for the first time in the ICJ's 1970 *Case Concerning Barcelona Traction, Light and Power Company, Limited (Belgium v Spain)* judgment,[10] it had not had any practical or substantive effect in any ICJ case.[11] Arguably, the ICJ had failed to exercise its full potential.

Accordingly, the most important legal development in the *Belgium v Senegal* judgment was the ICJ's formulation—for the first time—of a practical and substantive procedural effect arising from *erga omnes* obligations: that a common interest in the compliance with an *erga omnes* obligation is enough for *any* State to have standing to invoke the responsibility of another State for breaching such an obligation (provided the ICJ has jurisdiction). The majority was satisfied that the existence of a common interest of States Parties to the Torture Convention (1984) in the compliance with *erga omnes* obligations alone—specifically under Article 6(2) and Article 7(1)—sufficed to recognise both Belgium's *locus standi* and

[7] *Belgium v Senegal* (n 2) Dissenting Opinion of Judge ad hoc Sur, 611, para 21.

[8] See Andenas and Weatherall (n 6) 766.

[9] *Belgium v Senegal* (n 2) 450, paras 69–70; *Belgium v Senegal* (n 2) Declaration of Judge Owada, 470, paras 22–23; *Belgium v Senegal* (n 2) Separate Opinion of Judge Skotnikov, 482, para 8.

[10] *Barcelona Traction, Light and Power Company, Limited (New Application: 1962) (Belgium v Spain)*, Second Phase, Judgment, ICJ Rep 1970, 3, 32, paras 33–34 (5 February).

[11] See, eg, *Legal Consequences of the Construction of a Wall in the Occupied Palestinian Territory*, Advisory Opinion, ICJ Rep 2004 (9 July), pp 171–72, 199, paras 88, 155–57; *Case Concerning Armed Activities on the Territory of the Congo (New Application: 2002) (Democratic Republic of the Congo v Rwanda)*, Jurisdiction of the Court and Admissibility of the Application, Judgement, ICJ Rep 2006, 6, 31–32, 52, paras 64, 125 (3 February); *Case Concerning the Application of the Convention on the Prevention and Punishment of the Crime of Genocide (Bosnia and Herzegovina v Serbia and Montenegro)*, Judgment, ICJ Rep 2007, 43, 104, 111, paras 147, 162 (26 February).

the admissibility of Belgium's claims. This marks a significant shift in the way standing and admissibility, at least before the ICJ, has been traditionally understood.

In this respect, it is worth noting that, a decade earlier, the International Law Commission ('ILC') authoritatively codified the general legal interest in the compliance with an *erga omnes* obligation. The ILC's Draft Articles on Responsibility of States for Internationally Wrongful Acts (2001) entitle any State, other than an injured State to whom such obligation is owed, to invoke the responsibility of another State for breaching it (yet without clarifying which obligation is of an *erga omnes* nature).[12] The *erga omnes* nature of the obligation to extradite or prosecute under the Torture Convention (1984) now suffices to provide standing before the ICJ to any Party to which the obligation is owed to bring a claim against the offending State as a consequence of the *jus cogens* nature of the prohibition of torture.[13] The *Belgium v Senegal* judgment explicitly determined the legal effect of an *erga omnes* obligation and thereby consolidated the ILC's codification of a third States' entitlement to invoke State responsibility for the non-compliance with such an obligation.

Further, although the Vienna Convention on the Law of Treaties (1969) gave formal recognition to the *jus cogens* concept, the ICJ's judges had generally discussed it only in their separate and dissenting opinions.[14] The Judges of International Criminal Tribunal for the former Yugoslavia, in the *Furundžija* case, were the first to establish that the prohibition of torture had attained *jus cogens* status.[15] On the other hand, only in 2006 and in 2007, in the *Case Concerning Armed Activities on the Territory of the Congo (New Application: 2002) (Democratic Republic of the Congo v Rwanda)* and *Case Concerning Application of the Convention on the Prevention and Punishment of the Crime of Genocide (Bosnia and Herzegovina v Serbia and Montenegro)* respectively, did the ICJ's judges recognize the prohibition of genocide as a *jus cogens* norm. In the *Case Concerning Ahmadou Sadio Diallo (Republic of Guinea v Democratic Republic of the Congo)*, the ICJ's uncontroversial acknowledgment that the prohibition of inhuman and degrading treatment was among the rules of general international law 'which are binding on States in all circumstances, even apart from any treaty commitments',[16] brought its judges closer to considering the prohibition of torture to be equally binding on States in all circumstances.

The significance and authority of the *Belgium v Senegal* judgment in the affirmation of *jus cogens* norms is that, while in the *Case Concerning Ahmadou Sadio Diallo (Republic of Guinea v Democratic Republic of the Congo)* the ICJ did not fully explain its reasoning, this time the ICJ exhaustively articulated why the prohibition of torture had become a peremptory norm by determining that it 'is grounded in a widespread international practice and on the *opinio juris* of States'.[17] It noted that the prohibition appears in numerous international instruments of universal application, had been introduced into the domestic law of almost

[12] Draft Articles on Responsibility of States for Internationally Wrongful Acts, with commentaries, 2001, in Yearbook of the ILC (2001) Vol II, Part 2 (A/CN.4/SER.A/2001/Add.1) 126-29, Art 48.

[13] *Belgium v Senegal* (n 2) 449–50, 457, paras 67–70, 99.

[14] Vienna Convention on the Law of Treaties, 23 May 1969, 1155 UNTS 331 (1969), *entered into force* 27 January 1980, Arts 53 and 64. See *North Sea Continental Shelf Cases (Germany/Denmark; Germany/The Netherlands)*, Judgment, ICJ Rep 1969, 3, Separate Opinion of Judge Sørensen, 248 (20 February); *Belgium v Spain* (n 4) Separate Opinion of Judge Ammoun, 325, para 34.

[15] *Prosecutor v Furundžija*, Case No IT-95-17/1-T ICTY, Trial Judgment (10 December 1998) paras 144, 153–56.

[16] *Ahmadou Sadio Diallo (Republic of Guinea v Democratic Republic of the Congo)*, Merits, Judgement, ICJ Rep 2010, 639, 671, para 87 (30 November).

[17] *Belgium v Senegal* (n 2) 457, para 99.

all States, and that acts of torture were regularly and consistently denounced within national and international fora.[18]

Relevantly, two ICJ judges found, in dissenting opinions, that the majority had gone beyond what it was called upon to determine. Judge Abraham determined that the finding that the prohibition of torture was part of customary law and that it had even become a peremptory norm was 'clearly a mere *obiter dictum*', which the ICJ could have omitted without depriving its reasoning of any vital element.[19] Judge ad hoc Sur also characterized the references to *jus cogens* as *obiter dictum* that gave weight to 'a disputed notion, whose substance has yet to be established'.[20]

Obligation *aut dedere aut judicare*

The *Belgium v Senegal* judgment also held that, in terms of jurisdiction, at the date of the filing of the application before it, no dispute existed between the Parties as to Senegal's obligation to prosecute or extradite Habré for alleged crimes under customary international law. The only obligations referred to by Belgium and Senegal in their diplomatic correspondence leading up to the ICJ case were those under the Torture Convention (1984).[21] Therefore, the ICJ proceeded to consider the *aut dedere aut judicare* principle only within the rubric of the Torture Convention (1984) and emphasized that the 'Hague formula' was used in Article 7(1).[22] Moreover, when it referred to the obligation of a State Party to criminalize torture and to establish its jurisdiction over such conduct under the Torture Convention (1984), the ICJ employed wording similar to that in the ILC's Draft Code of Crimes against the Peace and Security of Mankind (1996), which included the obligation to extradite or prosecute individuals alleged to have committed war crimes, crimes against humanity, genocide or crimes against UN and associated personnel.[23]

In the *Belgium v Senegal* judgment, the ICJ unequivocally decided not to assign the same weight to extradition and submission for prosecution under the Torture Convention (1984). Rather, it expressly prioritized prosecution as an obligation under the Convention while extradition was an option offered to the States Parties.[24] The significance of the ICJ's judgment in determining the material scope and aspects relevant to the implementation of the obligation to prosecute or extradite cannot be overstressed, especially considering that, while Belgium and Senegal did not disagree on Senegal's duty to prosecute Habré, they disagreed about what constituted a breach of those obligations and what conditions they imposed. In addition, although formally confined to the Torture Convention (1984), the *Belgium v Senegal* judgment may also be relied upon to clarify the obligation to extradite or prosecute under other treaties that have followed the same 'Hague formula', since it served as the model for the relevant provisions included in

18 *Belgium v Senegal* (n 2) 457, para 99.

19 *Belgium v Senegal* (n 2) Separate Opinion of Judge Abraham, 477, para 27.

20 *Belgium v Senegal* (n 2) 605–06, para 4.

21 *Belgium v Senegal* (n 2) 444–45, 462, paras 53–55, 122(2). Judge Abraham and Judge ad hoc Sur dissented on this matter: *Belgium v Senegal* (n 2) 476–80, paras 21, 24–25, 31–39; *Belgium v Senegal* (n 2) 610, para 17.

22 *Belgium v Senegal* (n 2) 454–55, para 90.

23 Compare *Belgium v Senegal* (n 2) 451, para 75 to Draft Code of Crimes against the Peace and Security of Mankind, with commentaries, 1996, in Yearbook of the ILC (1996) Vol II, Part 2, 30–32, Art 9 (Obligation to extradite or prosecute). See also Andenas and Weatherall (n 6) 767.

24 *Belgium v Senegal* (n 2) 456, paras 94–95.

the Torture Convention (1984).[25] However, the 'Hague formula' does not explicitly address the issue of whether the obligation to prosecute is triggered once the alleged offender is present on the territory of the relevant State or once an extradition request is refused.[26]

A necessary prerequisite to enforcing an obligation to extradite or prosecute an alleged torturer present on the territory of a State is establishing jurisdiction over the crime and the individual concerned.[27] Here, the ICJ observed that the Torture Convention (1984) 'brings together 150 States which have committed themselves to prosecuting suspects in particular on the basis of universal jurisdiction'.[28] Such jurisdiction allows any State, in the absence of other bases of jurisdiction, to prosecute individuals for crimes regardless of where they were committed, who committed them, or against whom they were committed.[29] Considering the specific circumstances of the Habré case, the ICJ showed its support for the premise that universal jurisdiction is permissible and indispensable to the proper operation of the obligation to extradite or prosecute alleged torturers—especially when they are not prosecuted in the territory where the crime was committed.[30]

Additionally, the ICJ made it clear that the fulfilment of the obligation to extradite or prosecute requires States Parties to the Torture Convention (1984) to undertake necessary national measures to criminalize torture, investigate or undertake a preliminary inquiry and submit the case to prosecuting authorities or to extradite, if another State requests extradition. State authorities are then left to decide, based on the applicable domestic laws, whether to initiate criminal proceedings in light of the evidence available. It was also noted that national authorities must deal with such a case in the same manner as any other criminal matter of a serious nature under the law of the State concerned.[31]

As to the obligation to investigate, according to the ICJ, national authorities must start an investigation as soon as they have reasons to suspect that an individual that may be held responsible for acts subject to the obligation to extradite or prosecute under the Torture Convention (1984) is present on their territory.[32] The obligation to initiate and conduct a preliminary inquiry by drawing up a case file, establish facts and collect evidence, applies to the authorities of the State where the alleged crime was committed or of any other State where complaints have been filed in relation to the case. The State on whose territory the individual is present, in order to comply with its obligation to conduct an inquiry, must seek the cooperation of the authorities of the aforementioned States. Notably, an inquiry

[25] See *The Obligation to Extradite or Prosecute* [Aut Dedere aut Judicare], Report of the International Law Commission, Sixty-sixth Session (A/69/10) para 65(10), fn 440, in Yearbook of the ILC (2014), Vol II, Part 2 (forthcoming).

[26] See eg, Convention for the Suppression of Unlawful Seizure of Aircraft, 16 December 1970, 860 UNTS 105 (1970), *entered into force* 14 October 1971, Art 7.

[27] Referring specifically to the decisions of the Senegalese courts of 2000–2001 as to lack of jurisdiction, the ICJ recalled that, by virtue of Article 27 of the Vienna Convention on the Law of Treaties (1969), a State Party to a treaty may not invoke the provisions of its internal law as justification for its failure to perform a treaty (*Belgium v Senegal* (n 2), 460, para 113).

[28] *Belgium v Senegal* (n 2) 451, para 75.

[29] See H J Steiner, 'Three Cheers for Universal Jurisdiction—Or is it Only Two?' (2004) 5(1) Theoretical Inquiries in Law 199, 201–02

[30] *The Obligation to Extradite or Prosecute* (Aut Dedere aut Judicare), Second Report on the Obligation to Extradite or Prosecute *(Aut Dedere aut Judicare)* by Mr Zdzislaw Galicki, Special Rapporteur (A/CN.4/585) in Yearbook of the ILC (2007) Vol II, Part 1 (A/CN.4/SER.A/2007/Add.1) 72, para 3.

[31] *Belgium v Senegal* (n 2) 454–55, 456, paras 90–91, 94.

[32] ibid 454, paras 86, 88.

conducted on the basis of universal jurisdiction must be just as demanding in terms of evidence as when the State has jurisdiction by virtue of a link with the case in question.[33]

The ICJ also explained that the obligation to prosecute entails the submission of the case to national prosecuting authorities, which may or may not result in the initiation of criminal proceedings. The decision to initiate proceedings must be taken in the same manner as national authorities would for any alleged offence of a serious nature under its domestic law.[34] The *Belgium v Senegal* judgment further stressed that, once a complaint has been filed against the suspect, all the measures and actions necessary for the implementation of the obligation to prosecute must be taken without delay and within a reasonable time, though without explaining what constitutes 'reasonable time' or 'without delay'.[35]

The alternative obligation to extradite an alleged torturer must only be exercised to send the person to a State that, under Article 5 of the Torture Convention (1984), has jurisdiction to prosecute the alleged offender.[36] In this respect, it is worth noting that the ILC, relying on its own codifications and the jurisprudence of the European Court of Human Rights, observed that complying with the obligation to extradite cannot be substituted by informal forms of dispatching the suspect to another State.[37] Informal forms—such as deportation or rendition—fall short of important human rights safeguards, whereas the extradition legislation of most, if not all, States requires compliance with particular requirements, including double criminality, *ne bis in idem, nullem crimen sine lege*, speciality, and the non-extradition of the suspect to stand trial on the grounds of ethnic origin, religion, nationality or political views.[38]

The *Belgium v Senegal* judgment and the ICC's arrest warrants against former Sudanese President Al Bashir

A lot has been written on the ICC's arrest warrants against Al Bashir which accuse him of crimes against humanity, war crimes and genocide.[39] Much of the attention of commentators/academics[40] and domestic courts[41] had been focused on whether Al Bashir was entitled

[33] ibid 453, paras 83–84.

[34] ibid 455, 456, paras 90, 94.

[35] ibid 460, paras 114–15. See also Trent Buatte, 'The Time of Human Justice & the Time of Human Beings: *Belgium v. Senegal* & Temporal Restraints on the Duty to Prosecute' (2013) 45(2) George Washington International Law Review 349, 370.

[36] *Belgium v Senegal* (n 2) 461, para 120.

[37] *The Obligation to Extradite or Prosecute* (n 30) para 22, fn 474 (citing *Bozano v France*, App No 9990/82 (ECtHR, 18 December 1986) paras 52–60).

[38] *The Obligation to Extradite or Prosecute* (n 30) para 22, fn 474 (citing Article 12 (now Article 13) of the Draft Articles on the Expulsion of Aliens, in Yearbook of the ILC (2012) Vol II, Part 2 (A/CN.4/SER.A/2012/Add.1) 16, para 45.

[39] See *Prosecutor v Al Bashir*, ICC-02/05-01/09-1, Warrant of Arrest for Omar Hassan Ahmad Al Bashir (4 March 2009); *Prosecutor v Al Bashir*, ICC-02/05-01/09-3, Decision on Prosecution's Application for a Warrant of Arrest Against Omar Hassan Ahmad Al Bashir (4 March 2009); *Prosecutor v Al Bashir*, ICC-02/05-01/09-94, Second Decision on the Prosecution's Application for a Warrant of Arrest (12 July 2010); *Prosecutor v Al Bashir*, ICC-02/05-01/09-95, Second Warrant of Arrest for Omar Hassan Ahmad Al Bashir (12 July 2010).

[40] See Dapo Akande, 'The Legal Nature of Security Council Referrals to the ICC and its Impact on Al Bashir's Immunities' (2009) 7(2) Journal of International Criminal Justice 333; M J Ventura, 'Escape from Johannesburg? Sudanese President Al-Bashir Visits South Africa, and the Implicit Removal of Head of State Immunity by the UN Security Council in Light of *Al-Jedda*' (2015) 13(5) Journal of International Criminal Justice 995; Dire Tladi, 'The Duty on South Africa to Arrest and Surrender President Al-Bashir under South African and International Law: A Perspective from International Law' (2015) 13 Journal of International Criminal Justice 1027.

[41] See *Minister of Justice and Constitutional Development and others v Southern Africa Litigation Centre* (867/15) [2016] ZASCA 17 (15 March 2016) (Supreme Court of Appeal of South Africa); *Attorney General and Others*

to personal immunity *ratione personae*, a situation fuelled by the ICC's inconsistency in articulating why such immunity did not preclude his arrest and surrender to the ICC and a controversial ICC Appeals Chamber.[42] However, in April 2019, he was ousted in a coup and is thus now a *former* Head of State and, accordingly, is only entitled to functional immunity *ratione materiae*.

The fact that one of the underlying crimes alleged by the ICC is torture has also attracted less attention. Indeed, Pre-Trial Chamber I found 'reasonable grounds to believe that civilians belonging primarily to the Fur, Masalit and Zaghawa groups were subject to torture' by Sudanese forces in the Darfur region and issued its first arrest warrant for, *inter alia*, torture as a crime against humanity.[43] It would subsequently issue a second arrest warrant and find that there were 'reasonable grounds to believe that acts of […] torture […] were committed against members of the [Fur, Masalit and Zghawa] groups' and that this and other acts meant that 'the material element of the crime of genocide by causing serious bodily or mental harm […] [w]as fulfilled'.[44] This leads one to ask whether the principles espoused in the *Belgium v Senegal* judgment—particularly in regards to the obligation to extradite or prosecute—have any role to play vis-à-vis Al Bashir.

A customary obligation to prosecute or extradite?

On its face, there appears to be a direct impediment to the application of the ICJ's judgment: Sudan is not a State Party to the Torture Convention (1984).[45] Therefore, its provisions do not bind Sudan and, consequently, it can be argued that they are of no consequence. However, the mere fact that an obligation is found in a treaty does not mean that the obligation cannot have a separate—but parallel—customary basis.[46] Further, the ICJ has also stated that rules that were originally conventional in nature may convert into custom, and that in such cases 'the provision concerned should[] […] be of a fundamentally norm-creating character'.[47] Accordingly, the question of whether the obligation to extradite or prosecute under the Torture Convention (1984) is conventional *and* customary in nature, or only conventional, should be considered.

It is well beyond the scope of this chapter to comprehensively address the State practice and *opinio juris* necessary to identify a norm of customary international law. Nonetheless,

v Kenya Section of International Commission of Jurists, Civil Appeal No 105 of 2012 & Criminal Appeal No 274 of 2011 (16 February 2018) (Court of Appeal of Kenya).

[42] See *Prosecutor v Al Bashir*, ICC-02/05-01/09-397, Judgment in the Jordan Referral re Al-Bashir Appeal (6 May 2019); *Prosecutor v Al Bashir*, ICC-02/05-01/09-397-Anx1, Judgment in the Jordan Referral re Al-Bashir Appeal—Joint Concurring Opinion of Judges Eboe-Osuji, Morrison, Hofmański, and Bossa (6 May 2019); *Prosecutor v Al Bashir*, ICC-02/05-01/09-397-Anx2, Judgment in the Jordan Referral re Al-Bashir Appeal—Joint Dissenting Opinion of Judge Ibáñez Carranza and Bossa (6 May 2019).

[43] *Al Bashir*, Decision on Prosecution's Application for a Warrant of Arrest (n 39) 92, paras 104, 109. See also *Al Bashir*, Warrant of Arrest (n 39) 6, 8.

[44] *Al Bashir*, Second Decision on the Prosecution's Application (n 39) 28, paras 30–31. See also *Al Bashir*, Second Warrant of Arrest (n 39) 6–8.

[45] Sudan did, however, sign the 1984 Convention Against Torture.

[46] See *Military and Paramilitary Activities in and Against Nicaragua (Nicaragua v United States of America)*, Judgment, ICJ Rep 1984, 14, 424, para 73 (26 November).

[47] *North Sea Continental Shelf Cases (Germany/Denmark; Germany/The Netherlands)*, Judgment, ICJ Rep 1969, 3, 41–42, para 72.

the view that the requisite critical mass has already been reached with respect to torture is shared by numerous States,[48] academics[49] and has been expressed in judicial opinions.[50] Additionally, the Torture Convention (1984) has 166 States Parties—about 86% of UN Member States. Accordingly, in light of torture's *jus cogens* character,[51] its universal rejection and the norm-creating character of the Torture Convention (1984), it would not be unreasonable to assert that a customary obligation to extradite or prosecute exists as per the Torture Convention (1984).[52] Therefore, the *Belgium v Senegal* judgment could be applicable in cases of torture as defined in the Torture Convention (1984) if the obligation to extradite or prosecute under that treaty is part of custom. But Al Bashir is alleged to have committed torture as a crime against humanity and as genocide (ie causing serious bodily or mental harm), not under the Torture Convention (1984). This raises a question: is torture under the Torture Convention (1984) the same thing as torture as a crime against humanity and as genocide at the ICC?

Torture as a crime against humanity and as genocide at the ICC and under the Torture Convention (1984)

The definition of torture under the Torture Convention (1984)[53] is part of customary international law and its prohibition has attained peremptory (*jus cogens*) status.[54] Therefore, it makes no difference that Sudan is not a Party to the treaty in this respect. Yet, the elements of torture under the Torture Convention (1984) are different to torture when charged as an underlying international crime. Thus, the ICTY held that 'the public official requirement is not a requirement under customary international law in relation to the criminal responsibility of an individual for torture outside the framework of the Torture Convention.'[55] This is reflected in Article 7(2)(e) of the Rome Statute (1998), which defines torture as a crime against humanity as 'the intentional infliction of severe pain or suffering, whether physical or mental, upon a person in the custody or under the control of the accused; except that

[48] See *The Obligation to Extradite or Prosecute* (Aut Dedere aut Judicare), Third Report on the Obligation to Extradite or Prosecute (*Aut Dedere aut Judicare*) by Mr Zdzislaw Galicki, Special Rapporteur (A/CN.4/603) in Yearbook of the ILC (2008) Vol II, Part 1 (A/CN.4/SER.A/2008/Add.1) 128–29, para 98.

[49] See *The Obligation to Extradite or Prosecute* (Aut Dedere aut Judicare), Preliminary Report by Mr Zdzislaw Galicki, Special Rapporteur (A/CN.4/571) in Yearbook of the ILC (2006) Vol II, Part 1 (A/CN.4/SER.A/2006/Add.1) 266, para 40; M C Bassiouni, *International Extradition: United States Law and Practice* (6th edn, OUP 2014) 14, 21–22.

[50] See *Questions of Interpretation and Application of the 1971 Montreal Convention Arising from the Aerial Incident at Lockerbie (Libyan Arab Jamahiriya v United Kingdom)*, Provisional Measures, Order of 14 April 1992, ICJ Rep 1992, 3, Dissenting Opinion of Judge Weeramantry, 69 (14 April).

[51] See Thomas Weatherall, *Jus Cogens: International Law and Social Contract* (Cambridge University Press 2015) 347, 383.

[52] Belgium argued before the ICJ that, in addition to a treaty obligation to extradite or prosecute under the 1984 Convention Against Torture, a customary law obligation existed to extradite or prosecute persons accused of crimes against humanity, war crimes, and genocide, but did *not* claim a customary rule in regards to torture specifically. The ICJ dismissed this customary argument without addressing its merits (*Belgium v Senegal* (n 2) 444–45, paras 53–55). Notwithstanding, Judge Abrahams addressed the merits of Belgium's argument and held that an obligation *aut dedere aut judicare* had not acquired a customary basis (*Belgium v Senegal* (n 2) 476, 478–79, paras 21, 31–32). See also *Belgium v Senegal* (n 2) 610, 615, paras 18, 32.

[53] See 1984 Convention Against Torture Article 1.

[54] See *Prosecutor v Delalić and others*, Case No IT-96-21-T ICTY, Trial Judgment (16 November 1998) para 459; *Belgium v Senegal* (n 2) 457, para 99; *Prosecutor v Ntaganda*, ICC-01/04-02/06-1707, Second Decision on the Defence's Challenge to the Jurisdiction of the Court in respect of Counts 6 and 9 (4 January 2017) para 51.

[55] *Prosecutor v Kunarac and others*, IT-96-23 & IT-96-23/1-A ICTY, Appeal Judgment (12 June 2002) para 148.

torture shall not include pain or suffering arising only from, inherent in or incidental to, lawful sanctions'. Accordingly, torture as a crime against humanity at the ICC has no official capacity requirement.[56] Additionally, this torture definition—unlike under the Torture Convention (1984) or torture as a war crime at the ICC—does not require that the torture be committed for any specific purpose.[57]

Although the ICC has yet to precisely articulate the elements of torture as genocide (ie causing serious bodily or mental harm), Pre-Trial Chamber I has held that:

> [t]he underlying acts of genocide by inflicting bodily or mental harm[] [...] are identical to the underlying acts of the crimes against humanity included [...] as [...] torture [of] civilians [...]. [...] [I]n its determination of whether there are reasonable grounds to believe that the present underlying acts of genocide were committed, the Chamber may rely on its findings made with respect to the material elements of [...] torture [...] as long as there are reasonable grounds to believe that such acts were committed against members of the targeted group.[58]

Indeed, the same factual findings concerning torture as a crime against humanity were used to find reasonable grounds to believe that torture as genocide had been committed against the Fur, Masalit and Zaghawa groups.[59] Thus, the material elements of torture as a crime against humanity appear to be the same as torture as an act of genocide.

This reveals that in order to satisfy Article 1(1) of the Torture Convention (1984)—and thereby fall within the conduct to which a customary obligation to extradite or prosecute would apply—the allegations against Al Bashir must include two elements that were not required when the ICC's arrest warrants were issued: a public official requirement and a purpose requirement.[60] Concerning the former, as Al Bashir was an incumbent Head of State, this requirement is plainly satisfied. As for the latter, Article 1(1) of the Torture Convention (1984) lists purposes for which torture should be carried out: obtaining information/a confession, punishment, intimidation, coercion, or on discriminatory grounds. However, they are qualified with the words 'for such purposes as', which means that the list is not exhaustive and has led to the recognition of other purposes (eg humiliation and retaliation).[61]

To assess whether the prohibited purpose requirement is satisfied, we must ask *why* the alleged torture was committed. In this respect, Pre-Trial Chamber I is instructive:

[56] C K Hall and C Stahn, 'Article 7(1)(f)/Article 7(2)(e)—Torture as a Crime Against Humanity' in O Triffterer and K Ambos (eds), *The Rome Statute of the International Criminal Court: A Commentary* (3rd edn, Verlag C H Beck/Hart Publishing/Nomos 2016) 205, 273, margin nos 52, 135.

[57] *Prosecutor v Bemba*, ICC-01/05-01/08-424, Decision Pursuant to Article 61(7)(a) and (b) of the Rome Statute on the Charges of the Prosecutor Against Jean-Pierre Bemba Gombo (15 June 2009) para 195.

[58] *Al Bashir*, Second Decision on the Prosecution's Application (n 39); *Al Bashir*, Second Warrant of Arrest (n 39) paras 27–28.

[59] See *Al Bashir*, Second Decision on the Prosecution's Application (n 39) paras 29(ii), 30–31.

[60] It should be noted that torture as a crime against humanity at the ICC, as per Article 7(2)(e) of the Rome Statute (Rome Statute of the International Criminal Court, 17 July 1998, 2187 UNTS 3, (1998) 37 ILM 999, *entered into force* 1 July 2002), also requires the victim to be 'in the custody or under the control of the accused'. But since this is not required under Article 1(1) of the 1984 Convention Against Torture , it need not be considered further.

[61] See *Delalić* (n 54) para 470; *Furundžija* (n 15) para 162; *Prosecutor v Kvočka and others*, IT-98-30/1-T ICTY, Trial Judgement (2 November 2001) paras 141, 152, 157; UN Committee Against Torture, *VL v Switzerland* (Communication No 262/2005) UN Doc CAT/C/37/D/262/2005 (22 January 2007) para 8.10.

> there are reasonable grounds to believe that a core component of the GoS [Government of Sudan] counter-insurgency campaign ... was the unlawful attack on that part of the civilian population of Darfur—belonging largely to the Fur, Masalit and Zaghawa groups—perceived by the GoS as being close to the SLM/A [Sudan Liberation Movement/Army], the JEM [Justice and Equality Movement] and other armed groups opposing the GoS in the ongoing armed conflict in Darfur.[62]

The torture for which Al Bashir stands accused formed part of this attack that targeted the Fur, Masalit and Zaghawa groups.[63] Therefore, it appears that they were targeted because Sudan believed they were aligned with rebels that had taken up arms against it. While the ICC did not explicitly state that the torture was committed for any specific purpose, it is reasonable to conclude that it was a means to retaliate against, intimidate or punish the Fur, Masalit and Zaghawa groups for their perceived support of the rebels or on a discriminatory basis. This falls within the purpose requirement of the Torture Convention (1984).

The fact that Al Bashir is accused of torture pursuant to the provisions of the Rome Statute (1998) derives from the jurisdiction *ratione materiae* of the ICC. Nonetheless, it is submitted that, on its face, the ICC's torture allegations align with, or simultaneously satisfy, the definition of torture under the Torture Convention (1984). Consequently, Al Bashir's alleged criminal conduct would engage any emerging obligation to prosecute or extradite torturers under custom (or under the Torture Convention (1984) if Sudan were a State Party to that treaty).

Torture and Al Bashir's former Head of State immunity

Al Bashir, as the Head of State of Sudan, once enjoyed absolute (personal) immunity *ratione personae* before domestic courts under customary international law—even if accused of international crimes.[64] But since being deposed in a coup in April 2019, he is now a *former* Head of State that can only lay claim to functional immunity *ratione materiae*. His legal position is now similar to that of Habré—except that Chad waived any immunity to which Habré may have been entitled[65] and that Sudan, unlike Chad, is not a party to the Torture Convention (1984).

Here, the UK House of Lords' *Pinochet (No 3)* case is relevant. It held that Augusto Pinochet—the former Chilean Head of State—was not entitled to immunity *ratione materiae* on the basis of the Torture Convention (1984), and, in so doing, some judges also

[62] *Al Bashir*, Decision on Prosecution's Application for a Warrant of Arrest (n 39) paras 76, 83, 191 (see also para 215); *Al Bashir*, Second Decision on the Prosecution's Application (n 39) para 10. See also *Al Bashir*, Decision on Prosecution's Application for a Warrant of Arrest (n 39) Separate and Partially Dissenting Opinion of Judge Anita Ušacka, 105–06, para 22.

[63] See *Al Bashir*, Decision on Prosecution's Application for a Warrant of Arrest (n 39) paras 103–04, 109, 192, 215. See also *Al Bashir*, Warrant of Arrest (n 39) 6, 8; *Al Bashir*, Second Warrant of Arrest (n 39) 6–8; *Al Bashir*, Second Decision on the Prosecution's Application (n 39) paras 11, 29(ii), 30–31, 42(ii).

[64] See *Arrest Warrant of 11 April 2000 (Democratic Republic of the Congo v Belgium)*, Judgment, ICJ Rep 2002, 3, 20–22, paras 51, 53–55 (14 February).

[65] See *Belgium v Senegal* (n 2) 432, para 20. It was because of this waiver that the ICJ's judgment did not consider Habré's immunity.

relied on torture's international criminal and *jus cogens* status.[66] The underlying reasoning varied: that the commission of torture cannot be a State function to which immunity *ratione materiae* could apply; that customary international law rendered immunity *ratione materiae* inapplicable with respect to international crimes; and/or that the Torture Convention (1984) had itself removed any immunity for torture. Since then, the notion that immunity *ratione materiae* cannot be claimed in criminal cases for torture or other *jus cogens*/international criminal violations has been repeated by various courts, including the European Court of Human Rights[67] and the courts of Italy,[68] Switzerland,[69] Belgium,[70] Canada,[71] and The Netherlands.[72] ICJ judges have also recognized this trend.[73] These developments led the ILC's Special Rapporteur on the immunity of State officials from foreign criminal jurisdiction to state that '[t]he viewpoint whereby grave crimes under international law cannot be considered as acts performed in an official capacity, and immunity *ratione materiae* does not therefore protect from foreign criminal jurisdiction exercised in connection with such crimes, has become fairly widespread.'[74] One author has also posited that:

> according to the bulk of the case law [...] immunity *ratione materiae* is declined in cases when (former high-ranking) State officials face allegations of crimes pursuant to international law. Disapproval with this conclusion in domestic judgments is sparse. Accordingly, domestic case law contributes to customary international law to the effect that immunity *ratione materiae* from foreign criminal jurisdiction is denied in the context of crimes pursuant to international law. (Former high-ranking) State officials incur individual responsibility in criminal proceedings conducted in the courts of another State for crimes pursuant to international law.[75]

This is further reflected by the ILC's recent provisional adoption of Draft Article 7(1)(a)–(f) on the Immunity of State officials from foreign criminal jurisdiction which provides that '[i]mmunity *ratione materiae* from the exercise of foreign criminal jurisdiction shall not apply' with respect to genocide, crimes against humanity, war crimes, apartheid, torture, and enforced disappearances.[76]

[66] See *Regina v Bow Street Metropolitan Stipendiary Magistrate and Others ex parte Pinochet Ugarte* [1999] UKHL 3, [2000] 1 AC 147, 203–205 (per Lord Browne-Wilkinson), 246–48 (per Lord Hope), 261–63 (per Lord Hutton), 266–67 (per Lord Saville), 277–78 (per Lord Millett), 289–90 (per Lord Philips).

[67] See *Ould Dah v France*, App No 13113/03 (ECtHR, 17 March 2009) 463.

[68] See *Lozano (Mario Luiz) v Italy*, Case No 31171/2008 (24 July 2008) (Italy, Supreme Court of Cassation). See Antonio Cassese, 'The Italian Court of Cassation Misapprehends the Notion of War Crimes: The *Lozano* Case' (2008) 6(5) Journal of International Criminal Justice 1077.

[69] See *A (Nezzar) v Office of the Attorney General of Switzerland*, Case No BB.2011.140 (25 July 2012) para 5.3.5 (Switzerland, Federal Criminal Court).

[70] *Re Pinochet* (1998) 119 ILR 345 at 349 (Belgium, Court of First Instance, Brussels).

[71] See *Bouzari v Islamic Republic of Iran* (2004) 71 OR (3d) 675, para 91 (Canada, Court of Appeal for Ontario).

[72] See *Bouterse*, LJN: AA8395, R 97/163/12 Sv & R 97/176/12 Sv (20 November 2000) para 4.2 (The Netherlands, Amsterdam Court of Appeal) (overturned on other grounds: *Bouterse*, LJN: AB1471, 00749/01 CW 2323 (18 September 2001) (The Netherlands, Supreme Court).

[73] See *Democratic Republic of the Congo v Belgium* (n 64) Separate Opinion of Judges Higgins, Kooijmans, and Buergenthal, 88, para 85.

[74] *Immunity of State Officials from Foreign Criminal Jurisdiction*, Second Report on Immunity of State Officials from Foreign Criminal Jurisdiction by Mr Roman Anatolevich Kolodkin, Special Rapporteur (A/CN.4/631) in Yearbook of the ILC (2010) Vol II, Part 1 (A/CN.4/SER.A/2010/Add.1) 413.

[75] Ramona Pedretti, *Immunity of Heads of State and State Officials for International Crimes* (Brill Nijhoff 2015) 192. See also Weatherall (n 51) 317.

[76] Report of the International Law Commission, Sixty-ninth Session (A/72/10) 164, 171–73, 177–91, paras 74, 116–29, 141, in Yearbook of the ILC (2017) Vol II, Part 2 (forthcoming).

Because Al Bashir is only entitled to immunity *ratione materiae*, the fact that he has been accused of torture alone—not to mention crimes against humanity, war crimes, and genocide—appears to precludes his ability to claim immunity in any criminal-related proceedings, particularly in States other than Sudan. The fact that Sudan is not a party to the Torture Convention (1984) would not, on its face, be an impediment.

The obligation to prosecute or extradite and the 'third alternative'

A customary obligation to prosecute or extradite alleged torturers, when considered alongside the reality that Al Bashir only enjoys (functional) immunity *ratione materiae* and that the facts alleged by the ICC meet the definition of torture under the Torture Convention (1984), has consequences. For Sudan, it means that it is obliged to prosecute or extradite Al Bashir for torture. The same goes for States other than Sudan, should he be present on their territory.[77] But the *Belgium v Senegal* judgment made clear that the obligation to prosecute—at least under Article 7(1) of the Torture Convention (1984)—only entails '[t]he obligation to submit the case to the competent [State] authorities for the purpose of prosecution' and 'was formulated in such a way as to leave it to those [State] authorities to decide whether or not to initiate proceedings'.[78] However, before any prosecution commences, an investigation must first take place to determine if a case evens merits being submitted for prosecution at all.[79]

In the case of Al Bashir, the ICC's torture allegations—on facts that satisfy the (customary) definition of torture under the Torture Convention (1984)—should be taken into account. After all, if he is already being sought for torture beyond Sudan's borders, then this ought to be considered in deciding whether to prosecute. In this respect, the ICJ has explained that 'if the State in whose territory the suspect is present has received a request for extradition in any of the cases envisaged in the provisions of the Convention, it can relieve itself of its obligation to prosecute by acceding to that request', and clarified that this could occur 'on the condition that it is to a State which has jurisdiction in some capacity [. . .] to prosecute and try him.'[80] Here, such a request would not come from a State, but would come from an international court, namely, the ICC. Thus, Sudan—or any other State on which Al Bashir is present—faces a question: if it does not prosecute, would it fulfil an *aut dedere aut judicare* obligation by surrendering him to the ICC?

The ILC has considered the relationship between the obligation to prosecute or extradite and what has been described as the 'third alternative':

> [w]ith the establishment of the International Criminal Court and various *ad hoc* international criminal tribunals, there is now the possibility that a State faced with an obligation to extradite or prosecute an accused person might have recourse to a third alternative—that of surrendering the suspect to a competent international criminal tribunal.[81]

[77] If the relevant State is State Party to the 1984 Convention Against Torture, then their obligation arises from that treaty or, alternatively, if they are not, then the obligation would be based on custom.

[78] *Belgium v Senegal* (n 2) 455, paras 90–91.

[79] See Article 6(2) of the 1984 Convention Against Torture (n 3) which provides that a preliminary inquiry must be initiated as soon as the alleged torturer is present on the territory of the relevant State.

[80] *Belgium v Senegal* (n 2) 456, 461, paras 95, 120.

[81] See *The Obligation to Extradite or Prosecute* (n 30) para 65(27).

This was endorsed by Judge Xue in her dissenting opinion to the *Belgium v Senegal* judgment. She found that had Senegal surrendered Habré to what eventually became the Extraordinary African Chambers—which convicted Habré in May 2016[82]—such action could not be regarded as a breach of Senegal's obligations under the Torture Convention (1984), since 'such a tribunal [wa]s created precisely to fulfil the object and purpose of the Convention; neither the terms of the Convention nor the State practice in this regard prohibit such an option'.[83] The ILC also affirmed this approach, opining that 'the obligation to extradite or prosecute may be satisfied by surrendering the alleged offender to a competent international criminal tribunal'.[84] It suffices to say that surrendering Al Bashir to the ICC, if a State chooses not to prosecute, would be far from violating a customary obligation to prosecute or extradite torturers.

Conclusion

This chapter has endeavoured to show that the *Belgium v Senegal* judgment has the potential to be influential beyond its facts. This has been demonstrated in one particular instance: the ICC's arrest warrants against former Sudanese President Al Bashir. Based on torture's *jus cogens* character and the obligation to extradite or prosecute alleged torturers under the Torture Convention (1984), as well as the high number of States Parties to the Convention and the prevailing tide of legal opinion, it is warranted to assert that the obligation to prosecute or extradite alleged torturers is, or is becoming, part of customary international law. Moreover, the definition under the Torture Convention (1984) matches the torture alleged by the ICC. In these circumstances—all other things being equal—an ICC State Party has potentially a two-fold obligation if Al Bashir is present on its territory: arrest and surrender Al Bashir to the ICC pursuant to its obligations under the Rome Statute (1998) and a separate, but parallel, obligation to surrender/extradite him to the ICC as an alleged torturer (if the relevant State chooses not to prosecute) pursuant to either customary international law or under the Torture Convention (1984) (if the relevant State is a Party to this treaty). Those States that *are not* an ICC State Party—including Sudan—also have an obligation to surrender/extradite Al Bashir to the ICC if he is on their territory (in the event they do not prosecute), on the basis of a customary *aut dedere aut judicare* obligation with respect to torture.

Al Bashir's ultimate fate in Sudan is, at this time, unknown. Although it appears that Al Bashir will undergo some sort of domestic criminal process, it is not clear whether it will address Darfur crimes as alleged by the ICC. If it does not, this chapter suggests that Sudan may have an obligation to surrender him to the ICC for torture, despite the fact that Sudan is not an ICC State Party. Further, Al Bashir may not be able to escape this result by simply moving to a friendly State. The call of justice will haunt Al Bashir for the rest of his days.

[82] *Ministère Public c Habré*, Trial Judgment EAC (30 May 2016). *Procureur Général c Habré*, Appeal Judgment EAC (27 April 2017).

[83] *Belgium v Senegal* (n 2), Dissenting Opinion of Judge Xue, 583, para 42.

[84] See *The Obligation to Extradite or Prosecute* (n 30) para 65(34).

34

Victims as a Third Party

Empowerment of Victims?

Liesbeth Zegveld[1]

On the eve of the trial against the former president of Ivory Coast, Gbagbo, at the International Criminal Court (ICC) in January 2016, the ICC Prosecutor Fatou Bensouda told journalists 'that the purpose of the trial [...] is to uncover the truth through purely a legal process [...], for the sake of doing justice for the victims'.[2]

Victims are a key reason for international criminal trials. Trials are said to be held because of the great numbers of victims that the crimes have created. Perpetrators are prosecuted so victims can see justice being done.[3]

Yet when it comes to victims who want to claim their own rights before international criminal courts, the picture is less clear. These courts have struggled with how to deal with victims. Response to victims' participation in criminal trials has ranged from outright opposition, to reluctant acceptance, to apparent embrace. Even when there seems to be embrace, though, under the surface victims struggle to have their suffering and damage recognized. Victims are merely third-parties in the criminal trial. The charges are not their charges; they may not fit their damage. What is more, courts deal with victims collectively, denying them the individual attention their claims may demand. To make things worse, rather than applying the legal principle of accountability to victims' claims for damage, courts have a tendency to address victims' damage as a humanitarian problem that can be solved through humanitarian assistance.

Of course, prosecution of perpetrators is in and of itself valuable to victims. Victims generally wish criminals to be tried and punished. But victims also have different interests, interests of their own. For one thing: they have suffered damage. Are international criminal courts the right place of action to make them whole? Certainly, some international criminal courts have tried to accommodate the needs of victims. We are, however, a long way from full recognition of victims in these trials.

[1] This chapter is an adapted version of an article by the author that was previously published in the *International Criminal Law Review*, see: L Zegveld, 'Victims as a Third Party: Empowerment of Victims?' (2018) 19(2) International Criminal Law Review 321.

[2] International Criminal Court, Office of the Prosecutor, 'ICC Prosecutor's statement at press conference, ahead of the trial-start of the Prosecution's case against Messrs. Laurent Gbagbo and Charles Blé Goudé' (*Press Release*, 27 January 2016) <https://www.icc-cpi.int/Pages/item.aspx?name=otp-stat-27-01-2016> accessed 29 June 2019.

[3] See also, eg, the Preamble of the Rome statute: 'Mindful that during this century millions of children, women and men have been victims of unimaginable atrocities that deeply shock the conscience of humanity' (Rome Statute of the International Criminal Court, 17 July 1998, 2187 UNTS 3, 37 ILM 999 (1998), *entered into force* 1 July 2002).

Liesbeth Zegveld, *Victims as a Third Party* In: *The President on Trial*. First edition. Edited by: Sharon Weill, Kim Thuy Seelinger, and Kerstin Bree Carlson, Oxford University Press (2020). © Liesbeth Zegveld. DOI: 10.1093/oso/9780198858621.003.0035

International criminal tribunals accommodating victims

For a long time, victims did not play any role in international criminal tribunals. Victims were virtually absent at the Nuremberg International Military Tribunal (IMT). Hardly any victims were called to testify, let alone join as civil parties to receive reparation. Various reasons have been given for this exclusion. One is that the Nuremberg trials were dominated by American prosecutors, acting in the Anglo-American common law tradition.[4] Common law countries generally do not provide for victim participation and compensation in connection with criminal cases; in the common law system, any claims for compensation must be pursued via a civil lawsuit.

Reparation for victims of genocide was included in a draft of the Genocide Convention.[5] Ultimately, however, the proposed article was left out.[6] Drafters decided that redress and compensation should be part of the jurisdiction of an eventual genocide court.[7] It was agreed that such a court 'shall also be authorized to assess damages on behalf of persons found to have sustained losses or injuries as a result of the violation of this Convention by any High Contracting Party'.[8] However, as we know, a genocide court never saw the light of day.

The establishment of a permanent criminal tribunal then became a project of the International Law Commission (ILC).[9] Yet, when developing its draft statute in 1994, the Commission decided to delete an article on reparations, finding that a criminal court was not an appropriate forum for ordering reparations.[10]

In line with the ILC's view, the International Criminal Tribunal for the Former Yugoslavia (ICTY)[11] and the International Criminal Tribunal for Rwanda (ICTR),[12] the first international criminal tribunals after 1948, also lack jurisdiction to deal with compensation for victims. The victims of the crimes tried by these tribunals have no role in their own right

[4] Another reason is that at the time of the IMT 'there was a general lack of awareness/or disbelief of the full extent of the Nazi crimes, including the holocaust'. See SB Garkawe, 'The Role and Rights of Victims at the Nuremberg International Military Tribunal' in HR Reginbogen, CJM Safferling, and WR Hippel (eds), *Die Nürnberg Prozesse: Völkerstrafrecht seit 1945: Internationale Konferenz zum 60 Jahrestag* (KG Saur 2006) 86–93.

[5] Convention on the Prevention and Punishment of the Crime of Genocide, 9 December 1948, 78 UNTS 277, *entered into force* 12 January 1951; William A Schabas, *Genocide in International Law: The Crime of Crimes* (1st edn, Cambridge University Press 2000) 400; UN Economic and Social Council (ECOSOC), 'Draft Convention on the Crime of Genocide' (26 June 1947) UN Doc E/447, 5–13, Art XIII; the Netherlands agreed: 'The principle of awarding an indemnity in cases where this can be done, seems reasonable'. See ECOSOC, 'Prevention and Punishment of Genocide: Comments of Governments on the Draft Convention Prepared by the Secretariat' (22 April 1948) UN Doc E/623/Add.3.

[6] Schabas (n 5) 400.

[7] ibid; Article 6 of the Convention on the Prevention and Punishment of the Crime of Genocide calls for criminals to be tried 'by such international penal tribunals as may have jurisdiction'.

[8] ECOSOC, 'Draft Convention, Communications Received by the Secretary-General' (27 September 1947), UN Doc A/401, Art VII (as cited in H Abtahi and P Webb, *The Genocide Convention: The Travaux Préparatoires* (Brill 2009) 380).

[9] In 1948, the United Nations General Assembly (UNGA) invited the International Law Commission (ILC) 'to study the desirability and possibility of establishing an international judicial organ for the trials of persons charged with genocide'. See UNGA, Res 260, GOAR UN Doc A/RES/3/260 (9 December 1948).

[10] Draft Statute for an International Criminal Court with commentaries, 1994, in Yearbook of the ILC (1994) Vol II, Part 2 (A/CN.4/SER.A/1994/Add.l) 60, Art 47, paras 3–4. For the 1993 draft, see Annex: Report of the Working Group on a Draft Statute for an International Criminal Court, in Yearbook of the ILC (1993) Vol II, Part 2 (A/CN.4/SER.A/1993/Add.l) 125, Art 53(4).

[11] UN Security Council (UNSC) Res 808, UN SCOR, UN Doc S/RES/808 (22 February 1993) para 1.

[12] UNSC Res 955, UN SCOR, UN Doc S/RES/955 (8 November 1994) para 1.

before these tribunals. They only serve as witnesses and cannot claim compensation from those convicted of genocide.[13]

The fact that victims have rights was recognized, though. In its Resolution 827 (1993) of 25 May 1993 adopting the Statute of the International Criminal Tribunal for the former Yugoslavia, the Security Council decided that 'the work of the International Tribunal shall be carried out without prejudice to the right of victims to seek, through appropriate means, compensation for damages incurred as a result of violations of international humanitarian law'.[14] The idea was that they turn to domestic courts. Rule 106 of the Rules of both Tribunals stipulates that victims seeking compensation must apply to a national court or other competent body. In these domestic proceedings, the victims may avail themselves of judgments of the ICTY or ICTR.[15]

The Presidents (and judges) of the ICTY and ICTR thus recognized victims' general right to compensation. In fact, they at some point considered revisions of their Statutes to incorporate compensation for victims.[16] However, they ultimately rejected these amendments. Reportedly, they feared the additional workload and the significant impact such a possibility would have on the conduct of proceedings and the length of trial. The judges argued that the Tribunals' aim had consistently been to shorten trials and minimize the length of pre-trial detention, which is a fundamental right of the accused. Expanding the ICTR's mandate with compensation claims would in the ICTR's view 'not be efficacious, would severely hamper the everyday work of the Tribunal and would be highly destructive to the principal mandate of the Tribunal'.[17]

It was for this reason that the ICTY proposed that a mechanism, modelled on that of an international mass claim procedure, should be created. This was seen to be a much faster way to ensure that the rights of the victims were satisfied. It would also be fairer as it would, theoretically, cover all victims.[18]

Remarkably, while deciding that victims' compensation claims would not be dealt with by the ICTR and ICTY, the Gender Adviser of the ICTR advocated for a victims' compensation scheme to be adopted by the International Criminal Court.[19] And she did so successfully: in

[13] UNSC Res 827, UN SCOR, UN Doc S/RES/827 (25 May 1993). Rule 106 of the Rules of both Tribunals stipulates that victims seeking compensation must apply to a national court or other competent body. In these domestic proceedings, the victims may avail themselves of judgments of the ICTY or ICTR. See L Zegveld, 'Remedies for victims of violations of international humanitarian law' (2003) 85/851 International Review of the Red Cross 497, 523.

[14] UNSC Res 827, UN Doc S/RES/827 (25 May 1993) para 7.

[15] Zegveld (n 13) 523.

[16] UNSC, 'Letter dated 2 November 2000 from the Secretary-General addressed to the President of the Security Council' (3 November 2000) UN Doc S/2000/1063, Annex 'Letter dated 12 October 2000 from the President of the International Tribunal for the Former Yugoslavia addressed to the Secretary-General,' Appendix 'Victims' compensation and participation'; UNSC, 'Letter dated 14 December 2000 from the Secretary-General addressed to the President of the Security Council' (15 December 2000) UN Doc S/2000/1198, Annex 'Letter dated 9 November 2000 from the President of the International Criminal Tribunal for Rwanda addressed to the Secretary-General.' UNSC, Appendix 'Victims' compensation and participation' in UNSC, 'Letter dated 2 November 2000 from the Secretary-General addressed to the President of the Security Council' (3 November 2000) UN Doc S/2000/1063, para 46.

[17] UNSC, Annex 'Letter dated 9 November 2000 from the President of the International Criminal Tribunal for Rwanda addressed to the Secretary-General' in UNSC, 'Letter dated 14 December 2000 from the Secretary-General addressed to the President of the Security Council' (15 December 2000) UN Doc S/2000/1198, para 4.

[18] UNSC, Appendix 'Victims' compensation and participation' (n 16) para 48; UNSC, Annex 'Letter dated 9 November 2000 from the President of the International Criminal Tribunal for Rwanda addressed to the Secretary-General' in UNSC 'Letter dated 14 December 2000 from the Secretary-General addressed to the President of the Security Council' (15 December 2000) UN Doc S/2000/1198, para 15.

[19] ICTR, 'Paper by Elsie Effange-Mbella (Gender Adviser, Office of the Registrar, ICTR) on Support Measures to Victims and Witnesses Summoned to Appear Before the Tribunal' (ICTR Conference on Challenging Impunity,

contrast to the ICTY and ICTR, the ICC may award reparations to the benefit of individual victims.[20] It may do so directly against a convicted person.[21]

The Statute of the ICC is the first embodiment of the right of victims to reparations. This right covers harm caused by the commission of crimes falling under the ICC jurisdiction.[22] Apparently, the concerns expressed by the ICTY and ICTR, for example fears of serious trial delay, were not considered prohibitive by the drafters of the ICC Statute.

As for other international criminal courts currently operative, the picture is mixed. Victims can take part in the criminal proceedings before the Extraordinary Chambers in the Courts of Cambodia (ECCC) and claim reparation provided they are a victim of a crime within the jurisdiction of the Court.[23]

Similarly, victims were able to claim reparations before the Extraordinary African Chambers (EAC), which was established under an agreement between the African Union and Senegal to try international crimes committed under the regime of former Chadian President Habré. Articles 27 and 28 of the Statute provided the Chambers with the possibility to award collective and individual reparations to victims, either directly or through the Victims' Trust Fund. In addition, the Statute of the Special Tribunal for Lebanon stipulates that '[t]he Special Tribunal may identify victims who have suffered harm as a result of the commission of crimes by an accused convicted by the Tribunal'.[24] Subsequently, when the Tribunal has found the accused guilty, a victim may bring an action in a Lebanese or other national court or other competent body to obtain compensation, based on the Tribunal judgment, which shall be final and binding as to the criminal responsibility of the convicted person.[25]

Other international or internationalized courts are silent on the question of victims' reparations or they rely on domestic courts, noting national courts in their statutes as the fora where victims can present their claims after successful convictions by international courts.[26]

7-9 November 2006) para 27, available at <http://ictr-archive09.library.cornell.edu/ENGLISH/challenging_impunity/support_measures.pdf> accessed 21 December 2017.

20 Rome Statute (n 3) Art 75(1); See on reparation claims before the ICC, JB Jeangène Vilmer, *Réparer L'irréparable: Les Réparations aux victimes devant la Cour Pénale Internationale* (Press Universitaires de France, 2009).

21 Rome Statute (n 3) Art 75(2). Reparation may take the form of restitution, compensation, and rehabilitation (Rome Statute (n 3) Art 75(1); Rules of Procedure and Evidence, Official Records of the Assembly of States Parties to the Rome Statute of the International Criminal Court, First session, New York, 3–10 September 2002 (ICC-ASP/1/3 and Corr.1), Part II.A, r 95(1) (hereinafter ICC RPE)); UNSC, Appendix, UN Doc S/2000/1063 (n 16) paras 16-17; D Donat-Cattin, 'Reparations to victims' in O Triffterer and K Ambos (eds), *Commentary on the Rome Statute of the International Criminal Court: Observers' Note, Article by Article* (1st edn, Hart Publishing 1999) 967.

22 It should be noted that Art 75(6) of the Rome Statute (n 3) provides that its provisions on victims' reparations shall not 'be interpreted as prejudicing the rights of victims under national or international law'. Thus, their claims can be pursued in national and other fora.

23 The Extraordinary Chambers are regular Cambodian courts with international features, in particular in terms of the composition and applicable law. The ECCC's Statute and Rules of Procedure combine domestic and international law.

24 Attachment 'Statute of the Special Tribunal for Lebanon', UNSC Res 1757, UN SCOR, UN Doc S/RES/1757 (30 May 2007) (hereinafter STL Statute). See also chapters XXX

25 STL Statute (n 24) Art 17 provides that victims may present their views and concerns under certain conditions.

26 For example, The Special Court for Sierra Leone referred to domestic courts as instances where victims can submit reparations claims based on successful prosecutions. The successor of the ICTY and ICTR, UNMICT, follows its predecessors. See UN Mechanism for International Tribunals (MICT), Rules of Procedure and Evidence (8 June 2012) UN Doc MICT/1/Rev.2, as amended 26 September 2016, r 130. The War Crimes Chamber of

So, the overall picture presented is not one of sheer conviction and belief in victims' empowerment within international criminal courts. Some international criminal fora recognize victims' rights and sometimes also offer private causes of action to individual victims. However, these courts are still few in number. Many international criminal courts still deny access to victims or (partly) refer them to domestic courts.

Third party role

A first problem is victims' role as a third-party. Victims are external to the criminal procedure. They are extraneous. They cannot initiate a procedure nor can they terminate it. They do not determine the charges. This also means that they can never in a true sense assert their harms. The charges are not their charges, they may not entirely fit their damage. They are the prosecutor's charges, often burdened by many political choices. In the Lubanga case, for example, civilians targeted by Lubanga's troops could not officially be recognized as victims because the warlord was only convicted of enlisting and using child soldiers.[27]

Victims can only participate in the criminal trial to the extent they are allowed to by the Court. Whether the Court will allow them depends on whether victims succeed in convincing the Court that their interests are at stake and that they are linked to the legal issue or evidence at hand.[28] The Court must reach a separate decision on this question before it allows them to participate.[29] Victims' personal interests are not limited to issues of reparation,[30] but neither is it sufficient to have a general interest in the outcome of the case. Victims have been allowed to participate during the confirmation hearing of the charges. The court considered in this regard that the central interest of victims—namely their right to the truth[31] and justice, seeing the perpetrators being prosecuted and if convicted given an appropriate punishment—is closely connected to the issue of guilt or innocence.[32] But, the bottom line is that when and how the victims can present their views and concerns depends on the discretionary powers of the relevant chamber.

the Court of Bosnia and Herzegovina has also refrained from ordering compensations, despite its Criminal Procedure Code that allows for such orders in Art 198(2). See B Ivanišević, *The War Crimes Chamber in Bosnia and Herzegovina: From Hybrid to Domestic Court* (International Center for Transitional Justice 2008) 20–21.

27 *Prosecutor v Lubanga*, ICC-01/04-01/06-3129, Judgment on the appeals against the 'Decision establishing the principles and procedures to be applied to reparations' of 7 August 2012 (3 March 2015) para 186.

28 Rome Statute (n 3), Art 68(3).

29 ICC RPE (n 21) r 89(1) mentions opening and closing statements.

30 *Prosecutor v Lubanga*, ICC-01/04-01/06-1119, Decision on Victims' Participation (21 January 2008) para 98.

31 *Prosecutor v Katanga and Chui*, ICC-01/04-01/07-474, Decision on the Set of Procedural Rights Attached to Procedural Status of Victim at the Pre-Trial Stage of the Case (15 May 2008) para 32.

32 *Katanga and Chui* (n 31) para 42; Trial Chamber I in the Lubanga case also granted the victims whose personal interests were affected with various participatory rights, namely the right to consult the record of proceedings (*Lubanga*, Victims' Participation (n 30) paras 105–06), to question witnesses (ibid 108; ICC RPE (n 21) r 91(3)), to tender and examine evidence (*Lubanga*, Victims' Participation (n 30) para 108), to challenge the admissibility or relevance of evidence (ibid 108–09), and if appropriate granted the right to initiate procedures stating that it could include filing applications and requests when the personal interests of the victims were affected in accordance with Article 68(3) (ibid 118).

It is significant in this regard that the Statute speaks of 'interests' instead of rights. The use of the word rights is reserved for the rights of the accused.[33] Victims cannot invoke any rights under the Statute as they do not have any.[34]

If their interests are indeed at stake, it is for the Court to determine *at which stage* they may present their views and concerns. Victims are not allowed to intervene throughout the proceedings.[35] Article 68 ICC Statute stipulates that the intervention of victims must be conducted in a way 'which is not prejudicial to or inconsistent with the rights of the accused and a fair and impartial trial'. Whether the Court will allow victims to participate will therefore depend on the case at hand and its developments in court. If the criminal trial takes more time than anticipated, the time left for victims will be cut. Similarly, if there is a large number of victims, their time to present their views and concerns will also be reduced. Rule 86(b)(iv) STL RPE, stipulates that in deciding whether victims may participate, the pre-trial judge may consider 'whether the proposed participation would cause unnecessary delay and inefficiency in the proceedings'.

While views and concerns may be allowed throughout the criminal proceedings, victims' reparations claims are dealt with after the criminal proceedings. While one would assume that at this stage there is no risk of interference with the criminal trial, victims' participation in this stage is still limited. Article 75(3) of the ICC Statute provides that '[b]efore making an [reparation] order under this article, the Court may invite and shall take account of representations from or on behalf of the convicted person, victims, other interested persons or interested States.' Apparently, the Court can make an order for reparation without hearing the views of those who have suffered the damage. If the victims or their representatives do not present their views on reparation themselves, the Court can invite them to do so, but does not have to. This is even more remarkable if we realise that the Court may make a reparation order at its own motion, which means that the victims have no active role at all. They are mere objects of the proceedings rather than the subjects.

Also striking is the order of representations mentioned in article 75 paragraph 3: 'the convicted person, victims, other interested persons or interested States'. Strangely, victims are mentioned here after the convicted person. As it is their reparation claim one would expect them to be the first to be invited by the Court to present their claim.

In sum, the role of victims as mere third parties in the proceedings at the ICC, has severe implications on their participation in the trial. They have no rights, only interests. Whether and, if so, how, they are allowed to pursue those interests is fully in the hands of the Court.[36]

[33] Eg, Rome Statute (n 3) Art 64(2); Rome Statute (n 3) Art 75 (6) recognises that victims have rights but not in relation to the court proceedings: 'Nothing in this article shall be interpreted as prejudicing the rights of victims under national or international law.'

[34] The only provision referring to 'rights of victims' is ICC RPE (n 21), r 97(3).

[35] ICC RPE (n 21) r 89(1).

[36] Contrary to the case with victims before the ICC, victims' participation before the EAC was not limited by personal interests being affected. The victims before the EAC organized themselves as civil parties and as such they were fully recognized and enjoyed similar procedural rights as the defence. The victims before the EAC were not subjected to the discretionary powers of the Chamber, unlike the victims before the ICC. As a result, they knew what to expect before they organized themselves as civil parties.

Collective approach to victims

In addition to being mere third parties in the criminal proceedings, victims are dealt with collectively. They are represented collectively before the ICC and this Court may also award collective reparations. The argument underlying this approach is that it has to handle a large number of victims.[37] This would leave no other option than to throw victims' claims into one pile, in an effort to speed up the 'justice' process.

It is certainly true that victims reaching out to international criminal courts are often numerous. These courts try the most serious crimes, which are likely to have created a great many victims and thereby overwhelm the court. Financing these cases is difficult. They may also consume much of the court's time. Still, collective representation allows for the appointment of one legal team to represent large groups of victims, whereas individual representation would put large groups of lawyers in the courtroom.

But it must also be noted that international criminal courts have an explicit objective of reaching as many victims as possible. There is a wish to do justice to all victims, also those victims not before them.[38] During the reparations proceedings in the ICC's *Katanga* case, the trial chamber allowed additional victims who had not yet come forward to apply for reparations.[39]

While the ICC thus has an explicit aim to include as many victims as possible, the same is not true with regard to the accused. When dealing with genocide there are a great number of perpetrators. Here the Court has, however, taken measures to limit the number of perpetrators it can potentially try. It aims to only prosecute and try 'the most serious crimes'.[40] We know that international criminal courts are not capable of dealing with large numbers of accused. It is left to domestic criminal courts to try the remainder of the culprits. But why then try to include as many victims as possible, with no threshold regarding the damage or injuries that they have suffered?

The sheer number of victims leave no choice but to adopt a collective approach towards victims during trial.[41] Courts want to provide victims with a cheap, quick and relatively simple procedure for getting compensation for their losses. Collectivity goes much faster and does not result in too much additional workload or a significant impact on the conduct of the proceedings and the length of the trials. In the *Lubanga* case, the Appeals Chamber found that the Trial Chamber did not err in deciding to award reparations only on a collective basis, and not on an individual basis, and highlighted that the number of victims is

[37] Principles 8 and 13 of the Van Boven/Bassiouni Principles (Basic Principles and Guidelines on the Right to a Remedy and Reparation for Victims of Gross Violations of International Human Rights Law and Serious Violations of International Humanitarian Law, GA Res 60/147, GAOR, UN Doc A/RES/60/147 (16 December 2005)) indicate a comprehensive approach towards mass victimization, as it includes both individual and collective victims. Another mechanism is collective representation. Thus, if the ICC judges fear large numbers of victims invading the Court, they may interpret the articles in a way so as to narrow down the participation of the victims.

[38] The ICTY and ICTR did not want to deal with victims as they would never be able to over all of them (UNSC, Appendix, UN Doc S/2000/1063 (n 16) para 27).

[39] *Prosecutor v Katanga*, ICC-01/04-01/07-3546-tENG, Decision on the 'Demande de clarification concernant la mise en œuvre de la Règle 94 du Règlement de procédure et de preuve' and future stages of the proceedings (8 May 2015) para 19.

[40] Rome Statute (n 3) Art 1; See also Rome Statute (n 3) Art 5, 'The jurisdiction of the Court shall be limited to the most serious crimes of concern to the international community as a whole.'

[41] See also M Henzelin, V Heiskanen, and G Mettraux, 'Reparations to Victims Before the International Criminal Court: Lessons from International Mass Claims Processes' (2006) 17/3-4 Criminal Law Forum 317.

an important factor in determining that reparations on a collective basis are more appropriate. The Chamber said that there is no internationally recognized human right to the consideration of individual applications for reparations.[42]

It is a sure thing that dealing with many victims in lawsuits is expensive and time-consuming. Lawsuits can also be frustrating and even humiliating for the victims.[43] Nevertheless, the decision of the judges in the *Lubanga* case that reparations would only be collective brought disappointment on part of the victims. An accused has a face. A victim rarely has a face, be it even through their representative. He or she is usually referred to as a number.

Another consequence of this collective treatment is that the specific characteristics of individual victims' claims are lost. These claims do not receive court attention individually. In the *Lubanga* case, the Appeals Chamber observed: 'When only collective reparations are awarded . . . a Trial Chamber is not required to rule on the merits of the individual requests for reparations.'[44]

Another aspect of the collective approach to victims is their representation, which is also handled collectively. Once victims have been granted the right to participate, victims have the possibility to present their views with or without counsel. Article 68(3) ICC Statute does not require victims to have a legal representative. However, according the Rules of Procedure and Evidence, victims who have a legal representative will have more opportunities to participate during proceedings, pursuant to rule 91,[45] than victims who choose not be represented. In accordance with rule 89(1), victims may, in both instances, make opening and closing statements if the Chamber finds it appropriate.[46]

Rule 90 ICC Rules of Procedure and Evidence provides that 'a victim shall be free to choose a legal representative'. This freedom is however an empty shell. 'Where there are a number of victims the Chamber may, for the purposes of ensuring the effectiveness of the proceedings, request the victims or particular groups of victims, if necessary with the assistance of the Registry, to choose a common legal representative or representatives.'[47] This provision has led to the practice that the Registry has appointed a collective representative for large groups of victims.

Generally, victims bring their own legal representatives when they apply for participation. However, when the Court has appointed a collective legal representative, the individual legal counsel of victims will be excused.[48]

The Court has repeatedly stated that the right to choose legal counsel is not an absolute right and that it is subjected to paragraph 2 and 3 of rule 90 of the Rules of Procedure and

[42] *Lubanga*, Appeals Judgment on Reparations principles (n 27) para 155. See also *Prosecutor v Al Mahdi*, ICC-01/12-01/15-236, Reparations Order (17 August 2017) paras 141-142.

[43] D Luban, 'Settlements and the Erosion of the Public Realm' (1995) 83 Georgetown Law Journal 2619, 2621.

[44] *Lubanga*, Appeals Judgment on Reparations principles (n 27) para 7.

[45] For example, attending and participating during hearings and the possibility to question a witness, ICC RPE (n 21) ex rule 90, paras 1–2.

[46] *Prosecutor v Kony, Otti, Odhiambo, Lukwiya and Ongwen*, ICC-02/04-01/05-134, Decision on legal representation, appointment of counsel for the defence, protective measures and time-limit for submission of observations on applications for participation a/0010/06, a/0064/06 to a/0070/06, a/0081/06 to a/0104/06 and a/0111/06 to a/0127/06 (1 February 2007) paras 2–12.

[47] ICC RPE (n 21) r 90(2).

[48] *Prosecutor v Ruto, Kosgey and Sang*, ICC-01/09-01/11-249, Decision on Victims' Participation at the Confirmation of Charges Hearing and in the Related Proceedings (8 August 2011) paras 67 and 77; *Prosecutor v Muthaura, Kenyatta and Hussein Ali*, ICC-01/09-02/11-267, Decision on Victims' Participation at the Confirmation of Charges Hearing and in the Related Proceedings (28 August 2011) paras 79, 81 and 91.

Evidence.[49] In some cases, instead of referring to the fact that victims should have the opportunity to decide on a collective legal representative with the help of the Registry,[50] the Court has invoked regulation 80(1) of the Regulations of the Court, stating it is in the 'interests of justice' to appoint a collective legal representative or nothing at all.[51] Nevertheless, it should be pointed out that the Court has the responsibility to provide victims with adequate information on how they wish to be represented before the Court. But in practice victims are merely allowed to indicate on the victim's application form whether they agree with a collective legal representative.[52]

Victims thus lack the procedural capacity to bring claims through a representative of their own choice. Whether this is a problem may depend on individual cases. Clearly one representative for numerous victims cannot invest as many resources in factual investigation and legal research, which will influence the outcome of the case. Unfairness in a hearing is a difficult, fussy matter. Another consequence of collective representation is that it general leads to cases being pleaded in the absence of the victims. This makes it extremely difficult for victims to assess the fairness of their hearing and feel connected to the proceedings that usually take place on the other side of the world.

Passive versus active actors

After Lubanga was convicted, his judges issued, on 7 August 2012, the Court's first-ever decision on reparations. The Trial Chamber observed that:

> In the Chamber's view, reparations, as provided in the Statute and Rules, are to be applied in a broad and flexible manner, allowing the Chamber to approve the widest possible remedies for the violations of the rights of the victims and the means of implementation.[53]

This statement shows that the Chamber wished to bring as many victims as possible under the reparations scheme. The ICC Statute takes a similar approach. Article 75 lid 2 provides that reparations may be made 'to or in respect of, victims'. The words 'in respect of' show that reparation is not necessarily the consequence of a victim's specific demand for

[49] See for example *Prosecutor v Katanga and Chui*, ICC-01/04-01/07-1328, Order on the organization of common legal representation of victims (22 July 2009) para 11; *Prosecutor v Banda and Jerbo*, ICC-02/05-03/09-337, Decision on common legal representation (25 May 2012) paras 12–14.

[50] ICC RPE (n 21) r 90(2).

[51] *Prosecutor v Muthaura and Kenyatta*, ICC-01/09-02/11-498, Decision on victims' representation and participation (6 October 2012) para 60; *Gbagbo*, Decision on Victims' Participation (n 49) para 42; *Ruto & Sang*, Victims' representation and participation (n 50) para 44.

[52] *Prosecutor v Ongwen*, ICC-02/04-01/15-303, First Report on Applications to Participate in the Proceedings (18 September 2015) para 21. Human Rights Watch, *Who Will Stand for Us? Victims' Legal Representation at the ICC in the Ongwen Case and Beyond* (Human Rights Watch 2017) 30–37. The EAC Statute has included the same clause as regulation 80 of the ICC Court regulations, in the interest of justice (see *Statut des Chambres africaines extraordinaires au sein des juridictions sénégalaises pour la poursuite des crimes internationaux commis au Tchad durant la période du 7 juin 1982 au 1er décembre 1990*, 22 August 2012 [hereinafter EAC Statute]). Art 14(2) provides the victims the choice to form groups and to find a collective representative. However, the EAC Statute did not mention nor created the impression that victims could have individual representatives.

[53] *Prosecutor v Lubanga*, ICC-01/04-01/06-2904, Decision establishing the principles and procedures to be applied to reparations (7 August 2012) paras 179–80.

reparation. Rather reparations are regarded, at the ICC, as something that is granted to victims, ideally as many victims as possible.[54]

Indeed, a victim's claim is unnecessary to order reparations. In the *Lubanga* case, the Appeals Chamber ruled that collective reparations can be awarded irrespective of whether victims submitted a request for reparations and whether they participated in the trial proceedings.[55] This is because all victims are to be treated fairly and equally as regards to reparations. The Trial Chamber considered:

> given the uncertainty as to the number of victims of the crimes in this case—save that a considerable number of people were affected—and the limited number of individuals who have applied for reparations, the Court should ensure there is a collective approach that ensures reparations reach those victims who are currently unidentified.[56]

The Trial Chamber found that 'it would be inappropriate to limit reparations to the relatively small group of victims that participated in the Trial and those who applied for reparations'.[57] In the *Al Mahdi* case the Trial Chamber made a similar decision. It decided to set aside the individual applications for reparations because 'it has received only 139 applications during the reparations phase, despite determining that collective harm was suffered across Timbuktu (a city of approximately 70,000 people around the time of the attack)'. It set aside its own ruling on the applications with an administrative screening by the Trust Fund for Victims.[58]

Hence victims are the target of the reparation; they are the recipients. Reparation cases before the ICC are not so much concerned with victims' *rights*. Victims are treated as objects as opposed to subjects who can demand remedies.

It is true that victims can object to receiving reparation. They do need to give their consent, because, in the words of the Court 'reparations are entirely voluntary'.

> 160. The Appeals Chamber notes that, despite correctly recognising the voluntary nature of victims' participation in the reparation programmes, the Trial Chamber made their participation in such programmes dependent on whether the Trust Fund 'considers it appropriate'. The Appeals Chamber notes that, at the time of making applications for reparations, the victims either applied for individual awards or applied for a collective award, without knowledge of the kind of a collective programme that would be ultimately adopted. The Appeals Chamber therefore finds that it is necessary to seek the victims' consent when a collective award is made, consistent with the principle, identified by the Trial Chamber, that '[r]eparations are entirely voluntary'.[59]

But the words 'entirely voluntary' are strange words in a court of law, where legal disputes, between parties, are handled. It displays a view of victims as recipients rather than

[54] *Lubanga*, Appeals Judgment on Reparations principles (n 27) para 100. Also in *Lubanga*, Appeals Judgment on Reparations principles (n 27) para 70.
[55] *Lubanga*, Appeals Judgment on Reparations principles (n 27) para 151.
[56] *Lubanga*, Decision on Reparations principles (n 53) para 219.
[57] ibid 187.
[58] *Al Mahdi*, Reparations Order (n 42) paras 141–42.
[59] *Lubanga*, Appeals Judgment on Reparations principles (n 27) para 160.

as participants submitting a claim. They are offered something that they can refuse. They are not acting out of their own initiative, they are not demanding anything. Using this approach, victims are reduced to wounded, injured persons who have suffered damages, rather than a party submitting a claim that a court needs to adjudicate.

A reason to opt for collective reparations is to be as inclusive as possible. Read this observation of the Trial Chamber:

> 'reparations proceedings and reparations orders and programme's in favour of child soldiers, should guarantee the development of victims' personalities, talent and abilities to the fullest extent and, more broadly, they should ensure the development of respect for human rights and fundamental freedoms.'[60]

These may be the words of a social worker or psychologist. Certainly, these objectives—the development of victims' personalities, talent and abilities to the fullest extent -are highly respectable and no one could be against them. But that may be exactly the problem. In my view, they do not belong in a court of law. A court of law deals with disagreements between parties, over rights and obligations. These need to be weighed and determined. A court of law has to dispense justice, deal with legal disputes between parties and carry out the administration of justice in accordance with the rule of law.

A complicating factor in this respect is also the Court's efforts to avoid tensions between victims. The Trial Chamber considered that: 'individual reparations should be awarded in a way that avoids creating tensions and divisions within the relevant communities.'[61] It is a fact that compensation can lead to tensions and divisions. The Court is not in a position to deal with all victims, as it is not in a position to deal with all crimes and all perpetrators. This means that, by definition, there are victims who will be excluded. But it is debatable whether the Court should consider itself responsible for such tensions. If an individual is legally entitled to reparations, to what extent should the Court take into account community interests? Again, a conception of victims transpires as a large community at the cost of individual entitlements to reparation on the basis of the law and accountability.

What we are seeing is that rather than applying the legal principle of accountability to victims' claims for damage, their compensation is too often approached as a humanitarian or charity effort. The role of the Trust Fund for Victims within the ICC enhances this problem.

The ICC Trust Fund as an example

The ICC has the option of granting individual or collective reparation, concerning a whole group of victims.[62] If the Court decides to order collective reparation, it may order that reparation be made through the Victims' Trust Fund.[63] While the Court issues the reparation order, the Trust Fund is tasked with the implementation of this order.

[60] *Lubanga*, Decision on Reparations principles (n 53) para 213.
[61] ibid 220.
[62] ICC RPE (n 21) r 97.
[63] ICC RPE (n 21) r 98(3); Rome Statute (n 3) Art 75(2).

To avoid tensions between victims' communities, collective reparations through the Trust Fund is an attractive alternative for the Court. The Trust Fund tries to be as inclusive as possible. For example, civilians targeted by Lubanga's troops could not be officially recognized as victims because the warlord was only convicted of enlisting and using child soldiers. The director of the Trust Fund argued that this is why those communities should be included in a consultative process on reparations: to prevent reparations awards to victims from leading to 'more harm and jealousy'.

Another sensitive issue in both the *Lubanga* and *Katanga* cases is that, due to the specific charges for which these men were convicted, almost all victims are Hema. Other ethnic groups who also suffered are not formally recognized as victims. 'It is another reason why we prefer to have an approach of designing reparations in which not only victims, but also communities are consulted. To avoid problems that might even reignite the conflict', explains the director of the Trust Fund.[64]

However, as respectable as these objectives are, they also reveal a tension between the ICC and the Trust Fund. The Court is not the place to go to with the aim to reintegrate ethnic groups or communities. Proponents of a large role of the Trust Fund value peace over justice. I would argue, however, for justice over peace. The ICC is one of the very few institutions out there that can adjudicate. Leave peacebuilding to other bodies.

The Trust Fund may certainly be helpful as a fund providing assistance to victims, ie a fund to the 'benefit of victims'.[65] As the Trust Fund may be more flexible, not bound by narrowly defined legal principles, it is likely better equipped to deal with large number of victims. But the Trust Fund should not replace the ICC in the latter's responsibility regarding legal reparations. This is what is happening as the ICC does not rule on individual applications for reparations but leaves the identification of the victims to the Trust Fund. In the *Al Mahdi* case, the Trial Chamber considered:

> When the Court does not identify the beneficiaries, it falls to the TFV to establish a verification procedure to determine that any persons who identify themselves to the TFV are in fact members of the beneficiary group. The Chamber considers that proceeding in this manner is an alternative to an application-based process, whereby the Chamber assesses the reparation requests of identifiable beneficiaries filed pursuant to Rule 94 of the Rules.[66]

The ICC relinquishes its competence to rule on individual victims' claims to the Trust Fund. However, the Trust Fund is a humanitarian fund, providing material support, aiming to alleviate suffering. The work of the Trust Fund does not lead to a public standard setting. Judicial decisions do have that function of standard setting. Decisions of a court of law indicate which actions are considered socially and morally acceptable under the current legal system.[67] The Trust Fund cannot have that role. What is more, the Trust Fund lacks

[64] T Lingsma, 'A Banner Year for Victims' Reparations at the International Criminal Court?' (2015) 173 Intl Justice Tribune 3 <http://www.tjitske-lingsma.nl/wp-content/uploads/2013/02/A-banner-year-for-victims%E2%80%99-reparations-at-the-International-Criminal-Court-International-Justice-Tribune-173.pdf> accessed 22 December 2017.

[65] ICC RPE (n 21) r 98(5).

[66] *Al Mahdi*, Reparations Order (n 42) para 143.

[67] De Bock, *De toekomst van de civiele rechtspraak: Een pleidooi om de rechter niet te ontlasten* (Uitgeverij Parijs 2017) 14. For the pros and cons on private dispute settlement, see, eg, C Giabardo, 'Private Law in the Age of the "Vanishing Trial"' in K Barker, K Fairweather, and R Grantham (eds), *Private Law in the 21st Century* (Hart Publishing 2017) 547–60; E Thornberg, 'Reaping what we sow: anti-litigation rhetoric, limited budgets,

impartial and independent judges to decide on which reparations should be made and how these should be made. By referring victims' claims to the Trust Fund they are outside of the scope of justice, the rule of law and the public domain. Victims should not be excluded from this domain.[68]

It must be said that in this case, the instructions of the ICC were more specific than in other cases, as the Chamber—while recognizing the Trust Fund's 'general position to prioritise collective awards—ordered that the limited number of individual reparations should be prioritized during implementation', although it immediately downplayed this instruction by adding that the Trust Fund should only do so 'insofar as individual reparations do not hinder broader reconciliation or stigmatise individual victims vis-à-vis the community of Timbuktu'.[69]

Conclusion: Empowerment of victims?

Various international criminal courts deal with victims differently. There has been outright opposition to victims' participation in criminal trials, reluctant acceptance, and apparent embracement. However, even when there seems to be embrace, such as by the ICC, under the surface victims struggle to get their rights and the damage they have suffered recognized.

Compared to the rights of the accused, and the administration of the prosecution, the victims lag far behind. This is understandable to a certain extent. The logic of criminal tribunals has established civil rights for victims. The functioning and the capacity of these tribunals are determined by their objective to try and convict perpetrators of international crimes. Victims are a side matter that these tribunals wish to include in the margins of their functioning.

The ICC jurisprudence on victims is still developing. The ICC ruling in the *Katanga* case is better than the judgment of the Trial Chamber in *Lubanga*, since *in Katanga* the reparation was also awarded to individual victims. The Appeals Chamber in the *Lubanga* case drew reparations more into the legal domain by articulating principles on reparations.

and declining support for civil courts' (2011) 30 Civil Justice Quarterly 74; Luban (n 43); O Fiss, 'Against Settlement'(1984) 93(6) Yale Law Journal 1073; M Loth and E Mak, 'The Judicial Domain in View—Figures, Trends and Perspectives' (2007) 3(1) Utrecht Law Review 75; H Genn, 'Why the Privatisation of Civil Justice is a Rule of Law Issue' (36th F A Mann Lecture 2012); H Genn, *Judging Civil Justice, The Hamlyn Lectures 2008* (Cambridge University Press 2010).

[68] De Bock (n 67) 16.

[69] See *Al Mahdi*, Reparations Order (n 42) paras 29 and 140. The EAC also had to deal with numerous reparation requests, but they did not recoil from what the EAC had set out to do, namely to do justice. The civil parties requested both collective and individual reparations. The EAC awarded individual reparations (See *Le Procureur c Hissène Habré*, Appeal Judgment EAC (27 April 2017) paras 857–75), after all victims were identified (*Le Procureur c Habré*, Civil Decision EAC (29 July 2016) para 52 (hereinafter Reparations Judgment)) and categorized per crime (*Habré*, Reparations Judgment paras 57–68; see *Ministère Public c Habré*, Trial Judgment, Annexes 1–7 (30 May 2016)). The EAC made a distinction between victims of sexual violence, arbitrary execution, enforced disappearance, torture, or murder. Additionally, it distinguished between direct and indirect victims. The indirect victims had to provide proof that a member of the family was a victim (*Habré*, Reparations Judgment) para 67).

SECTION C

CAPTURING THE JUDICIAL PROCESS: ACTORS AND DYNAMICS

One central dynamic of ICL is who is in and who is out, ie which actors are included, and how they occupy their procedural role. This section considers this question through examination of victims, witnesses, and the possible reach of the law. The section begins with Eric Stover and Stephen Cody's chapter discussing their work with victims before international criminal tribunals. Stover and Cody consider the possible benefits of ICL trials to address victims' perceptions regarding procedural fairness and the legitimacy of trials. Christopher Sperfeldt examines the particular problem of victim satisfaction through his chapter considering reparations. Next Sarah Williams examines the *amicus curiae* brief drafted for the EAC regarding sexual violence in order to theorize the appropriate role of such briefing in enabling silenced voices to participate in international criminal tribunals. The possibility of affording greater legal protections to victimized groups is the topic of Patricia Sellers and Jocelyn Kestenbaum's chapter, which examines the doctrinal avenues for the recognition and prosecution of 'sexualized slavery'. Nancy Combs' chapter considers a parallel question, that of witnesses and their protection. Witnesses before international criminal tribunals are sometimes twice victimized, first by the trauma they lived through and second by dangers associated with participating in international trials; Combs explores these dynamics.

35

'We Will Not Go Away'

The Participation of Victims in International Criminal Tribunals

Stephen Cody and Eric Stover

'Today I feel ten times bigger than Hissène Habré.'
- Souleymane Guengueng, Victim and Activist.[1]

Introduction

The conviction of Hissène Habré before the Extraordinary African Chambers, or EAC, on 30 May 2016 marked a hard won victory for victims who suffered under the ex-Chadian dictator's regime.[2] Without their perseverance, it is unlikely the trial would have come to pass.[3] For twenty-five years, Chadian victims' organizations, in partnership with Human Rights Watch and other human rights organizations, assiduously investigated and documented Habré's crimes, presented their findings before international and regional commissions, and lobbied governments to ensure that justice would prevail. As Reed Brody, a former Human Rights Watch lawyer, said shortly after the verdict was read: 'Today will be carved into history as the day that a band of unrelenting survivors brought their dictator to justice . . . It is a big joy, a big day. A victory for victims.'[4]

Yet the journey for Chadian victims wasn't an easy one. Once it became known that victims' associations were documenting Habré's crimes, his supporters set out to thwart their efforts. Jacqueline Moudeina, a Chadian lawyer, narrowly survived an assassination attempt in 2001 by one of Habré's aides because of her work representing victims.[5] Other survivors, like Souleymane Guengueng, left prison deeply scarred by years of torture and

[1] Human Rights Watch, 'Chad's Ex-Dictator Convicted of Atrocities' (*Human Rights Watch*, 30 May 2016) <https://www.hrw.org/news/2016/05/30/chads-ex-dictator-convicted-atrocities> accessed 25 June 2019.

[2] We use the terms 'victim' and 'survivor' interchangeably throughout this chapter and also use the term 'victim participation' to include victims of serious international crimes who participate in trial proceedings either as victim-witnesses; civil parties (in French, *parties civiles*) in the civil law tradition; or as 'victim participants' as defined by the Rome Statute of the International Criminal Court.

[3] Reed Brody, 'Bringing a Dictator to Justice' (2015) 13 Journal of International Criminal Justice 209, 209–17.

[4] Ruth Maclean, 'Chad's Hissène Habré found guilty of crimes against humanity' *The Guardian* (London, 30 May 2016) <https://www.theguardian.com/world/2016/may/30/chad-hissene-habre-guilty-crimes-against-humanity-senegal> accessed 25 June 2019.

[5] See Marlise Simons, 'Lawyer Outlasts Grenade and Terror to Bring Ex-Leader of Chad to Trial' *New York Times* (New York, 19 July 2015) <https://www.nytimes.com/2015/07/19/world/africa/surviving-grenade-and-terror-to-bring-chads-ex-leader-to-trial.html?action=click&contentCollection=Africa&module=RelatedCoverage&region=EndOfArticle&pgtype=article> accessed 25 June 2019.

Stephen Cody and Eric Stover, *'We Will Not Go Away'* In: *The President on Trial*. First edition. Edited by: Sharon Weill, Kim Thuy Seelinger, and Kerstin Bree Carlson, Oxford University Press (2020). © Stephen Cody and Eric Stover.
DOI: 10.1093/oso/9780198858621.003.0036

abuse.[6] Upon his release, Guengueng was expelled from Chad. Undeterred, he and several fellow survivors went on to interview hundreds of former prisoners and the widows and relatives of those killed by Habré's political police, the Documentation and Security Directorate, or DDS.[7] Another survivor-turned-activist, Clement Abaifouta, developed severe post-traumatic stress disorder after spending four years in a DDS prison where he was forced to bury hundreds of detainees in mass graves just outside the prison's walls.[8] Despite his disorder, he went on to become the President of the Chadian Victims' Association, or AVCRP, which played a leading role in facilitating the participation of victims, known as 'civil parties' (in French, *parties civiles*), in the Habré trial.[9]

More than 4,000 civil parties participated in the Habré trial. Of these, sixty-nine testified in court as either 'direct' or 'indirect' victims.[10] Direct victims had suffered brutalities at the hands of Habré's military and police, while indirect victims were those who had lost loved ones. Unlike witnesses, who only spoke at the proceedings if called on by the prosecution or defence, civil parties were able to present evidence, make closing statements, and receive reparations.[11]

One of dozens of direct victims who testified in the trial was a welder named Robert Hissein Gambier who spent five years in a DDS prison. Holding two sticks in the air, he demonstrated to the judges how his torturers used them to squeeze his head like a vise.[12] 'It was like seeing clouds. I saw torturers below me and from above. Everything was down below me. Even the room was below me.'[13] On another day, four women—two of whom were fifteen at the time of their imprisonment—told the court how soldiers had used them as sex slaves in a camp in northern Chad.[14]

Beyond the occasional news story about civil parties who testified at the Habré trial, little is known about the experiences of the thousands of others who engaged with the court: What motivated these men and women to testify? What did they think of the court and the behaviour of the judges, prosecutors, and defence attorneys? Was the process fair and the verdict adequate? Did they see the act of engaging with the court in strictly personal

[6] Dionne Searcey, 'He Helped Topple a Dictator. In New York, He's Another Face in the Crowd' *New York Times* (New York, 6 January 2017) <https://www.nytimes.com/2017/01/06/world/africa/souleymane-guengueng-chad.html> accessed 25 June 2019.

[7] ibid.

[8] Clement Abaifouta, 'Forgiveness does not come easy after this kind of suffering, but we are working on it' (*Justice Hub,* 17 April 2017) <https://justicehub.org/article/clement-abaifouta-forgiveness-does-not-come-easy-after-kind-suffering-we-are-working-it> accessed 14 March 2018.

[9] Human Rights Watch, 'Hissène Habré Trial: Witness Hearings Ending' (*Human Rights Watch*, 13 December 2015) <https://www.hrw.org/news/2015/12/13/hissene-habre-trial-witness-hearings-ending> accessed 14 March 2018. ['Some 4,500 victims joined the procedure as civil parties, represented by legal teams, most of whose members are Chadian lawyers.']

[10] Amnesty International, 'Chad: Hissène Habré Appeal Closes dark chapter for victims' (*Amnesty International*, 27 April 2017) <https://www.amnesty.org/en/press-releases/2017/04/chad-hissene-habre-appeal-ruling-closes-dark-chapter-for-victims/> accessed 14 March 2018. ['The trial against Hissène Habré opened on 20 July 2015, and 69 victims, 23 witnesses and 10 expert witnesses testified during the proceedings.']

[11] Charles P Trumbull IV, 'The Victims of Victim Participation in International Criminal Proceedings' (2008) 29 Michigan Journal of International Law 777, 778.

[12] France Médias Monde, 'Procès Habré: le témoin qui "court plus vite que le mort"' *RFI Afrique* (Dakar, 30 October 2015) <http://www.rfi.fr/afrique/20151030-habre-proces-senegal-torture-dds-detenu-court-plus-vite-sabagalmoute> accessed 14 March 2018.

[13] Thierry Cruvellier, 'The Trial of Hissène Habré' *New York Times* (New York, 15 February 2016) <https://www.nytimes.com/2016/02/16/opinion/the-landmark-trial-of-hissene-habre.html> accessed 14 March 2018.

[14] Reed Brody, 'Victims Bring a Dictator to Justice: The Case of Hissène Habré' *Brot für die Welt* (June 2017) 16–17 <https://www.brot-fuer-die-welt.de/fileadmin/mediapool/2_Downloads/Fachinformationen/Analyse/Analysis70-The_Habre_Case.pdf> accessed 14 March 2018.

terms or did they see it as contributing to a greater good? Have they suffered any repercussions because of their testimony? To answer these questions, a systematic interview survey would need to be conducted with a large cohort of civil parties.

Lacking such a survey, we try in this chapter to provide an overview of the historical, procedural, and psychosocial aspects of victim participation in international criminal tribunals based on our own studies[15] of victim-witnesses at the International Criminal Tribunal for the former Yugoslavia (ICTY)[16] and the International Criminal Court (ICC),[17] civil parties at the Extraordinary Chambers in the Courts of Cambodia (ECCC),[18] and victim participants in ICC cases in Democratic Republic of Congo, Ivory Coast, Kenya, and Uganda.[19] We conclude the chapter with several recommendations of studies that could be conducted with civil parties and representatives of local victims associations and human rights groups who engaged with the EAC so as to better understand their interactions with the court and how those experiences affected their lives and their views of justice.

Victims in international criminal justice

Victim participation in international criminal trials has been uneven. Historically, prosecutors often have sidelined victim testimony in favour of documentary or physical evidence or assumed that justice for victims equated to retributive punishment of offenders.[20] In recent decades, however, victims have become more active contributors in criminal investigations and proceedings.[21] Victim participation at all stages of the Habré trial, for example, suggests a growing trend towards greater victim inclusion in international and national criminal trials. As such, it is incumbent on court personnel, as well as international justice

[15] The Human Rights Center also conducted several population-based surveys on the attitudes about justice and social reconstruction in five post-war countries. These studies include: *Iraqi Voices: Attitudes Toward Transitional Justice and Social Reconstruction* (May 2004); *Forgotten Voices: A Population-Based Survey on Attitudes about Peace and Justice in Northern Uganda* (July 2005); *When the War Ends: A Population-Based Survey on the Attitudes about Peace, Justice, and Social Reconstruction in Northern Uganda* (December 2007); *Living with Fear: A Population-Based Survey on the Attitudes about Peace, Justice, and Social Reconstruction in the Eastern Democratic Republic of Congo* (August 2008); *So We Will Never Forget: A Population-Based Survey on Attitudes about Social Reconstruction and the Extraordinary Chambers in the Courts of Cambodia* (January 2009); *Building Peace, Seeking Justice: A Population-Based Survey on Attitudes about Accountability and Social Reconstruction in the Central African Republic* (August 2010); *Transitioning to Peace: A Population-Based Survey on Attitudes About Social Reconstruction and Justice in Northern Uganda* (December 2010); and *After the First Trial: A Population-Based Survey on Knowledge and Perceptions of Justice and the Extraordinary Chambers in the Courts of Cambodia* (June 2011). See also Eric Stover and Harvey Weinstein (eds), *My Neighbor, My Enemy: Justice and Community in the Aftermath of Mass Atrocity* (Cambridge University Press 2004).

[16] Eric Stover, *The Witnesses: War Crimes and the Promise of Justice in The Hague* (U Penn Press 2005).

[17] Human Rights Center, University of California, Berkeley School of Law, *Bearing Witness at the International Criminal Court: An Interview Survey of 109 Witnesses* (June 2014).

[18] Eric Stover, Mychelle Balthazard, and K Alexa Koenig, 'Confronting Duch: Civil Party Participation in Case 001 at the Extraordinary Chambers in the Courts of Cambodia' (2011) 93 International Review of Red Cross 503.

[19] Human Rights Center, University of California, Berkeley School of Law, *The Victims' Court? A Study of 622 Victim Participants at the International Criminal Court* (November 2015).

[20] Luke Moffett, 'The role of victims in the international criminal tribunals of the Second World War' (2012) 12 International Criminal Law Review 245, 249.

[21] Claire Garbett, 'From Passive Objects to Active Agents: A Comparative Study of Conceptions of Victim Identities at the ICTY and ICC' (2016) 15 Journal of Human Rights 40; Jonathan Doak, *Victims' Rights, Human Rights and Criminal Justice: Reconceiving the Role of Third Parties* (Hart, Oxford 2008); T Markus Funk, *Victims' Rights and Advocacy at the International Criminal Court* (OUP 2010); Christoph Sperfeldt, 'Cambodian civil society and the Khmer Rouge Tribunal' (2012) 1 International Journal of Transitional Justice 149.

researchers and practitioners, to better understand the diverse needs of victims and how they can be best supported before, during, and after trials.[22]

Victim participation in criminal trials has been more typical in countries with civil law traditions than in those with common law traditions. In most common law systems, including the United States and United Kingdom, victim participation in proceedings is largely limited to that of being a witness or being able to present victim impact statements at sentencing. By contrast, victims participating in civil law systems in continental Europe and many countries in Latin America and Africa and Asia can assume a much larger role by initiating proceedings against an accused, applying to join a criminal prosecution as a civil petitioner (*constitution de partie civile)*, and/or seeking compensation or other forms of reparations for harms suffered. Because many international criminal tribunals draw from both common law and civil law traditions, they historically have had to decide which of these two models of victim participation to adopt or whether to create a hybrid alternative of the two.[23]

In the aftermath of World War II, the Allied powers modelled the Nuremberg and Tokyo tribunals on common law courts. At Nuremberg, the chief prosecutor, Justice Robert H. Jackson, called thirty-three witnesses to testify, of whom only a few were victim-witnesses. While survivor testimony would have humanized the trial, Jackson feared that survivors' stories could be too horrific to be believed and could jeopardize the prosecution of Nazi leaders.[24] He instead sought to make his case with extensive documentary evidence from the Third Reich's own archives.[25] Similarly, at the Tokyo tribunal, Allied prosecutors relied heavily on documentary evidence largely because of 'the logistical problems in locating and bringing witnesses from overseas.'[26]

Victims played significant roles in several high-profile trials after Nuremberg, including national proceedings in Israel in 1961 against SS officer Adolf Eichmann[27] and in France in 1983 against former Gestapo leader Klaus Barbie.[28] In the Barbie case, the court defined the term 'victim' fairly broadly. Victims included 'not only the direct objects of systematic racial and religious persecution, but also those who opposed such persecution by any means. Thus, [even] Resistance members, as soldiers fighting Nazism ... could be deemed victims of crimes against humanity.'[29] French courts adopted this expansive definition of what constituted a 'victim', or civil party, in subsequent trials of Paul Touvier, a leader of a Vichy-run paramilitary group, and Maurice Papon, a police official in the Prefecture of Bordeaux.[30]

22 Laurel E Fletcher and Harvey M Weinstein, 'Violence and Social Repair: Rethinking the Contribution of Justice to Reconciliation' (2002) 24 Human Rights Quarterly 573, 588.

23 Stephen Smith Cody and Eric Stover, 'The Role of Victims: Emerging Rights to Participation and Reparation in International Criminal Courts' in Philipp Kastner (ed), *International Criminal Law in Context* (Routledge 2018) 317–35.

24 Robert H Jackson, *The Nürnberg Case* (Alfred A Knopf 1947).

25 Telford Taylor, *The Anatomy of the Nuremberg Trials: A Personal Memoir* (Alfred A Knopf 1992) 148.

26 Yuma Totani, *The Tokyo War Crimes Trial: The Pursuit of Justice in the Wake of World War II* (Harvard University Asia Center 2008) 121.

27 Deborah E Lipstadt, *The Eichmann Trial* (Schocken Books 2011).

28 Alain Finkielkraut, *Remembering in Vain: The Klaus Barbie Trial and Crimes against Humanity* (Columbia University Press 1992).

29 Michael E Tigar and others, 'Paul Touvier and the crime against humanity' (1995) 30 Texas International Law Journal 285, 295.

30 ibid. See also Leila Sadat Wexler, 'Reflections on the Trial of Vichy Collaborator Paul Touvier for Crimes Against Humanity in France' (1995) 20 Law and Social Inquiry 191.

Much to the chagrin of victims' rights advocates, neither the Statutes nor the Rules of Procedure and Evidence of the UN ad hoc international criminal tribunals for Rwanda and the former Yugoslavia, established in 1993 and 1994, respectively, provided victims with specific 'rights.' In addition, budgetary shortfalls at these tribunals in their early years restricted their ability to provide adequate support services to witnesses.[31] While witnesses at the Yugoslavia tribunal reported that they valued the chance to participate in criminal cases, a significant number also said they 'faced social, economic, and other repercussions as a result of their testimony, and there was a small, but critical group of witnesses who faced security threats before and after they testified'.[32]

The adoption of the Rome Treaty establishing the International Criminal Court in 1998 triggered a seismic shift in the relationship between victims and international justice. The ICC's statute allowed victim participants, largely through their legal representatives, to comment on the court's decision to open an investigation, admit or reject a case, narrow or broaden the scope of charges against an accused, make submissions to the chambers or question witnesses during proceedings, or comment on the nature and extent of reparations, so long as the presentation was done 'in a manner which is not prejudicial to or inconsistent with the rights of the accused and a fair and impartial trial'.[33] These 'rights' or 'entitlements' meant that victims would now be primary agents in international criminal justice—or so it was hoped.

This expansion of victims' rights has benefits for victims and prosecutors alike.[34] Victims can help prosecutors acquire new information, such as the location of mass graves or clandestine prisons, which, in turn, can help establish the elements of a crime, and provide essential linkage evidence to documentary and physical evidence.[35] Increased victim participation in court proceedings can also lead to greater victim interaction with local human rights and support groups, as well as the formation of new victim-centred organizations.

For example, a survey of 222 civil parties who testified at the Extraordinary Chambers in the Courts of Cambodia (ECCC) found that majority of respondents (88.1%) felt very well supported by the assistance they received from the victims' associations and other support groups, including the Transcultural Psychosocial Organization (TPO) and the Human Rights and Development Association (ADHOC). These organizations provide legal and psychosocial support services, including a hotline, to civil parties participating in ECCC proceedings. Many of the respondents reported that they had received little or no assistance

[31] Stover, *The Witnesses* (n 16) 136–41.

[32] Kimi King and others, *Echoes of Testimonies: A Pilot Study into the Long-Term Impact of Bearing Witness Before the ICTY* (U North Texas and the Victims and Witness Section at the ICTY 2016) 20 <http://www.icty.org/x/file/About/Registry/Witnesses/Echoes-Full-Report_EN.pdf> accessed 25 June 2019.

[33] See Rome Statute of the International Criminal Court, 17 July 1998, 2187 UNTS 3, 37 ILM 999 (1998), *entered into force* 1 July 2002, Art 68(3). See also Salvatore Zappalà, 'The Rights of Victims v. the Rights of the Accused' (2010) 8 Journal of International Criminal Justice 137.

[34] Jonathan Doak, 'Victims' rights in criminal trials: prospects for participation' (2005) 32 Journal of Law and Society 294; J-Anne Wemmers, 'Where Do They Belong? Giving Victims a Place in the Criminal Justice Process' (2009) 20 Criminal Law Forum 395; E Stover and Harvey Weinstein (eds), *My Neighbor, My Enemy: Justice and Community in the Aftermath of Mass Atrocity* (Cambridge University Press 2004).

[35] Valentina Spiga, 'No Redress Without Justice: Victims and International Criminal Law' (2012) 10 Journal of International Criminal Justice 1377; Hans-Peter Kaul, 'Victims' Rights and Peace' in Thorsten Bonacker and Christoph Safferling (eds), *Victims of International Crimes: An Interdisciplinary Discourse* (Springer 2013) 223–29.

for the harms they had suffered under the Khmer Rouge prior to engaging with these organizations.[36]

Once organized, victims are in a better position to advocate for other transitional justice mechanisms, including truth commissions, local justice mechanisms, memorials, and reparations programs. ICC victim outreach meetings in Uganda and Kenya, for example, have provided opportunities for victims to meet and discuss efforts to seek support for reconstruction and memorial projects from government agencies and donor organizations. Victim participation also helps to ensure that legal proceedings far from the sites of mass violence stay moored to local experiences of violence and the gravity of personal loss remains at the forefront during trials.[37]

Victim participation programs at international criminal tribunals are not without controversy. Trial observers and defence counsel, as well as judges and prosecutors, frequently argue that victim participation violates the rights of the accused to a fair trial.[38] In *Eichmann in Jerusalem*, Hannah Arendt betrays her impatience with the 'endless sessions' of survivor testimonies that occupied half the court's agenda. The trial, she writes, degenerated 'into a bloody show, a rudderless ship tossed about on the waves', where 'witness followed witness and horror was piled on horror'.[39] Other observers were highly critical of the number of civil parties and their lawyers who appeared in the Touvier and Papon trials (there were thirty-four lawyers in the Touvier case). Many of the civil parties, these observers said, failed to draw any link between their own suffering and the fate of their family members and the actions of the accused.[40] For its part, the ICC has sought to avoid these pitfalls with mixed results. Even when the number of victim participants who appear in court proceedings is limited, their attorneys can enter motions that cause excessive delays.[41] Moreover, victim participation can place a strain on limited court resources as court staff must develop outreach and education programs, recruit legal counsel, and work with national and local officials to facilitate participation.

Victims' needs

Most victims of mass atrocities have survived or witnessed killings, rape, torture, inhumane imprisonment, forced expulsion, and the destruction of their homes and villages. For many, testifying in an international trial requires an act of great courage, especially when perpetrators still live in their communities. Yet the act of telling one's story in a trial can be fraught with unanticipated consequences.

[36] Judith Strasser and others, *A Study about Victims' Participation at the Extraordinary Chambers in the Courts of Cambodia of Cambodia and Gender-Based Violence under the Khmer Rouge* (Transcultural Psychosocial Organization, September 2015) 12.

[37] Claire Garbette, 'The Truth and the Trial: Victim Participation, Restorative Justice, and the International Criminal Court' (2013) 16 Contemporary Justice Review 193.

[38] Zappalà (n 33).

[39] Hannah Arendt, *Eichmann in Jerusalem: A Report on the Banality of Evil* (Penguin Books 1977) 8–9.

[40] Nancy Wood, 'The Papon Trial in an "Era of Testimony"' in R J Golsan (ed), *The Papon Affair: Memory and Justice on Trial* (Routledge 2000) 97.

[41] Mirjan Damaska, 'What Is the Point of International Criminal Justice?' (2008) 83 Chicago-Kent Law Review 329; Mirjan Damaska, 'The Competing Visions of Fairness: The Basic Choice for International Criminal Tribunals' (2010) 36 North Carolina Journal of International Law and Commercial Regulation 365.

During the Habré trial, for example, some of the women who testified had never spoken publicly about the sexual violence they had suffered and thus exposed themselves to potential repercussions and stigmatization back in their home communities. Indeed, one survivor, Khadidja Zidane, who had testified that Habré had raped her, later told *The Guardian* that upon returning to Chad she had been threatened with death, physically attacked by strangers on the street, and abused in her own home. 'When I came back from Dakar', she said, 'people came to my house and insulted me and shouted: "Whore. You went to Dakar to testify. Something will happen to you this year." '[42]

In a 2010 Human Rights Center survey of twenty-one of the twenty-two civil parties who testified in the trial of Kaing Guek Eav (alias 'Duch'), the Khmer Rouge commander of the infamous Toul Sleng prison, we found that most of them had formed strong supportive bonds with one another. During the course of the trial, the civil parties established the Victims Association of Democratic Kampuchea (or Ksem Ksan Association), one of the first such organizations in Cambodia. One respondent told us:

> [F]or me, personally, I couldn't talk about my suffering ... but meeting other civil parties it allows me to talk about it ... We've build friendships. And now we take care of each other ... There is a kind of self-help between victims ... and perhaps it helps to keep alive the memory of our family and ... help to prevent the return of such crimes.

Victims who testify in international criminal trials may not realize how profoundly they have been affected by the violent crimes they experienced or witnessed and the extent to which testifying can trigger past memories of those painful events. Violence often affects a victim's physical and psychological well-being. It can also dig deep into the psyche and undermine a victim's sense of safety and control. There is always the danger that disturbing memories and sensations can surface and overwhelm a survivor of violent crimes.

To make matters worse, international trials, like criminal trials, have the potential to produce the unexpected at any state of the proceedings. Either side may present evidence designed to challenge a victim participant's or witness's credibility. This constant state of uncertainty can place them in an intimidating position and throws the therapeutic benefit of bearing witness into doubt.

International criminal tribunals have a moral and often statutory obligation to ensure that outreach and education programs, protective measures, security arrangements, and psychosocial services are in place for victims and witnesses.

Outreach and education

Court outreach and education is the backbone of victim participation in international criminal trials. Yet our studies suggest that victim participants often lack sufficient information

[42] Ruth Maclean, '"I told my story face to face with Habré": courageous rape survivors make history' *The Guardian* (London, 18 September 2016) <https://www.theguardian.com/global-development/2016/sep/18/hissene-habre-chad-dictator-couragous-rape-survivors-make-history> accessed 25 June 2019. See also Kim Thuy Seelinger, 'Hissène Habré's rape acquittal must not be quietly airbrushed from history' *The Guardian* (London, 10 May 2017) <https://www.theguardian.com/global-development/2017/may/10/hissene-habre-acquittal-not-airbrushed-from-history-khadidja-zidane-kim-thuy-seelinger> accessed 25 June 2019.

to make informed decisions about their participation in legal proceedings.[43] For example, many ICC victims we interviewed, particularly in rural locations, believed the court operated primarily as an aid organization, rather than as a criminal court.[44] Few of these victims understood that participation in ICC meetings and proceedings had no bearing upon reparations decisions. Some even reported that they expected individual compensation for their participation. Effective victim participation thus requires that victims understand their rights to participation and reparation as well as a court's limitations, particularly with regard to direct assistance.[45]

Our 2015 study of ICC victim participants also found several factors that influenced *who* ended up registering as a victim participant. First, court outreach efforts often favoured men and more affluent victims. Several female victim participants told us that they were unable to attend court outreach events outside of their villages because they had to care for their children. Second, limited education and outreach programs in local languages and dialects reduced participation of non-English and non-French speaking victims. The language barrier also tended to favour the participation of more affluent victim participants with higher levels of education. Finally, victims who lived in more easily accessible locations, such as urban centres, had more regular contact with tribunal officials and thus better access to information about the court. These victims also had better access to newspapers and radios and were able to follow developments in court proceedings. The social dynamics of victim outreach requires further study, but evidence suggests that cultural, educational, and financial differences among victims significantly impact victims' participation in international justice.[46]

We do not know how victims' unequal access to justice impacts trials or reparations proceedings. More study is needed to understand barriers to victims' participation, particularly among women and the rural poor. Meanwhile, tribunal personnel should work to ensure that populations of victim participants mirror the universe of survivors whenever possible, and continue to ask the question: who is missing? Victim participation must not replicate social hierarchies and inequalities. Outreach and education programs can help to ensure that affected communities have equal access to information about cases and make informed decisions about their own legal participation.

Witness support, security, and protection

Courtrooms are hardly safe and secure environments for recounting traumatic events.[47] The adversarial nature of trial proceedings can result in unexpected events in the courtroom. A long repressed memory or sight of a photograph of a loved one can devastate even

[43] Human Rights Center, *The Victims' Court?* (n 19) 3.

[44] ibid 3.

[45] Carla Ferstman, 'The Participation of Victims in International Criminal Court Proceedings: A Review of the Practice and Consideration of Options for the Future' (*Redress*, October 2012) 24.

[46] Human Rights Center, *The Victims' Court?* (n 19) 74.

[47] David Mendeloff, 'Trauma and Vengeance: Assessing the Psychological and Emotional Effects of Post-Conflict Justice' (2009) 31 Human Rights Quarterly 592; Phuong N Pham, Harvey M Weinstein, and Timothy Longman, 'Trauma and PTSD Symptoms in Rwanda: Implications for Attitudes Toward Justice and Reconciliation' (2004) 292 Journal of American Medical Association 602; Judith Lewis Herman, 'The Mental Health of Crime Victims: Impact of Legal Intervention' (2003) 16 Journal of Traumatic Stress 159.

the most confident witness. Before testifying witnesses may worry about how they are going to perform on the stand or feel trepidation about confronting the accused. Some victim participants report feeling a heavy burden as they attempt to represent deceased family members in the presence of the accused. Before testifying in the Duch trial, for example, a female respondent wanted the accused to apologize for the death of her father at Toul Sleng prison. But she found what he said in the courtroom deeply disappointing:

> When I saw the accused I felt tense. But after we spoke and he accepted responsibility for the death of my father, it helped me release my tension. But then, in the end, he said he wasn't sure if I was my father's daughter. That really upset me. Why did he have to say that?[48]

Some victim participants and witnesses fear retribution after testifying in court. Even when using pseudonyms, or face and voice-altering technologies, they remain concerned about their safety. They are well aware that defendants often maintain active networks of supporters, some in high places, back in their communities. In the case of the Yugoslavia tribunal, for example, government authorities in the former Yugoslavia were largely responsible for the security of witnesses during the pre-trial and post-trial stages. Yet, these officials, especially in the tribunal's early years, paid little attention to such safety issues. Our study of eighty-three victim-witnesses found that while the majority said that on balance testifying before the ICTY had been a positive experience, and most said they would testify again. Of these, however, several stipulated that they would only testify again if afforded better protection on returning home.[49]

Victims' fears of testifying can be further compounded by the formality and adversarial character of legal proceedings.[50] The psychological toll of testifying can be particularly high for sexual violence survivors, children, and other vulnerable victims and witnesses. Many survivors of sexual violence, for example, fear for their safety and may face stigma once they return to their communities.[51] It is important therefore that tribunals establish Victims and Witnesses Sections and include staff with expertise in trauma, including trauma related to crimes of sexual violence.

In our study of 109 ICC witnesses the vast majority spoke highly of the services provided to them by the court's Victim and Witness Unit (VWU).[52] Respondents gave especially high marks to the counselling staff and their round-the-clock availability.[53] Many respondents, however, were concerned for their safety once they returned home. 'Now that I have completed my testimony, I hope the ICC does not abandon us', said one witness. Another noted: 'My life will look like the life of somebody who has enemies.' When witnesses return

[48] Stover, Balthazard, and Koenig (n 18) 528.

[49] Stover, *The Witnesses* (n 16) 100–03.

[50] Article 67(e) of Rome Statute gives defendants rights to 'examine, or have examined, the witnesses against him or her and to obtain the attendance and examination of witnesses on his or her behalf under the same conditions as witnesses against him or her . . .']

[51] See, for example, Kim Thuy Seelinger, Helene Silverberg, and Robin Mejia, 'The Investigation and Prosecution of Sexual Violence' (May 2011) Working Paper of the Sexual Violence and Accountability Project, Human Rights Center, University of California, Berkeley School of Law, 41–50 <https://www.law.berkeley.edu/wp-content/uploads/2015/04/The-Investigation-and-Prosecution-of-Sexual-Violence-SV-Working-Paper.pdf> accessed 15 June 2019.

[52] Human Rights Center, *Bearing Witness at the International Criminal Court* (n 17) 5.

[53] ibid 44.

home, the VWU does provide services to ensure their security. However, because of the need to safeguard confidentiality, the study was unable to access the effectiveness of these measures.[54] Additional research is needed to more fully evaluate long-term protection mechanisms provided by the ICC and other tribunals.

Participating in courtroom proceedings can be isolating for many victims. Most must leave family and friends and travel long distances to unfamiliar places in order to testify in trials. At the ICC, the VWU tries to mitigate these concerns through a number of procedures, which could be replicated in other national and international courts. Before traveling to The Hague, witnesses and victim participants are given a brochure and shown a video that explains what to anticipate at the court. These materials describe everything from the layout of the city and its weather to the trial process. Before traveling each witness undergoes a 'fit-to-travel' check, or medical check-up, to ensure that air travel will not pose a health risk. Potentially vulnerable witnesses also undergo a preliminary psychological assessment. If the assessment indicates witness vulnerability, a VWU psychologist schedules a full vulnerability assessment. Observations and conclusions of this secondary assessment, including recommendations for special measures, are submitted to the Chamber. Based on the report, the Chamber then decides on the capacity of the witness to testify as well as the use of any special measures.[55]

Tribunals also need to be attentive to victim and witness desires to travel with companions or dependents, particularly when the testifying witness is the primary caretaker of young children or nursing an infant. In general, ICC witnesses travel to The Hague without family or friends largely because of the costs involved. Only in exceptional cases have witnesses been allowed to travel with companions. For witnesses with small children and infants, the ability to stay together can be crucial to enabling the witness to testify. On occasion, witnesses will request to bring non-dependents to accompany them, especially if it is the witness's first trip abroad. In all of the cases, the VWU will analyse whether the request is reasonable given the court's limited budget.[56]

Our studies have found that victims, whether testifying as witnesses or victim participants, have a compelling need to tell their story and for their account to be recognized and acknowledged. In addition, many victims yearn to understand *why* defendants—who often are their fellow citizens and in some cases neighbours—had committed, or let their subordinates commit, such abominable acts. Yet witnesses generally are not encouraged to give expansive accounts or provide opinions about how they perceive or interpret events.[57] This is because the law is only interested in 'restrictive facts' and rarely gives quarter to expansive and nuanced story-telling.[58] In contrast to more restorative mechanisms, such as truth commissions or community-based justice mechanisms, criminal trials intentionally narrow questions of accountability to the defined elements of specific crimes. It's important

[54] ibid 62.
[55] ibid 12.
[56] ibid 21.
[57] Sara Kendall and Sarah Nouwen, 'Representational practices at the International Criminal Court: The gap between juridified and abstract victimhood' (2013) 76 Law and Contemporary Problems 235; Laurel E Fletcher, 'Refracted Justice: The Imagined Victim and the International Criminal Court' in Christian De Vos, Sara Kendall, and Carsten Stahn (eds) *Contested Justice: The Politics and Practice of International Criminal Court Interventions* (Cambridge University Press 2015).
[58] Martha Minow, *Between Vengeance and Forgiveness: Facing History after Genocide and Mass Violence* (Beacon Press 1998) 25–51.

to remember that even when victims have an overall positive experience in court, they may be disappointed that they could not present a fuller picture of events or they may experience moments of distress or negative feelings in response to some questions.

We need to understand more about the lasting impact of criminal prosecutions on the victims and witnesses who participate in proceedings. Victims' long-term feelings and recollections of trial may depend on their overall experience working with the tribunal and whether or not they find the outcome adequate to justify their participation and sacrifice. Unfortunately, longitudinal surveys of witnesses and victim participants are rarely conducted. This is especially true for witnesses who live in remote or insecure regions where tribunal personnel rarely venture. Given this concern, tribunals should incorporate survey-related practices that ensure the ongoing evaluation of witness experiences, with particular attention given to vulnerable witnesses and those in protection programs. Scholars have shown that witnesses who receive no post-trial follow-up often report feeling 'abandoned'.[59]

Local partnerships

International criminal tribunals are not humanitarian or development organizations, and they must be transparent with survivors about the limitations of what they can do. Few tribunals have sufficient resources to adequately address victims' psychosocial or material needs. Efforts to conduct outreach and education program can be hamstrung by finite budgets, and even witness protection programs can fall short of meeting the long-term needs of victim-witnesses. But there are good reasons for tribunals to avoid getting involved in relief or development actions. Direct aid from tribunals can create or exacerbate intergroup tensions in post-conflict settings or raise expectations that tribunals will deliver ambitious reconstruction well beyond their capacity. Additionally, direct support to victims can undermine public perceptions of judicial autonomy and impartiality, and ultimately the legitimacy of a tribunal.

Working with local partners can help to assuage some of these concerns and still allow the court to support victims and facilitate their participation in cases. Tribunals should explore partnerships with a variety of organizations, including local civil society organizations, national government bodies, and international donor and humanitarian organizations. While tribunals must preserve their legal autonomy and wall off criminal investigations and prosecutorial activities from such partnerships, these relationships present significant opportunities to increase victim inclusion, generate goodwill, and support post-conflict transitions in affected communities.

After the verdict

Victims in the Habré case reported feelings of elation when the chambers announced its guilty verdict and sentenced Habré to life in prison.[60] But survivors' feelings about trials and

[59] Catherine C Byrne, 'Benefit or Burden: Victims' Reflections on TRC Participation, Peace And Conflict' (2004) 10 Journal of Peace Psychology 237.

[60] Maclean, 'I told my story face to face with Habré' (n 42).

their own participation of them can change over time, sometimes in profound ways. Elation at a conviction can give way to more complex feelings of disappointment and even resentment when witnesses and victim participants return to their war-torn communities with little hope for economic improvement.

More research is needed into the long-term needs of witnesses and victim participants who participate in international criminal trials. Yet, courts, as a general practice, almost never collect *long-term* information from those who participate in judicial proceedings, including their attitudes about the court, verdict, or harms they may have suffered. As a result, we know little about how victims fare in the long-run following trials. Indeed, victims may face threats, assaults, relationship changes, or job losses as consequences of their participation in trials and tribunal personnel would likely never know.

Victims often have expectations for what a trial will achieve and how a tribunal will support them after a verdict is reached. Many presume that convictions will result in individual or collective compensation. And when courts fail to meet victims' expectations, they may feel abandoned or even betrayed, and thus their views of trials and criminal justice may change radically.

But why should tribunals—and the EAC in particular—care about the post-verdict experiences of witnesses and victim participants? After all, tribunals, which are often strapped for cash, are not designed to be social engineering institutions—nor should they be. Tribunals, principally through indictments and verdicts but also by having investigators on the ground, have both positive and negative impacts on the political and social life of the countries and regions where they hold jurisdiction. Recall the arrest, in March 2001, of Serbian ultranationalist and former president Slobodan Milošević in Belgrade and his transfer to stand trial in The Hague. His arrest caused considerable turmoil, including massive demonstrations in support of the fallen nationalist inside Serbia and the Republica Serbska and in Bosnia and Herzegovina.[61] Tribunals, of course, can't control such outcomes. What tribunals can—and should—do is put in place mechanisms, in collaboration with university research centres and local support and advocacy organizations, to monitor the welfare of witnesses and victim participants from the pre-trial phase through the post-trial phase.

The presence of Tribunal investigations on the ground can also impact communities in profound ways. In the late 1990s, for example, the ICTY dispatched teams of forensic investigators to the former Yugoslavia to exhume mass graves of thousands of persons who had gone missing during the Balkan conflict. The investigators were drawn from more than forty countries and interacted daily with family members, family organizations of the missing, and local government officials. The investigators had two principal objectives. The first was to collect physical evidence of mass killings through the identification and determination of the manner and cause of death of victims. The second was to return the remains of the deceased to the families for proper burial. This effort was eventually taken over by the International Commission of Missing Persons, which, working with local family organizations, established a regional DNA database to help with the identification efforts.

[61] Eric Stover, Victor Peskin, and Alexa Koenig, *Hiding in Plain Sight: The Pursuit of War Criminals from Nuremberg to the War on Terror* (University of California Press 2016) 161–66.

Today, memorials for the dead can be found at mass gravesites throughout the region.[62] Independent of criminal prosecutions such work can help to provide answers to survivors about the fate of disappeared loved ones and support transitional justice processes in affected communities.

Reparations for victims are another means by which tribunals can support survivors and their communities after conflict. In recent decades, reparations have evolved to include rights not only to restitution, but also to individual compensation and rehabilitation. The ICTY and ICTR, for example, included only restitution provisions, and so failed to provide redress to victims for wrongful deaths and other serious crimes.[63] However, the statutes of most modern tribunals, including the ICC and EAC, now contain more robust reparations provisions that permit judges to order both individual and collective reparations.[64] These legal innovations can have profound implications for victims and their communities. On the one hand, reparation processes provide victim participants with a more authoritative representation of their interests during and after the trial. On the other hand, reparations can raise the expectations of victims. For example, after the collapse of the Habré regime in 1992, thousands of victims have sought reparations for his crimes. Under immense pressure from victims groups, the Chadian Commission of Inquiry was formed to develop a reparations program. It recommended a range of reparations, most of which were never implemented. Victims then pressured the new Chadian government to provide reparations. When that effort failed, they turned to the EAC.[65]

The quest of reparations raises a number of questions: How do the civil parties in the Habré trial view this glacial pace in the actual awarding of court-mandated reparations? How do the thousands of other victims who did not register as civil parties or were deemed ineligible for one reason or another feel about not being included in the court's ruling in favour of reparations? And how will the civil parties feel if institutions fail to raise the necessary funds?

These are not purely academic questions.[66] Many commentators have hailed the EAC as a model for future African courts mandated to deal with serious international crimes.[67] Moreover, if the ICC's complementarity efforts to promote domestic trials involving serious international crimes ever takes hold, we may see more national and regional courts being established with provisions for individual and collective reparations without fully understanding how they may be perceived by victims and their communities. For this reason, as

[62] Eric Stover and Rachel Shigekane, 'Exhumation of Mass Graves: Balancing Legal and Humanitarian Needs' in Eric Stover and Harvey Weinstein (eds), *My Neighbor, My Enemy: Justice and Community in the Aftermath of Mass Atrocity* (Cambridge University Press 2004) 85–103.

[63] Liesbeth Zegveld, 'Victims' Reparations Claims and International Criminal Courts: Incompatible Values?' (2010) 8 Journal of International Criminal Justice 79, 87–8.

[64] Kristin Kalla and Peter Dixon, 'Learning from the TFV's Second Mandate: From Implementing Rehabilitation Assistance to Reparations, Fall 2010 Programme Progress Report' (ICC Trust Fund for Victims, 2010; Nader Iskandar Diab, 'Challenges in the Implementation of the Reparation Award against Hissein Habré: Can the Spell of Unenforceable Awards across the Globe be Broken?' (2018) 16 J Intl Crim Justice 141.

[65] Christoph Sperfeldt, 'The Trial Against Hissene Habré: Networked Justice and Reparations at the Extraordinary African Chambers' (2017) 21 International Journal of Human Rights 1243; Nader Isdandar Diab, 'Challenges in the Implementation of the Reparation Award against Hissein Habré: Can the Spell of Unenforceable Awards across the Globe by Broken?' (2018) 16 Journal of International Criminal Justice 141.

[66] Diab (n 64).

[67] Celeste Hicks, 'The Trial of Hissene Habré and What it Could Mean for Justice in Africa' (*Justice in Conflict*, 27 March 2018) <https://justiceinconflict.org/2018/03/27/the-trial-of-hissene-habre-and-what-it-could-mean-for-justice-in-africa/> accessed 14 March 2018.

well as potential security and welfare issues that can arise following trials, tribunals must continue to assess the long-term needs of witnesses and victim participants.

Conclusion

We argue in this chapter that international criminal tribunals, whether based in The Hague or in the countries and regions where mass atrocities took place, should strive to operate as independent legal institutions unaffected by international and national politics. At the same time, they have a duty to victims and witnesses to make the process of testifying in trials as safe, respectful, and dignified an experience as possible. They also have a responsibility to monitor the welfare of victims and witnesses throughout the trial process and, in partnership with local organizations and research centres, access how court actions are affecting communities torn apart by war and political violence.

As the world community turns increasingly to international criminal justice to respond to mass atrocity, we must shed the grandiose assumption that 'revealing is healing' and acknowledge that testifying in a criminal trial can have both good and ill effects. Testifying can be a positive experience for victim participants and witnesses under some conditions.[68] Ongoing assessment of those conditions during investigations, prosecutions, and reparations can improve victims' perceptions of procedural fairness and also the legitimacy of tribunals.

It is also imperative that tribunals establish programs to protect victims and witnesses and monitor their security and welfare. These programs should include staff with expertise in trauma and an understanding of the cultural, political, and security dynamics of the conflict situations under investigation. Some individuals and groups may require particular types of support to feel safe and secure working with criminal tribunals. In some national jurisdictions, for example, special precautions and procedures have been developed to protect vulnerable legal participants, especially children, the disabled, and survivors of sexual violence.

Since the establishment of the ICTY in 1993, we have learned a great deal about the interactions between international criminal tribunals and victims and witnesses and their communities. Yet more research is needed in a number of areas. First, we need to better understand the experiences of women who testify before international tribunals. Our research has shown that women participate in ICC trials at rates far lower than men.[69] It is important to assess why this is, and to identify ways of improving the ability of women to testify in proceedings. Anecdotal evidence suggests, for example, that prosecutors may be less likely to ask women to testify, except in cases dealing with sexual violence.[70]

Second, we need to develop better procedures for informing victims and their communities about a court's limitations, especially if it has the mandate to issue reparations. This is a herculean task, especially as many victims see courts as their last resort, the place where

[68] See, for example, David Mendeloff, 'Trauma and Vengeance: Assessing the Psychological and Emotional Effects of Post-Conflict Justice' (2009) 31 Human Rights Quarterly 593; Raquel Aldana, 'A Victim-Centered Reflection on Truth Commissions and Prosecutions as a Response to Mass Atrocities' (2006) 5 Journal of Human Rights 107.

[69] Human Rights Center, *Bearing Witness at the International Criminal Court* (n 17) 38.

[70] ibid 27.

they can be heard and receive justice but also obtain funds to rebuild their lives and communities. Yet court-ordered reparations are far from straightforward.[71] They depend on the rulings of judges, who may provide for reparations or deny them. Reparations come in many forms ranging from financial compensation to collective reparations including funds for development projects, building monuments in memory of victims, and vocational training programs for the children of victims. Reparations are often dependent on the resources of the accused and the ability to access those funds or may be overseen by trust funds supported by financial contributions from governments. Moreover, individuals and communities affected by mass violence may not agree on which form of reparations best suits their needs. Such disagreements may exacerbate existing tensions. All of these factors suggest that further research needs to be conducted to better understand the challenges courts face in implementing reparation programs.

Finally, more research needs to be conducted on how international criminal tribunals, principally through the Registry and Office of the Prosecutor, can work collaboratively with victim associations and other local organizations to meet the needs of victim participants and witnesses. Our studies suggest that these organizations are a tremendous—and often untapped asset—for international criminal tribunals. They can facilitate outreach efforts; help victims with the bureaucratic demands of traveling to a court to testify; distribute informational brochures about a court's procedures and limitations; update victims and witnesses about case developments; and help coordinate the access of researchers who wish to interview victim participants and witnesses about their opinions and attitudes about their interaction with courts. Yet, to date, few systematic studies have focused on local organizations that perform all or some of these functions. We hope that many of these voids in our understandings of victims' experiences of international justice will be filled in the coming years.

[71] Peter J Dixon, 'Reparations, assistance and the experience of justice: Lessons from Colombia and the Democratic Republic of the Congo' (2015) 10 International Journal of Transitional Justice 88.

36

Reparations and the Habré Trial in Context

Christoph Sperfeldt

Introduction

One of the interesting features of the Extraordinary African Chambers (EAC) is that its victim participation scheme allows individual victims of crime to submit claims for reparations.[1] The promise that reparations can be delivered through international criminal justice has now been around for more than two decades, but the first practice has only emerged in the last few years. The adjudication of the first reparations claims before the International Criminal Court (ICC) and the Extraordinary Chambers in the Courts of Cambodia (ECCC) has been arduous and revealed disagreement within and outside these courts over the nature, extent and purpose of reparations in an international criminal justice framework.[2] Considerable uncertainty surrounds whether these reparations schemes can live up to expectations placed upon them. It is in this context that an examination and a comparative discussion of the EAC's approach to reparations might provide some fruitful insights.

Claims and aspirations for reparations have been around since the fall of the Habré regime. In 1992, the Chadian Commission of Inquiry recommended a range of reparative measures.[3] Most of these recommendations were never followed up. Local victim associations called on Chad's government to compensate victims. In 2005, the *Association des Victimes de Crimes et Repressions Politiques* (AVCRP) even presented the government with a draft law on victim compensation, which was not taken up by the legislator.[4] While the Chadian government acknowledged, in 2013, that victims could be compensated, it has not taken any serious steps to set up a state-sponsored reparations program.[5]

The EAC statutory reparations provisions blend the Senegalese civil party system with selective borrowing from the ICC's reparations mandate. Yet, these provisions remain ambiguous and do not provide a functioning, lone-standing framework for an effective reparations order. It was thus no surprise that the EAC judges, when ordering reparations, relied

[1] This chapter builds upon and expands an earlier article published at Christoph Sperfeldt, 'The Trial against Hissène Habré: Networked Justice and Reparations at the Extraordinary African Chambers' (2017) 21 International Journal of Human Rights 1243–60.

[2] See for instance Conor McCarthy, 'Victim Redress and International Criminal Justice: Competing Paradigms, or Compatible Forms of Justice?' (2012) 10 Journal of International Criminal Justice 351–72; Luke Moffett, 'Reparations for Victims at the International Criminal Court: A New Way Forward?' (2017) 21 International Journal of Human Rights 1204–22; and Liesbeth Zegveld, 'Victims' Reparations Claims and International Criminal Courts' (2010) 8 Journal of International Criminal Justice 79–111.

[3] 'Les Crimes et Détournements de l'ex-Président Habré et de ses Complices', Rapport de la Commission d'Enquête Nationale du Ministère de la Justice (Paris, L'Harmattan, 1993), 98–99. (hereafter Commission of Inquiry Report)

[4] Human Rights Watch, 'Chad: The Victims of Hissene Habre Still Awaiting Justice' (2005) 30. Available at <https://www.hrw.org/reports/2005/chad0705/> accessed 22 December 2017

[5] See Human Rights Watch's Q&A on the Habré trial at <https://www.hrw.org/news/2016/05/03/qa-case-hissene-habre-extraordinary-african-chambers-senegal#17> accessed 21 December 2017.

Christoph Sperfeldt, *Reparations and the Habré Trial in Context* In: *The President on Trial*. First edition. Edited by: Sharon Weill, Kim Thuy Seelinger, and Kerstin Bree Carlson, Oxford University Press (2020). © Christoph Sperfeldt.
DOI: 10.1093/oso/9780198858621.003.0037

mainly on the framework they were familiar with from domestic practice. In this chapter, I examine the reparations process in the Habré trial and bring it into conversation with the experience of other international(-ized) criminal courts with a reparations mandate, most notably the ICC and the ECCC—the latter being the only other hybrid criminal court with a civil party scheme.

The EAC's reparations framework

The EAC Statute provides for the participation of direct and indirect victims of crime as *parties civiles*, based on similar provisions in Senegalese criminal procedural law.[6] Like with other countries following the civil law tradition, the civil party system allows for reparations claims to be made in the framework of the criminal trial. Yet, the EAC Statute broadens these provisions in two important ways. First, the Statute under Article 27(1) stipulates that reparations measures 'shall include restitution, compensation and rehabilitation'.[7] Second, Article 28 concerns provisions for the establishment of a Trust Fund for the benefit of victims,[8] which suggests that the drafters were mindful of incorporating provisions into the Statute that allow for a more flexible approach to reparations beyond the strict boundaries of the criminal trial. This is visible in provisions enabling external voluntary contributions to the Trust Fund and the award of reparations to 'victims', whether or not they participated in the proceedings.[9]

The trial judgment on reparations (2016)

Reparations were the last issue addressed at trial. After rendering the criminal judgment against Habré on 30 May 2016, the EAC Trial Chamber took less than two months to consider and rule on civil parties' reparations submissions. The Trial Chamber received two civil party reparations claims—one by civil parties associated with the *Association des Victimes de Crimes du Régimes de Hissène Habré* (AVCRHH) then representing 4,733 victims, and one joint submission by the AVCRP and the *Reseau des Associations des Droits de l'Homme du Tchad* (RADHT), then representing a total of 3,850 victims.[10]

[6] Civil parties may be formed at any stage during the investigative stage, and victims may choose to form groups with joint representatives. See Art 14 of the EAC Statute.

[7] EAC Statute, Art 27 (1) and (2). This language is similar to the one used in the ICC Rome Statute (Art 75(2)). Other provisions under Art 27 also seem to be adapted directly from the Rome Statute with little change. Art 27(3) on the possibility of observations by convicted person, victims, and other interested persons or States is similar to Art 75(3) in the Rome Statute; and Art 27(4) on the preservation of victims' rights under national and international law is identical to Art 75(6) in the Rome Statute.

[8] See EAC Statute, Art 28 (1) and (2). Art 27(2) states that the EAC 'may order that the award for reparation be made through the Trust Fund', indicating the EAC can use the Trust Fund as an intermediary for a reparations order.

[9] EAC Statute, Art 28(1) and (2).

[10] Reparations Submission by Civil Parties Abaifouta et al., *Ministère Public c. Hissein Habré*, 10 June 2016 (hereafter Reparations Submission Abaifouta et al); and Reparations Submission by Victim Groups AVCRP and RADHT, *Ministère Public c. Hissein Habré*, 10 June 2016 (hereafter Reparations Submission AVCRP and RADHT).

Preparing for reparations

In interviews with lawyers and victim representatives before the trial proceedings in mid-2015, it was obvious that not much thought had gone into the reparations claim—the focus was visibly on the criminal trial.[11] The Habré trial is here no exception compared to other mass atrocity trials that combine criminal action with reparations. The reasons for late action on reparations at these courts are manifold, including judges' respect for the presumption of innocence and civil party lawyers' focus on the criminal proceedings. Indeed, reparations remain a secondary issue, subordinated to the criminal trial. As a result, both courts and victim lawyers are frequently underprepared for reparations, leaving little time for consultations with participating victims and a more thorough consideration of the many complex issues involved with conceiving reparations in the aftermath of mass atrocities.

At the reparations stage, the transnational advocacy coalition around Human Rights Watch and the *Association Tchadienne pour la Promotion et la Defense des Droits de l'Homme* (ATPDH) facilitated the involvement of more specialized expertise on reparations, such as from Redress.[12] Efforts to establish a trust fund gained momentum after the conclusion of trial hearings, but a proactive strategy from civil party representatives and enthusiasm among decision-makers was lacking. The EAC administration was working against a tight budget and timeline to complete the trial, and the donor committee did not seem to be motivated to assist with a mechanism that would require additional funding.[13]

Yet, some limited consultations with Chadian civil parties took place between the Closing Hearings and the pronouncement of the judgment in 2016.[14] One of the most significant differences between the Habré trial and the first cases at the ICC and the ECCC is that civil party participation at the EAC could rely on well-organized victim associations in Chad which—in conjunction with local and international NGOs—were able to gather and channel civil parties' inputs into the court process. This has also aided the reparations process, mainly by providing civil parties with a more authoritative and coherent representation of their interests during and after the trial.

Defining the beneficiaries of reparations

At the EAC, civil party status is the main entry point for survivors to claim reparations.[15] A range of legal parameters determine whom courts recognize as 'victims', including limited jurisdiction, selective investigations and prosecutions, procedural obstacles (eg awareness among survivors, evidentiary requirements) and judicial findings. Applying these parameters to the broad universe of victims in a given atrocity situation, such as Chad, gradually narrows the numbers of 'legal victims'.[16] These legal categories are important, as

[11] Interview with civil party lawyer, Dakar, 21 July 2015.

[12] See also Redress, 'Time to Repair the Harm to the Victims of the Habré's Regime', press release, 30 May 2016.

[13] Telephone interview with court observer, 21 March 2016.

[14] The AVCRHH reported consultations, including by way of twenty-three civil party focal points. See Reparations Submission Abaifouta et al (n 10), paras 28–29.

[15] For more on the ECCC reparations experience refer to Christoph Sperfeldt, 'Collective Reparations at the Extraordinary Chambers in the Courts of Cambodia' (2012) 12 International Criminal Law Review 457–89.

[16] Kendall and Nouwen refer to this as a 'pyramid of juridified victimhood'. See Sara Kendall and Sarah Nouwen, 'Representational Practices at the International Criminal Court: The Gap between Juridified and Abstract Victimhood' (2013) 76 Law and Contemporary Problems 235–62.

they determine eligibility for reparations before international(-ized) criminal courts. In its judgement, the Trial Chamber declared admissible only claims from victims it was able to identify and for which it had received some form of verification.[17] This included those who were heard during the EAC's investigative missions to Chad (around 2,500) or appeared before the judges during hearings, as well as those who produced some form of identification documents or notary statements. The judgment provided various annexes with names of eligible civil parties, but did not provide a total number of eligible civil parties.

Calculating the compensation

Both civil party claims had expressed a preference for individual financial compensation. For the purpose of calculating the compensation requests, civil party lawyers borrowed from mass claims processes and categorized victims into groups on the basis of the nature of the harm they suffered.[18] Two of the five suggested sub-groups of direct victims specifically dealt with the harm suffered by victims of sexual violence. AVCRHH's lawyers requested for those victims a higher amount of compensation than they had demanded for other victims of torture, also to cover costs for physical, mental and reproductive health care.[19] In addition, civil parties affiliated with the AVCRHH asked to complement monetary compensation with some collective reparations measures, including development projects in survivors' communities, monuments at massacre sites, inclusion of the Habré period into the teaching curriculum in schools, declaring the day of the EAC guilty verdict as a memorial day, and building educational and training centres for the victims' children in various communities.[20] The defence did not provide any substantive comments on these reparations claims.[21] Adjusting the proposed victim categories, the Trial Chamber, in its judgment, granted compensation to admissible victims as follows: CFA 20 million for each victim of sexual violence; CFA 15 million for victims of arbitrary detention and torture, prisoners of war and survivors of massacres; and CFA 10 million for indirect victims.[22] The judges rejected all proposed collective measures.

The appeals judgment on reparations (2017)

The civil parties appealed the reparations order, lamenting in particular issues relating to civil party admissibility, uncertainties with the compensation order and the rejection of

[17] *Ministère Public v Hissein Habré* (Judgment), civil judgment rendered on 29 July 2016, published in conjunction with criminal judgment, paras 43–53 (hereafter Trial Reparations Judgment).

[18] These included the categories of direct victims—with five sub-categories relating to arbitrary detention and torture, victims of rape in detention, victims of sexual slavery, victims of massacres, and prisoners of war—and indirect victims. Reparations Submission Abaifouta et al (n 10), paras 33–36.

[19] Reparations Submission Abaifouta et al (n 10), paras 126–46.

[20] Reparations Submission Abaifouta et al (n 10), paras 147–52.

[21] The defence argued in its late submission that the Trial Chamber was irregularly constituted and as such civil claims should be discontinued. See Order by the Trial Chamber to Declare Inadmissible the Defence Submission on Civil Interests, *Ministère Public c. Hissein Habré*, 5 July 2016.

[22] At the time of writing, CFA 20 million and CFA 15 million converted to approximately US$34,000 and US$25,000 respectively. It remained unclear whether the compensation was to be made by way of a trust fund, which was not mentioned in the judgment. See also Trial Reparations Judgment (n 17), paras 59–68.

collective reparations.[23] Through its more reasoned decision, pronounced in conjunction with the appeals judgment on 27 April 2017, the Appeals Chamber addressed most of the civil parties' grounds of appeal.[24]

Civil parties appealed the fact that the Trial Chamber failed to provide such a number and thus left ambiguous the exact number of beneficiaries of reparations. The Appeals Chamber remedied this omission and provided a more detailed assessment of the claims on the basis of additional information provided by the civil parties. The appeals judges eventually recognized a total of 7,396 civil parties, both direct and indirect victims, but declared inadmissible the claims of another 3,489 individual victims.[25] At the same time, the appeals judges recognized the limitations of the criminal trial and left an opening for the Trust Fund to engage with other victim populations beyond the civil parties at trial. More specifically, the judges invited the Fund to consider any additional evidence brought forward by rejected civil parties and applications for reparations from victims who had not participated in the trial.[26]

In determining the admissibility of civil parties, the Appeals Chamber relied to a great extent on jurisprudence from Case 001 at the ECCC, whose civil party system the judges found to bear great similarities with the EAC's own civil party scheme.[27] Yet, the judges did not consider the ECCC's much more flexible handling of civil party admissibility in its second case.[28] Still, the participation of such a large number of civil parties in a distant court—without much support from the EAC itself, and against great logistical challenges—can be considered an achievement. These participation outcomes, larger than in any case before the ICC or ECCC to date, were only possible due to the more structured representation provided by Chadian victim associations.

Furthermore, the appeals judges largely confirmed the compensation amounts set by the Trial Chamber, but in addition also calculated the total liability and ordered Habré to pay over CFA 82 billion (almost US$140 million) to the civil parties.[29] Considering that the EAC ended its operations in mid-2017, the Appeals Chamber instructed the Trust Fund to implement the compensation order.[30] Hence, the final outcome was a substantial reparations order against Hissène Habré that left open many questions regarding its implementation.

[23] Appeals Reparations Submission by Civil Parties Abaifouta et al, *Ministère Public v Hissein Habré*, 5 December 2016 (hereafter Appeals Reparations Submission Abaifouta et al); and Appeals Reparations Submission by Victim Groups AVCRP and RADHT, *Ministère Public c. Hissein Habré*, 5 December 2016 (hereafter Appeals Reparations Submission AVCRP and RADHT).

[24] *Le Procureur Général c. Hissein Habré* (Appeals judgment), 27 April 2017, 226 (hereafter Appeals Reparations Judgment).

[25] ibid 226.

[26] ibid paras 607–09.

[27] ibid paras 657–58.

[28] See the ECCC Pre-Trial Chamber's finding of a 'collective injury' when admitting a larger number of previously rejected civil parties back into Case 002. 'Decision on Appeals against Orders of the Co-Investigating Judges on the Admissibility of Civil Party Applications', *Case File No. 002/19-09-2007-ECCC/OCIJ*, D404/2/4, 24 June 2011.

[29] Appeals Reparations Judgment (n 24), paras 938–39.

[30] ibid paras 607–10.

Individual vs collective reparations

One of the dilemmas for (internationalized) criminal courts with a reparations mandate is how to deal with the effects of their limited, exclusionary participation schemes. Those considering more broadly the societal implications of reparations at the ICC and the ECCC tried to compensate these perceived shortcomings by proposing modalities that would benefit broader victim constituencies. Collective reparations in particular have often been regarded as the most appropriate and feasible answer to the reparations conundrum in international criminal justice—at times against the expressed preferences of victim participants. The ECCC, whose mandate is limited to collective and moral reparations only, and the Trial Chamber in the Lubanga case chose such pathways.[31]

Unlike some of their colleagues at the ICC and the ECCC,[32] the EAC judges refused to consider broader reparations measures known from a context of state responsibility, such as certain types of satisfaction or more far-reaching guarantees of non-repetition. Instead, they settled early on an accountability-based conception of reparations inherent in the traditional civil party claim, with its focus on reparations to the victims before the court. Noting the persistence of harm largely at the individual or family level and citing a general lack of confidence in communal or state structures, civil parties themselves had expressed a strong preference for individual monetary compensation.[33] With the establishment of a trust fund still under way, the EAC judges did what they knew best from their domestic practice: they simply calculated Habre's liability and ordered reparations against the convicted person for the exclusive benefit of the identified civil parties before them.

The EAC reparations judgments bear a certain similarity the ICC's approach in the aftermath of the 2015 appeals reparations judgment in the Lubanga case. Yet, both the ICC and the ECCC have frequently stressed the imperative of expectation management and remained therefore hesitant to engage discussions about individual monetary compensation. This has gradually changed with the ICC eventually giving in to victims' preference for monetary awards and adopting a symbolic compensation approach in the Katanga and Al Mahdi cases.[34]

In addition to compensation, civil parties affiliated with the AVCRHH had also asked to set aside 30 per cent of the claimed amount to finance collective reparations measures, including various development projects in survivors' communities, monuments at massacre sites, inclusion of the Habré period into the school curriculum and declaring the day of Habré's verdict as a memorial day.[35]

The Trial Chamber rejected all collective reparations requests, mainly on the grounds that they lacked specificity and did not provide sufficient detail—such as costs, exact location of monuments or precise nature of development programs—that would have allowed

[31] *The Prosecutor v Thomas Lubanga Dyilo*, 'Decision Establishing the Principles and Procedures to Be Applied to Reparations' (Reparations Decision) (2012) ICC-01/04-01/06-2904. See also Sperfeldt, 'Collective Reparations' (n 15).

[32] See also Marissa Brodney, 'Implementing International Criminal Court-Ordered Collective Reparations: Unpacking Present Debates' (2016) 1 JOXCSLS 1–35.

[33] See Reparations Submission Abaifouta et al (n 10), paras 30–31.

[34] In both cases, ICC judges ordered a symbolic payment of US$250 to eligible victims. See *Prosecutor v Germain Katanga*, 'Order for Reparations Pursuant to Article 75 of the Statute' (Reparations Judgment) ICC-01/04-01/07-3728-tENG, 24 March 2017.

[35] Reparations Submission Abaifouta et al (n 10) para 148, 49.

the judges to assess their feasibility.[36] Moreover, the Chamber rejected all measures that would have required an involvement or consent of the Chadian state, including those relating to school education and the public commemoration day. The judges argued that the Chadian state was not party to the proceedings, and it was therefore unable to impose obligations on the state.[37] The EAC trial judges' reasoning for rejecting collective measures is strikingly similar to the way ECCC judges had dealt with such claims in Case 001.[38]

The EAC Appeals Chamber essentially agreed with the Trial Chamber ruling, but made the additional effort of seeking the views of the Chadian state on collective reparations.[39] The final judgment merely noted that 'the Chadian government did not respond favourably to the collective reparations solicited by the civil parties'.[40] The Appeals Chamber then rejected the civil parties' appeal, concluding that it could not order collective awards that infringe on the sovereignty of the Chadian state and whose feasibility appears hypothetical and uncertain.[41] Nevertheless, the appeals judges recognized the importance of collective reparations and therefore invited the Trust Fund to work with the victim associations on their realization.[42]

Responsibility for reparations: The convicted person

A central tenet of accountability-based conceptions of reparations is the responsibility and liability of convicted persons for reparations. Here also lays one of the dilemmas: Not only are convicted persons' assets never enough to afford relief for the harm caused by mass atrocities, but often these assets are also out of reach. Civil party lawyers had highlighted the importance of ordering compensation independently of the availability of funds.[43] In ordering compensation purely on the basis of harm and thus above and beyond the known assets of the convicted person, the Trial Chamber arguably followed domestic practice, and is similar to the stance adopted by the ICC in the Lubanga case. Yet, the approach diverts from the practice at the ECCC, where judges resisted issuing what they called 'fictitious awards'—awards that, even if symbolically important, would be substantively void with little prospect for implementation and therefore frustrate victims.[44]

Early in the proceedings, in 2013, the EAC investigating judges had ordered the identification and preservations of Habré's assets.[45] The Trial Chamber later noted

[36] Trial Reparations Judgment (n 17), paras 69–70.

[37] ibid, para 71.

[38] See ECCC Supreme Court Chamber, 'Appeals Judgment' [2012] Case File No. 001/18-07-2007-ECCC/SC (hereafter ECCC Case 001 Appeals Judgment).

[39] On 18 January 2017, the EAC Appeals Chamber sent a letter to the Chadian Ministry of Justice to invite observations by the Chadian State. It received a response on 18 April 2017. Appeals Reparations Judgment (n 24), paras 863–65.

[40] ibid para 843.

[41] ibid para 848.

[42] ibid paras 612 and 847.

[43] Reparations Submission Abaifouta et al (n 10), paras 153–57.

[44] The ECCC judges justified this as follows, 'it is of primary importance to limit reparations to such awards that can realistically be implemented so as to avoid the issuance of orders that, in all probability, will never be enforced and would be confusing and frustrating for the victims'. ECCC Case 001 Appeals Judgment (n 38), para 667.

[45] Trial Reparations Judgment (n 17), paras 65 and 73. It has been claimed that Hissène Habré took considerable public assets within him when he fled from Chad.

that Senegalese authorities had confiscated one property in Dakar and two bank accounts.[46]

The EAC investigating judges' action to preserve Habré's assets, including for reparations purposes, was swifter than that of its peers at the ICC or ECCC—also because it could rely on powers under Senegalese criminal procedural law that other courts lacked. Despite all the rhetoric in international criminal justice surrounding the importance of convicted persons' liability for reparations, only limited capacities are devoted to investigating the assets of defendants. Most accused in the first cases at the ICC and the ECCC have been declared indigent.[47] Against this background, the EAC's record of securing at least some assets for reparations purposes is respectable. In fact, the value of these frozen assets, estimated in media reports and by observers at below US$ 1 million,[48] is comparable to the funds made available so far by the ICC Trust Fund for Victims for reparations in the Katanga case. Still, Habré's known and other personal assets potentially located in future are likely to fall drastically short of what is needed to satisfy the EAC's reparations order.

Responsibility for reparations: The state

Victim representatives in (internationalized) criminal trials therefore also try to raise notions of state responsibility for reparations. At the EAC, the AVCRP, and RADHT asked the Trial Chamber in their reparations submission to declare the Chadian state responsible for reparations, so that it could contribute to reparations.[49] Similar to the matter of collective reparations, the Trial Chamber rejected these requests on the basis that the Chadian state was not party to the proceedings.[50] The EAC Statute also limits jurisdiction to natural persons only.[51]

Whilst the Chadian state has contributed to the costs of the EAC and even pledged to provide some funds to the future Trust Fund,[52] it has so far resisted acknowledging its broader responsibility for reparations. What is more, in 2014, the Chadian government had asked to join the proceedings before the EAC as a civil party on the grounds that the state had suffered harm when Habré pillaged the country.[53] Thus, rather than taking responsibility as a state for the crimes committed by the former regime, the Chadian government portrayed itself as a victim of these crimes. The EAC judges refused to admit the application, as these

[46] It is also believed that Habré might hold further assets in Europe. Such assets could be reclaimed through requests under mutual legal assistance, an avenue not pursued by the EAC or Senegalese authorities. The Appeals Chamber suggested that such tasks might fall onto the Trust Fund, including monitoring Habré's financial situation. Appeals Reparations Judgment (n 24), 226.

[47] An exception is here the Bemba case, where some assets were confiscated. See more at Manuel Galvis Martinez, 'Forfeiture of Assets at the International Criminal Court' (2014) 12 Journal of International Criminal Justice 193–217.

[48] Various media reports and observers estimated the value of the property at around EUR 700.000. Author's interview with international NGO staff, 29 May 2015.

[49] Reparations Submission AVCRP and RADHT (n 10), 16.

[50] Trial Reparations Judgment (n 17), paras 75–76.

[51] EAC Statute, Art 10(1).

[52] So at N Diab, 'Challenges in the Implementation of the Reparation Award Against Hissein Habré: Can the Spell of Unenforceable Awards across the Globe Be Broken?' (2018) 16 Journal of International Criminal Justice 141–63.

[53] The Chadian government claimed that Habré stole an estimated CFA 7 billion (about EUR 10 million) from the treasury. Nathalie Magnien, 'Chad Can't Be a Civil Party in Habre Case, Rules EAC', International Justice Tribune, 10 September 2014.

crimes went beyond the Court's jurisdiction.[54] The Chadian state's attempt has little precedent in international criminal law. The Rwandan government sought, in 1998, to join the Bagosora case at the International Criminal Tribunal for Rwanda (ICTR) as *amicus curiae* and to make submissions in relation to restitution of property and assets allegedly taken by the accused. The ICTR judges denied the request arguing that the Prosecutor's indictments did not allege that the accused unlawfully took property.[55]

The Chadian state's responsibility also became the subject of proceedings in domestic courts. A Chadian court in N'Djamena unexpectedly convicted, on 25 March 2015, a number of former high-ranking security agents of Habré's regime.[56] The judgment included a comprehensive reparations order, granting CFA 75 billion in total to around 7,000 civil parties participating in the trial. Declaring the Chadian state 'civilement responsable', the judgment stipulated that 50 per cent of the amount be carried by the state and 50 per cent by the convicted persons.[57] While none of these measures have been implemented so far, the order itself was a stunning turn-around in a domestic context where all previous attempts at justice for the victims of Habré's regime vis-à-vis the Chadian state had stalled.[58] More than two years later, in November 2017, 7,000 victims filed a complaint against the Chadian government before the African Commission on Human and Peoples' Rights, claiming that the government failed to comply with the judgment and its international obligations.[59]

Establishing a trust fund

Whilst a trust fund was part of the EAC's statutory reparations framework, it had not yet established when the Trial Chamber delivered its reparations order. As a consequence, the Fund does not feature in the EAC's first reparations order, which did not stipulate the procedures for implementing the ambitious reparations award.[60] The civil parties and victim advocates asked the Appeals Chamber to rectify this shortcoming and to put the Trust Fund at the core of operationalizing reparations at the EAC.[61]

The EAC Appeals Chamber followed the appellants' arguments and made a number of rulings that set the Trust Fund at the centre of implementing reparations in the aftermath

[54] Trial Reparations Judgment (n 17), para 81.

[55] *The Prosecutor v Theoneste Bagosora et al*, 'Decision on Amicus Curiae Request by the Rwandan Government', Case No ICTR-98-41-T, 13 October 2004. Belgium had made similar unsuccessful requests to the ICTR to intervene on behalf of Belgian citizen affected by the crimes. See *The Prosecutor v Theoneste Bagosora*, 'Decision on the Amicus Curiae Application by the Government of the Kingdom of Belgium', Case No ICTR-96-7-T, 6 June 1998.

[56] *Ministère public et Ismael Hachim et autre contre Saleh Younous, Warou Fadoul Ali et Autres*, Arrêt Criminel, Répertoire No 01/15, 25 March 2015.

[57] In addition, the court ordered that a memorial be established within a year for those who were killed under the Habré regime and that the former DDS premises in the capital be turned into a museum. See *Ministère public et Ismael Hachim et autre contre Saleh Younous, Warou Fadoul Ali et Autres*, Arrêt Criminel, Répertoire No 01/15, 25 March 2015.

[58] See Human Rights Watch, 'Tchad: Le gouvernement n'a toujours pas indemnise les victimes du régime de Hissene Habré', 24 March 2016. Available at <https://www.hrw.org/fr/news/2016/03/24/tchad-le-gouvernement-na-toujours-pas-indemnise-les-victimes-du-regime-de-hissene> accessed 21 December 2017.

[59] *Clement Abaifouta and 6,999 Others v Republic of Chad*, Communication to the African Commission on Human and Peoples' Rights, assisted by the Association Tchadienne pour la Promotion et la Défense des Droits de l'Homme (ATPDH), The Redress Trust (Redress), Human Rights Watch (HRW), 10 November 2017.

[60] See Diab, 'Challenges in the Implementation of the Reparation Award' (n 52).

[61] See appeals submission of Abaifouta Clement et al, para 64. See also Redress, 'Demande d'autorisation de présenter une soumission d'amicus curiae concernant la question des réparations', Submitted to EAC Appeals Chamber, 8 February 2017.

of the Habré trial. Among others, the judges tasked the Fund with implementing the individual reparations order and further ruled that all frozen assets and relevant judicial records, including civil party files, be turned over to the Trust Fund.[62] The judges stressed that all assets be exclusively used for reparations purposes and not for the Fund's operational costs.[63] The Chamber also invited the Fund to collaborate with the civil parties, the Chadian government and other interested organizations on the implementation of collective reparations. Thus, the implementation of the EAC's court-ordered reparations now fully hangs on an institution that so far only exists on paper.

The Trust Fund was formally created by resolution under the auspices of the African Union (AU) in July 2016.[64] At the time of writing, the Fund's parameters and its statute are still being debated. Drafts of the statute foresee a mixed Board of Directors with members from the AU, the Chadian government, victim representatives and Chadian civil society. Following the dissolution of the EAC in Dakar, the Trust Fund's secretariat is likely to be based in N'Djamena, which would require additional agreements between the AU and Chad.

In establishing a trust fund to implement reparations for the victims of the Habré regime, the EAC seems to have followed the ICC model. Yet, the example of the ICC Trust Fund for Victims also shows that voluntary contributions will not simply plug the gap in funding reparations. Funding judicial reparations, and even more so financial compensation, does not easily attract donors who are more inclined to fund humanitarian and development programs. Moreover, whilst the establishment of the Trust Fund might provide catalytic opportunities for more comprehensive reparations in Chad, civil parties chose a risky strategy when putting all hope into a new institution that still has to become operational. It makes the disbursement even of the existing assets contingent on the establishment and functioning of the Fund and has so far only delayed further action on reparations.

Conclusion

The experience with reparations at the EAC has shown some old and some new challenges. Whilst the transnational advocacy coalition achieved its primary goal of putting Habré on trial, the final outcome regarding reparations is less certain. Combining criminal action with reparations in a mass atrocity trial is still a novel experiment. The EAC struggled with many of the same challenges encountered by the better-resourced ICC and ECCC. The EAC judges dealt with these matters much swifter than their international peers, especially when compared to the multi-year long reparations proceedings at the ICC. Yet, much more work is required post-EAC, if victims are not to end up with a 'fictitious award' that only exists on paper.

One of the more innovative aspects of the EAC is that it attempts to deliver reparations through a universal jurisdiction trial that concerns cross-border interactions. In this context, reparations are awarded in one state, but have to be implemented in another state.

[62] Appeals Reparations Judgment (n 24), paras 613–14.

[63] ibid para 614.

[64] In resolution Assembly/AU/Dec.615 (XXVII), 'Décision sur l'affaire Hissein Habré', adopted at the AU summit in Kigali, 17–18 July 2016, the African Union decided to establish a trust fund and to organize a donor conference to solicit voluntary contributions.

Whilst the EAC put forward an ambitious reparations order, it never had the power to enforce this order in Chad.[65] The observations from the EAC suggest that universal jurisdiction trials will prove most effective on reparations, if they have access to some of the defendant's assets and can count on minimal cooperation by the state concerned. Yet, universal jurisdiction trials are unlikely to deliver large-scale reparations in far-away countries beyond the boundaries of their jurisdiction. There is a need to recognize both the potential and the clear limitations of recasting mass atrocity trials as a site for realizing reparative justice ambitions.[66] Scholars have identified a pressing need to look beyond criminal courts in the pursuit of reparations for victims of mass atrocities.[67]

Sarah Williams suggested that 'we should not expect the EAC to achieve much beyond the trial of Habré, as it is not intended or designed to achieve wider transitional justice goals in Senegal or Chad'.[68] The experience of the EAC thus far indicates that court-ordered reparations are unlikely to have a broader transformative impact if they are restricted to financial compensation, target only a narrow constituency of survivors and do not address the responsibility of the state. Indeed, the refusal so far of the Chadian government to take responsibility for the enduring legacy of the Habré regime and ownership of the trial's outcomes, including reparations, limit the EAC's impact in Chad. The most important impact of the process has perhaps come from its side-effects, most notably the emancipation and empowerment of survivors and their associations.

Looking into the future, however, it is clear that the requirements of an anti-impunity campaign are rather different from those of a platform in support of local aspirations for reparations. International justice campaigners and lawyers will need to look to expertise and strategies that are more familiar from development work. Both insights will be needed to deliver on a longer-term and context-specific reparations and justice agenda in Chad. From this perspective, the trial against Habré was perhaps more a start than an end point.

65 'Accord de coopération judiciaire entre la République du Sénégal et la République du Tchad pour la poursuite des crimes internationaux commis au Tchad durant la période du 7 juin 1982 au 1 décembre 1990', 3 May 2013.

66 I agree on this point with Sara Kendall who put forward similar arguments at Sara Kendall, 'Beyond the Restorative Turn: The Limits of Legal Humanitarianism' in Christian De Vos, Sara Kendall, and Carsten Stahn (eds), *Contested Justice*: The Politics and Practice of International Criminal Court Interventions (Cambridge University Press 2015) 352–76.

67 See Luke Moffett, 'Reparative Complementary: Ensuring an Effective Remedy for Victims in the Reparations Regime of the International Criminal Court' (2013) 17 International Journal of Human Rights 368–90.

68 Sarah Williams, 'The Extraordinary African Chambers in the Senegalese Courts: An African Solution to an African Problem?' (2013) 11 Journal of International Criminal Justice 1140.

37

Hybrid Courts and *Amicus Curiae* Briefing

Sarah Williams[1]

Introduction

Submissions by *amicus curiae* have influenced the process and judicial outcomes of international and hybrid criminal tribunals, including the International Criminal Court (ICC). *Amici* can improve the quality and accuracy of judicial decision-making by providing additional expertise that may not otherwise be available to the judges. *Amici* may also make arguments on behalf of those not otherwise represented in proceedings. Thus, by enabling a broader range of actors to participate and different interests to be voiced in proceedings, *amici* interventions may contribute to enhancing the legitimacy of the institution itself. The potential influence of an *amicus curiae* submission was evident at the Extraordinary African Chambers (EAC). Several international criminal law practitioners and academics submitted an *amicus* brief to the Chambers highlighting the need to include crimes of sexual and gender-based violence in the charges to be considered by the Chambers (the SGBV brief).

This contribution explores this brief and its impact in the Habré trial. To do so, it first places this brief in the broader context of the role of the *amicus curiae* in international criminal tribunals. Second, it explores how civil society actors have used *amicus curiae* briefs to highlight the experiences and needs of women and girls affected by conflict and failures by tribunals to investigate and prosecute sexual violence in other international criminal tribunals. Next, the contribution outlines the history of the SGBV brief, its drafters and content, and then attempts to determine the influence of the brief on the Chambers and the outcomes of the trial. In conclusion, the contribution recognizes the role of this, and other *amicus curiae* submissions, in progressing charges of sexual violence. However, it also highlights the limits of this mechanism. The contribution recommends the inclusion of a specific provision and procedure for *amicus curiae* in the rules of future tribunals, irrespective of the local legal tradition, to safeguard the integrity and transparency of trials.

The Amicus Curiae in international criminal tribunals

The term *amicus curiae* means literally 'friend of the court' in Latin. The concept enables actors who are not a party to proceedings (third parties) to provide information that is relevant, but which may not otherwise be brought before the court.[2] *Amici* cannot lead

[1] This research was supported under Australian Research Council's *Discovery Projects* funding scheme (project DP 140101347). The views expressed herein are those of the author and are not necessarily those of the Australian Research Council.

[2] Samuel Krislov, 'The Amicus Curiae Brief: From Friendship to Advocacy' (1963) 72 Yale Law Journal 694, 694.

Sarah Williams, *Hybrid Courts and* Amicus Curiae *Briefing* In: *The President on Trial.* First edition. Edited by: Sharon Weill, Kim Thuy Seelinger, and Kerstin Bree Carlson, Oxford University Press (2020). © Sarah Williams. DOI: 10.1093/oso/9780198858621.003.0038

evidence or question witnesses, are not entitled to appeal or to respond to the submissions of the parties or other *amici*, and are generally restricted to the provision of written submissions on defined topics.[3] All international criminal tribunals, including the ICC, formally provide for the submission of *amicus curiae* observations through their Rules of Procedure and Evidence (Rules).[4] The *amicus curiae* mechanism is discretionary, with participation by the leave or invitation of the Chamber.

Tribunal Rules provide little guidance to Chambers in exercising this discretion—other than that the observations should be 'desirable' or 'would assist' the Chambers in determining an issue. Given the focus of proceedings on individual criminal responsibility, there is clear recognition that the participation of *amici* should not be at the expense of the expediency and efficient operation of the trial or the fair trial rights of the accused. Moreover, *amici* are generally limited to providing submissions on legal issues, rather than factual information, as the production of evidence is for the prosecution and defence. *Amici* should also not make arguments addressing the individual criminal responsibility of a particular accused, as determining criminal responsibility is the core function of the judges, based on evidence provided by the parties.

Gender, civil society, and amicus curiae in international criminal tribunals

There has been a long history of civil society involvement in the Tribunals, including participation as *amicus curiae*.[5] The *amicus* brief has also been a useful tool for promoting issues surrounding the prosecution of sexual and gender-based violence in international criminal tribunals. Gender justice organizations—particularly the Coalition for Women's Human Rights in Conflict Situations and Women's Initiatives for Gender Justice (WIGJ)—have influenced the approaches of the ICTY, ICTR, and ICC in relation to prosecuting sexual and gender-based violence, even though the *amicus curiae* applications were not always accepted.

One of the most frequently mentioned cases of a civil society *amicus curiae* submission having had considerable impact was in the case of *Akayesu* before the ICTR.[6] The original

[3] For extensive discussion of the role and practice of the *amicus curiae* in international criminal tribunals, see Sarah Williams, Hannah Woolaver, and Emma Palmer, *The Amicus Curiae in International Criminal Justice* (Hart 2019, forthcoming); Sarah Williams and Hannah Woolaver, 'The Role of the *Amicus Curiae* before International Criminal Tribunals' (2006) 6 International Criminal Law Review 151.

[4] Rules of Procedure and Evidence, Official Records of the Assembly of States Parties to the Rome Statute of the International Criminal Court, First session, New York, 3–10 September 2002 (ICC-ASP/1/3 and Corr.1), part II.A, r 103; International Tribunal for the Prosecution of Persons Responsible for Serious Violations of International Humanitarian Law Committed in the Territory of the Former Yugoslavia since 1991, 'Rules of Procedure and Evidence' (8 July 2015) IT/32/Rev.50, r 74; International Criminal Tribunal for Rwanda, 'ICTR Rules of Procedure and Evidence' (13 May 2015) r 74; Special Court for Sierra Leone, 'Rules of Procedure and Evidence' (31 May 2012) r 74; Extraordinary Chambers in the Courts of Cambodia, 'Internal Rules' (Rev 3), as revised on 16 January 2015, r 33; Special Tribunal for Lebanon, Rules of Procedure and Evidence (20 March 2009) STL-BD-2009-01-Rev.9, as amended and corrected 3 April 2017, rr 97, 131, and 176.

[5] For further discussion, see: Mark Ellis, 'NGO Intervention in Court Proceedings through Amicus Curiae Briefs' in Linda Carter, Mark Ellis, and Charles Halloh (eds), *The International Criminal Court in an Effective Global Justice System* (Edward Elgar 2016); Sarah Williams and Emma Palmer, 'Civil Society and Amicus Curiae Interventions in the International Criminal Court' (2016) Acta Juridica 40.

[6] Anne-Marie de Brouwer, *Supranational Criminal Prosecution of Sexual Violence: The ICC and the Practice of the ICTY and the ICTR* (Intersentia 2005); Rhonda Copelon, 'Gender Crimes as War Crimes: Integrating Crimes Against Women into International Criminal Law' (2000) 46 McGill Law Journal 217, 225–26.

indictment in *Akayesu* incorporated charges of genocide for killings but not the rapes and other acts of sexual violence against women and girls perpetrated as part of the genocide.[7] The ICTR Trial Chamber, in particular Judge Pillay, having recognized the potential indicators of sexual violence questioned certain witnesses testifying before the Chamber, ultimately revealing evidence of sexual violence and the role of the accused in relation to it.[8] In the light of this emerging evidence, a group of women's organizations—the Coalition for Women's Human Rights in Conflict—submitted an *amicus curiae* brief arguing that the ICTR Trial Chamber could and should correct the Prosecutor's failure to charge rape in the *Akayesu* case.[9] The Coalition had been established in 2006 'specifically to monitor the ICTR and ensure that it protected the rights and interests of women appearing before the Tribunal'.[10] The brief argued that the Chamber should exercise its inherent supervisory jurisdiction to invite the Prosecutor to amend the charges to include sexual violence as war crimes, crimes against humanity and as an act of genocide.[11]

The Trial Chamber accepted the brief, placed it on the case file and served it on the parties.[12] The Prosecution subsequently sought to amend the indictment to include sexual violence, although the Prosecution claimed that the brief was not the impetus for this change.[13] The Prosecution suggested that it had already been considering evidence of sexual violence and reconsidered the charges based on further evidence that emerged during testimony linking the accused to crimes of sexual violence.[14] The Trial Chamber granted leave to amend the indictment. Further factual allegations concerning sexual violence were incorporated into the amended indictment and three additional charges—of rape and other inhumane acts as crimes against humanity and outrages upon human dignity in particular rape, degrading and humiliating treatment and indecent assault as a war crime—were included.[15] Sexual violence then became a prominent feature of the prosecution case, ultimately leading to conviction of Akayesu for rape and other inhumane acts as crimes against humanity and genocide, with the judgment specifically recognizing that acts of rape and sexual violence could constitute prohibited acts for genocide, particularly where rape may impact upon births within the group.[16]

Despite the Prosecution's assertion, it is probable that the *amicus* brief did have some influence. The Chamber referred to the brief in its decision 'noting the interest shown in this

[7] *Prosecutor v Akayesu*, ICTR-96-04-0003, Indictment (13 February 1996).

[8] For further discussion see Beth van Schaack, 'Engendering Genocide: The Akayesu Case before the ICTR' in Deena R Hurwitz, Margaret L Satterthwaite, and Doug Ford (eds), *Human Rights Advocacy Stories* (Thomson Reuters/Foundation Press 2009) 193, 198–200. See also *Prosecutor v Akayesu*, ICTR-96-4-TRA000010/1, Transcript (27 January 1997).

[9] Coalition for Women's Human Rights in Conflict Situations, 'Amicus Brief submitted to the International Criminal Tribunal for Rwanda respecting the Amendment of the Indictment and Supplementation of the Evidence to Ensure the Prosecution of Rape and Other Sexual Violence within the Competence of the Tribunal' (17 June 1997). Note that this brief is not part of the official online records of the *Akayesu* case. For a discussion of the probable influence of this brief, see de Brouwer, *Supranational Criminal Prosecution of Sexual Violence* (n 6), 294–95; Copelon, 'Gender Crimes as War Crimes' (n 6) 225.

[10] van Schaack, 'Engendering Genocide' (n 8) 201.

[11] Coalition for Women's Human Rights in Conflict Situations, 'Amicus Brief' (n 9) para 3.

[12] As detailed by van Schaack, 'Engendering Genocide' (n 8) 202.

[13] *Prosecutor v Akayesu*, ICTR-96-4-TRA000025/1, Transcript (17 June 1997) 8.

[14] ibid 6; van Schaack, 'Engendering Genocide' (n 8) 202. This claim was also evident in a 2016 film outlining the history of the *Akayesu* case, which interviewed key prosecution officials. See *The Uncondemned* <http://www.theuncondemned.com/> accessed 15 January 2018.

[15] *Prosecutor v Akayesu*, ICTR-96-4-1, Amended Indictment (17 June 1997).

[16] *Prosecutor v Akayesu*, ICTRY-96-4-T, Judgement (2 September 1998) paras 507, 508.

issue by non-governmental organizations, which it considers as indicative of public concern over the historical exclusion of rape and other forms of sexual violence from the investigation and prosecution of war crimes'.[17] Certainly, key gender advocates and commentators considered the brief to have been significant in changing the outcome of the trial.[18] The resulting Trial Chamber judgment in *Akayesu* significantly developed the law concerning sexual violence, recognizing for the first time that sexual violence can be prosecuted as constituting part of genocide and highlighting the links between sexual violence and torture.[19]

This experience influenced the actions of the Women's Caucus for Gender Justice (WCGJ) at the negotiations for the adoption of the Rome Statute of the International Criminal Court. The WCGJ used the history of the *Akayesu* proceedings to justify the inclusion of judges and other personnel with special expertise in sexual violence, in particular against women and children, and for recognition of a broader range of sexual violence crimes in the Rome Statute and of the link between sexual violence and other crimes, in particular torture, in the Elements of Crimes.[20] In addition, the WCGJ viewed inclusion of a provision in the ICC Rules that would enable *amicus curiae* submissions to be an essential tool for allowing civil society actors to place the issue of sexual and gender-based violence—as well as other important issues—on the court's agenda.[21]

This proved to be an astute argument, with an *amicus curiae* submission featuring in the first case before the ICC, that of Thomas Lubanga. In a story echoing that of the *Akayesu* proceedings at the ICTR, despite evidence of widespread sexual violence in the Democratic Republic of the Congo (DRC) perpetrated by Lubanga's forces, the first ICC Prosecutor, Louis Moreno O'Campo, brought charges only concerning the war crimes of conscripting and enlisting children under the age of fifteen and using them to participate actively in hostilities. In 2006, several NGOs, including WIGJ, FIDH, and Human Rights Watch, attempted to expand the charges brought at the ICC against Lubanga to include sexual violence by writing to the ICC Prosecutor,[22] but without success. WIGJ also presented to the Prosecutor a dossier of testimony from victims of sexual violence.[23] The next effort by WIGJ was to apply to appear as *amicus curiae* in Lubanga's confirmation of charges hearing,[24] seeking to make submissions on the proper role of the Pre-Trial Chamber in the determination of charges. Similar to the brief submitted in *Akayesu*, WIGJ argued that there was a broad supervisory duty on the part of the Pre-Trial Chamber that would extend to asking the Prosecutor to include other crimes in the charges. The organization also argued for a

[17] ibid para 417.

[18] de Brouwer, *Supranational Criminal Prosecution of Sexual Violence* (n 6); Coalition on Women's Human Rights in Conflict Situations, 'RWANDA: Akayesu Sentencing a Victory for Women's Rights' <https://www1.essex.ac.uk/armedcon/story_id/000054.pdf> accessed 15 January 2018; van Schaak, 'Engendering Genocide' (n 8).

[19] *Akayesu*, Judgement (n 16). See also Valerie Oosterveld, 'Gender-sensitive Justice and the International Criminal Tribunal for Rwanda: Lessons Learned for the International Criminal Court' (2005) 12 New Eng J Intl & Comp L 119.

[20] Oosterveld, 'Gender-sensitive Justice' (n 19).

[21] Louise Chappell, *The Politics of Gender Justice at the International Criminal Court* (OUP 2015) 60.

[22] International Federation for Human Rights, 'Concern about Your Communication of June 28, 2006 Informing the Pre-Trial Chamber of the Temporary Suspension of Your Office's Investigation in the Case against Mr. Thomas Lubanga' (*FIDH*, 31 July 2006) <http://www.fidh.org/spip.php?article3622> accessed 15 January 2018.

[23] Louise Chappell, 'Conflicting Institutions and the Search for Gender Justice at the International Criminal Court' (2014) 67 Political Research Quarterly 183, 188.

[24] *Prosecutor v Lubanga*, ICC-01/04-01/06-403, Request Submitted Pursuant to Rule 103(1) of the Rules of Procedure and Evidence for Leave to Participate as Amicus Curiae in the Article 61 Confirmation Proceedings (7 September 2006).

broader definition of victim and thus participation at Article 61 proceedings (ie not just linked to those crimes in arrest warrant), and asked the Prosecutor to investigate sexual and gender-based violence and to include such violence in the charges. The Prosecutor and defence counsel for Lubanga opposed the application.

The Pre-Trial Chamber refused to accept WIGJ's application to submit an *amicus curiae* brief because, by this stage, the case against Lubanga was confined to the existing charges and 'therefore, the Request has no link with the present case'.[25] Instead, the Pre-Trial Chamber invited WIGJ 'to re-file their request for leave to submit observations in the record of the DRC situation'.[26] In other words, the Chamber suggested that WIGJ apply to act as *amicus curiae* within the broader Pre-Trial process, rather than in the *Lubanga* case specifically, where charges were already laid. WIGJ subsequently obliged, but this request was also rejected.[27]

However, the failure to have the brief accepted does not mean these efforts had no impact. As the trial developed, testimony revealed evidence of sexual violence, and various actors attempted to draw attention to this element of the conflict. In 2009, the victims' legal representatives applied to have the facts re-characterized to include charges of sexual slavery and cruel and inhuman treatment under Regulation 55.[28] While a majority of the Trial Chamber accepted this application,[29] the Appeals Chamber overturned that decision on appeal.[30] This effectively precluded recognition of SGBV crimes in either the judgment or sentencing, although Judge Odio Benito continued to raise the issue in questioning.

Ultimately, perhaps due to the criticism directed at the OTP, the Prosecutor attempted to bring sexual violence into the charges of enlisting, conscripting and using child soldiers, arguing that sexual violence at the hands of their commanders was a key aspect of the daily experience of girl child soldiers and that 'active participation in hostilities' should be read expansively so as to include this experience.[31] As the Trial Chamber judges rejected this approach,[32] it could not formally incorporate the sexual violence into conviction or sentence. However, the judgment on conviction and sentencing recognized that such violence had occurred and criticized the Prosecutor's failure to include charges of sexual and gender-based violence initially or to request an amendment of the charges subsequently.[33]

[25] *Prosecutor v Lubanga*, ICC-01/04-01/06-480, Decision on Request Pursuant to Rule 103(1) of the Statute (26 September 2006).

[26] ibid.

[27] *Situation in the Democratic Republic of the Congo*, ICC-01/04-373, Decision on the Request Submitted Pursuant to Rule 103(1) of the Rules of Procedure and Evidence (17 August 2007).

[28] *Prosecutor v Lubanga*, ICC-01/04-01/06-1891, Joint Application of the Legal Representatives of the Victims for the Implementation of the Procedure under Regulation 55 of the Regulations of the Court (22 May 2009); Sienna Merope, 'Recharacterizing the Lubanga Case: Regulation 55 and the Consequences for Gender Justice at the ICC' (2011) 22 Criminal Law Forum 311.

[29] *Prosecutor v Lubanga*, ICC-01/04-01/06-2049, Decision Giving Notice to the Parties and Participants that the Legal Characterisation of the Facts may be Subject to Change in Accordance with Regulation 55(2) of the Regulations of the Court (14 July 2009).

[30] *Prosecutor v Lubanga*, ICC-01/04-01/06-2205, Judgment on the Appeals of Mr Lubanga Dyilo and the Prosecutor Against the Decision of Trial Chamber I of 14 July 2009 Entitled 'Decision Giving Notice to the Parties and Participants that the Legal Characterisation of the Facts may be Subject to Change in Accordance with Regulation 55(2) of the Regulations of the Court' (8 December 2009).

[31] See, eg, *Prosecutor v Lubanga*, ICC-01/04-01/06-2748-Red, Prosecution's Closing Brief (01 June 2011) para 139; *Prosecutor v Lubanga*, ICC-01/04-01/06-T-107-Eng, Transcript (26 January 2009) 11.

[32] *Prosecutor v Lubanga*, ICC-01/04-01/06-2842, Judgment Pursuant to Article 74 of the Statute (14 March 2012) para 913.

[33] *Prosecutor v Lubanga*, ICC-01/04-01/06-2901, Decision on Sentence Pursuant to Article 76 of the Statute (10 July 2012) para 60.

The *Lubanga* case showed the dangers of limited charging for sexual and gender-based violence or excluding such charges altogether. Chappell has detailed the gender (in)justice cascade resulting from these decisions, with victims of sexual violence subsequently not entitled to reparations as there was no link to the crimes for which the accused was convicted.[34] However, the case shows the value of civil society intervention in trials, with the criticism directed at the Prosecutor no doubt influential in subsequent decisions to include charges in other cases and in the adoption of a specific policy on sexual and gender-based violence in 2016.[35] In particular, *Lubanga* shows the utility of the *amicus curiae* mechanism, even if an application is not ultimately successful, in drawing attention to sexual violence and in keeping the pressure on court actors to recognize and prosecute such violence.

Yet, there are two dimensions that limit the impact of an *amicus* brief where the issue is failure to investigate or to charge sexual violence. First, an application to file an *amicus* brief can generally only be filed before Chambers (including in certain institutions investigating judges), which means applications cannot be made before judicial proceedings are commenced. The Prosecutor will have made many of the decisions concerning the scope of investigations and the selection of charges before this stage—as in *Lubanga*, this will lead to an *amicus* application being rejected as irrelevant or not timely. Second, Chambers have held—often at the behest of the Prosecution—that the determination of the scope of the investigation and the charges is a matter within the discretion of the Prosecutor and is not a decision for the Chambers. This too will likely lead to an application by an *amicus* being rejected as there is no issue before the Chambers that can be assisted by the provision of the *amicus* submissions. Before the SGBV brief, the briefs in *Akayesu* and *Lubanga* appeared to be the outliers in terms of influencing the prosecution or a Chamber. In the ICTR, the same Coalition attempted to file an *amicus* submission in the proceedings concerning *Ntagerura, Bagambiki, and Imanishiwme*, again seeking the amendment of the original indictments to include sexual violence charges. However, the Chamber rejected the application in the face of opposition by the Prosecution, who claimed that this was a matter solely for the discretion of her office.[36]

Civil society actors have submitted few briefs on gender and sexual violence to ICC Chambers. One instance of note is the intervention of the WIGJ as *amicus* in the Bemba proceedings. The Prosecution had sought the confirmation of charges against Bemba for murder, rape and torture as crimes against humanity and the charges of murder, torture, rape and outrages upon personal dignity and pillaging as war crimes. Charges of torture (as a crime against humanity) and of outrages upon personal dignity (a war crime) were based on acts of rape and other sexual violence. At the confirmation of charges hearing, the Pre-Trial Chamber rejected this cumulative approach to charging and refused to confirm the charges of torture and outrages upon personal dignity, which it argued were supported

[34] Louise Chappell, 'The Gender Injustice Cascade: 'Transformative' Reparations for Victims of Sexual and Gender-Based Crimes in the *Lubanga* case at the International Criminal Court' (2017) 21 International Journal of Human Rights 1223.

[35] International Criminal Court, the Office of the Prosecutor, 'Policy Paper on Sexual and Gender-Based Crimes' (June 2014) <https://www.icc-cpi.int/iccdocs/otp/OTP-Policy-Paper-on-Sexual-and-Gender-Based-Crimes--June-2014.pdf> accessed 15 January 2018.

[36] *Prosecutor v Ntagerura, Bagambiki and Imanishimwe*, ICTR-99-46-T, Decision on the Application to File an Amicus Curiae Brief According to Rule 74 of the Rules of Procedure and Evidence Filed on Behalf of the NGO Coalition for Women's Human Rights in Conflict Situations (24 May 2001).

by the same conduct and subsumed by the separate charge of rape.[37] The Prosecution appealed that decision.[38] The WIGJ applied to file observations as *amicus curiae* in support of the appeal, addressing cumulative charging and its impact on the fair trial rights of the accused.[39] A single judge approved the WIGJ request.[40] In its filing, WIGJ observed that, while the Pre-Trial Chamber had correctly identified the test for cumulative charging, it had misapplied that test on three occasions and, as a result, the decision on the confirmation of charges created 'unintentional adverse effects on gender' and violated Article 21(3) of the Rome Statute.[41] Although the Chamber ultimately rejected the appeal, it summarized and engaged with the submissions made by WIGJ in its decision.[42]

Another instance, significant for the early stage of proceedings in which is arose, was the filing by WIGJ in the Bangladesh/Myanmar proceedings before ICC Pre-Trial Chamber I, that is, before the Prosecutor had opened a preliminary examination. In April 2018, the ICC Prosecutor filed a request with the PTC for a ruling on jurisdiction, seeking confirmation from the Chamber that the ICC could exercise jurisdiction where at least one element of a crime had been committed on the territory of a state party to the Rome Statute. The request concerned allegations of deportation of members of the Rohingya from Myanmar (not a state party) to Bangladesh (a state party). Several civil society organizations sought—and were granted—leave to participate, some as *amicus curiae* and others as representatives of victims, including women and girls.[43] In the *amicus curiae* submission of WIGJ, together with Naripokkho, Ms Sara Hossain, and the European Center for Constitutional and Human Rights,[44] the amici addressed how 'sexual and gender-based violence can be appraised within the crime of deportation or forcible transfer'.[45] While this issue we technically not relevant to the issues raised by the proceedings (the brief would have been more appropriate at a later stage of proceedings), the Chamber—referring to the observations of the *amici*—indicated that other forms of violence, including sexual violence, could constitute the expulsion element of deportation.[46] There have also been several successful filings

[37] *Prosecutor v Bemba Gombo*, ICC-01/05-01/08-424, Decision Pursuant to Article 61(7)(a) and (b) of the Rome Statute on the Charges of the Prosecutor Against Jean-Pierre Bemba Gombo (15 June 2009) para 190.

[38] *Prosecutor v Bemba Gombo*, ICC-01/05-01/08-427, Prosecutor's Application for Leave to Appeal the Decision Pursuant to Article 61(7)(a) and (b) on the Charges against Jean-Pierre Bemba Gombo (22 June 2009).

[39] *Prosecutor v Bemba Gombo*, ICC-01/05-01/08-447, Request for Leave to Submit Amicus Curiae Observations Pursuant to Rule 103 of the Rules of Procedure and Evidence (13 July 2009).

[40] *Prosecutor v Bemba Gombo*, ICC-01/05-01/08-451, Decision on Request for Leave to Submit Amicus Curiae Observations Pursuant to Rule 103 of the Rules of Procedure and Evidence (17 July 2009). A request by the International Women's Human Rights Law Clinic, on behalf of proposed *amici* consisting of UN torture and women's human rights experts and human rights advocates, was rejected.

[41] *Prosecutor v Bemba Gombo*, ICC-01/05-01/08-466, Amicus Curiae Observations of the Women's Initiatives for Gender Justice Pursuant to Rule 103 of the Rules of Procedure and Evidence (31 July 2009) paras 38–40.

[42] *Prosecutor v Bemba Gombo*, ICC-01/05-01/08-532, Decision on the Prosecutor's Application for Leave to Appeal the 'Decision Pursuant to Article 61(7)(a) and (b) of the Rome Statute on the Charges of the Prosecutor Against Jean-Pierre Bemba Gombo' (18 September 2009).

[43] See Global Rights Compliance, ICC-RoC46(3)-01/18-9, Submission on Behalf of the Victims Pursuant to Article 19(3) of the Statute (30 May 2018).

[44] Pre-Trial Chamber I, ICC-RoC46(3)-01/18-15, Decision on the 'Joint Request for Leave to Submit Amicus Curiae Observations pursuant to Rule 103 of the Rules' (11 June 2018).

[45] Women's Initiatives for Gender Justice and others, 'Joint Observations Pursuant to Rule 103 of the Rules', ICC-RoC46(3)-01/18, para 12.

[46] Pre-Trial Chamber I, ICC-RoC46(3)-01/18, Decision on the 'Prosecution's Request for a Ruling on Jurisdiction under Article 19(3) of the Statute' (6 September 2018) para 61.

concerning the need for a transformative and gender-sensitive approach to reparations under Article 75 of the Rome Statute.[47]

The ICTY and the ICTR also received a few—but not many—applications by potential *amici* concerning sexual and gender violence, mainly concerning protective measures for victims.[48] The Special Court for Sierra Leone (SCSL), despite an open approach to *amicus* briefs and cases that raised important SGBV legal issues,[49] did not receive any briefs on gender issues or sexual violence, which is surprising. The ECCC has delivered a number of important rulings with relevance to sexual violence during the Democratic Kampuchea era (1975–1979), for example a decision as to the status of rape as a distinct crime against humanity in 1975[50] and the status of the third, extended form of joint criminal enterprise in customary international law by 1975.[51] Given their similar temporal jurisdiction, such decisions may also have proved influential for the EAC. In fact, the SGBV brief expressly attempted to distinguish the ECCC decision on rape by providing additional evidence of customary international law that was not made available to the ECCC Chambers.[52] Although the ECCC Internal Rules allow *amicus* submissions, and some *amicus* submissions were received from academics on the joint criminal enterprise issue,[53] until relatively recently there was no interest from women's groups or international NGOs in submitting briefs on issues connected to SGBV. This is interesting, in that the ECCC replicated many of the failings of the ICTR, the ICC, and other tribunals in relation to the investigation of sexual violence and charges did not initially include sexual violence.[54] Following the inclusion of

[47] See, eg, *Prosecutor v Lubanga,* ICC-01/04-01/06-2876, Observations of the Women's Initiatives for Gender Justice on Reparations (10 May 2012); *Prosecutor v Katanga,* ICC-01/04-01/07-3554, Redress Trust Observations Pursuant to Article 75 of the Statute (15 May 2015).

[48] See, eg, *Prosecutor v Furundzija,* Case No IT-95-17/1-T ICTY, Amicus Curiae Brief on Protective Measures for Victims or Witnesses of Sexual Violence and Other Traumatic Events, Submitted on Behalf of the Centre for Civil and Human Rights, Notre Dame Law School (6 November 1998).

[49] The SCSL adopted a specific practice direction (Special Court for Sierra Leone, 'Practice Direction on Filing Amicus Applications Pursuant to Rule 74 of the Rules of Procedure and Evidence of the Special Court for Sierra Leone' (20 October 2004)), encouraged the submission of amicus filings, and made extensive use of briefs filed. See Ellis, 'NGO Intervention' (n 5) and Williams and Palmer, 'Civil Society and Amicus Curiae Interventions' (n 5).

[50] *Prosecutor v Ieng Sary,* Criminal Case File No 002/19-09-2007-ECCC/OCIJ (PTC75), Decision on Ieng Sary's Appeal Against the Closing Order (11 April 2011) para 369; see also *Co-Prosecutors v Kaing Guek Eav alias Duch,* Criminal Case File No 001/18-07-2007-ECCC/SC, Appeal Judgement (3 February 2012) paras 177-178; Sarah Williams and Emma Palmer, 'The Extraordinary Chambers in the Courts of Cambodia: Developing the Law on Sexual Violence' (2015) 15 International Criminal Law Review 452; Rachel Killean, 'An Incomplete Narrative: Prosecuting Sexual Violence Crimes at the Extraordinary Chambers in the Courts of Cambodia' (2015) 13 Journal of International Criminal Justice 331.

[51] *Co-Prosecutors v Ieng Thirith and others,* Criminal Case File No 002/19-09-2007-ECCC/OCIJ (PTC38), Decision on the Appeals Against the Co-Investigative Judges Order on Joint Criminal Enterprise (JCE) (20 May 2010); see also *Co-Prosecutors v Nuon Chea and others,* Criminal Case File No 002/19-09-2007/ECCC/TC, Decision on the Applicability of Joint Criminal Enterprise (12 September 2011); *Co-Prosecutors v Khieu Samphân and Nuon Chea,* Criminal Case File No 002/19-09-2007-ECCC/SC, Judgment (23 November 2016).

[52] *Hissène Habré:* Amicus Curiae Brief of the Human Rights Center at the University of California, Berkeley, School of Law, and International Experts on Sexual Violence Under International Criminal Law, 'Rape and Other Forms of Sexual Violence as Crimes Against Humanity, War Crimes and Torture Under Customary International Law' (8 December 2015) 17–19 <https://www.law.berkeley.edu/wp-content/uploads/2015/04/MICUS-CURIAE-BRIEF-OF-THE-HUMAN-RIGHTS-CENTER-AT-THE-UNIVERSITY-OF-CALIFORNIA-BERKELEY-SCHOOL-OF-LAW-AND-INTERNATIONAL-EXPERTS-ON-SEXUAL-VIOLENCE-UNDER-INTERNATIONAL-CRIMINAL-LAW-Eng.pdf> accessed 18 January 2018 (hereinafter 'SGBV Brief').

[53] *Amicus* briefs were submitted by Professor Antonio Cassese, Professor Kai Ambos and the McGill Centre for Human Rights and Legal Pluralism at the Pre-Trial stage.

[54] Emma Palmer and Sarah Williams, 'A "Shift in Attitude"? Institutional Change and Sexual and Gender-Based Crimes at the Extraordinary Chambers in the Courts of Cambodia' (2017) 19 International Feminist Journal of Politics 22.

charges of forced marriage, there were some briefs filed, including one concerning forced marriage.[55]

The SGBV brief in the Habré trial

Context to the brief

This section focuses on the context to the SGBV brief and shows how the SGBV brief follows the tradition of using an *amicus curiae* brief to attempt to persuade the Chambers to prompt the inclusion of charges to address SGBV. Several contributions to this volume, as well as other authors, have documented the complex history of the establishment of the EAC and the Hissène Habré to trial. Contributors have also outlined the difficulties in drawing attention to sexual violence, with the indictment not including charges concerning sexual violence.

The EAC Statute includes several provisions that enable prosecution of SGBV, in particular: Article 6(a), which recognizes the crimes against humanity of rape, sexual slavery, enforced prostitution, enforced sterilization, or any other form of sexual violence of comparable gravity; Article 6, incorporating the definition of genocide; Article 7(1)(b), the war crime of torture or inhuman treatment, including biological experiments, or wilfully causing great physical or mental suffering; Article 7(2)(a), violence to life, health and physical or mental well-being of persons, in particular murder as well as cruel treatment such as torture, mutilation or any form of corporal punishment; Article 7(2)(e), outrages on personal dignity, including rape; and Article 8, torture. However, the judicial investigation largely excluded allegations of sexual violence. Thus, when Habré was indicted on 2 July 2013, the indictment did not incorporate acts of sexual violence. Unlike the ICC, there was no requirement in the instruments establishing the EAC for judges or court personnel to have experience in investigating sexual violence. Most key participants, including judges, were not familiar with international provisions on sexual violence crimes or best practice on collating evidence of such crimes. Given this history and context it is not surprising that sexual violence was omitted from the investigation. The EAC therefore had a similar issue to other tribunals in that it had failed to prioritize SGBV in its investigations and charges.

However, the EAC Rules, being based on the civil law system found in Senegal, permitted victims to participate in proceedings as civil parties, represented by a team of civil party lawyers. As with the ECCC, it was the inclusion of civil parties and their lawyers that enabled the extent and nature of sexual violence during Habré's regime to come to light. Habré's trial commenced on 20 July 2015. In October 2015, several civil parties testified as to systematic rapes perpetrated by Habré's soldiers and security forces and by Habré himself.[56] The testimony of four women revealed how women, including young girls, had been sent to camps

[55] *Khieu Samphân and Nuon Chea*: Amicus Curiae Brief on Forced Marriage, Criminal Case File No 002/19-09-2007-ECCC/TC (29 September 2016).

[56] ibid. See also Human Rights Watch, 'Senegal: At Hissène Habre Trial, Sexual Slavery Accounts' (*Human Rights Watch*, 22 October 2015) <https://www.hrw.org/news/2015/10/22/senegal-hissene-habre-trial-sexual-slavery-accounts> accessed 23 January 2018. Trust Africa also produced daily summaries of testimony: summaries of the relevant court days (19–22 October 2015) are available at Truth Africa, 'The Extraordinary African Chambers Monitor' (19 April 2016) <http://www.trustafrica.org/en/resource/news/item/3212-extraordinary-chambers-monitor> accessed 22 January 2018.

and used as sexual slaves for soldiers in the Chadian army. One civil party, Khadidja Hassan Zidane, testified that Habré had himself raped her four times in the Presidential Palace. This testimony dramatically 'surfaced' the sexual violence perpetrated during the regime. The civil party lawyers filed a request with the Chambers to amend the indictment to include charges relating to sexual violence. Seventeen organizations wrote an open letter to the Chambers criticizing the failure to include sexual violence charges in the indictment.[57] The issue attracted the attention of the media and other actors who pushed for inclusion of SGBV charges.[58] It was as part of this 'catch up' drive to try to amend the charges to include sexual violence that the SGBV brief was filed with the Chambers, after parties observing the trial contacted the team at the Human Rights Centre.[59]

Content, authors, and impact of the brief

The SGBV brief, entitled 'Rape and Other Forms of Sexual Violence as Crimes Against Humanity, War Crimes, and Torture under Customary International Law', was drafted by the Human Rights Centre at the University of California, Berkeley, School of Law and sixteen 'international law experts on sexual violence under international criminal law'.[60] The brief draws on the US tradition, also evident in jurisdictions such as South Africa, of expert briefs being drafted by one *amici* and 'signed on to' by a significant number of academics and practitioners. In international criminal tribunals, this practice is relatively rare, with most briefs and applications submitted by a few actors working together, rather than large coalitions. However, the number of contributors to the SGBV brief was quite small when compared to some briefs in national legal systems, particularly the US. While collaborative briefs may not necessarily be discouraged at the ICC (the practice of the ICC is neutral as to whether the number of signatories matters), as they are arguably more efficient than numerous repetitive submissions by different *amici*, a significant trend towards this pattern is not likely.

The Rules for the EAC—which are based on Senegalese procedural law—do not incorporate a provision on *amicus curiae*, most likely as the mechanism is not formally recognized in the Senegalese legal system. There was thus no legal framework for the submission of *amicus* briefs to the Chambers. The absence of formal recognition of the *amicus* mechanism within a national legal system is not prohibitive of *amicus* briefs being accepted or considered: particularly in civil law jurisdictions, briefs have been accepted by national courts even in the absence of a formal power to do so. In common law and international jurisdictions, the ability to allow an *amicus* submission is considered part of a tribunal's inherent power to manage its own procedures.

[57] 'Open Letter to the Extraordinary African Chambers in the Courts of Senegal' (*Refugee Rights*, October 2015) <http://refugee-rights.org/wp-content/uploads/2015/10/Open-letter-sexual-violence.pdf> accessed 22 January 2018.

[58] See, eg, Celeste Hicks, 'Lawyers press for Chad's Hissène Habré to face sexual slavery and rape charges' *The Guardian* (22 December 2015) <https://www.theguardian.com/global-development/2015/dec/22/chad-hissene-habre-lawyers-sexual-slavery-rape-charges-trial> accessed 23 January 2018.

[59] Kim Thuy Seelinger, 'Rape and the President: The Remarkable Trial and (Partial) Acquittal of Hissène Habré' (2017) 34 World Policy Journal 16.

[60] SGBV Brief (n 52).

The SGBV brief was filed with the Chambers on 8 December 2015, accompanied by a motion requesting leave to file the brief. The motion referred to the inherent powers of the Chamber and the growing practice in other international tribunals or in national institutions of accepting submissions. The brief partly echoes the practice in other institutions in stating that the *amici* 'hope *to assist* this Court in meeting its responsibility to adjudicate acts of rape, sexual slavery, and other forms of sexual violence committed under the Habré regime' (emphasis added),[61] but it does not explicitly address how it intends to do so, the expertise of the *amici* (amici are merely listed by title and affiliation) or the relationship between this brief and the submissions of the parties, including civil parties, all factors *amici* in other institutions would normally be required, or at least advised, to address in their application. However, without access to party submissions it is often challenging for amici to show how their submissions avoid duplication or will address other issues. This brief was the only *amicus curiae* brief filed with the Chambers during the *Habré* trial. The brief was reported in an article in The Guardian, which linked to the brief itself, thus allowing the parties and other interested actors to utilize its expertise and maintaining the public attention on this issue.[62]

Consistent with the absence of an articulated legal basis for accepting the brief and the uncertainty of its status, the Chambers did not formally accept the brief, although the President of the Chambers acknowledged receipt and commented that the brief would 'be an extremely helpful resource in his and the other judges' deliberations'.[63] The parties apparently had access to the SGBV brief, presumably as the brief was in the public domain, being accessible on the Centre's website, which meant that, while the parties were not given a formal opportunity to respond to the brief, they could—and did—engage with the substantive arguments made by the *amici* in their own submissions. Given that, as is detailed further below, the brief influenced the Chambers' decision, the uncertain status of the SGBV brief may have had implications—albeit limited—for the fair trial rights of the accused. It also arguably affected the procedural integrity of the trial and undermined the transparency of the Chambers' decision-making. Moreover, it also raises a question as to why the SGBV brief was required, given it must have duplicated or at least complemented the submissions of the victims' lawyers, and whether the experts coordinated with the victims' lawyers or the prosecution. As the brief was filed before final submissions of the parties, the legal advice could have been provided directly to the parties for incorporation in their submissions. However, there may well have been value in supporting the requests made by the victims' lawyers through a submission relying on the expertise and status of the *amici* and, for the victims' representatives, avoiding a direct criticism of the Chambers.

In terms of the content of the brief, the intention here is not to critique the legal arguments made, but to provide observations on their nature and consistency with briefs in other institutions. The SGBV brief starts with an articulation of the normative position of the *amici*, who are 'deeply concerned by the allegations of rape and other forms of sexual violence raised in the proceedings of this case',[64] including allegations concerning Habré as

[61] ibid para 4.
[62] Hicks (n 58).
[63] ibid; see also Kim Thuy Seelinger 'The Landmark Trial Against Dictator Hissène Habré' (*Foreign Affairs*, 2016) <https://www.foreignaffairs.com/articles/chad/2016-06-16/landmark-trial-against-dictator-hiss-ne-habr> accessed 29 June 2019.
[64] SGBV Brief (n 52) para 2.

a direct perpetrator. The submission then highlights that the *amici* will assist the Chambers by sharing 'their professional understanding of the ways acts of rape and other forms of sexual violence constituted crimes under customary international law at the time of the Habré regime'.[65] Unlike at other tribunals, where a CV or other form of statement of expertise or interest may be required, there is no further attempt to explain the expertise or experience of the *amici*, or why it was required to supplement the submissions of the parties. This is not to dispute the qualifications of the *amici* in this area; rather, it merely highlights that the Chambers may not have separately validated the expertise and the need for assistance, nor did the parties have a formal opportunity to do so.

The *amici* then specify the aim of the submission: '*Amici* urge the revision of the charges to reflect the full scope and gravity of the sexual violence described by the victims'.[66] This is based on Senegalese procedural law, which did permit judges the power to recharacterize charges based on the available evidence. The brief is more closely linked to the facts than many other *amicus* briefs, which are often limited to submissions on specific legal issues. Here, a summary of relevant facts is included, namely the facts and testimony that the *amici* suggest support the responsibility of the accused for various crimes of sexual and gender based violence. This is unusual, and would in other institutions have been potentially fatal to an *amicus* application, as Chambers are careful to distinguish between *amici* providing assistance and *amici* suggesting factual and legal conclusions from the evidence. There is little attempt on behalf of the *amici* to appear independent or impartial by focusing on legal elements; rather, it is evident throughout the brief that prosecution for SBGV is the clear goal of the brief. In this sense the brief is more similar to a party submission, and aligned closely to the demands for prosecution from victims and their lawyers.

The focus of the legal analysis in the SGBV brief is the state of customary international law concerning crimes of sexual violence between 1982 and 1990. This was required to allow the Chambers to include charges without violating the *nullum crimen* rule. In particular, the brief concludes that customary international law at the time of the regime supports the classification of rape and other forms of sexual violence as crimes against humanity, torture and war crimes, as included in the EAC Statute.[67] In reaching this conclusion, the SGBV brief provides a clear and systematic survey of the relevant history and jurisprudence of these crimes under customary international law. However, it is striking to note how simplified the brief is, in that it does not assume basic knowledge and explains central concepts of international law, for example, explaining how a rule of customary international law is formed and stating that the Geneva Conventions and Additional Protocol I 'make up the backbone of international humanitarian law'.[68] In many ways, this is an educational document—drafted by an international NGO and international academics and practitioners—directed at national judges lacking familiarity with the relevant international legal provisions and jurisprudence. It may also have been intended to serve as a blueprint for the relevant parts of the judgment and, to a more limited extent, an advocacy document in that it supported and informed the broader efforts to draw attention to sexual violence during the Habré regime.

[65] ibid 4.
[66] ibid.
[67] ibid 145–46.
[68] ibid 22.

In terms of the impact of the SGBV brief, the Chamber eventually decided to re-characterize the facts and include charges concerning sexual violence and in the judgment found the defendant was convicted of rape and torture as a crime against humanity in respect of rapes that occurred in detention centres.[69] The judgment recognized that the prolonged servitude of women and girls in detention could constitute slavery as a crime against humanity.[70] The Chamber also convicted Habré of torture as a separate crime, based on the rapes perpetrated in detention centres.[71] While Habré was convicted of war crimes including inhumane treatment and torture, the war crimes sections of the judgment do not address sexual violence directly.[72] In addition, the Chamber found that Habré had personally raped one witness, Zidane.[73] The decision was welcomed as an important contribution to ending impunity for sexual violence, including the first instance where a former head of state had been convicted of personally committing rape.[74] However, while the conviction in relation to the other sexual violence charges was upheld on appeal, this conviction for rape as a direct perpetrator was overturned on appeal for procedural reasons, with the Appeals Chamber holding that as evidence of these rapes had only emerged during the trial, this evidence was new and could not be re-qualified.[75]

In the absence of rules addressing the ability to file *amicus* submissions, the legal status of the brief was uncertain. The impact of the brief is hard to determine, as multiple factors may have led to the inclusion of these additional charges, including the submissions of the victims' legal representatives, the evidence that had emerged in testimony, renewed prosecution efforts to focus on sexual violence, and the growing interest in seeing sexual violence investigated. It is difficult to isolate the influence of the SGBV brief separate from these possible causal factors. Yet, the brief clearly had some impact, as the reasoning, structure and sources in the brief were reflected in important places in the judgment.[76] Key actors, including the *amici* themselves, believed that the SGBV brief did influence the judges and their decision and contributed to a process that turned the *Habré* trial from another failure to recognize and prosecute SGBV crimes into a qualified success.[77] Inclusion of charges concerning sexual violence also led to specific reparations addressed to victims of sexual violence.[78]

69 *Ministère Public c Hissène Habré*, Trial Judgement EAC (30 May 2016).

70 ibid from para 1482.

71 ibid from para 1539, especially from para 1571 and from para 1801 regarding torture.

72 ibid from para 1783 (torture as a war crime) and from para 1737 (inhumane treatment).

73 ibid 719-36.

74 See, for example, UN Women, 'Statement on the Conviction of Hissène Habré' (*UN Women*, 31 May 2016) <http://www.unwomen.org/en/news/stories/2016/5/ed-statement-on-conviction-of-hissene-habre> accessed 23 January 2018.

75 *Procureur c Hissène Habré*, Appeal Judgement EAC (27 April 2017) paras 417–531. See also Seelinger, 'The Landmark Trial Against Dictator Hissène Habré' (n 63).

76 The structure of the section of the trial judgment on sexual violence follows a similar structure to the SGBV brief, ie slavery, then sexual slavery. The judgment also draws on many of the same judicial decisions referred to in the SGBV brief, for example drawing on the ICTY decision of *Kunarac* to establish that '*Les violences sexuelles causent necessairement une douleur ou des souffrances aigues, physiques ou mentales, et justifient ainsi leur qualification d'actes de torture*' ['Sexual violence necessarily gives rise to severe pain or suffering, whether physical or mental, and in this way justifies its characterisation as an act of torture.']. See *Habré*, Trial Judgement (n 69) para 1552. This was the *same passage* quoted by the *amici*: SGBV Brief (n 52) 83.

77 One expert mentioned that the SGBV brief was the most successful example of a brief that came to mind, in an interview for our study on the amicus curiae in international criminal justice.

78 For a further discussion of reparations, see Christoph Sperfeldt, 'The Trial against Hissène Habré: Networked Justice and Reparations at the Extraordinary African Chambers' (2017) 21 International Journal of Human Rights 1243.

Conclusion

The influence of the SGBV brief in the *Habré* trial continues the history of civil society actors attempting to use the *amicus curiae* mechanism as a tool to highlight experiences of sexual and gender-based violence and to ensure investigation and prosecution of such crimes. Dolidze highlights the potential of civil society actors using the *amicus curiae* brief to serve as norm entrepreneurs to promote an international law norm.[79] This contribution shows clearly that various actors have attempted to use the *amicus* brief in several international criminal tribunals to promote the norm of investigation and prosecution of sexual violence crimes. While those briefs have not always been formally accepted, or even if accepted may not demonstrate much direct influence on judicial outcomes, they have contributed to highlighting the issue of sexual violence and created pressure for institutions to address these previously neglected crimes.

The SGBV brief certainly had some influence on the judgment and helped to advance the norm of prosecution for sexual violence in the EAC. However, in the case of Habré (as indeed with the briefs in *Akayesu* and *Lubanga*), it is better to consider the brief as part of a 'transitional justice network' that operated to push the Chambers towards including charges concerning sexual violence.[80] The influence of the brief should not be considered in isolation from other factors, including the emerging testimony of sexual violence, initiatives by victims and their legal representatives to push the Court to recognize sexual violence and the broader advocacy campaign mounted to bring attention to this issue. As seen in other tribunals, given that acceptance of an *amicus* brief is within the discretion of the Chambers, it is rare that submitting an *amicus* brief alone will lead to changes in charging, particularly in those institutions such as the ICC where prosecutorial discretion in this area is paramount. In fact, initiatives by victims and their representatives, both formally in legal proceedings but also in making their views known to the Prosecutor through other means, are more likely to be effective than an *amicus* brief.

The absence of a legal framework for the acceptance of *amici* applications also aided the 'influence' of the brief, but may have had negative implications for the fair trial rights of the defence and the transparency of the proceedings. Unlike at other tribunals, the brief was not subject to a formal process that enabled its relevance and appropriateness, as well as the expertise and possible interest(s) of the *amici*, to be assessed before the brief was accepted. The SGBV brief had an uncertain legal status. This meant that the parties were not given an opportunity to respond formally to the submission of the brief (although they could respond to the substance of the brief in their own pleadings), yet the brief appears to have had some influence on the judicial decision-making process. Given the partisan style of the brief, which supported prosecution for SGBV, not allowing an opportunity for the defence to object to the brief arguably prejudiced Habré's fair trial rights. Moreover, the SGBV brief was directed to judges with little experience of international crimes and no history or expertise with prosecuting sexual violence, with limited resources for independent legal research, and probably also unfamiliar with the role of *amici*. Those factors made it more likely that the judges would rely on the brief. This suggests that other internationalized

[79] Anna Dolidze, 'Bridging Comparative and International Law: *Amicus Curiae* Participation as a Vertical Legal Transplant' (2015) 26(4) European Journal of International Law 851.
[80] See Sperfeldt (n 78).

tribunals should incorporate a provision on *amicus curiae* submissions into the Rules, even if the national legal system does not recognize or have a formal procedure for such briefs, to make the process at least somewhat clear, consistent and transparent. Judges and personnel on such tribunals, as well as potential *amici*, would also benefit from practice directions or other forms of guidance as to what is required to submit a brief, the requirements for the nature and structure of the brief, the process to be followed, and the circumstances in which a brief will be accepted. This will all enhance the fairness, transparency, and legitimacy of the proceedings and, ultimately, the institution itself.

38

'Sexualized Slavery' and Customary International Law

Patricia Viseur Sellers and Jocelyn Getgen Kestenbaum

Introduction

The Hissène Habré trial[1] and appellate[2] judgments represent watershed legal decisions rendering long-denied justice to victims of the brutal Chadian regime. Delayed charges of credible sexual violence[3] inflicted upon both males and females[4] challenged the judges of the Extraordinary African Chambers ('EAC') in Senegal. Legal characterizations of sexual assaults ultimately attributed to Habré represent significant jurisprudential advancements on rape, sexual slavery, and torture as international crimes.

The EAC's observations acknowledge that sexual slavery constitutes part of the *actus reus* of enslavement as crime against humanity and of slavery as a war crime.[5] While agreeing with the Chambers that sexual slavery is anchored in customary international law, this Chapter deepens the inquiry into the international legal prohibition of sexual slavery. The authors posit that, in fact, the 1926 Convention to Suppress the Slave Trade and Slavery ('1926 Slavery Convention') proscribed what is identified as 'sexual slavery' because sexualized violence is and always has been part and parcel of both *de jure* (legal) and *de facto* (customary) forms of slavery.[6]

[1] *Ministère Public c Hissène Habré*, Trial Judgment EAC (30 May 2016).

[2] *Le Procureur c Hissène Habré*, Appeal Judgement EAC (27 April 2017).

[3] See Reed Brody, 'Victims Bring a Dictator to Justice: The Case of Hissène Habré' *Brot für die Welt* (June 2017) 16–17 <https://www.brot-fuer-die-welt.de/fileadmin/mediapool/2_Downloads/Fachinformationen/Analyse/Analysis70-The_Habre_Case.pdf> accessed 11 September 2018 (recounting that victims' and Human Rights Watch reports told of Habré's policy of enslavement, which included transferring women to military camps where officers and guards detained and raped them). Additionally, the EAC found that prison guards forced women to have sex in exchange for access to basic necessities, such as water and medicine. See Kim Thuy Seelinger, 'Rape and the President: The Remarkable Trial and Partial Acquittal of Hissène Habré' (2017) 34 World Policy Journal <https://www.law.berkeley.edu/wp-content/uploads/2015/04/World-Policy-Journal-2017-Seelinger-16-22-2.pdf> accessed 5 April 2018.

[4] *Habré*, Trial Judgment (n 1) 610–20.

[5] The authors posit that, more precisely, *sexual violence* or *sexualized violence*—as opposed to 'sexual slavery'—is part of the *actus reus* or indicia of slavery and enslavement.

[6] The term 'forms of slavery' has been used in different contexts to mean either *de jure* or *de facto* slavery, or to mean the various institutions and practices that meet the definitional elements of slavery, ie institutions and practices in which perpetrators exercise any and all powers attaching to the right of ownership over victims. For example, the 1926 Slavery Convention calls for 'the complete abolition of slavery in *all its forms*' (The Convention to Suppress the Slave Trade and Slavery, 25 September 1926, 60 LNTS 253, *entered into force* 9 March 1927, Art 1(1) (emphasis added)). Also, the 1956 Supplementary Convention and Additional Protocol II to the Geneva Conventions prohibits slavery and the slave trade 'in *all their forms*' (Supplementary Convention on the Abolition of Slavery, the Slave Trade, and Institutions and Practices Similar to Slavery, 30 April 1956, 226 UNTS 3, *entered into force* 30 April 1957, preamble; Protocol (II) Additional to the Geneva Conventions of 12 August 1949, 8 June 1977, *entered into force* 7 December 1978, Art 4(2)(f)). Here, we refer to 'forms' as *de jure* or *de facto* slavery in the various institutions and practices in which these forms manifest. The important point for our purposes is that whether you consider 'forms' to mean *de jure* and *de facto* slavery, or the manifestations of these forms in

Patricia Viseur Sellers and Jocelyn Getgen Kestenbaum, *'Sexualized Slavery' and Customary International Law* In: *The President on Trial*. First edition. Edited by: Sharon Weill, Kim Thuy Seelinger, and Kerstin Bree Carlson, Oxford University Press (2020).
 DOI: 10.1093/oso/9780198858621.003.0039

Accordingly, the Habré Trial Chamber might have refined its distillation of sexual slavery as customary international law by noting that it as an intractable component of slavery, which was outlawed in the 1926 Slavery Convention. Sexual slavery, often mischaracterized as a recent or modern *form* of slavery, demands a more astute legal articulation. This Chapter clarifies the law on slavery, asserting that sexual violence or assaults on sexual integrity are integral to *de jure* and *de facto* forms of slavery. The authors endeavour to reorient the legal discussion toward a more nuanced, multidimensional understanding of the crimes of slavery and enslavement.

Part II of this Chapter focuses on the EAC's treatment of sexual violence and the crime of sexual slavery throughout the course of the Habré trial. Part III examines the customary law bases of slavery as an atrocity crime, maintaining that the 1926 Slavery Convention is the proper place to begin such inquiries and to receive such grounding. Then, Part IV asserts that 'sexualized slavery'—consisting of acts of sexualized violence—comprises the *actus reus* or indicia of slavery whether it be *de jure* or *de facto* slavery; thus, when present, sexual violence and sexual integrity harms cannot be decoupled from manifestations of slavery. Part V concludes by suggesting legal and practical rationales—including correcting course in codified international criminal law—to reintegrate sexual violence and sexual integrity harms into our conceptualization of slavery as an international crime.

Sexual slavery in the Hissène Habré trial

The investigating magistrates' original referral order to the EAC in the Hissène Habré trial recognized evidence of sexual violence, such as rapes against detained women, sexualized torture against male prisoners and sexual violence against children.[7] Despite overwhelming proof of sexual violence, the resulting charges did not contain any explicit allegations of sexual and gender-based crimes.[8] Notwithstanding these omissions, victim-witnesses testified at trial that Habré and his agents detained them in secret prisons as sex slaves, perpetrating against them additional horrific acts of violence—including rapes, genital injuries, beatings, stabbings, forced nudity, electric shocks on sexual organs and forced contraception (ie being forced to take birth control pills).[9] In the wake of this testimony, civil society groups urged the Trial Chamber to address fully the sexual violence, and international law experts filed an *amicus curiae* brief to aid the EAC in its legal analysis of potential charges.[10]

institutions and practices today, 'sexual slavery' is not a 'form' of slavery; rather, sexualized violence is part and parcel of *de jure* and *de facto* forms of slavery in all the institutions and practices in which slavery exists.

[7] Habré, Trial Judgment (n 1) 1480.

[8] ibid 96–97.

[9] Seelinger, 'Rape and the President' (n 3); Testimony of Fatimé Sakine [22 October 2015] Trust Africa, 'The Public Prosecution v. Hissène Habré - Summary of the Thirty-First Hearing Held on 22 October 2015' <http://www.trustafrica.org/images/ICJ_reports/EAC-%20Trial%20Hearing%20Report%20-%2022nd%20October%20 2015%20-%20English.pdf> accessed 4 April 2018; Testimony of Garba Akhaye [28 September 2015] Trust Africa, 'The Public Prosecution v. Hissène Habré—Summary of the Sixteenth Hearing Held on 28 September 2015' <http://www.trustafrica.org/images/ICJ_reports/EAC-%20Trial%20Hearing%20Report%20-%2028th%20 September%202015%20-%20English.pdf> accessed 5 April 2018; Testimony of Katouma Deffalah [Tuesday 20 October 2015] Trust Africa, 'The Public Prosecution v. Hissène Habré—Summary of the Twenty-Ninth Hearing Held on 20 October 2015' <http://www.trustafrica.org/images/ICJ_reports/EAC-%20Trial%20Hearing%20 Report%20-%2020th%20October%202015%20-%20English.pdf> accessed 5 April 2018.

[10] *Hissène Habré*: Amicus Curiae Brief of the Human Rights Center, University of California, Berkeley, School of Law, and International Experts on Sexual Violence Under International Criminal Law, 'Rape and Other Forms

Toward the close of trial, the EAC notified the parties of its duty to characterize the entirety of the criminal conduct, inclusive of sexualized and gender-based violence.[11] The victims' representatives then submitted a motion to the EAC, requesting that the Chambers consider sexual violence charges.[12] As a result, the EAC 're-qualified' the evidence and amended the charges to include rape and sexual slavery as crimes against humanity under Article 6(a) of the EAC Statute.[13] Further, the EAC rightly characterized the charges of war crimes and the autonomous crime of torture under Article 8 to comprise sexual violence acts committed against male and female detainees.[14]

On 30 May 2016, the EAC convicted Habré of rape and sexual slavery as crimes against humanity and of torture as both a war crime and a stand-alone crime.[15] The judgment declared that Habré was liable, not only for the rapes and sexual slavery his subordinates committed, but also for the rapes he directly perpetrated.[16] To establish that sexual slavery occurred, the Court intoned that:

> ... [T]he Chamber is satisfied that the soldiers at the camp exercised the powers associated with property rights over them. The Chamber is also convinced that the military men deliberately forced the females to have sex with them. There is no doubt that [the soldiers] were conscious that the females, held captive in the camps, over a long period of time, with no ability to escape, had no autonomy over their lives, and that [the soldiers] exercised power over [the victims] such that, in reality, they were under their complete control, including control over their reproductive capacity.[17]

Thus, the Trial Chamber found that Habré was the 'maestro of the orchestra of a repressive system'[18] and culpable for the sexual violence because he was 'aware that women [and men] were held in a climate of generalized and institutionalized violence ... in a state of extreme vulnerability, without any protection. He also knew that they were interrogated and monitored by male state agents who used daily, and with impunity, violence against the detainees.'[19] In light of the evidence, the EAC concluded that Habré knew or should have known that his subordinates would rape detainees under their complete control.[20]

of Sexual Violence as Crimes Against Humanity, War Crimes and Torture Under Customary International Law' (8 December 2015) <https://www.law.berkeley.edu/wp-content/uploads/2015/04/MICUS-CURIAE-BRIEF-OF-THE-HUMAN-RIGHTS-CENTER-AT-THE-UNIVERSITY-OF-CALIFORNIA-BERKELEY-SCHOOL-OF-LAW-AND-INTERNATIONAL-EXPERTS-ON-SEXUAL-VIOLENCE-UNDER-INTERNATIONAL-CRIMINAL-LAW-Eng.pdf> accessed 5 April 2018.

11 *Habré*, Trial Judgement (n 1) 1481.
12 ibid 168.
13 ibid 179.
14 ibid 1565. The trial judgment explains the EAC's ability to 're-qualify' the acts. It cites to the French law that inspired the Senegalese law, the practice of the Extraordinary Chambers in the Courts of Cambodia (ECCC), and the practice before the International Criminal Court (ICC). Evidence can be re-qualified, as long as the accused is duly informed (ibid 160–68). The judgment holds that sexual violence evidence can be the subject of requalification (ibid 178).
15 ibid 536. Article 6 of the EAC Statute includes '*esclavage sexuel*', or 'sexual slavery', in 6(a) under crimes against humanity and '*reduction en esclavage*', interpreted as 'enslavement' later in 6(f).
16 ibid 536.
17 ibid 1536 (authors' translation).
18 ibid 2155.
19 ibid 2159.
20 ibid 2160 (authors' translation). '[T]he crime of sexual slavery is charged in this case and its prohibition was foreseeable to the Accused at the time it was committed' (ibid 1498).

On appeal, the EAC upheld Habré's conviction for crimes against humanity of sexual slavery and rape, and for the sexualized torture that his agents perpetrated.[21] The Appeals Chamber, however, overturned Habré's conviction for the four rapes and acts of torture that he allegedly perpetrated himself against Khadidja Hassan Zidane.[22] Despite the Appellate Chamber's finding that the victim-witness testimony was credible, the Court ruled that the investigating judges had not considered these sexual assaults in the *ordonnance de renvoi*; therefore, any change at that stage would have consisted of modifying (read supplementing)—not re-characterizing—the facts in the *ordonnance de renvoi*.[23] Indeed, Khadidja Hassan Zidane's recounting of these incidences came to light only after the trial began.[24] Thus, the Court procedurally could not include the sexual violence perpetrated by Habré himself among the evidence eligible for re-qualification, and, consequently, those rapes could not be the basis of the amended charges nor of any ensuing conviction.[25]

Despite the meaningful--yet partial[26]--redress, the re-qualification of sexual and gender-based crimes recalibrated the narrative of Habré's ruthless reign by situating long-term, systematic sexual violence and slavery among the regime's most horrific crimes. Moreover, this consideration allowed for further judicial scrutiny of sexual slavery's proscription under international law. The case called upon the Trial Chamber to assess the legal status of sexual slavery at the time of the Habré regime. In other words, was sexual slavery a crime during the 1980s under international law? The Chamber rightly responded unequivocally in the affirmative. To reach the conclusion that the safeguards of *jus cogens* and customary international law condemned sexual slavery as a crime against humanity and a war crime at the operative time,[27] the Trial Chamber meticulously reviewed the applicable law.

The Trial Chamber noted first that customary law recognized the prohibition of slavery around 1926 to 1930,[28] and second that custom was evinced in the charters of the international military tribunals established after the Second World War that enumerated individual criminal liability for enslavement.[29] Likewise, the EAC recognized that slavery or enslavement found berth in Control Council Law No. 10 and in the provisions of the Nuremberg Principles.[30] The Chambers also acknowledged that the International Law Commission's Draft Code of Crimes Against the Security and Peace of Mankind dated the inclusion of its enslavement provision to at least the 1950s.[31] The Court cited to jurisprudence of the International Criminal Tribunal of the former Yugoslavia (ICTY) and the Extraordinary Chambers in the Courts of Cambodia (ECCC) as conclusive evidence of the crime against humanity of enslavement's customary status,[32] given that their exercise of jurisdiction was limited to crimes under customary law.

21 *Habré*, Appeals Judgement (n 2) 229.
22 ibid.
23 ibid 522–26, 529–31.
24 Seelinger, 'Rape and the President' (n 3).
25 *Habré*, Appeals Judgment (n 2) 527–28; Seelinger, 'Rape and the President' (n 3).
26 *Habré*, Appeals Judgment (n 2) 531.
27 *Habré*, Trial Judgment (n 1) 1483.
28 ibid 1484. Under the 1926 Slavery Convention, 'slavery' is defined as 'the status or condition of a person over whom any or all of the powers attaching to the right of ownership are exercised' (1926 Slavery Convention (n 7) Art 1(1)).
29 *Habré*, Trial Judgment (n 1) 1485.
30 ibid 1486.
31 ibid 1487.
32 ibid 1487–88.

To determine the international customary law basis of sexual slavery, the Trial Chamber appraised the international criminal jurisprudence. First, the Court examined *Prosecutor v. Kunarac et al.*, an ICTY case in which the Tribunal convicted several accused for enslavement as a crime against humanity based upon the defendants' sexual control of detained Bosnian Muslim females during the war in the former Yugoslavia.[33] The Habré Trial Chamber cited to the *Kunarac* judgment's reasoning that enslavement could comprise acts of a sexual nature[34] and that such sexual control could be the means by which to carry out enslavement.[35] The Trial Chamber further noted that the ECCC confirmed in its arrest warrant in *Prosecutor v Duch* that the exercise of sexual control could be considered part of the customary law of enslavement.[36] Accordingly, the Court concluded that international customary law recognized sexual slavery as a factual indicator of the crime of enslavement.

Turning its gaze on international humanitarian law, the Habré Trial Chamber scrutinized national military cases emanating from the Second World War and found that sexual slavery was perpetrated in many venues, including detention camps.[37] The Chamber noted the Batavia Temporary Military Court's case of Colonel Shoichi Ikeda for crimes committed in Dutch colonized Indonesia.[38] The Military Court convicted Ikeda for the abduction and forced prostitution of thirty-five Dutch female detainees who Ikeda coerced into sexual service of Japanese soldiers in a brothel.[39] The Trial Chamber also relied on analysis from the Appendix to the Report of the Special Rapporteur on Contemporary Forms of Slavery, observing that, by the 1940s, international customary law proscribed the wartime sexual slavery endured by the so-called 'comfort women' of the Second World War.[40]

Moreover, the EAC noted Geneva Convention provisions--in particular Common Article 3 and Article 28 of the Fourth Geneva Convention--that prohibit rape and sexual slavery as *jus cogens* norms.[41] The Chambers cited international jurisprudence, such as the Guatemalan *Sepur Zarco* case and the ICTY's *Furundžija* case to support these findings.[42] The Trial Chamber cogently ascribed the wartime prohibition of sexual violence under customary international humanitarian law as descending from the Lieber Code, the 1907 Fourth Hague Convention, and Control Council Law No 10.[43] Given the bevy of customary norms, international jurisprudence, treaty law, commentary and scholarly writings, the Trial Chamber concluded that, under international humanitarian law, sexual slavery, indeed, is a type of slavery.[44]

The Habré judgment's customary law grounding of sexual slavery as both a crime against humanity and a war crime—even if not convicting Habré of sexual slavery as a war crime—is commendable. Most significant is the Trial Chamber's pronouncement that

[33] ibid 1490.
[34] ibid.
[35] ibid 1491.
[36] ibid. *Co-Prosecutors v Kaing Guek Eav alias Duch*, Criminal Case File No 001/18-07-2007/ECCC/TC 147–54, Judgment (26 July 2010).
[37] *Habré*, Trial Judgment (n 1) 1493.
[38] ibid 1493.
[39] ibid.
[40] ibid.
[41] ibid 1494–95; *Prosecutor v Ntganda*, ICC-01/04-02/06 51, Second Decision on the Defense's Challenge to the Jurisdiction of the Court in respect of Counts 6 and 9 (15 June 2017).
[42] *Habré* Trial Judgment (n 1) 1494–95.
[43] ibid 1496.
[44] ibid 1497.

'sexual slavery ... is an element to take into account to determine whether there was enslavement and the duration during which the powers of ownership have been exercised.'[45] This Chapter, however, interrogates whether customary international law proscribed sexual slavery as a determinant of ownership earlier, under the 1926 Slavery Convention. If so, the crime that is now codified as 'sexual slavery,' begs reconsideration. The authors proffer that physical and psychological sexual violence acts were (and are) interconnected and inseparable from *de jure* chattel slavery or *de facto* slavery. Thus, mischaracterizing sexual slavery as recent or as modern slavery ignores the historical realities of enslavement and misconstrues the legal breadth of the abolition of slavery.

Slavery in all its forms under the 1926 Slavery Convention

Consistent with the Habré Trial Chamber's analysis, the authors recognize that the prohibition against slavery, enslavement, and the slave trade is a non-derogable,[46] *jus cogens* norm[47] with attendant *erga omnes* obligations.[48] Under international law, slavery was prohibited in times of war and peace; by 1945, twenty-six international instruments codified the prohibition of slavery and slavery-like practices.[49] Bassiouni posited the customary law basis of slavery crimes and similar practices, noting that:

> The cumulative effect of these [numerous international law] instruments established that slavery, slave-related practices and forced labor, were before 1945, prohibited under conventional international law, and ... also establish the customary international law basis

[45] ibid 1504. The authors agree with the Habré Trial Chamber's observation and, as demonstrated below, offer that the more precise legal determination is that sexualized violence is an act that is evidence, or *indicia*, of slavery, which is present whenever the perpetrator exercises powers attaching to the right of ownership over a person. For a detailed analysis, see Section IV, *infra*.

[46] Universal Declaration of Human Rights, GA Res 217A (III), UN GAOR, 3rd Session Part I at 71, UN Doc A/810 (10 December 1948) Art 4 ('No one shall be held in slavery or servitude; slavery and the slave trade shall be prohibited in all their forms.'); International Covenant on Civil and Political Rights, 16 December 1966, 999 UNTS 171, *entered into force* 23 March 1976 (Art 8(1): 'No one shall be held in slavery; slavery and slave-trade in all their forms shall be prohibited.' Art 8(2): 'No one shall be held in servitude.' Art 8(3)(a): 'No one shall be required to perform forced or compulsory labour.'); European Convention for the Protection of Human Rights and Fundamental Freedoms, 4 November 1950, 213 UNTS 221, *entered into force* 3 September 1953 (Art 4(1): 'No one shall be held in slavery or servitude.' Art 4(2): 'No one shall be required to perform forced or compulsory labour.'); American Convention on Human Rights, 22 November 1969, OAS/Ser.K/XVI/1.1, Doc 65, Rev 1, Corr 1, *entered into force* 18 July 1978 (Art 6(1): 'No one shall be subject to slavery or to involuntary servitude, which are prohibited in all their forms, as are the slave trade and traffic in women.' Art 6(2): 'No one shall be required to perform forced or compulsory labor.'); African Charter on Human and Peoples' Rights, 27 June 1981, OAU Doc CAB/LEG/67/3/Rev 5, *entered into force* 21 October 1986 (Art 5: 'Every individual shall have the right to the respect of the dignity inherent in a human being and to the recognition of his legal status. All forms of exploitation and degradation of man particularly slavery, slave trade, torture, cruel, inhuman or degrading punishment and treatment shall be prohibited.').

[47] Anthony D'Amato, *The Concept of Custom in International Law* (Cornell University Press 1971); Alfred Verdross, 'Jus Dispositivum and Jus Cogens in International Law' (1966) American Journal of International Law 55, 58–59; Gay J McDougall, *Contemporary Forms of Slavery: Systematic Rape, Sexual Slavery and Slavery-like Practices during Armed Conflict*, UN Doc E/CN/Sub.2/1998/13 (22 June 1998) para 46 (hereinafter McDougall Report).

[48] *Barcelona Traction, Light and Power Company, Limited (New Application: 1962) (Belgium v Spain)*, Second Phase, Judgment, ICJ Rep 1970, 3, paras 33–34 (5 February). McDougall Report (n 47) 74; M Cherif Bassiouni, 'International Crimes: *jus cogens* and *obligatio erga omnes*' (1996) 59(4) Law and Contemporary Problems 63.

[49] M Cherif Bassiouni, 'Enslavement as an International Crime' (1991) New York University Journal of International Law and Policy 445; McDougall Report (n 47) 46; M Cherif Bassiouni, *Crimes Against Humanity: Historical Evolution and Contemporary Application* (Cambridge University Press 2011) 378.

for the prohibition of these practices and for their inclusion as part of 'crimes against humanity'.[50]

The first international attempt at codifying the universal prohibition of slavery and the slave trade, the 1926 Convention to Suppress the Slave Trade and Slavery (1926 Slavery Convention), however, defines slavery as 'the status or condition of a person over whom any or all of the powers attaching to the right of ownership are exercised.'[51] The 1926 Slavery Convention includes either 'status' or 'condition' in the definition and actually enlarged the prohibition to govern *de jure* slavery (evidenced by legal title) and *de facto* slavery (evidenced by customary practice).[52]

To grasp the scope of slavery's operative definition, the 1926 Slavery Convention's preparatory works,[53] as well as Viscount Cecil's Temporary Slavery Commission Report[54] are informative. Cecil's Report accompanying the proposed 1926 Slavery Convention demonstrates that slavery's operative definition is the exercise of 'powers attaching to the right of ownership'.[55] Thus, the factual and legal understanding of the 1926 Slavery Convention encompasses the exercise of powers of ownership based upon sexual access to an enslaved person—what is today referred to as 'sexual slavery'. As the Habré Trial Chamber observed, sexual slavery is a factor in determining the occurrence of enslavement.[56] In other words, sexual slavery is slavery when powers attaching to the right of ownership are exercised. Consequently, sexual slavery is not a distinct *form* of slavery; rather, any and all forms of slavery, whether *de jure* or *de facto*, can be—and often are—inclusive of sexual slavery whenever sexualized violence is integral to the exercise of powers attaching to the right of ownership over a person.

The objective of the League of Nations—which included several Colonial powers who engaged in slavery and other widespread exploitative labour practices—was narrowly tailored toward ending legal (ie *de jure*, or chattel) slavery and the slave trade.[57] Notwithstanding this narrow aim, independent expert-members of the Temporary Slavery Commission recommended a broad definition of slavery that encompassed nearly all contemplated forms of human exploitation.[58] In 1925, the Temporary Slavery Commission set forth that 'debt slavery', the enslaving of persons disguised as the adoption of children, and the acquisition of girls by purchase disguised as payment of dowry, etc. constituted slavery whenever the definitional element of slavery--exercising any or all of the powers of ownership--were met.[59]

50 ibid 378; M Cherif Bassiouni, *Crimes Against Humanity in International Criminal Law* (Springer Netherlands 1992) 299.

51 1926 Slavery Convention (n 6) Art 1(1).

52 I/A Court HR, *Trabalhadores Fazenda Brazil Verde v Brazil*: Amicus Curiae Brief submitted by Helen Duffy, Human Rights in Practice (4 March 2016) <http://rightsinpractice.org/Brazil-Verde-Slavery-Amicus.pdf> accessed 5 April 2018.

53 Jean Allain, *The Slavery Conventions: The Travaux Préparatoires of the 1926 League of Nations Convention and the 1956 United Nations Convention* (Brill 2008); Jean Allain, 'A Legal Consideration of Slavery in Light of the *Travaux Préparatoires* of the 1926 Convention' (2006) paper presented at the Twenty-First Century Slavery: Issues and Responses Conference, The Wilberforce Institute for the Study of Slavery and Emancipation (WISE)).

54 League of Nations, *Slavery Convention: Report presented to the Assembly by the Sixth Committee* (1926) A.104.1926.VI (hereinafter Temporary Slavery Commission 1926 Report).

55 ibid; Allain, 'Legal Consideration of Slavery' (n 53) 11.

56 *Habré*, Trial Judgment (n 1) 1504.

57 Temporary Slavery Commission 1926 Report (n 54).

58 Jean Allain, *The Law and Slavery: Prohibiting Human Exploitation* (Brill 2015) 423–24.

59 League of Nations, *Annex: Draft Convention, League of Nations Official Journal (Special Supplement 33) Records of the Sixth Assembly: Text of Debates* (1925) 439; see also Temporary Slavery Commission's Second Session Minutes, (1925) para 55 <http://biblio-archive.unog.ch/Dateien/CouncilMSD/C-426-M-157-1925-VI_

The following year, Cecil similarly hinged slavery's definition on the elements now expressed in Article 1 of the 1926 Slavery Convention. He recognized that 'slavery in all its forms', or in any form, required the demonstration of exercising any power attached to the right of ownership over an individual,[60] even in cases that did not require legal ownership (*de facto* slavery). Conversely, when the conditions did not evidence the exercise of powers attaching to the right of ownership, then such acts would not constitute slavery.[61] Cecil's report proffered that '[a] legislative text which, as far as practicable, covers all offences against the liberty of the individual by a single, comprehensive sentence seems preferable to one attempting to enumerate all possible forms [ie manifestations] of slavery.'[62] The Temporary Slavery Commission's 1925 Report stated:

> In order to eradicate practices restrictive of liberty so far as they may occur in connection with marriage, concubinage, and adoption, the first object should be to strengthen the law so as to enable the courts to repress all abuses, and, secondly and more especially, to take measures in order that everyone should be fully aware that the status of slavery is in no way recognised by law.[63]

The Commission's intent was to outlaw any demonstration of powers attaching to the right of ownership over a person, crafting the definition in such a way that any exercise of powers of ownership would comply with the general, inclusive definition of slavery[64] and contemplating future novel ways in which slavery might manifest. Accordingly, sexual acts that domestic slaves were compelled to perform owing to their enslaved status would come within

EN.pdf> accessed 4 April 2018 (hereinafter Temporary Slavery Commission Second Session Minutes). Among the concerns Viscount Cecil addressed in the Report was the sale of children and servants in Hedjaz. The following passage illustrates the situation: 'The Temporary Slavery Commission is informed on authority which it regards as entirely trustworthy that many of the slaves of foreign origin in the Hedjaz are either young girls from the Far East who come as pilgrims or are smuggled for sale; or are persons coming from various countries accompanying their parents or masters in the pilgrimage to Mecca. The former case would seem to merit the attention of the Commissions concerned with the traffic in women, but there appears to be no doubt that they are sold as slaves. It is understood that certain Governments in the Far East insist that all persons, before sailing for the Hedjaz, shall provide themselves with passports. It seems desirable that this procedure should be more generally adopted. As regards the second case, it also seems desirable that some restriction should be placed on the taking of children or young persons to the Hedjaz and that all persons travelling as servants of or as attendants on pilgrims should be given freedom papers and registered at the port of embarkation'. ibid, 38–39.

60 Temporary Slavery Commission 1926 Report (n 54) 1–2.

61 Allain, *The Law and Slavery* (n 58) 423–24.

62 Temporary Slavery Commission 1926 Report (n 54) 25.

63 The Second Session meeting minutes of the Temporary Slavery Commission in 1925 describe that 'concubinage' fits squarely within the intended meaning of slavery as it is distinguished from wives. Children are born to a master who are not free and thus the freeing of two people, the woman and the child, is of issue. This was stated within a discussion of outlawing sexual slavery. Also, Sir F Lugard added that, with regard to concubines, those who bore children to their masters were set free and were considered to be free born. Children of concubines shared inheritance with the children of free-born wives. The result of freeing the concubines was that the children would become bastards and lose their inheritance and the women would degenerate into the position of 'kept women'. The Legal Adviser to the Sudanese Government vouched for this statement of Koranic law. Temporary Slavery Commission Second Session Minutes (n 59) 62.

64 Allain, *The Law and Slavery* (n 58) 423–24. Neither the Commission nor subsequently the drafters of the 1926 Slavery Convention, however, intended to outlaw what was forced labour; drafters found that, although evidence of constrained conditions existed, no powers of *de jure* or *de facto* ownership were exercised over persons. Jean Allain, 'The Definition of 'Slavery' in General International Law and the Crime of Enslavement within the Rome Statute,' Guest Lecture Series of the Office of the Prosecutor (2007) 5–6 <https://www.icc-cpi.int/NR/rdonlyres/069658BB-FDBD-4EDD-8414-543ECB1FA9DC/0/ICCOTP20070426Allain_en.pdf> accessed 4 April 2018.

the definition. The drafters' key concept was to condemn the exercise of powers attaching to the right of ownership, regardless of the nature of the acts that masters forced slaves to perform.

Prompted by the 1925 Temporary Slavery Commission Report, the ensuing modification to the 1926 Slavery Convention draft is singularly significant. The 1926 Slavery Convention omitted language of the types of slavery, such as 'domestic slavery and similar conditions', from the text.[65] Unsurprisingly, the drafters deemed it too limiting to qualify specific manifestations of slavery, preferring to emphasize the abolition of slavery *in all its forms*.[66] This revision is consistent with the drafters' intent to eradicate any and all slavery falling under the article 1(a) definition.[67]

The next question is this: How did the legal understanding of the 1926 Slavery Convention encompass the factual exercise of powers of ownership based upon sexual access to an enslaved person—what today is referred to as 'sexual slavery'? Part IV below advances, as pleaded by *amici* in the Habré case, the basis for sexual slavery as *indicia* of slavery, irrespective of its forms and, therefore, also as an atrocity crime under customary international law.

'Sexualized slavery' as slavery under customary international law

Recent international criminal law instruments have codified 'sexual slavery' as a standalone crime, partially due to the failures of adequate acknowledgement, investigation, prosecution, adjudication, and redress for victims and partially due to a misconception of slavery. Wartime female slavery, which often includes sexualized violence, has received pithy legal attention, even with the increased focus on conflict-related sexual and gender-based violence. Wartime male sexualized slavery remains almost completely unaddressed. The Tokyo Tribunal's failure to prosecute perpetrators for the enslavement of tens of thousands of 'Comfort Women' constitutes a lamentable omission in the annals of international law's ability to redress mass atrocity crimes.[68] Even today, criminal conduct referred to as 'sexual slavery' struggles against invisibility and impunity. The need to re-qualify the initial charges in the Habré case starkly illustrates this problem.

Assaults on sexual integrity often have been an innate aspect of the crime of slavery.[69] United Nations Special Rapporteur Gay McDougall has found that the 'term "sexual" is ... not to denote a separate crime. In all respects and in all circumstances, sexual slavery

[65] At the time of the drafting of the 1926 Slavery Convention, drafters used the term 'domestic slavery' to refer to 'non-Western slavery', 'African Slavery', 'indigenous slavery', or slavery as practiced in the colonies of Africa (as opposed to imported slavery practices of European powers in the trans-Atlantic slave trade). See Susan Miers, *Britain and the Ending of the Slave Trade* (Africana Publishing Corporation 1975) 118.

[66] Allain, 'The Definition of "Slavery"' (n 64) 5–6 (emphasis added).

[67] ibid.

[68] Patricia Viseur Sellers, 'Wartime Female Slavery: Enslavement?' (2011) 44 Cambridge International Law Journal 115, 118; Kelly Dawn Askin, *War Crimes Against Women: Prosecution in International War Crimes Tribunals* (1st edn, Martinus Nijhoff Publishers 1997) 73–775.

[69] Orlando Patterson, *Freedom in the Making of Western Culture* (Basic Books 1991) 50–51 (noting that circa 700 BCE, the Greek city-states would capture enemy females in order to replenish the slave population that was overwhelmingly female); Orlando Paterson, 'Trafficking, Gender and Slavery: Past and Present' in Jean Allain (ed), *The Legal Understanding of Slavery: From the Historical to the Contemporary* (1st edn, OUP 2012).

is slavery'.[70] Notably, neither the 1926 Slavery Convention nor the 1956 Supplemental Convention specifies that slavery be restricted to a certain sex or gender, nor does it proscribe a particular purpose for which a person is enslaved.[71] Any person, regardless of sex, age, or other status, can be enslaved. A slave is enslaved irrespective of labour, work, or service exerted from them, meaning that a person can be enslaved and not be required to perform any toil. Slavery is the status or condition to which a person is reduced.

Under international law, the predominant concept of slavery emerged as a result of the trans-Atlantic and East African Slave Trades. Slavery was characterized as an institution based upon chattel. Chattel slavery was *de jure* slavery that recognized the legal title or ownership of persons. Chattel slavery inherently included all proprietary rights over a slave's body.[72] Ownership over slaves extended to whatever labour or service that masters forced slaves to render; thus, slave ownership included complete sexual and reproductive proprietorship.[73]

Sexual access and reproductive control may be the *indicia* of the slavery in question. Although much historical research remains ongoing, the practice of chattel slavery in North and South America and the Caribbean from the seventeenth to the nineteenth centuries was rife with disregard for the sexual integrity of female and male slaves alike.[74] Slave auctions, for example, would advertise and sell both female and male slaves referred to as 'breeders' based on their perceived or real abilities to reproduce and bear children who would be born into slavery.[75] Slaveholders bred child-slaves through their sexual ownership over female and male slaves.[76] Breeding slaves allowed for masters to increase their wealth and slave labour force.

In addition to breeding, slaveholders themselves impregnated, raped, sexually mutilated slaves; ordered the sexual assaults of slaves; conducted sexual medical experiments on slaves, or otherwise abused slaves sexually.[77] Slave brothels or the housing of 'fancy [slave] girls' existed for owners' and associates' sexual entertainment.[78] State laws that prohibited the legal recognition of rape of female slaves reinforced sexual ownership.[79] Whether evidenced by breeding, impregnation, rapes, selling of sexual access, sexual mutilation, or

[70] McDougall Report (n 47) 30. The authors go further, arguing that sexual slavery is not a 'form' of slavery at all; rather, sexualized violence, including attacks on sexual integrity, is part of the *actus reus* of slavery *in all its forms*.

[71] Sellers, 'Wartime Female Slavery' (n 68) 123.

[72] Daina Ramey Berry, *The Price for Their Pound of Flesh: The Value of the Enslaved, from Womb to Grave, in the Building of a Nation* (Beacon Press 2018).

[73] Minutes of the Temporary Slavery Commission's 17th Meeting show that M Roncagli interrogated: 'Was it also certain, as had been said, that the only object of slavery in Africa was to obtain labour? It enslaved the whole material and moral life of the individual. It could not therefore be concluded that at the present time slavery only existed for the purpose of obtaining labour' (Temporary Slavery Commission Second Session Minutes (n 59) 87).

[74] See Peter Kolchin, *American Slavery* (Penguin History 1995) 124–25.

[75] Sellers, 'Wartime Female Slavery' (n 68) 122; Donna Wyant Howell, *I Was a Slave: True Life Stories Dictated by Former Slaves in the 1930's, Book Four: The Breeding of Slaves* (Am Legacy Books 1996) 11–12.

[76] Ramey Berry, *The Price for Their Pound of Flesh* (n 72).

[77] House slaves were exposed to sexual violence. See, eg, Diana Ramey Berry, *Swing the Sickle for the Harvest is Ripe: Gender and Slavery in Antebellum Georgia* (University of Illinois Press 2007) 37.

[78] Tiye A Gordon, *The Fancy Trade and the Commodification of Rape in the Sexual Economy of 19th Century U.S. Slavery* (2015).

[79] From the US Colonial period through Abolition, many states penalized the rape of female slaves. Although impunity was the norm, slave owners could sue offenders if offenders damaged slave owners' proprietary interests. See A Leon Higginbotham, Jr, *In the Matter of Color: Race and the American Legal Process: The Colonial Period* (OUP 1978) 282.

other violations of sexual integrity,[80] exercising powers over the reproduction and sexual integrity of slaves was inherent to chattel (*de jure*) slavery.

Sexual access through—and rules for access to—'sexual wives', such as in Zanzibar, the East African Slave Trade, or Arab slavery, provide further examples of sexualized violence as inherent in Eastern institutions of slavery.[81] Today, the Islamic State ('IS') has revived the past practice of legal enslavement of women and girls, which includes sexual access under specific conditions as part of the group's assertion of the Caliphate in Iraq and Syria.[82] According to IS publications, fighters have captured, sorted, sold, or gifted Yazidi women and children as 'spoils of war' or *sabaya*.[83] The IS Committee for the Buying and Selling of Slaves has organized the Yazidi slave markets and allowed a local committee and commander to preregister IS fighters before placing their bids to purchase slaves.[84] Enforced rules on reselling Yazidi women or girls as slaves prohibit slave trading between brothers and require that slaves complete a menstrual cycle to demonstrate they are not pregnant prior to sale.[85] Such regulations delimiting sexual access to a slave and controlling a slave's reproduction demonstrate sexualized violence as integral to and permissive as part of enslavement.

Indeed, sexual slavery--or, more precisely, sexual violence and attacks on sexual integrity--have been understood under customary international law to fall squarely within the *actus reus*—the exercise of any or all powers attaching to the right of ownership—of slavery as an atrocity crime well before its enumeration in the Rome Statute. In the East African Slave Trade, sexual ownership of female slaves, either as sexual wives or as concubines, constituted an ingrained feature of society.[86] The British colonial negotiations with the Zanzibar sultanate to abolish slavery in Zanzibar, hesitant to disrupt family structures, carved out an exception for concubines with regard to the scheduled manumission of slaves. Slavery was abolished in 1897. Nonetheless, an intentional, ten-year hiatus in outlawing the enslavement of sexual wives or concubines prolonged the status of these female slaves until

[80] For a discussion on using female slaves in the US to conduct medical experiments often without anesthesia to develop surgical procedures, including fistula and other gynaecological maladies, see Harriet A Washington, *Medical Apartheid: The Dark History of Medical Experimentation on Black Americans from the Colonial Times to the Present* (Doubleday Press 2006) 64–68.

[81] Abdulaziz Y Lodhi, *The Institution of Slavery in Zanzibar and Pemba* (Cambridge University Press 1973) 20. For example, social science defines slavery as the control of one person (the slave) by another (the slaveholder). Control transfers agency, freedom of movement, access to the body, and labour and its products and benefits, from the slave to the slaveholder, and violence supports and sustains such control. The aim of this control is primarily economic exploitation, but also may include sexual use or psychological benefit. See K Bales, *Disposable People: New Slavery in the Global Economy* (University of California Press 1999) 6; Kevin Bales, 'Slavery in its Contemporary Manifestations' in Jean Allain (ed), *The Legal Understanding of Slavery: From the Historical to the Contemporary* (1st edn, OUP 2012) 285.

[82] Report of the UN Human Rights Council (HRC), *'They came to destroy': ISIS Crimes Against the Yazidis*, UN Doc A/HRC/32/CRP.2 (15 June 2016) 55. The United States, Syria and Iraq are all states parties to the 1926 Slavery Convention.

[83] UN HRC Report, *'They came to destroy'* (n 82) 75.

[84] ibid 58.

[85] ibid 75.

[86] Lodhi (n 81) 20; Jonathon Glassman, 'Racial Violence, Universal History, and Echoes of Abolition in 20th Century Zanzibar' in Derek R Peterson (ed), *Abolitionism and Imperialism in Britain, Africa, and the Atlantic* (Ohio University Press 2010); League of Nations, *Report of the Temporary Slavery Commission*, A.19.1925.VI (1925) para 58 ('The custom of *concubinage under Moslem law and according to certain local practices is, on the contrary, much more likely to lead to slave-dealing*, since the acquisition of a concubine is generally effected by means of payment of a sum of money by whatever name—"present" or "dowry"—it may be called, which in this case is, in fact, a real purchase.') (hereinafter Temporary Slavery Commission 1925 Report).

1909.[87] The foregoing illustrates that sexual and reproductive access always has been contemplated as part of the *actus reus* of slavery under the 1926 Slavery Convention definition.

Take the Temporary Slavery Commission's 1925 Report, for instance, in which experts found that, '[a]ccording to the Koranic law, if strictly observed, a free woman cannot be a concubine ... The abolition of the legal status of slavery gives to the concubine the right to claim her freedom.'[88] Finally, under the institution and practice of slavery, a master had unfettered sexual access to a slave whether or not such power was exercised.[89] Indeed, for female slaves or their children to become kin in many kinship-based societies would have been unfathomable due to the nature of some strict hereditary kingdoms.[90] Sexual access, therefore, was an absolute right as an exercise of power of ownership.

In 1950, the UN Secretary-General appointed an Ad Hoc Committee on Slavery to suggest ways of eradicating slavery.[91] In its second Report in 1951, the Committee recommended adopting a supplementary convention to the 1926 Slavery Convention that would be 'more precise than that instrument in defining the exact forms of servitude dealt with [in the 1926 Slavery Convention]'.[92] Resisting this recommendation, the Secretary-General reiterated the inclusive purpose of general language in the 1926 Convention, quoting again the Cecil Report, that the 1926 Convention 'applies not only to domestic slavery but to all those conditions mentioned by the Temporary Slavery Commission ... ie, "debt slavery", the enslaving of persons disguised as the adoption of children, and the acquisition of girls by purchase disguised as payment of dowry, etc'.[93] That 'sexual slavery' was never mentioned as a specific addition demonstrates an understanding that sexual and reproductive access to and use of enslaved persons was accepted as an inherent and integral aspect of slavery—either a power attaching to the right of ownership or an indication of enslavement.

Additional evidence of sexualized slavery as an integral part of the prohibition of slavery is the UN Secretary-General's 1953 Memorandum, which considers the characteristics of the powers attaching to the right of ownership in the definition of slavery.[94] The Secretary-General included that the 'master may use the individual of servile status, and in particular

[87] Elke E Stockreiter, 'British Perceptions of Concubinage and the Patriarchal Arab Household: The Reluctant Abolition of Slavery in Zanzibar, 1890s–1900s' (2015) Slavery and Abolition 721, 727–29. For a discussion of similar legal redress of female concubine slaves in the context of colonial Nigeria, see also Paul E Lovejoy, 'Concubinage and the Status of Women Slaves in Early Colonial Northern Nigeria' (1988) Journal of African History 245 <http://www.jstor.org/stable/182383> accessed 7 August 2018.

[88] Temporary Slavery Commission 1925 Report (n 86) 59 ('*According to the Koranic law, if strictly observed, a free woman cannot be a concubine.* Concubines have a status which gives them certain privileges: for instance, a concubine cannot be repudiated if she bears a child to her master, a concubine having in this respect a more privileged position than a wife. Her children are free and share the inheritance with the children of the free-born wife.'), 60 ('*The abolition of the legal status of slavery gives to the concubine the right to claim her freedom*, though she may remain with her master if she wishes.').

[89] In the 1800s and early 1900s in the Great Lakes region of Africa, female slaves were used for reproduction to meet demands for labour needs, or to perform domestic chores as 'cook wives'. Henri Mêdard and Shane Doyle (eds), *Slavery in the Great Lakes Region of East Africa* (Ohio University Press 2007) 31–33.

[90] ibid 181.

[91] UN Economic and Social Council, Res No 238(IX) (20 July 1949); Jean Allain, *The Law and Slavery* (n 58) 431.

[92] UN Economic and Social Council, *Report of the* Ad Hoc *Committee on Slavery*, Second Session, UN Doc E/AC.33/13 (4 May 1951) 16–17.

[93] Temporary Slavery Commission 1925 Report (n 86) 439.

[94] UN Economic and Social Council, Report of the Secretary-General, *Slavery, the Slave Trade, and other forms of servitude*, UN Doc. E/2357 (27 January 1953) 28 (hereinafter UN Secretary-General's 1953 Report); Allain, 'The Definition of "Slavery"' (n 64) 13.

his [or her] capacity to work, in an *absolute manner, without any restriction* other than that which might be expressly provided by law'.[95]

Furthermore, Article 1 of the 1956 Supplementary Convention on the Abolition of Slavery, the Slave Trade, and Institutions and Practices Similar to Slavery (1956 Supplementary Convention) prohibits four enumerated servile statuses—debt bondage, serfdom, forced marriage, and child exploitation—'whether or not they are covered by the definition of slavery contained in Article 1 of the Slavery Convention'.[96] Thus, the 1956 Supplementary Convention expressly finds that any of these enumerated—or any other—statuses where the powers attached to the right of ownership are exercised is covered under the 1926 Slavery Convention.[97] The 1956 Supplementary Convention does not directly prohibit sexual slavery because it does not need to prohibit specific *indicia* of or acts that evidence slavery. The explicit mention of certain forms of slavery in the 1956 Supplementary Convention serve to increase the visibility and emphasize the enforcement of particular persistent manifestations of slavery but did not prohibit any new forms of enslavement. The definition of slavery persists as hinging on the exercise of any and all of the powers attaching to the right of ownership over another person.

The ICTY's *Kunarac* case exemplified a form of ownership illustrating customary international law: the accused held sixteen victims for months in captivity and subjected them to rape, including multiple gang rapes.[98] Here, the ICTY clarified that the work or tasks slaves are forced to perform may be factors or *indicia* to determine whether the crime of enslavement occurred, but do not constitute per se the elements of the crime of enslavement under customary international law.[99] According to the Court, factors indicative of enslavement include *inter alia* control of sexuality and forced labour.[100]

While enumeration of sexual slavery as a separate crime in statutes, such as the EAC statute or the Rome Statute, *does* emphasize its visibility and initiates momentum toward its eradication, this more contemporary legal separation may hinder a fuller comprehension of slavery in all of its dimensions. Sexual access is inherent in—or at times is the *raison d'être* of certain forms of—slavery. Historically, as explained *supra*, the slavery endured by females and males in the New World often enmeshed manual labour, sexual access, and reproductive control under powers exercised by a perpetrator-slave owner.[101] The specific codification today in international criminal law tends to decouple hard manual slave labour, often misconceived of and conflated with the term chattel slavery, from physical or psychological sexual violence that a 'manual' slave must endure. Such decoupling can be problematic in that it fails to understand the nature of slavery in all its forms, and that sexualized violence is but one mechanism of exercising control (ie powers attaching to the right of ownership) over a person.

[95] UN Secretary-General's 1953 Report (n 94) 28 (emphasis added). The phrase 'other than that which might be expressly prohibited by law' could include rules for enslavement. The IS enslavement of women and girls as *sabaya*, for instance, includes specific prohibitions as to who may be enslaved, for example, by religious belief, status, and age, which is largely based on when a slave may be raped or otherwise accessed sexually. IS D.013, IS D.014 (n 82); UN HRC Report, '*They came to destroy*' (n 81) para 55.

[96] Allain, *Travaux Préparatoires* (n 52) 18.

[97] ibid.

[98] *Prosecutor v Kunarac, Kovač and Vuković*, IT-96-23-T & IT-96-23/1-T, Trial Judgment (22 February 2001).

[99] ibid 542–43.

[100] ibid 543.

[101] Sellers, 'Wartime Female Slavery' (n 68) 115.

The desuetude of redressing slavery based upon sexual access and violence results partly from a legally and practically misguided extraction of sexual slavery from the crimes of slavery and enslavement. Even if pragmatically successful in combating impunity for sexual and gender-based crimes in international criminal law in the short term, such a divergence from customary international law must be corrected going forward to avoid long-term fragmentation of the international law on slavery. The Rome Statute's confusing enumeration of both enslavement and sexual slavery as a crime against humanity, and its omissions of enslavement under war crimes while listing sexual slavery, are incoherent, yet not dispositive of the customary law basis of sexualized violence--what is characterized today as 'sexual slavery'--as part of the prohibition of the crime of slavery.[102] Understandably, this divergence may cause uncertainty as to whether there are additional elements for prosecutors to prove under a 'sexual slavery' charge; the operative element, however, remains whether the accused exercised any or all powers attaching to the right of ownership over the victim. Causing a slave to be held out for a sexual act is evidence toward proof of sexual integrity violations of the slave, which is *indicia* of exercising powers of ownership over a person.

The Habré judgment: Positive steps towards clarity

In light of the discussion above, the recognition of sexual violence and attacks on sexual integrity as part of the customary international law safeguard on slavery is indelible. Given that an act of a sexual nature--what is enumerated in some international instruments as 'sexual slavery'--has been recognized as indicia of slavery and part of customary international law since 1926, sexual slavery was an international crime under customary international law during the time of the Habré regime.

Regrettably, the EAC overlooked an opportunity to deepen further a legal understanding of slavery in international law. Sexual violence and attacks on sexual integrity are essential indicia of slavery. Such a legal pronouncement would have lent itself to combating both male and female slavery in times of armed conflict or other atrocious political settings. Moreover, it would have assisted in increasing visibility for, among other victims, child-slaves born enslaved as a result of sexualized slavery. The bifurcation of sexual slavery and enslavement in the EAC Statute, similar to the Rome Statute's enumeration of these as separate crimes, is troublesome since it seemingly denudes the crimes of slavery and enslavement of their long-accepted indicia comprised of attacks on sexual integrity.

Finally, Habré's conviction might have delivered a more refined gendered analysis of the sexual enslavement that occurred in Chad, thus helping to clarify the crime's place in customary international law generally. Specifically, the Court might have examined the gender dimensions of slavery, including what is now codified as 'sexual slavery', by explaining the ways in which female and male slaves experience slavery. These nuanced analyses are

[102] Additionally, the drafters of the Rome Statute notably omitted the customary war crime of the 'slave trade' and, as a consequence, muddled what could be understood as 'slave trading' under enslavement as a crime against humanity. The problem with this conflation is that, in systems crimes like slavery, many perpetrators engage in different aspects of the crimes. Inadvertently, the practical consequence of enslavement encompassing both the crimes of slavery and the slave trade can serve to under-emphasize the prosecution and punishment of perpetrators who trade in slaves, but do not exercise powers of ownership and, thus, do not engage in the practice of slavery or slaveholding.

fundamental to rectifying discriminatory application of the law on slavery. A lack of further exploration of sexual slavery as the *actus reus* or indicia of any and all forms of slavery under customary international law, for instance, generally neglects gendered roles of women, girl, men, and boy-victims of sexualized violence and slavery. As a legal matter, recognizing the customary international law basis of sexual slavery also allows for the redress for men and boys—boy soldiers or 'Bacha bazi' in Afghanistan, for example—under slavery as a war crime and enslavement as a crime against humanity. In the Habré case, this lack of gendered recognition, as it relates to females, was detrimental to the Chadian and international communities' understanding of the scope and scale of Habré's ruthless reign.

39

Witness Protection

Nancy Amoury Combs[1]

Introduction

Witness protection has long been a contentious and expensive component of domestic criminal trials,[2] and it is an even more contentious and expensive component of international criminal trials of genocide, war crimes, and crimes against humanity. In many international criminal cases, the prosecution's case is based exclusively or almost exclusively on witness testimony.[3] Thus, if witnesses are not willing to testify, then the prosecution's case will necessarily fail.[4] Indeed, the last few years have seen several high-profile international criminal prosecutions disintegrate when witnesses recanted their inculpatory pre-trial statements and refused to testify. Prosecutors accused defendants and their associates of intimidating the witnesses;[5] victims, NGOs, and even judges lamented their inability to bring the alleged wrongdoers to justice.[6] But the defendants and their associates denied the accusations, the witnesses remained firmly unwilling to testify, and the defendants walked free.

Given the tremendous importance of witnesses to international criminal cases and given the ease with which defendants can credibly threaten harm to those witnesses, one might assume that the international criminal tribunals do everything necessary to provide witnesses with whatever level of protection they need in order to assure their safety and thereby enable them to testify. The international criminal tribunals do spend vast sums—in both financial and human resources—to provide top-quality witness protection, but there are countervailing considerations in the form of fairness to defendants that place limits on the efforts they can and should undertake. Anonymous witnesses are safer witnesses, to be sure, but they are also witnesses whose testimony cannot be adequately investigated or scrutinized by defence counsel. Witnesses who are relocated to peaceful nations are assuredly safer witnesses, but offering relocation provides those witnesses an incentive to fabricate whatever inculpatory testimony is necessary to get themselves on the witness stand and (thereby) out of their war-torn homelands.

Any in-depth examination of international criminal law is apt to reveal a series of compromises. Typically, these compromises mediate between the idealistic principles that

[1] I am grateful to Nathan Mehta for excellent research assistance. Any mistakes are my own.

[2] For a summary description of domestic witness protection systems, see Chris Mahony, *The Justice Sector Afterthought: Witness Protection in Africa* (2010) 5–7.

[3] See Markus Eikel, 'Witness Protection Measures at the International Criminal Court: Legal Framework and Emerging Practice' (2012) 23 Criminal Law Forum 97, 98; Goran Sluiter, 'The ICTR and the Protection of Witnesses' (2005) 3 Journal of International Criminal Justice 962, 963–64.

[4] Likewise and arguably more problematic: when defence witnesses are too fearful to testify, then international criminal tribunals run a real risk of convicting the innocent.

[5] See Susanne D Mueller, 'Kenya and the International Criminal Court (ICC): Politics, the Election and the Law' (2013) 8 Journal of East African Studies 25, 34–35.

[6] ibid 34.

Nancy Amoury Combs, *Witness Protection* In: *The President on Trial*. First edition. Edited by: Sharon Weill, Kim Thuy Seelinger, and Kerstin Bree Carlson, Oxford University Press (2020). © Nancy Amoury Combs. DOI: 10.1093/oso/9780198858621.003.0040

courts and legal officials aim to defend and the grimy political realities that surround efforts to prosecute political and military leaders who still command armies, police forces, and treasuries. An examination of witness protection in international criminal law also reveals compromises, but these compromises more often mediate between two principled positions that international courts appropriately and simultaneously seek to uphold. On the one hand, witnesses must be protected from violence. On the other hand, the rights of the accused must be safeguarded. That means that witness protection measures must be calibrated to provide just enough disguise, concealment, or distance to prevent harm to the witness without undermining the defendant's ability to elucidate relevant facts, raise appropriate questions about the witnesses' testimony, and generally present a robust defence. And the protection measures certainly should not provide an independent incentive to become a witness in the first place. If witness protection could be measured out in teaspoons, then the careful calibration I have just described might take place. In the messy world of post-conflict justice, by contrast, international criminal tribunals have at various times over-protected and they have under-protected. They have developed legal doctrines on the fly, only to reverse course and develop different doctrines in later cases. Witnesses have lied and witnesses have died. Witness protection stands as among the most crucially important yet excruciatingly difficult tasks that international criminal tribunals undertake. In the following pages, this chapter will explore the witness protection path that international criminal law has forged in seeking to gain *accurate* testimony, from witnesses who *live* to tell the tale, in trials that are *fair* to the accused.

Witness protection: The need, the rules, and the precedents

In the *Tadić* case, the International Criminal Tribunal for the former Yugoslavia (ICTY) launched the modern wave of international criminal justice. As the first case decided by an international criminal tribunal since the Nuremberg and Tokyo Tribunals, *Tadić* broke new ground on a variety of substantive and procedural issues. One of the most controversial precedents the *Tadić* judgment set, however, concerned witness protection. The *Tadić* case was heard while the conflict in the former Yugoslavia was still raging, so the Prosecution sought a series of protective measures, maintaining that they were needed to allay the fears of witnesses and convince them to testify.[7] Many of the prosecution's requested protections were uncontroversial, but one highly controversial measure the prosecution sought was to present witnesses whose identities would not be revealed to the defendant. Though one Trial Chamber judge dissented, a majority acceded to the prosecution's request, and permitted certain witnesses to testify anonymously so long as five requirements were met.[8] This precedent—though ground-breaking—had no lasting impact. Whether the ICTY was stung by the storm of academic criticism the decision provoked[9] or was chagrined after the

[7] *Prosecutor v Tadić*, Case No IT-94-1 ICTY, Decision on the Prosecutor's Motion Requesting Protective Measures for Victims and Witnesses (10 August 1995) 5.

[8] ibid 62–66, 76–85.

[9] See, eg, Natasha Affolder, 'Tadić, the Anonymous Witness and the Sources of International Procedural Law' (1998) 19 Michigan Journal of International Law 445, 493–94; Paul Hoffman, 'The Dusan Tadić Trial and Due Process Issues' (1997) 19 Whittier Law Review 313, 314–15; Monroe Leigh, Editorial Comment, 'Witness Anonymity is Inconsistent with Due Process' (1997) 91 American Journal of International Law 80; Patricia M Wald, 'Dealing with Witnesses in War Crimes Trials: Lessons from the Yugoslav Tribunal' (2002) 5 Yale Human

defence proved that one of the Tadić witnesses who had not been granted anonymity had perjured himself[10] is not clear, but the ICTY never again permitted a party to present the testimony of an anonymous witness. And neither has any other international tribunal.

Perhaps the *Tadić* Chamber swung the pendulum too far in favour of protecting witnesses, but there is little question that witnesses in international criminal cases are in great need of protecting. By 1996, the International Criminal Tribunal for Rwanda (ICTR) had barely begun its work, yet a United Nations report found that 99 witnesses had been murdered by Hutu extremists as a consequence of their cooperation with the tribunal.[11] ICTY witnesses, similarly, have turned up dead,[12] and legions more—at all of the tribunals, including the International Criminal Court (ICC)—either live in terror following their testimony or refuse to testify at all because they or their families have been threatened with violence.[13] But it is likewise true that some witnesses lie,[14] and certain witness protection measures unquestionably impair defence efforts to identify their perjury.

Most scholarship on witness protection focuses on the protection afforded to witnesses when they testify at trial, but to be effective, witness protection efforts must begin well before any individuals have even been identified as witnesses. Merely speaking to international criminal tribunal investigators can endanger the local population, particularly when the conflict in question is on-going, and the security situation is unstable. For this reason, international criminal tribunal investigators often must undertake extraordinary efforts to approach potential witnesses without exposing them, as it were.[15] At the ICC, for instance, these efforts have included 'identify[ing] safe sites for interviews; secur[ing] discreet transportation for investigators and witnesses; provid[ing] for the contingency of moving witnesses to safe locations without attracting attention; and even check[ing] the relationships of drivers and hotel owners with the suspects'. In addition, witness protection must continue long after the trial ends and even potentially after the tribunal finishes its cases and closes its doors.[16]

Rights and Development Journal 217, 222–23 (describing the 'furor' ignited in the American Bar Association as a result of the decision).

[10] See Hoffman, 'The Dusan Tadić Trial' (n 9) 315; Richard Blystone and Reuters, 'War Crimes Tribunal Jeopardized by Witness Tampering' *CNN* (The Hague, 25 October 1996) <www.cnn.com/WORLD/9610/25/war.crimes> accessed 29 June 2019.

[11] See P J Magnarella, *Justice in Africa: Rwanda's Genocide, its Courts and the UN Criminal Tribunal* (Ashgate Publishing 2000) 74.

[12] See Matthew Brunwasser, 'Death of War Crimes Witness Casts Cloud on Kosovo' *New York Times* (Prizren, 6 October 2011); B92, 'Details of Statement by one of Haradinaj Witnesses who Died' (11 April 2017) <www.b92.net/eng/news/politics.php?yyyy=2017&mm=04&dd=11&nav_id=100993> accessed 29 June 2019.

[13] See Mahony, *Afterthought* (n 2) 26; Michael P Sharf and Ahran Kang, 'Errors and Missteps: Key Lessons the Iraqi Special Tribunal can learn from the ICTY, ICTR, and SCSL' (2005) 38 Cornell International Law Journal 911, 939; Balkan Insight, 'Can the New Kosovo Court Keep Witnesses Safe?' (20 January 2016) <http://www.balkaninsight.com/en/article/can-the-new-kosovo-court-keep-witnesses-safe--01-20-2016> accessed 29 June 2019

[14] See Nancy Amoury Combs, *Fact-Finding Without Facts: The Uncertain Evidentiary Foundations of International Criminal Convictions* (Cambridge University Press 2010) 130–66.

[15] See Office of the Prosecutor, 'Report on the activities performed during the first three years (June 2003–June 2006)' (ICC 12 September 2006) 7 <www.icc-cpi.int/NR/rdonlyres/D76A5D89-FB64-47A9-9821-725747378AB2/143680/OTP_3yearreport20060914_English.pdf> accessed 29 June 2019; see also Mahony, *Afterthought* (n 2) 72-75 (discussing challenges facing ICTR prosecutors).

[16] See, eg, Valerie Oosterveld, 'The International Criminal Court and the Closure of the Time-Limited International and Hybrid Tribunals' (2010) 8 Loyola University of Chicago International Law Review 13.

Turning to the witness protection measures that are taken during trial, they may be broadly classified as (1) those aiming to conceal the witnesses' identity from the public; and (2) those aiming to protect witnesses from the defendant. Although both sets of measures implicate the defendant's fair trial rights, those in the former category tend to generate less controversy. For that reason, in some tribunals, it has become so routine for witnesses to testify under pseudonym that virtually no witnesses are identified by name.[17] Likewise, the international tribunals commonly use voice distortion and screens to prevent the public from identifying the witnesses.[18] These measures are particularly valuable for witnesses who have been victims of sexual violence. Many such witnesses are deeply reluctant to testify because they reside in communities in which the mere reporting of rape can leave victims vulnerable to rejection, ridicule, and stigmatization.[19]

Finally, the tribunals use *in camera* proceedings to conceal the identity of witnesses from the public. Ideally, Trial Chambers would use this measure sparingly and go *in camera* only to prevent the disclosure of certain, specific testimony that threatens to reveal the witness's or family's identity. Although some Trial Chambers do employ very targeted use of *in camera* proceedings, in other cases, large portions of the testimony are held *in camera*,[20] prompting claims that the tribunals are violating the defendants' right to a public trial.[21] Trials that are not sufficiently available to the public also undermine the tribunals' efforts to educate local communities and create a historical record of the atrocity. Indeed, some have claimed that excessive use of *in camera* proceedings negatively impacts the Tribunal's credibility and legitimacy.[22]

Measures that conceal the witness's identity from the defendant are far more controversial because they have the potential to more seriously impair the defendant's fair trial rights. As noted, the ICTY initially was willing to accept testimony from witnesses whose identities were never revealed to the defendant, but it abandoned that practice and no subsequent tribunal took it up. What all of the tribunals have authorized, however, is the delayed disclosure of witness identities to the defence. In the tribunals' early years, the rules of procedure and evidence permitted the prosecution to keep witness identities confidential until

[17] See Sluiter, 'The ICTR' (n 3) 967, 976. Such measures are authorized by Rome Statute (Article 57(3)) and the rules of procedure and evidence (rule 87). Rome Statute of the International Criminal Court, 17 July 1998, 2187 UNTS 3, 37 ILM 999 (1998), *entered into force* 1 July 2002, Art 57(3); Rules of Procedure and Evidence, Official Records of the Assembly of States Parties to the Rome Statute of the International Criminal Court, First session, New York, 3–10 September 2002 (ICC-ASP/1/3 and Corr.1), part II.A, r 87.

[18] See Colin T McLaughlin, 'Victim and Witness Measures of the International Criminal Court: A Comparative Analysis' (2007) 6 Law and Practice International Courts and Tribunals 189, 196–98, 200–02; Patricia M Wald, 'The International Criminal Tribunal for the Former Yugoslavia Comes of Age: Some Observations on Day-To-Day Dilemmas of an International Court' (2005) 5 Washington University Journal of Law and Policy 87, 109.

[19] See, eg, Florence Mumba, 'Ensuring a Fair Trial Whilst Protecting Victims and Witnesses—Balancing of Interests?' in Richard May and others (eds), *Essays on ICTY Procedure: In Honour of Gabrielle Kirk McDonald* (2001) 359, 361; Human Rights Watch, 'Struggling to Survive: Barriers to Justice for Rape Victims in Rwanda' (Report, 29 September 2004) 29–30; Amnesty International, 'Sierra Leone: Getting Reparations Rights for Survivors of Sexual Violence' (Report, AI-Index AFR 51/005/2007 7, 1 November 2007).

[20] See International Justice Monitor, 'New Lubanga Witness To Give All Testimony In Camera' (24 March 2010) <www.ijmonitor.org/2010/03/new-lubanga-witness-to-give-all-testimony-in-camera/> accessed 29 June 2019.

[21] See Christine Kunst, *The Protection of Victims and Witnesses at International and Internationalized Criminal Courts—the example of the ECCC* (2013) 192; see also Wald, 'Dealing with Witnesses' (n 9) 223–24 (observing that the combination of witness protection measures employed by the ICTY raises questions about whether the Tribunal is upholding the defendant's right to a public trial).

[22] See Mahony, *Afterthought* (n 2) 50-51.

some point before the trial began.[23] This practice proved insufficiently protective, however, because international criminal trials are so lengthy and often feature dozens of prosecution witnesses. As a consequence, witness identities that were revealed directly before the trial began often were revealed months or even years before the witness actually testified and thereby provided defendants ample time to threaten or harm witnesses.[24] As a consequence, in recent years, the tribunals have revised their rules to provide for 'rolling disclosure'; that is, disclosure of the witness's identity that only occurs a short time before the witness is actually scheduled to testify.[25] Different tribunals require disclosure at different times,[26] but defence counsel uniformly complain that the mandated periods does not provide them sufficient time to adequately prepare to cross-examine the witnesses.[27]

Perhaps the most effective measure that tribunals can employ to protect witnesses is to provide them with new identities and relocate them far from the conflict zone where they face so many threats. Despite its effectiveness, the ICC has labelled relocation a measure of 'last resort',[28] and offers it only to witnesses who satisfy stringent requirements.[29] Typically, relocation has been reserved for witnesses who are both particularly crucial to the prosecution's case and who face particularly potent threats as a consequence of their testimony.[30] Many of the witnesses who fulfil these dual standards are insider witnesses; that is, witnesses who were once close associates of the defendants but who now are prepared to testify against them—so long as they are adequately protected.[31] Insider witnesses are often critically important to the prosecution's case because they can connect high-level defendants—who did not themselves kill, rape or torture anyone—with their subordinates or associates who did. Insider witnesses are also at considerable risk of retaliation both because they are considered traitors for betraying the cause for which they once fought, and because their identities are more easily ascertainable despite the use of pseudonyms and voice distortion, due to the content of their testimony. It should come as no surprise, then, that it is the testimony of insider witnesses that is often held entirely *in camera*.

The ICC has observed that relocation should be used sparingly because it 'significantly impacts on and disrupts the life' of the witness.[32] Although this observation is undoubtedly true, it is equally true that many witnesses ardently desire the 'disruption.' Indeed, one ICTY prosecutor revealed that prosecutors 'often fudge on telling a potential witness about the full range of protective measures. I mean, if you did that, the system would be clogged with witnesses demanding to be relocated to another country'.[33] Likewise, trials at the Special

[23] See Sangkul Kim, 'The Witness Protection Mechanism of Delayed Disclosure at the Ad Hoc International Criminal Tribunals' (2016) 9 Journal of East Asia and International Law 53, 58.

[24] ibid 73; McLaughlin, 'Victim and Witness Measures' (n 18) 195.

[25] For a more detailed discussion of rolling disclosure, see Kim, 'Witness Protection Mechanism' (n 23) 58.

[26] See Kim, 'Witness Protection Mechanism' (n 23) 68–72.

[27] See, eg, *Prosecutor v Katanga*, ICC-01/04-01/07, Public redacted version of the Decision on the Protection of Prosecution Witnesses 267 and 353 of 20 May 2009 (2009) 21; Sluiter, 'The ICTR' (n 3) 973.

[28] Silvana Arbia, 'The International Criminal Court: Witness and Victim Protection and Support, Legal Aid and Family Visits' (2010) 36 Commwealth Law Bulletin 519, 522.

[29] See Eikel, 'Witness Protection Measures' (n 3) 125–26.

[30] See *ICTY Manual on Developed Practices: Prepared in conjunction with UNICRI as part of a project to preserve the legacy of the ICTY* (UNICRI 2009) 202.

[31] See Hassan B Jallow, 'The OTP-ICTR: Ongoing Challenges of Completion,' Guest Lecture Series of the Office of the Prosecutor (1 November 2004) 6 <www.icc-cpi.int/NR/rdonlyres/669ECEA9-E48A-4540-B56A-9D49B10770DA/0/Jallow_presentation.pdf> accessed 29 June 2019.

[32] Arbia, 'Protection and Support' (n 28) 522.

[33] Eric Stover, *The Witnesses: War Crimes and the Promise of Justice in the Hague* (University of Pennsylvania Press 2005) 78.

Court for Sierra Leone featured several insider witnesses who reportedly were delighted to testify because doing so made them potentially eligible for relocation.[34] The tribunals are able to accommodate only a tiny proportion of witnesses who desire relocation, however, because the costs of relocation are so high.[35] Moreover, defence counsel understandably worry that its availability will provide potential witnesses incentives to falsely inculpate defendants.[36] Given that international criminal trials have featured witnesses willing to lie on the stand in the hopes that they will be eligible for benefits as meagre as a sink and some building materials,[37] it is reasonable to fear that the promise of a new life in a safe, economically developed location would motivate false, inculpatory testimony.

Challenges and observations

The final section of this brief tour of witness protection measures will centre on certain overarching observations along with a discussion of the challenges faced by those seeking to balance the legitimate aims of witness protection and fair trial rights.

First, although space constraints have required me to treat witness protection somewhat monolithically, witness protection is by no means a one-size-fits-all endeavour. The fact is, optimal protection measures will depend not only on the needs of particular witnesses, but also on the nature and timing of the conflict, the location and features of the tribunal prosecuting the atrocities and the popular support enjoyed by the accused, among other factors. This book's focus on hybrid international-domestic tribunals provides a useful lens through which to consider the various factors relevant to witness protection.

For instance, experience shows that tribunals located in the states where the conflict took place may need to be more sensitive to witness protection issues than courts located thousands of miles away. On the one hand, many consider hybrid tribunals' in-state location to be one of their key benefits.[38] But that very location—for all of its positive aspects—may render hybrid tribunal witnesses more vulnerable to attack.[39] In reporting on the hybrid Special Court for Sierra Leone (SCSL), for instance, Human Rights Watch observed that '[l]ocating the Special Court in Sierra Leone ... present[s] challenges for the protection of witnesses not faced by the ICTY and the ICTR.'[40] The SCSL sought to respond to these difficulties in innovative ways,[41] but there is no question that locating a hybrid tribunal in

[34] See Combs, 'Fact-Finding' (n 14) 141 (discussing the relocation desires of former Brigadier General John Tarnue and George Johnson).

[35] Eikel, 'Witness Protection Measures' (n 3) 126–28.

[36] See Caroline Buisman, 'Delegating Investigations: Lessons to be Learned from the Lubanga Judgment'(2013) 11 Northwestern Journal of International Human Rights 30, 98–103.

[37] See Combs, 'Fact-Finding' (n 14) 141.

[38] See, eg, Laura A Dickinson, 'The Promise of Hybrid Courts' (2003) 97 American Journal of International Law 295, 310 ('[T]he functioning of hybrid courts in the local community ... may contribute to the broader dissemination (and adaptation) of the norms and processes of international human rights law.'); ibid, 302–03 (noting that fully international tribunals may suffer from diminished legitimacy due to 'the physical distance between the tribunal and the local population').

[39] Amy E DiBella, 'Witnessing History: Protective Measures at the Special Court for Sierra Leone' in Charles Chernor Jalloh (ed), *The Sierra Leone Special Court and its Legacy* (2013) 423, 433–34.

[40] See, eg, Human Rights Watch, *Bringing Justice: The Special Court for Sierra Leone: Accomplishments, Shortcomings, and Needed Support* (Report, 8 September 2004) <https://www.hrw.org/report/2004/09/08/bringing-justice-special-court-sierra-leone/accomplishments-shortcomings-and> accessed 29 June 2019.

[41] For instance, the tribunal created 'safe houses' to house protected witnesses (ibid).

the state where the crime took place can exacerbate witness protection challenges. Indeed, two of the most recent hybrid tribunals—the Special Tribunal for Lebanon and the Kosovo Specialist Chambers—had to be situated in The Hague precisely because their creators were not convinced that witnesses could be adequately protected if the tribunals were held their trials in Lebanon[42] or Kosovo.[43]

To be sure, the location of the hybrid tribunal is not the only factor relevant to the need for witness protection. The hybrid Extraordinary Chambers in the Courts of Cambodia (ECCC) is located in Phnom Penh, but it is prosecuting octogenarian defendants for crimes that took place more than forty years ago, in a country that has been peaceful for many years.[44] It should come as no surprise, then, that, compared to the other tribunals—hybrid or fully international—relatively few ECCC witnesses received protective measures.[45] Moreover, different populations of witnesses, even testifying before the same tribunal, sometimes generate different protective needs. For instance, although the ICTY had to make efforts to protect witnesses from all ethnic groups, witnesses from Kosovo seemed especially likely to face threats and intimidation.[46] Indeed, virtually all of the ICTY's Kosovar Albanian defendants were acquitted,[47] most amid accusations that they had intimidated prosecution witnesses into recanting their inculpatory testimony.[48]

The size of the witness's locality is also relevant to the witnesses' need for protection, regardless of the type of tribunal that is prosecuting the crimes. The ICTR, for instance, had difficulty concealing the identity of its witnesses because most Rwandans reside in small communities where everyone knows everyone else. Thus, one would not need to engage the services of Sherlock Holmes to recognize that when an individual—who previously had never travelled beyond the locality—was collected by a UN vehicle and then returned without explanation a week later, then that individual very likely travelled to the ICTR to testify. As Andrew Trotter observes, 'small communities and tight family and community

[42] Adam Taylor, 'The U.N.'s Tribunal in Lebanon Has Cost Millions and Made no Arrests. Now the Journalists Are on Trial' *Washington Post* (Washington, DC, 1 April 2015) <www.washingtonpost.com/news/worldviews/wp/2015/04/07/the-u-n-s-tribunal-in-lebanon-has-cost-millions-and-made-no-arrests-now-the-journalists-are-on-trial/?utm_term=.a8f7a0f99a9f> accessed 14 January 2018 ('In Lebanon, where police officers investigating Hariri's death have been killed and security concerns led to the tribunal setting up its office in the Netherlands, concern about the fate of witnesses is even more fraught.').

[43] *Balkan Insight* (n 13) (observing that 'one of the main reasons why the [new Kosovo Relocated Specialist Judicial Institution will have some of its sessions outside Kosovo is the failure of all previous international missions and the Kosovo government itself to protect witnesses').

[44] See Kunst, 'Protection of Victims and Witnesses' (n 21) 199.

[45] *Co-Prosecutors v Kaing Guek Eav alias Duch*, Criminal Case File No 001/18-07-2007/ECCC/TC 147–54, Judgment (26 July 2010) para 54.

[46] See Brunwasser, 'Death of War Crimes Witness' (n 12) (noting that the ICTY's *Haradinaj* case featured an especially large proportion of witnesses who received protection measures). The ICTY has suggested that witness intimidation was a particular problem in Kosovo as a result of its 'small communities and tight family and community networks which made guaranteeing anonymity difficult.' Indeed, the 'parties themselves agreed that an unstable security situation existed in Kosovo/Kosova ... was particularly unfavorable to witnesses.' *Prosecutor v Haradinaj and others*, Case No IT-04-84*bis*-T ICTY, Judgement (3 April 2008) para 6.

[47] The ICTY acquitted Fatmir Limaj and Isak Musliu (see *Prosecutor v Limaj and others*, Case No IT-03-66-T ICTY, Judgment (30 November 2005)), along with Ramush Haradinaj, Idriz Balaj, and Lahi Brahimaj (see *Prosecutor v Haradinaj and others*, Case No IT-04-84*bis*-T ICTY, Judgment (29 November 2012)). Indeed, two of the latter three defendants were acquitted twice! See *Prosecutor v Haradinaj and others*, Case No IT-04-84-T ICTY, Judgment (3 April 2008) (overturned on appeal); *Prosecutor v Haradinaj and others*, Case No IT-04-84-A ICTY, Judgment (19 July 2010). The only Kosovar Albanian to be convicted was Haradin Bala. See *Limaj and others* (n 40).

[48] See 'A Second Witness in Haradinaj et al. Case Arrested for Contempt of Court' (ICTY Press Release, 23 November 2007) CT/MOW/ PR1197e.

networks [make] guaranteeing anonymity difficult'.[49] SCSL witnesses who resided in Freetown, by contrast, were not as likely to be identified. For these and other reasons, as Chris Mahony put it, 'a geopolitical and historical understanding of the situation is particularly important when considering the threat to witnesses and the protective measures to be adopted in response'.

Even when international tribunals possess a nuanced understanding of witness needs, they face myriad challenges in protecting them. Lack of adequate resources stands as one particularly potent challenge. Everything about international criminal trials is extraordinarily expensive,[50] and providing effective protection for witnesses of mass atrocities is no exception. In 2017, the ICC budgeted $11 million for its Victims and Witnesses Unit,[51] and other tribunals have spent similarly large amounts.[52] Despite this, commentators frequently describe the tribunals' witness units as under-resourced and less capable of providing appropriate protection than they should be.[53] Hybrid tribunals are particularly likely to be starved for funds,[54] and their resource constraints invariably impair their ability to protect witnesses.[55]

Lack of resources not only poses a direct challenge to the efficacy of witness protection schemes, but it indirectly impairs them as well. International courts have no police forces of their own, so they must rely on domestic police and security units to provide witnesses with the requisite protection. Security forces in developed nations might be up to the task of adequately protecting international criminal witnesses residing their territory, but the impoverished and underdeveloped states where many atrocities occur frequently lack the

[49] Andrew Trotter, 'Witness Intimidation in International Trials: Balancing the Need for Protection against the Rights of the Accused' (2012) 44 George Washington International Review 521, 535; see also Iva Vukušić, 'Successes and Failures of Transitional Justice in BiH: The Case of the ICTY' in Soeren Keil and Valery Perry (eds), *State Building and Democratization in Bosnia and Herzegovina* (Ashgate Publishing Limited 2015) 151, 155 ('Witness protection is . . . difficult to implement in a country where many witnesses live in small communities and where word about neighbors testifying travels quickly.').

[50] See, eg, Nancy Amoury Combs, *Guilty Pleas in International Criminal Law: Constructing a Restorative Justice Approach* (Stanford University Press 2006) 28–29.

[51] See Assembly of States Parties, *Proposed Programme Budget for 2017 of the International Criminal Court* (17 August 2016) ICC-ASP/15/10 163.

[52] See, eg, UN Secretary General, *Budget for the International Tribunal for the Prosecution of Persons Responsible for Serious Violations of International Humanitarian Law Committed in the Territory of the Former Yugoslavia since 1991 for the Biennium 2002–2003* (23 October 2001) UN Doc A/56/495 paras 42(a), 42(a)(iii), 42(c)(i), 42(f)(ii), 42(f)(v)(a–c); Wald, 'Dealing with Witnesses' (n 9) 219.

[53] See, eg, Human Rights Watch, *Courting History: The Landmark International Criminal Court's First Years* (Report, July 2008) 150–151; Shana Eaton, 'Sierra Leone: The Proving Ground for Prosecuting Rape as a War Crime' (2004) 35 Georgetown Journal of International Law 873, 893–94.

[54] See Sara Kendall, 'Marketing Accountability at the Special Court for Sierra Leone' in Charles Chernor Jalloh (ed), *The Sierra Leone Special Court and its Legacy* (Cambridge University Press 2013) 387, 403 (noting that the 'Court faced struggles in securing funding throughout its lifespan'); Dickinson, 'Promise' (n 38) 307 (noting that 'a lack of resources has proven to be the most serious problem' for hybrid tribunals); David Cohen, 'Seeking Justice on the Cheap: Is the East Timor Tribunal Really a Model for the Future?' (August 2002) 61 *AsiaPacific Issues* <https://www.eastwestcenter.org/publications/seeking-justice-cheap-east-timor-tribunal-really-model-future> accessed 14 January 2018. See also 'UN General Assembly Approves US$ 15.5 Million Funding Reserve' (ECCC, 23 May 2014) <https://www.eccc.gov.kh/en/articles/un-general-assembly-approves-us-155-million-funding-reserve> accessed 14 January 2018 (noting that both international donors and the Cambodian government have failed to meet the ECCC's funding shortfall).

[55] See Human Rights Watch, *Bringing Justice: The Special Court for Sierra Leone: Accomplishments, Shortcomings, and Needed Support* (Report, 8 September 2004) < https://www.hrw.org/report/2004/09/08/bringing-justice-special-court-sierra-leone/accomplishments-shortcomings-and> accessed 29 June 2019; Christine Evans, *The Right to Reparation in International Law for Victims of Armed Conflict* (Cambridge University Press 2012) 112–13 ('The Serious Crimes process in East Timor was completely under-funded given its task and lacked earmarked funding . . . Despite provisions to the contrary, no witness protection measures were provided during the prosecutions.').

capacity to provide protection for vulnerable witnesses in their own domestic criminal trials, let alone for international criminal trials.[56]

Although additional money would unquestionably buy additional protection, many of the challenges that witness protection units face stem as much from political obstruction as from financial limitations. As just noted, international courts must rely on state actors to provide security, but in many cases, the state in question is, at best, unsympathetic to the goals of the prosecution, and at worst, affirmatively desires to obstruct it—in part through witness intimidation. The ICC saw its efforts to prosecute the President and Deputy President of Kenya dissolve, for instance, when 'a circle of officials within the Kenyan administration' allegedly threatened prosecution witnesses into withdrawing from the case.[57] And even if state officials do not actively engage in witness intimidation themselves, their efforts to protect witnesses may vary considerably depending on their political interests. According to defence counsel, for instance, the government of Rwanda—which strongly supported genocide prosecutions—expended little effort to protect Hutu defence witnesses.[58] Likewise, in the former Yugoslavia, the political interests of the state or local officials within the state had a great deal to do with how much protection the ICTY could expect that witness to receive from his or her government.[59]

A final, related challenge concerns the appropriate response when witness protection orders are flouted. It is not uncommon for defendants and their associates to reveal the names of protected witnesses,[60] thereby exposing them to danger. Post-revelation contempt proceedings have often reached unsatisfactory conclusions, and limited alternative options exist for punishing these breaches, not least because resource scarcity renders contempt proceedings a distant second priority when in competition with a genocide trial.[61] For that reason, tribunals have made greater efforts to prevent violations by extending the scope of protective measures at the outset.[62]

Conclusion

Witness protection exemplifies all that is so impossibly challenging about international criminal law. International criminal tribunals absolutely must protect witnesses—the bread and butter of their trials—both from actual and perceived threats. Witness protection,

[56] See Mahony, *Afterthought* (n 2) 11–13, 20.

[57] Human Rights Watch, *ICC: Kenya Deputy President's Case Ends* (5 April 2016) <www.hrw.org/news/2016/04/05/icc-kenya-deputy-presidents-case-ends> accessed 29 June 2019.

[58] See Beth S Lyons, *The Evolution of a Partisan: Observations of a Criminal Defense Attorney at the ICTR* (BePress 2010) 1, 15, 17–18 <https://works.bepress.com/beth_lyons/> accessed 29 June 2019; Sluiter, 'The ICTR' (n 3) 970-71.

[59] See Kitty Felde and others, 'The Prosecutor v. Dusko Tadić' (2011) 13 American U Intl L Rev 1441, 1450–51 (comments of Michail Wladimiroff).

[60] See, eg, *Prosecutor v Seselj*, Case No IT-03-67-R77.2 ICTY, Decision on Allegations of Contempt (21 January 2009) 6; *Prosecutor v Blaškić*, Case No IT-95-14-A ICTY, Order for the Immediate Cessation of Violations of Protective Measures for Witnesses (2 December 2004); *Prosecution v Brima and others*, Case No SCSL-04-16-T, Order Regarding the Disclosure of the Identity of a Protected Witness TF1-081 (8 March 2005); *Prosecution v Taylor*, Case No SCSL-12-01-T, Judgment in Contempt Proceedings (19 October 2012) 36. Even the prosecution can accidentally reveal the names of protected witnesses. See 'Laurent Gbagbo Case: ICC Judge Apologises after Witnesses Named' *BBC* (London, 8 February 2016) <www.bbc.com/news/world-africa-35526267> accessed 29 June 2018.

[61] See Sluiter, 'The ICTR' (n 3) 971.

[62] ibid.

then, is both a moral imperative and a practical necessity for institutions that want to continue having trials. But international criminal tribunals absolutely cannot allow protective measures to hamper the defendant's ability to contest the charges against him. Witnesses testify inaccurately sometimes—on purpose or by accident—and it is only through careful, painstaking investigations that defence counsel can identify and highlight that inaccurate testimony: careful, painstaking investigations that may be impeded by robust witness protection measures. Protecting the defendant's right to contest the testimony against him, then, is both a moral imperative and a practical necessity for institutions that want to adhere to human rights norms and convict defendants only on the basis of accurate, appropriately scrutinized testimony. And international criminal tribunals must mediate between these conflicting moral imperatives and practical necessities without sufficient funds and while relying on external police power that is sometimes inadequate and sometimes deployed to frighten rather than protect witnesses.

The international criminal tribunals have developed a large body of mostly consistent, mostly principled precedent designed to mediate between the needs of victims who are in danger of retaliatory violence and the needs of the defendants who are in danger of unjust convictions. This chapter has not had the space to examine the specifics of this body of precedent, but given the conflicts and constraints under which the tribunals operate, it generally stands as a reasonable effort to act consistently with moral imperatives while taking account of practical necessities.

The problem we currently face is that victims are dealt with merely as persons who have suffered. Does this have to do with the political image of the courts? That their explicit aim is *to do justice to the victims*? In view of victims' weak legal position at the ICC, one must wonder if they are somehow being used by the Court. Victims are not dealt with as persons that have rights, and should be able to claim their rights. However, trials and judgments are necessary. They are painful last resorts, but they are necessary. We have to deal with large scale traumas and damage that are at the basis of the existence of international criminal courts. We need standard setting and law-making. Not mere humanitarian aid or a kind of settlement approach. That means that we need trials.[63] This may lead us to think beyond the current organization of the ICC and forces us to start thinking about setting up a victims' claims chamber at the ICC. With specialized judges.

[63] Luban (n 43) 2621–22.

SECTION D

THE POLITICAL AND ITS INTERACTION: CAPTURED INSTITUTIONS?

International criminal law is not neutral, and those who practice, theorize, and are impacted by it do not stand in a neutral position towards it. Law's legitimacy is rooted in objectivity, however, so a great deal of theory regarding ICL, particularly its doctrine and procedure, positions it as objective. The contradiction between law as objective, neutral, and self-regulated and legal institutions as political bodies is not unique to international criminal law but rather is omnipresent in law itself.

This final section considers the interaction between institutions, legal doctrines, and politics. Pierre Hazan frames the Habré case in its geopolitical and temporal context. From this case overview, he further considers central challenges to transitional justice today. Justice Richard Goldstone is among the first architects of international criminal justice. He offers a bird's eye position in his chapter, considering Africa's relationship to international justice via its fraught contestation of the ICC. Mia Swart examines the potential for a broad, African application of universal jurisdiction, the normative approach which enabled the Habré trial, in other African courts. Finally, William Schabas, a seminal scholar of the ICC from its inception, looks at this long twentieth century of international criminal law to contextualize the twenty-first century's possibilities and challenges.

40

Hissène Habré, the Little Bird on the Branch, and the Challenges of International Criminal Justice

Pierre Hazan

The judicial process that led to the ex-president of Chad, Hissène Habré, being judged twenty-six years after his overthrow was an 'interminable legal and political soap-opera' as Desmond Tutu perceptively remarked. The trial, held in Dakar in 2016, and concluding with a sentence of imprisonment for life for 'crimes against humanity, war crimes, and crimes of torture' for the ex-dictator, was a historic one on many levels. It set important precedents in the struggle against impunity in Africa and testifies to the slow construction of a system of global justice. It also gives a foretaste of even greater challenges that criminal justice in Africa must meet.

The trial of the ex-dictator of Chad was historic for at least three reasons: it was the first time that the African Union had created a Regional Criminal Court. It was also the first time that a former head of state was judged in an African country other than his own for massive human rights violations. It was also the first time that a former head of state was condemned for rapes that he himself had committed. Such is the importance that the Habré trial constituted in the combat against impunity on the African continent.

It is tempting to analyse the creation of the Extraordinary African Chambers (EAC) and the trial of Hissène Habré (HH) that ensued as the product of international norms and standards. That, however, would be far too hasty. In this text, I will demonstrate that the Chadian ex-dictator's trial was only held thanks to a singular conjunction of judicial and political factors. More precisely, the case against Habré was solid, but the creation of the EAC was, essentially, the product of a power struggle created and won by HH's victims and international human rights organizations. This in and of itself questions the respective places of law and politics in the processes of transitional justice.

It would also be tempting to compare the popular legitimacy of the EAC with that of the International Criminal Court (ICC). This often-made argument is not wrong. The proximity of the victims to the place of judgment is an important factor in the appropriation of justice. Similarly, on a continent that experienced the brutality of colonization, the idea of a Court that judges in the name of universal human rights but which is located in The Hague, the capital of a former colonial power (even if the Netherlands had no colonial possessions in Africa), certainly worked against the ICC.

The attitude of African governments that laid the foundation of the EAC while criticizing the ICC can be explained by a single factor: by deciding to judge Hissène Habré, the member governments of the African Union were agreeing to judge a 'has-been', a fallen dictator out of power for more than a quarter of a century and most of whose crimes dated

Pierre Hazan, *Hissène Habré, the Little Bird on the Branch, and the Challenges of International Criminal Justice* In: *The President on Trial*. First edition. Edited by: Sharon Weill, Kim Thuy Seelinger, and Kerstin Bree Carlson, Oxford University Press (2020).
 DOI: 10.1093/oso/9780198858621.003.0041

to the beginning of the 1980s. In other words, the EAC presented no threat or dangerous precedent to current political or military leaders, with perhaps the exception of the president of Chad, Idriss Déby, as will be discussed later. The Habré trial was one thus for the history books, much as France had in 1987 judged Klaus Barbie, former head of the Gestapo in Lyon, four decades after the events. In that sense, the trial of Hissène Habré only partially reflected contemporary challenges to international criminal justice and to truth commissions. Without minimizing its scope, this trial reflected a world that no longer existed, that of human rights violations committed by an African dictator during the Cold War, and not the political environment in which the ICC now operates.

A media and political campaign, as much as a judicial one

It is nonetheless striking to note that, even if the trial was one for the history books, the prosecution of Hissène Habré was dauntingly complicated to organize. The pursuit of the ex-dictator stretched out over some fifteen years, encountering countless obstacles until the EAC were finally created. The struggle against impunity was arduous even though nothing current was at stake except for the symbolic targeting of an exiled dictator with very limited support, basically only that of Abdoulaye Wade, president of Senegal from 2000 to 2012.

In 2001, HRW already had the 'smoking gun': irrefutable documentary evidence of the crimes committed by the Habré regime that permitted the reconstruction of the chain of command, including lists of victims and orders signed by Habré himself. Reed Brody, Olivier Bercault, and I[1] had found, to our stupefaction and in an indescribable disorder, the archives of terror in the 'Swimming Pool', the former headquarters of the Direction de la Documentation et de la Securité, the political police better known by its acronym, the DDS. Despite that, it took fifteen years to bring the ex-dictator to trial. The lessons from this endless pursuit were profound as they demonstrated essentially that the struggle to hold Habré accountable even in a case with no real contemporary import was as much a politico-media combat sport as a simple question of legal ground. No African government wanted to crack open the door, however slightly, to the possibility of indicting former heads of state.

The big wings of little birds

Note first of all the formidable determination of Hissène Habré's victims, who in 1991 created the Association of Victims of Crimes and Political Repression in Chad (AVCRP). It won a superficial victory in 1992 with the publication of a report by the Chadian National Board of Enquiry, which estimated the number of victims of the Habré regime at 40,000 and recommended criminal proceedings against the ex-dictator, then in Dakar, and against his régime's security apparatus. The promise of this victory remained unfulfilled. Despite that, the victims' association remained mobilized up to the 2016 trial, collecting statements

[1] At the time I was accompanying Reed Brody and Olivier Bercault of HRW as a journalist when we entered the 'Swimming Pool'. The film I was then making, *Chasseur de dictateur—Hunting Dictators*, shows the archives of the DDS as we discovered them, ARTE/RTS/RTBF http://www.film-documentaire.fr/4DACTION/w_fiche_film/10191_1. The Chadian authorities authorized HRW to make copies of the documents, which were essential in consolidating the future indictment, even if at the time no tribunal had officially been applied to judge Hissène Habré.

from survivors, identifying those who perished, and continuing to press the authorities for justice. Without the AVCRP, nothing would have come to fruition. The victims incarnated the struggle against impunity in Chad, providing uncontestable legitimacy that was reinforced by their representation by Chadian lawyers, particularly Jacqueline Moudeina and Delphine Djraibé. Even though this made it difficult to do so, Hissène Habré's supporters and partisans of sovereignty sought to convince African public opinion that, essentially, the desire to try an ex-president was the product of a neo-imperialist judiciary from the United States and Europe.

A coalition was created around the legitimacy of the AVCRP. It regrouped Chadian organizations, notably the Chadian Association for the Promotion and Defense of Human Rights (APPDH); international human rights organizations, particularly Human Rights Watch (HRW) where Reed Brody was a key figure; and the International Federation for Human Rights (FIDH). One of the General Secretaries of the FIDH, Sidiki Kaba, was for a time one of the lawyers of Habré's victims in Dakar, before becoming many years later the Senegalese Minister for Justice, in 2013. As soon as he was appointed he wholeheartedly supported setting up the African Extraordinary Chambers, underlining the close ties between the world of non-governmental organizations, the legal world, and the political world. In an ironic historical twist, the legal proceedings initiated against Habré in 2000 in Senegal failed due to the opposition of the head of state, Abdoulaye Wade, a Habré supporter. Fifteen years later, the same legal proceedings were successful because they were supported by the Senegalese government. Both cases are far from the separation of powers described by Montesquieu.

This coalition, and particularly the alliance between the Chadian victims, HRW, and the FIDH was therefore incredibly productive, with the victims providing indispensable legitimacy and the NGOs providing legal, political and media expertise, as well as funds to wage an almost planet-wide legal battle.

Thus Human Rights Watch put emblematic victims such as Souleymane Guengueng and Clément Abaïfouta in the international media spotlight. Tortured to the point of blindness, Souleymane was one of the few to emerge alive from the killing cells. He swore that if he survived that hell, he would devote all his energy to having the ex-dictator convicted of his crimes. Souleymane, Clément, and a few other victims incarnated that combat. Souleymane often described himself as being as powerless as 'a little bird on a branch', but he became, he said with justifiable pride, 'greater than Hissène Habré ever was' because he finally obtained justice.

The image of 'the little bird on a branch' evokes the vulnerability of the former victim, even if he ends up regaining both his liberty and the solid anchoring of the tree's roots. The image is lovely but misleading. I in no way want to minimize the determination and courage of the victims, without whom nothing would have been possible. Still, this was first and foremost a legal, social, and political battle of almost planetary proportions. To note only the most salient actors and episodes of this search for justice: Habré's victims were joined by Chadian human rights NGOs; then the expertise of Human Right Watch was able to mobilize funds from American foundations to launch an international campaign to bring Habré to justice; then first the Senegalese and the Belgian legal systems were called on to judge Habré on the principle of universal competence; then the United Nations Committee Against Torture in Geneva intervened to request on several occasions that Senegal try Habré; and then finally a ruling by the International Criminal Court in The Hague came to the same conclusion![2] Not until presidential elections in Senegal were the final political barriers to a trial removed and Chadian and western promises of financing were made could the decision of the African Union to create the Extraordinary African Chambers in Senegalese jurisdictions final come to fruition. The little bird spread vast wings ...

Realpolitik in Chad and international NGO strategies on human rights

Throughout the pursuit for Habré up to his trial, one question remained unanswered: how would the government of Chad respond? In the 2000s it was in a complicated position. President Idriss Déby had ousted Hissène Habré on 1 December 1990 (at the time of writing, Idriss Déby was still in power in N'Djamena), but he was Habré's chief of staff from 1984 to 1985. On one hand, the president of Chad wanted Habré to be condemned: this would further legitimate his taking power. On the other hand, he distrusted the idea of justice that he did not control, fearing—legitimately or not—that he, too, could be accused of crimes committed during the Habré regime. In addition, President Déby kept a number of individuals in charge of his predecessor's security apparatus in place, individuals who had been responsible for massive human rights violations. So the Chadian government would doubtless have preferred to avoid a trial. However, when the international political and media campaign to bring Habré to justice grew to international proportions, it decided to support it officially, all the while trying to insure that its own interests would not be threatened. Though in 2000 seventeen of Habré's victims filed a complaint against the former directors, heads of services, and members of the Direction de la Documentation et de la Sécurité (DDS), the first trial was not held until 2015, just when the EAC were being progressively put into place. Thus only when Chad had decided to become the principle financial backer of a Habré trial in Senegal (taking care not to demand Habré's extradition so that he could be judged on Chadian soil) did it organize the trials of some twenty former DDS chiefs, who were convicted of murder, torture, kidnapping, and arbitrary detention, with sentences from seven years to life in prison. Among the condemned were two DDS heads that the EAC wanted to judge, but which N'Djamena's regime preferred to punish—belatedly—by itself.

During the fifteen long years of Habré's pursuit, the ambiguous attitude of the Chadian authorities forced HRW to work strategically and make compromises, namely by keeping the Chadian president out of the discussion as much as possible in order to ensure his fullest cooperation in the proceedings against Habré. HRW knew exactly what to expect: the organization had published a report in 2015 noting the forty-one former DDS members still employed by the Chadian security services, demonstrating not only the impunity from which they benefitted under the Idriss Déby regime, but also the fact that they were still in the same role! To avoid compromising the case against Habré and the indispensable collaboration with the regime in N'Djamena (even if only to ensure that that the victims would be able to testify before the EAC in Dakar), HRW refrained from criticizing it too loudly.

Thus the Chadian authorities were able to achieve their objectives: the sitting president was left alone during the Habré trial in 2016. For some fifteen years, between the turn of the

[2] Questions relating to the obligation to prosecute or extradite (Belgium v Senegal), http://www.icj.Cij.org/docket/files/144/17065.pdf.

millennium to the 2016 trial, and then the 2017 appeal, they held to a consistent line: try Habré but only Habré.

Media battle

One area of confrontation in the Habré case was that of image in the media. In many respects, it was decisive as it shaped the attitudes of African and European governments. The African governments, via the African Union, had the legitimacy to create an *ad hoc* regional criminal tribunal—legal but nonetheless without precedent—while the European governments offered both political and financial support.

In its communication strategy, HRW was able to 'translate' the legal battle to try Habré for western opinion. This was not a foregone conclusion. Except possibly in France, only a tiny percentage of the European and American populations had ever heard of Hissène Habré or would have been capable of situating Chad on a map of Africa. Given that, Habré had to be depicted with a vocabulary that could be understood throughout the world. HRW made the decision to dub Habré the 'African Pinochet'. This gave a double advantage: at the end of the 1990s, nearly the entirety of western public opinion considered Pinochet to be the example par excellence of the Latin-American dictator whose crimes finally caught up with him, thanks to an arrest warrant issued by a Spanish judge—and even though the former Chilean general was then in the United Kingdom. By juxtaposing Habré with the Chilean dictator, HRW was able not only to depict him as a war criminal in the eyes of the western media and therefore of African and European governments, but also, most importantly, to justify the construction of a global justice system by using the principle of universal jurisdiction. For defenders of human rights, the Pinochet precedent could not remain an isolated example. It was thus strategically important for HRW that there be a new 'Pinochet' case. This became the function of the Habré case, with the hope that universal jurisdiction would be activated by an African country, Senegal, to avoid traditional accusations of judicial neo-imperialism.

In the Habré case, the battle for the western media was won by HRW and FIDH but remained in doubt for some time in Senegal, for the ex-dictator—at least before the trial opened—was able to call on his connections. In the image game, Habré presented himself as a pious, humble man, attending the mosque every Friday in a crisp, white boubou, financing a local Senegalese football club, taking a local wife, and especially presenting himself as the victim of a neo-imperial justice by an American organization headquartered in the Empire State Building, a name symbolic of the scope of American power and even its arrogance. Ultimately it was the discourse of the victims which slowly brought Senegalese public opinion to see the justice of trying Habré. The battle that Souleymane Guengueng and his companions won was, at the same time, a battle the International Criminal Court had lost: that of legitimacy. Never had the ICC put forward the image of a victim or managed to represent itself to the public as embodying the fight against impunity. The Court had raised the hopes of African civil society but had never been able to capitalize on that initial wave of interest.

From the Habré case to contemporary challenges

The Habré trial showed how an essentially internal Chadian affair[3] could, under pressure initiated by local victims associations, be transformed into a regional and even international one, ultimately adjudicated under the auspices of the African Union in an ad hoc tribunal in another country 3,000 kilometres away. The image of the 'little bird on a branch' reflects the sentiments of a victim, but not the reality of a pursuit that encompassed N'Djamena, Dakar, Brussels, Geneva, The Hague, Paris, New York, and Addis Ababa.

The Habré trial also bears witness to the importance of civil societies, the role of international media, the judicial expertise provided by international NGOs, the respective weights of states (from Belgium to Senegal) and of the United Nations, and the legitimacy and political and financial support of regional institutions and the African and European Unions. Ultimately, the Hissène Habré trial is not so much the product of a judicial institution, but rather of an epic political and judicial battle that was played out over fifteen years and on three continents.

But the Habré trial also illustrates limits. One of the hopes of Chadian human rights activists was that it would help make the N'Djamena regime more democratic. It didn't. Similarly, other governments and particularly France and the United States, which for years had supported Hissène Habré as a bastion against Muammar Gaddafi, were never investigated during the trial of their former protégé. They were, like the current president of Chad, left alone. Habré's victims waited for reparations for years. The Dakar decision went in their favour as the ex-dictator was sentenced to pay them some 120 million euros. However, as he doesn't have the funds, his victims are unlikely to see any of it.

The Habré trial was nonetheless a trial for the history books and remains significant both as a precedent and as a symbol—even if it was held at a moment when international criminal justice was confronted with more formidable challenges than those encountered by the complicated Habré affair!

The foundations of the fight against impunity which were laid during the 1990s were at the time part of a desire to mark a return to a state of law and democracy, with the end of apartheid in South Africa, communist regimes in central and eastern Europe, and military dictatorships in Latin America. In the 2000s, and particularly in Africa with the exception of Tunisia, many countries had to deal with deep structural crises whose violence, even when it took the shape of religious extremism, was simply the expression of an infinitely deeper evil, one deeply rooted in the long age of colonization. These crises were reinforced by bad government, poverty, and the incapacity to furnish basic services including education and health.

Such critical situations in Africa challenge the State itself. Some countries, like the Central African Republic, Mali, and Nigeria, lost control of part or even most of their territory to armed groups. Other, like Somalia, imploded. The ICC and its mechanisms of transitional justice have been called upon in several of these contexts, where conflicts continue to rage. Hence the problematic challenge of this new mission for justice at a global scale: to intervene during the conflict to punish those who commit war crimes but also to reconcile populations.

[3] With the exception of a certain number of Libyan prisoners of war, nearly all the victims were Chadian.

Even without evoking the very real danger of political instrumentalization, how can the ICC and its transitional justice mechanisms be adapted to situations of violence and conflict? To what extent can they truly protect victims and lay the foundations of a state of law when the State itself is collapsing or otherwise incapable of exercising its sovereignty? How can judicial mechanisms be integrated into peacekeeping operations or peace accords? What connections can be made between the mechanisms of justice and the questions of governance, security, and disarmament? Such daunting questions take stock of the risks to peace and security in Africa, as entire areas, particularly the Sahel and the Great Lakes regions, are unstable and in the throes of violence.

In the post-Cold War period, the struggle against impunity was carried on by dozens of NGOs in countries on different continents. It was this popular pressure on governments that made possible the drafting of the ICC's statutes and its being put into place. This mobilization then waned, partly because of the bureaucratic functioning of the ICC and its first prosecutor's inadequate penal strategy, but especially because the fight against impunity was unable or unwilling to face challenges due to structural causes of conflict and violence. It could no longer, as in the 1990s, simply denounce human rights violations committed by authoritarian regimes. Rather, it had to deal directly with situations where the State itself was questioned because of its inability to offer either basic services or a future for the young people who represent two-thirds of its population.

The result: the social contract between the citizen and the State is weakened if not broken, in particular in regions where as a consequence trafficking and violent ideologies take hold. The example of the countries of the Sahel is eloquent. The evils are known: poverty, corruption, and bad governance combine, worsened by the incoherent policies of European countries that, on one hand, finance programs that reinforce the capacities of a State of law and, on the other, make locking down borders a condition of financial support—without recognizing that blocking immigration creates conditions of greater political and social instability. Ultimately it is the legitimacy of the State, including its judicial system, that is called into question.

Ultimately it is the legitimacy of the State, including its judicial system, that is called into question.

The great lesson of the Habré affair is that legitimacy is never a given. It is constructed by conviction, by engagement, by the mobilization of victims and civil society actors in both Africa and the west, and by the role of the media and human rights instruments, be they local, regional, or international. It is their synergy, their interaction, and their dynamism which can shift the balance of power and allow a space of justice to emerge. The issue of legitimacy is today at the heart and future of the struggle against impunity, even though its challenges have never been more formidable.

41

The ICC and Africa

Richard Goldstone

Introduction

The relationship between Africa and the International Criminal Court (ICC) is a complex and complicated one. There is a tension between the strong desire of most African states and their people to bring justice to the victims of war crimes and the perceived bias against Africa arising from the fact that all but one of the eleven situations before the ICC relate to African states. The problem is exacerbated by the failure of the Security Council to refer to the ICC egregious cases of war crimes committed on other continents and particularly in Sri Lanka and Syria. This chapter discusses the politics of the relationship between the ICC and Africa and how the optics have changed during the first fifteen years of the active life of the ICC. The chapter concludes with considerations for the future of the ICC in Africa and highlights the importance of positive complementarity.

Early support for the ICC

The Rome diplomatic conference called in the middle of 1998 received warm support from many African countries. For many years the continent had been plagued by the commission of serious war crimes. The egregious genocide committed in Rwanda during 1994 was fresh in the minds of African delegates who attended the meeting in Rome. There was a universal call from victims for justice.

One of the most appealing provisions of the Rome Statute was the recognition of the sovereignty of the nations who might ratify the Statute. In effect, the ICC is a court of last resort and primacy is granted to domestic courts provided they are willing and able to investigate and prosecute crimes that fall within the jurisdiction of the ICC. This is known as 'complementarity' and it is a foundational principle that underlies the jurisdiction of the ICC.[1] It is designed to ensure that whenever possible suspected war criminals are investigated and tried by the courts of the suspects' own nation.

It also appealed to African states that the jurisdiction for the ICC was prospective, ie limited to the investigation and prosecution of crimes that were committed after the date on which the Rome Statute came into operation, ie 1 July 2002 or the date on which a nation ratifies the Statute.[2]

In respect of personal jurisdiction, the ICC may exercise its jurisdiction against nationals of States that have ratified the Rome Statute or nationals of any State for crimes alleged

[1] The Rome Statute for the ICC, art 17(1).
[2] ibid, art 11.

Richard Goldstone, *The ICC and Africa* In: *The President on Trial*. First edition. Edited by: Sharon Weill, Kim Thuy Seelinger, and Kerstin Bree Carlson, Oxford University Press (2020). © Richard Goldstone. DOI: 10.1093/oso/9780198858621.003.0042

to have been committed in a country that has ratified the Rome Statute.[3] In addition, the Security Council may refer a situation to the ICC under the peremptory provisions of Chapter VII of the United Nations Charter.[4] Such a referral may include nationals of any member state of the United Nations.

South Africa joined Canada as a leader of the so-celled 'like-minded nations' that actively encouraged all States to support the ICC. It successfully encouraged most of the other members of the Southern African Development Community to ratify the Rome Statute. After the inception of the jurisdiction of the ICC, it was African governments that referred their own situations for investigation by the Prosecutor of the ICC. The first was Uganda,[5] followed by the Democratic Government of the Congo,[6] the Central African Republic,[7] and Mali.[8] This was an unexpected development as it had been assumed that the first investigations would be initiated by the Prosecutor using his or her own powers.[9]

Referrals by the Security Council were considered highly unlikely in the face of the veto power of the United States and the strong opposition to the ICC exhibited by the administration of President George W Bush. One of the last acts of President Bill Clinton on 1 December 2000 was to sign the Rome Statute and thus commit the United States to take no act inconsistent with it.[10] On 6 May 2002 the US severed its relationship with the ICC and the Bush Administration 'unsigned' the Rome Statute.[11]

It came as a pleasant surprise for the ICC and its supporters when, in March 2005, the Bush Administration abstained from voting against the resolution referring to the ICC the situation in the Darfur region of Sudan.[12] Then, in February 2011, the US voted in favour of an unanimous Security Council resolution referring the situation in Libya to the ICC.[13] At the time of this writing there are eleven situations before the ICC. One of them, Georgia, is not in Africa. Only three of the African situations have resulted from the Prosecutor using her or his own powers, namely in December 2010 with regard to Kenya,[14] in October 2011 with regard to Côte d'Ivoire[15] and in November 2017 with regard to Burundi.[16]

[3] ibid, art 12.

[4] ibid, art 13(b).

[5] See: ICC, Situation referred to the ICC by the Government of Uganda, International Criminal Court 2004, available at https://www.icc-cpi.int/uganda

[6] See: ICC, Situation referred to the ICC by the DRC Government, International Criminal Court 2004, available at https://www.icc-cpi.int/drc?ln=en

[7] See: ICC, Situation referred to the ICC by the CAR Government, International Criminal Court 2004 https://www.icc-cpi.int/car?ln=en

[8] See: ICC, Situation referred to the ICC by the Government of Mali, International Criminal Court 2014 https://www.icc-cpi.int/mali

[9] The Rome Statute of the International Criminal Court, article 15(1)

[10] See: ICC, Statement by US President Bill Clinton, authorizing the US signing of the Rome Statute of the International Criminal Court, ICCnow.org 2000, available at http://www.iccnow.org/documents/USClintonSigning31Dec00.pdf

[11] See: BBC, US renounces world court treaty, BBC 2002 http://news.bbc.co.uk/1/hi/1970312.stm

[12] UN Security Council, 31 March 2005 resolution 8351. See: http://www.un.org/press/en/2005/sc8351.doc.htm

[13] UN Security Council, 26 February 2011 resolution 10187. See http://www.un.org/press/en/2011/sc10187.doc.htm

[14] See: ICC, ICC Prosecutor opens *proprio motu* investigation, ICC 2010, available at https://www.icc-cpi.int/kenya?ln=en

[15] See: ICC, Côte d'Ivoire accepts ICC's jurisdiction, ICC 2003, available at www.icc-cpi.int/cdi?ln=en

[16] See: https://www.icc-cpi.int/

The politics changed

On 4 March 2009, President Omar Al-Bashir of Sudan became the first head of state to be charged by the ICC. He joined President Slobodan Milosevic of Serbia, who was indicted by the United Nations International Criminal Tribunal for the former Yugoslavia, President Jean Kambanda of Rwanda who was indicted by the United Nations International Criminal Tribunal for Rwanda and President Charles Taylor of Liberia, who was indicted by the Special Court for Sierra Leone.

During the presidency of Al Bashir, there were serious outbreaks of violence in the Darfur region of Sudan between the Janjaweed militia, the Sudanese Liberation Army (SLA), and the Justice and Equality Movement (JEM). In this civil war it is estimated that over 200 000 civilians were killed, and some 2.5 million people out of a total population of 6.2 million in Darfur were displaced.[17] Al-Bashir faces charges of genocide and crimes against humanity.

On 6 September 2009, using his own powers, the Prosecutor of the ICC referred the situation in Kenya to a Pre-Trial Chamber, seeking authorization to investigate crimes committed in that country in the aftermath of the general election held in December 2007. Some 1,200 people died and about 500,000 were displaced. In March 2011, charges of crimes against humanity were brought against Uhuru Kenyatta, William Ruto and four others. After the 2013 general election, Kenyatta became the President and Ruto became the Deputy President of Kenya.

Al Bashir and Kenyatta encouraged member states of the African Union to oppose the indictment by the ICC of sitting heads of state. They complained that it was inconsistent with the exercise of their important domestic duties and obligations. The African Union passed a number of resolutions in support of head of state immunity and some of those resolutions were specifically in protection of Al Bashir. In 2010 the African Union declared that it would not cooperate with the ICC in seeking to arrest Al Bashir. Those moves were intensified when Kenyatta and Ruto came before the ICC. The Kenyan Government stated that ICC was a neo-colonial institution 'targeting Africans'.

In light of the cases that came from African Governments themselves and then from the Security Council, this allegation of bias was both unfair and without justification. However, the negative perceptions of many in Africa were fuelled by the absence of situations in non-African countries coming before the ICC. The situation in Georgia is still in the investigation stage and no indictments have yet been sought by the Prosecutor. More recently, a pre-trial chamber authorized the Prosecutor to investigate serious war crimes alleged to have been committed by senior officials in Burundi. And, authorization was sought by the Prosecutor to launch a formal investigation into alleged war crimes committed in Afghanistan. After reserving its judgment on the last-mentioned application for some eighteen months, in a highly contested and controversial decision delivered on 12 April 2019, Pretrial Chamber II refused to allow the Prosecutor to proceed with the investigation.[18]

The perception of bias against Africa remains, and is aggravated by the fact that egregious war crimes have been committed in non-African states and have not come to the ICC. The

[17] See: UNICEF, Darfur—overview, UNICEF 2004, available at https://www.unicef.org/infobycountry/sudan_darfuroverview.html

[18] See: ICC, SITUATION IN THE ISLAMIC REPUBLIC OF AFGHANISTAN, ICC 2009, available at https://www.icc-cpi.int/CourtRecords/CR2019_02068.PDF

Afghanistan decision fuels this perception. The most serious war crimes were committed in Sri Lanka and Syria. The failure to refer them to the ICC lies with the Security Council. Neither Sri Lanka nor Syria have ratified the Rome Statute and without a Security Council referral, the ICC has no jurisdiction with regard to either of those countries. Threatened vetoes from Russia and China prevented the Security Council from referring either of those situations to the ICC. This failure certainly justifies the perception that the international community is treating the investigation of serious war crimes in an unequal and unfair way. But, with the exception of the Afghanistan decision, the fault does not lie with the ICC.

The African campaign reached the Security Council where Kenya was unsuccessful in its attempt to persuade the Council to use powers conferred upon it by the Rome Statute to order the deferral of the trial against Kenyatta and Ruto. In this regard it should be recalled that head of state immunity for what are today called 'atrocity crimes' was denied by the terms of the London Agreement that established the Nuremberg Tribunal at the end of the Second World War. That approach to head of state immunity is also to be found in the laws that govern all modern international criminal courts.

In 2016 the campaign against the ICC led to three African countries issuing notices of withdrawal from the Rome Statute—they came from Burundi, The Gambia, and South Africa. The motives of the first two were not difficult to ascertain. Both Burundi and The Gambia were governed by repressive dictators who did not wish the ICC to investigate the commission of crimes for which they might be held personally responsible. In 2016, President Yahya Jammeh of The Gambia lost the general election to Adama Barrow. Jammeh tried to cling to power but the African Union and, more importantly, ECOWAS, refused to recognize his illegal claim to remain in office. Eventually, on 19 January 2017, Senegalese troops entered The Gambia at the behest of ECOWAS and with the consent of the Security Council. On 21 January 2017 Jammeh agreed to step down and went into exile in Equatorial Guinea. One of the first decisions taken by the newly installed President Barrow was that the notice of withdrawal from the Rome Statute would be recalled. The withdrawal by Burundi has become effective. However, the crimes now being investigated by the ICC in Burundi were allegedly committed prior to the withdrawal by Burundi having become effective. Under the Rome Statute, the Court retains its jurisdiction in respect of those crimes.[19]

South Africa was a different case. Its notice of withdrawal was a consequence of its courts holding that the Government was acting in violation of the South African Constitution and domestic implementing legislation by failing to have arrested President Al Bashir when he visited Pretoria in July 2016 to attend a Ministerial meeting of the African Union. Indeed, the Government had allowed Al Bashir to flee the country in violation of the terms of an order by the High Court. The ICC subsequently convened a trial chamber to determine whether South Africa had acted in violation of its international obligations under the Rome Statute in failing to have arrested Al Bashir. In July 2017 the Chamber held that indeed it had done so. However, some months before, the South African courts held that the Government's notice of withdrawal under the Rome Statute was itself unconstitutional and that the power to take such action rested with parliament and not the executive. It ordered the government to immediately withdraw its notice. The withdrawal was also inconsistent with the provisions

[19] Article 127(2) of the Rome Statute provides that the withdrawal of a States Party 'shall not ... prejudice in any way the continued consideration of any matter which was already under consideration by the Court prior to the date on which the withdrawal became effective.'

of the domestic implementing legislation.[20] The government had already introduced legislation to repeal the implementing legislation. In consequence of the court order, both the notice of withdrawal and the repeal legislation were withdrawn. Whether Parliament will proceed along the path of withdrawal remains to be seen. It should be noticed that the South African government decision to withdraw from the Rome Statute was based upon domestic political considerations and not from any expectation that any South African might be suspected of committing a crime falling within the jurisdiction of the ICC.

It now appears that what was feared as being the beginning of successive withdrawals from the Rome Statute by African states has been halted, with only that of Burundi proceeding.

An African solution to African problems

In chapters that follow, there is discussion on proposed African regional mechanisms to investigate and prosecute war crimes in Africa in an African court. Suffice it to say here that those efforts have thus far failed to materialize. The ICC remains the only court with jurisdiction to investigate and prosecute international crimes committed on the African continent in the absence of the exercise of domestic jurisdiction by African courts having jurisdiction, ie application of the principle of complementarity.

Generally speaking, the African objections to the ICC have been a top-down rather than a bottom-up process. It should not be forgotten that Al Bashir is charged with genocide, crimes against humanity including murder, rape, torture, and pillage. Al-Bashir's removal from power in a military coup raises the expectation that he might end up on trial before the ICC. That some African heads of state wished to protect him is somewhat difficult to understand. Some of them no doubt wished to protect themselves from suffering the problems faced by Al Bashir or, until the withdrawal of the charges against them, by Kenyatta and Ruto. It is difficult to carry the burden of a head of state when concerned about international warrants of arrest. Presumably that is what motivated Kenyatta and Ruto to appear voluntarily before the ICC whilst doing everything possible at home to limit the availability of evidence required by the Prosecutor to establish their guilt. It was those efforts that, in the end, left the Court with little option but to withdraw the charges.

The fate of the Kenyan charges demonstrates yet again how reliant any international court is upon cooperation from governments. These courts have no other means of enforcing orders or requests made by them.

It should also not be forgotten the ICC case against the Kenyan defendants would not have materialized if the Kenyan Parliament had followed the advice of its own commission of inquiry (the Waki Commission), namely to establish a domestic mechanism to investigate and prosecute crimes committed with regard to the 2007 elections. If that had happened, complementarity would have precluded the ICC from exercising jurisdiction. It should also be noted that the ICC has successfully brought charges of serious crimes against defendants in those cases where the domestic authorities have cooperated with it. Cases that come to mind are those from the Democratic Republic of the Congo and Mali.

[20] Implementation of the Rome Statute for the International Criminal Court, 27 of 2002.

Conclusion

The future of the ICC in Africa will depend upon political factors. The most important of these is the sensitivity to any invasion of the sovereignty of African states. Having regard to the colonial history of the Continent that is not difficult to understand. The Prosecutor of the ICC could well ameliorate some of the negative perceptions in Africa by adopting policies that are usually referred to as 'positive complementarity', ie assisting domestic prosecutors use domestic courts to prosecute international crimes committed by nationals of those states and, by doing so, oust the jurisdiction of the ICC. To that end the ICC might consider the establishment of offices in relevant countries primarily designed to assist domestic prosecutions. If and when there are regional courts with jurisdiction over crimes within the jurisdiction of the ICC, similar assistance might be offered. Whether pursuing positive complementarity ultimately eases the burden of domestic or regional courts will depend not only on political factors but also on the extent to which the budget of the ICC will allow it to follow such a policy. I have no doubt that it would be money well spent. No effort should be spared by those who support international criminal justice to strengthen the relationship between the ICC and the African Union and individual African nations.

The relationship between the ICC and African states would also be enhanced if the Security Council could be persuaded to use its Chapter VII powers in a more even-handed way. Where it is prevented from acting because of the threatened use of the veto by one or more of the five permanent members of the United Nations, the unfairness of such partial protection of war criminals should be highlighted by those members of the Security Council who might be in favour of a referral of a situation to the ICC.

The fact that the withdrawal from the Rome Statute by Burundi is the only one from Africa still standing[21] should be recognized by the organs of the ICC as an opportunity for more dialogue with the African Union and its members.

[21] On 17 March 2019, Philippines withdrew from the Rome Statute.

42

The African Pinochet? Universal Jurisdiction and the Habré Case

Mia Swart

For all the excitement generated by the concept of universal jurisdiction, there have been very few instances of prosecutions on the basis of universal jurisdiction in Africa.[1] Moreover, even in Europe, the heartland of universal jurisdiction, the application of this form of jurisdiction has been on a sharp decline—in spite of ambitious universal jurisdiction legislation adopted in countries such as Belgium and Germany. In this landscape, the 'successful' prosecution of the Hissène Habré case is of particular significance, especially given the highly contested field of international criminal justice in Africa. It is preferable for states to prosecute international crimes themselves. The reality, however, is that the political climate in states in the direct aftermath of mass atrocities is rarely conducive to domestic prosecutions of international crimes.

Can the successful Habré case help to turn the tide in favour of universal jurisdiction, ie, can there be a 'Habré effect' similar to the 'Pinochet effect'? In the African context, there are a few modest instances suggesting the answer might be yes. First, the chapter will consider the requirements for a successful universal jurisdiction prosecution in the African context. One of the restraints that posed an obstacle to Senegal's attempts to exercise universal jurisdiction was the argument that this form of jurisdiction violates the principle against the retroactive application of criminal law. This chapter will show that the Dakar Court of Appeal and the ECOWAS Community Court of Justice erred in basing their refusal to prosecute Habré on the principle against retroactivity. Second, the chapter will consider what 'Habré effect' we might be seeing in the wake of the *Habré* case. The so-called Zimbabwe torture docket decision of the South African Constitutional Court,[2] which like the *Habré* case can be regarded as an exceptional instance of a prosecution under universal jurisdiction, represents one of the few other universal jurisdiction success stories on the African continent.[3]

[1] F Jessberger, 'On behalf of Africa: Towards the Regionalisation of Universal Jurisdiction' in G Werle and M Vornbaum (eds), *Africa and the International Criminal Court* (Springer 2014) 167.

[2] *South African Litigation Centre and another v National Director of Public Prosecutions and others* [2012] ZAGPPHC. An important distinction between the Habré case and the Zimbabwe torture docket case is that the Habré case matured to the point of an actual conviction whereas the Zimbabwe torture docket case was merely a symbolic breakthrough in the sense that the South African Constitutional Court ordered the South African National Prosecuting Authority (NPA) to investigate the allegations of crimes against humanity by the Mugabe regime. To date, however, the NPA has however failed to prosecute the alleged perpetrators.

[3] A Cassese, 'Foreword to Symposium on the Twists and Turns of Universal Jurisdiction' (2006) 4 Journal of International Criminal Justice 559–60.

Mia Swart, *The African Pinochet? Universal Jurisdiction and the Habré Case* In: *The President on Trial*. First edition. Edited by: Sharon Weill, Kim Thuy Seelinger, and Kerstin Bree Carlson, Oxford University Press (2020).
DOI: 10.1093/oso/9780198858621.003.0043

Universal jurisdiction and the Habré case

The lack of a general treaty on universal jurisdiction and the scarcity of jurisprudence complicates arriving at a single definition of universal jurisdiction. Although there is no generally accepted definition of universal jurisdiction in conventional or customary international law,[4] it is generally agreed that universal jurisdiction is a form of jurisdiction which requires no territorial or national nexus to the alleged act or actors over which the state legitimately may claim authority.[5]

Universal jurisdiction therefore allows the assertion of jurisdiction regardless of 'any nexus the [S]tate may have with the offense, the offender, or the victim'.[6] Some argue that the 'only basis' for exercising universal jurisdiction is the 'assumption that the prosecuting state is acting on behalf of all states'.[7] The Princeton Principles[8] reflect this idea in defining universal jurisdiction in paragraph 1(1):

> [C]riminal jurisdiction based solely on the nature of the crime, without regard to where the crime was committed, the nationality of the alleged or convicted perpetrator, the nationality of the victim, or any other connection to the state exercising such jurisdiction.

The limits of scope and applicability of universal jurisdiction remain strongly contested, however.[9] The 2002 *Arrest Warrant* decision of the ICJ confirmed the uncertainties about the application of the principle of universal jurisdiction. The conservative position taken by the ICJ, in which it prioritised immunity over the exercise of universal jurisdiction, was severely criticized by many commentators.[10] In the years following the ICJ's *Arrest Warrant* decision,[11] commentators have identified a decline[12] or even demise of universal jurisdiction. Yet as Jessberger notes, more states have the legislative instruments to prosecute on the basis of universal jurisdiction than ever before.[13] Therefore it is overall fair to say that there is a slow, gradual increase in the use of universal jurisdiction as a basis for prosecutions.[14]

[4] R O'Keeffe, 'Universal Jurisdiction: Clarifying the Basic Concept' (2004) Journal of International Criminal Justice 735, 744.

[5] RB Baker, 'Universal Jurisdiction and the Case of Belgium: A Critical Assessment' (2009) 16 ILSA Journal of International and Comparative Law 141, 142.

[6] C C Joyner, 'Arresting Impunity: The Case for Universal Jurisdiction in Bringing War Criminals to Accountability' (1996) 59 Law and Contemporary Problems 153, 165.

[7] ibid.

[8] See https://lapa.princeton.edu/hosteddocs/unive_jur.pdf.

[9] B Broomhall, 'Universal Jurisdiction: Myth, Realities and Prospects: Towards the Development of an Effective System of Universal Jurisdiction' (2001) New England Law Review 404.

[10] A Cassese 'When may senior state officials be tried for international crimes? Some comments on the Congo v Belgium case' European Journal of International Law 13 4 (2002); S Wirth 'Immunity for Core Crimes? The ICJ's judgment in the *Congo v Belgium* case' European Journal of International Law 13 4 (2002); M Spinedi, 'State responsibility v Individual Responsibility for international crime: *Tertium Non Datur*?' European Journal of International Law 13 4; M Swart, 'DRC v Belgium: A Step Backwards?' South African Public Law 17 (2002); K Trapp, *State Responsibility for International Terrorism* 98, 99. See also the Dissenting Opinion of Judge ad hoc van den Wyngaert (*Democratic Republic of Congo v Belgium*) (2002) ICJ.

[11] *Democratic Republic of Congo v Belgium*, ICJ, 14 February 2002, ICJ Reports 2002 3.

[12] See IBA Manual 'International Criminal Law Manual' on 343 that states: 'In academic literature there is much talk of the decline of universal jurisdiction since the Arrest warrant case before the ICJ and the subsequent alteration of Belgian legislation'.

[13] Jessberger (n 1).

[14] See Maximo Langer, 'Universal Jurisdiction is not Disappearing' (2015) 13 Journal of International Criminal Justice 248. See also Y Han, 'The Individualisation of War' 31 August 2017 in https://iow.eui.eu/2017/08/31/rebirth-universal-jurisdiction/

The emergence of universal jurisdiction

Belgium was one of the first countries to take the lead in practising universal jurisdiction, with its law of 16 June 1993.[15] The War Crimes Act granted Belgian courts jurisdiction over war crimes, crimes against humanity, and genocide, regardless of where in the world they took place. When first enacted, the Belgian law was the most extensive and far-reaching attempt of a state sanctioning universal jurisdiction.[16] Belgium subsequently tried a four Rwandan genocide suspects under this law—the first trial based on the 1993 War Crimes Act.[17]

In the face of increasing pressure and criticism over its universal jurisdiction law,[18] Belgium amended the law in 2003, requiring that the accused must be either a Belgian citizen or resident.[19] By amending its law, Belgian's position on universal jurisdiction became as restrictive as that of most European countries. Many were of the view that the Belgian Parliament's repeal of its landmark universal jurisdiction statute was a step backwards in the global fight against the worst atrocities.[20]

The case against Habré

Universal jurisdiction over the Habré case centred on the crime of torture. Universal jurisdiction over torture offences is set forth in Article 5, para 2 of the 1984 Torture Convention, according to which 'each State Party shall [...] take such measures as may be necessary to establish its jurisdiction over [torture] offences in cases where the alleged offender is present in any territory under its jurisdiction and it does not extradite him [...].' This means that States are obliged to establish jurisdiction over torture offences absent any nexus of these offences with their territory, except the presence of the offender.[21] One of the most

[15] *Loi modifiant la loi du 16 juin 1993 relative à larépression des violations graves du droit international humanitaire et l'article 144ter du Code judiciaire.*

[16] Roozbeh Baker, 'Universal Jurisdiction and the Case of Belgium' (2009) ILSA Journal of International and Comparative Law 16. https://www.asil.org/insights/volume/6/issue/13/belgian-jury-decide-case-concerning-rwandan-genocide

[17] Four Rwandans, the so-called 'Butare Four', were tried under Article 4 of the Belgian War Crimes Act. The accused were Sister Gertrude (nee Consolata Mukangano) and Sister Maria Kisito (nee Julienne Mukabutera), two Benedictine nuns accused of collaborating with Hutu militia to kill Tutsis as well as Vincent Ntezimana, a professor at the National University of Rwanda, and Alphonse Higaniro, a factory owner. This trial ended in a conviction. *ASIL Insights* 25 May 2001 available at https://www.asil.org/insights/volume/6/issue/13/belgian-jury-decide-case-concerning-rwandan-genocide

[18] In June 2003, US Defense Secretary Donald H Rumsfeld threatened Belgium that it risked losing its status as host to NATO's headquarters if it did not repeal the law. See 'Belgium: Universal Jurisdiction Law Repealed' Human Rights Watch 1 August 2003 available at https://www.hrw.org/news/2003/08/01/belgium-universal-jurisdiction-law-repealed See also 'Belgium's Genocide Law - Why Belgium is changing its law against genocide' (*The Economist*, 17 April 2003).

[19] Wet tot wijziging van de wet van 16 Juni 1993 betreffende de bestraffing van ernstige schendingen van het internationaal humanitair recht (which can be translated as 'Act amending the 1993 Act Concerning the Punishment of Grave Breaches of International Law').

[20] Interestingly, the Habré case was one of the cases already investigated by Belgium before the amendment. The case was lodged by Belgian citizens of Chadian origins who took advantage of Belgium's progressive position on universal jurisdiction. In 2002 a Belgian investigating judge went to Chad in 2002 to investigate and collect evidence for the case. At the time Belgium was a particularly suitable jurisdiction because its universal jurisdiction law allowed for trials *in absentia*.

[21] Cedric Rygaert 'Universal Jurisdiction over Torture: a state of affairs' Institute for International Law Working Paper no 66 (2005).

contested aspects of universal jurisdiction, and not only with respect torture offences, concern the presence requirement.[22]

The facts and background to the Habré case are discussed extensively in other contributions to this volume. The Senegalese courts initially refused to exercise universal jurisdiction when a civil suit was lodged in Dakar. The civil suit was based on universal jurisdiction mandated by article 5 (2) of the Torture Convention of which Senegal was a party.[23]

On 4 July 2000 the Dakar Court of Appeal dismissed the case on the basis that 'Senegalese courts do not have competence over acts of torture committed by a foreigner outside of Senegalese territory'.[24] This ruling was both at odds with the Pinochet precedent as well as Senegal's obligations under articles 5 to 7 of the Torture Convention, however. While recognizing that the Torture Convention obliged Senegal to establish its jurisdiction, it pointed out that that the legislative branch had neglected to insert the offense of torture in the list of crimes giving rise to extraterritorial jurisdiction (Article 669 of the Code of Criminal Procedure). Given the peculiarities of criminal justice, a certain procedural formalism was required, namely the incorporation of universal jurisdiction over the indeed universal incrimination of torture. In the absence of such incorporation, Senegalese courts would have no universal jurisdiction over torture offences.

On 20 March 2001 the Senegalese Court of Cassation ruled that the Senegalese courts lacked the competence to prosecute Habré. In September 2005 the Belgian Judge Fransen issued an international arrest warrant for Habré and Belgium requested Habré's extradition from Senegal.[25] Belgium could justify exercising universal jurisdiction in this case since three of the twenty one plaintiffs were Belgian nationals.[26] The case was further facilitated by the fact that Chad waived any claim for immunity for Habré. Belgium issued a warrant of arrest for Habré on the charges of torture and crimes against humanity. But Senegal refused to extradite Habré to Belgium and approached the AU for assistance.

The AU decided that a Committee of Eminent African Jurists was to consider all aspects of the *Habré* trial as well as the options available for this trial'.[27] Importantly, the Committee had to make 'concrete recommendations on ways and means of dealing with issues of similar nature in the future'.[28] This meant that the Committee made recommendations not only on the *Habré* case but also on the wider issue of how to deal with future cases of a similar kind. The Committee decided that Senegal was in the best position to try Habré because of Senegal's obligations under the Torture Convention. The Committee stated that if Senegal could not do so then any another African state who is party to the Torture Convention could prosecute Habré.[29]

[22] See Tim Kluwen, 'Universal Jurisdiction in Absentia before Domestic Courts prosecuting international crimes: a Suitable Weapon to fight impunity?' (2017) 8 Goettingen Journal of International Law 7–38

[23] R O'Keeffe, *International Criminal Law* (2015) 397.

[24] See the translation by Reed Brody, 'The Prosecution of Hissene Habré—An African Pinochet' (2000–2001) 35 New ER LR 321.

[25] Ellen Lutz 'Prosecutions of Heads of State in Europe' in Ellen Lutz and Catlin Reiger (eds), *Prosecuting Heads of State* (2009) 38.

[26] ibid 37.

[27] See *Decision of the Hissene Habre Case and the African Union*, Assembly/AU/Dec.103 (VI) (24 January 2006), para 3.

[28] ibid paras 4 and 5.

[29] See Report of the Committee of Eminent African Jurists on the Case of Hissene Habre, paras 27–33.

The Habré effect

The paradigmatic example of an assertion of universal jurisdiction over international crimes is the *Pinochet* case. The Ex Chilean dictator Augusto Pinochet was arrested by the London Metropolitan Police on an international arrest warrant issued by the Spanish issuing magistrate Balthazar Garzon.[30] It was alleged that Pinochet was responsible for the murder of Spanish citizens during the military regime in Chile. The Crown Prosecution Service requested Pinochet's extradition to the Spain. Pinochet was ultimately tried in the United Kingdom.[31]

In *Pinochet*, the House of Lords held that Pinochet could not invoke immunity before British courts because torture does not form part of a leader's official functions. As Langer writes: 'There is no question that the *Pinochet* case is the most well-known contemporary example of an assertion of universal jurisdiction over core international crimes; no universal jurisdiction case has had such notoriety and impact since'.[32] Universal jurisdiction is generally considered as rising to its peak with the arrest of Augusto Pinochet in London in 1998.[33]

The *Habré* case was the first use of the Pinochet precedent outside of Europe.[34] One important similarity between the two cases was that both cases were about the crime of torture to the exclusion of other crimes such as crimes against humanity and political killings.[35] An interesting difference between the two cases is the fact that whereas head of state immunity formed a core defence in the *Pinochet* case, it was not raised in the *Habré* case. One reason for this could be the fact that Chad waived Habre's immunity in 2002.[36]

What the Pinochet and Habré precedents confirm is that only those dictators who have lost support at home in their place of refuge as well as internationally will face prosecution.[37] As Mennecke states, the ultimate test would be whether states will accept universal jurisdiction as a matter of law and practice, not only when it is politically opportunistic.[38] Penrose is of the view that the relevance of the Pinochet precedent is confined to perpetrators living in exile.[39] In light of the reality of limited state practice, the prevailing reality is still that states are reluctant to interfere in the affairs of another state.

30 A Gattini 'The *Pinochet* Cases' Oxford Public International Law available at https://opil.ouplaw.com/view/10.1093/law:epil/9780199231690/law-9780199231690-e859 accessed on 7 July 2019.

31 ibid.

32 M Langer, 'Universal Jurisdiction is not disappearing: The shift from "Global Enforcer" to "No Safe Haven"' (2015) 13(2) Journal of International Criminal Justice 205.

33 ibid.

34 Brody (n 24) 334.

35 ibid.

36 'Q&A: The Case of Hissene Habre' Human Rights Watch 3 May 2016 available at https://www.hrw.org/news/2016/05/03/qa-case-hissene-habre-extraordinary-african-chambers-senegal

37 Mary Margaret Penrose, 'It's good to be the King: Prosecuting Heads of State and former Heads of State under International Law' (2000) 39 Columbia Journal of Transnational Law 214.

38 M Mennecke 'The African Union and Universal Jurisdiction' in Jalloh and Bantekas 12.

39 Penrose (note 74) 215.

Zimbabwe Torture Docket case

The Zimbabwe Torture Docket case is one of very few examples of a domestic African court exercising extraterritorial jurisdiction under its domestic legislation implementing the Rome Statute.

The genesis of the Torture Docket case was a docket presented by the *Southern Africa Litigation Centre (SALC)* to the Priority Crimes Litigation Unit of the South African National Prosecuting Authority (NPA) on 14 March 2008. The docket contained evidence of acts of torture committed in Zimbabwe following a raid on Harvest House—the headquarters of the opposition Movement for Democratic Change—on 28 March 2007. The docket further alleged that the torture was *systematic* and took place as part of *an attack against the civilian population, pursuant to a State policy*. This elevated the torture to the level of crimes against humanity. The docket named senior security and government officials that allegedly bore individual criminal responsibility for these crimes under the doctrine of command responsibility. According to the docket, these individuals regularly visited South Africa on both official and personal business. On this basis SALC requested the authorities investigate, and if necessary prosecute, the crimes under section 4 of the Implementation of the Rome Statute of the International Criminal Court Act (Implementation Act)[40] on the basis of universal jurisdiction.

Section 4(3)(c) of the Implementation Act extends jurisdiction to a person who 'after the commission of a crime' is present on the territory of the Republic—thereby providing South Africa with conditional universal jurisdiction.[41] In the Zimbabwe Torture Docket case the Constitutional Court stated that the Implementation Act deems that all crimes contemplated by that Act, wherever they are committed, are committed in South Africa.[42]

More than a year later, in June 2009, the Acting National Director of Public Prosecutions informed SALC that it did not intend to investigate the alleged crimes. SALC applied to the North Gauteng High Court for an order setting aside the decision not to investigate. SALC argued that the National Prosecuting Authority and the South African Police Services had a duty to investigate under the Implementation of the Rome Statute of the International Criminal Court and South Africa's international law obligations. The High Court granted the order. The National Commissioner of the South African Police Services and the Acting National Director of Public Prosecutions appealed to the SCA, which held that under the ICC Act, the South African Police Service Act and the Constitution of the Republic of South Africa, the South African Police Services had a duty to investigate the allegations of torture.

The National Commissioner of the South African Police Services subsequently approached the Constitutional Court for leave to appeal against the Supreme Court of Appeal's decision. The Constitutional Court granted the leave to appeal but dismissed the appeal and in a unanimous judgment in which the Court concluded that the South African Police Services must investigate. They reasoned that they had a duty to do so under the Constitution, the ICC Act and South Africa's international law obligations (in this regard the court made reference to the principle of universal jurisdiction and a number of international crimes, including those which exist even in the absence of binding international

40 Act 27 of 2002.

41 See Dugard and Abrahams 'Foreign Policy and International Relations' 2002 Annual Survey 140.

42 P 222 f–g.

treaty law). The court further concluded that SAPS has a duty to investigate where Zimbabwe was either unwilling or unable to investigate and if, on the facts and circumstances of the particular case, an investigation would be reasonable and practicable.

The court explained why States should be able to conduct such investigations:

> This approach is to be followed for several valid reasons. Requiring presence for an investigation would render nugatory the object of combating crimes against humanity. If a suspect were to enter and remain briefly in the territory of a State party, without a certain level of prior investigation, it would not be practicable to initiate charges and prosecution. An anticipatory investigation does not violate fair trial rights of the suspect or accused person.[43]

The Court then proceeded to hold that SAPS not only had the right to open a universal-jurisdiction investigation into torture in Zimbabwe, it had an *obligation* to do so—a remarkable position for the Court to take.[44] The Court however imposed two limitations on that obligation. The first limitation is that the territorial State must have failed to prosecute the international crimes in question. The Court stated:

> [This] limitation arises from the principle of subsidiarity ... [T]he principle of non-intervention in the affairs of another country must be observed; investigating international crimes committed abroad is permissible only if the country with jurisdiction is unwilling or unable to prosecute and only if the investigation is confined to the territory of the investigating State. Simply put, we may not investigate or prosecute international crimes in breach of considerations of complementarity and subsidiarity.[45]

The Court stated that the second limiting principle is that there must be 'anticipated presence' of the suspect in South Africa:

> The second limiting principle is practicability. Before South Africa assumes universal jurisdiction it must consider whether embarking on an investigation into an international crime committed elsewhere is reasonable and practicable in the circumstances of each case. That decision must be made in the light of all the relevant circumstances. None of these factors alone should be dispositive of the enquiry.[46]

The Court held that South Africa has very wide powers to prosecute foreign officials, even Heads of State, in its domestic courts, powers that reach beyond even that of the International Criminal Court. The South African Constitutional Court stated that sometimes 'perpetrators can only be brought to justice through the application of universal jurisdiction'.[47]

[43] *South African Litigation Centre* (note 5) para 48.

[44] Kevin John Heller 'Huge Win in the Zimbabwe Torture Docket Case' (*Opinio Juris*, 2014) available at http://opiniojuris.org/2014/10/30/huge-win-zimbabwe-torture-docket-case/

[45] *South African Litigation Centre* (note 5) para 33.

[46] ibid para 63.

[47] *National Commissioner of the South African Police Service v Southern Africa Human Rights Centre* (Judgment) [30 October 2014] ZACC para 32.

The Zimbabwe Torture Docket case was the first case in which the meaning of the provisions in the Implementation Act was fleshed out. The case was remarkably progressive for a jurisdiction such as South Africa with a history of neglect for international law. The case shows how the ICC can strengthen domestic prosecution of crimes committed in a non-state parties such as Zimbabwe. The Implementation Act was used as a powerful legal foundation for exercising universal jurisdiction—interestingly the Constitutional Court did not apply it in the context the Rome Statute was primarily drafted for (ie the context of the ICC regime) but to a context outside that regime. This is an exciting and innovative application of the Implementation Act that might not have been envisaged when the South African Parliament passed the implementing legislation but that has put South Africa at the forefront of implementing universal jurisdiction in Africa. In light of the reluctance governments and courts have displayed worldwide (and specifically in Africa) to exercise universal jurisdiction *in the absence of empowering legislation*, using Acts designed to implement and domesticate the Rome Statute for the purpose of exercising universal jurisdiction should be encouraged. Max du Plessis describes the Zimbabwe Torture docket case as a case which shows how domestic legislation could allow for universal jurisdiction as a complement to the work of international criminal tribunals and the ICC. He describes this as a 'new level of complementarity'.[48] This mechanism of exercising complementarity by exercising universal jurisdiction is particularly relevant to non-state parties. The mechanism can be viewed either as a form of unintentional complementarity or as an innovative way to exercise universal jurisdiction outside of the framework of the ICC.

It is to be hoped that the strong language which the Constitutional Court used against torture and the acknowledgment of the fact that torture is a *ius cogens* crime will inspire South African lawyers to urgently litigate on the many instances of torture that occur *within* South Africa.

One of the most serious concerns is that of enforcement of decisions such as the one obtained in the Zimbabwe Torture Docket case. The South African National Prosecuting Authority (NPA) has let South Africans down before in deciding not to prosecute. Examples of this would be the *Wouter Basson* case[49] of the South African Constitutional Court in which the NPA decided not to prosecute Basson after the court gave the NPA the go-ahead to do so.

Ravalomanana case

In 2012 the South African National Prosecuting Authority announced that it would investigate the individual criminal responsibility of the ousted former President Marc Ravalomanana, who had by then been exiled from Madagascar and was residing in South Africa. The NPA was approached by a group called the Association of the Martyrs of Antananarivo Merrina Square as well as citizens of the State of Madagascar. NPA made it clear that it would investigate the conduct of a foreign citizen for events removed from South Africa, with no obvious territorial or personal link to the state, other than

[48] M du Plessis 'The Zimbabwe Torture Docket Decision and Proactive Complementarity' ISS Policy Brief 81 (2015) file:///C:/Users/mswart/Downloads/PolicyBrief81%20(9).pdf

[49] *S v Basson* 2005 (12) BCLR 1192 (CC).

Ravalomanana's presence on its soil.[50] Unlike Zimbabwe, Madagascar is a party to the Rome Statute.[51] The ICC has not yet opened a preliminary examination into the events Madagascar, however.

Ravalomanana has been charged *in absentia* with murder and attempted murder for the ordering of the shooting of protesters outside his presidential palace on 7 February 2009, killing 71 people and injuring 698 people. The South African case was initiated by Malagasy litigants (specifically the Association of the Martyrs of Antananarivo Merrina Square and citizens of the State of Madagascar) who charged Ravalomanana for crimes against humanity for the same incident.[52]

Ventura has suggested that South Africa's investigation can be described as being horizontally complementary to Madagascar's unwillingness, inability or inaction.[53]

In light of the fact that there has been no issue of a warrant for arrest for Ravalomanana, it does not seem as if the South African prosecuting authority (NPA) is prioritising this case. Ravalomanana seems to have benefitted from the national reconciliation process in Madagascar.[54] In 2018, he ran for the presidency in a closely contested vote; his opponent was declared the winner by court ruling in 2019.

Conclusion

The EAC was described as a court that would try Habre 'on behalf of Africa'.[55] For many reasons, including the ongoing tension between the African Union and the International Criminal Court, the future of international criminal justice depends on the viability of domestic prosecutions through mechanisms such as universal jurisdiction. Clearly, it cannot be left to the International Criminal Court to combat all international crimes, especially in light of the obligations *erga omnes* that arise for all States to act in instances where the core international crimes are committed.

Unlike notions such as Responsibility to Protect, universal jurisdiction cannot be described as a 'trend' which is popular or unpopular at any given point. Universal jurisdiction, rather, should be understood as part of the *obligation* to prosecute international crimes under international law—an obligation which long precedes the Statute of the International Criminal Court. The Habré trial is a victory for those who believe Africa can effectively prosecute war crimes and for those who believe that the European hegemony in war crimes prosecution can be successfully challenged.

[50] See Manuel Ventura 'Complementarity and Universal Jurisdiction: South Africa's ICC Act and the Domestic Investigation of Extraterritorial International crimes' in S Casey-Maslen (ed) *The War Report* (2012)

[51] Madagascar became an ICC state party on 14 March 2008.

[52] See Bob Dewar, Simon Massey, and Bruce Baker 'Madagascar Time to Make a Fresh Start' Chatham House 2013 4 available at https://www.chathamhouse.org/sites/default/files/public/Research/Africa/0113pp_madagascar.pdf

[53] Ventura 13. See also 'NPA Called on to Probe Crimes outside SA' IOL available at https://www.iol.co.za/sundayindependent/npa-called-on-to-probe-crimes-outside-sa-1268181.

[54] 'Madascar's ex leader Ravalomanana freed from house arrest' Modern Ghana https://www.modernghana.com/news/362826/madagascars-ex-leader-ravalomanana-freed-from-house-arrest.html

[55] *Decision on the Hissène Habré Case and the African Union*, Assembly/AU/Dec. 03(VI), 2 August 2006, § 5(ii), available online at http://www.hrw.org/en/news/2006/08/02/decision-hiss-ne-habr-case-and-african-union (last visited 13 December 2010).

The *Habré* case reveals both the potential and limitations of universal of jurisdiction in Africa. Under the right conditions, the prosecution of crimes by a neighbouring state is a highly desirable alternative to national or international prosecution. Such prosecution is in the spirit of Cassese's conception of universal jurisdiction as 'the only alternative to the impunity resulting from insistence on jurisdiction by the territorial or national state.

43
Main Challenges and the Future of International Criminal Law

William Schabas

International criminal law as we know it began almost exactly a century ago. It has been through three periods of vigorous development punctuated by prolonged intervals of virtual dormancy. The first two such periods followed the great wars of the early twentieth century. They are sometimes referred to, in shorthand, as 'Versailles' and 'Nuremberg'. The third period began in the early 1990s and has not yet run its course. Whether an abrupt decline followed by another protracted lull awaits cannot be known. We are haunted by the past. There is no certainty that the historic pattern will repeat itself any more than there is a guarantee of uninterrupted dynamism. Mark Twain said history doesn't repeat itself but it often rhymes. The quotation, like so many other aphorisms attributed to the great American writer, is probably apocryphal. *Pace* Mark Twain, history is not poetry but nor is it geometry. It does not always move in straight lines. Martin Luther King spoke of 'arcs of justice'. But even if the lines are curved sometimes they have jagged edges.

The centrepiece of each of these three periods has been an international tribunal: the International Criminal Court, the International Military Tribunal and, although it was never actually established, the 'special tribunal' pledged by Article 227 of the Treaty of Versailles. Unfortunately, other hugely significant developments, mainly at the national rather than the international level, have tended to be overshadowed or overlooked. For example, in discussions of the dramatic revival of international criminal justice during the 1990s, the establishment of the ad hoc tribunals for the former Yugoslavia and Rwanda as well as the International Criminal Court invariably feature prominently. Yet one of the most glittering moments of that period, the arrest and attempted extradition of Chilean tyrant Augusto Pinochet, took place at the national level. Similarly, history may well record the trial and conviction of Hissène Habré as the defining event of international justice in the past decade, one marked by the closing of the three ad hoc tribunals, the stagnation of the Special Tribunal for Lebanon and the existential crisis confronting the International Criminal Court. This concluding essay attempts to address some challenges to the future of international criminal justice that are raised by the Habré proceedings.

The 'time factor' in international justice

The Grand Chamber of the European Court of Human Rights, in a 2015 judgment dealing with criminal prosecution for denial of the Armenian genocide, spoke of the 'time factor'. 'Whereas events of relatively recent vintage may be so traumatic as to warrant, for a period of time, an enhanced degree of regulation of statements relating to them, the need for such

William Schabas, *Main Challenges and the Future of International Criminal Law* In: *The President on Trial*. First edition. Edited by: Sharon Weill, Kim Thuy Seelinger, and Kerstin Bree Carlson, Oxford University Press (2020).
DOI: 10.1093/oso/9780198858621.003.0044

regulation is bound to recede with the passage of time', wrote the majority of the Chamber.[1] More recently, when a Pre-Trial Chamber of the International Criminal Court denied the Prosecutor authorization to conduct an investigation into the *Situation in Afghanistan*, it invoked 'the significant time elapsed between the alleged crimes and the Request'.[2] Referring to events that took place almost 15 years ago, the Pre-Trial Chamber said that '[t]he very availability of evidence for crimes dating back so long in time is also far from being likely'.[3] The Pre-Trial Chamber considered this 'time factor' to be significant in assessing the likelihood of successful prosecution.

These controversial holdings of two of the most prestigious international tribunals are troubling. They suggest a resistance to justice for historic abuses that is inconsistent with such special rules as the prohibition of statutory limitation for international crimes.[4] In so many contexts, justice and accountability require digging deeply into crimes of the relatively distant past, like those of Hissène Habré. Temporal factors were not without importance in the lengthy judicial saga of the *Habré* case. In 2010, immediately prior to a donors' meeting as efforts to prosecute Habré appeared to have gathered decisive momentum within Senegal, the Court of Justice of the Economic Community of West African States (ECOWAS) issued a bizarre ruling declaring that the relevant domestic legislation violated the principle of legality because it had retroactive effect. The Court said that the prosecution of Hissène Habré breached Article 11(2) of the Universal Declaration of Human Rights as well as Article 7(2) the African Charter of Human and People's Rights. The Court held that 'international custom' required the establishment of ad hoc or special jurisdictions for the prosecution of international crimes, and that this could not be done before the ordinary courts of Senegal ('*la Cour relève que la mise en œuvre du mandat de l'Union Africaine doit se faire selon la coutume internationale qui a pris l'habitude dans de telles situations de créer de juridictions ad hoc ou spéciales*').[5] The Court cited no authority for the mysterious 'international custom' that it claimed to have identified. Indeed, there would appear to be none, except for the Court's decision itself. The whole idea was strangely contradictory with the message in the preamble of the Rome Statute 'that it is the duty of every State to exercise its criminal jurisdiction over those responsible for international crimes'. Habré's lawyers gloated that this was the end of any hope for prosecution. But within a few months, the African Union had found a solution, embarking on the establishment of 'extraordinary chambers' within the Senegalese justice system.

The *nullum crimen sine lege* issue has plagued international criminal justice since its earliest days. When the first international prosecutions were contemplated, at the Paris Peace Conference in 1919, the Commission on Responsibilities said that 'premeditation of a war of aggression ... is conduct which the public conscience reproves and which history will condemn' but that it could not be considered 'an act directly contrary to positive

[1] *Perinçek v Switzerland* [GC] no 27510/08, § 250, 15 October 2015.

[2] *Situation in Afghanistan* (ICC-02/17), Decision Pursuant to Article 15 of the Rome Statute on the Authorisation of an Investigation into the Situation in the Islamic Republic of Afghanistan, 12 April 2019, para 91.

[3] ibid, para 93.

[4] For example, Rome Statute of the International Criminal Court, (2002) 2187 UNTS 3, Art 29. Also: Question of the punishment of war criminals and of persons who have committed crimes against humanity, UN Doc A/RES/2392(XXIII); Convention on the non-applicability of statutory limitations to war crimes and crimes against humanity, (1970) 754 UNTS 73; European Convention on the Non-Applicability of Statutory Limitation to Crimes against Humanity and War Crimes, CETS 82.

[5] *Affaire Hissène Habre c. République du Senegal*, no ECW/CCJ/APP/07/08, arrêt no ECW/CCJ/JUD/06/10, 18 November 2010, para 58.

law'. Doubtful that waging aggressive war could have been deemed an international crime in 1914, when the First World War began, the Commission advised against prosecution based upon 'the acts which brought about the war' but said that in the future 'penal sanctions should be provided for such grave outrages against the elementary principles of international law'. When the Commission proposed prosecution for breaches of the 'laws and principles of humanity', the American negotiators, Robert Lansing and James Brown Scott, protested. They argued that this was a moral standard, and that such breaches were not recognized in the laws applicable at the time. They insisted that 'an act could not be a crime in the legal sense of the word, unless it were made so by law, and that the commission of an act declared to be a crime by law could not be punished unless the law prescribed the penalty to be inflicted'.[6]

The issue returned at Nuremberg in 1945. Even before the trial had begun, lawyers for the Nazi defendants filed a motion challenging the indictment because the charge of crimes against peace, which had never before been codified, was 'repugnant to a principle of jurisprudence sacred to the civilized world, the partial violation of which by Hitler's Germany has been vehemently discountenanced outside and inside the Reich'. They noted that the maxim 'is precisely not a rule of expediency but it derives from the recognition of the fact that any defendant must needs [sic] consider himself unjustly treated if he is punished under an ex *post* facto law'.[7] According to the Nuremberg judgment, 'it is to be observed that the maxim *nullum crimen sine lege* is not a limitation of sovereignty, but is in general a principle of justice'. The French version of the judgment is more qualified: '[n]ullum crimen sine lege *ne limite pas la souveraineté des États; elle ne formule qu'une règle généralement suivie*'. The judgment continues: 'To assert that it is unjust to punish those who in defiance of treaties and assurances have attacked neighbouring states without warning is obviously untrue, for in such circumstances the attacker must know that he is doing wrong, and so far from it being unjust to punish him, it would be unjust if his wrong were allowed to go unpunished ... [The Nazi leaders] must have known that they were acting in defiance of all international law when in complete deliberation they carried out their designs of invasion and aggression.'[8]

Outside the criminal courtroom, retroactivity issues also arise in a more political context. Acts perpetrated long ago, for which criminal prosecution is not an option because there are no living suspects, are nevertheless denounced not only as atrocities or human rights violations but as international crimes. Sometimes the purpose is merely hortatory although a subtext involving claims of compensation is often present. Here, there seems to be a window of human history dating back a few hundred years, but not longer, when such claims are entertained. Thus, nobody wastes much energy trying to argue that charges of crimes against humanity, war crimes or genocide be sustained against the Romans for the rape of the Sabine women, or the Athenians for the massacre at Milos described and defended by Thucydides, or the religious leaders responsible for the Spanish inquisition. On the other hand, claims based upon colonialism, racial discrimination and the slave trade in recent

[6] 'Violations of the Laws and Customs of War, Reports of Majority and Dissenting Reports of America and Japanese Members of the Commission on Responsibilities, Conference of Paris, 1919' (1920) 14 American Journal of International Law 95, 118, 120, 145. See also William A Schabas, *The Trial of the Kaiser* (Oxford University Press 2018).

[7] Motion adopted by all defense counsel, 19 November 1945, (1948) 1 IMT 168–70.

[8] Two Hundred and Seventeenth Day. Monday, 30 September 1946, (1948) 22 IMT 411, p 462.

centuries retain some salience. The Declaration adopted at the 2001 Durban Conference on Racism states that 'slavery and the slave trade are a crime against humanity and should always have been so, especially the transatlantic slave trade ...' Note the enigmatic phrase 'should always have been so'. There was really nothing innovative about describing slavery and the slave trade as crimes against humanity, a label used in this context as early as the eighteenth century. At the time of the French revolution, Condorcet wrote that '*l'esclavage est regardé universellement ... comme un crime de lèse humanité*'.[9]

The malleable approach to the *nullum crimen* objection at the Nuremberg trial may have hardened with its codification in international human rights law. Nevertheless, in applying the norm, human rights tribunals have tended to the same flexibility, rejecting the militant positivism proposed by the Nuremberg defendants. The European Court of Human Rights has frequently held that uncodified crimes may be prosecuted by national courts provided that they are sufficiently foreseeable and accessible.[10] This is not really all that different from the remarks of the International Military Tribunal, cited above. Similar thinking is reflected in case law of the modern-day international criminal tribunals. In one of the more detailed treatments of this issue, a Trial Chamber of the International Criminal Tribunal for the former Yugoslavia was asked to declare that the concept of superior responsibility as a mode of liability amounted to retroactive law. It turned to the case law of the European Court of Human Rights, noting that Article 7 of the European Convention 'allows for the "gradual clarification" of the rules of criminal liability through judicial interpretation'. The Tribunal held that it was 'not necessary that the elements of an offence are defined, but rather that general description of the prohibited conduct be provided',[11] citing in support several rulings of the European Court, including one of the spousal rape decisions, which it quoted *in extenso*. Subsequently, the Appeals Chamber of the Special Court for Sierra Leone relied upon this passage in its discussion of *nullum crimen* in the child soldier case.[12]

A year after the *Hadžihasanović* ruling, the Appeals Chamber of the International Criminal Tribunal for the former Yugoslavia invoked the words of the International Military Tribunal to the effect that *nullum crimen* was 'first and foremost a "principle of justice"'. Also citing the European Court, the Tribunal's Appeals Chamber said that it did not prevent a court from interpreting and clarifying the elements of a particular crime nor did it preclude the progressive development of the law by the court. The Appeals Chamber referred again to the European Court's position that the concepts of 'foreseeability' and 'accessibility' of a norm will greatly depend on 'the content of the instrument in issue, the field it is designed to cover and the number and status of those to whom it is addressed'.[13] But the determination is not always straightforward, as the Grand Chamber of the European Court of Human Rights demonstrated in *Vasiliauskas v Lithuania*, a case concerning retroactive application of a definition of the crime of genocide that goes beyond that of the 1948 Convention to include political groups.[14] The Grand Chamber divided by the narrowest

[9] Nicolas de Condorcet, *Oeuvres completes de Condorcet*, Paris, Vol XI (Paris 1804) p 197.

[10] *CR v United Kingdom*, 22 November 1995, § 42, Series A no 335-C.

[11] *Proecutor v Hadžihasanović* et al (IT-01-47-PT), Decision on Joint Challenge to Jurisdiction, 12 November 2002, para 58.

[12] *Prosecutor v Norman* (SCSL-2004-14-AR72(E)), Decision on Preliminary Motion Based on Lack of Jurisdiction (Child Recruitment), 31 May 2004, para 25.

[13] *Prosecutor v Milutinović* et al (IT-99-37-AR72), Decision on Dragoljub Ojdanić's Motion Challenging Jurisdiction—*Joint Criminal Enterprise*, 21 May 2003, paras 37, 38, 68.

[14] *Vasiliauskas v Lithuania* [GC], no 35343/05, ECHR 2015.

of majorities, eight to seven, finding a violation of Article 7 of the Convention. A few years later, a seven-judge Chamber of the Court appears to have reversed the decision.[15]

The right to historical truth

The 'time factor' is intimately bound up with the 'right to truth'. In 1986, the Inter- American Commission on Human Rights observed that 'every society has the inalienable right to know the truth about past events, as well as the motives and circumstances in which aberrant crimes came to be committed, in order to prevent repetition of such acts in the future'.[16] In his 1997 report to the United Nations to the Sub-Commission on the Protection and Promotion of Human Rights, Louis Joinet wrote:

> This is not simply the right of any individual victim or his nearest and dearest to know what happened, a right to the truth. The right to know is also a collective right, drawing upon history to prevent violations from recurring in the future. Its corollary is a 'duty to remember' on the part of the State: to be forearmed against the perversions of history that go under the names of revisionism or negationism, for the history of its oppression is part of a people's national heritage and as such must be preserved. These, then, are the main objectives of the right to know as a collective right.[17]

Joinet listed the 'right to truth' as Principle 1 in the Set of Principles for the Protection and Promotion of Human Rights through Action to Combat Impunity, where it was presented as a right of a 'people' rather than of individuals: 'Every people has the inalienable right to know the truth about past events and about the circumstances and reasons which led, through the consistent pattern of gross violations of human rights, to the perpetration of aberrant crimes.' Joinet said that full and effective exercise of the right to the truth 'is essential to avoid any recurrence of such acts in the future'.[18] In the French version, he wrote: '*Chaque peuple a le droit inaliénable* . . . '. Principle 2, entitled 'The Duty to Remember', stated that '[a] people's knowledge of the history of their oppression is part of their heritage'.[19]

Inevitably, the past—indeed, the rather distant past—surfaced as an issue at the Durban Conference on Racism, Racial Discrimination, Xenophobia and Related Intolerance in September 2001. The Declaration adopted by the Conference emphasized that 'remembering the crimes or wrongs of the past' and 'telling the truth about history' were 'essential elements for international reconciliation and the creation of societies based on justice, equality and solidarity'. The Declaration stressed 'teaching about the facts and truth of the history of humankind from antiquity to the recent past', all of this 'with a view to achieving a comprehensive and objective cognizance of the tragedies of the past'.[20] It referred specifically to slavery, the slave trade, the transatlantic slave trade, apartheid, colonialism, and

[15] *Drėlingas v Lithuania*, no 28859/16, 12 March 2019.
[16] Inter-American Commission on Human Rights, Annual Report, 1985–86, OEA/Ser.L/V/II.68, Doc 8 rev 1, p 193.
[17] Final report prepared by Mr Joinet pursuant to Sub-Commission decision 1996/119, UN Doc E/CN.4/Sub.2/1997/20/Rev.1, para 17.
[18] ibid, Annex II, Principle 1.
[19] ibid, Principle 2.
[20] UN Doc A/CONF.189/12 and Corr 1, chap I, para 106.

genocide, and indicated the relationship between these historic abuses and those of the present day. It also alluded to 'dark chapters in history'.[21]

Louis Joinet's early discussion of the right to truth did not point to specific provisions of the Universal Declaration of Human Rights or the main human rights treaties. Nevertheless, his remarks were situated in a discussion of impunity where two fundamental rights, the right to life and the prohibition of cruel, inhuman or degrading treatment, are of particular importance. In this context, the European Court of Human Rights has developed the notion of a 'procedural dimension' to these rights.[22] States have a duty to investigate violations of these fundamental rights even if they are not themselves directly responsible as perpetrators. The procedural obligation of the right to life, set out in Article 2 of the European Convention of Human Rights, has been held to be 'separate and autonomous' from the substantive obligation.[23]

According to the European Court of Human Rights, the procedural obligation entitles victims, their families and heirs to know the truth about circumstances associated with a violation of the right to life, especially when this is linked to a large scale or massive violation of fundamental rights. For example, it has stressed the importance of this 'in the event of widespread use of lethal force against the civilian population during anti-Government demonstrations preceding the transition from a totalitarian regime to a more democratic system'.[24] Although the issue arises in the context of individual rights, there is some authority in the Court's jurisprudence for the recognition of a broader collective or social dimension to this right to know the truth. In one decision, the Court framed the importance of an investigation into events in light not only of the rights of the individual applicants but 'in view also of the importance to Romanian society of knowing the truth about the events of December 1989'.[25]

In *El Masri v 'former Yugoslav Republic of Macedonia'*, where government complicity in 'extraordinary renditions' by the Central Intelligence Agency was involved, the Grand Chamber of the European Court of Human Rights underscored 'the great importance of the present case not only for the applicant and his family, but also for other victims of similar crimes and the general public, who had the right to know what had happened'.[26] In a concurring opinion in that case, several judges noted that the right to truth was implicit in the European Convention, in particular within the procedural obligation of Articles 2 (right to life) and 3 (prohibition of torture and inhuman or degrading treatment or punishment), although they argued that it was best approached from the perspective of Article 13 (right to a remedy). They wrote:

> In practice, the search for the truth is the objective purpose of the obligation to carry out an investigation and the raison d'être of the related quality requirements (transparency, diligence, independence, access, disclosure of results and scrutiny). For society in general, the desire to ascertain the truth plays a part in strengthening confidence in public institutions

[21] ibid, para 101.
[22] *McCann and others v United Kingdom*, 27 September 1995, §§ 157–64, Series A no 324.
[23] *Šilih v Slovenia* [GC], no 71463/01, § 159, 9 April 2009.
[24] *Association '21 December 1989' and others v Romania*, nos 33810/07 and 18817/08, § 106, 24 May 2011.
[25] ibid, § 130. Also: *Şandru and Others v Romania*, no 22465/03, § 79, 8 December 2009; *Vasiliaulskas v Lithuania* [GC], no 35343/05, Dissenting Opinion of Judge Ziemele, § 27, 20 October 2015.
[26] *El Masri v former Yugoslav Republic of Macedonia* [GC], no 39630/09, § 191, ECHR 2012.

> and hence the rule of law. For those concerned—the victims' families and close friends—establishing the true facts and securing an acknowledgment of serious breaches of human rights and humanitarian law constitute forms of redress that are just as important as compensation, and sometimes even more so. Ultimately, the wall of silence and the cloak of secrecy prevent these people from making any sense of what they have experienced and are the greatest obstacles to their recovery.[27]

In *Abu Zubaydah v Poland*, which concerned complicity of Polish authorities in the torture of a prisoner who was being transferred to Guantanamo by the United States Central Intelligence Agency, a Chamber of the Court wrote: '[W]here allegations of serious human rights violations are involved in the investigation, the right to the truth regarding the relevant circumstances of the case does not belong solely to the victim of the crime and his or her family but also to other victims of similar violations and the general public, who have the right to know what has happened.'[28] Another decision of the European Court, referring to the killings by soldiers during the conflict in Northern Ireland, insisted upon the importance of a 'reasoned decision available to reassure a concerned public that the rule of law had been respected'.[29] Granting an application based upon Article 3 of the European Convention, a Chamber of the European Court said it appreciated the fact that descendants of the Polish officers murdered by the Soviets at Katyń had 'suffered a double trauma: not only had their relatives perished in the war but they were not allowed, for political reasons, to learn the truth about what had happened and forced to accept the distortion of historical fact by the Soviet and Polish Communist authorities for more than fifty years'.[30]

Do the principles prohibiting statutory limitation of crimes against humanity and war crimes provide legal muscle to help pry open the door to the more distant past in such a way that ordinary procedural and jurisdictional limitations do not apply in the same inflexible manner as they may when so-called ordinary crimes are concerned. This is an issue that does not arise, at least not in the same way, as long as the right to truth is confined to the victims themselves or to their next of kin. From the perspective of individual victims, the right presumably exists only as long as they or their offspring are themselves alive.[31] Perhaps the right can even be transmitted to one or more succeeding generations. But when the right is associated with the 'people's knowledge of the history of its oppression', and when it is 'aimed at preserving the collective memory from extinction' because it is 'a collective right, drawing upon history to prevent violations from recurring in the future', can there be any logical basis for a temporal limitation on its scope?

Yet a 2013 ruling by a sharply divided Grand Chamber of the European Court of Human Rights imposed a form of statutory limitation on the right to truth, barring the door to claims based upon the procedural obligation if the actual loss of life occurred prior to the adoption of the European Convention on Human Rights in November 1950.[32] In *Janowiec and others*

[27] ibid, Joint Concurring Opinion of Judges Tulkens, Speilmann, Sicilianos, and Keller, § 6.

[28] *Abu Zubaydah v Poland*, no 7511/13, § 489, 24 July 2014.

[29] *Kelly and others v United Kingdom*, no 30054/96, § 118, 4 May 2001.

[30] *Janowiec and others v Russia*, nos 55508/07 and 29520/09, § 156, 16 April 2012.

[31] In right to life cases, under some circumstances the European Court of Human Rights will give standing to the next of kin where the victim is no longer alive: *Fairfield and others v United Kingdom* (dec.), no 24790/04, 8 March 2005.

[32] William Schabas, 'Time, Justice, and Human Rights: Statutory Limitation on the Right to Truth?', in Nanci Adler (ed), *Understanding the Age of Transitional Justice: Crimes, Courts, Commissions, and Chronicling* (Rutgers University Press 2018) 37–55.

v Russia, the Grand Chamber held that it could not consider the 'underlying values' exception if the loss of life had taken place prior to 4 November 1950, the date when the European Convention on Human Rights was signed at the Palazzo Barberini in Rome. It said that 'a Contracting Party cannot be held responsible under the Convention for not investigating even the most serious crimes under international law if they predated the Convention'.[33] In the judgment of the seven-member Chamber, the Russian judge wrote that the European Convention on Human Rights had 'arisen out of a bloody chapter of European history in the twentieth century' but that it was drafted as part of a process of reconstructing post-war Europe and 'not with the intention of delving into that black chapter'.[34]

The very substantial dissenting opinion of Judges Ziemele, De Gaetano, Laffranque and Keller harshly criticizes the majority for turning a 'long history of justice delayed into a permanent case of justice denied'.[35] The majority's decision 'closes the Court's door to victims of any gross human rights violation that occurred prior to the existence of the Convention', they wrote.[36] The dissenters said that the Court has failed 'to fulfil the role for which it was intended: to provide a Court that would act as a 'conscience' for Europe'.[37] It is hard to be a 'conscience' if one refuses to even consider the past. Indeed, where else does 'conscience' come from if not the past?

Victims and their concerns

One of the more significant innovations in international criminal law since its revival in the early 1990s has been the place given to victims. Obviously victims have always been present in the criminal trial process. Until quite recently, in international war crimes prosecutions, their role has been an essentially passive one, as witnesses. Important initiatives have aimed to provide for both enhanced active participation in the proceedings themselves and an independent role as a party with a view to claiming reparation from those convicted. The Habré trial stands out in this respect. Not only were victim representatives robustly involved in the trial, they also secured for the victims a very substantial award of reparations. An important component is unfulfilled, however. Despite reports that Habré left Chad with huge assets, the monetary judgment against him is and seems likely to remain unenforced. Inspired by the example of the Rome Statute, the African Union has created a Trust Fund in the hope that voluntary contributions from wealthy countries may fill the gap and make reparations a reality for victims. But if the example of the International Criminal Court is any guide, the generosity of European benefactors will tend to the symbolic. To date the Habré Trust Fund is no more than a chimera.

In international law, the focus on victims can be traced to the 1985 Declaration of Basic Principles of Justice for Victims of Crimes and Abuse of Power of the United Nations General Assembly. Under the heading 'Access to justice and fair treatment', the Declaration

[33] *Janowiec and others v Russia* [GC], nos 55508/07 and 29520/09, § 151, 21 October 2013.

[34] *Janowiec and others v Russia*, nos 55508/07 and 29520/09, Joint Concurring Opinion of Judges Kovler and Yudkivska, 16 April 2012.

[35] *Janowiec and others v Russia* [GC], nos 55508/07 and 29520/09, Joint Partly Dissenting Opinion of Judges Ziemele, De Gaetano, Laffranque, and Keller, 21 October 2013, § 36.

[36] ibid, § 33.

[37] ibid.

states that '[t]he responsiveness of judicial and administrative processes to the needs of victims should be facilitated by … Allowing the views and concerns of victims to be presented and considered at appropriate stages of the proceedings where their personal interests are affected'.[38] Furthermore, under 'Restitution' the Declaration says that '[o]ffenders or third parties responsible for their behaviour should, where appropriate, make fair restitution to victims, their families or dependants'.[39] These principles were reaffirmed in 2005 by the General Assembly in the Principles and Guidelines on the Right to a Remedy and Reparation for Victims of Gross Violations of International Human Rights Law and Serious Violations of International Humanitarian Law, prepared by the late Cherif Bassiouni.[40]

The 1985 Declaration and the ideas that it set out influenced the drafters of the Rome Statute. At the early stages, however, victim issues were of little significance. The two key innovations of the Rome Statute, participation in proceedings and reparations, initially received virtually no attention whatsoever in the drafts of the International Law Commission.[41] The possibility that the Court might be able to order reparations was considered only very briefly by the Commission.[42] In its final report on the draft statute to the General Assembly, the International Law Commission concluded that an international criminal court was not the appropriate forum for a matter 'best left to national jurisdictions and to international judicial cooperation agreements, of which there is a growing network'.[43] The report of the Ad Hoc Committee of the General Assembly, which met in 1995, contains four perfunctory references to victims, including a suggestion that they be allowed to trigger the Court's jurisdiction,[44] that consideration be given to their protection,[45] and that they be entitled to restitution of property and compensation.[46]

A vision of a court with both civil and criminal jurisdiction, able to convict and award damages, emerged in the early sessions of the Preparatory Committee. There were several proposals[47] including a rather seminal draft from France.[48] Egypt proposed authorizing active participation of victims in proceedings for the purpose of claiming compensation.[49] A more substantial, consolidated text was developed during the fourth session of the Preparatory Committee, in August 1997,[50] inspired by proposals from New Zealand.[51] By the time that the Rome Conference convened, the guiding principles of victim participation in proceedings and reparations that had been rejected by the International Law

[38] UN Doc A/RES/40/34, para 6(b).

[39] ibid, para 8.

[40] UN Doc A/60/147.

[41] Yearbook of the International Law Commission, 1994, UN Doc A/CN.4/SER.A/1994/Add.l (Part 2), p 58.

[42] Tenth report on the draft Code of Crimes against the Peace and security of mankind, by Mr Doudou Thiam, Special Rapporteur, UN Doc A/CN.4/442, para 51.

[43] Yearbook of the International Law Commission, 1994, UN Doc A/CN.4/SER.A/1994/Add.l (Part 2), p 60.

[44] Report of the Ad Hoc Committee on the Establishment of an International Criminal Court, UN Doc A/50/22, para 117.

[45] ibid, para 181.

[46] ibid, para 188.

[47] Preparatory Committee 1996 Report, Vol I, para 282. Also: Preparatory Committee 1996 Report, Vol II, p 224.

[48] Working Paper Submitted by France, UN Doc A/AC.243/L.3.

[49] Proposal Submitted by Egypt for Article 43, UN Doc A/AC.249/WP.11.

[50] Revised Abbreviation Compilation, UN Doc. A/AC.249/1997/WG.4/CRP.9; Decisions Taken by the Preparatory Committee at its Session Held from 4 to 15 August 1997, UN Doc A/AC.249/1997/L.8/Rev.1, pp 36–37.

[51] Proposal by New Zealand on Article 43, Non-Paper/WG. 4/No.19; Amended Proposal by New Zealand on Article 43, Non-Paper/WG. 4/No.19/Rev. 1; UN Doc A/AC.249/1997/WG.4/CRP.9.

Commission had gained wide acceptance. What became Article 68 of the Rome Statute was discussed in the framework of a Canadian proposal that recognized the role of legal representatives of the victims, leaving the modalities to the Rules of Procedure and Evidence.[52] The significance of Article 75, which authorizes the Court to award reparations, was justified as an effort at repairing a shortcoming of the ad hoc tribunals.[53] The role of the Trust Fund for Victims, addressed in Article 79 of the Rome Statute, broadened as the reparations agenda gained momentum. Nevertheless, its placement in Part VII, entitled penalties, tends to indicate that using the Trust Fund to assist victims of international crimes outside the context of criminal convictions was not seriously considered by the drafters. This is confirmed by the observations of early commentators on the Statute.[54]

The developments were heralded by commentators. The adoption of the Rome Statute, wrote Claude Jorda and Jérôme de Hemptine, 'appears to mark a new step forward and to fill those gaps; victims are accorded the double status denied to them by the provisions setting up the ad hoc tribunals'.[55] Writing in the first edition of the *Triffterer Commentary*, in 1999, David Donat-Cattin said that '[t]he movement of NGOs, individuals and Governments supporting the respect and full realization of victims' rights through criminal justice found in the ICC process unique opportunity to advocate the further codification of victims' rights in international law'.[56]

When the Court became operational, the three rather modest provisions in the Rome Statute took on proportions that were larger than many delegates to the Rome Conference could ever have imagined. Legal representatives of victims not only appeared at most of the Court's hearings, they participated very actively, generating submissions and motions on issues going well beyond the reparations issue. Judges devoted huge amounts of time to assessing victim applications. Many years before the Court ever entered a conviction, the Trust Fund for Victims was funding projects in situation countries, acting more like an overseas development NGO than an institution for the enforcement of sentences. More than fifteen years after the entry into force of the Statute, what are the results?

Despite the large footprint left by victim representatives during the trials, in terms of filings and interventions, the value added by having a third party at the trial is quite underwhelming. As a general rule, the victim representatives do little more than echo the Prosecutor. Nobody seems to know the real cost of victim participation, an issue of some significance given concerns about the Court's budget and its allocation of resources.[57] Of course, there are the direct expenditures involving salaries for the victim lawyers and staff. But a real audit of the cost of victim participation also needs to take into account the added length to the proceedings, including the time taken by all participants to read and often respond to the submissions. Judges, prosecutors and defence counsel all assume additional

52 Canada: proposal regarding Article 68, UN Doc A/CONF.183/C.1/WGPM/L.58/Rev.1.

53 UN Doc A/CONF.183/SR.6, para 74 (France).

54 Mark Jennings, 'Article 79', in Otto Triffterer (ed), *Commentary on the Rome Statute of the International Criminal Court, Observers' Notes, Article by Article* (Nomos 1999) 1005–07.

55 Claude Jorda and Jérôme de Hemptinne, 'The Status and Role of the Victim', in Antonio Cassese, Paola Gaeta, and John RWD Jones (eds), *The Rome Statute of the International Criminal Court: A Commentary*, Vol II (Oxford University Press 2002) 1387–88.

56 David Donat-Cattin, 'Article 75', in Otto Triffterer (ed), *Commentary on the Rome Statute of the International Criminal Court, Observers' Notes, Article by Article* (Nomos 1999) 869–88, 871–72.

57 *Situation in the Islamic Republic of Aghanistan* (ICC-02/17), Decision Pursuant to Article 15 of the Rome Statute on the Authorisation of an Investigation into the Situation in the Islamic Republic of Afghanistan, 12 April 2019, para 95.

burdens in terms of time because of this third party whose real contribution seems quite inconsequential. Too often, the discussion of victim participation takes place at an entirely abstract level, where it is hard to argue with the claim that the proceedings may be somewhat enriched by their contribution. But that cannot be the issue. The question that needs to be asked is whether the value that they add to the proceedings justifies the very considerable expense involved.

Reparations have been awarded in three cases but against indigent defendants. Much of the great disappointment with the ultimate acquittal of Jean-Pierre Bemba on appeal was attributable to the fact that he was a wealthy man, the first convicted person who might be capable of paying out large sums to victims. Alas, it seems likely that the only way the existing reparations judgments can be paid is from the limited assets of the Trust Fund for Victims. A little over a quarter of a million euro has been generated in fines imposed by the Court, in the proceedings against Jean-Pierre Bemba and his legal team for tampering with witnesses. Otherwise, the income of the Trust Fund is almost entirely composed of voluntary contributions from wealthy States in the Global North, some of it earmarked for special projects. But over the years the cost of running the Trust Fund has sometimes even exceeded the income of the Fund itself. If it were a business required to pay its expenses from its income, it would have gone bankrupt many years ago.

And what of the individual victims, who were the justification for the whole project? They appear to be as overlooked as they were twenty-five years ago. For all of the tens of millions that have been consumed by the victim-related parts of the Statute, the total payout to individual victims stands at $US 250 each for about 300 victims of the Bogoro massacre[58] and amounts yet to be specified for loss of income to a small number of residents of Timbuktu who earn their living from the religious monuments that were destroyed in 2012.[59] That cannot be much because the monuments were rebuilt within a few years.

Of course, the eastern Democratic Republic of the Congo has millions of victims of the armed conflict that is comprised by the situation before the Court. The same is true of Mali. These victims only benefit from 'collective reparations' and 'assistance projects' which are of limited scale, given the resources of the Trust Fund. They would benefit more if the money were given to reputable NGOs with competitive overheads, although then the projects would not be branded 'ICC'.

Can any reasonable person think that the alleged 'gaps' in the legal framework of the ad hoc tribunals to which Jorda and de Hemptinne referred have now been filled? And there seems little likelihood of significant change in the foreseeable future. Victim participation and reparations was a seductive idea in the 1990s. Many sceptics were won over or were at least willing to give the proposals a chance to prove themselves and show their merit. The whole business has proven to be a damp squib, a costly and distracting enterprise whose main financial beneficiaries are well-heeled professionals paying off their mortgages.

The real problem with reparations, as I see it, is that criminal justice is not and never was a very good vehicle for addressing the victims of mass atrocity or, for that matter, crime in general. True, some justice systems combine criminal justice with civil claims. But these,

[58] *Prosecutor v Katanga* (ICC-01/04-01/07), Order for Reparations pursuant to Article 75 of the Statute, 24 March 2017, para 226.

[59] *Prosecutor v Al Mahdi* (: ICC-01/12-01/15), Reparations Order, 17 August 2017, para 81. See Francesca Capone, 'An Appraisal of the *Al Mahdi* Order on Reparations and Its Innovative Elements: Redress for Victims of Crimes against Cultural Heritage' (2018) 16 Journal of International Criminal Justice 645.

by and large, involve individual lawsuits that are only taken when defendants have visible means of paying an important judgment so as to justify the expense of the litigation itself. They reflect a rather archaic vision of the role of private law that was developed at a time when there was little expectation the State was responsible for the welfare of its citizens. As the Appeals Chamber has explained, Article 75 of the Rome Statute establishes 'a legal system of establishing *individual* criminal liability for crimes under the Statute'.[60]

Modern human rights law changes all of that. The United Nations Human Rights Committee recently confirmed, in General Comment 36, adopted in late 2018, 'States parties should take appropriate measures to address the general conditions in society that may give rise to direct threats to life or prevent individuals from enjoying their right to life with dignity. These general conditions may include high levels of criminal and gun violence, pervasive traffic and industrial accidents, degradation of the environment, deprivation of land, territories and resources of indigenous peoples, the prevalence of life threatening diseases, such as AIDS, tuberculosis or malaria, extensive substance abuse, widespread hunger and malnutrition and extreme poverty and homelessness'.[61] In other words, victims shouldn't need to go to a criminal court in order to obtain relief from the consequences of war and atrocity.

Long ago, socially progressive governments, whether of inquisitorial or adversarial judicial traditions, began to abandon private litigation when mass claims were involved in favour of no fault regimes. Worker's compensation, introduced in Germany almost a century and a half ago, was probably the first such initiative. A worker injured on the job makes a claim to an administrative body in a simple procedure, with no need to hire a lawyer, to advance costs (and pay them if the claim is unsuccessful) or to worry about the solvency of the defendant. In so-called civil law countries, when businesses are prosecuted for causing injury due to dangerous working conditions, there is no *partie civile*. That's because the victim is indemnified whether or not the perpetrator is convicted, indeed, whether or not those responsible are even charged with a crime. Similar schemes have been introduced in many countries for victims of violent crime, medical injury and even automobile accidents.

The legal profession generally disdains such initiatives, insisting on the benefits of courtroom litigation as the best way to provide reparation to victims. In no fault compensation schemes, the role (and income) of the legal profession is greatly diminished or eliminated entirely. More money goes to the victims, and it is distributed more equitably. When such matters are left in private hands, much of the money never finds its way to the real victims. Rather, it sticks to the fingers of lawyers. Isn't this more or less what has happened at the International Criminal Court too?

To argue that the International Criminal Court is not an effective mechanism for the delivery of reparations to victims of international crimes is certainly not to argue that victims of international crimes should be denied reparations. In any case, there is no real need to debate this because individual victims at the International Criminal Court don't appear to get anything anyway. Admittedly, the Court awards modest 'collective reparations', paying these out of a Fund financed by voluntary contributions rather than the litigation process

[60] *Prosecutor v Lubanga* (ICC-01/04-01/06 A A 2 A 3), Judgment on the appeals against the 'Decision establishing the principles and procedures to be applied to reparations' of 7 August 2012, 2 March 2015, para 65 (emphasis in the original).

[61] General comment No 36 (2018) on Article 6 of the International Covenant on Civil and Political Rights, on the right to life, UN Doc CCPR/C/GC/36, para 26.

itself. But the two prongs of 'collective reparations' and 'assistance' appears to be a distinction without a difference. Why not, then, completely disconnect the reparations process from the criminal justice system?

The wealthy States who fund the reparations process will not like that idea. A genuine no-fault reparations or compensation system for victims of international crimes will cost several orders of magnitude more than the modest and little more than symbolic amounts they bequeath to the Trust Fund. Linking reparations for victims to litigation at the Court is a way to ensure that the contributions of governments remain paltry. For example, recently the Netherlands contributed €70,000 to the Trust Fund for Victims.[62] The money was earmarked to pay for the individual reparations awarded to the residents of Bogoro in the *Katanga Reparations Decision*. This is very generous of the Netherlands, which has benefited financially from hosting the Trust Fund for Victims. Activities related to the Trust Fund have surely brought a lot more than €70,000 to the Dutch treasury in the form of taxes related directly or indirectly to the work of the Fund. But its government would not even want to contemplate the sums required to make a meaningful contribution to reparations for all victims of armed conflict in the Democratic Republic of the Congo.

Concluding comments

As these words are written, in June 2019, the future of international criminal law seems uncertain. Supporters of the great project express anxiety in a manner not seen for decades. The great temporary institutions of the 1990s and the first decade of the century are essentially closed, their work completed. In their place, at the international level, is the faltering International Criminal Court. Fifteen years ago, the International Criminal Tribunal for the former Yugoslavia, the International Criminal Tribunal for Rwanda and the Special Court for Sierra Leone were thriving. Their courtrooms were busy. Visitors to The Hague, Arusha and Freetown could be confident of attending one or more trials on almost any given day, just as they would at the local courthouse. Today, the three beautiful new courtrooms of the International Criminal Court stand empty most of the time. Rarely is more than one of the three ever in use at the same time, Over the past twelve months, the Appeals Chamber has issued only three decisions, a major but quite unnecessary judgment on the immunity of Omar Al-Bashir and two rather summary rulings on whether or not to release Gbagbo and Blé Goudé following their acquittal by a Trial Chamber. One ad hoc tribunal remains active, although that is a generous way of describing its work. The Special Tribunal for Lebanon is concluding an unbearably lengthy trial, considering that no defendants were present. It looks to be the most expensive moot court in history. The newest of the international tribunals, the Kosovo Specialist Chambers, has been operational in principle for more than two years but has yet to even name a defendant, let alone actually begin proceedings.

The excitement, to the extent that there is any, is with new investigative mechanisms in the Middle East, the International Impartial and Independent Mechanism which is gathering evidence for eventual prosecutions in Syria and a similar initiative in Iraq. These bodies appear to be slaking the thirst of unemployed professionals. Whether they will make

[62] Report to the Assembly of States Parties on the projects and the activities of the Board of Directors of the Trust Fund for Victims for the period 1 July 2017 to 30 June 2018, ICC-ASP/17/14, para 99.

any realistic contribution to future prosecutions remains a matter of speculation. Banking of evidence for trials that may take place sometime in the future is an attractive notion but it remains untested. The rights of the defence may not be protected at an acceptable level. There will be challenges to the admissibility of such evidence. Prosecutors may feel it too risky to proceed with cases based upon evidence that they have not themselves assembled.

The malaise within the international criminal justice system cannot be fully understood outside of the context of attacks on multi-lateral institutions coming from political leaders and their movements that are colloquially described as 'populist'. There are frequent allusions to the crises of the 1930s. But there is an important difference between today's circumstances and the situation prior to the Second World War. The world is now blessed with highly developed international institutions that were created in reaction to the Second World War and designed to prevent its recurrence. As Robert Jackson said in his opening address at the Nuremberg Trial, '[t]he wrongs which we seek to condemn and punish have been so calculated, so malignant, and so devastating, that civilization cannot tolerate their being ignored, because it cann6t survive their being repeated'.[63]

It is beyond doubt that there has been a sea change in practice at the national level. Peace agreements without provisions addressing issues of impunity and accountability are today unthinkable. Domestic legislation has evolved dramatically, responding to pressure from human rights monitoring bodies. Civil society is deeply committed to criminal justice as a necessary response to atrocity. No longer can the perpetrators of atrocity dismiss the prospect of accountability. We may not yet be able to say that there is a real likelihood such people will be brought to book. But unlike the situation that prevailed a quarter of a century ago, justice is now a real possibility. If any tyrants need to be reminded of this, they might think about the fate of Hissène Habré. To that extent, in the words of William Butler Yeats, the world has been changed, changed utterly.

[63] 'Second Day, 21 November 1945' (1948) 2 IMT 95, 98–99.

Index

Note: *For the benefit of digital users, indexed terms that span two pages (e.g., 52–53) may, on occasion, appear on only one of those pages.*
Footnotes are indicated by n. after the page number.